THE TRIALS OF
NINA McCALL

THE TRIALS
OF NINA
McCALL

Sex, Surveillance, and the

Decades-Long Government Plan

to Imprison "Promiscuous" Women

SCOTT WASSERMAN STERN

BEACON PRESS
BOSTON

BEACON PRESS
Boston, Massachusetts
www.beacon.org

Beacon Press books
are published under the auspices of
the Unitarian Universalist Association of Congregations.

21 20 19 18   8 7 6 5 4 3 2 1

This book is printed on acid-free paper that meets the uncoated paper
ANSI/NISO specifications for permanence as revised in 1992.

Text design and composition by Kim Arney

Library of Congress CIP Data is available for this title.
ISBN 9780807042762 (e-book) | ISBN 9780807042755 (hardcover)

To my grandparents: Deborah and Marvin Wasserman,
and the late Bernice and Cyril Stern

And also to the thousands of women
whose freedom was stolen, but who fought back

CONTENTS

Author's Note

THIS IS A TRUE STORY. Every character really existed, and every event really happened. All the dialogue can be found in original sources (letters, transcripts, newspaper articles, diaries, archival records, and so forth), as indicated in the endnotes. I have preserved all original spellings and grammatical usages.

As I was writing this book, I struggled over a number of decisions regarding terminology, and I will explain three of these here. First: Nina. In the original draft of this book, I referred to its protagonist, Nina McCall, as "McCall." I chose to do this because I wanted to be respectful to her and it struck me as the most respectful possible convention. However, this choice forced me to refer to her mother, Minnie McCall, as "Minnie," which, to some degree, defeated the purpose. Later in the book, Nina got married, then remarried, her last name changing both times, which further complicated matters. Finally, I felt that calling her by her first name would create a sense of intimacy between her and the reader. For these reasons, I have chosen to refer to Nina and her family members by their first names.

Second, I originally used the term "venereal disease" (and "VD" for short) rather than "sexually transmitted infection" (and "STI"). I initially chose to do this because pretty much all of the characters in this book used the phrase "venereal disease," which was the convention until relatively recently. However, I came to feel that "sexually transmitted infection" was not only more medically accurate but also less stigmatized. I have, however, retained "venereal disease" whenever quoting someone who said it or wrote it.

Third, and finally, I labored over how to refer to people who sell sex. In many recent works, authors have chosen to use the term "sex worker," rather than the more familiar "prostitute." After much thought, I chose to use "prostitute" in this book for a couple of reasons. "Sex worker" is a broader term (it also encompasses escorts, strippers, exotic dancers, adult film actors, phone sex operators, and others), while "prostitute" is more specific and indisputably better known. In addition, many of the former prostitutes and sex workers' rights advocates with whom I spoke throughout the course of my research want to reclaim the word "prostitute." (One told me she preferred the word "whore.") Most told me they cared far less about the words I used and far more about the story I told.

I hope this story is worth it.

"Young Lady, Do You Mean to Call Me a Liar?"

NINA MCCALL'S DECISION to go to the detention hospital, the government would later claim, was entirely voluntary. She had, after all, been given a choice in the matter. And though the choice mortified her, though she did not fully understand its ramifications, though she was barely eighteen years old, and though, when she tried to take back her decision, she was told it was too late, her signature at the bottom of a three-paragraph-long voluntary commitment order was all the Michigan authorities needed to claim that she had imprisoned herself in the Bay City Detention Hospital of her own free will.

It was Thursday, October 31, 1918.[1] The weather in the small town of St. Louis, Michigan, was fair, with just a hint of wind coming from Lake Michigan to the west. Winter had not yet truly arrived in central Michigan, notorious for its biting cold, though light flurries were forecasted for the next evening.[2] St. Louis residents were still able to bask in the last, flickering vestiges of autumn before yet another hard winter.

Nina McCall was, to use the old cliché, just minding her own business. That morning, she had been walking around St. Louis's business district, which consisted of just a few blocks of stores, mere minutes from the home Nina shared with her brother and mother. The business district sat on flat, dusty land, bounded to the north and west by the meandering Pine River. To the east was the grand Park Hotel, and to the south was Washington Street, the road up which Nina had probably walked to get into town that day. Handsome brick and clapboard buildings with hand-painted gable signs loomed over passersby, exuding that friendly small-town charm.[3] Little drugstores and garages peppered streets with names like West Saginaw, North Pine, North Mill, and West Center Avenue.[4] Nina entered the St. Louis Post Office at about 10:00 a.m.[5]

As she was exiting the post office, Nina locked eyes with Louis N. Martin, St. Louis's deputy sheriff.[6] Martin, a Republican and the owner of a livery stable in his early forties, was not wholly unfamiliar to Nina. She had met him several times over the past five years; indeed, she had even been inside his West Saginaw Street home when she "chummed" with Martin's teenaged daughter, Bernice.[7] But the sight of the deputy sheriff surely made Nina uneasy. Over the past few days, Nina had seen Martin talking to four or five "girls" on the streets of St. Louis. They were girls Nina did not recognize. Martin, ever businesslike, never one to casually converse with women around town, was suddenly chatting with girls left and right. One day he was talking with two girls together at a familiar street corner, the next it was one girl on her own. He had talked to some right outside the post office Nina had just exited. The girls, Nina recalled, "acted so funny." Then some of them got into Martin's car with him, and they drove away. It was all so strange.[8]

And now Martin was approaching her. The two exchanged words, and Martin told Nina that she would have to report to the office of health officer Thomas Carney for an "examination."[9] It is unclear whether he told her that Carney, and possibly other government officials, believed Nina had a sexually transmitted infection—syphilis or gonorrhea. Carney would have to examine Nina to verify whether or not she was a carrier of these dreaded, stigmatized conditions. And he would have to do it immediately.[10]

Nina abandoned whatever she had been planning to do around St. Louis's business district and walked home. For the past week, home had been above a garage on West Washington Street owned by a young St. Louis businessman.[11] Ever since Nina's father, Abe, had died in 1916, the family had been moving around rural Gratiot County quite a bit. They had returned to St. Louis, where Nina had attended school on and off as a girl, so that Nina's mother, Minnie, could care for her own ailing father, John.[12]

For Minnie, October 31 had started just like any other day. She had eaten breakfast and done some chores around the house, washing the clothing, changing the bed linen, "and that sort of thing."[13] Then she heard her daughter coming up the stairs. She could hear that Nina was crying. Minnie asked her daughter what had happened. The sobbing Nina told her mother that she had been ordered to go with Martin to Dr. Carney's office. The two talked it over, and Minnie decided to accompany Nina to the examination. Nina and her mother walked a couple blocks away from their house, past the greenhouse, down the road toward Alma, which lay a mere three miles away. Along the road, at about 10:30 a.m., they met Martin, who drove the two women the rest of the way to the office of Dr. Thomas J. Carney.[14]

Carney, a physician in his late forties, originally from New York, was serving as Alma's beleaguered health officer, devoting much of his time and energy to instituting some of the harshest (and least popular) methods to combat the influenza epidemic in all of Michigan.[15] Martin pulled up in front of his office and told the McCalls to wait in the car; he went up and, about five minutes later, came back to fetch mother and daughter. The first person Nina saw upon entering Carney's office was Miss Howell, the "office girl." Then Dr. Carney himself breezed past Nina and Minnie without saying a word. It was the first time either of them had ever seen him.[16]

For the next hour or so, the two women sat in the waiting room. Minnie later remembered that they both cried the entire time.[17] Finally, at about 11:30 a.m., Carney returned, and Nina and Minnie followed him into his office. Carney told them that Nina had been "reported" to him—that "somebody had complained." Carney said she would have to submit to a medical examination. Nina asked what the examination was for, and Carney replied that it was for "venereal disease." Both mother and daughter objected vociferously.[18]

"I knew I wasn't diseased," Nina recalled years later.[19]

"I didn't want her to have it of course," Minnie added, "and I objected to it. I said so."[20]

Nina said she would not submit. Carney said she would. And back and forth it went. Finally, he told her it was the law. He was the health officer; he had this authority. Either Nina would submit or she would be sent to the house of correction, the dismal, iron-barred prison in Detroit. Or, Carney added (in Nina's words), "I would be forced to submit to an examination."[21]

Finally, Nina agreed. Minnie and a nurse, Miss Olson, accompanied Nina into an examination room. Olson laid Nina on a standard operating table and put a sheet over her. Then Carney came in. Prone as she was, Nina couldn't see the doctor, and he did not tell her what he was about to do. The eighteen-year-old had never before had a gynecological examination. The deafening silence of the examination room was only broken by the sounds of sobbing coming from Nina and her mother.[22]

Carney inserted a speculum into Nina's vagina and probed with both the instrument and, most likely, his fingers.[23] Nina was, she later recalled, "just scared to death all the time. I was afraid."[24] The examination took about five minutes. Carney took slides of something Minnie could not see and then left the room with these. Nina and Minnie walked back to the waiting area. For a few minutes, mother and daughter waited for the doctor to come back. Nina began experiencing pain in her groin. Just moments later—Nina estimated less than three minutes, Minnie "just a few"—Carney returned. With an affected phrasing befitting his officialdom, Carney announced, "I find this girl slightly diseased." Nina had been infected with gonorrhea, Carney claimed, for about two years—since she was sixteen years old.[25]

Again, Nina and her mother objected. Nina stated it just could not possibly be true. Minnie started with more restraint. "You don't mean to tell me she has a bad disorder?" she asked. Carney replied, "I didn't say so, I said she was slightly diseased." Minnie told the health officer that she did her daughter's washings and had found no evidence of a sexually transmitted infection.

Carney repeated his line about Nina being "slightly diseased." Nina insisted she had never been with a man. Carney said he wasn't accusing her of having been with a man, just of being "slightly diseased." If Minnie's recollection is to be believed, he added, with stunning inaccuracy, "There were other ways to get it."[26]

When Nina continued to tearfully insist that she had no such infection, Carney turned on her and thundered, with all the authority of his position and his gender, "Young lady, do you mean to call me a liar?"

"Yes sir," Nina shot back, "if you say I am diseased."[27]

But it was no use. Nina would have to get treated, the health officer told her. And in order to do that, she would have to be locked away somewhere. Minnie asked Carney where that would be, and he responded, the Bay City Detention Hospital. Neither mother nor daughter had ever heard of it. Minnie asked if she couldn't just take her daughter home and have her "doctored" from there. Carney replied that the expense would be too great for the single mother—perhaps $200. Minnie told Carney she would "do most anything to keep the child with me." Nina said she could get a job to help pay for the treatments. But Carney said this wasn't an option. Either Nina would go to Bay City, or he would be forced to put up a placard outside the McCall residence.[28]

"VENEREAL DISEASE," the placard would read in all capital letters. "No Person shall ENTER or LEAVE this House Until this Card is officially REMOVED. The Removing or Defacing of this Notice without written authority from the Board of Health IS PUNISHABLE BY FINE OR IMPRISONMENT. By Order of the Board of Health." The placard would be large. And red. Carney told Nina and her mother that everyone would surely see it, and that he would personally see to it that the text was readable and noticeable.[29]

Nina and Minnie both knew they couldn't have the placard outside their home. This was a time when few newspapers would even print the words "venereal disease." Both mother and daughter writhed at the thought of such a "disgrace" brought literally to their doorstep. Nina knew she wasn't infected, but the shame was worse than the lie. She asked Carney what Bay City was. He told her it was a "detention hospital." Nina had never heard of such a thing. "I supposed it would be a hospital like other hospitals," she remembered later.[30]

Carney also told her she would be there for about six weeks and that patients could go "down town a couple of times a week." Both of these statements were untrue. Carney added another option: Nina could, instead, go to the dreaded house of correction. And then, according to Nina's recollection, he again subtly insinuated the specter of physical force. If he wanted, he could ignore her choice and simply force Nina to go to Bay City.[31]

Reluctantly, having never heard of Bay City before and still not understanding what it was, just a few hours after she had been visiting the post office completely unaware that her life was about to change forever, Nina agreed to be committed to the Bay City Detention Hospital. It was a decision she would almost immediately regret and attempt to take back just days later. But she had made her "choice," Carney and others told her, and now she would have to live with it.[32]

TERRIFYING THOUGH IT SURELY WAS TO HER, Nina McCall's apprehension, examination, and incarceration were hardly out of the ordinary. Indeed, for much of the twentieth century, tens, probably hundreds, of thousands of American women were detained and subjected to invasive examinations for sexually transmitted infections (the exams usually conducted by male physicians). These women were imprisoned in jails, "detention houses," or "reformatories"—often without due process—and there treated with painful and ineffective remedies, such as injections of mercury. They were locked in buildings that often had barbed wire, armed guards, or both.[33] At least one woman called the facility in which she was to be held a "concentration camp."[34] Some of these imprisoned women were beaten or otherwise abused; some were sterilized. These women—and, in spite of many ostensibly gender-neutral laws, they were nearly all women—were incarcerated as part of a government campaign known as the "American Plan." Initially conceived at the start of World War I to protect soldiers from sexually transmitted infections (STIs) and prostitutes (because prostitutes were believed to nearly always carry STIs), and later expanded to reach into American communities at large, the American Plan became one of the largest and longest-lasting mass quarantines in American history. Though the American Plan also involved less repressive tactics— such as sex education—it was the Plan's repressiveness and its reliance on stereotypes that had the strongest impact on people's lives.

Federal, state, and, most often, local officials enforced the American Plan from the 1910s through World War II and beyond. Empowered by hastily passed state and national laws, federal bureaucrats partnered with local law enforcement officials and representatives of private organizations to scour the streets looking for any woman whom they "reasonably suspected" of carrying an STI. These officials detained countless women, examined them without their consent, and locked up those who tested positive—as well as a number who didn't, but who were deemed sufficiently "immoral" or "promiscuous" to pose a threat to soldiers anyway. Though no historian has ever asserted this before, the American Plan operated more or less continuously in some places during the 1920s, 1930s, and 1940s. During World War II, it was reinvigorated on a national level, though local officials had never truly ceased to round up and lock up women for having STIs or being suspected of prostitution. In some places, officials continued to enforce the Plan into the 1950s, 1960s, and 1970s.

Though it is remembered by a handful of historians, most people have simply never heard of the American Plan. That the US government instituted a system of surveillance to watch women, that officials arrested these women, often denied them due process, and then imprisoned and abused them, that this went on for decades—these facts are simply not widely known. The American Plan has been forgotten.

THE PLAN'S ORIGINS were far from recent and far from American. Its history is one of tacit government support of prostitution, of brutal government repression of prostitution, of brilliant bureaucrats conceiving novel cures for STIs, of crowds of thousands demanding an end to a hated epidemic. To understand this history, one must trace the evolution of the American Plan from the nineteenth century into the twentieth, from a collection of isolated, disparate attempts to crack down on prostitution and STIs into a muscular, relatively unified, national program. For decades before World War I, communities were arresting women suspected of sexual impropriety, subjecting them to examinations and forcibly treating those found to be infected with syphilis or gonorrhea. The American Plan always operated first and foremost on a local level—and it varied from region to region, city to city, year to year—but without the federal government and the nation's entrance into the Great War, the Plan would never have been as massive or as pressing an imperative.

As the United States entered World War I, and millions of young men gathered in military training camps across the nation, the cries of local doomsayers, describing the terrors of STIs, alarmed an entire nation. Suddenly, syphilis and gonorrhea were more than just a threat to the nation's health; they were a threat to these young men—a threat to national security. Congress passed a law enabling the federal government to detain, isolate, or quarantine those with STIs who might pose a threat to the military. When it quickly became clear that only a fraction of infected soldiers and sailors had contracted STIs after joining the military—most infections had originated in their supposedly pure hometowns—officials suddenly had the rationale to expand the American Plan into cities and towns across the country. The federal government dispatched bureaucrats around the nation to spur local officials to stalk suspicious women and to influence local judges to convict these women virtually without question. The federal government also pushed each of the states to pass their own laws—based on "model laws" the feds happily distributed—to empower local officials to examine anyone whom they "reasonably suspected" of carrying an STI, and detain that person until the results of the examination were known. Assuming the detained woman tested positive, she could be imprisoned without a trial for an indeterminate sentence until she was "cured" or rendered "noninfectious." In all, tens of thousands of women were incarcerated and abused under the early American Plan, this at a time when no effective treatment existed for syphilis or gonorrhea.

Following the end of World War I, there was a push to maintain the American Plan as a national program, but natural tight-fistedness and newfound medical opposition to state involvement in health care killed this effort. Nonetheless, states and cities continued to arrest, examine, and imprison young women—for decades. No historian has ever described the American Plan, as such, after the early 1920s, but evidence suggests that officials continued to subject thousands upon thousands of women to its abusive practices through the 1920s and 1930s. When, in the early 1940s, the nation entered another world war, federal authorities hastily assembled to recreate a national program to prevent the spread of debilitating STIs among the troops. Federal officials called on many of the creators of the World War I–era American Plan for advice and leadership. Once again, federal agents, state authorities, municipal police, and private investigators watched, followed, approached, examined, and imprisoned women whom they considered suspicious. Once again, tens of thousands of women spent time behind bars. Once again, the brunt of the work was done by local officials who had never truly stopped enforcing the Plan, though this time many women were held in federally run facilities, known as "rapid treatment centers."

After the end of World War II, the enforcement of the American Plan slowed across the nation. However, it did continue in some locales for decades—as late as the 1970s. And the laws originally passed under the Plan outlasted even that late date. Authorities referred to them in the 1980s and 1990s to justify the quarantine of another group of individuals with a stigmatized infection: those with HIV/AIDS. Each of these laws remains on the books, in some form, to this day.[35]

ON JUNE 1, 1920, two women and three men walked into court to face their adversaries. Weather reports called for showers, possibly thunderstorms.[36] Despite the weather, the entourage made their way to Ithaca, Michigan, home of the Gratiot County Courthouse, an imposing, sandstone structure with a high clock tower and manicured grounds. The younger of the two women was there to sue three government officials in an attempt to force them to stop harassing her. She had spent months behind bars, months on the lam, and months undergoing brutal, poisonous "medical treatments" at the behest of a state agent. She wanted this treatment to stop. The three men with her were her lawyers. The young woman, just nineteen years old, would be the first to testify. Her testimony would reveal her shame, her fury, and her deep conviction that what the state was doing to her was wrong. Her name was Nina McCall.

OVER THE DECADES of the American Plan's existence, dozens of women would sue government officials in an attempt to win their freedom, seek damages for mistreatment, or force ongoing mistreatment to stop. This was Nina McCall's method of resistance, but it was not the only method of resistance. Other women incarcerated under the Plan—hundreds, probably thousands of them—would escape from the detention facilities in which they were held. Others would riot and destroy their sites of incarceration; many would burn these buildings to the ground. Still others would go on hunger strikes or use the press to call attention to the conditions under which they suffered.

It is these acts of resistance that historians have covered the least. It is the voices of these women that have been most effectively ignored or silenced.

This book is the first to focus attention on these women for more than just a passage or a chapter. It tells a story with many different components: a national yet locally run, half-century-long American Plan; the "progressive" men who created and ran the Plan; the remarkable professional women who also created and ran the Plan, but who later turned against it with impotent fury; the religious leaders, journalists, and activists who resisted the Plan with limited success; and the thousands upon thousands of women who were the Plan's victims, its antagonists, and its survivors.

Using these women's few surviving words, attempting to understand their actions, finding their voices lost in the banal drone of government reports, one can attempt to reconstruct their lives. Who were they? Why were they treated this way? What were their lives like in captivity? What were their lives like after captivity? How did they perceive the treatment they were subjected to? How did these women survive?

The woman whose life is featured most extensively in this book is Nina McCall. Nina's extraordinary testimony at trial gives insight into what at least one incarcerated woman saw behind bars. Nina discussed how she felt—when she was ashamed and when she was defiant. Nina's story exemplifies the divide between what officials claimed was going on and what was actually going on. It shows that many women held under the American Plan had an awareness of the mass arrests occurring around them. It shows that women uneducated in medicine could understand the serious ramifications of surrendering to the best medical practices of the time. It not only confirms that women's voices were censored, but describes how exactly officials imposed such censorship. Finally, it closely charts what drove women to resistance, and the varied forms that this resistance took.

Nina McCall spent nearly three months in captivity in the Bay City Detention Hospital. Inside, she was forced to endure inhumane (and ineffective) medical treatments. Her days were filled with scrubbing floors and washing dishes; her nights were spent sharing a bed with another woman in a small room. After Nina was released, a state agent followed and harassed her, forcing her to continue taking the agonizing mercury injections, on threat of reincarceration. Unable to tolerate the pain any longer, Nina eventually decided to sue the government. She needed this cruel mistreatment to stop.

Nina McCall's story is one of oppression and humiliation. Her story is one of abuse, one of fear, and even one of murder. Yet it is also a story of one woman's refusal to silently submit to injustice. Hers is a story of chutzpah. Certainly, not all women incarcerated under the American Plan could resist in ways as overt as Nina did, yet simply by continuing to live their lives upon release—continuing to work, to have sex, to fall in love, to thrive and to struggle and to survive—they resisted as well. They resisted a philosophy and a narrative that insisted that women were uniquely immoral, diseased, and defective, unable to determine the direction of their own lives, the identities of their friends and partners, and their places in the world. They fought back.

Government officials took Nina McCall from her home, examined her without consent, imprisoned her, stalked her, and abused her. Then, as Shakespeare might put it, the most unkindest cut of all: they forgot her.

Modern scholars have a duty to try to correct this final injustice, for it is the only one we can even attempt to address at this late date. A century after Nina's incarceration, her story—and the story of thousands of women like and unlike her—remains untold.

Chapter 1

"WILLING TO GO TO JAIL FOR SUCH A CAUSE"

IT WAS THE AUTUMN OF 1872 in the north of England, and as the tendrils of smoke began to curl up through the rafters, Josephine Butler knew she was about to die. The windows were too high to jump out of, and Butler—along with the other women present in the hayloft—was hemmed in by enemies, with "no possible exit." The jeers of men burst through the loft. Looking down, Butler saw them, "head after head of men with countenances full of fury." Bundles of straw in the storeroom below had been set ablaze. Butler and the other women in attendance realized to their horror that they were stuck; they were trapped "like a flock of sheep surrounded by wolves," as Butler put it. Her activism, she reflected, "had stirred up the very depths of hell." She and the other women said nothing, for no one would have been able to hear them above the roar of the flames and the taunts of the men. All this, Butler surely thought, for trying to speak out against the laws that governed prostitution![1]

Butler, with her dark, silky hair, high cheekbones, slightly dreamy eyes, and spine of pure steel, was one of the most famous women in England. She had come of age as an activist speaking out against British laws that forced prostitutes to register with the government and allowed the state to detain suspected prostitutes, examine them for sexually transmitted infections, and then imprison them for treatment. For years, Butler had traveled the country, evangelizing against these laws. In Kent, in Carlisle, in Liverpool, in Birmingham, in dozens of other cobblestoned villages and smoky cities, she spoke before masses of grimy workingmen, imploring them to rise up with the fire of rebellious peasant forebearers. She spoke before packed audiences of women, likening the "permanent class of harlots" to an "army of martyrs" and proclaiming that the laws endanger "the honour of all women."[2] She even traveled to jails and detention hospitals and communed directly with imprisoned women, offering counsel and eliciting testimony through the iron bars.[3]

Butler was certainly no stranger to threats. Members of Parliament had denounced her personally, calling her "worse than the prostitutes"; members of her own family had literally turned their backs on her.[4] Once, at a meeting in Colchester, she was pursued by a mob of ruffians supposedly led by a brothel keeper. Fearful yet cool, Butler had removed her hat and gloves, disguised herself with an old shawl, escaped the meeting hall through a side window, and hid behind a stack of bacon in a grocery store's closet.[5]

The day that she found herself surrounded by fire and hostile men, Butler had come to the British town of Pontefract—a military station—fully aware that she would face opposition. That fall of 1872, Butler and her political allies were trying to unseat a local politician who was in favor of the prostitution laws. Butler had been forced to hold her meeting in the hayloft because its owner was the only local man brave enough to give her a venue at which to speak. Butler had thought the loft would be safe, but when she first arrived, she found the floor coated with cayenne pepper, which irritated the attendants' eyes and mouths. After a woman washed away the pepper as best she could, Butler began to talk, but no sooner had she started than the smoke rose up, heralding her imminent demise. The fire roared. The men advanced, swearing hideously as they moved closer. Butler simply prayed. Just as the men were about to grab her, a "young Yorkshire woman, strong and stalwart, with bare muscular arms," charged them. Protected by other workingwomen, Butler decided to make a dash. She ignored the stairs and the flames and jumped out the loft's trapdoor in one bound. Finding herself unscathed, Butler escaped into the still, moonlit night.[6]

UNDERGIRDING THE PASSIONS that flared in Pontefract that day was a stark political debate, one so extreme that its partisans considered it to be tantamount to the mid-nineteenth-century struggle over slavery. This debate had become a battle in England, one that raged for years. And that battle was only a small one in the great war over prostitution and STIs—of which the "American Plan" might be considered the most violent, though certainly not the final, skirmish.

The debate was this: should government authorities accept prostitution as an inevitability and try to make it safer for all involved, or should they attempt to annihilate it? On the former side, proponents supported "regulationism," the idea that prostitution was inevitable, so, in order to minimize the supposed harm to health or morality it could inflict, prostitutes should be carefully regulated so that they would remain free from infection and operating far from respectable citizens. On the opposing side were advocates of "abolitionism," which insisted that prostitution should never be allowed to exist in any form, even if the women themselves were uninfected or geographically isolated. Implicit in both sides of the debate was the flawed assumption that prostitutes disproportionately (or, according to some "experts," exclusively) spread STIs.

Though various governments had regulated prostitution on and off for millennia, the first time an attempt at regulation was coupled with an organized effort to control STIs was in the France of Napoleon Bonaparte, the brilliant, brutal, repressive, sexually repressed emperor (who had, in fact, lost his virginity to a prostitute).[7] Beginning on March 3, 1802, Parisian officials pioneered a system whereby all prostitutes would register with the police and live in a specific section of their city.[8] The *police des moeurs*, or morals police, would hunt down women if they refused to cooperate. Every week or two, the prostitutes had to report to a large room with straw mattresses, divided into stalls, so that officials could scrutinize their genitals for signs of STIs. If the officials determined they were infected, the prostitutes could be imprisoned, without due process or a criminal conviction, in grim, filthy prisons.[9] There, they would be injected with mercury—the most common treatment of the day. By the time *police des moeurs* hit the Paris streets, physicians had long abandoned medieval treatments, such as barraging patients with laxatives and bloodletting, or slicing open a pigeon or a frog and wrapping it around an infected penis.[10] Yet mercury was only negligibly more effective. It may have killed the organism that caused infection, but it could also (and often did) kill the patient. It could not cure syphilis or gonorrhea, but it did expose the patient to the risk of mercury poisoning. Mercury treatments caused, among other things, throbbing pain, kidney damage, inflammation or ulceration of the mouth, and terrible skin rashes. Eventually, it could stunt growth, affect the memory and basic mental functioning, bring about deafness or blindness, and result in death. Mercury's painful and dangerous side effects nearly always outweighed any benefits the treatment could bring.[11]

Gonorrhea is an ancient disease. Chinese and Middle Eastern texts from more than five thousand years ago appear to mention it; Leviticus alludes to it quite clearly; Julius Caesar was vexed by a gonorrhea outbreak among his soldiers.[12] It is a gloriously variable condition: it can present with lesions; burning or painful urination; white, yellow, or green discharges from the penis; vaginal bleeding; increased vaginal discharge; anal itching; painful bowel movements; or swelling. If left untreated, it can cause pain, sterility or infertility, meningitis, and various heart conditions; infected women can give birth to blind babies; and, if it spreads to the bones or joints, it can even lead to death.[13] Syphilis, on the other hand, appears to be far more modern in its origins. One of the first times it popped up in recorded history was in 1494, when Charles VIII of France invaded Italy and army physicians noticed—"out of a blue sky," in the words of one historian—a confounding spate of pustules on the penises of his troops. Within five years, this condition had spread all across Europe. This time line has led many to conclude that Columbus's sailors brought the disease back from the New World, although that hypothesis is by no means definitive.[14] In any event, syphilis can present with sores, nodules, strange rashes all over the body, and inflammation; if left untreated, it can return, often decades later, in its latent phase, causing grotesque physical deformities, numbness, paralysis, blindness, or even dementia.[15] Until the middle of the nineteenth century, no one knew for certain that syphilis and gonorrhea were separate diseases; most doctors assumed they were strains of the same venereal scourge.[16] Certainly, there were no cures.

Regulationism—or the "French Plan," as it became known—spread like a syphilitic rash; what began with a single, painless sore, isolated in one particular place, gradually evolved into an indistinct eruption of reddish spots. So faint it was hard to notice, it slowly began to cover the hands, the feet, the limbs, the back, until the patient was completely engulfed. First, it spread all across France. Then, as Napoleon's Grand Army—gaining men as it conquered Europe—reached the Netherlands early in the 1800s, it forced the Dutch to adopt regulationism.[17] The French Plan also invaded the minds of policy makers. In 1843, Russia adopted regulationism; Spain did likewise in 1845. Scandinavia, Hong Kong, and most central European countries had adopted regulationism by the middle of the nineteenth century. Japan and Argentina followed suit a little later.[18] In Italy, Count Cavour—the country's great, ruddy-faced prime minister—was impressed with the French Plan and successfully pushed his legislature to adopt it in 1860. Opposition arose among the radicals, as well as liberals, and Pope Pius IX himself wrote to King Victor Emmanuel, pleading with him not to legalize the "patented merchandise of human flesh." The opposition accomplished little.[19]

The French Plan was far from perfect. Poor women were more likely to be forced by circumstance into prostitution and thus were disproportionately likely to be imprisoned.[20] Furthermore, countless prostitutes declined to register. In France, these women were known as *insoumises* or *clandestines*, and the police hunted them relentlessly. This led to numerous women who were not prostitutes falling under the long, muscular arm of the law. Authorities followed women through the streets, hoping to see them enter or exit a brothel, or consort with known prostitutes. Prolonged "suspicious" behavior was enough to merit arrest, as was another citizen denouncing a woman as a prostitute (or even as a carrier of an STI). Regulations directed the police to distinguish between prostitutes and women who simply deviated from conventional sexual norms; they often failed to do so.[21] Every day, the police went on "women hunts."[22] Any woman who was arrested was tested, and any woman who tested positive for an STI was assumed to be a prostitute and imprisoned as such. She was, forever after, a prostitute in the eyes of the law, and she would have to register with the police upon her release to avoid further sanctions. Furthermore, any woman arrested for promiscuity or lewdness had to register as well. The registry grew to include girls as young as ten. All this was done without warrants and without the act of prostitution being defined in any legal statute as a crime. Men were never arrested or examined or imprisoned in this manner.[23]

These practices—of arresting women suspected of being prostitutes or having STIs, of arresting those suspected of defying sexual norms, of abusing them—spread along with the French Plan itself. From Rotterdam to Berlin, police stalked "suspicious" women, arresting and testing them. Over a twenty-four-year period in Bologna, more than 50 percent of the women forcibly examined proved to be neither prostitutes nor infected.[24]

In 1864, at the urging of physicians from the Continent, the British Parliament quietly passed the first of the Contagious Diseases (CD) Acts, which sought to regulate prostitution in the kingdom.[25] Under this "English Plan," women whom authorities deemed "suspicious"—initially just those near military bases, but later women across a vast swath of the country—could be arrested, tested for STIs, and imprisoned in "lock hospitals" for treatment. Even outside lock hospitals, these women were made to live in certain heavily watched areas. Plainclothes policemen walked the streets, detaining "suspicious" women; and, as the historian Judith Walkowitz noted, the CD Acts largely affected poor, working-class, and immigrant women, those simply "suspected of promiscuous behavior."[26] Imprisoned women faced bad food, poor ventilation, excruciating and ineffective mercury treatments, and "an intense religious atmosphere and coercive discipline," in Walkowitz's words.[27] A small yet vocal group of reformers—led by Josephine Butler—was outraged by the CD Acts and battled unrelentingly for their repeal.[28] Brilliantly tapping into the passions of religious, feminist, and antislavery activists, Butler composed a "Ladies' Appeal and Protest," signed by thousands of prominent women. Butler and her cohort were especially offended by the highly invasive examinations and treatments, administered by male physicians. Members of Parliament were terrified by the "revolt of women."[29]

Abolitionists believed that prostitution—the "social evil"—was a sin and a moral outrage, and they largely blamed male exploiters for the existence of the sex trade and the spread of STIs. They believed the French and English Plans caused extramarital sex, sexual infection, and the abuse of women. Abolitionists sought to abolish "State regulated vice," as well as all other forms of vice; they wanted to close brothels, punish male exploiters of women, and "reform" the prostitutes themselves (sometimes this involved incarcerating them). Most fundamentally, they wanted to create a culture that held men and women to the same standard of sexual morality—neither should be allowed to have sex outside marriage.[30] To accomplish this, abolitionists often campaigned with a fiery vocabulary of morality, religion, and good versus evil. Their prophetess was Butler, who barnstormed England. Breathless accounts in newspapers, magazines, and an avalanche of pamphlets beamed stories of Butler's protests around the world.[31]

And so the debate between regulation and abolition was exported to the United States. As in Europe, regulationists had the upper hand in late-nineteenth-century America. In 1870, the city of St. Louis—the one in Missouri—enacted an ordinance empowering the board of health to register and inspect prostitutes.[32] Days later, New York physicians lauded the law and called on their legislators to do the same.[33] In 1871, a regulationist bill actually made it through the legislature, though it never received the governor's signature.[34] A similar bill nearly passed in San Francisco; if Susan B. Anthony hadn't been in town to denounce it, it might have.[35] In Chicago, the Common Council discussed the St. Louis ordinance at length and tried throughout the 1870s to copy it.[36] The council was foiled only when the wife of one of its members insisted that her husband introduce an identical bill—except that it substituted the word "man" for "woman." That, of course, was unacceptable.[37] A delegation from Cincinnati actually visited St. Louis and returned home determined to replicate its regulations; a group of "influential citizens" obtained some anti–CD Act pamphlets from England and distributed them to defeat it.[38] Washington, DC, tried to copy the St. Louis ordinance not just once but three times. When, in 1874, a Miss Edson discovered that such a bill was working its way through Congress, she flew from her home and worked feverishly through the night, rousing congressmen from their beds and haranguing newspaper editors. In the end, her opposition was successful, though, according to two male abolitionists, "these efforts cost her her life; she soon fell ill from over-exertion, and died—a martyr to our cause."[39]

Even where officials did not attempt to legalize prostitution through regulationism, they institutionalized it through "tacit acceptance," in the words of historian Neil Shumsky, by creating "red-light districts," where prostitutes were known to operate openly. The districts were named for the glowing red lanterns that sometimes signified the presence of the brothels—brothels that were ignored, though all too often frequented, by the police. "By 1900," according to Shumsky, "nearly every large American city, and many smaller ones, too, possessed a recognized and well-known red-light district where prostitution flourished."[40] Sometimes these districts were racially segregated; sometimes they were located in black neighborhoods or Chinatowns because white customers felt "freer" and more anonymous there.[41] New York had its Tenderloin district and Chicago its Levee; San Francisco had two districts: the Barbary Coast, where the rooms were less spacious, the drinks less potent, and the women "less desirable"; and the Upper Tenderloin, where pianos tin-kled as patrons enjoyed fine dining, cultured conversation, and, above all, discretion.[42] One of the most famous red-light districts was New Orleans's Storyville—an explosion of bars and brothels constructed in a dizzying pas-tiche of gaudy, clashing architectural styles.[43] It was in the cribs of Storyville that a young man named Louis Armstrong first blew his horn.

Yet abolitionists struck back. European abolitionists, including Josephine Butler, traveled to the United States to raise money and awareness for their cause.[44] In 1874, St. Louis clergy began preaching against the city's regula-tionist ordinance in earnest; the reverends gathered a group of young vir-gins, dressed them all in white, and "literally marched them to the statehouse doors," as two historians put it. Shortly thereafter, the ordinance was hastily repealed.[45] In 1876, desperate abolitionists successfully stopped the Ameri-can Medical Association from endorsing regulationism.[46] Because of such passionate efforts, no regulationist law, other than that of St. Louis, passed in the United States. And in England, abolitionist forces, led by Butler, success-fully pressured Parliament to suspend the clause of the CD Acts demanding compulsory examinations of suspected women in 1883. Yet when it came to outright repeal of the acts, Parliament would continue to stall.[47]

THAT YEAR, a few thousand miles away geographically, but a million miles away culturally, Nina McCall's story began as so many other stories have—with a pilgrimage.

On March 30, 1883—a cloudy day with a gust coming in from the north—a fifty-year-old Canadian man signed a piece of paper and became a United States citizen.[48] The man's name was John Henry McCall. He had been born in Charlotteville Center, a medium-sized Ontario village about as far south as one could go before sinking into Lake Erie.[49] Six years before, in 1877, John had come south to the United States, bringing with him his wife, Barbara (ten years his junior), and their children: George, fifteen; John Jr., thirteen; Charles, twelve; Abraham, nine; Robert, eight; James, six; Daniel, four; and Mary, two. Both of John's parents had also been Canadian, also born and raised in Charlotteville Center, but Barbara was from Scotland. John, Barbara, and their eight children settled in Gratiot County, Michigan. Less than a year later, Barbara would give birth to another daughter, Charity, and then, a year after that, to Francis, a son.[50]

"I, John McCall," the paper read, "solemnly swear that it is bona fide my Intention to become a CITIZEN OF THE UNITED STATES, and to Renounce Forever, all Allegiance and Fidelity to each and any Foreign Prince, Potentate, State or Sovereignty whatsoever, and particularly the Queen of Great Britain of whom I have been a subject." John signed the oath with his loopy though not illegible cursive.[51]

Gratiot County had first been surveyed a half century earlier in 1831, just two years before John McCall's birth. A group of white settlers, led by Captain Charles Gratiot—a handsome West Point graduate and military engineer—had set out to study the wilderness of central Michigan. As David McMacken, the foremost historian of the county, has written, "They navigated through the woods, crossed streams and rivers, and slogged through swamps with their measuring instruments as they identified township lines."[52] One of these townships would eventually be known as Bethany, a small, nearly square patch of land with a few narrow waterways—Pine River, Bush Creek, Taylor Drain—flowing lazily from the northeast corner to the southwest. It was to Bethany Township that the McCall family moved in the late 1870s.[53]

John purchased a farm in Bethany—eighty acres of unsettled land worth around $1,000. By 1880, nearly all of it remained covered with forest, but John had acquired $40 worth of farming implements and $130 worth of livestock— apparently a handful of oxen and a milk cow.[54] The livestock produced milk and meat that could feed his family; any extra milk could be sold to a nearby cheese factory for some cash.[55] John may have just been starting out, but he could hardly have picked a more promising place. As the historian Kathleen Anne Mapes noted, "farmers in Gratiot were considered some of the wealthiest in the state. They practiced diversified agriculture, growing a mixture of winter wheat, corn, oats, clover, beans and potatoes." The ground was fertile, resting comfortably along the basin created between the Saginaw and Grand River watersheds. It was flat land—remarkably flat, with no more than a foot of elevation for miles and miles. Dense pine forests blanketed much of it— "the finest and most perfect pines to be found anywhere," as one county historian modestly put it. Lumber became an important regional industry, and every spring Gratiot Countians would enjoy the music of laborers shipping millions of feet of pine logs down the aptly named Pine River. There were also swamps nearby, useless for farming, full of "aggravating, clinging, trailing, tearing, ripping vines." But much of the rest of the county land produced bounteous harvests.[56]

One of the neighboring farms was owned by another Canadian immigrant, John Scott, and his New York–born wife, Adaline. The Scotts were a generation younger than the McCalls, and, compared with the sprawling McCall clan, their household was modest. In 1880, they had just two young daughters: Della, seven, and Minnie, nine.[57]

In such close proximity, lumped together in the rural isolation of Gratiot County, it was inevitable that the Scott girls and the McCall brood would mingle. They probably played together, socialized together, walked their parents' lands together. Most likely neither strayed too far from home, as Gratiot County still had a bit of a wolf problem in those days and wild bears were "quite plentiful," in the words of the county historian.[58] At some point, the acquaintance or friendship between Minnie Scott and Abraham McCall would blossom into something greater. Decades later, after they had married, Minnie would give birth to their first child, a daughter. They would name her Nina.

DURING THE LATE nineteenth and early twentieth centuries, tens of millions of men, women, and children did exactly what the McCall and Scott families did: they immigrated to the United States. "Wide open and unguarded stand our gates," lamented the American poet Thomas Bailey Aldrich in 1895. "And through them presses a wild motley throng." For much of the nineteenth century, about 2.5 million immigrants per decade had come ashore in America, and they mostly came from familiar places like England, Ireland, Scandinavia, and Germany. But the late nineteenth century brought with it industrialization, and millions of people left farms and hamlets, crossed borders, even crossed oceans, and arrived seeking jobs in the United States, famed around the world as a land of opportunity. Between 1880 and 1890, immigration to America jumped to 5.25 million. After a small dip in the next decade, immigration exploded between 1900 and 1910 to an astounding 8.8 million.[59]

These new immigrants were different from those who had come in decades past. They were southern and eastern Europeans, often somewhat darker in skin tone than their northern and western European neighbors. They were frequently Catholics or, more loathed still, Jews. These immigrants—twenty-two million of them between 1890 and 1920—came from Russia, Poland, Italy, Hungary, places too often plagued by crushing poverty, omnipresent disease, and religious repression. If we had stayed, many Italian immigrants were known to remark, "we would have eaten each other." By 1914, nearly one in five American residents was a European immigrant who had arrived in the last quarter century; by the next year, 60 percent of the American labor force had been born in another country.[60]

To some, this was cause for concern. "O Liberty, white Goddess!" the poet Aldrich cried. "Is it well / To leave the gates unguarded?" Government officials believed immigrants disproportionately brought in and spread STIs, and they examined and excluded any migrants showing obvious symptoms (though, as it turned out, they discovered very few infected individuals).[61] Furthermore, many feared these immigrants might bring in their foreign customs and alien practices, including a concept known as "white slavery"—that is, the forced trafficking of young white women for prostitution. The term had been coined by the writer (and noted antiregulationist activist) Victor Hugo, author of

Les Misérables and *The Hunchback of Notre Dame*, to distinguish between the "slavery of black women," which had been "abolished in America," and the "slavery of white women [that] continues in Europe."[62] In the early 1880s, tales of white slavery had begun popping up all over England, enrapturing the British press and enflaming the excitable public. Immigrants were often painted as the villains of these tales. The narrative quickly became standard: a young, innocent, "respectable" white woman is kidnapped or tricked into sexual slavery after being offered some innocuous job; she is then drugged and taken to a far-off land, where she is subjected to unthinkable cruelties, always including an invasive examination for STIs. Some are stripped of their own clothing, their hair, their teeth, even their names. In one of the most widely circulated stories, an abducted Englishwoman in Brussels had her vagina surgically enlarged to make her body a tourist attraction.[63]

Lurid tales of widespread trafficking became common on both sides of the Atlantic—tales that were wildly exaggerated. These fantastical narratives reflected a hatred of immigrants—traffickers were "a fraternity of fetid male vermin (nearly all of them being Russian or Polish Jews)"—a noxious anti-Semitism—"It is an absolute fact that corrupt Jews are now the backbone of the loathsome traffic"—and, above all, a fear of women's newfound sexual independence.[64] Yet, even so, these tales were powerful.

As it happened, the white slavery issue was the greatest gift the abolitionist campaign could have asked for. The hated Contagious Diseases Acts took a serious hit on July 6, 1885, when journalist William T. Stead published a fabulously inflammatory article in the *Pall Mall Gazette*, entitled "The Maiden Tribute of Modern Babylon."[65] In order to expose what he claimed was a massive, international trafficking ring dealing in young white women, Stead went through the motions of "purchasing" Eliza Armstrong, a girl of thirteen, and forcing her into a life of prostitution. In reality, Stead ensured that Armstrong was safe, but the apparent ease with which he accomplished his goal and the fire of his pen enflamed virtually all of England. Stead claimed that the police were women's abusers-in-chief, complicit in the white slavery trade. "The power of a policeman over a girl of the streets," he wrote, "although theoretically very slight, is in reality almost despotic."[66] Humiliated, the police arrested Stead. Yet an estimated 250,000 men and women assembled in Hyde Park—that massive, green rectangle in central London—screaming and shouting and waving hands and flowers and banners, demanding an end to the traffic in women and girls. The crowd reminded Josephine Butler of "revolution days in Paris."[67]

Stead's white slavery revelations began to convince the public and members of Parliament of the corruption and complicity of the authorities enforcing the CD Acts. The fervor from the "Maiden Tribute" forced Parliament to finally, formally repeal the CD Acts in 1886.[68] Queen Victoria gave her assent on Butler's birthday. Butler, learning of this while abroad in Italy, wrote, "So *that* abomination is dead & *buried*. Praise the Lord!"[69]

The repeal of the CD Acts revealed the dark side and ultimate paradox of abolitionism—after state regulations were destroyed, what to do with the prostitutes themselves? The answer, it would seem, was to stigmatize, criminalize, and institutionalize them (while doing little to their clients). Following repeal, British police obtained what the historian Judith Walkowitz termed "far greater summary jurisdiction over poor working-class women and children" in the name of suppressing brothel prostitution.[70] The Criminal Law Amendment, an abolitionist law passed in 1885 that sought to protect women from white slavery and exploitation by raising the age of consent, imposed harsh penalties for street solicitation and brothel operation and empowered the police to search brothels on a whim. This made life harder for those forced to sell sex, further rendering them outcasts and pushing them to become "more covert and furtive."[71] The CD Acts may have been dead, but state interference in the lives of sexually active, working-class women was far from over.

SOMETIME IN 1910, a family of four in Michigan gathered up all their worldly possessions and left the farming life behind forever.[72] This family—mother, father, daughter, and son—joined millions of other Americans around the turn of the century, leaving the countryside for the bustling new cities, thick with opportunity and pollution. The city to which this family traveled, though, was more of a village. In 1910, St. Louis, Michigan, was home to just 1,940 souls.[73]

For the past decade, the McCall family had lived on a small, rectangular farm in the south of Bethany Township, resting in a crook of the curving Bush Creek, just south of the Pere Marquette railroad tracks.[74] Abraham McCall, the father, and Minnie Scott McCall, the mother, had married some years before, apparently when Abe, as he was known, was about twenty-one and Minnie was eighteen.[75] They had moved to a farm that shared a border with Abe's father John's farm directly to the north; Minnie's father John's farm was just a few plots to the west.[76] It is impossible to know what kind of man Abe was— no words of his own survive, and he exists today only in a scattered handful of historical records. Yet perhaps it is telling that sometime between 1894 and 1900, his elderly, widowed father chose to live with him, in spite of nine other children, most living nearby.[77]

Abe was likely the family member who tilled the land; Minnie probably cooked and cleaned, and quite possibly helped till the land as well. On September 2, 1900, Nina McCall entered the world.[78] Two years later, a brother, Vern, arrived.[79] Were there other children? Testifying on her daughter's behalf two decades later, Minnie told the court she had "two children who are living."[80] Whether this was an innocuous turn of phrase or subtle evidence of terrible pain is simply unknowable. Only Vern and Nina are listed with their parents on the 1910 census.[81]

Young Nina probably grew up playing in the trickling Bush Creek out back, though this is, of course, speculation. We know that she went to school regularly during the first decade of her life.[82] Children in Gratiot County would often walk several miles to get to school, except in the winter, when they could sometimes catch sleigh rides from passing farmers. The youngsters would arrive at the brick schoolhouse carrying their lunches in tin syrup or lard buckets. The lunches consisted of food that had been made on the farms—bread and butter sandwiches, sometimes with a slice of pork, cookies and cake, apples, applesauce or canned fruit, and boiled eggs in springtime. Kids would trade their food, and during the noon hour they got to play outside; the boys sometimes organized baseball teams and competed against neighboring schools. In May, accompanied by their teacher, the students could go look at flowers in the nearby woods.[83]

Gratiot children—Nina included, most likely—also helped farm their parents' land. This was hard work—the "soil was wet in the spring from the melted snow and abundant rains," recalled Gratiot native Addie Hill, who was born five years before Nina. "It was almost impossible to get rid of the water." Farmers wielded shovels or used horse-drawn plows to try to eliminate the constant wet. When the county finally started digging drainage ditches in about 1910, they took up a considerable amount of space and were financed by a tax increase. This "caused some neighborhood quarrels," remembered Hill.[84] Many farmers grew grain, which, until the advent of the horse-drawn reaper, had to be cut by hand with a cradle—an intimidating tool with a long blade to sever the stalks and wooden tines to catch it. It was a slow, arduous process.[85] Nearly all rural children had chores of one kind or another; usually boys had to help their fathers in the field, while girls assisted in the house and garden.[86]

Labor on the farms was divided sharply along the line of gender. In some places, farm girls had to stay home from school on Mondays to assist their mothers with the washing.[87] The introduction of electricity would eventually make laundry, clothes-making, and cleaning less physically demanding, but during the years that Nina was growing up in Bethany Township, these tasks remained trying.[88] One Midwestern farmwife, writing in 1905, recorded that she arose at 4:00 a.m., dressed and combed her hair, started a fire in the kitchen stove, swept the floors, made breakfast, strained the morning's milk, and filled her husband's lunch pail, all before 5:30 a.m. After her husband left, she drove the cattle into the pasture and tended to the other livestock, feeding the hogs and chickens; then she straightened the bed. Hopefully, she could grab a "mouthful of food" before 7:15 a.m., when it was time to wash and dress the children. She hoed the garden in the heat of the day until lunch, then tended to the shrubs and the flower bed, pulling tomatoes, sweet potatoes, or cabbages. The rest of the day was more tending to animals, more feeding and bathing the children, more cleaning, then scrubbing the dishes and bed. "All the time that I have been going about this work I have been thinking of things I have read," she wrote, "and of other things which I have a desire to read, but cannot hope to while the present condition exists"—that is, her extreme busyness.[89] Because of illness, absence, or death, young girls like Nina often had to stand in for their mothers.[90] Some girls who were eldest children were assigned the role of "father's boy" and would help in the fields until any younger brothers were old enough; Nina could have been one of these "father's boys."[91]

Nonetheless, life for young Midwestern farm women—such as Nina—was exciting. During these years, women began joining female civic societies and even radical political parties.[92] Every summer, Gratiot County women and their families could expect a visit from a band of brightly dressed gypsies.[93] These women also began dating, receiving jewelry, cards, or even pets from "wild" young men; the sedate courtship of their parents gave way to the furtive, exciting dating of a new age—dalliances might occur behind barns, on horseback, in the woods, or, most daring of all, on trips to faraway cities.[94] Yet this meant life for these women was dangerous as well. Women who were perceived as promiscuous were subject to gossip and ostracism; women who had children out of wedlock often found that their communities were unwilling to support such "illegitimate" spawn.[95] Rural women who were raped in these years might even face consequences for their "delinquency." When one rural Midwestern woman, around the turn of the century, claimed she had been assaulted and impregnated, the district attorney asked her why she had allowed such a thing to happen; when she tried to bring formal charges against the assailant, the district attorney called her a "bad girl" and charged her with "having sexual relations with other young men."[96]

Sadly, no contemporary record exists to document any aspect of Nina's childhood. All we know for certain is that when she was about ten years old, her family moved to nearby St. Louis, Michigan, four miles from Minnie's birthplace.[97] St. Louis—the central-most town in Michigan—had been founded some seventy years earlier by Lutheran missionaries hoping to convert the nearby Chippewa people. It was known mostly for a bubbling mineral spring that was said to have healing powers. Such luminaries as Civil War general Joseph Hooker and detective Allan Pinkerton came to bathe in the spring, hoping to cure paralyzed limbs; US Supreme Court justice Salmon Chase arrived by carriage a few years later, trying to stave off senility. Tourism quickly became the town industry; hotels sprang up, private homes transformed overnight into boarding houses, and railroad tracks were hastily laid.[98] The McCall family settled on West Washington Street, not too far from the spring. It was a small town, just 3.5 square miles—nowhere was that far from the spring. No longer a farmer, Abe went to work in a local hardware store.[99]

Nina McCall grew up in a rapidly changing world. Just as she and her family left, a telephone line came to the farmers of Bethany Township.[100] Technology was likewise advancing all across the country—the internal combustion engine, alkaline battery, radio transmitter, steam turbine, continuous tractor tracks, airplane, and automobile—including Ford's Model T—all came of age during the same decade as Nina. Largely as a result of this technological seismic shift, more Americans than ever moved to the nation's cities to work in factories or the department stores selling mass-produced commercial goods. The number of women working outside the home jumped from 5.3 million to 7.6 million between 1900 and 1910, increasing nearly 50 percent.[101]

In the 1910s, young women moved from farms to cities in droves, seeking jobs as shop girls, cosmetologists, nurses, or secretaries.[102] As more and more women entered the workplace (to say nothing of universities), more and more women decided to demand political power and forge lives different from those lived by their mothers and grandmothers. Rates of premarital sex rose sharply. Dances became more intimate; clothing became more revealing. City streets—dense with pool halls, dance halls, nightclubs, cabarets, bars—beckoned. "I was dazzled by the glamour of the white lights and the music and dancing on Broadway," one young woman, new to New York, recalled.[103] Single women relocating to cities often moved into lodging houses where they were closely supervised by dowdy matrons; others, rejecting this stifling arrangement, pooled their money and moved in together. Even women living with their parents started dating. And, as the historian Joanne Meyerowitz documented in her study of Chicago, somewhere between one in five and one in six female workers in the city lived alone. They were called "women adrift."[104]

Some women were forced by grueling poverty into prostitution. Nonwhite and immigrant women in particular were excluded from the mainstream labor market and often had no choice but to work in the sex industry.[105] Many other women chose prostitution willingly, deciding to use their sexuality to attain financial independence, to liberate themselves from overbearing family, and even, as the historian Cynthia M. Blair put it, to assert "self-respect." One Kentucky woman recalled that she had first entered the sex trade when she "decided to start merchandising sex instead of giving it away. . . . I was a sex merchant . . . [t]o make money and acquire the better things in life." Once, when an antiprostitution activist asked a crowd of prostitutes if any would rather do housework for a living, they laughed at him. "What woman wants to work in a kitchen?" one shouted back. Still others departed from prior sexual mores in ways that blur the line between dating and sex work; prostitution was not, nor has it ever been, a clearly defined category, and in 1910, a greater number of American women than ever before were exchanging sexual or romantic favors for "theater tickets, dance hall admissions, and late-night dinners at the automat," as the historian Elizabeth Clement wrote. These women became known as "charity girls."[106]

These changing sexual mores, and the changing societal roles that women demanded and attained, truly spurred the movement against prostitution and STIs—and, a few years later, the American Plan. Reformers—both men and women—didn't know what to make of these new, young, predominantly working-class women; certainly, they had to be protected from white slavers, exploitative bosses, predatory lovers, and, more than anything else, themselves—their own desires, dreams, and choices.[107]

THE HYSTERIA OVER WHITE SLAVERY—and the police's apparent complicity in it—had sounded the death knell for regulationism. Who would trust the cops to regulate such a system? As the nineteenth century became the twentieth, many European countries repealed their systems of regulation.[108] American medical journals, acting almost as one, embraced abolitionism.[109] The shuttering of regulated districts often forced prostitutes out of female-run brothels and onto the streets; sex work became more common, more criminalized, and more likely to feature a business model that took control away from women and placed it in the hands of exploitative men.[110]

The epic showdown between regulationism and abolitionism appeared to be over, but some regulationists fought on. By the turn of the twentieth century, many physicians had crafted a new system, known somewhat derisively as "neoregulationism." Proponents of neoregulationism still wanted to control prostitution and STIs, but through public health mechanisms, rather than by police supervision. Instead of having police—so susceptible to graft and abusive behavior—register prostitutes, court officials could hand convicted women over to the board of health, which could ensure their treatment and keep the registry. The foremost advocates of neoregulationism were physicians; as the historian Alain Corbin noted, neoregulationism "was above all a manifestation of the efforts of the medical profession to develop its power and exert its authority."[111]

This was a thrilling time for doctors. In the late nineteenth century, scientists had begun to believe that infinitesimally small organisms called germs, as opposed to noxious fumes or imbalanced humors, caused disease. The famed

German doctor Robert Koch had made history when he isolated the bacterium that caused anthrax in 1876. In 1879, Albert Neisser—later a champion of regulationism—discovered the bacterium that caused gonorrhea. In 1905, two German scientists managed to isolate a corkscrew-shaped bacterium from the labia of a young woman: it was the syphilis microbe. The next year, one of Koch's protégés, August von Wassermann, developed a moderately reliable test for early-stage syphilis—known thereafter as the Wassermann test. Finally, in 1909, Paul Ehrlich—a bearded, bespectacled, obsessive, alcoholic protégé of Koch—announced that he had discovered an effective treatment for syphilis. Ehrlich's "magic bullet," as it came to be known, was a compound of arsenic—the favorite poison of murderers. Physicians quickly discovered that Salvarsan, as the drug was branded, was moderately effective but monstrously toxic in humans. It could be injected no more than once a week, and even then, it led to painful, sometimes fatal, side effects. Kidneys failed around the world. Few patients could tolerate the whole complement of injections (which sometimes took two years to deliver). Ehrlich frantically began trying to develop a less poisonous version; in 1912, he released Neosalvarsan— less toxic but also less effective. Three years later, Ehrlich died in disgrace.[112] Nonetheless, Wassermann's and Ehrlich's discoveries provided public health officials with the tools to put neoregulationism into practice. In this exciting age of discovery, doctors were more convinced of their own omniscience than ever before.[113]

In America, neoregulationism began in New York City. There, on September 1, 1910, the city opened the Women's Night Court in the Jefferson Market Courthouse, a Greenwich Village building with a signature clock tower and an elaborate jumble of roofs, gables, and red-brick trimmings.[114] The Women's Night Court was the creation of the new Page Law (named for its principal author, state senator Alfred Page), which was intended to reform New York's antiquated and needlessly complicated court system. The Page Law established a centralized court for all women charged with "morals offenses" in Manhattan and the Bronx, staffed by special magistrates interested in women's issues, social workers, psychologists, and probation officers. One provision, the hated Section 79—proposed by a male physician with ties to German regulationists, and buried deep within the Page Law—provided that any woman convicted of vagrancy, prostitution, or similar offenses would be examined (by a female physician) for STIs. Those found to be infected would be imprisoned and treated by the state, usually in the cramped and dingy workhouse. In full view of an ogling audience, court officials would immediately drag convicted women into a small side room with an eight-foot-high board dividing it in half. On one side, a patrolman took the women's fingerprints; on the other side, a female physician poked and prodded the women's vaginas. Examined women would be held for twenty-four hours, no matter their sentence, to await the results of the STI test.[115] As historian David Pivar has written, "The Page Law definition of vagrancy was so loose that almost anyone walking New York streets could be classified as a vagrant."[116]

From the very first day of the operation of the Women's Night Court, prominent female reformers protested its existence, as well as Section 79. Edith Houghton Hooker—a brilliant, irreverent, radical suffragist and one of the first women ever admitted to the medical school of Johns Hopkins University—stood outside the courthouse on September 1, 1910, and declared, "We intend to start a regular campaign against this court, and we will come down here in large numbers to protest. We may be arrested, but we do not care about that. I for one shall be willing to go to jail for such a cause."[117] Joining Hooker in opposition were dozens of women's organizations and abolitionist groups, decrying the sexism of the program, and also its supposed tacit sanction of prostitution (by making it "safer" for men to sleep with prostitutes).[118] Women on the ground also fought back. Female activists noted that "there were many women who fainted and resisted, and several cases which were held over for twenty-four hours because of protracted fainting fits and hysteria before they could be examined."[119] One woman—whom the New York Tribune labeled "a fat Jewess"—screamed for half an hour because she "could not stand it to stay in one place as that"—the workhouse, for STI treatment—for "two months."[120] Many of the city's physicians, however, supported Section 79; they felt that they had the ability, and should have the authority, to treat infected women and stop the spread of STIs.[121] Salvarsan had become available in New York just as Section 79 became law.[122]

Edith Hooker quickly found a woman named Adelina Barone who had been convicted of "disorderly conduct," examined for STIs, and thrown into the gray granite workhouse—with its small, dark cells, bucket toilets, and cold stone floors—and she financed a lawsuit on Barone's behalf, challenging the new law. In June 1911, the New York Supreme Court struck down Section 79.[123] Thus, the first attempt at neoregulationism in the United States failed. Yet the war between abolitionists and neoregulationists was bound to continue; years later, Hooker would be one of the American Plan's most vociferous opponents, and several New York physicians would be among its most prominent supporters.

The battle moved to California. Just a few months before Section 79 was struck down, the city of San Francisco opened a "Municipal Clinic" on the outskirts of its Barbary Coast red-light district, in a one-story building with a white sign outside reading "Municipal Clinic, For Women Only."[124] Prostitutes—thousands of them—had to submit to medical examinations (by white-uniformed male physicians) at least twice a week, paying fifty cents each time for the privilege. New women were photographed and entered into a registry. By 1912, physicians were performing Wassermann tests for syphilis, in addition to closely scrutinizing the genitals. Those women who tested negative were given certificates attesting to their lack of infection. Those who tested positive had to "go into retirement" while they were treated with weekly injections of Salvarsan (for syphilis) or vigorous cleanings and lancings of the genital glands (for gonorrhea). Those who refused could be prosecuted or physically forced to undergo an examination.[125] Police court judges began sending women merely arrested—not convicted—for vagrancy, disorderly conduct, or other similarly vague charges to the clinic for compulsory examinations and, if necessary, forced treatments.[126]

As in New York, women's clubs and anti–white slavery advocates fought the clinic from the outset.[127] Women on the ground also opposed it. In one rare surviving statement, a woman recalled being horrified when a "nasty oily" man took her picture, being humiliated by the leering crowd of men who would watch the prostitutes go into the clinic, and being terrified of missing one of her examinations, lest "two regular police officers" be dispatched to find her and "force her" to report to the clinic. "I will never forget that procession of 'girls,'" she later wrote, "fat and thin, light and dark, young and old." And they charged *her* money for this! It was "the biggest graft in the country."[128] Yet physicians and public health officials continued to support it.[129] Eventually, the clinic's opponents persuaded San Francisco's famously louche mayor, James "Sunny Jim" Rolph, to order the police to stop checking prostitutes to see if they had certificates of cleanliness, which effectively killed the clinic. By September 1913, it had closed its doors.[130]

For those seeking a more moderate, palatable version of neoregulationism, they only had to look as far as Sacramento. There, a short, portly academic named William F. Snow was promoting what one historian would later call "a pragmatic middle-ground between these extremes": abolitionism and neoregulationism.[131] Snow had been born in 1874, educated at Stanford University and Cooper Medical College, and become the secretary of the state board of health in 1909.[132] As a newly minted doctor in a California clinic, Snow had once treated a young man who had contracted syphilis in San Francisco's red-light district, and the "tragedy" of the boy's case stayed with him even in his powerful new post.[133] In 1911, Snow led California to become the first state in the union to require physicians to report all cases of STIs, male or female, to the state. He also pushed, successfully, for the state legislature to add gonorrhea and syphilis to the list of diseases whose carriers state health officials could quarantine (though at the time, quarantine was meant to be a last resort, and it would hardly ever be invoked for STIs before World War I).[134] Snow's policy was a kind of moderate neoregulationism, neither condemning prostitution nor explicitly tolerating it, yet vesting public health officials with the authority to treat or quarantine STI carriers. The reporting policy made him a national celebrity and inspired a number of other states, including New York, to pass laws imitating it.[135]

"MR. FOREMAN, and gentlemen of the additional Grand Jury," read out the plump, mustachioed judge one wintry day in 1910, "it is your duty to make an investigation."

The judge was facing twenty-three New Yorkers in suits and ties. These twenty-three men worked in fields ranging from publishing to dry goods, from coffee to paper; many sold real estate. They were all there, the judge announced, to investigate the white slave trade in New York City. They were not there to look into isolated cases of prostitution, but rather to discover if an "organized traffic in women exists in this city."[136] The jury's foreman was a slender, square-jawed, thirty-something named John D. Rockefeller Jr., who just happened to be the son of the wealthiest man in history. Born in 1874, Rockefeller had been a finicky, moralistic child. He had gone to Brown for college because it was a Baptist school; there, one classmate heckled him as being "without one redeeming vice." Before the judge recruited him into service, the young Rockefeller had been proving himself to be a terrible businessman; he had just invested $1 million in what turned out to be a scam. However, he was becoming increasingly interested in philanthropy: how to give away some of his growing mega-fortune? Rockefeller and his father had been fascinated by the problem of prostitution for years; the two had given money to groups that investigated the sex trade; Junior had even given $10,000 to support Paul Ehrlich's syphilis research. This was motivated by Junior's abiding religious faith and Victorian sense of morality combined with his compulsive desire for order. Hoping to escape from his father's shadow and publicly separate himself from the scandal-tinged Standard Oil Company, the young Rockefeller had agreed to investigate white slavery.[137]

Rumor had it that Rockefeller had been appointed foreman because Tammany Hall political bosses believed him to be an ineffectual patsy. Much to their horror, the youthful millionaire proved otherwise. In the words of his biographer, Rockefeller "threw himself into it with his characteristic vigor and thoroughness."[138] Arrayed in an imposing semicircle, he and his fellow jurors questioned scores of witnesses. The jury was supposed to sit for only one month, but Rockefeller insisted that it sit for five.[139] Rockefeller's grand jury would come to exemplify a new reality of the fight against prostitution and STIs in the second decade of the twentieth century: private citizens were beginning to take the lead.

The point of neoregulationism was to take the power out of the hands of the police and place it in those of public health authorities. The problem with neoregulationism was that the cops still had to be involved. Someone had to arrest prostitutes who refused to show up for examinations or remain for treatment; someone had to find women who weren't prostitutes but were having extramarital sex. Private citizens, convinced that the police were corrupt and in bed—literally as well as figuratively—with the prostitutes, pimps, and procurers, decided that they would have to step up and take the place of those boors in blue.

In the 1890s, a bearded New York reverend with a booming voice founded the Society for the Prevention of Crime, one of the first private organizations to undertake antiprostitution work. Members of the society started conducting illegal raids on private properties, breaking into gambling dens and brothels, swinging sledgehammers, waving axes, and firing pistols into the air.[140] In 1900, fifteen prominent New Yorkers anointed themselves the "Committee of Fifteen" and dispatched investigators to go undercover to converse with mothers, young girls, and candy shop owners, kick in doors, and work in tandem with the (crooked) police to secure arrests. Committee of Fifteen investigators focused their attention on working-class and immigrant neighborhoods such as Chinatown, Little Italy, and the Lower East Side, and sought out women to ensnare. They frequently ventured through alleys festooned with clotheslines, ringing with the music of a dozen tongues, and upstairs with women, into cramped tenements or sordid hovels. There is reason to believe they even slept with the women they were there to police.[141]

In 1902, the Committee of Fifteen issued a report on prostitution in New York entitled *The Social Evil* and then promptly ceased to exist. *The Social Evil* rejected regulationism yet ardently wished for some method by which prostitutes might be tracked and forcibly treated—STIs being "usually directly or indirectly traceable to prostitution."[142] The Committee of Fifteen was resurrected in 1905, shorn of one titular member, as the Committee of Fourteen.[143] Once again, this committee employed a corps of private investigators—usually unemployed Greeks or Jews who could blend in at immigrant watering holes. These investigators gambled and drank on the job, and possibly slept with some of the women (and men—"fairies," as they called them) they were there to observe. Departing from Fifteen precedent, the Fourteen deployed female investigators "in war paint"—makeup—to understand streetwalking most effectively.[144] Glimpsing women unaccompanied by men, or women smoking cigarettes with "skirts up-high" was enough for Fourteen investigators to decide to follow them. Investigators carefully recorded their findings and then tipped off the police and district attorney's office as to the presence of women they deemed prostitutes; they even accompanied police on raids, assisting with arrests.[145] The Committee of Fourteen was vocally in favor of Section 79, on medical grounds, and racial segregation, on moral grounds—the moral grounds being antimiscegenation.[146]

One of the most important financial backers of the Committee of Fourteen was John D. Rockefeller Jr.[147] The 1910 grand jury on which he had served failed to find any evidence of a white slave trade, but it did uncover considerable prostitution in New York; Rockefeller was hooked.[148] Intrigued by the "social evil," he reached out to prominent antiprostitution groups and eventually even founded his own organization, the Bureau of Social Hygiene, to investigate the causes of prostitution and sex trafficking.[149] He hired private investigators to work with the New York Police Department, "apprehending those operating in and connected with the traffic in girls and women."[150] But he still felt that his contributions were inadequate, and more broadly speaking, the many private groups combating prostitution and white slavery (many reliant on Rockefeller money) were too balkanized.[151] On the one side were the religious and often female-led groups that investigated white slavery, urged local officials to crack down on prostitution, and remained resolutely abolitionist. On the other side were groups that fell under the umbrella of "social hygiene"; these groups believed that STIs could be combated through open discussion, sex education, and the promotion of sexual continence.[152] The social hygienists were mostly physicians, and many were thus neoregulationists.

Rockefeller had grown up watching his father promote efficiency by consolidating different groups; he set out to do the same with the groups fighting prostitution and STIs.[153] All throughout 1912 and 1913, Rockefeller labored to bring the abolitionists and the neoregulationists together. He and his associates called and traveled; they begged and they pushed.[154] He had "most interesting and strenuous" conversations with social hygienists who didn't trust abolitionists, and with abolitionists who didn't trust social hygienists.[155] Rockefeller's influence over the two camps was considerable, since he was contributing thousands of dollars to both—a fact he wielded like a cudgel yet was assiduously trying to keep from the press.[156]

Eventually, Rockefeller engineered a truce between the abolitionists and neoregulationists. At the Fourth International Congress on School Hygiene, a conference on sex education and hygiene in schools held in Buffalo, New York, from August 25 to August 30, 1913, Rockefeller united the largest abolitionist group and the largest social hygiene collective. He had convinced the leaders of the two groups that they could simply continue their earlier work under one roof: abolitionist personnel could continue vice investigations and legislative lobbying, and the social hygienists could keep advocating public discussion of STIs and compulsory reporting.[157] At 2:00 p.m. on August 27, following what one Rockefeller associate called "somewhat warm debate," the assembled abolitionists and neoregulationists decided to form a single, new organization, the American Social Hygiene Association (ASHA). At its head would be none other than William F. Snow.[158] He would now be the general in the national campaign against vice. He left his California post and moved to New York.[159]

Mostly through Rockefeller's generosity, the ASHA rented offices, founded a journal, and set up a traveling educational exhibit.[160] It lobbied state governments to pass antiprostitution laws; it sent its own investigators to compile evidence of the evils of red-light districts and then presented these findings to the government.[161] The new organization simultaneously adopted the fiery antiwhite slavery, antiprostitution rhetoric of the abolitionists and the neoregulationist goals—sex education, compulsory reporting, expanded (and sometimes mandated) treatments—of the social hygienists. In 1915, the new association faced its first major test. The Panama-Pacific International Exposition, a world's fair to be held in San Francisco, was going to draw tens of millions to that city, and Snow and his colleagues feared an influx of prostitution and promiscuous sex. ASHA leaders in New York conferred with Rockefeller associates and members of the Committee of Fourteen, and they dispatched a number of ASHA workers to San Francisco.[162] In preparation, ASHA investigators launched a top-secret investigation into prostitution in San Francisco; the association's western division chief sent undercover workers—including his own wife—to look into conditions.[163]

Once the exposition started, a slight, bespectacled ASHA official named Bascom Johnson sent out "detectives" to scrutinize prostitution in the exposition's vicinity.[164] Led by Johnson himself, the ASHA's detectives and field agents went undercover and entered buildings they thought might be brothels, "without ringing or knocking."[165] They spent their nights following around young women with painted cheeks, low-cut dresses, or any other features that Johnson and his coworkers considered suspicious.[166] It was, in retrospect, excellent practice for this private organization, dedicated to wiping out prostitution and STIs.

As historian David Pivar summed it up, "The American Social Hygiene Association maintained a loose partnership with the public health movement with the war"—the upcoming World War I—"providing an unprecedented opportunity for greater cooperation. What resulted was a major experiment in social and venereal control equal in significance to Prohibition. Plans for this joint venture, the 'American Plan,' were completed in the ASHA New York offices."[167]

Chapter 2

"LESS FORTUNATE SISTERS"

ON THE FIRST DAY of the Fourth International Congress on School Hygiene—the 1913 meeting at which the American Social Hygiene Association was founded—Burton S. Teeft, the commissioner of schools in Saginaw, Michigan, stood up and declared, "My home is a city having schools that rank second to none in the state; and I say this with pride, not with boasting." Yet Teeft also admitted that he was "astonished at the great variety" of schools in Saginaw. Some were well constructed and modern, with functioning heating systems, new blackboards, and "closely observed toilet rooms." Others, however, were cramped, dilapidated, and crumbling. Moreover, when he examined the pupils, Teeft discovered, "Defects of vision, teeth, breathing, and vitality and mentality were everywhere found."[1]

If these were the students in schools that ranked "second to none in the state," one only wonders what they must have looked like just one county over in Gratiot, where, in 1913, Nina McCall was a pupil.

Decades before, back when St. Louis was barely a town, its schoolhouse had to be smeared with dirt in warm weather, the better to keep out the mosquitoes. "At that time the wild beasts had not been exterminated and it was not always safe for children to be out alone," wrote one historian of the town. "Some of the larger pupils walked five miles through the wilderness to get to the school. Every child seemed to have a different book. All were old books, some of them Canadian."[2] By the time the McCalls moved to St. Louis in 1910, things had improved considerably. The town had erected a permanent grammar school (located just beyond the city lines, in Bethany Township) in 1879; it was a handsome brick building with a bell tower. A stout, four-story high school became reality a few years later, near the center of town. It was, by all accounts, a top-notch facility, situated in a beautiful grove of trees, with a spacious library, several laboratories, and special rooms for students who opted for an agricultural course of study. In 1913, the high school had teachers for math, science, Latin, German, English, history, music, drawing, business, and agriculture.[3]

A thirteen-year-old Nina McCall would have been in eighth grade in 1913. The eighth-grade teacher was a young woman named Edna Duff, who had graduated from the St. Louis schools herself just six years before. However, as

Nina's mother later asserted, after the family moved to St. Louis, Nina's school attendance was "not steady."[4] She would never complete the eighth grade.[5] Though Michigan had a compulsory education law, this was not terribly uncommon.[6] The previous school year, in 1912, there were 380 children of school age in Bethany Township and the town of St. Louis; only 261 attended school. Thirty-one of these were enrolled in the eighth grade.[7]

One wonders how Nina spent her days, if not in school and no longer on a farm. There is no evidence that she held a job at this point in her life.[8] She could have spent her time at St. Louis's leafy, oak-lined park, sitting on one of its many benches or admiring the ten-pound cannon. She could have gone with friends to the town's man-made lake or its tidy business district, perhaps ducking into one of St. Louis's two bakeries or three drugstores. She might have gazed longingly at the newest hats in Stylerite Parlors or the fine dresses in William Schmidt's tailor shop. She might have spent her mornings in the market or her afternoons in the Presbyterian, the Methodist Episcopal, the Protestant Episcopal, or the Baptist churches. (The Catholics made do without a church of their own.) She may even have walked the town's brand-new streets, freshly draped with telephone wires. St. Louis had possessed no paved roads until 1913, when seven blocks (including one on Washington Street) received a layer of fresh black asphalt. The residents were so pleased that plans were immediately drawn up to pave a dozen more blocks the next year. Electric streetlights arrived the same year as the paving, and suddenly Mill Street, and then others, glowed in the evenings. Charming little pillars topped with four spherical light bulbs enchanted passersby.[9]

Perhaps, though, Nina McCall simply stayed home. St. Louis was a town that had known its share of tragedies. Around the turn of the century, citizens had been devastated when a St. Louis mother shot and killed her four- and five-year-old sons in the cellar of their home and then took her own life. A few years later, an eight-year-old was killed when his older brother accidentally shot him with a revolver.[10] In 1911, just a year after the McCall family moved there, the "great hailstorm" blew in from the north and decimated the city. "Coal-black clouds hung heavily from the sky," recorded one newspaper. "Then underneath them there began to sway back and forth what appeared to be a mass of foam. . . . The wind swooped down, ever increasing, until it blew at the rate of a small hurricane." Suddenly, the "whole sky seemed to drop," and hail as large as chicken eggs began pelting the earth—one piece measured thirteen inches. Roofs caved amid a fusillade of ice bullets, homes flooded, and entire orchards and farms were denuded of life.[11] Another newspaper noted that on Washington Street, where the surely terrified McCalls resided, the homes "were a sorry sight with not a whole pane of glass in a single window."[12] And then there were the fires. Every couple of years back in Bethany, a barn had gone up in flames, but in St. Louis, the conflagrations were more frequent and more destructive. The first nine months of 1913 saw three large blazes, the first destroying a junk shop and its contents, the second devastating three buildings in the north of town, and the third consuming a barn and two cars.[13]

Yet, all things considered, St. Louis was not a terrible place to grow up. "The location of the village as to health, beauty and convenience is all that could be desired," remarked one local attorney in 1913.[14] Its land was fertile, its homes well made, and many citizens thrived in the lumber trade, the salt markets, the beet sugar industry, or mineral spring–related tourism. It was a close-knit small town. "I knew practically everybody in St. Louis," Nina Mc-Call later recollected.[15] Abe McCall spent three years in St. Louis working for the prosperous St. Louis Hardware Company before switching jobs in 1913 to work at a grain elevator.[16] His wife, Minnie, found time to become an officer of the Rebekahs, a female service organization dedicated to the Golden Rule.[17] Perhaps Abe joined the local chapter of the YMCA, which set up a "lounging place for idle boys"—perfect for Nina's younger brother, Vern.[18]

It's worth mentioning that lounging, for idle girls, was a bit more dangerous. Failing to attend school was a crime, and young women (like Nina) who did so could be sentenced to the State Industrial Home for Girls in Adrian—Michigan's reformatory for girls. For decades, state laws had endowed authorities with the power to commit girls between the ages of ten and seventeen to the home until they turned twenty-one for being truant or, more commonly, for "being a disorderly person," which was vaguely defined as "frequent[ing] saloons," "lounging upon the public streets," or "attend[ing] any public dance, skating rink or show" without a parent's permission. This law did not apply to young men.[19]

The hundreds of girls sentenced to Adrian every year were not privileged: more than half of them appear to have had immigrant parents, and only two—of 314 inmates in 1914, of whom the average age was around sixteen—had made it past the eighth grade. The vast majority of these young women had been sentenced for various "morals" offenses, such as being "Vicious and immoral" or "Using vile, indecent, profane and obscene language." Upon arriving at the home, new inmates were subjected to a barrage of medical tests, including a gynecological examination for STIs; those who tested positive were forced to undergo painful and ineffective treatments. Periodically, "experts" from the State Eugenics Commission came to the home to give the inmates rudimentary IQ tests. In 1913 and 1914, of 385 girls tested, only 25 were mentally "normal," in the opinion of the experts. Girls whom the experts deemed "feebleminded"—that is, of so low an IQ that they were unreformable—could be transferred to the Michigan Home and Training School at

Lapeer for a longer sentence, sometimes even for life. The IQ tests led the State Industrial Home for Girls' superintendent to recommend to the state legislature a "Woman's Reformatory" for "those too old to be classed as juveniles"—those inmates whom she felt needed to remain even longer behind bars.[20]

The inmates at Adrian spent their days performing physical labor; from 1913 to 1914, the women made 1,469 school aprons, 222 kitchen aprons, 1,437 aprons with sleeves, 4,730 hemmed handkerchiefs, 2,130 hemmed towels, 5,334 napkins, 1,790 pairs of underpants, 1,089 blue print dresses, and literally tens of thousands of doilies, cloths, and bags that the state sold commercially. The women were also instructed in "domestic science, art needlework, sewing and dressmaking."[21] Such toil was considered women's work, and it was meant to teach the inmates how to be proper young ladies.[22]

The State Industrial Home was certainly known to residents of St. Louis. Of the 314 young women committed there in 1913 and 1914, 43 came from Gratiot County.[23] The home's existence was a constant threat to young women: be chaste and obedient—or else.[24]

JUST AS NINA MCCALL CAME OF AGE, institutions much like the State Industrial Home for Girls—"reformatories" as they were called—were proliferating across the nation.

The history of women controlling and being controlled by state institutions is a long one. There had been female prisoners in early America, but very few of them; for the most part, they had been neglected, ignored, and thrown away to rot in dark, dank, dripping cells.[25] Yet, as the nineteenth century passed, and as more and more women were arrested and imprisoned, a generation of female reformers "took up the cause of women prisoners as their special mission," in the words of historian Estelle Freedman. In the mid-nineteenth century, these women began visiting prisons; later, they started creating organizations to aid female prisoners. After the Civil War, perhaps empowered by their war work as nurses and administrators, women began demanding authority over penal institutions for women.[26] Nineteenth-century female reformers viewed imprisoned women as their "fallen" sisters—women who had strayed from the proper moral path but who could be reformed.[27] In order to reform these wayward women, female activists founded "reformatories"—state prisons that could morally uplift fallen women, teaching them "proper," non-promiscuous sexual mores. The first separate women's reformatory was founded in Indiana in 1873; others followed in Massachusetts in 1877 and New York in 1887 and 1893.[28] Other nineteenth-century women founded maternity homes or rescue shelters to care for—and morally reform—their "less fortunate sisters."[29]

Reformatories, one historian noted, "expanded state surveillance and control of working-class female youths."[30] Women might be reincarcerated if they engaged in "promiscuous" sex.[31] Nonetheless, the reformatories were created with the best of intentions, and they typically attempted to train inmates in academic, domestic, and vocational arts and eliminated corporal punishment.

One of the most influential reformatories in the nation was the Reformatory for Women in Bedford Hills, New York, a cluster of brick cottages scattered among the steep, secluded hills of Westchester County.[32] Bedford had been created to serve as a model, utopian reformatory; it housed women convicted in New York City of vagrancy, disorderly conduct, prostitution, and "incorrigibility." At Bedford, the khaki-uniformed inmates laid cement walks, planted gardens, milked cows, cared for pigs, and put on plays; instructors taught the inmates stenography, typing, or bookkeeping; the reformatory's superintendent instilled in the inmates proper middle-class values, including abstinence and good manners at teatime. (One woman, facing a sentence to Bedford, dismissed all this as "a lot of sweatshop work and praying.") The superintendent also attempted to study the inmates, determining how many were "mentally subnormal."[33] This last interest led her to write to John D. Rockefeller Jr., requesting funding for a "careful scientific study" of the women.[34] Rockefeller assented and provided the money to build the Laboratory of Social Hygiene at Bedford, at which staff conducted physical and eugenic tests on the inmates. Laboratory staff claimed that this research determined that virtually all women convicted of "morals" offenses were infected with STIs and were mentally "defective."[35] This research would be cited by those wishing to lock up women for decades to come.[36]

In 1910, blacks represented just 2 percent of New York's population but 13 percent of Bedford's, reflecting the racism of the criminal justice system.[37] In describing the black inmates, Bedford administrators wrote of the "true African type . . . inclined to be somewhat vicious looking" and of "typical African cunning calculating eyes," reflecting a more personal racism.[38] Yet Bedford was something of an anomaly in that it had any black inmates at all, since many reformatories accepted only white women. In response, some pioneering black female activists proudly created their own reformatories; interestingly, these activists forced inmates to conform to the same Victorian standards of respectability as their white counterparts.[39]

One female prison reformer who would later play an important role in the American Plan, and who had also long relied on Rockefeller's money, was a tall woman with prematurely silver hair named Maude Miner. In the 1910s, Miner was in her early thirties, part of a generation of new, elite women—schooled at Smith, Wellesley, or Bryn Mawr—who were demanding access to graduate education as well as the vote; they were often religious in inclination yet quietly subversive. These women believed it was their duty to help their less fortunate sisters. Miner had gone to Smith, then Columbia, and then became one of New York City's first female probation officers in 1906.[40] It took barely a year for her to be thoroughly demoralized by the places incarcerated women were held—dirty, with mattresses strewn all across the floor, drunken women muttering in the crowded darkness. So, in 1908, she opened Waverley House, a "detention house"—essentially a reformatory, but intended to be only temporary. With the financial assistance of a sympathetic John D. Rockefeller Jr., Waverley would house hundreds of women over the next few years.[41] Its workers instructed the inmates in sewing, housework, and hat-making, as well as Victorian sexual ethics.[42] Upon arriving, inmates were interrogated about their family and sexual histories; they were subjected to primitive IQ tests, and were scrutinized for STIs. Of the first 151 women held in Waverley House, 50 tested positive and were held for treatment.[43] In finding women who might benefit from Waverley, Miner targeted immigrant and Jewish women in particular, believing them to be inherently defective.[44] She promoted the "detention house" model all over the country, yet another way to lock up those deviant women.[45]

The early years of the twentieth century were a time when women—well, some women—were gaining power. College-educated, mostly white women were rapidly becoming superintendents, probation officers, and other court officials—occasionally even police officers and judges.[46] Within just a few more years, many of these women—including Maude Miner—would play key roles in the American Plan.

ALL WAS QUIET ON THE SOUTHWESTERN FRONT. The 12 officers and 341 soldiers guarding the tiny American base at Columbus, New Mexico, were sleeping peacefully, with little prospect of anything interesting to interrupt the cool night of March 8, 1916. After all, who would want to attack this insignificant, indisputably ugly little hamlet? A treeless, grassless, windswept desert town, pockmarked with adobe houses, hotels, stores, a bank, and a post office, Columbus baked by day beneath the vernal sun. But this night, around 4:00 a.m., hundreds of armed bandits crept into town. After an American scout spotted them, there was a furious gunfight, the flashes of bullets providing the only light. Eventually, the Mexicans retreated, but not before 18 Americans and 105 Mexicans were killed.[47] This raid, engineered by the infamous Mexican general Pancho Villa in response to the abuse of Mexicans at the US border, was one of the first foreign attacks on American soil since the War of 1812 a century before.[48] It put Woodrow Wilson, the president who had "kept us out of war," in a bind. Though naturally inclined toward peace, he was facing an upcoming election, and the nation wanted blood. Wilson called on newly appointed Secretary of War Newton Baker, who was rumored to be a pacifist.[49] Baker, in turn, appointed Brigadier General John J. Pershing to lead an expedition to ferret out Villa's band of followers.[50]

Pershing's expedition quickly developed a reputation for debauchery and disorder. The thousands of troops who hastily swarmed into the Southwest loved to drink and dance with women, the newspapers claimed. They had little else to do, as Villa had disappeared deep into the unfamiliar Mexican wild, and Pershing was reluctant to follow. All along the border, large concrete or wooden homes were erected to accommodate women who followed the National Guard there. STIs were rampant. In an attempt to solve what he called the "woman problem," Pershing (who as a young man had contracted gonorrhea himself—twice) instituted a system of tightly controlled, racially segregated, and centrally regulated prostitution. The rate of infection dropped, but reformers were up in arms about the apparent sanction of prostitution. Furthermore, many of the soldiers refused to use the regulated brothels, preferring to venture out on their own.[51] American public health officials believed the border's "moral problem" was "very greatly complicated by having a large Mexican population."[52]

By July, the situation had become intolerable to the nation's leading anti-STI activists. So, early that hot summer month, William F. Snow, general secretary of the ASHA, along with the secretary of the Rockefeller Foundation (who was also an ASHA member), and a YMCA executive, came to Washington, DC, and met with Secretary of War Baker. They all agreed that something had to be done, and they all agreed on the man to do it: Raymond Fosdick.[53] Fosdick was one of the Progressive movement's rising stars—a high-ranking New York municipal reformer by the time he was just twenty-six, and a man who had traveled around the world investigating, among other things, prostitution. He had been born in 1883, studied at Princeton under Woodrow Wilson (where he delighted in Wilson's "dialect stories, told in Scotch, Irish, or Negro accents"), and had close professional ties to Rockefeller and the ASHA. He was young, smart, and idealistic.[54]

Quickly, Baker telegraphed Fosdick, summoning him to his office. The two had become friendly during Woodrow Wilson's presidential campaign, and they remained on good terms. Baker, a small, frail man with a habit of tucking one foot under himself as he perched behind a mammoth desk, posed a simple question. Could Fosdick go down to the Mexican border and see if things were truly as bacchanalian as he had heard? "Let's get the exact facts," the secretary of war told the reformer. Feeling a sense of duty, Fosdick accepted on the spot, and a week later, he was in San Antonio, eager to attack this new project with his trademark intensity.[55] There was no federal money to pay for his trip, so Rockefeller would fund it.[56]

For five weeks, Fosdick traveled down the dusty roads of the Southwest, stopping at San Antonio, Brownsville, Mercedes, Llano Grande, Donna, Pharr, McAllen, Mission, Laredo, El Paso, Columbus, Douglas, and Nogales. By the end of his travels, Fosdick was terrified by what he had seen.[57]

In every major city he visited, he noted, there were red-light districts, and "the presence of the army has caused a considerable increase in the number of prostitutes and generally in the size of the restricted districts." "Indeed," he wrote Baker in his report, "there are grounds for the belief that large numbers of prostitutes from all over the country are flocking to such centers as San Antonio, Laredo and El Paso." Alcohol use was staggering. Street solicitation was becoming more and more flagrant. And STI rates would only continue to climb. To remedy this cocktail of terrors, Fosdick suggested that the military scour the streets, looking for "the cheaper grades of prostitutes." Municipal police could also be recruited for this task. "Army officials should under no circumstances tolerate and even sanction such farcical examination of prostitutes," Fosdick wrote. Even the availability of STI treatment was dangerous, as it led the soldiers to believe their actions were safer than they actually were.[58]

"I am conscious that the foregoing suggestions will not bring ideal conditions," Fosdick wrote toward the end of his report. "They appeal to me only as next steps for the immediate future. What is needed is a well thought out policy for the army on this most complex problem."[59]

Riding back to New York on a hot, dust-choked train, Fosdick reflected on everything he had seen. Obviously prostitution and liquor were problematic. And he felt he had raised important points in his report. But Fosdick also began to dwell on other realities of life in a military camp. There was no fun, anywhere. There were no newspapers, no picture shows, no pool tables, no sports equipment, no home-cooked meals—there were only a handful of saloons and a haphazard row of tents, filled with prostitutes.[60]

That summer, Fosdick and Baker held several long conferences in Baker's grand office, with it tall western windows and a fresh pansy perpetually atop the wooden desk.[61] Together they sat—Fosdick, all thin limbs and earnestness, Baker, with a tiny foot tucked under his body, the other dangling—and discussed STIs and prostitution and the problems posed by libido and ennui.[62] "We thought we were talking about the Mexican border," Fosdick reflected years later. "In fact, although we were unaware of it, we were discussing ways and means of normalizing the life of the American soldier in the greatest war in which the United States, up to that time, had ever been involved."[63]

THE SUMMER OF 1916 did not pass peacefully for the McCall family. Abe had left his job at the hardware store a few years before; he had been working in a grain elevator for the better part of three years. Once a farmer himself, he now handled the crops others raised for a living. The work was physical. He wanted something more. That summer, Abe traveled without his family to Detroit, finding a job in one of the factories springing up across the Midwest.[64] Like so many men around the region, he dropped a shovel or a pitchfork or a plow and picked up everything to move to a city and work on an assembly line.

For such men, Detroit in particular was the place to be. Immigrants from around the world were streaming into the Motor City to work in the sooty new automobile factories that were just beginning to feel the truly mad frenzy of demand. In 1900, Detroit produced barely four thousand cars; twenty years later, annual production would be almost two million. About half the cars for the whole country were made in Detroit, and that percentage was only shooting higher and higher. Smaller factories closed as the larger corporations began eating them alive. Stores for the workers burst up from the ground in explosions of wood and plaster, while new telephone wires soared overhead. Gritty exhaust hung in the air like ambivalent birds. Meanwhile, alcohol was not yet prohibited in Detroit, and it was perhaps helping to fuel the increasingly contentious battles between management and labor unions. Strikes, accidents, and ethnic strife were facts of daily life. Every shift change, the streets bustled with ashen-faced men holding lunch pails, well-dressed managers' wives holding parasols to shield themselves from the fumes, immigrants speaking every conceivable tongue, and, everywhere, construction. The highpoint for the construction of new buildings in Detroit was 1916; that year alone, the city added more than sixteen thousand buildings, each stretching higher or wider than the last.[65]

"He went down there to work," his wife, Minnie, recalled years later. "He wanted to go down there and see if he could better himself."[66] Abe stayed in Detroit for about six weeks, probably working in an automobile factory; about half the city's industrial laborers did.[67] But soon he became quite ill. He had no choice but to return to St. Louis.[68] At some point around this time— whether in St. Louis or Detroit or elsewhere we do not know—he sought out treatment from a chiropractor, eschewing traditional medical care, but to no avail. When Abe collapsed while dining on September 7, 1916, Minnie hurriedly summoned W. E. Barstow, a medical doctor. Barstow suspected that his patient was suffering from the perforation of an intestinal ulcer, most likely caused by an episode of typhoid. Thirty minutes after midnight on September 8, Abraham McCall died. He was just forty-eight years old.[69]

Abe left behind a widow, a fourteen-year-old son, and Nina, whose sixteenth birthday had been just six days earlier. Nina went to school when she could. All in all, the summer of 1916 was not a bad time to be an American teenager, even during days made tough by economics and personal tragedy. Affordable motion pictures were entering their "golden decade," and they were proliferating across the country, their beautiful stars gaining more fame and esteem with each passing day. Radios crackled and soda fountains gleamed with exciting possibility. Jazz and fast dancing attracted those who were able to get out of the house, and even though many students worked after school, more and more teenagers—even less-privileged teenagers—were actually able to stay in school until graduation. In June, President Wilson signed a bill incorporating the Boy Scouts of America. Six months later, Paramount released *Snow White*, a romantic, melodramatic silent film that enraptured and inspired another Midwestern teenager—a fifteen-year-old named Walt Disney. Billy Murray—the popular singer with the strong jaw—released "Pretty Baby" that year and told every woman in America, "Oh, I want a lovin' baby, and it might as well be you."

Just like millions of other young people, Nina McCall was living a life enriched and upended in these turbulent years of urbanizing, industrializing, socializing, and militarizing, of changing technology, changing lifestyles, and changing mores. For Nina, though, just like tens of thousands of other women, the true turbulence had yet to begin.

Chapter 3

"Waging War on the Women"

ONE EVENING, deep in the heart of central Michigan, Nina McCall walked home. "I was about 16 or 17," she recalled a few years later. "It was about nine o'clock at night too when I got home. I was with a fellow from Alma that I knew before, riding in a car. There was two of us girls and two boys and they stopped and told us what we had to do and we got up and walked home. We did not submit to them. I got home about nine o'clock."[1] Nina's memory is the only evidence of this episode. It is worth remembering she had every reason to defend her virtue—that she did not "submit" to male advances. Yet, accuracy aside, it is a telling episode. "This is the only time that I ever walked home," Nina insisted.[2] True or not, she felt she had to insist it was a onetime occurrence. Boys and girls in a car together, out at night—this was enough to merit suspicion. And to be suspicious was to be labeled dangerous. Perhaps someone had seen her in the car that night.

WOODROW WILSON WAS NERVOUS. This would be, he knew, one of the defining moments of his life. It was April 2, 1917, and a light rain blanketed the nation's capital, falling gently from a sky of deepening blue. Anticipation was in the air. The president had driven up Washington's wide boulevards to the floodlit Capitol that evening for one simple reason: to ask Congress to declare war. Wilson, normally so self-assured, had to pause for a moment in a side room to compose his long, sallow features. He stared hard at himself in a mirror. Once his trembling stopped, he made his way toward the grand chamber of the House of Representatives. It was time. "Gentlemen," boomed the Speaker at precisely 8:32 p.m., "the President of the United States!" The crowd rose as one. Everywhere, there were well-dressed men applauding: congressmen, cabinet officials, Supreme Court justices, diplomats, bureaucrats. It was a sea of black broadcloth, spotted with occasional flashes of color; someone had handed the senators little silk flags.[3]

Wilson spoke calmly, without rhetorical flourish, not forcefully but with clarity.[4] Every member of his audience could recollect all of the days that had led up to this one. The German acts of aggression; the fires of war careening through unmilitarized waters; the (correct) German cries that the United States was bankrolling its enemies; and then, in late February, the revelation that Germany was attempting to conspire with an admittedly uninterested Mexico to attack—attack!—American soil. The whole world was engulfed in war. Security, Wilson told the crowd, was impossible. "The world," Wilson said, "must be made safe for democracy." This was to be the line that would go down in history. Senator John Sharp Williams, the skinny old Southerner with the angry eyebrows, heard the phrase in spite of his deafness and began to clap. The entire gallery followed, bursting into thunderous applause.[5]

Continuing in his measured tone, Wilson asked Congress to send millions of American men to take part in the greatest, bloodiest conflict the world had ever seen. Four days later, Congress would comply. Cynics would later point out—and provide substantial evidence—that the arms industry—which stood to profit if the United States intervened in Europe—had considerable influence over American foreign policy, that American bankers had lent billions of dollars to England and her allies, and that these bankers had pressured Wilson to protect their loans.[6] For the moment, though, these voices were silent, or else silenced by nationalistic zeal. America was fighting to make the world safe for democracy!

Raymond Fosdick was inspired.

"THOSE OF US WHO crowded into the Capitol on the evening of April 2, 1917—and few of us are left," Fosdick wrote in his autobiography in 1958, "to hear Woodrow Wilson deliver his great war address before the joint session of Congress will never forget the impact of his moving eloquence." The speech electrified Fosdick. The seasoned investigator, so recently returned from viewing scenes of debauchery among troops stationed along the Mexican border, was moved by the "mood of dedication and crusade" that the speech created. "Before us stretched a shining prospect, and it seemed as if our generation by some divine providence had been specially chosen for great and determining events."[7]

Excited, and working quickly now, Fosdick and Newton Baker began to put Fosdick's year-old report into practice; they crafted an organization that would come to be called the Commission on Training Camp Activities. First things first, the CTCA needed members. "I am appointing a commission under the chairmanship of Mr. Raymond Fosdick," Baker wrote in mid-April to a few, select recipients, "to have charge in an advisory way of recreational activities in military camps and to study and suggest the manner of police regulations in their environments. I should be very happy indeed to have you accept membership on this commission, if your time permits." The recipients were all white men, all fabulously educated—they were YMCA officials and promoters of the "playground movement," some of the most prominent reformers in the country.[8] The commission's establishment was supported by a subcommittee of the Council of National Defense—an organization that had been created in 1916 to ready the country for war in the event it was forced to abandon its neutrality—with the ASHA's William F. Snow as its secretary. That April, Snow's subcommittee recommended that the Navy and War departments "take steps toward the prevention of venereal infections through the exclusion of prostitutes within a zone surrounding all places under their control, and by the provision of suitable recreational facilities, the control of the use of alcohol drinks, and other effective measures."[9]

On April 26, a cloudy day in the nation's capital, with the temperature inching up toward 50 degrees, seven men walked into an imposing office building on Connecticut Avenue, nestled between Farragut Square, McPherson Square, and Lafayette Square, within spitting distance of the White House.[10] The men were there for the commission's first meeting, to be held at 9:30 a.m. The seven settled around a table and began to hash out just what exactly the CTCA would do. They decided the commission would focus on four main lines of activity: (1) amusement and recreation within the camps (including reading rooms, game rooms, motion picture exhibitions, dramatics, and singing); (2) athletic activities; (3) the mobilization of recreational and social agencies outside the camps to provide "wholesome recreation and social life" for men on leave; and (4) the "regulation, inspection and control of public amusement resorts in the neighborhood of the camps." They agreed to reach out to the ASHA and Committee of Fourteen, among other groups, which would send investigators to scrutinize moral conditions around training camps and report the results to the CTCA. Two of the men would coordinate recreational activities with the YMCA; one man would liaise with college athletic leaders; another man would develop the idea of dramatic productions; yet another would help obtain motion pictures to show at camps. Fosdick and Malcolm McBride, a Cleveland industrialist, were put in charge of "restrictive measures in the communities surrounding the camps."[11]

"Restrictive measures." For the next two years, Fosdick would revolutionize the meaning of that slightly ominous phrase. He had not forgotten the profusion of STIs on the Mexican border. He had not forgotten the flagrancy of the prostitution. To prevent these evils, he would do everything in his power, which was quite a lot, as it turned out.

Decades later, Fosdick looked back and reflected: "I would have preferred to have the positive side of our work"—the education, the recreation—"take precedence over the negative aspects"—the policing—"but there was no choice, and we were launched into a resounding battle."[12]

There were still a few nuts and bolts to be worked out, however. On May 1, less than a week after the CTCA's first meeting, Senator Wesley Livsey Jones, a jowly Republican legislator from Washington and a vocal supporter of Prohibition, introduced an amendment to the Selective Service Act, the bill that would draft millions of American men into service. Jones's amendment, which, he made clear, was presented with the support of the CTCA and Council of National Defense, would allow the secretary of war "during the present war to do everything by him deemed necessary to suppress and prevent the keeping or setting up of houses of ill fame, brothels, or bawdy-houses within such distance as he may deem needful of any military camp."[13] This was not a controversial move. Fosdick had testified previously and clued the Senate in about the conditions along the Mexican border.[14] The senators abided by Jones's wish and immediately adopted the amendment, which came to be known as Section 13, without a debate or a roll call. The Senate also added another amendment onto the bill, Section 12, which endowed the secretary of war with similar authority to suppress alcohol.[15] On May 16, the House approved the bill, Sections 12 and 13 included; the Senate did likewise the next day. On May 18, President Woodrow Wilson signed it into law.[16]

Within a matter of months, Baker would write to the mayors of every large city in the country, informing them that Sections 12 and 13 applied within a five-mile radius—the so-called "moral zone"—of every military installation. The secretary of war made clear that it was the responsibility of local officials to enforce the "absolute repression" of alcohol and prostitution within these zones, and even outside the zones if such "vices" were reachable to soldiers or sailors. "This policy involves, of course, constant vigilance on the part of the police."[17]

In April 1917, the US Army was, in the words of historian Robert Ferrell, "not much of a force." It was a "miniscule organization with an aging officer corps and no experience in modern war. . . . it was so weak that the European belligerents did not consider it a military force—among armies of the world it ranked seventeenth." The day Wilson signed the declaration of war, if the War Department really tried, it could have sent overseas just twenty-four thousand soldiers, with enough ammunition to last a day and a half. Before America's entrance into the war, the president hadn't really cared about the army. It was a "quiet, sleepy place," a calm respite for old, gray-haired soldiers to dawdle until they could draw their pensions. Until quite recently, the army had been dominated by ancient Civil War veterans, chewing plug-cut tobacco and swapping stories of Gettysburg, Shiloh, and Ulysses S. Grant. From this pitiful excuse for an army, German officials felt they had nothing to fear.[18]

But with the Selective Service Act, this all changed. All across the country, war was on. By the middle of the summer, nearly two million men had been called to report for duty. Many of these men, about 10 percent of them, were black, and they were rigidly separated from whites.[19] The leader of all the troops was to be none other than John J. Pershing. To house, feed, and train these draftees, the War Department established sixteen cantonments in the northern states; the department also created sixteen National Guard camps in the southern states. The northern cantonments consisted of about twelve hundred hastily constructed wooden buildings each, including officers' quarters, recreation facilities, miles of barracks, thousands of acres of drill grounds, and a base hospital of a thousand beds. (The camps in the South consisted mostly of tents, and thus cost only one-quarter as much.) The men arrived by rail, on endless rows of train cars, hot, crowded, and with insufficient food, winding their way through the muggy countryside. Thousands of these trains had YMCA representatives on board, hard at work establishing friendly relations with soldiers—the better to inculcate them with proper, Christian morality.[20]

Upon arrival, drafted men received uniforms, a cot, and the promise of $25 a month in pay.[21] They also received a physical. Because of the sheer quantity of men arriving at cantonments, chaos and confusion ensued, and the military had to rely primarily on volunteer doctors, many of whom had received just a day or two of hasty training in how to conduct the physicals. Amid the tests for eyesight and flat feet and the like, the doctors examined the young men for STIs. The men sat on specially constructed stools, and the doctors inspected the groin area, palpated the scrotum, closely scrutinized the penis, took smears from the urethra, washed their hands, and repeated on the next man in line. Syphilis or gonorrhea was enough for a man to avoid the draft, and rumors began to spread that men were intentionally getting themselves infected.[22] Few would guess that, months later, the results of these physical examinations would propel authorities to dramatically expand the scope of the burgeoning American Plan.

BACK IN MICHIGAN, Abraham McCall's death had left his family without its primary breadwinner. Five years later, his widow, Minnie, would proudly assert that she and Abe had owned the home in which he had died. She managed to hold on to the house for more than a year after his death, until the fall of 1917. Then, she and her two children, Nina and Vern, moved to the small town of Alma just a few miles away. The family of three lived in half of a stand-alone house on Grover Avenue, where, presumably to supplement their savings, they had a boarder "for a while."[23] Nina's already unsteady school attendance ceased altogether when they moved to Alma.[24]

Grover Avenue, the McCalls' new home, bordered a part of town known as Millerville. Millerville was the closest thing Alma had to a red-light district—

the streets were poorly paved, the houses doubled as brothels, and considerable carousing took place there. It was only a block away from Alma's largest factory. "There got to be a saying that when the whistle blew at the plant, the whistle blew at the whorehouse," recalled historian David McMacken.[25] This was the neighborhood where a newly idle Nina could easily have ventured.

These were exciting times. "One by one the young men in our community were being called into service," recalled one Gratiot County woman.[26] Within days of the declaration of war, nine young men in Alma—mostly high school students—left town on a Pere Marquette train to Saginaw, where they enlisted in the navy. The town held a celebration in their honor, with red, white, and blue bunting decking the windows of shops on the main street. One of the physicians who conducted the physical examinations of enlisting men was Alma's health officer, Thomas Carney.[27]

Soon, Gratiot County had formed a three-man draft board, and hundreds of Gratiot citizens enlisted or were drafted into service.[28] With millions of men heading off to war, there were gaping holes in the labor market, and women were beginning to plug these holes with enthusiasm. Some stood behind shop counters and manned cash registers; others donned overalls and caps and hammered or soldered with the best of them, sparks flying, grease splashing.[29] In Alma, the local factories started hiring women to work in the office; soon, the bosses had no choice but to put the women on the assembly line.[30]

For those women too young to work full-time, meanwhile, the entrance into the war marked a turning point in the time line of teenage sexual liberation. As the historian Susan Ferentinos noted, "The *number* of young people experiencing physical intimacy and the *age* at which they began to do so changed around World War I. More people were exploring their sexuality before marriage; and they were doing so at a younger age than their parents had." More and more teenagers were "petting," a trend most unsettling to their elders.[31]

Trains arrived every day in Battle Creek, Michigan, a little more than a hundred miles from the McCalls' home in Gratiot County. Battle Creek housed the new, hurriedly constructed army cantonment, Camp Custer.[32] Located on loamy ground about six miles southeast of Battle Creek proper, the cantonment was situated in a rich wilderness that was also plagued by occasional sandstorms.[33] Even before the barracks were completed, the YMCA had established a hut on site.[34] By July, thousands of young men were stationed in Camp Custer, there to train hard six hours a day, march in the surrounding countryside, swim in nearby Eagle Lake, and, perhaps, meet the local women just a few miles away. Alcohol was banned in the town of Battle Creek, and "city officials are making every effort to co-operate with the military officials in keeping the city a proper place into which the 40,000 drafted men may be sent," one newspaper reported in late July.[35] Still, as one of the

CTCA's first field investigators, Walter Clarke, reported to Fosdick that summer, city officials believed "there has been an influx of immoral women into Battle Creek in preparation for the establishment of the cantonment here." There were reports of prostitutes attempting to buy houses.[36] For young men away from home for the first time, these were surely thrilling times indeed.

The thrill even reached small, provincial Alma—Nina McCall's new home. That summer the residents gathered to form the largest crowd in the town's history to see Billy Brock, the "Ace of the Air," fly his famous aeroplane; they successfully fought to acquire a baseball team from nearby Saginaw; and they saw three of Michigan's most notorious bandits arrested on city grounds. The gang of bandits, which had robbed more than fifty establishments over the past four months (including several in the nearby village of St. Louis), was perhaps more emblematic of the exciting times than most bands of brigands: the three arrested members included two women, one only fourteen years old. Young girls were doing all sorts of crazy things, many residents surely thought.[37]

LATE THAT SUMMER, agents of the federal government began fanning out across the country, spreading the command to repress prostitution like gospel.

In May, the ASHA had voted to assign two men—Walter Clarke, an intrepid young man fresh out of Harvard, and Bascom Johnson, who had so carefully scrutinized conditions in San Francisco—to work with the CTCA.[38] Though the ASHA would continue to pay their salaries, the two men would hit the streets on behalf of the commission, finding information about prostitution, STIs, alcohol, and drugs near every military camp they could reach. Their activities would mark the beginning of the CTCA's fieldwork—work that would later bring federal bureaucrats into direct contact (and conflict) with the nation's young women. The ASHA also voted to authorize William F. Snow "to carry out the plan for the employment of additional investigators."[39] In July, Snow relocated to Washington, the better to work closely with the CTCA.[40]

Bascom Johnson was a forty-year-old ASHA attorney whose scrawny, bespectacled visage belied a vital athleticism. As a prep schooler, he had won track and field competitions across New England, and he had broken the intercollegiate pole vault record while a freshman at Yale. In 1900, he represented the United States at the Paris Olympics; then he went on to law school at the University of Pennsylvania. After serving as an inspector at the federal Indian bureau, Johnson became a celebrated white slavery investigator. He drew on this experience as he set off immediately as one of the CTCA's first two field agents.[41] He began by walking up and down the seedy streets of San Francisco, ducking into fine hotels and tawdry bars, inquiring into the availability of liquor and women and reporting his findings back to Fosdick.[42]

Then he was off to Montgomery, Alabama, where he successfully pushed the city council to pass ordinances aimed at restricting prostitution, and New Orleans, where he helped to strong-arm the city's mayor into closing the notorious Storyville red-light district and arresting any remaining prostitutes.[43] Then Douglas, Arizona, and Alexandria, Louisiana; both of these closed their red-light districts as well.[44]

It is impossible to know how the residents of these red-light districts felt about officials shuttering their homes and destroying their livelihoods, but the response of a group of Washington, DC, prostitutes to that city's closure of its red-light district might offer a hint. "We must live somehow. We are human," they wrote in a powerful letter. "How many citizens will give employment to women of our class?"[45]

"How many of the women in your church would accept us into their homes—even to work?" one San Francisco prostitute asked a minister who was trying to close that city's red-light district. "You would cast us out—where to? There isn't one among us here who would not quit this life for decent work." One prostitute, she recounted, "wrote to her brother, a Methodist preacher, for help. He answered 'trust in the Lord.'"[46]

In October 1917, Johnson was promoted. His investigations and exhortations had produced "[s]uch satisfactory results," in the words of one CTCA report, that Fosdick decided to replicate them across the country. On October 1, Fosdick officially created the Law Enforcement Division within the CTCA.[47] At its head, he appointed Johnson.[48] Johnson suggested that the CTCA recruit young men—mostly lawyers—to staff the new division. Very quickly, he had some forty men working under him.[49]

Johnson and Fosdick divided the country into ten districts and put a supervisor in charge of each. Beneath that supervisor would be the field representatives. The job of the field representatives would be to investigate the presence of alcohol, prostitution, and general female promiscuity in a given area. Often, these investigators would go undercover, dressed in civilian clothes. They would be instructed to focus on the black sections of town in particular. They were empowered to threaten municipal authorities, police officials, and even judges into closing red-light districts and arresting "suspicious" women, locking up those found to be prostitutes. Cities that refused to comply could be placed "out of bounds" for soldiers, thus threatening economic prosperity, or an entire military installation could be moved. Or, as happened in Philadelphia, the CTCA could simply take over the city's police department. The field representatives were not supposed to make arrests themselves—though, as we shall see, this rule was sometimes flouted.[50]

The field representatives' on-the-ground tactics would prove to be startlingly, devastatingly successful. In San Francisco, when one CTCA field agent encountered resistance from local judges, reluctant to incarcerate women convicted of prostitution or similar offenses, he wrote threatening letters to the judges. When he raised the specter of San Francisco's military bases being removed, the judges folded quickly.[51] As 1917 continued, the San Francisco Police Department's morals squad increased its "repressive measures" targeted at young women.[52] "Much as we dislike waging war on the women," that field agent wrote to William F. Snow, "we are all of the opinion that the only way to prevent a larger influx of these women, when the camp is running full strength, is to have them, when convicted, given *jail sentences* [emphasis in original]."[53]

The CTCA's field staff was assisted by agents of the Bureau of Investigation—an arm of the Justice Department that would later be known by a different name: the Federal Bureau of Investigation.[54] FBI agents walked the streets and arrested women for violating Section 13 in cities as varied as Houston, Philadelphia, and San Francisco.[55] In some cities, agents focused particularly on the "Negro section" of town.[56] Private organizations in Chicago, San Francisco, Oregon, and elsewhere were also deputized to detain women.[57] In New York City, Committee of Fourteen agents helped arrest suspected prostitutes, and they quickly expanded their work to include Buffalo, Syracuse, Long Island, Atlantic City, and Allentown, Pennsylvania, as well.[58] These private groups also disproportionately policed nonwhite neighborhoods.[59]

The Committee of Fourteen continued to rely on Rockefeller money, and it wasn't the only group to do so. Indeed, John D. Jr. basically bankrolled the American Plan at the federal level. For the fiscal year bridging 1917 and 1918, the Rockefeller Foundation donated $145,000 to the ASHA (the equivalent of over $2.5 million in today's dollars), and Rockefeller personally gave an additional $5,000, making the association almost entirely financially dependent on the young millionaire.[60] In June, the foundation pledged up to $100,000 to support the CTCA, ASHA, and "other similar organizations that may be named by Mr. Fosdick."[61] Meanwhile, by the fall of 1917, prominent ASHA members—including Snow, Fosdick, and Johnson—were already in federal jobs. Within a matter of months, every single other member of the ASHA's staff—hundreds of individuals—would join the CTCA.[62] In order to save the federal government money, the Bureau of Social Hygiene (funded almost entirely by Rockefeller) paid Fosdick's salary, while the ASHA paid the salaries of Snow, Johnson, and many others; the association paid field secretaries assigned to the CTCA $3,000 apiece. "This cozy arrangement saved the taxpayers money," historian Abigail Claire Barnes wrote. "It also helped the American Social Hygiene Association continue its work under the aegis of a governmental agency."[63]

AND IT WASN'T JUST MALE FEDS. Beginning during these same consequential months in the early autumn of 1917, women too got in on the action.

Back in July, Maude Miner—the silver-haired head of Waverley House detention home—had written to Fosdick about the need for "protective work" for women—work to stop women from becoming prostitutes in the first place. Over the next several months, Fosdick kept receiving "serious complaints" about "young girls who were not prostitutes, but who would probably be to-morrow, and who were diseased and promiscuous." They had to be stopped. By September, Fosdick had decided to create a section within the CTCA to focus on "protective work" for women. To this Committee on Protective Work for Girls (CPWG), Fosdick appointed Miner, Martha Falconer (a prominent reformatory matron and ASHA member), Vera Cushman (an important YWCA official), Abby Rockefeller (the wife of John D. Jr.), and Ethel Sturges Dummer, a wealthy Chicagoan who had provided the money for a "detention home" for "delinquents" in the Second City.

Born in 1866, raised in Chicago, Ethel Dummer—who had heavy brows, a straight, aristocratic nose, and soulful eyes—had come of age as an activist by raising money to support child labor laws and juvenile courts.[64] She, for one, mulled over the appointment for a few days. The committee could be a cover to repress young women, not protect them. Eventually, Dummer wrote back to Fosdick: "The work you offer is somewhat appalling." Nonetheless, she added, "it is of great importance, and, feeling sure that under Maude Miner it will be not merely repressive, but constructive in a large way, I will serve on the committee on Protective Work for Girls."[65] For the moment, Dummer was alone in her doubts about the committee.

The women of the CPWG began meeting on the third floor of 130 East Twenty-Second Street in New York City, a sturdy office building just a block from the tree-lined, private Gramercy Park.[66] They started recruiting women to serve as protective officers—to hit the streets and look for women in need of protection. Dummer herself traveled to Camp Devens, in Massachusetts, to inspect conditions for women, while Miner journeyed to the Midwest.[67] They didn't trust the official statistics, so they decided to find out what was happening themselves or through the efforts of loyal female investigators.[68] They appointed investigators for communities ranging from New Jersey to California to Texas. Fosdick, for one, wanted a dozen female "protective officers" in New York City alone.[69]

The whole point was to be less punitive than the rest of the CTCA. Of course, the obvious tension was that, in order to prevent women from falling into a life of vice, the CPWG wanted to reform women, and in order to reform them, it would have to lock them up. From the very beginning, the CPWG's members described their work as, first and foremost, "secur[ing] increased facilities for the protection and care of girls" or "securing cottages and deten-tion homes where girls may be placed instead of in jails."[70] They expanded the work of the federal government from policing suspected prostitutes to polic-ing any woman suspected of having sex outside marriage.

In the first days of their work on the CPWG, its leaders hoped to "con-duct their work on an individual basis, with protective officers functioning as case workers for endangered girls," to quote historian Linda Sharon Janke.[71] Though these female workers would be empowered to arrest young women, it was not a tactic they would be encouraged to use. But, as Janke recounted, two factors forced these female officers to change their tack and embark on a system of mass arrests and incarcerations. First, Fosdick would not give the CPWG sufficient funds to hire enough protective workers to implement the individualized casework model. (The wealthy Dummer was funding the CPWG herself within a few months.)[72] Second, the women with whom CPWG protective workers interacted did not appear to be victimized girls who could be reformed; rather, they appeared to be actively rejecting middle-class sexual mores and "would require strict monitoring, controls on their be-havior, and potential incarceration."[73] As a female CTCA official would recall later, "Six months' work on the basis of protecting the supposedly good girl proved that the problem was really with the delinquent girl."[74]

Within a matter of months, Miner had dispatched seventy-five female protective workers into the field, assigning one or two to each training camp community in the country. Miner appointed four (later five) district supervi-sors to oversee the protective officers. Significantly, CPWG officials also depu-tized hundreds of other local women within camp communities to assist in protective efforts. They appointed black officers to work with black women and Hispanic officers to work with Hispanic women; it appears CPWG offi-cial Martha Falconer even supported appointing Jewish officers to work with Jewish women. These women traipsed along city pavement, looking for girls "in need of protective care, and those who are becoming delinquent," as Miner put it, but they also inspected dance halls, movie theaters, and amusement parks. They supervised female employees in camp laundries, shops, and post offices. They sought to intervene before a woman became a prostitute. One CPWG worker hid in the bushes of Boston Common, lying in wait to catch young women walking with soldiers. If a girl appeared "in danger" of falling into prostitution, the protective officer would go to her home and interrogate her mother. Yet, if a female employee or passerby appeared to be suspicious, protective officers could arrange to have her examined for STIs. Those em-ployees whom they determined to be infected were promptly fired.[75] There is no evidence of any employers resisting calls to fire infected employees.

In Battle Creek, Michigan, not too far from Nina McCall in Alma, a CPWG supervisor made a survey of the town and found, to her dismay, that the dance halls were unsupervised, the movies were uncensored, and the curfew law was unenforced. She secured the appointment of a protective officer there who was "given police power" by local authorities.[76]

Women deemed in need of reformation could also be imprisoned. CPWG officials hated the idea of women spending time in jails, so they pushed for the establishment of special "detention houses," in the model of Waverley House, to hold women gone astray. CPWG efforts resulted in the creation of special institutions to imprison so-called immoral women in places as far flung as San Antonio, Texas; Spartanburg, South Carolina; Pensacola, Florida; and Tacoma, Washington.[77] These detention houses were supposed to be temporary, not long-term.[78] Yet infected women could also be committed to reformatories, which were, by definition, for long-term moral reform. Several members of the CPWG, including Martha Falconer, had been affiliated with reformatories, and the CPWG spurred the creation of several new ones.[79] CPWG protective workers even arrested and ensured the incarceration of women who were not prostitutes but were, rather, simply considered wayward.[80]

Indeed, the CPWG contributed a great deal to the American Plan tactic of imprisoning women. As one federal official wrote in 1922, "The committee on protective work for girls, the first Federal organization to engage in work for girls in the war situation, saw the great need of the detention houses in the camp towns and succeeded in popularizing the idea."[81] Through the CPWG, prominent female reformers not only joined their male counterparts in detaining, examining, and incarcerating women on a mass scale, but also helped shape—and expand—the campaign.

IN SPITE OF THE frenetic activity within the federal government, officials knew that the brunt of the American Plan's enforcement would have to happen at the local level.

Such local work began on July 21, 1917, a somewhat windy day in San Francisco, when men from all over the state gathered in the beautiful, ornate San Francisco Board of Supervisors' chamber.[82] The California State Board of Health had collaborated with the War Department to organize this meeting to discuss how to make STI control in California more effective. The federal and state officials shared a fear: that prostitutes, as well as merely promiscuous women, were infecting the troops. This wasn't simply a threat to morality; it was a threat to the war effort. The officials decided they would have to hold a meeting. They would have to decide what to do about the "girl problem."

Everyone was present. Seated beneath sparkling chandeliers and gilt friezes, there were representatives from every city and county in the Bay Area, including mayors, city and county health officers, chiefs of police, and sheriffs. There were representatives from the army, navy, US Public Health Service (USPHS), and four members of the state board of health. Only one of the officials was a woman.[83] At 10:30 a.m., the meeting was called to order by San Francisco mayor Sunny Jim Rolph. Seated on Rolph's right was a colonel in the army, and on his left was an official from the navy.[84]

By the end of the meeting, the group had unanimously adopted seven resolutions. These called for prostitution to be "vigorously and continuously" suppressed, for local health officers to investigate rumors of infected women, and for the instruction of young people "in the advantages of a clean life and the dangers from venereal diseases." One resolution read, "Prostitutes brought to the attention of the police or health authorities are to be examined; and all persons, male and female, capable of spreading venereal diseases are to be isolated, under the provisions of the Public Health Act or local ordinance, and treated at public expense as long as there is danger in the opinion of the health officer, of their exposing others."[85] Recalling the meeting several months later, Wilbur Sawyer, the Harvard-educated secretary of the state board of health, seemed to forget the gender neutrality of this resolution, tellingly claiming that the attendees had "recommended that all low women be examined and if infected, that the women be quarantined in hospitals and treated just as in cases of any communicable disease."[86] Secretary Sawyer promised to send a copy of the resolutions to every municipal and county official in California, and to urge them, whether or not they were present at the conference, to "do their utmost" to follow them.[87]

Inspired by these resolutions, the California State Board of Health met bright and early on September 1, 1917, and formally adopted "rules and regulations . . . for the prevention of venereal diseases." These included instructing all city and county health officers to appoint inspectors and "ascertain the existence of, and immediately investigate, all suspected cases of syphilis . . . and gonococcus infection." They were to examine all "persons reasonably suspected" of having STIs and "isolate such persons whenever . . . isolation is necessary to protect the public health." They were to do this without a trial, a conviction, or even a semblance of due process. Isolated persons were not to be released until they were "non-infectious." The state's Bureau of Venereal Diseases (to which the board had just given an official office) was to issue Salvarsan to the state's hospitals, and these hospitals were instructed to appoint female physicians to examine female patients.[88] Such a plan, as one public health official wrote, made California "the first state in the Union to attack the problem actively."[89]

It was a sweeping set of resolutions, expanding the repressive campaign beyond the areas surrounding military bases—couched, for the most part, in gender-neutral language. After all, the regulations called for the examinations of all "persons reasonably suspected," not just women. Yet the next line in the regulations was, "Owing to the prevalence of such disease among prostitutes all such persons may be considered within the above class"—that is, reasonably suspected.[90] At the time, prostitution was defined as a crime of which only women could be guilty. Male prostitutes were often harassed and arrested, but this was for cross-dressing, sodomy, crimes against nature, or the like; they could not be charged with prostitution, per se. Furthermore, men patronizing prostitutes were not guilty of prostitution either, so they were not automatic STI suspects in the same way accused prostitutes were. The consequences of this language would become clear almost immediately.[91]

By September 6, just five days later, officials in San Francisco and across California were already detaining and examining "suspected" women, but not men.[92] Four days after that, on September 10, a woman in San Diego attempted to challenge her quarantine in court. This was perhaps the first legal challenge to the American Plan, and—as if to prophesy the fate of future legal challenges to the Plan—it went nowhere fast. Just two days later, on September 12, Sawyer, the secretary of the state board of health, talked the woman's lawyers into dropping the case.[93]

One lawyer, upon hearing of California's plan years later, exclaimed, "Why, a woman or a girl could be kept in prison under that regulation for years without trial!"[94]

The California practices were justified by a number of faulty assumptions. The first was that prostitutes and promiscuous women were nearly always sexually infected. Relying on studies such as those conducted at Bedford Reformatory, experts declared that some 90 percent of prostitutes were infected.[95] A poster tacked up by the New York Board of Health claimed that 95 percent of prostitutes and "easy women" were infected.[96] The second was that women bore the responsibility for spreading these infections. "Men take more precautions," declared a high-ranking federal public health official. "Women are very negligent. . . . One woman will infect ten men for every one woman that one man will infect."[97] Indeed, the perception that women were disease spreaders was so pervasive that, as the historian George Chauncey recounted, "Some gay men interested in sex with 'straight' men also portrayed themselves as less dangerous than women by arguing that there was no chance they would infect the men with the venereal diseases women were thought to carry."[98]

This plan—with its sexist assumptions and blatant disregard for due process—would soon be copied by every other state in the union. First up: Michigan.

Chapter 4

"REACHING THE WHOLE COUNTRY"

JACKSON, MICHIGAN, home to the state's first prison, and the corset-making capital of the country, was about to be host to the state's first-ever conference on STIs. It was an exciting time to be in this small city in the south of the state.

The attendees gathered at 2:00 p.m. on September 12, 1917, in the auditorium of Jackson's public library, a stout, two-story building with towering windows and columns. There were physicians, educators, pastors, labor leaders, military officials—about fifty people in all. They included Richard M. Olin, the secretary of the state board of health; several officials from the University of Michigan; and the state food commissioner. The chief of police of Bay City, where Nina McCall would later be held, showed up. Governor Albert Sleeper himself was supposed to attend, but he was called back from the road—some war emergency, apparently.[1]

Less than two weeks earlier, Jackson's health officer had been discussing STIs with the city's mayor; the deleterious effects of these maladies would be exacerbated, the two men agreed, by the influx of young men into military service. The mayor recommended that the health officer call a conference, a suggestion that the health officer heeded with relish. "There is no precedent for such a gathering," the health officer wrote to the invitees, "but never have the dangers ahead for our whole social structure been so clearly apparent." He acknowledged that, for "the first time in history, a determined stand has been taken by the authorities"—in the form of Raymond Fosdick's CTCA—but it was not enough. "We must act quickly and together."[2]

Jackson's health officer opened the meeting by stressing its importance. He was followed by an Ann Arbor reverend, and then Dr. William F. Martin, the physician at Battle Creek and a close associate of William F. Snow. "The germ which lies in venereal diseases," Martin confidently told the crowd, "is a far greater enemy than the Germans." After Martin came a CTCA official who had been stationed at Battle Creek for seven weeks. He claimed that prostitutes were bad enough, but the real danger lay in "young girls, 13 to 16 years of age, who think they are doing their bit by being of service to soldiers."

The speaking went on and on. Board of Health Secretary Olin spoke; the regent of the University of Michigan spoke.[3] A prominent female reverend took her turn to address the women of Michigan, speaking directly to the nation's "daughters"—none of whom were actually present—on behalf of the nation's "mothers." "We beg you, as American women, to do your bit in this terrible war and let the soldiers alone."[4]

At one point, a University of Michigan pathologist stood and read the resolutions adopted on September 1 by the California State Board of Health—the ones that called for the examination of "persons reasonably suspected" and the isolation of those found infected, all without due process—and urged the assembled men and women to recommend these resolutions to the Michigan State Board of Health. The attendees agreed with the pathologist and followed his recommendation to a T; they recommended to the governor that he appoint a committee of prominent citizens to recommend the resolutions to the board. "I am sure that considerable good was accomplished," Martin wrote to his comrade Snow about that decision, "especially along the lines of an effort pointing towards the quarantining of venereal diseases."[5]

The attendees ended up endorsing not just the idea of a recommending committee, but also a set of resolutions focused on prostitution. "Prostitution is to be suppressed vigorously and continuously," they resolved. Furthermore, "Prostitutes brought to the attention of the police or health authorities are to be examined; and all persons, male or female, capable of spreading venereal disease are to be isolated under the provisions of the public health act." STIs should be made reportable, they decided, and sexual abstinence should be promoted.[6]

Michigan was on its way.

THINGS MOVED QUICKLY FROM THERE. Governor Sleeper appointed the requested committee, which met on September 28 and promptly wrote a letter back to the governor. "Your Commission does not harbor the illusion that venereal disease can be eradicated from the state by any program it might suggest," they wrote. "However, it is the unanimous opinion of its members that a great deal can be done to reduce the danger of venereal infection to our soldiers and to the civil population." The committee recommended making STIs reportable, isolating infected soldiers in military hospitals for treatment, isolating infected women in "detention hospitals"—they wrote nothing explicitly about infected male civilians—and expanding the five-mile "moral zone" Newton Baker had created. The governor forwarded these recommendations to the state board of health, instructing the board to eradicate STIs "as much as possible."[7]

A month later, on October 11, the seven men composing the Michigan State Board of Health met in a Detroit office building. After a quick vote, they decided that the board's secretary, Olin, would contact every doctor in the state and instruct them that STIs were now to be considered reportable.[8] "Each physician *must* report all cases of gonorrhea or syphilis coming to his attention, together with the source of infection," Olin would write. "With this information, the State Board of Health will apprehend the person transmitting the disease, place them in a hospital and treat them at state expense." Olin's closing was significant, considering the sexism that would infect the enforcement of his order—"Yours fraternally," he signed.[9] He attached to the letter five blank forms that the physicians were to fill out and send in when they came across a patient with an STI.[10]

Finally, at a special meeting of the board several weeks later, late on the evening of November 20, the members voted to formally declare syphilis and gonorrhea "to be dangerous communicable diseases," and thus to employ investigators to find cases of STIs and to provide suitable places for quarantine and treatment.[11] What Olin had written to the state's physicians now had the backing of law: STIs would officially fall under the state's ten-year-old quarantine law, and health officers had the power to lock up carriers. Furthermore, the day before, Olin had met with members of the State Pharmaceutical Association and State Rexall Club—two organizations representing 90 percent of Michigan's druggists—and gotten the groups to agree that their members would no longer sell treatments for STIs without medical prescriptions. Thus, infected persons could not attempt to treat themselves.[12]

In the days that followed, Olin organized meetings across the state to convince both doctors and druggists to join the state board of health's crusade. At one point, he traveled to Saginaw, a bustling town bisected by the heavily polluted Saginaw River, to drum up support.[13] Saginaw was not even fifty miles from Nina McCall's hometown of St. Louis. In less than two weeks, Olin had received about a hundred letters from physicians throughout the state—"and only one out of that number has anything but commendation for our plan." In the two months following the state board's decision, doctors reported 1,650 cases of STIs to the state.[14]

Nothing in any of the decisions by the state board of health was facially discriminatory. All of the regulations governing reporting, arrest, quarantine, and treatment were gender-neutral. Perhaps Michigan women had nothing to fear. Yet, at the same time, the state defined prostitution as a crime of which only women could be guilty.[15] And, as it turned out, enforcement would be discriminatory even for women not charged with prostitution.

THE FIRST OF THE CTCA'S FIELD representatives in Michigan was a tall man of average build, with dark brown eyes and black hair. Just thirty years old, a native of Kentucky, he had avoided the draft by claiming ill health. Ironically, he was an employee of a Battle Creek sanitarium, where he was known to lead "laughing exercises"—"Here is the exercise. Try it, repeating each word four times. Ho! Hoo! He! Hi! Ha! Hah! Haw!" His name was Edwin K. Piper.[16]

Piper's boss at the sanitarium, a man named John Harvey Kellogg, had been warning CTCA officials about Battle Creek for months. He claimed prostitution, alcohol, and STIs were rampant, and were largely ignored by the city administration. This was a threat to the troops! Kellogg had warned Bascom Johnson of this in person, but Johnson felt he couldn't rely on Kellogg's verbal warnings alone.[17] He needed investigations. Another CTCA official whose ear had been bent by Kellogg wrote wistfully, "I wish we might have sent here a federal detective, who would put a big scare into the city administration. . . . At present this is being done by volunteers. If you will take this vice situation up with Mr. Fosdick, I am sure that his men can help us."[18]

In mid-October 1917, the official got his wish. William F. Snow—by then a major in the Army Sanitary Corps, just like many members of the CTCA's Law Enforcement Division—chose Piper to represent the army's new Section on Combating Venereal Diseases, as the section's man in Camp Custer. Snow also instructed Piper to report to Fosdick "for direction and authority for action."[19] Piper quickly became a lieutenant in the Army Sanitary Corps, a field representative in the CTCA, and he began reporting weekly to both Snow and Johnson.[20] It was Piper's job to investigate—and investigate he did.

In the first days of November, shortly before Olin wrote his vaguely threatening letter to the state's doctors, Piper presented himself to the major general in charge of Camp Custer, at Battle Creek. The major general told the young lieutenant that he was interested in cooperating with him, though Piper received a somewhat frostier reception when he met with the camp's surgeon later that day. Next he surveyed the town of Battle Creek.[21] Battle Creek had been Piper's home for years, but now he was looking on it with new, stern eyes. And how it had changed! By the middle of the summer, there were already nearly a thousand men stationed at Camp Custer. They put up electric lights and hung telephone wire. The government paid $50,000 to pave a road from the camp to Battle Creek proper.[22] With the completion of the road, the soldiers were connected to Battle Creek and the state beyond. When Camp Custer officials tested the men, they found truly terrifying results. A full 10 percent of them had STIs. "Their condition was so serious," the meeting minutes of the Michigan State Board of Health later noted, "that many were rejected and others put under medical treatment in military hospitals at a tremendous expense to the Federal Government."[23] Thus, men, too, were being treated in government facilities, though there was no talk of morally reform-ing them while in captivity. Furthermore, they were not forced to perform labor inside these hospitals (though they did forfeit their pay).[24]

Piper concluded his first report on November 10. He had found that the uniformed police of Battle Creek were too lax in arresting suspected pros-titutes, though there were plainclothes police who were encouragingly ac-tive. The prosecuting attorneys were similarly enthusiastic, while the mayor was less impressive. One man whom Piper consulted, a professor, estimated that there were three hundred "street solicitors active" in the city. Piper began compiling a list of places he would inspect: dance halls, hotels, lodging houses, skating rinks, social clubs, private enterprises, and on and on. He began meet-ing with civil and military authorities. He started "observing the streets in order to investigate suspicious type[s] and report violators." He concluded by recommending that the CTCA "concentrate on 'free lance' prostitution until it is cleaned up."[25] He also began scheduling trips to other Michigan cities. The CTCA's work there would not stay confined to military areas for long.

Piper took to his field investigations with uncommon vigor. Though he was based out of Battle Creek—taking up offices in the city hall—Piper criss-crossed the state, meeting with mayors, health officers, military authorities, and chiefs of police. He planned a "sweeping investigation" of prostitution and liquor cases across all of Michigan. During the months of November and December, Piper personally created a citizen's committee to combat vice in Kalamazoo, advised Bay City officials on their campaign to "clean up" vice, and personally "[o]pened [the] vice crusade in Saginaw." He cajoled police officials to arrest young women, pushed district attorneys to prosecute them, and urged mayors to shut down red-light districts. He arranged lectures on morality for thousands of soldiers. He created a "geographical directory" of local prostitutes, which he updated lovingly. He took time to scour dance halls and skating rinks.[26]

It was through the actions of men like Piper that the CTCA helped pro-mote and expand the repression of prostitution, and the American Plan, around the country. Yet there appears to have been no aspect of investigat-ing he enjoyed more than walking the streets at night, looking for women to detain.

Piper routinely joined Camp Custer's provost marshal, proceeding care-fully down the dark streets of the town. He would help take "suspicious" women into custody and demand that health officials examine them for STIs.[27] After Piper excitedly told Bascom Johnson that "we" made the arrests and asked permission to hire a "small staff of intelligent privates or non-commissioned officers who will work on the streets at night under my direction," Johnson was forced to put him in his place.[28] "It was my understanding that you had already been informed that you have no power to make arrests," Johnson wrote in late November. "Wherever evidence of the violations of the law come to your notice, you should place such evidence before the proper authorities, requesting them to take action. Your chief function in law enforcement is to secure action by these authorities and to coordinate wherever possible the activities of the Military Police, local police, and the Department of Justice, in securing law enforcement."[29] In other words, there were plenty of authorities arresting women already. Nonetheless, in the weeks that followed, Piper continued his own on-the-ground investigations virtually every night. He continued scrutinizing rooming houses, ordering raids, ordering arrests, and even securing evidence for the police or Bureau of Investigation.[30]

In mid-December, a CTCA higher-up visited Michigan to monitor Piper's progress. "Lieutenant Piper is doing excellent work and is rapidly organizing various forces," he reported back to headquarters. The CTCA administrator was so busy, on account of his investigations and meetings, that he had no time to inspect the text of Michigan's statutes and board of health resolutions. "But from what I learned," he concluded in his report, "they are admirably suited to compel examination, quarantine, and internment of all persons venereal[ly] diseased."[31]

Yet to William F. Snow, they weren't enough.

BILL SNOW, as his friends called him, was worried. One can easily imagine his fleshy forehead wrinkled with concern. The organizations he had come to Washington, DC, to work with—especially the CTCA—were too narrow in their focus: they were only concerned with wiping out prostitution, drunkenness, and STIs in the areas around military bases. But, during the long summer of 1917, the short and stumpy Snow had learned something that troubled him deeply: the medical examinations of drafted men had revealed that most STIs originated not near military bases, but in the draftees' hometowns. As many as five in six infections came from the hometowns; in some camps, one in four draftees arrived at the military bases already infected. This knowledge filled Snow with a sense of urgency. Something had to be done, and that something—whatever it was—could not just be confined to the five miles around military areas. Somehow, he had to "reach every community of any size within a fifty or hundred mile radius of every camp and cantonment in this country," one associate later wrote. "To all intents and purposes, this meant reaching the whole country, and at the earliest moment possible."[32] This was a daunting task, yet Snow would not be deterred. In fact, he was known to be so relentless and indefatigable that during this period, he acquired a new nickname: "The Driven Snow."[33]

Snow still ran a subcommittee on STIs within Woodrow Wilson's Council of National Defense; fellow members included Raymond Fosdick, Bascom Johnson, Jerome Greene (of the ASHA and Rockefeller Foundation), Walter Clarke (the CTCA's first field investigator, besides Johnson), and Hugh Cumming (a US Public Health Service surgeon who, in a few years, would be surgeon general). Snow obtained for the committee some ASHA offices in New York, and its members, led by Snow, embarked on an ambitious letter-writing campaign. They sent thousands and thousands of letters and pamphlets to individuals in more than nine hundred communities across the country. They drew up a list of thousands of prominent doctors, lawyers, and businessmen and wrote to each and every one of them, cluing them in about "the single greatest menace to our National health and efficiency," as the form letter went: syphilis and gonorrhea.[34]

In December, Snow sent a letter to every state board of health in the country. "What is being done within the camps and in communities in the vicinity of [military] camps," he wrote, "is insufficient." Most infections came from civil life. This necessitated "a direct attack on venereal diseases as a public health measure." Snow attached to his letter the plans for attacking STIs from two states and one city "which have impressed us as being especially well-prepared." One of the states was Michigan. "We call particular attention to the program adopted in California," he continued. It was California's plan, after all, that first ordered the examination of "persons reasonably suspected" and the incarceration of those found infected. Snow asked each state board to send him a progress report.[35]

Less than a month later, Surgeon General Rupert Blue sent a telegram, a letter, and a memorandum to health officers in every state in the country. Together, these communiqués demanded that the states quarantine infected persons, as well as "[t]hose who are careless or willful in the distribution of these infections through promiscuity." Furthermore, "all persons arrested" (apparently for any crime) were to be examined for STIs.[36] Every governor in the nation received a memorandum calling for "the suppression of prostitution" and "the arrest and examination of prostitutes and the isolation and treatment in public institutions of those affected." Still further, the memo demanded "the commitment to institutions of non-diseased prostitutes for industrial training and for the commitment of all feeble-minded prostitutes to custodial care." Just how such measures would eliminate STIs was left unstated.[37]

All of these missives received a "hearty and universal response," in the words of one US Public Health Service official. Indeed, state officials began writing to the federal government, requesting specific wording for laws they could pass.[38]

Snow looked to California for help. He convinced his old friend Wilbur Sawyer, secretary of the California State Board of Health, to leave Sacramento and join Bascom Johnson in Washington to craft the requested law.[39] On January 22, 1918, Sawyer resigned his post on the state board of health, received a wristwatch, and arranged to journey to the nation's capital by train.[40] He arrived at 11:00 p.m. on January 31—cold, behind schedule, and probably already pining for his wife. In the months to come, he would write her frequent, ardent love letters.[41] Five days after arriving, on February 4, Sawyer received a telegram that his brother's only daughter had been run over and killed by an electric train, two days before her seventh birthday. So dedicated was Sawyer to his work that he stayed in Washington and missed the funeral.[42]

Sawyer and Johnson would work well together. Both had begun battling STIs in California; both were bald, bespectacled elites. They quickly began working on "the preparation of models for state legislation, regulations for state boards of health and city ordinances for venereal disease control," as Sawyer put it.[43] Throughout February and March, they studied laws across the country, refining and perfecting a "model law" and drawing up model "rules and regulations" as well. With the help of Snow, they collected at least three copies of "all laws, ordinances, and health regulations, now in force and those planned or projected, providing for (1) the reporting of venereal diseases and (2) the quarantine of persons infected with these diseases when necessary for the protection of the public health, (3) the prevention through other measures of venereal diseases."[44] They buried themselves in paper, drowned themselves in ink, became conversant in the language of laws.[45]

By the end of March, Sawyer and Johnson were done. They had created what one official called "a 'model law' to serve as a board of health regulation, or still better, as a state law for the control of venereal diseases."[46] On March 29, 1918, the US Public Health Service published the model law, which included twelve recommendations (borrowing heavily from the California State Board of Health's regulations):

1. Venereal diseases to be reported (by name, not merely number).
2. Patients to be given information concerning the nature of their diseases and the necessity for treatment until cured.
3. Investigation of cases with the view of obtaining information as to the sources of infection: "Local health officers are hereby empowered and directed to make such examinations of persons reasonably suspected of having syphilis, gonorrhea, or chancroid. [Chancroid was another STI that officials feared at the time, though it was far less common than syphilis or gonorrhea. It is characterized by painful open sores on the genitalia.] . . . Owing to the prevalence of such diseases among prostitutes and persons associated with them, all such persons are to be considered within the above class."

4. Provision for the protection of others from infection by venereally diseased persons by means of:
5. Quarantine of such infected persons who by their habits are a menace to others;
6. By measures to fix the responsibility of a person about to be released from quarantine so that he or she should be compelled to continue treatment until cured.
7. Conditions which make it possible to preserve secret the name of the person having venereal disease so long as such person does not menace the public by his habits.
8. Prohibition of drug stores' prescribing for venereal diseases.
9. The spread of venereal diseases to be declared unlawful.
10. Prostitution declared a prolific source of venereal disease and its repression to be considered a public health measure.
11. Certificates of freedom from venereal diseases prohibited.
12. Records to be secret.[47]

State health officers flooded the USPHS offices with positive responses and appeals for help implementing the suggestions. The office received so many responses, in fact, that a surgeon stationed in Leavenworth, Kansas, was called back to headquarters and reassigned to run the USPHS's legislation campaign.[48]

To further push the states along, on April 3, Attorney General Thomas Watt Gregory—a thin, severe Mississippian—wrote a letter to every US attorney in the country. The government was "engaged in an aggressive and organized campaign against the spread and for the cure of venereal diseases," he wrote, "and as prostitution is a prolific source of these diseases, this campaign includes both the suppression of prostitution, and the medical examination, quarantine and cure of prostitutes afflicted with such diseases." He continued:

> You are, therefore, instructed in the cases of all persons arrested under the foregoing section and regulations, to arrange for the immediate reporting of all such persons to the local or State health authorities, in order that these authorities may have opportunity, under local health laws, to cause medical examinations of such persons to be made and to enforce such health laws, regulations, or ordinances relative to quarantine, treatment and other disease control measures. Pending the examination, isolation and treatment by the health authorities, the prosecution should be suspended, to be resumed when the health authorities discharge the defendant from the hospital or other institution to which she may have been sent by them.

In other words, infected women would be locked up without trials. If local officials refused to cooperate, Gregory wrote to the US attorneys, report them to the federal government.[49] He concluded with an attachment assuring the US attorneys that the constitutionality of this scheme was "clear."[50] That same day, Gregory sent another letter to all US district judges, urging them not to interfere with the examinations, deferred prosecutions, or incarcerations sans due process. Prostitution, he wrote, was "a prolific source of venereal disease." The attorney general felt, therefore, "that my Department, as well as my courts, should do all within their power to minimize this evil."[51]

States began adopting the model law and regulations with alacrity. One of the first states to do so was New York, where an ASHA official working with the CTCA sought the reintroduction of "Old Clause 79."[52] The head of the Committee of Fourteen keenly remembered the battles of years past and favored a different strategy. "I cannot agree with you that this is a time when we can secure a re-adoption of Clause 79 of the Inferior Criminal Courts Act," he wrote to the ASHA man. "The opposition to the clause which resulted in the case, as a result of which it was held to be unconstitutional, came from the suffrage group and there is no reason to believe that the group would be any more receptive at this time to an amendment which must necessarily seem to the average person to oppress the women more than the men." Rather, he thought that "pressure should be brought to bear upon the Health Commissioner" so that he would designate any woman "suspected of prostitution to be a venereal suspect and to require that she submit to the taking of a Wasserman test."

"In other words," he concluded, "the proceedings should be on the basis of health and not as a criminal offense."[53] With extensive lobbying from the CTCA, New York passed such a health law just a few weeks later.[54] State and local officials began locking hundreds of infected women in a number of institutions, including many established reformatories, such as the storied Bedford Reformatory.[55]

ON FEBRUARY 8, 1918, a chilly, snowy day with temperatures hovering around 10 degrees, Richard M. Olin, secretary of the Michigan State Board of Health, held a conference in the office of Bay City mayor Robert Mundy.[56] Bay City was a thriving city of nearly fifty thousand people, built along the Saginaw River, which flowed into Saginaw Bay, which became Lake Huron.[57] It had also been home to a red-light district for more than four decades.[58] All of the city's heavyweights were present that day: the chief of police, the sheriff, several city councilmen, and Dr. J. A. Keho, the secretary of the local board of health. Olin, who was by now devoting himself to the antivice campaign essentially full-time, had come to Bay City to advise local officials about how best to combat STIs and prostitution.[59] Two months before, at the urging of CTCA field representative Edwin Piper, Bay City officials had ordered a "clean up" of the city.[60]

A pudgy man with blue eyes and light hair, Olin had been born forty-two years earlier in New York. He had come to Michigan decades before this wintry day, after attending the medical school of New York University, and he had worked for several years as a physician in Battle Creek. Now he was the secretary of the state board of health, in charge of evangelizing its policies all across Michigan.[61] And Olin was proud of his state. "Camp Custer is more free from vice contamination than any other cantonment in this country," he told his Bay City audience, somewhat hyperbolically. "This condition is due to a big campaign that has been undertaken to protect the soldier boys from disease, and we are proud of the fact that Michigan was the first to grapple with the menace and point the way to other states." But Olin also emphasized that there was work yet to be done—reform work. "Our purpose is not only to eradicate communicable social diseases as far as possible," he said, "but likewise to place women back on their feet so that they may make an honest respectable livelihood for themselves, and the state is going to help them to do so."[62] In spite of the state's gender-neutral law concerning those "communicable social diseases," Olin was clearly more preoccupied with infected women.

Olin had just hired Katharine Ostrander, a Hull House veteran and the daughter of the chief justice of Michigan's supreme court, as the director of the social service department for the state board of health. Her job would be to "assist women who are being treated in the venereal disease hospitals maintained by the state board of health to obtain employment."[63] Enthusiastic, Ostrander had written to Raymond Fosdick on January 23, asking for help.[64] Two days later, Edwin Piper was transferred out of Michigan to a military base in Alabama.[65] It was a time of great change in the Michigan anti-STI campaign when Olin went to Bay City to speak.

Gazing out before his expectant audience that chilly February day, Olin complimented Bay City's antivice work thus far and noted approvingly that the city already had a "well equipped detention hospital," as one newspaper put it. This detention hospital had been built in 1911 to house patients with other contagious diseases, such as smallpox, scarlet fever, and diphtheria.[66] Could Bay City not use this detention hospital to house sexually infected women from other cities across the state? To sweeten the deal, Olin named a "liberal price to be paid [to the city] for such accommodations." Mayor Mundy and health officer Keho seemed to approve of the plan and said they would take it under advisement.[67]

By this time, detention facilities for infected women were a major concern, in Michigan and in the rest of the country. In early January, after Olin had written to physicians that the state's "plan is to apprehend and place in hospitals . . . all carriers of these diseases that are liable to infect others," Detroit had set aside fifty beds for venereally infected persons, and another fifty had been contributed by Ann Arbor.[68] But it wasn't enough. The spacious and underutilized Bay City Detention Hospital looked, to Olin, very appealing. Whether Bay City officials decided to heed his request would have important ramifications for women across Michigan—including a certain seventeen-year-old in Alma.[69]

On the national stage, Fosdick was thinking along the same lines as Olin. He was vexed by "the question of the custody and rehabilitation of the girls whose commitment to institutions was found necessary," as he later put it. "The jails were full, and the local authorities were unable to handle those sent to them by the courts." Fosdick recalled a particularly depressing visit to a dilapidated internment facility for infected women in Newport News, Virginia. Inspecting the facility's interior, Fosdick was appalled to find that "every single inch of floor space on three floors was covered with mattresses in an attempt to provide for the inmates."[70]

But he knew what to do. Fosdick decided to request funds to construct detention houses for infected women. Inside these detention houses, of which Maude Miner's Waverley House was an early prototype, women could be held while authorities examined them for STIs and inspected their social and sexual backgrounds. Women in need of greater reformation, or medical treatment, could be held in more long-term facilities: reformatories, such as Bedford Hills in New York, which could not only treat women but also teach them proper morality. Fosdick ran this idea by Miner and Bascom Johnson, and both approved.[71]

When formulating this plan, Fosdick kept his keen eye on one particularly pressing situation. "In South Carolina," he wrote, "where there are three camps and a Navy yard there is no reformatory for girls. An urgent request comes from the Governor of South Carolina to aid in establishing such a reformatory. A bill to provide for it is now before the State Legislature. If help can be secured for the erection of a building, assurance is given that the bill will be passed and provision made for its maintenance."[72]

Mere days after Fosdick drafted his request for funds, South Carolina would be home to a dramatic emergency that would painfully illustrate just how much detention houses and reformatories were needed.

And just one day after Olin approached Bay City officials about using their detention hospital to imprison infected women from across Michigan, on February 9, the city and the state board of health reached an agreement.

Physicians from across the state could send women to the Bay City Detention Hospital, and, in exchange, the city would receive from the state $15 per patient, per week—a tidy sum.[73] And a motivation to lock up as many women as possible. As the *Bay City Times Tribune* noted, "This pays all the expense connected therewith and leaves a nice profit for the city besides."[74]

CAMP SEVIER, located a handful of miles outside Greenville, South Carolina, was a tidy collection of row after row of identical, triangular tents, surrounded by telephone poles, long wooden administrative buildings, and a smattering of sparse trees.[75] Ever since the men of the 30th Infantry Division had arrived there for training in the humid summer of 1917, thousands of young women had flocked to the camp, and to nearby Greenville, to work in the laundry, the mess hall, the hospital, or the neighboring businesses.[76] This had terrified town officials, as well as bureaucrats back in Washington. These women might infect the soldiers![77]

Then, in February 1918, either fifteen, nineteen, or twenty-four "girls"— reports of the exact number varied—were arrested for violating Section 13 of the Selective Service Act—the section that empowered the federal government to ban prostitution around training camps. After a trial in federal court, the girls were sentenced to a year's imprisonment. Yet South Carolina lacked suitable facilities, so the judge, the local district attorney, or the Justice Department—reports varied yet again—ordered that they serve out their sentences in the National Training School for Girls in the nation's capital. Arriving in DC, officials discovered the training school was filled to capacity. Finally, officials found space for the girls in the Massachusetts Reformatory for Women at Framingham, a massive stone building that had been in operation since 1877.[78] The Massachusetts Reformatory, which sat on thirty leafy acres and provided such amenities as iron bedsteads and "private rooms," was more than nine hundred miles from the girls' homes in Greenville.[79]

Who were these girls? A CPWG memo from February 20, 1918, suggests that most of them were poor; several had been working in factories since the ages of eight or nine. The CPWG was aware that some were not prostitutes or even sexually infected: Juanita Wright, a twenty-year-old "Indian girl," had committed the crime of simply living with a soldier. And most of the "girls" truly were girls—Lois Sarratt, "immoral since eleven years of age . . . leading life of prostitution since thirteen years of age" was just fifteen; Marie Gosnell, arrested some twenty-five times, a sexually infected prostitute (according to the report, at least), was only thirteen.[80] These descriptions fit neatly within a stunning pattern among professional reformers and protective workers of the time: to record for any infected woman the age of her first "sex offense" or "sex delinquency," as reports tellingly phrased it. The age listed for a first "of-fense" or "delinquency" was often as low as seven.[81] Reformers saw what they expected to see. A seven-year-old girl was not a victim; she was a delinquent.[82]

The South Carolina episode vividly illustrated to the War Department "the lack of institutional facilities for the handling of the camp-girl problem," as one female federal official put it. Because of this incident, later in February President Wilson allotted $250,000 from his National Security and Defense Fund, a multimillion-dollar wartime cash reserve for the president to disburse at his discretion, for the construction of new facilities for "the custody and re-habilitation of girls and women who proved to be a menace to the health and morals of the men in training," in the words of the same official. To oversee this massive construction effort, Fosdick would create a Section on Reforma-tories and Detention Houses within the CTCA.[83]

Significantly, Fosdick placed the new section under Bascom Johnson's Law Enforcement Division of the CTCA, not Maude Miner's CPWG. Fosdick appointed at its head Martha Falconer, formerly the matron of a reformatory and a member of the CPWG.[84] The section would oversee the construction of new facilities to house infected women or women imagined as otherwise dan-gerous. Fosdick didn't stop there. In late March, he decided to fold William F. Snow's subcommittee on STIs into the CTCA to focus on sex education for soldiers and civilians.[85]

WATCHING ALL THIS, Maude Miner despaired. More and more, she was wor-ried. And she was angry. She and Falconer just didn't see eye to eye. While Miner, the head of the CPWG, wanted to protect young women from falling into a life of vice, Falconer was far too interested in law enforcement work. Miner wanted to use the $250,000 to intervene before women turned to vice, or house them only temporarily; Falconer wanted to hold young women long term in order to "reform" them.[86]

Martha Falconer—an idealistic, middle-aged Quaker from Philadel-phia—wanted to ensure that a situation like that in South Carolina never oc-curred again, so she set to work funding or constructing reformatories with a vengeance. Not every city had an isolation facility already available, as Bay City did. Starting in April 1918, and over the following two years, Falconer would disburse almost half a million dollars to construct twenty-three new detention houses and four new reformatories, as well as expand sixteen ex-isting detention institutions. A lot of this money went toward transforming brothels into internment facilities.[87] "With large reception rooms, many bed-rooms, and a disproportionately high number of bathrooms," wrote the his-torian Mara L. Keire, "brothels made ideal detention houses. Government contractors usually only needed to fit the brothel with an infirmary and add a high wall topped with barbed wire to complete the conversion."[88] A majority of these detention facilities had barbed wire, armed guards, or both. Over those two years, these institutions housed eighteen thousand women—women who had been arrested by CTCA officials, military police, local police, and municipal, state, and federal public health authorities.[89] And this number says nothing of the women incarcerated in institutions that did not receive federal funding, such as the Bay City Detention Hospital. Some of these local institutions, like the one in Bay City, held only women detained under the American Plan, while others, like Bedford, held women detained under the Plan together with other women (convicted of offenses like prostitution, disorderly conduct, and vagrancy).

Significantly, Falconer chose to lavish money on the South and give local officials carte blanche to use it; she also left them in charge of the new institutions. Thus, she funded racial segregation. Back in the city of Greenville, South Carolina, for instance, Falconer funded a renovated detention house for white women, but incarcerated black women still had to languish in the "stockade"—a single, unhygienic room. In nearby Spartanburg, there was a detention home for whites, but black women detained under the American Plan were sent to jail, where they were whipped mercilessly.[90] Some federally funded institutions were supposed to admit nonwhite women, but local authorities chose to keep them all white.[91]

Miner saw all this happening before it even started. In February 1918, she had written to Fosdick, urging him to focus on the social work aspect of addressing the "girl problem" and expressing her hope that the federal government could be a "powerful positive force among girls."[92] When Fosdick failed to heed her request, Miner objected in a more irrevocable way. On April 9, 1918, she resigned. "Believing that I can be of greater service to the girlhood of the country by withdrawing from the Commission at this time," she closed, "I beg to be released."[93] Fosdick quickly wrote back, praising Miner for "mapp[ing] out the work for us," which she probably did not take as the compliment he had intended.[94]

Fosdick had missed the point. In a private letter, Miner wrote to Ethel Sturges Dummer that she had "realiz[ed] that the protection of girls was not really the thing which was sought by the Commission."[95] She was right. In April, Fosdick decided to reorganize the CTCA and formally change the role of the CPWG. It was placed under the Law Enforcement Division, along with Falconer's division. As historian Nancy Bristow dryly noted, "This section soon changed its name to the Section on Women and Girls"—eliminating the word protective—"perhaps because it did so little protective work."[96] As the summer of 1918 progressed, the female agents oversaw the construction of detention houses and supervised the implementation of "reasonable suspicion" laws.[97]

Miner returned to New York, where she resumed her positions supervising both Waverley House and the Girls' Protective League, a local agency. Ironically, many women detained in New York under the American Plan were incarcerated in Waverley House. Girls' Protective League workers, meanwhile, had been given police power by the mayor and enthusiastically engaged in the kind of maternal "protective work" Miner had tried to get the CPWG to do—attempting to better young women's lives but also sometimes sending them to institutions like Waverley House, for their own good, of course.[98]

The CTCA's reorganization was no mere bureaucratic machination; it represented a deliberate reorientation of the CTCA's purpose. Snow's scheme to expand the American Plan beyond the borders of military zones had been institutionalized. More workers were under the umbrella of "law enforcement" than ever before. No longer were female field-workers or reformatory matrons expected to save vulnerable, reformable young women. First and foremost, they were expected to get those deviant, delinquent, dangerous girls off the streets.

IT WAS AROUND THIS time that Alma, Michigan—many miles from the nearest military base—began to be flooded with soldiers. They arrived by the dozens, riding the Pere Marquette railroad straight into town. That all of these soldiers were gathering in this small, rural community might seem confusing—until one hears the tale of the Republic Motor Truck Company, a true American Cinderella story.

Founded in 1913 by an Alma inventor who wanted to mass-produce this noisy new vehicle, Republic was besieged by orders from the very start. "The work force quickly grew from 30 to 100," wrote the historian David McMacken. "Then to 200." The company's founder adopted Henry Ford's assembly-line process, and Republic's factory expanded pretty much continuously. "By 1916, the undreamable had happened. Republic Truck had become the largest exclusive manufacturer of trucks in the world. Alma was awash in money. . . . Every ninth truck in America was a Republic." Hundreds of workers rushed in to work for Republic; they crowded into every available room in Alma and neighboring St. Louis. New homes sprang up. To accommodate the company, Alma paved its roads and installed a sewage system. The city constructed a new school, Republic School, which stands to this day.[99]

When Newton Baker's War Department decided to order tens of thousands of trucks for the soldiers in Europe, Republic was one of the lucky companies to be blessed with government business. More and more workers crowded into Alma and nearby St. Louis to build the canopy-covered Liberty trucks, which were sturdy even though they lacked both doors and windshields. At peak production, perhaps two thousand of the town's eight thousand residents worked for Republic on one long shift; the factory couldn't be illuminated at night. Eventually, one of these workers would be Nina's younger brother, Vern. When it became clear that the trucks would be difficult to transport by train, the soldiers were sent to Alma. There, young troops who had grown up riding horses took classes to learn how to drive and take care of the trucks; two men were assigned to each truck, and they drove them from Alma to the East Coast in forty-truck conveys, where the trucks were disassembled, boxed, and shipped to France.[100]

It took weeks to complete all these trucks, however, and the soldiers had free time on their hands. Bored young men took to walking up and down Superior Street. This was dangerous. Desperate to keep the troops on the straight and narrow, the town organized chaperoned dances in the Republic factory's cafeteria. "But," recounted McMacken, "at the same time, girls arrived. And with the girls came the clap." Soon, horrified Almans were witnessing young ladies accompanying the soldiers up and down Superior Street. The town fathers knew they had to do something about this behavior. According to later reports, the War Department also became interested in the alarming presence of young women in Alma.[101]

On May 16, 1918, an editorial appeared in the *Alma Record* entitled "Action Is Needed." The weekly newspaper demanded that the city council immediately take "drastic action" and pass an ordinance to "do away with the present state of affairs in the city, where men now seem to think that they are privileged to accost ladies and young girls at any time of day or night and invite them to go out for a good time." But this ordinance wasn't just to protect the women; it was to protect the troops. "The presence of so many men in the city at the present time, including a number of soldiers, is said to be bringing women of an unsavory reputation into the city frequently," continued the editorial. "[T]he city must meet such problems."[102]

That same day, the *Record* ran a brief article suggesting that the city was, to some extent, already meeting the sticky situation head on. "It is understood that Dr. T.J. Carney, head of the health department of this city, is determined that some of the existing conditions here shall cease at once," reported the newspaper, a tad euphemistically, "and as a result several parties have been ordered to clean up their premises within the next few days. Arrests will follow if the orders are not obeyed, it is reported."[103]

Dr. Thomas J. Carney was more than just the local health officer; he was a man on a mission, a doctor with an almost messianic devotion to protecting the public health. He had been born in 1869 in Watkins Glen, New York, and raised on a homestead that had belonged to the Carneys for half a century. He attended a seminary and preparatory school, and then matriculated to Cornell and to Long Island Medical College. After practicing at New York's Women's Hospital and elsewhere for several years, he moved to Alma in 1915, to accept a position as city health officer—"a job no other physician wanted," as one newspaper put it. Alma was growing rapidly in those days, and the town was far from sanitary. "Summer breezes carried a pungent odor in Alma that summer," one journalist recalled. Garbage was everywhere, as were cow and horse dung; Almans were selling unpasteurized milk to their neighbors. "He soon found himself in a maelstrom of anger from citizens who for years had gotten away with these unsanitary conditions at their homes," wrote McMacken. Carney ordered the townsfolk to clean up their privies, their waste, and their animals' droppings. Known to bring a fist down on his desk to emphasize a self-righteous point, Carney made many, many enemies, yet he persisted. Carney was, by nature, a rule follower, and he was obsessed with public health.[104]

It was this obsessiveness that would later result in the incarceration of dozens of young women, including Nina McCall—and then, just a little thereafter, in Carney himself being practically run out of town.

JULY 9, 1918, was a glorious day in the nation's capital. The weather was perfect—clear and cool, with gentle breezes rippling the Potomac. While DC was usually a veritable swamp in the summer, the cool spell was making it, in the words of the *Evening Star*, "a regular summer resort."[105] Washingtonians out on the street enjoying the day might have glimpsed a hopeful headline from newsstands: "Smashing Blow Again Delivered Against Huns."[106]

One development that did not make the front page, but that was no less significant, occurred that day when President Woodrow Wilson signed into law the Army Appropriations Act of 1919—the bill funding the army for the next year. This law included an amendment known as the Chamberlain-Kahn Act, which had passed both houses of Congress unanimously and without debate the previous month.[107]

The Chamberlain-Kahn Act did many things: it created an "Interdepartmental Social Hygiene Board," to consist of the secretaries of war, the navy, and the treasury; the surgeon general of the United States; and the surgeons general (that is, chief medical officers) of the army and navy. The new board was in charge of disbursing money to the states from a $1 million fund appropriated by the act, to be used "for the purpose of assisting the various States in caring for civilian persons whose detention, isolation, quarantine, or commitment to institutions may be found necessary for the protection of the military and naval forces of the United States against venereal diseases." The act further set aside $1 million for the states to use "in the prevention, control, and treatment of venereal diseases," $100,000 to be paid to universities for research on STIs, and $300,000 for developing "effective educational measures in the prevention of venereal diseases." (This money would be appropriated each year for two years.) Finally, the act created the Division of Venereal Diseases within the USPHS to study STIs, help states prevent STIs, and eliminate the spread of STIs across state lines.[108]

This law was the result of months of dreaming and scheming. The original act had been written by an associate of William F. Snow's, with Snow's input.[109] After a thick-necked, brutish congressman from Seattle proposed a far more draconian bill calling for a nationwide network of "detention and internment stations and hospitals" for prostitutes and infected women, as well as female adulterers and promiscuous women, Snow and his colleagues revised their bill to make it match that more repressive version, adding the language about internment facilities.[110] Snow, Bascom Johnson, and others then appeared before Congress to lobby for it.[111] When they heard a rumor that Jeanette Rankin, the only female member of Congress, was going to oppose the bill, they dispatched an ally to meet with Rankin and assuage her fears.[112] Finally, the act sailed through.

The new Division of Venereal Diseases consisted of a growing staff of earnest young medical officers, each with either two silver bars or one gold leaf emblazoned across his chest. Soon, in dozens of states, these young officers would be allowed to run state bureaus of venereal diseases directly. From these positions, they would lobby for the "enforcement by state and municipal officials of laws and ordinances directed against prostitution in all its phases," as well as "the establishment and management of institutions for the rehabilitation of venereally infected persons."[113] The division also employed black officers "to present this program to their own race."[114] The new Interdepartmental Social Hygiene Board, meanwhile, was armed with millions of dollars it could disburse to the states. With Snow as its secretary, the board announced that in order for states to qualify for any of the cash, they would have to pass a law making STIs reportable, making the transmission of STIs illegal, mandating "cooperation with local civil authorities in their efforts to suppress public and clandestine prostitution," and agreeing to cooperation in the "isolation and treatment in detention hospitals of infected persons who are unable or unwilling to take measures to prevent themselves becoming a menace to others."[115] Thus, not only did the board—and by extension the federal government—fund the American Plan locally, it also used its money to pressure states into enforcing it. In 1918, Michigan received $30,544.47 from the board.[116]

By the middle of 1918, officials in virtually every state in the union were hard at work detaining, examining, and locking up suspicious women. In

Texas and in Massachusetts, in Florida and in Montana, in communities with military camps and in those without, in communities with a federal official present and in those without, women were routinely denied due process and imprisoned in jails, detention homes, and reformatories for nothing more than having a medical condition.

Officials even enforced the American Plan outside the continental United States. In Puerto Rico, for instance, Howard Kern—the island's white, Harvard-educated, Wilson-appointed attorney general—launched an island-wide campaign to "cleanse prostitutes from every town and barrio." At the urging of American officials (including the surgeon general), Kern announced that "suspect" women would be detained and forcibly examined for STIs. In the months that followed, police all across Puerto Rico captured more than a thousand working-class women, often simply for having nonmarital sex, and then had them examined; men were never treated like this. Infected women were held in disgusting cells while they were treated. As the historian Eileen Suárez Findlay recounted, "Across the island, women reformers leaped to help in surveillance activities as their counterparts had done in the United States." Elite women established "feminist police" forces in San Juan, Arecibo, and Mayaguez to search for suspected women.[117]

Authorities also enforced the American Plan, at least to some extent, in the many other places the United States had power—that is to say, its imperial holdings. Health officials in the territory of Hawaii adopted Plan laws as early as April 1918, though it is unclear how closely they were followed.[118] Americans in the Dominican Republic were more enthusiastic in their efforts to round up suspected prostitutes and jail women with STIs, though, as the historian Rebecca Lord documents, such efforts were not launched in earnest until late 1919, because of the "slow pace of . . . or even passive resistance by" Dominican authorities.[119] American officials attempted to repress prostitution in the Panama Canal Zone, ordering the Panamanian authorities to deport more than three hundred black migrant women they accused of prostitution and infecting American soldiers with STIs. (The Panamanians refused.)[120] The Americans were more effective in the Philippines, successfully demanding that local authorities shutter the brothels and deport a number of alleged prostitutes.[121]

Not only did the Plan influence conditions in America's colonial holdings, but those holdings influenced the Plan. A number of the Plan's most important federal administrators had begun their careers as public health officers in the Philippines, Panama, Hawaii, and elsewhere, and this service shaped their conceptions of public health, darker-skinned peoples, and themselves. These men routinely imposed quarantines on the natives of these lands and carefully scrutinized their daily lives; one senior Plan administrator got his start decades earlier by dictating the manner in which Filipinos were allowed to defecate. These white men returned to the United States believing they had the ability, and the burden, to impose "proper" behavior on others—especially those with darker skin.[122]

WITH ALL OF THE SOLDIERS flocking to Michigan, and to Alma in particular, it was inevitable that Nina McCall would come across some of them. "In the summer of 1918," she recalled, "there were a great many soldiers in Alma. I seen them there; I knew they were there. I had heard about them being there and I seen them sometimes." Years later, Nina would deny knowing too many military men, but she would admit to being acquainted with Lloyd Knapp, a young painter and soon-to-be soldier who lived nearby.[123] With hundreds of new female field-workers walking around—to say nothing of male federal agents and scores of local officials—such an association was dangerous.

There was a great fear in 1918 that opportunistic women were hastily marrying soldiers left and right. "Young girls in their teens have been married to one, two or three soldiers," Martha Falconer wrote in alarm.[124] That summer, the War Department sent a questionnaire to eighteen large cities, inquiring into whether soldiers were marrying prostitutes. Federal agents claimed that the results uncovered 108 soldiers marrying prostitutes, 54 soldiers marrying non-prostitutes but marrying too hastily, 36 soldiers marrying women whom the agents believed were only in it for the money, and 31 soldiers entering "bigamous marriages." This result was disturbing, though not disturbing enough to justify an ordinance that the War Department was seriously considering at the time: that "no soldiers in camp should be permitted to marry without the consent of his commanding officer, such consent only to be given after some investigation of the case."[125] The fear of soldiers marrying young women was so pervasive that when Ethel Sturges Dummer's own daughter telegraphed her parents in December of 1917, announcing her engagement to a young officer, she began, "Please do not think this war hysteria."[126]

Nina was almost one of those dreaded brides. On May 11, 1918, Nina and Lloyd Knapp filed for a marriage license. They never returned to complete the paperwork, and thus were never married, but it is likely they continued to associate.[127] Nina later claimed that she had not slept with Knapp and that her mother had been against her marrying him. He was just "a boy that lived up near our home."[128] Nina's relationship with Knapp—who was drafted later that summer—would become a central question at her trial.[129]

Sometime that June, Nina, along with her mother, Minnie, and her younger brother, Vern, moved yet again. Minnie's elderly father, John, was "poorly"— his health was not good—and Minnie decided to relocate her family "back to my father's [home] to look after him—to help him, in St. Louis." For a time, the McCall family lived with John Scott and Minnie's younger sister, Della. A few months later, the McCalls would move out, into rooms above a garage on West Washington.[130] After moving to St. Louis, Nina claimed, she saw even less of the soldiers. "I wasn't in Alma very much, I did not come to Alma very frequently that summer and fall," she would testify. In the end, such denials wouldn't matter. Her association with Knapp was apparently more than enough to label her suspicious in the eyes of those with power.

NINA HAD LEFT ALMA JUST IN TIME. Late that summer, only a few weeks after she and her family packed their bags, the city started arresting young women simply on the suspicion of being promiscuous or infected.

In mid-July, Alma's police chief received a complaint that Treva Franklin and Effie Marvin, each roughly sixteen or seventeen years of age, had "learned the lure of the life of the red lights." The police watched the two young women very closely for two weeks and saw them hanging around with soldiers. Yet the police chief could "discover nothing that would enable him to hold the girls," reported the *Alma Record*. "His line of action was determined as a result. Monday evening both of the girls were picked up and following an examination as to their condition they were taken to Ithaca and are now held in the detention rooms at the court house." The two young women were examined by health officer Thomas Carney, who pronounced them infected with STIs. For almost week, they remained behind bars in the Gratiot County Courthouse.[131]

Likely because of this case, Secretary Olin hastened to Alma the next day and deputized Carney as an official "medical inspector" empowered to enforce the American Plan.[132] In the coming weeks, some two dozen women and girls in Alma were similarly detained and examined, some as young as fourteen.[133] The case of Franklin and Marvin, though, stands out as especially notable. It led to a front-page story in the *Alma Record* and, in the words of historian David McMacken, "caused quite a stir throughout the county."[134] Following several days of incarceration, the two managed to escape the detention rooms at the courthouse, after the county clerk mixed up his paperwork and accidentally granted them their liberty.[135] A week after that, Marvin was picked up again and sent away for treatment. She was sent to the Bay City Detention Hospital.[136]

Effie Marvin, Treva Franklin, and the thousands of other women detained and examined during these years all shared two things in common: their gender and the fact that government officials had a "reasonable suspicion" that they were infected.

This standard was incredibly flawed—it was vague and informed by the whims and personal preferences of the (usually male) individuals applying it. In California, for example, a health officer and a lawyer were once arguing over the broadness of the "reasonable suspicion" mandate. The health officer exclaimed, "I can come out to your home at any time and examine your wife!" The lawyer responded quickly, "Try it! I assure you your body would be so full of shot that you could not drag it off my premises!"[137] Around the same time, one young woman in California, a cashier supporting her infirm father, was propositioned by a soldier; when she refused the man's advances, he threatened to "get her had." Later, after the soldier acquired an STI from another woman, he claimed it was the poor cashier who had infected him. She was detained and examined. Even though she was ultimately pronounced uninfected, she still spent time behind bars, lost her job, lost her reputation, and was eventually forced to live with prostitutes.[138]

Personal relationships with authority figures—such as Nina had with Deputy Sheriff Martin, the father of her friend—could doom women to incarceration. One CTCA agent recounted the tale of a young woman in El Paso, "one of the worst offenders in the city, especially as a source of infection for soldiers; she is a distant relative by marriage of Sheriff Orndorff, and to protect the family name I believe he contemplates keeping her in jail most of the time in the future."[139]

In Kansas, hundreds of women were detained under the American Plan and then, upon admission to that state's detention hospital, interviewed. The records of these interviews—though terse and undoubtedly parsed by the ideology of the recorder—are a stunning revelation of what could actually constitute "reasonable suspicion." One woman, for instance, was arrested and examined for defending a friend from the police; another woman was detained for no apparent reason mere hours before her wedding.[140] One woman owed rent to a former sheriff, who had her taken in on suspicion when she could not afford to pay; another was arrested after changing jobs, when her former boss vengefully reported her to the health officer.[141] One woman was arrested after her car broke down; another was examined after volunteering to be a witness against men accused of stealing a car.[142] The presence of alcohol often led to women's internments: one was arrested for pouring an acquaintance's alcohol out the window of a car, while another was prescribed whiskey by her doctor to treat tuberculosis; when the police found the liquor on her, they brought her in.[143] One woman was forcibly examined after just being on a date with a man who was drinking.[144]

Many women were simply in the wrong place at the wrong time. One woman was with a female acquaintance when the cops came for the acquaintance; her husband had reported her to the health officer. For good measure, the police took in the other woman too.[145] A great many women were detained and examined just for the misfortune of being in the same room as a man who was being arrested. In each of these cases, the men (whether they had an STI or not) were released after a few days, while infected women invariably ended up at the detention hospital.[146] One Wichita woman was arrested when the place where she and her husband were staying was raided and the police asked her to produce a marriage license; she didn't have it with her. She telegraphed her family and was easily able to obtain a copy of the certificate, but her blood had already been tested, and health officials had pronounced her infected.[147]

Race also played a role in the arrests, and law enforcement officials went out of their way to target nonwhite women. One CTCA official stationed in Columbus, New Mexico, wrote that he suspected many of the black women in the city were "really prostitutes, but it is very difficult to get evidence against them." Still, he consoled himself with the thought that "[s]ome, if not all, of them sell liquor occasionally and can be arrested in this way."[148] This same official worried about the "lax sexual morals of the Negro race," even among married black women. Noting that 263 black soldiers in Columbus had wives, he wrote, "It is inevitable that some of these wives are of easy virtue and far from faithful to their husbands."[149]

It is important not to sympathize only with the so-called "innocent" victims—to do so would reinforce the stigmatization of infection and female sexuality. Countless women admitted to (as their captors recorded it) having "led an immoral life," and they believed this had led the health officers to take them in.[150] These women were not a reformer's idealization of Victorian womanhood, but rather were human, and thus flawed. "I was insulted by a Jew while I was on the street and I struck and was arrested," one woman recalled. "I was examined and failed to pass."[151] Another woman blamed her infection on her husband, who "ran with negro women."[152] Yet many of their interviews also reveal trauma and tragedy. One woman reported that she had to resort to prostitution "to support my baby and myself," while another admitted to "hustling" because she "needed money for doctor bills."[153] One woman said she believed she had acquired her STI after being raped by her uncle at the age of eight.[154] Another stated, "The only time I was ever immoral was when I was drugged and attacked by 3 men."[155]

It was this loose definition of "reasonable suspicion" that would ultimately ensnare eighteen-year-old Nina McCall.

ON SEPTEMBER 23, 1918, a woman named Ida Peck arrived in the city of Alma. She was moving. For Peck, constant relocation was not at all unusual;

before coming to Alma, she had lived in Lansing for three months, in Battle Creek for one year, in Owosso for three years, in Saginaw for nine years, in Pontiac for six years, and in Caro for ten years. She had been born in Holly, a small village spotted with lakes in Michigan's southeast. Peck's vocation had changed as frequently as her residence: in Caro, she had taught school; in Battle Creek, she had run a rooming house; in Pontiac, she had worked for the state asylum; in Lansing, she had cared for her ailing father; in Saginaw, she had been a private nurse—unregistered—and also the "fore-lady of a match factory"; in Owosso, she had been a nurse yet also found time to do "some social work among the poor."[156]

Yet on September 23—a cool, cloudy day—Peck was moving on yet again; like Napoleon, she followed her star.[157] And it had led her to Alma—and to Thomas Carney. Upon arriving in town, Peck went straight to Carney, the local health officer, to inquire into an opening for a welfare worker. "A welfare worker is one who looks after the girls," she later explained. Carney saw to it that the city hired her, and she started work on September 26. From then on, Peck worked closely with Carney, monitoring young women and carefully reporting their movements back to him. "I watched the girls, yes sir, I did," she would testify in her unusual speaking style, "suspicious ones, of whom we were suspicious, those that raised a suspicion in my mind. I did not watch the boys. Just the girls."[158] Many of the girls she reported to Carney ended up hauled in for an examination and then were sent away to the Bay City Detention Hospital. Peck was in charge of transporting them.[159]

Peck's work complemented Dr. Carney's, yet she later insisted that she did not take orders from him. She decided which "girls" to follow based on her own instincts.[160] But the relationship between Peck and Carney raises some interesting red flags and suggests a closeness beyond the confines of professionalism. "I went to Dr. Carney's about the first of January, 1919, to room," Peck would later testify. "I visited there before that. I occasionally stayed there over night, two or three times. That was previous to my going there to room."[161]

In any event, on October 4, barely a week after starting the job, Peck transported a group of supposedly infected women to Bay City for the first time. On the trip, or so she would testify, she first heard the infected women say a name: Nina McCall. Peck didn't know her. The next day, back in Carney's office, Peck chose not to mention Nina. "I kept still," as she later put it. But from that day in the autumn of 1918, Nina was being watched.[162]

Chapter 5

"It Was Too Late"

AND THEN IT HAPPENED. On that brisk October 31, 1918—Halloween—Deputy Sheriff Louis Martin detained Nina McCall in St. Louis and took her to the office of health officer Thomas Carney, about three miles away. Carney probed her vagina, pronounced her "slightly infected" with gonorrhea, and told her she would have to go to the Bay City Detention Hospital. Nina refused. Carney threatened, cajoled, and outright lied about conditions at the detention hospital. Finally, as Nina recalled, "I submitted to going to Bay City. I agreed to go if I had to, if it was necessary." Carney told her to return to his office the next morning, where he would have "papers" for her to sign. Nina and her mother, Minnie, boarded a bus back to St. Louis.[1]

Surely, as the bus trundled east, over a bridge spanning the Pine River and through the flat, brown fields of central Michigan, Nina wondered who was responsible for her sorry lot. Welfare worker Ida Peck, for one, later claimed she had not set this chain of events in motion. She had never told Carney about Nina, even after hearing of Nina's indiscretions, she would testify.[2] Yet if not her, then who? How did Carney, and thus Martin, learn of Nina in the first place? Carney told Nina that he'd had Martin out looking for her for the past four or five weeks.[3] Was it her association with Lloyd Knapp, or was it something else?

This is destined to remain a mystery, in part because of the paltriness of law enforcement records from the time, and in part because Nina was never formally arrested or charged—the police took her into custody without a warrant and she later signed a voluntary commitment order. The notes of the CTCA field representatives in Michigan at this time do not survive, nor do reports of any military police officers or Bureau of Investigation agents stationed there. Yet it is possible that agents of the federal government were the ones to initiate Nina's captivity. The federal government had been interested in Alma and nearby St. Louis ever since soldiers started arriving in town to drive Republic trucks.

When Nina got off the bus and entered her home, she noticed that there was dark blood staining the seat of her pants—a result of the examination to which she had just been subjected.[4]

——————

THE FOLLOWING MORNING, November 1, 1918, Nina returned to Carney's Alma office, braced for whatever the doctor told her next. What Carney did end up telling her, though, was that the nurse who was to take Nina to Bay City was sick and that Nina should return that afternoon instead. When Nina dutifully presented herself a few hours later, Carney told her to return the next day. The next day, he told her she would have to return the following day. And on and on—for seven days.[5]

Every morning Nina awoke and made the trek to Alma. Every day, she traipsed back home. She went alone to Carney's office every day except one, when an aunt accompanied her—presumably, for moral support, though Nina did not give the reason.[6] Nina's mother never returned to Dr. Carney's office; Minnie had been in poor health for the past several years, and as Nina later recalled, the "shock" of her daughter's examination triggered a relapse. "Her health has been bad enough so that I have worried about her very much," Nina would testify.[7] Other residents of Alma continued going about their daily lives, probably failing to notice the eighteen-year-old in their midst that week. According to newspaper social pages, a number of Alma residents were off visiting or traveling that week, likely getting such visits out of the way in advance of the cold months to come.[8]

Finally, on November 6, another fair day with winds blowing in from the west, Nina arrived at Carney's office at about 9:00 a.m., and found Carney there, along with two female coworkers: Miss Olson, the nurse, and Miss Howell, the "office girl." Today was going to be the day, Carney announced. As Nina later recounted, "When I went in there in the morning I begged of Dr. Carney to put the sign [placard] up and let me stay home." Carney, unfazed, replied (in Nina's recollection), "It was too late." Nina would recall that she broke down and began crying, telling the health officer between sobs that her mother's health was "bad" and that she simply must stay. Once again, Carney told her it was too late—"that I would have to go." And besides, "you won't mind it," he added.[9]

Fifteen minutes after Nina got there, Ida Peck, the welfare worker, arrived, and Carney told Nina that this would be the woman who would transport her to Bay City. Peck had indeed been ill the past couple of weeks, but now she was ready to take Nina to the detention hospital.[10] Carney handed Nina a rolled-up sheaf of papers and told her to head over to the law office of James Kress, the county clerk. Nina asked what the papers were, and Carney "said it was about Bay City," Nina remembered. He did not elaborate. Nina exited the health officer's office and walked alone through the brisk morning air to Kress's office, which sat above a nearby drugstore. Kress, she found, was not present; he had buried his wife just days before and had six children left at home.[11] Nonetheless, someone else in the office summoned a notary public to meet with the young woman who, in all likelihood, still had tears drying on her face.[12]

"Do you know what is in these papers?" he asked her.

Just "what Dr. Carney has told me about obeying the orders at Bay City," Nina replied.[13]

Apparently satisfied with that response, the notary told Nina to sign the papers. There were three in all. The first read, "Nina M. McCall, being duly sworn deposes and says she has been given a choice of remaining in her own home in quarantine or becoming a patient of detention hospital and that she voluntarily consents to becoming a patient of said hospital." The second was an acknowledgment that she had been diagnosed "with a dangerous communicable disease commonly known as gonorrhea," and that she was voluntarily committing herself to the Bay City Detention Hospital. The third was an official commitment order signed by Carney, which Nina countersigned.[14] The "voluntary" language of these forms blatantly contradicted reality; Carney's behavior in giving Nina a "choice" had been highly coercive at best, and then, that very morning, Nina had repeatedly told Carney that she wanted to remain in her own home, and he had refused. Furthermore, Nina later maintained that the notary had never "duly sworn" her and that the forms had never been explained to her.[15]

After signing the papers, Nina walked back to Carney's office. It was time to leave, the health officer told her, summoning Miss Howell along with a driver. Nina asked if she could return home first; she had on her mother's coat, and she wanted to retrieve her own clothes. Carney assented but told Howell not to let Nina out of her sights. The two women were driven back to St. Louis, to the rooms over the garage that Nina shared with her mother and brother. Walking up the stairs and through the door, Nina and Howell encountered Minnie. "I have got to go, Mama," daughter told mother. "This lady"—Howell—"was with her all the time," Minnie later recalled. "There was no time when I had [an] opportunity to speak to her alone." Nina only stayed in the apartment a few minutes, just long enough to collect her clothes, and then she and Howell left. Minnie would not see her daughter again for nearly three months.[16]

Howell and the driver delivered Nina to the St. Louis train depot. When a train pulled up, Nina saw that Peck and Carney were both on it. Carney got off the train to rejoin his "office girl" and driver, but Peck only came to the steps and beckoned to Nina to join her. Nina climbed on board, and, a few moments later, the train set off—winding its way northeast, over plodding rivers and endless fields, toward Bay City.[17]

———————

THE MEDICAL EXAMINATION for gonorrhea that Nina bore at the cold hands of Thomas Carney was not at all unusual for a young woman during the age of the American Plan. Indeed, it was one of the defining features of the repressive regime.

For generations, young women entering facilities ranging from jails to juvenile detention homes to reformatories had faced such invasive STI testing, usually at the hands of male doctors. Women merely charged with certain crimes, such as prostitution, vagrancy, and various other morals offenses, were treated likewise. The gonorrhea examinations themselves were often nightmarish and painful, especially at a time before most women underwent routine gynecological tests.[18] The physician would usually insert his fingers into a woman's vagina to secure smears, which would later be examined under a microscope for signs of gonorrhea, the most common STI. He could also use a long steel instrument called a speculum. Witnessing one such examination in mid-1918, Katharine Bushnell, a California activist highly critical of the American Plan, noted that when the physician removed the speculum, it was covered with bright red blood. "I do not know," Bushnell wrote a few days after observing the examination, "and did not think to ask, whether the blood was secured on purpose, or simply because the patient was carelessly handled."[19] Surgeon General Rupert Blue advised physicians to use their fingers, the speculum, and then an additional probe, wound with cotton, "inserted . . . and rotated several times," just to be thorough.[20] Often, doctors also checked to see if the young women were virgins.[21]

Josephine Butler, and generations of her followers, had objected to these examinations as unsanitary and degrading, a form of rape.[22] British abolitionists rejected the use of the speculum as a "steel penis."[23] Bushnell thought likewise. "In a word, the process is simply masturbation by the hand of the doctor," she wrote in 1918. "This is the modern scientific way of examining for gonococci. And the girls merely 'suspected' of wrong-doing are to be put through this! God have mercy on us!"[24] The "girls," themselves, agreed. One married woman, after spending several hours behind bars until an examination showed her to be uninfected, recalled: "At the hospital I was forced to submit to an examination just as if I was one of the most degraded women in the world. I want to say I have never been so humiliated in my life."[25] Yet under the American Plan, any woman whom authorities "reasonably suspected" of carrying an STI could be subjected to such an examination, usually before any sort of trial (if ever one was held). In some locales, any and every woman detained for any crime would be tested for STIs.[26]

Men were never treated this way in any systematic manner. In Michigan, between July 1, 1918, and June 30, 1919, 1,121 people (including Nina McCall) were "hospitalized at the expense of the State" because the authorities believed they had STIs. Forty-nine were men; 1,072 were women.[27]

Significantly, these tests were highly unreliable. The accuracy of visually inspecting microscopic slides for the gonorrhea organism presupposed that physicians would take the time and care to examine these carefully—something many doctors, including, possibly, Dr. Carney, did not do. And even when physicians were scrupulous, the preparation of the slides was subject to technical problems, and the presence of other bacteria could lead to a false diagnosis.[28] Nonetheless, in spite of these problems and concerns, medical authorities insisted on the reliability of their examinations. The entire American Plan depended on accurate diagnostics.[29]

And government officials could be blasé in their dismissals of civil rights or humanitarian concerns. "It is common knowledge," wrote one (male) Los Angeles judge, "that in the majority of cases persons who are not afflicted with these diseases are not objectionable to having examination made in the proper way and under the proper circumstances to ascertain whether they have the disease."[30]

AFTER NINA'S TRAIN pulled into the Bay City station that fair November 6, she and Peck found that there was no one there to meet them. Peck phoned the police station, and a uniformed policeman—the city's chief—was dispatched to pick the two women up. It took him about fifteen or twenty minutes to get there, but the detention hospital was a healthy distance from the station, and Peck did not relish walking there. The chief pulled up, the two women piled into his unmarked car, and he drove them to the Bay City Detention Hospital.[31]

Heading east about a mile along Columbus Avenue, away from the Saginaw River, the trio quickly reached a three-story brick building. This was to be Nina's home for the next several months. The detention hospital had opened on December 12, 1911, in the wake of a devastating smallpox outbreak. It was designed to treat patients with smallpox, as well as other infectious diseases, including scarlet fever and diphtheria. The hospital sat on eight acres of land in the south of town and bordered several residential homes, as well as the St. Stanislaus Kostka Cemetery, its handsome headstones jutting out of the lumpy, green earth. It had a capacity of fifty patients and featured "modern equipment," as the *Journal of the American Medical Association* noted approvingly at the time.[32] It operated quietly and uncontroversially for the next several years, under the superintendence of Sarah Mulholland, a white woman in her midfifties.[33] The detention hospital took contagious patients other institutions wouldn't touch. And then, in February 1918, the city agreed to take women with STIs from all across Michigan. By the end of May, the state had incarcerated 443 infected women, many of them in Bay City; by November 1, the day after Nina was arrested, that number had very nearly doubled, reaching 883.[34]

Peck and Nina arrived at the detention hospital at about 1:00 p.m. At the door, Peck introduced Nina to Mary Corrigan, the hospital's matron. Corrigan had been born thirty-six years earlier, in Bay City, to an American father and Canadian mother, both of Irish descent.[35] For most of the last two decades, she had been a nurse in Bay City.[36] She had moved to the detention hospital in April 1917, nearly a year before it began to house women with STIs.[37] Nina left her suitcase in Corrigan's office and ate a presumably lonely lunch. Afterward, several of the inmates took Nina upstairs. Peck stayed for about two hours before heading home on an afternoon train. She would later testify that Nina "did not appear frightened or terrified . . . did not appear to be under any duress or restraint of any sort."[38] Nina's rebuttal, as well as some measure of common sense, would cast serious doubt on this claim. Following supper that evening, a nurse showed Nina where she was going to sleep. Nina retrieved her suitcase and walked to the bedroom. The room had two beds; she was to share these with three other women. "It was just a little small room with one window in it," she remembered years later.[39]

As she lay there, alongside a stranger on this small bed in this small room, perhaps Nina reflected on her isolation. Few people even knew where she was. "I didn't tell anybody that I had to go to Bay City because I was ashamed of it, it was a disgrace to me," she would later claim. She had confided her secret only in her mother and two aunts.[40] She was all alone.

IT WAS, as the *London Daily Express* memorably put it, the "greatest day in history." At 11:00 a.m. on November 11, 1918—the fated eleventh hour of the eleventh day of the eleventh month (of the fourth year of the world's bloodiest war)—the armistice German leaders had signed six hours before in a French general's private train car went into effect. Church bells tolled all across Europe. World War I was over.

The end of the Great War, CTCA chairman Raymond Fosdick later wrote, "was upon us almost before we could grasp what was happening. The fighting seemed to be over, but the big problem of delay and demobilization loomed ahead of us."[41] There would be no rest for Fosdick and the other federal administrators of the American Plan. Millions of soldiers would now be streaming home, and they would have to be protected from vice. Two days after the signing of the armistice, Secretary of War Newton Baker sent a telegram to governors and mayors across the country, informing them that "the War Department is determined to return soldiers to their families and to civil life uncontaminated by disease."[42] The only question that remained was how—how to retain the imperative of the American Plan without the powerful impetus of military necessity.

This was a pressing issue. "The vicious elements will try to take advantage of the national feeling of relaxation and jubilation which peace ushers in," one CTCA official would write a week after the armistice. "Prostitution and venereal disease must not obtain a new foothold. The war made it possible to take this problem from the darkness into the light. We must *keep* the limelight of public opinion focused on it."[43]

In St. Louis and Alma, Michigan, all thoughts were of their men coming home. The two towns had held "the greatest celebration" in their history on November 8 at the impending prospect of peace, which the newspapers had informed them was just days away. Five thousand people marched for four hours in a parade two miles long. A St. Louis band led the procession, and observers clanged their hard hats and dinner pails with excitement. As the sky darkened, bonfires lit up the horizon, as did a burning effigy of the kaiser. One hundred war trucks, filled with everyone from Red Cross workers to suffragists—"girls and boys driven wild with the glorious news"—drove triumphantly in the parade. The trucks had been built by Republic Motor Truck Company—the company whose operations had attracted soldiers, and possibly the scrutiny of young women, a few months before.[44]

Bay City had also seen days of celebrations leading up to the armistice. But nothing could dwarf the wild jubilation of November 11. Whistles all across the city blew at about 3:00 a.m. that morning to announce peace. Even before daylight, crowds began to gather in the streets. A parade was hastily planned, and hundreds of trucks and automobiles, teeming with screaming humanity, drove through town. A huge bonfire illuminated the marchers. The Bay Citians had brought "every noise-making device imaginable." This was triumph.[45]

Lying in the bed she shared in the detention hospital on the outskirts of town, Nina McCall may have heard the whistles or the shouting. She may have glimpsed the light of the bonfire through her window. She may have considered whether the armistice would change anything at all.

A FEW DAYS INTO NINA'S CAPTIVITY—possibly on that fateful November 11—a nurse took a syringe, plunged it into Nina's arm, withdrew a vial or two of blood, and sent the blood off to a state laboratory. The nurse did not tell Nina why she was drawing her blood.[46] For the past several years, state public health officials had been receiving vials of blood from every corner of Michigan and performing Wassermann tests—the most common method of detecting syphilis—on the blood, free of charge.[47] By the time Nina was incarcerated at Bay City, the state was testing thousands of samples of blood a year; the November Nina's imprisonment began, her blood sample would be just 1 of 678 tested by the state.[48]

Such blood tests were a routine part of the intake procedure at most of the facilities where women were interned under the Plan. Indeed, sometimes the initial medical examination could be far worse. A medical intake record from a woman incarcerated in New York contained the note: "Hymen admits more than 2 fingers easily. Vagina of medium length and width. Cervix rather short." Another contained a graphic description of the woman's breasts.[49]

Often, the Wassermann blood tests were accompanied by primitive IQ tests. These tests, developed by a French psychologist in the early years of the century, consisted of a barrage of questions of increasing difficulty. The test's creators had given the test to what they believed were thousands of representative persons, against whom each of the test's subsequent takers would be compared. Thus, if a person got as many questions correct as the average thirteen-year-old, that person was said to have a mental age of thirteen.[50] Psychologists back on the Continent realized that the test's questions advantaged children from wealthier backgrounds, yet psychologists in America introduced it widely and without reservations.[51] By the second decade of the century, the test had infiltrated the American educational system, measuring with its supposed impartiality the intelligence of thousands of bemused schoolchildren and countless captive "delinquents." After the United States entered World War I, the army utilized it with particular zeal—and with troubling consequences. It was widely believed that college-educated draftees intentionally sabotaged the tests in order to avoid service. When, to the consternation of higher-ups, data revealed that the median scores of blacks and whites were virtually identical, the army revised the test so that blacks would score lower, thus confirming racial biases.[52] In few places were the tests used more faithfully—or more problematically—than in institutions for supposedly deviant young women.

In Bay City, as in every other institution for infected women in Michigan, a staff psychologist questioned each woman upon intake and then administered an IQ test. "Every girl under supervision," Katharine Ostrander, the state board of health's director of social services, said early in 1919, "we know where she works, who her friends are and how she puts in her time. . . . While the girl is in the hospital, we grade her mentally, and make a detailed social investigation. . . . Her mental grading helps us in determining what she can do." Evaluating the data from the last three months (thus, with Nina as a data point), Ostrander found that 75 percent of the women were "mental defectives to some degree," with 45 percent "testing below 12 years." To psychologists, a mental age below twelve made a woman "feebleminded"—that is to say, irrevocably mentally deficient.[53] (Experts sometimes employed the assumption that "the average intelligence of persons of the negro race is two years below that of persons of the white race."[54]) Experts at the time felt that the feebleminded caused poverty and crime, and since these experts believed feeblemindedness was inherited, the feebleminded perpetuated their condition as well.[55] When the psychologist graded a woman feebleminded, the consequences could be dire. "We are locking up," Ostrander continued, "just as many feebleminded girls as we can."[56]

Feeblemindedness was more than just a mental condition; it was an indicator of morality. The greatest experts of the age firmly believed the feebleminded were, in the words of historian Wendy Kline, "destructive to the morals of the community and future progeny."[57] Thus, in their minds, there was an undeniable link between feeblemindedness and prostitution. Most of the experts thought that anywhere from 33 to 97 percent of prostitutes were feebleminded; the average estimate seemed to be around 50 percent.[58] During these years, about one out of every twenty-five women detained under the American Plan—for being "reasonably suspected" of carrying an STI—was placed directly into "feebleminded institutions," as opposed to detention homes, reformatories, or jails.[59] Even as sympathetic an incarcerator as Maude Miner believed that "[f]eeblemindedness is an important factor in the girl problem" and lamented the lack of institutions for the feebleminded.[60]

In Michigan, women detained as "reasonably suspected" of having an STI who were then determined to be feebleminded could be subject to years of imprisonment in the state Home and Training School at Lapeer.[61] Nina later claimed that she could not remember having had "an examination as to mental conditions or an interview with a psychologist in Bay City."[62] It is possible that, amid the barrage of tests and trauma, she simply forgot about the eugenic procedures. Or it is possible that Bay City's administrators were just derelict in their duties. In any event, had she been given the IQ test and been found to be "feebleminded," Nina could have lost more than just her liberty. All across the country, supposedly feebleminded women were being sterilized.

The crux of the idea was that the morally or intellectually degenerate could pass on their failings to their children, and so they had to be stopped. As one promoter put it, sterilization would "ultimately eradicate these people that are undermining our civilization."[63] The result of this logic was generations of men, women, and children—all supposedly defective in one way or another, be it epilepsy or insanity or moral degeneracy—subjected to castrations, tubal ligations, vasectomies, and salpingectomies, all against their will. These were surgeries to alter or to excise, delicate little organs clipped or tied or plucked out. Though doctors had begun performing such operations in sporadic (and legally murky) fashion several decades earlier—the nation's first eugenic sterilization law had been proposed in Michigan in 1897, and the first passed in 1907, in Indiana—it wasn't until roughly 1918 that physicians started to see sterilization "as the most effective way of combating race degeneracy," as Kline put it.[64] Broader and more stringent sterilization laws were passed across the country. In 1917 alone, six states passed new laws calling for the sterilization of "defectives" and "the feebleminded," joining more than a dozen others.[65] Defective, feebleminded—such labels were vague for a reason. In some institutions, infected prostitutes who "tested normal" on IQ tests were still deemed sufficiently deviant or abnormal to be sterilized. Promiscuous sexual behavior likewise could justify the cruel surgeries.[66] And, as the historian Harriet Washington wrote, blacks were "staggeringly overrepresented in the ranks of the sterilized."[67]

By the time Nina McCall was incarcerated, dozens of states were dealing harshly with the "feebleminded"—often institutionalizing them for life, or sterilizing them. A eugenic sterilization law had passed in Michigan in 1913, but when the state tried to utilize it—sterilizing an unwed mother in a 1916 test case—the Michigan Supreme Court ruled the law unconstitutional because it applied only to individuals in state institutions, rather than to the public as a whole.[68] Thus, Nina was never in danger of sterilization, per se. Yet, in other states, an unknown number of women incarcerated under the American Plan—perhaps hundreds—went under the state's knife.[69] Though sterilization laws usually applied to both men and women, because of the stereotypes and stigmas surrounding female sexuality and STIs, women were far more likely to be classified as deviant or subnormal, and thus to face sterilization. In Georgia, for instance, women were deemed feebleminded three times as often as men were. Sterilization laws, in the words of historian Barbara Meil Hobson, were "aimed primarily at the female habitual moral offender."[70]

SAFE FROM STERILIZATION, though certainly not from abuse, Nina McCall settled into life in the Bay City Detention Hospital. A nurse assigned Nina to wash dishes, and her time became devoted to toil. Soapy water, wrinkled fingers, spotted dishes—these became the objects of her existence. Then, the nurse tasked her with washing the operating room floor one week and scrubbing the bathroom the next. One week the operating room, one week the bathroom, and on it went.[71] According to Superintendent Corrigan, changing up the women's duties was part of the philosophy of Bay City.[72] The work was purely domestic, and that was the point. Nina's imprisonment—as with the imprisonment of women across the nation—was meant to "reform" her, and to reform young women one had to teach them a skill. "In one school," wrote a female reformer a few years later, after surveying reformatories across the nation, "at 5.30 A.M. a bell tolls, three hundred girls start to work scrubbing, or report to laundry, dairy and bakery."[73] Sewing, scouring, sweeping the stairs—these tasks composed the daily existence of Nina and her fellow inmates. Every once in a while, one of them would be asked to help out in the kitchen.[74] But much of this work was for naught in the modern, industrial world. "Emphasizing nineteenth-century domesticity," historian Nancy Bristow wrote, "the work programs did little to prepare them for life on the outside."[75] The true purpose of the labor, another historian posited, was to make female inmates "hardworking, deferential, and chaste."[76] Even when the labor expanded beyond the purely domestic, it often served to reinforce traditional gender roles. In Massachusetts, for instance, the reformatory for delinquent men manufactured beds, furniture, and the like, while the reformatory for women focused on "needle industries," creating pillow cases, sheets, and nurses' uniforms over the course of an eight-hour day.[77]

Down on her hands and knees, scrubbing, Nina surely considered the building that held her. It was three stories high, featuring new pipes within and new fire escapes without.[78] It had many windows.[79] The inmates' dining room was in the basement, while the dormitory was on the third floor. This dormitory consisted of rooms that were a spartan white, with iron bedsteads and taut bed linen. Bay City's newspaper proudly boasted of the detention hospital's homey touches: "There is a phonograph, two or three pianos, good furniture, rugs and linoleum, and everything gives evidence of cleanliness."[80]

In all these ways, Bay City could be painted as an exemplary internment facility. Like many of the reformatories of the era, it sought to provide a more nurturing alternative to jails. Yet, bent low and washing dirt away, perhaps Nina dwelt on the detention hospital's less positive aspects. She later recalled that she and her fellow inmates subsisted on a monotonous diet of red beets and potatoes "and such stuff as that."[81] Corrigan would admit, "If vermin was prevalent among the inmates at that time, I don't remember but I would not doubt it."[82] Nina's movements were harshly restricted; even to go outside, she had to ask permission. There was a ditch in front of the building, and the inmates knew they could not go beyond it. When women went outside without approval or strayed in front of the ditch—and Nina recalled several instances when this happened—they were disciplined. "I know of punishment being accorded them," Nina gravely testified.[83]

The details of this punishment are obscured by the dense fog of history, but evidence from other American Plan institutions reveals that it could be brutal indeed. In Bedford Hills, New York, the reformatory designed to be an exemplar of progressive compassion, inmates at this time were punished in ways reminiscent of medieval torture. "Young women," a state report read in 1920, "who had transgressed the rules . . . were handcuffed with their hands behind their backs and fastened to the cell grating by another pair of hand-cuffs attached to those on their wrists so that, in some cases, their toes, or the balls of their feet, only touched the floor; and while suspended, their faces were dipped into pails of water until subdued."[84] This was far from unique. When Miriam Van Waters, an idealistic female prison reformer, surveyed similar institutions for women across the country, she found that corporal punishment was not at all uncommon:

> Flogging is still practised in nearly half of the institutions studied. The most frequent causes of flogging are running away and sex perversions. Starvation, or limited diet is found in two-thirds, the restricted diet last-ing from a period of a few days to a period of months. Solitary con-finement in black cells is still used. Isolation behind bars, or within steel cages is found; some form of segregation or "meditation" being almost universal. Other punishments are cold-water baths, doses of drugs that produce nausea, drenching the body with a stream from a fire hose, ty-ing up and other forms of physical restraint. Shaving the heads, suspen-sion from school, deprivation of medical attention, and nameless and terrible punishments are still found, survivals of the spirit of retaliation, fear and stupidity.[85]

Superintendent Corrigan would later insist that she and her staff used "no method of physical restraint," and that the "girls had the freedom of the grounds"—that is, provided "they could be trusted."[86]

A closed door and outside ditch barrier were decidedly tame compared with many of the other American Plan institutions; only two of Bay City's rooms even had barred windows.[87] Meanwhile, a majority of the women's re-formatories and detention houses that received federal funding during these years secured their prisoners with barbed wire, armed guards, or both.[88] Los Feliz Hospital, in Los Angeles, was surrounded by barbed wire and forced the women trapped within to perform hard physical labor.[89] Another reforma-tory, the Live Oak Farm, a suburban institution situated in a "fine building" on twenty acres outside San Antonio, was fortified with one hog fence eight feet high and then a taller fence four feet beyond; in between the two fences was a dense entanglement of barbed wire.[90]

Perhaps, then, Nina McCall had it easy. Yet even if she hadn't, it would be impossible to know today, for Nina's ability to communicate with the outside world about conditions at Bay City was startlingly restricted. When she received letters from her mother and aunts, she noticed that they "were always opened and read before I got them."[91] If she tried to respond to these letters with anything too revealing, "it wouldn't have went out." If she tried to inform her mother what was going on, "the letters were destroyed."[92] Again, this treatment was troubling but not unusual. Across the country, mail was censored—as in the case of a Massachusetts reformatory that intercepted "[l]ove notes of unclean tone" between two inmates.[93] In Bedford Hills, inmates had to sign a form authorizing the superintendent "to open, read, deliver, destroy, retain or return" any mail they received.[94] And most of these institutions did not permit visitors, further limiting contact with family, friends, or allies.[95]

Institutions such as the Bay City Detention Hospital were supposed to be enlightened alternatives to jails. Yet, all too often, such institutions were all but indistinguishable. Indeed, Jefferson County, Kentucky, used a jail and a reformatory interchangeably, and in Columbia, South Carolina, a reformatory opened literally on the floor above the jail.[96] Even in Michigan, authorities at the State Industrial Home for Girls (in the town of Adrian) claimed that for years they had worked to provide "a home and training school for delinquent girls," but now the "war conditions" had forced them to serve merely as "a hospital for interning and treating cases of venereal diseases."[97]

Nina's desire to leave this place of labor, of restrictions, of red beets and potatoes, was undiminished. Every three or four days, she asked Superintendent Corrigan if she could go home. Corrigan's answer was always the same.[98]

Chapter 6

"Why Should a Woman Be Imprisoned for a Disease?"

OUTSIDE THE WALLS of the detention hospital, the winds continued to blow, competing for dominance with chilly rains and occasional sprinklings of frost. The temperature in Bay City stayed stubbornly above freezing, and, indeed, all across the country, fair weather prevailed. Winter remained a threat, distant for now, yet hovering menacingly just beyond the flat horizon.[1]

About two weeks into her captivity, when the results of her Wassermann test made their way back to Bay City, Nina McCall was told they were "4 plus."[2] This result, in the words of one medical text from the time, "is absolutely diagnostic of syphilis."[3] Or, as a judge from Oregon wrote mere days after Nina was interned, "a result of four-plus is unquestionable."[4] In fact, experts now know that the Wassermann test could have the astoundingly high false positive rate of 25 percent.[5] But as far as the authorities at Bay City were concerned, Nina McCall had syphilis; it was unquestionable. Indeed, the report that accompanied Nina's test results emphasized that while a positive result on the Wassermann test "strongly indicates syphilis," a negative result "does not necessarily exclude syphilis."[6]

"And when the report came back positive 4 plus it was explained to you what that meant?" a lawyer would later ask Nina.

"They simply told me I had to take shots; they told me for syphilis," Nina would reply. "And they began giving me the hypodermic injections in my arm."[7]

Health officer Thomas Carney had told Nina that she had gonorrhea; he'd said nothing about syphilis. Yet now the authorities were telling her that she had that other, arguably even more stigmatized, STI. On or about the day that the "4 plus" test results arrived, the nurse, Miss McMann, led Nina into the detention hospital's operating room—a room Nina had previously scrubbed clean. There, the nurse took out a small tube, about the size of Nina's little finger. Nina could clearly read the word "mercury" written on it. Nurse McMann placed the mercury in a syringe and injected it into a vein in Nina's arm. Her treatment had begun.[8]

Nina would continue to receive injections of mercury on a weekly basis, either from a nurse or from Dr. J. A. Keho, Bay City's health officer and the secretary of the city's board of health. Over time, the process became a painful part of Nina's regular routine. After about a month, Nina also began receiving other injections—she called these "shots," as opposed to "mercuries"—but she could not identify what exactly the "shots" were.[9] It is almost certain that the "shots" were Salvarsan or Neosalvarsan, the treatments developed by famed German scientist Paul Ehrlich nearly a decade before. Ehrlich had believed Salvarsan to be a "magic bullet," a miraculous cure for syphilis, a disease many had thought incurable. Yet Salvarsan and Neosalvarsan were, quite literally, derived from poison, and they were toxic—even fatal—if not administered precisely.[10]

American physicians had faith in these drugs' efficacy, even intentionally flouting patent law and manufacturing their own supplies of the drugs—rebranded as arsphenamine or neoarsphenamine—when the Germans refused to sell the Allies Salvarsan and Neosalvarsan after the war began.[11] Nonetheless, they were aware that even in their less toxic forms, and even if administered carefully, the arsenic-based treatments were only moderately effective and could cause convulsions, liver damage (resulting in jaundice), dermatitis, abdominal pain, vomiting, and necrosis at the site of the injection. By the time Nina was receiving these injections, many physicians had decided to interspace injections of the arsenicals with injections of mercury. This apparently diminished the severity of the side effects, but it also exposed patients to a new danger: mercury poisoning. Mercury, we now know, could not cure syphilis.[12]

As a result of her toxic treatments, Nina "suffered physical pain," as she bluntly put it. "My arm"—where she received the injections—"swelled so that it was so full I couldn't hardly move it nor anything."[13] Over time, the arm became "sore and lame. It affected my sleep." Furthermore, "I suffered with my mouth; my teeth get sore and loose, they were so loose that they could bend them any place. They had never been that way before."[14] Her hair started to fall out.[15] She endured all this even as she was expected to continue scrubbing dishes and floors.

In this respect, Nina's experience was similar to that of thousands of women across the nation. Examining the American Plan in Seattle, one historian recorded:

> Intravenous Salvarsan treatments were administered on a separate floor, often by force. Treatment regimens for syphilis were aggressive. Some women received as many as nineteen shots of Salvarsan. . . . Testimony showed that some were on crutches as a result of rigorous treatment, and

that many had trouble with their backs and were carried out of the treatment room. A nurse told one visitor that the quarantine was the "rottenest institution they had ever been associated with, or had ever known, it was absolutely a disgrace to any city in any civilized country."[16]

Another historian quoted a physician stating that only in the 1930s did doctors realize "that mercury plus arsenic treatment may have killed as many patients as syphilis."[17] Surely young women incarcerated under the American Plan died as a result of these poisonous treatments. However, as the records concerning the institutions in which these women were held are nearly nonexistent, the evidence of these deaths is very thin. Some government reports recorded deaths at American Plan internment facilities, but they did not record the causes of death.[18] It is one of the cruelest mysteries of the Plan. As the historian Abigail Claire Barnes wrote at the beginning of her excellent dissertation, "At this stage it is not known how many were given the treatments, the number that died, or even the exact number of people who were put into detention. Much research remains to be done."[19]

ON NOVEMBER 30, yet another gray, cloudy day, Ida Peck arrived back in Bay City. She came early that morning, bringing along with her a few new inmates for the detention hospital.[20] She stuck around for a few hours, and, though it had not been her primary motive for going, she stumbled across Nina McCall. The two chatted for ten or fifteen minutes. In Peck's recollection, Nina did not complain. "I asked her how she was getting along there," the social worker recalled. "She said she was doing fine." Peck claimed that Nina had no complaints—not about "manual labor" or "red beets and potatoes" or medical treatment or anything. "She said that she was treated nice by Miss Corrigan and said that she liked all the nurses."[21]

Nina would only recall the visit with a few terse sentences. She remembered asking Peck when she would be allowed to come home. "Well, she told me I would be coming home pretty soon she thought. She never said anything more to me about it."[22]

Both women would distinctly remember Nina inquiring about her mother. "I asked her how mama was doing," Nina would later testify. She was concerned with her mother's ever-fragile health and asked Peck to check in with Minnie McCall. She also wanted Peck to let her mother know that she was "getting along all right"—recall that Nina could not write to her mother uncensored. Further, she wanted Minnie to come visit, to "come down and see her, come down and spend the day with her," as Peck put it. Peck promised she would repeat the comments to Minnie soon.[23]

True to her word, Ida Peck ventured into small St. Louis just a few days later. She visited Minnie, in her few rooms above the garage on West Washington Street, not far from the center of town. "She had seen Nina and was to come and see me," Minnie later recalled. "She said that she had been down and seen her at the hospital at Bay City." Minnie did not mention anything about being invited to visit her daughter, and, indeed, she never would make the trip to Bay City. Years later, Minnie would remark of Peck's visit, "She came at her own invitation, I guess."[24]

Two weeks later, on December 14, Peck returned to the detention hospital, and again she ran into Nina. "I asked her how mama was," Nina remembered, "and she told me that mama was alright."[25] For Peck, their brief visit was so uneventful that she could not even recall what the two had discussed.[26]

Rather, Peck was focused on the Bay City Detention Hospital itself. She had come to deliver a few new inmates, and while she was there, she took a couple of hours to look around. "I went through it and looked it over, into the different rooms and apartments and so forth." She walked up and down the stairs, traipsing through the living rooms, kitchen, and dining rooms (the one for the staff and the one for the inmates). She sampled the food. She inspected the sleeping quarters. It seems likely that she spoke with the detention hospital's employees, including a cook, a laundress, a nurse, and Superintendent Mary Corrigan. And she looked in on the inmates themselves.[27]

No inmate records survive from Bay City—not a single scrap or shred of paper. Yet in trial testimony a few years later, Superintendent Corrigan estimated that there were "between 60 and 65 patients" in the detention hospital while Nina was there.[28] A letter to Bay City's mayor in late 1918 indicated that the number was fifty-nine.[29] Either way, this was over the hospital's stated capacity of fifty. Subsequent evidence suggests that Bay City inmates were overwhelmingly young, disproportionately of immigrant descent, and entirely white. (It appears that the Bay City Detention Hospital did not accept nonwhite inmates.)[30] The women came from all across Michigan, though other records indicate that nearly half came from Bay City itself.[31] Presumably, this was a matter of convenience; perhaps the detention facilities in Detroit or Ann Arbor or Adrian likewise incarcerated a disproportionate share of their own citizens.

The homogeneity of the Bay City Detention Hospital's population belies a core reality of the American Plan: nonwhite, working-class, and immigrant women were disproportionately harmed by the Plan at every stage, from arrest and examination to incarceration, sterilization, and punishment. Part of the reason for this was that racist hiring and employment practices shunted nonwhite, nonbourgeois women into the sex industry, since in many cases jobs as full- or part-time prostitutes, nude models, or burlesque dancers were the only jobs they could get.[32] Even within the prostitute community, non-white, working-class, and immigrant women were more likely to have the rougher jobs walking the streets, and in more notorious, more heavily policed neighborhoods, thus subjecting themselves to heightened risk of arrest.[33]

Yet, economic realities aside, the police, federal investigators, and public health authorities—mostly white, middle-class men—also consciously chose to disproportionately harass women who did not look or sound like them. Federal and ASHA officials enthusiastically warned that nonwhite women were less moral, intent on infecting soldiers, and that blacks in particular were a "syphilis soaked" race.[34] "[N]egro women," wrote one official, "exercise little or no care in protecting themselves or in caring for themselves in the matter of gonorrhea."[35] "We have a large negro population," echoed a Louisiana mayor, "and as you well know the female of this race are unmoral."[36]

Because of these racist assumptions, CTCA officials encouraged police to target black communities.[37] Indeed, across the country, military officials began prohibiting soldiers from "visiting sections of town populated by negroes" and arresting any soldier "talking to, or in company with, negro women."[38] In Kansas, blacks were 3 percent of the population but made up nearly a third of women locked up under the American Plan; furthermore, nearly all of them were working class—servants, domestics, and the like, with little access to education.[39]

Once detained, nonwhite women were far more likely to be sent to less desirable institutions, in large part because many of the privately run reformatories—supposedly more enlightened alternatives to jails—refused to take them. Black inmates were forced to live "in dirt and disease, sleeping on ragged greasy mattresses on concrete floors and eating food prepared in the most unsanitary manner," recorded one observer.[40] Even when sent to the same institutions, nonwhite women were more likely to be relegated to less desirable rooms.[41] Along the border, in El Paso, Mexican and Mexican American women were not only arrested far more often but also often remained behind bars for STI treatments for up to six months, while the average detention for other women was ten to thirty days. Of these Mexican women, the darker their skin, the more likely they were to be held in detention.[42]

Once behind bars, the racist logic went, nonwhite women were no longer a threat to soldiers or other innocent young men, but they could corrupt reformable young white women. Reformatory administrators feared that "the colored girls are extremely attractive to certain white girls," and blamed interracial lesbian relationships for rioting and other forms of unrest within the reformatory. Same-sex relationships were apparently quite common in American Plan institutions. Administrators believed that black women were the aggressors in such relationships, and they sought to segregate reformatories and other detention facilities as a result. Responding to fears of "race suicide"—interracial relationships—and the strife that such relationships would supposedly engender, the superintendent of Bedford Hills separated black and white inmates. Black inmates were punished especially harshly.[43] A CTCA report from Pensacola, Florida, expanded upon this logic, noting, "The segregation of colored prostitutes is favored on sanitary as well as racial grounds as they are believed to be more generally infected with venereal disease."[44] San Antonio's Live Oak Farm went yet another step further, maintaining separate dormitories not just for blacks and whites; Mexicans too were separated.[45]

As Ida Peck gazed at the sea of young, white faces in the detention hospital, pausing for no more than a few minutes to chat with Nina, she likely missed one small fact of life for Nina—the young woman from St. Louis had made a friend. At some point after she arrived, Nina came across Mary Loudenslager, a woman with whom she had been acquainted back home in St. Louis, but not someone she had known well. Loudenslager was another Michigan native, another young white woman accused of having an STI. Loudenslager was more than a decade older than Nina, and she had already been married and divorced, yet apparently the two women formed a bond in captivity. This bond would prove pivotal to Nina's life after she was released from Bay City.[46]

ON DECEMBER 2, Raymond Fosdick and his fellow commissioners met to discuss the future of the CTCA. They decided that all of the commission's staff should vacate their posts by February 1, 1919, at the absolute latest, so that they could be replaced by military personnel. They wanted the military to entirely take over the CTCA so that it could become "a permanent institution." Secretary Baker replied with complete agreement. "The splendid work which the Commission has done," he wrote back a few days later, "must be perpetuated not only until the period of demobilization is over, but is of such tremendous value that it should be continued in some permanent form for the future benefit of whatever army we will maintain on a peace footing."[47]

A few weeks later, the men of the CTCA gathered in their offices at Eighteenth Street and Virginia Avenue and officially accepted Fosdick's plan.[48] In the coming weeks, they would iron out the details of how exactly to accomplish his plan. The positive, or recreational, elements of the CTCA's work—the baseball games, sing-alongs, moving-picture shows, and wholesome entertainment for soldiers—were quickly transferred to the army.[49] But the negative, or repressive, elements of the commission's work had somewhat more trouble finding a home. There was no branch of the military to take over the duties of supervising law enforcement activities, of spurring local officials to round up and lock up young women. The Law Enforcement Division—as well as its subsidiaries, including the Section on Women and Girls—remained in limbo for several months. To be sure, they were not without support; the Rockefeller Foundation had agreed to donate $310,000 for "the Law Enforcement and Social Hygiene Divisions" to fund their work through June 30, 1919.[50] But this was not a long-term solution.

Eventually, they would settle on the Interdepartmental Social Hygiene Board. The board, after all, had been created to centralize federal action in "assisting the various States in caring for civilian persons"—that is, women— "whose detention, isolation, quarantine, or commitment to institutions" could protect the military from STIs; it was the logical successor to the CTCA's repressive divisions. A federally overseen American Plan would continue.

This was not happy news for everyone.

RECLINING ON HER SHADED PORCH, in her family's vacation home on the affluent, slender peninsula of Coronado, California, Ethel Sturges Dummer began to fret. She had spent the past several months recuperating from tuberculosis, away from Washington, away from the CTCA, but she had stayed up-to-date by reading regular reports from coworkers in the field. She had quickly come to believe that the young women that her own employer imprisoned were being "treated with entire lack of sympathy or understanding." Sitting just up her lawn from the sailboats gliding through the Glorietta Bay, Dummer recalled a visit years earlier to an Illinois industrial school for girls. There, she had witnessed "little girls" confined behind iron bars. "What on earth are such children doing here?" Dummer asked the school's matron. The matron replied, "They have had sex experience and must not be permitted to mingle with other children lest they contaminate them." Dummer's "whole soul rebelled" at such treatment—not, it should be pointed out, because sexually active children were being incarcerated, but because they were being incarcerated "without the psychological adjustment enabling them to carry on." Dummer wanted true moral reform for such girls and women, and she wasn't alone.[51] Maude Miner had resigned because of the CTCA's repressiveness. Jessie Binford, another CTCA official—the district supervisor for the central United States—had begun writing Dummer despairing letters; "at the present," one read, "I feel completely discouraged about it all."[52]

Well, Dummer wasn't going to stand for it much longer. That December, she informed one of the CTCA's West Coast officials that she would "like to finance a law-suit against the hospital for one of the inmates." "I think it shocked him somewhat," she wrote of the encounter, with evident pleasure. "Why should a woman be imprisoned for a disease when the man, as responsible, goes scot free? Why should women be held in the bondage of prostitution because city councils and boards of health are bound up with vice rings? If the world is striving for freedom, is it not time to demand for women not alone political but social rights?"[53]

In the months that followed, Dummer, Miner, Binford—indeed, virtually all of the women within the federal government—would turn against the American Plan. They would decide to destroy it.

IN SPITE OF THE ROUNDS of painful injections—the syringes filled with mercury or arsenic poking into her veins—Nina McCall had not forgotten that she had been committed to Bay City in the first place because of gonorrhea, not because of syphilis. Yet for more than five weeks—from early November until mid-December, right around when Peck came to visit for the second time—Nina received no treatment for gonorrhea. Apparently, this was partly due to neglect on the part of Bay City administrators, but mostly to Nina's own initiative. When health officer J. A. Keho arrived at the detention hospital and stationed himself in the operating room to treat the women, Nina would simply fail to report to him. "I would not go into the operating room to take [the gonorrhea treatments]," she later recalled. "I guess they didn't notice. Miss McMann used to say, 'Well it is immaterial to me. It don't make any difference to me whether you take them or not; if you don't take them you won't get out.' I never refused; I just simply would not go into the operating room when it came time to take them."[54] Perhaps Nina feared the treatments would hurt, or perhaps she simply didn't trust their efficacy.

When Superintendent Corrigan was later asked if it was true that Nina had no gonorrhea treatment for five weeks, she replied, "I don't hardly think such a thing would be possible," but she admitted that her memory was uncertain and that she was not directly involved in the treatment of Nina, or of any of the other inmates.[55]

That Nina never refused treatment was only partially true. She did refuse to take the medicated douches the Bay City authorities handed out most evenings. "I never took them," she would testify. "I was supposed to take them."[56] Douching with water mixed with compounds of silver or iodine was among the more common treatments for gonorrhea at the time. Indeed, in Los Angeles's Los Feliz Detention Hospital, the city gave over ten thousand douches to the roughly two hundred women incarcerated there in 1918. As the historian Jennifer Lisa Koslow recounted, "these treatments led to interesting consequences. In 1918, the city engineer was brought in to study 'the discharge of sewage into cesspools which [were] located in the property across from the hospital.' He determined that 'due to the large amount of water discharged from said hospital, and to the nature of the soil,' the city needed to build a sewer."[57] Instead of taking these medicated douches—which, we now know, had little to no curative value—Nina took just clear-water douches, and even these she did not take regularly.[58]

Yet the first time that an authority directly asked her—around the start of her sixth week in captivity—Nina dutifully reported to Dr. Keho to be treated.[59] The male doctor topically applied Argyrol—a silver protein—and probably other silver compounds to Nina's vagina. Again, this was a common treatment for gonorrhea, and one without many curative benefits. In other detention facilities, physicians went a step further and even injected these chemical compounds directly into the urethra, a treatment that offered no benefits, only dangers. And treatments could be more gruesome still. In one American Plan institution in San Francisco, officials coerced imprisoned women with gonorrhea into submitting their bodies to "experimental surgeries."[60] As the historian Allan Brandt dryly wrote, "Until the advent of the sulfa drugs in the late 1930s, Ricord's dictum held true: 'A gonorrhea begins and God alone knows when it will end.'"[61]

In the weeks that followed, Nina would only receive this topical treatment once more, bringing the number of gonorrhea treatments she received to a grand total of two.[62] Even if she had received more regular treatment, of course, it likely would have had little effect on any STI she had. Yet it is worth noting that, in spite of the lack of effective treatment for either syphilis or gonorrhea, many of the nation's most marginalized women—prostitutes—were at least as informed as the nation's physicians when it came to preventing STIs. As the historian Elizabeth Alice Clement noted, "A vibrant culture surrounding prostitution kept some of them informed of methods to prevent disease." Many practicing prostitutes insisted their clients wear condoms, or would only perform oral sex; others inspected clients for the telltale signs of syphilis or gonorrhea. Still others took medicated douches or even injections themselves, and they generally sought to keep their genitals clean.[63]

BAY CITY SAW A WHITE Christmas that year, but just barely. After weeks of unseasonably warm weather, snow had finally begun halfheartedly falling in mid-December.[64] Yet the soft, white remnants had melted in the week leading up to the yuletide, and the snow returned only at the last minute, coming down amid strong northerly winds on the evening of December 24.[65] The *Bay City Times Tribune* buttressed its cheerful description of Santa's sleigh arriving in town with a banner headline declaring, "Merry Christmas to you!" and a chirpy article about a local grocer stuffing the stockings of impoverished youngsters.[66] This was partially offset, however, by a bordering article reporting 102 new influenza cases across Michigan. "High mortality continues to feature the influenza reports," the paper soberly announced.[67]

For Nina McCall, the Christmas season was likely more memorable because of the influenza than because of any holiday cheer. Even though the Michigan State Board of Health had given Superintendent Corrigan $1.00 per inmate to fund some "Christmas entertainment," Nina was miles away from her family, cut off from her ailing mother and young brother.[68] And right about this time, the dreaded scourge of influenza struck the Bay City Detention Hospital. The hospital saw thirty cases; even Superintendent Corrigan was afflicted.[69] And the flu was no ordinary ailment during that warm winter. The notorious influenza pandemic of 1918 would, by the time it finally flamed out in early 1920, affect perhaps one-third of humanity, or 500 million people. Fifty million would die. More than a quarter of all Americans—about 25 million people—would acquire the infection.[70]

The pandemic first struck America early in 1918, but it was mild enough to be "indistinguishable from the annual irritant," in the words of historian Nancy Bristow. It wasn't until late August that it truly reared its ugly head. What began with two or three sailors carrying the infection into Boston had become two thousand infected sailors within two weeks. The flu spread quickly from there. It was far more virulent than any strain in living memory, striking with astounding swiftness and quickly suffocating its victims with floods of fluid. As Bristow put it, "By the end of October 1918"—just as Nina McCall was approached by Sheriff Martin—"from Buffalo to Birmingham, from Pittsburgh to Portland, Americans were drowning in a sea of disease."[71]

The infection moved from person to person, leaping across entire states and regions. It reached Michigan in the last days of September; the first reports reached Richard M. Olin of the state board of health on October 1. By mid-October, Olin knew of well over four thousand cases statewide. Witnessing the devastation back East (and around the globe), he knew he had to act decisively. On October 18, Olin instituted what became known as the "ban," closing churches, dance halls, movie theaters, billiard rooms, bowling alleys, "and all places of amusements"; he also forbade funerals and other mass public gatherings "of any kind."[72] Governor Albert Sleeper publicly backed this order the following day.[73] In Bay City, stores closed for weeks, and authorities extinguished the streetlights downtown to discourage citizens from simply wandering around.[74]

On October 23, Thomas Carney, Alma's health officer, turned his attention to the home of Albert Worden, a twenty-year-old white laborer who'd been born and raised in Alma. Worden had been the first reported case of influenza in Alma, and it was obvious that he was desperately ill. Carney had

ordered Worden to be quarantined in his home, and he had placed a placard outside Worden's house, declaring "Influenza." Yet on October 23, the
Worden family called in another doctor who diagnosed young Albert with
typhoid fever and changed the sign to read "No Influenza." Carney's office
was "besieged on all sides by queries as to what it intends to do," the *Saginaw News* reported. "It is expected that arrests will be made within the next
24 hours." Instead, after speaking with Olin on the telephone, Carney opted
to call in state troops to surround the Worden house in order to ensure that
the quarantine was not broken. The following day, Worden became the first
Alma resident to die of influenza. Carney would continue to be rigid when it
came to the matter of quarantine.[75]

During the months of October, November, and December, Olin's state
board received 116,302 reports of influenza, resulting in 6,745 deaths.[76] By
early January, newspapers could happily announce, "Reports to the state
board of health on the influenza situation Friday seemed to indicate that the
crest of the second epidemic has been passed. . . . [T]he total was . . . the low-
est number reported in the past two weeks."[77] The infection had spared no
one, from lowly young women to esteemed government officials. Schools had
closed across the state, and quarantine orders had been common. Yet the citizens of Alma felt particularly victimized. It appears that they were less than
pleased at the guards surrounding the house of a dying native son, as well as
the threat such force conveyed. So on December 4, 1918, Carney submitted his
resignation to Alma's mayor. At a special evening meeting of the city council,
the resignation was accepted "with practically a unanimous vote," the *Saginaw
News* noted, "as a result of the feeling which has been created over some of the
orders issued from the health officer's office during the influenza epidemic."[78]
The position of health officer had been so poisoned by Carney's tenure that
the city had trouble finding a doctor to replace him.[79]

And so the man who had ordered the capture and incarceration of Nina
McCall saw his public career come to an ignominious end. His harsh behavior toward influenza reveals much about his behavior toward other dreaded,
stigmatized maladies—STIs—and their carriers. Yet his ouster came too late
for Nina McCall. She was already in the Bay City Detention Hospital by the
time Carney resigned. And right around Christmas, Nina herself contracted
the flu virus. She remained in bed for a week.[80]

ON JANUARY 20, 1919, Rupert Blue, the US Surgeon General, sent a thick
packet of papers to the Michigan State Board of Health. "Inclosed [*sic*] here-
with are standard forms of laws relating to prostitution and venereal disease

prepared by the Law Enforcement Division of the War Department Commission on Training Camp Activities," he wrote. "Reports from United States Public Health Service officers in the field indicate that gratifying progress is being made to bring up to the attention of legislators the need for proper laws and the appropriation of funds to carry on the venereal control program."[81] This was the second time in two weeks that the board of health had been sent a copy of the CTCA's "model law."[82]

The first time had been a few days before, after Michigan health officials had forwarded a copy of a "proposed bill for the control of venereal diseases" to the CTCA, asking for comment. A CTCA official had written back, saying that the bill was "excellently drawn," but that it was incomplete. He attached to his letter a copy of the model law and noted, "A comparison of your bill and the Act which we propose, will show that certain matter contained in Sections 3 and 4 are not contained in your bill. It may be desirable to incorporate these provisions in your bill."[83] Section 3 of the model law provided a mechanism for shutting down brothels, while Section 4 dealt with the "Control of Venereal Disease." Among other things, this section declared syphilis, gonorrhea, and chancroid to be "contagious, infectious, communicable and dangerous to the public health" and empowered state, county, and municipal officials to "make examinations of persons reasonably suspected of being infected with venereal disease" and "isolate or quarantine persons infected with venereal disease" when the officials deemed it "necessary to protect the public health."[84]

Olin, Michigan's stout, harried state board of health secretary, immediately got to work rewriting the bill. He would labor for weeks at his broad wooden desk, bathed in the light of the tall, square window behind him.[85] Olin would also consult officials from the state's Division of Venereal Diseases. The division had recently sent literature about its work and the dangers of STIs to every state legislator in Michigan, and it had another mailing on the way. By January 27, a new bill was ready.[86] It had adopted the language of the "Control of Venereal Disease" section of the CTCA's model law almost word for word—it declared syphilis, gonorrhea, and chancroid to be "dangerous, communicable and infectious diseases" and empowered state and local officials to "make an investigation of any suspected cases of syphilis, gonorrhea or chancroid" and to impose isolation or quarantine if necessary. It even copied the harshest language of the model law: "For the purpose of this act, all persons known to be common prostitutes, or reasonably suspected and believed to be such and all inmates of houses of ill fame shall be deemed to be suspected cases."[87]

No doubt Surgeon General Blue and the CTCA were pleased. By the end of 1918, STIs were "subject to report and quarantine in forty-one states," in the words of one federal report.[88] Olin's bill would become law in just a few months—but not before overcoming a few hurdles.[89]

THE SKY ABOVE was dotted with clouds as Dr. Gardener M. Byington made his way to the Bay City Detention Hospital.[90] It was January 27, 1919, a Monday. Byington was a busy man—he was the director of the state board of health's Division of Venereal Diseases, in charge of planning the division's statewide campaign against STIs. He had been appointed director just a month before, at the suggestion of Surgeon General Blue, and his salary of $10 a month was paid by the US Public Health Service.[91] Even though he was brand-new, Byington was already facing immense federal pressure to lobby the state legislature for appropriations; if he could not successfully obtain state funding to combat STIs and their carriers, he was told, he would lose his federal funding.[92] He also maintained his medical office in tiny Charlotte, Michigan, in the south of the state, and he had an infant son crying at home.[93]

Yet Byington made time to visit Bay City in person. He was one of just a handful of physicians who had the authority to examine the detention hospital's inmates and see if they had been cured of their STIs. Byington had been coming to the detention hospital regularly for the past week, even as he dashed off letters to battle for funds in the state legislature and placate his anxious bosses in the US Public Health Service.[94] He was accompanied on his trips to Bay City by J. A. Keho, the local health officer who had given Nina McCall her only gonorrhea treatments, as well as another male physician. The whole week leading up to January 27, Byington had been examining the inmates, one after another. These examinations had led to many of the inmates being discharged.[95]

Byington's presence that past week had been novel, but Keho was a fixture in the detention hospital. Among his regular duties was to examine the women and see if they were still infectious. Often he was joined by a coworker, and, as Superintendent Mary Corrigan remembered, the two frequently had their work cut out for them. "For a time when we had a crowd it was too much for one and [the two physicians] alternated," Corrigan later recalled, "they would take turns; they divided up; some would have half the crowd and some would have the other half."[96]

On January 27, it was Nina's turn to be tested. She walked into a room and found herself face-to-face with Byington, Keho, and another male physician. "I understood the purpose of Dr. Byington being there was to determine and pronounce me cured," she would recall. Yet she also remembered informing the doctor that she'd had virtually no treatments for gonorrhea. Assuming her recollection is correct, Byington didn't seem to care. For the past week, he and the other two doctors had been taking vaginal smears from Nina on a daily basis, using their cold, steel instruments, or perhaps their fingers. "[T]he three of them gave the examination together," she would later testify, "eight times in eight days running." They would then examine these smears to look for evidence of remaining gonococci. January 27 was to be the last such test. Around this time, a physician or nurse also extracted a sample of Nina's blood and sent it to the state laboratory in Lansing to be tested for syphilis.[97]

Two days later, on January 29, 1919, Mary Corrigan received a slip of paper. "This is to certify," it read, "that Nina McCall who has been quarantined at Detention Hospital for the reason that she was infected with syphilis and gonorrhea, has been found upon examinations made January 27, 1919 to be at present free from the diseases in the infectious stage. . . . Nina McCall is hereby released from quarantine."[98]

Corrigan got on the phone and informed Ida Peck that Nina was about to leave.[99] One of the nurses gave Nina enough money for train fare, and she set off on her own, ostensibly a free woman.[100] It is impossible to know what was going through her head as the Pere Marquette train car chugged south and west, yet it would be hard to imagine that Nina predicted what she would find back in St. Louis. Nina returned to her mother's house, yet she was coming back to a home she no longer knew. About a week before Nina got back, her mother, Minnie, had remarried, to a man from Alma named Henry Van Norman. For decades, Henry had been a farm laborer, but it appears that he too had recently begun working for Republic Motor Truck. He had previously been married and divorced. Nina had known him from before, but it was still likely something of a shock.[101]

And that, it would seem, was that. By the time she was released, Nina had been behind bars for nearly three months. Yet this time frame raises an intriguing question: did she ever have an STI in the first place? One wonders, for instance, how could Nina have tested positive for gonorrhea one day and then, just three months later, be deemed noninfectious after just two treatments and at a time when there was no effective treatment at all for gonorrhea? And could Nina truly have been free from syphilis, considering the limitations of the existing treatments, as well as the fact that Carney later told her that Bay City had not given her "the right kind" of mercury?[102] The trickiness of such questions is only compounded by the imprecision of the diagnostic tests. Even if we were to believe that she truly had syphilis and gonorrhea when Carney examined her, and that the two infections had coincidentally advanced to latent and noncontagious stages on their own—which was certainly possible—for this time line to fit the timing of Nina's examination and incarceration exactly would have had to be a remarkable coincidence.

Chapter 7

"We Will Get Even Yet"

ON JANUARY 29, 1919, Nina McCall returned home to St. Louis and gingerly settled into her new old life. She was living in her mother's house, along with her brother, Vern, and her brand-new stepfather, Henry Van Norman. She spent her time looking for a job—without success.[1] She continued to worry about her mother's fragile health.[2] She may have glanced at the newspapers and noticed a story that was enrapturing and appalling the citizens of Michigan. Had Nina picked up any major paper and perused it for a moment or two, she would have encountered a story of dozens of young women, abused and accused, all because authorities thought they had STIs. Perhaps she even felt some sense of solidarity with these women, who were imprisoned 130 miles due south in Adrian.

Newspapers across the state described the conditions in the Michigan State Industrial Home for Girls at Adrian, where there were steel bars on the windows, no equipment for recreation, freezing baths (for those lucky enough to get baths), and a disgusting, hopelessly outdated hospital. Some women were refused clothing and had to stay in bed, naked. The home was overcrowded and understaffed, with one nurse for sixty-five infected women. Even worse was the "heavy rule of 'silence'"—except for a handful of minutes each day, inmates were not allowed to speak or even to smile at one another.[3] Disturbingly, the silence rule was all too common in American Plan institutions.[4]

Olin, secretary of the state board of health, heard of the brewing scandal and hastened to Adrian himself. He took one look at the home's dismal hospital, swiveling his great bald head to take in the squalor, and exclaimed, "I might be arrested."[5]

On January 29, 1919, the very day Nina returned home, the newspapers announced that state legislators would begin holding hearings on the home the following week.[6]

ABOUT A WEEK AFTER Nina came back from Bay City, just as this story of discrimination and cruelty was exploding across the state, welfare worker Ida

Peck showed up uninvited at the McCall residence.[7] The conversation Peck and Nina had would later be a point of heated contention. Peck recalled that Nina told her she was "glad she was cured" in the detention hospital.[8] Nina remembered nothing of the sort. Yet both women agreed on the point of Peck's visit: "I had gone to call on her at that time in reference to coming up to Dr. Carney's office and taking further treatments," Peck claimed.[9] "She told me to report to Dr. Carney's office for mercuries," Nina would testify.[10]

In Nina's memory, Peck asked her if she'd received a "slip for after-treatments" from the Bay City authorities. Nina replied that she had not. Peck told her that she should have—"all the rest of the girls had them." But, Nina objected, she had tested negative for both syphilis and gonorrhea. That was the only reason she'd been released. Why should she need more treatments? Peck replied (in Nina's telling), "they always took them; that the girls should take one every so often." Furthermore, "She said I had to obey or they would send me to the House of Correction."[11] Peck would deny making the threat.[12] Nina would claim that Peck told her she had go in for treatment every five days; Peck could not remember having specified the frequency.[13]

And so Nina began making a regular trek southwest, roughly following the bends of the Pine River, back to Carney's Alma office. Surely she realized she was retracing with nauseating repetition the daily journey she'd been forced to make in the week before her incarceration. Only this time, Carney was no longer the county health officer; he'd been forced to resign his position because of his heavy-handed tactics toward infected individuals. Still, she had to report to him.

On the first of these visits, Carney ushered Nina into a private room. Once they were alone, he asked her "what kind of mercury they gave me at Bay City." Nina described it for him, and Carney told her—disturbingly—that "they didn't give me the right kind." Just what the doctor meant by that is unclear. In any case, he removed a syringe—containing, he told her, a "different kind" of mercury—and injected it into the young woman before him. Nina then returned home.[14]

Then, the pain began. Her body started to ache. "I was always so lame," Nina recalled.[15] Minnie began noticing that the site of the injections "would swell and turn very red and painful."[16] Just as the lameness would begin to fade, Nina would have to go back to Carney's for another injection. "Every time I would go over for one I would beg of him not to give me another one," Nina later testified. "He told me I would have to take 48."[17]

The agonized, desperate young woman still could not find work. After three weeks at home—and two weeks of injections—she decided to move to Mt. Pleasant, an appropriately pleasant village of a few thousand souls just twenty miles north of St. Louis.[18] Nina went there because she'd found a job in a Mt. Pleasant restaurant, perhaps serving the young people more privileged than herself who attended nearby Central Michigan University. For a few days, she worked at this restaurant. Yet she was so scared of being imprisoned in the house of correction that she made a quick trip back to Alma to get her "treatment" from Dr. Carney. And then, after just a week at the restaurant, someone told the restaurant owners that she'd spent time in the detention hospital. "Somebody reported I had been to Bay City," Nina would testify. "I would not stay on account of what they said. They said I had syphilis up there." Humiliated, she returned to St. Louis, jobless once again.[19]

Finding employment remained Nina's primary concern in the days after she got back. She had to live; she had to eat. Yet the matter of released women finding suitable employment was also one that deeply interested the authorities. For decades, those who ran reformatories for women had attempted to find jobs for their released charges—proper, ladylike jobs, that is. Women were taught domestic skills, such as sewing, cooking, or cleaning, and then expected to get domestic positions upon release.[20] As the historian Nicole Hahn Rafter noted, "one out of every five inmates of New York's Albion reformatory held a blue-collar job before incarceration, but nearly all were paroled to domestic positions. The women's reformatory movement kept women from competing with male workers but not from supplementing their labor."[21] Of course, there was a dark side to shunting women into these positions. For one thing, it reinforced the sexist division of the labor market, pushing women into menial, poorly paid, physically demanding positions. Revealing racist as well as sexist sensibilities, the Houston women running the Dorcas Home for Colored Girls essentially bound released women to white families to work as domestics.[22] And forcing women into domestic jobs also allowed reformatories to maintain control over them. Reformatories sometimes requested that employers scrutinize the released inmates, reporting back on their behavior and morality.[23] Changing jobs without prior permission could result in a woman being reincarcerated.[24]

This paternalistic system was supposed to protect women, to find them *some* means of supporting themselves, but often it failed to do even that. "Our plan is to apprehend and place in hospitals designated by the State Board of Health all carriers of these diseases that are liable to infect others," Olin had written a few months earlier. "If we place these people in hospitals at the time of their discharge, they are to be offered employment by social workers employed for that purpose."[25] Nina had been offered no such employment.

THE REVELATIONS about the home in Adrian kept getting worse and worse. All through the month of February 1919, witnesses appeared at the legislature's hearings, and every one of them exposed something more shocking than the last. The women who ran the home had often disciplined the inmates by turning hoses on them, or locking them in solitary confinement for three- or four-week stretches, often with reduced rations to boot.[26] There were about seventy-five inmates behind the steel bars who were overdue for release.[27] Some of the inmates themselves appeared to show appalled legislators the scars or open wounds on their fingers from the washing, ironing, and laundry work they were forced to do.[28]

Eventually, Governor Albert Sleeper himself made his way to Adrian and drank in the despair. Just a few days later, the governor demanded the resignations of the entire board of trustees and announced replacements.[29] The state legislature issued a report condemning the conditions at the home and demanding "[a]dequate appropriations . . . to place the school on a higher plane not only for the present, but for all time."[30]

Remarkably, even as these revelations rocked Michigan, members of the state board of health did not appear to doubt the policies that had exacerbated the problems at Adrian in the first place: their demands that the state imprison hundreds of women with STIs in penal institutions, some of which were clearly incapable of handling the additional traffic.

Olin had conducted a hasty investigation of conditions at Adrian and found that, as one newspaper summarized, the "medical attention for girls suffering from venereal diseases at the Adrian home was wholly inadequate." The problem, Olin believed, was not with the idea of locking up these women, but that the state had not appropriated enough money to do it right.[31]

Late on the evening of February 21, as the legislature was still finishing up its hearings, the board of health held a conclave in Olin's Lansing office, a room with gleaming wooden furniture and drab walls.[32] Present were Olin; a handful of board members; the director of the Division of Venereal Diseases, Gardener M. Byington; the director of protective work for women, Katharine Ostrander; and the board's president, Victor C. Vaughan, the esteemed former president of the American Medical Association. "I have asked these people"—Byington and Ostrander—"to come in and go over the work so that you men would know something about what we are doing," Olin told the board members. He turned the floor over to Ostrander.

"We have treated and have under supervision about 1,300 patients," Ostrander proudly began, "about 1,200 of these are women and 80% of these are street women." For the next hour or so, the men of the board bombarded her with questions. "How do you get hold of these girls?" Vaughan asked her. "They are reported through police departments and they report one another. We picked up one in Marquette and picked up sixteen the next day that she told us of," Ostrander replied.

"How do you lay hands on them?" Vaughan asked.

"We persuade them to be examined. If they won't be persuaded and we believe from reputable sources that they are on the streets, we quarantine them, with a placard over the door and they stay quarantined until they prove to us they are not diseased."

It emerged that Ostrander had forty-five field-workers investigating under her, and that these women were integral to the "persuasion" process.

Have the girls "been seduced by the soldiers?" Vaughan asked.

"No. I would say seduced by their own emotions," Ostrander replied.

"You are finding plenty of hospital rooms?" Vaughan questioned.

"We could use more," Ostrander responded, "although the hospitals are doing very nicely."[33] Perhaps much of the state, reading daily of the horrors at Adrian, would have begged to differ. Perhaps Nina would have had something to say about that.

Yet when, a month later, Olin visited the Bay City Detention Hospital in person, he came to a similarly upbeat conclusion. Beginning at 7:30 a.m. on the clear, chilly morning of March 21, Olin toured the detention hospital with an entourage of local dignitaries.[34] He exclaimed over the phonograph, the bed linen, and the general cleanliness of the place. Then he repaired to the basement dining room for a light lunch. Mayor Robert Mundy asked Olin to describe the state's methods to combat STIs for the other visitors, and Olin happily complied. "It is a great deal of satisfaction to come to Bay City," he began, "for the co-operation that has been afforded the state board of health here by your officers has not been equaled by any other city in the state. They have done everything we have asked and even more."

"This work was originally started to assist the United States government in caring for the soldiers," Olin continued. "You have all read what venereal diseases cost." So his board of health had made STIs reportable and had set out to imprison and treat infected "girls." He told his listeners that the state had treated "1,400 cases"—one hundred more than when Ostrander had given her presentation just one month before.

"I want to say that no city in the state of Michigan has given the state board of health the genuine co-operation we have found right here in Bay City," he reiterated genially toward the end of the lunch. "Your mayor and your chief of police, Mr. Davis, have supported us at all times. This hospital has done a highly satisfactory work. Many fine ladies of your city have assisted us. We have passed through this hospital 167 cases and we have 37 here now."[35]

Such praise would surely prove embarrassing when, in just a few months, one of the detention hospital's inmates sued the state of Michigan. And it would prove even more embarrassing when, just a few months after that, the detention hospital closed in disgrace, under a cloud of scandal.

AFTER RETURNING TO St. Louis from Mt. Pleasant, Nina McCall stayed put until March, when her whole family relocated to Alma. They apparently moved back to their house on Grover Avenue, on the east side of town.[36] Nina applied for work, but had no more success than she'd had in St. Louis.[37] "She was employed during the time I lived in Alma very little," recalled Minnie, who also did not have a job during this period. Seventeen-year-old Vern began working for the Republic Motor Truck Company, the dominant local industry. In the newly open postwar world, Republic was raking in money by exporting trucks abroad—most to Australia and Cuba—and it needed all the labor it could get. It appears that Henry Van Norman did not move with his new wife, perhaps foreshadowing the marital problems that were to come.[38] Nina continued going to Dr. Carney's for treatment, continued taking the poisonous mercury injections.

This whole time, Ida Peck kept calling on the McCalls. Every so often, perhaps once a week, she would arrive at their doorstep and check to make sure that Nina was still taking her injections. She came before Nina went to Mt. Pleasant, while she was away, after she'd returned, and even after the family moved to another city. She interacted with Nina's mother and met Van Norman, Nina's stepfather. Peck would later claim that their interactions were amicable, and that Nina even consulted her before going to Mt. Pleasant. "I told her it would [be alright] as far as I was concerned, I thought. She could do as she pleased as long as she was decent," Peck recalled.[39] Minnie would later claim that she heard Peck repeatedly threaten her daughter.[40] Nina herself was even more frank in her recollections of Peck. "She was just hounding the life out of me," she would later testify, "chasing me day and night."[41]

This dynamic—the stalking of released women—was an integral part of the American Plan. As with so much else, it had been pioneered decades earlier in reformatories, like New York's Bedford Hills.[42] When the women running many of these and other reformatories—like Maude Miner, Martha Falconer, and Jessie Binford—moved to the federal government, they took this philosophy with them. "In conversation they individually assure you, 'Sure, I've had my lesson. When I get out I'm going to get a job and stick to it!'" wrote Falconer, shortly after being appointed director of the CTCA's Section on Reformatories and Houses of Detention. But Falconer believed so many of these inmates fell back into old lives as prostitutes or sinners. She felt the solution was "established social service work to follow up cases after they leave the hospital."[43] Thus, under the American Plan, most women were incarcerated for "indeterminate sentences"; they would be held until they were cured and/or deemed reformed, and then released on parole.

As part of the parole system, reformatories and detention houses across the country required released inmates incarcerated under the Plan to send regular letters to the staff or, more commonly, dispatched women like Ida Peck to continue to monitor the women.[44] Women who behaved in ways contrary to their former captors' expectations risked being labeled "parole violators," and thus subjecting themselves to reincarceration. A woman could be labeled a parole violator for such transgressions as marrying without the reformatory's permission, disregarding curfew, disobeying their parents, running away from home, wearing makeup or seductive clothing, casually dating men, and, of course, turning to prostitution.[45] Black women were held to an especially stringent standard.[46] Released women were often dragged back behind bars for sexual behavior that displeased social workers or probation officers.[47] Other former inmates could even inform on women who engaged in questionable behavior.[48]

"Now, no matter how nice a young man comes along after you get out you will not be able to marry him," the superintendent of Bedford Hills had told one woman being paroled from the reformatory. "You will have to make your own living and support yourself, because you can't marry another man. Do you understand that?"

"Yes'm," the woman replied.[49]

For many women, this treatment proved grating, and studies suggest that nearly half of all released inmates violated their parole.[50] Eventually, Peck's visits became so intolerable that Nina made a shocking, and irrevocable, decision. She would do almost anything, it turned out, to get the harassment—and the mercury injections that came with it—to stop.

THE LEGISLATIVE SESSION of 1919 was proving to be one of the most productive—and contentious—in Michigan's history. For the past few months, the 32 senators and 100 representatives—130 Republicans, 2 lonely Democrats—had met in their gilded chambers in Lansing, arrayed in curving crowds of sturdy desks, beneath glittering chandeliers and surrounded by rectangular pillars, to do battle.[51] "While there has been a lot of petty quibbling," noted one reporter, "and while at times some of the legislators have acted more like small boys than statesmen, the program of constructive legislation stands out more prominently this year than in any previous session since 1907."[52]

The legislators had first convened at precisely noon, on January 1, 1919, in the state capitol, which, at the time, housed most of the government. The capitol was a beautiful, Italianate edifice with a soaring white dome, floors of Vermont marble, and woodwork of true Michigan pine. The House met in the north wing; the Senate gathered in the south. While the clerks of the House and Senate were calling the members to order that January 1, Governor Albert

Sleeper was being sworn in for his second term just a few rooms over, in an intimate ceremony with a mere handful of friends present—the influenza crisis had ruled out an elaborate inauguration. The next day, at 3:00 p.m., the corpulent, mustachioed governor addressed both houses of the legislature.[53] His speech was all about the war—how it had taxed, but also united, the assembled men. "During the past year," he said at one point, "the campaign against venereal disease, carried on by the state board of health, has been financed as a war measure from the state war fund. The board has placed under quarantine those so afflicted who were jeopardizing the health and morals of our young men at the military camps in Michigan. Women in need of medical attention have received scientific treatment and efforts have been made to give them clean and profitable employment." Even though the war was now over, "It is highly important that this work continue," he went on. The feds had disbursed to Michigan over $30,000 last year, Sleeper announced. Surely the legislature could add at least $100,000.[54]

The legislature would do him one better. On March 5, Representative Fred Dunn of Highland Park, an avowed eugenicist, introduced the bill that Olin had drafted—with help and guidance from the CTCA—two months before.[55] This bill appropriated $150,000 a year for two years, for anti-STI work; it required physicians to report patients with STIs and made those who did not, subject to imprisonment. It empowered the board of health to investigate "any suspected cases of syphilis, gonorrhea or chancroid" and any women "reasonably suspected" of being prostitutes, and to imprison and forcibly treat them, if necessary.[56]

A little more than a month later, the Dunn bill finally came to the floor of the House. On April 9, Dunn tried to get the House to vote on it, but, as one journalist put it, the bill was "put over for the day owing to the opposition from a number of members. They regarded it as unnecessarily strong."[57] The opposition was led by Representative Aaron Miles, a cigar manufacturer from Big Rapids.[58] That session, Miles had introduced a bill mandating equal pay for equal work by men and women in Michigan.[59] This apparently progressive legislator felt that the Dunn bill "was too drastic and too easily susceptible of misuse." At his urging, on April 10, the House voted to eliminate the provision of the bill allowing health officials to force those who were simply "reasonably suspected" of carrying an STI to yield to examination. The amended bill unanimously passed the house later that day.[60] Even though the House had eliminated the "reasonably suspected" clause, it had allowed the board of health's quarantine power to remain untrammeled. Furthermore, the board had the power to adopt its own rules and regulations regarding the implementation of the bill—a provision that would prove to be highly significant. Twelve days later, on April 22, the Senate passed the Dunn bill as well.[61]

Nationally, there was some resistance to bills like this one. Throughout early 1919, Alice Stone Blackwell, a prominent feminist and suffragist, denounced measures like the Dunn bill as "worse than useless," "ineffective," and "unfair," allowing the health officer to become "an irresponsible dictator in matters of health."[62] As Blackwell cannily noted, "The bills introduced in this country do not specify women. They say 'Any Person'; but the prime object is to get the power to shut up such women, and to keep them from infecting men."[63] She concluded one March 1919 article by exhorting her readers, "Women should do their best to kill them"—the bills, that is.[64] Around the same time, in California, Blackwell's friend Katharine Bushnell—an activist who opposed the American Plan—heard that a bill to create a reformatory for women (like the one in Adrian) had been introduced in the state legislature. She rushed to the capitol and lobbied legislators hard, issuing a pamphlet that dropped like a "bombshell," in the words of one newspaper, much to the horror of a CTCA representative sent there to usher the bill to passage.[65] "When you build that farm, build one for the men, too," another prominent woman told the legislature.[66] Yet, in Michigan, and across the country, little meaningful opposition arose. And even where it did—as in California—it proved unable to stop the American Plan laws from passing. The California bill passed two days after the Dunn bill.[67]

By the end of the 1919 session, the Michigan legislature had passed 445 laws—a new record. It had enhanced the state's workmen's compensation law, strengthened the state's prohibition law, and created a state police force. It had passed a bill abolishing the state board of health and creating in its place a department of health; the governor would soon announce that the inaugural health commissioner would be none other than Richard M. Olin. The legislature had also passed a bill appropriating half a million desperately needed dollars for the State Industrial Home for Girls at Adrian. And, most relevantly to the American Plan, the legislature had passed the Dunn bill.[68] A few weeks later, Governor Sleeper would sign it into law.[69]

"This bill," editorialized the *Detroit Free Press* on April 27, "while it sounds radical merely empowers the state board of health to continue what it has been doing throughout the war, under the war-born arbitrary power of the war department."[70] Laws like this would be the instruments through which local officials would extend the American Plan decades beyond World War I. By 1921, one would be on the books in every state in the union, and well over two hundred cities besides.[71]

APRIL 28, 1919—the day after the *Free Press* dismissed the Dunn bill's "radicalism"—turned out to be Nina McCall's wedding day. As Nina later stated, she had rather abruptly decided to get married for "protection"—protection from Ida Peck: "I got married to get away from her."[72] Perhaps if she had a husband, she would appear respectable; perhaps if she had a husband, she could be immune from suspicion; perhaps if she had a husband, Peck would have to leave her alone. So that day, in St. Louis, she was joined in the bonds of matrimony with a man named Clare Rock, a twenty-year-old laborer, another white Michigander. It was not a happy day for the bride. Nina appears not to have had any family or friends present; the witnesses were both relatives of S. B. Ford, the Methodist minister who performed the ceremony.[73]

That evening—Nina's wedding night—she and Rock stayed in her mother's house in Alma.[74] It was probably in her bedroom that Nina came to a sickening realization: Rock would provide her with no protection. That very night, as Nina later testified, Rock told his new wife "[h]e just simply married me because I had been in Bay City; he thought he could do just as he pleased. . . . He wanted to take me to Detroit; he wanted me to make his living by having—."[75] The rest of the sentence was omitted from Nina's trial transcript. The uncensored text strongly implies, however, that Nina's imprisonment in Bay City had convinced Rock that he could, in essence, prostitute her for his own profit. Nina would never assent to allowing herself to be exploited like this. "I told him I would not live with him under the conditions he wanted me to live under," she would recall.[76]

The following morning, April 29, the newlyweds made their way to Mt. Pleasant, the village twenty miles away where Nina had briefly worked in a restaurant.[77] Just why they did this is unclear, though the reason may well have been Ida Peck. According to Nina's testimony at trial, Peck was irate that Nina had had the gall to marry without her consent; she had confronted Minnie on the very day of the wedding and threatened to send her daughter to the house of correction.[78] Peck would admit that this meeting took place, but claim that she did not remember threatening Nina's mother.[79] In any event, the newly minted Mr. and Mrs. Rock left Alma on the morning of their first full day of married life.

Rock had family in Mt. Pleasant, but, according to Nina, he was adamant that they not find out about his new bride. There is no reason to believe Ernest and Olive Rock—Clare's parents—were anything other than respectable, working-class people: a carpenter and a housewife.[80] Rock told Nina that she could not stay the night with him at Mt. Pleasant's Park Hotel—"he got a room at the hotel and didn't want me to go to the hotel with him because he was afraid his folks would know it."[81] A room at the Park Hotel was an affordable $3.00 a night ($3.50 if you wanted a bath), but Mt. Pleasant had another hotel, the Bennett House, just two blocks away and boasting home-cooked meals.[82] When Nina found to her dismay that the Bennett House was all sold out, she was apparently forced to seek assistance from the hotel's clerk. The clerk brought her to "an old lady's house," where Nina spent the night.[83]

The next morning, Rock left his wife behind and departed for Detroit. "He told me he was going to Detroit with another woman," Nina remembered.[84] Clare Rock was many things, but a romantic and a faithful husband were obviously not among them. Rock was gone from about noon until 6:00 p.m. that day. During that time, Nina stayed in Mt. Pleasant, and in a propitious coincidence, she ran into an acquaintance of hers. On that windy, drizzly Wednesday, she came across Mary Loudenslager, the friend she'd made in the Bay City Detention Hospital.[85] Loudenslager, a thirty-one-year-old fellow Gratiot County native, was a worldlier woman than Nina by far. She'd been married for twelve years, from 1906 until her husband accused her of adultery in 1918, and the couple divorced. Following the divorce, Loudenslager had lost custody of her two children and, just weeks later—probably as a result of the divorce and the accusation of adultery—found herself thrown into the detention hospital.[86] She had been released shortly after Nina, and now the two women were reunited.[87] That evening, Rock returned—without his female companion. "I guess she had left him," Nina later reflected.[88] Yet, that night, Nina and the solo Rock still did not share a room. Rock stayed in the Park Hotel; Nina managed to secure a room in the Bennett House, and Loudenslager stayed with her.[89]

The details have been blurred by the passage of time, but it appears that the next morning, on May 1, Nina and Rock left Mt. Pleasant and returned to Alma. Perhaps tellingly, they left on the same train but did not sit together. Mary Loudenslager came with them and probably did sit with Nina. The troika arrived in Alma after the short journey, and Rock and Nina took a taxi to Nina's mother's house; Loudenslager waited at the depot. At Minnie's house on Grover Avenue, Nina and Rock picked up their bags. They did not linger long. The taxi drove Nina, Rock, and their luggage back to the depot—where they picked up Loudenslager—and then on to Ithaca, another small town less than ten miles away.[90] At the Ithaca train station, husband and wife parted ways. Rock boarded a train for Detroit. Nina and Loudenslager decided to return to Mt. Pleasant, where they stayed at the Bennett House again.[91]

Either that night or the next day, Nina received a message from her Aunt Della, her mother's sister, informing her that "Miss Peck had been after mamma. She had been hounding the life out of her." Peck had told Minnie that Nina must take her treatments, or else she would be committed to the house of correction. "I thought it was time to move from Mt. Pleasant if I didn't want to go to the House of Correction."[92] She was desperate. "I didn't have any protection from the man I married."[93] Miss Peck was relentless. So Nina McCall decided to exercise the one option she felt remained.

She fled.

———————

THIS TACTIC—flight—was one familiar to women held under the American Plan. Abruptly detained in brutal institutions for crimes many insisted they had not committed—or insisted were not crimes at all—hundreds, probably thousands, of these women attempted escape. Of 450 women locked up in one year at the City Farm—a joyless institution in Houston surrounded by a high board fence and barbed wire—53 escaped.[94] The Hospice, a similarly austere female-run detention facility in Jacksonville, Florida, witnessed a remarkable eighty escapes in just two years, from 1919 to 1921.[95] Women escaped from the Alabama State Training School for Girls at a rate of about one per week.[96] Perhaps Nina had read in the press—or otherwise heard through the grape-vine—of the spate of escapes in her own home state of Michigan. Of the first 391 women incarcerated under the Plan in Michigan, 22 escaped.[97] Six of these escapes were from the Bay City Detention Hospital itself.[98]

Sometimes, women escaped in ways that revealed their desperation—or their fury. In Seattle, detained women attempted escape by subduing their captors in sheets, by leaping out windows, and by breaking through plate glass.[99] One day, just a few weeks after Nina McCall's wedding, in Los Angeles's Los Feliz Hospital, five inmates passed unnoticed through the kitchen door during the appointed supper hour. The five women, three black and two white, eluded Mrs. Garrett, the formidable chief matron of Los Feliz, and the armed guards that patrolled the hospital's grounds, to make their way to the barbed wire fence that surrounded the perimeter. Using a butcher's knife and pair of shears they had likely taken for protection as well as for practical use, the women sawed away at the fence. They hacked a passage through the wire and escaped into the night, into the City of Angels.[100]

Detention house and reformatory administrators reacted to such escapes by redoubling their harshness. States passed laws that specifically addressed escaped women—a Connecticut statute called for recaptured inmates to be returned to their sites of incarceration and "disciplined in such manner as the board of directors may determine."[101] One woman, who escaped a few years later from a California reformatory, found herself handcuffed and thrown in "the dungeon" for twelve days upon her return.[102] And while the administrators of Los Feliz Hospital—which saw 12 percent of its inmates escape in its first year of operation—at first attempted to dissuade escapes by shortening the average period of forced treatment from ten weeks to five, after that failed to stanch the flow of flights, the administrators responded by heightening surveillance at the institution. The increase in guards and scrutiny did diminish escapes, but, significantly, it could never prevent them entirely.[103]

JUST DAYS AFTER Nina made the fateful decision to flee, the *Social Hygiene Bulletin*, a monthly publication put out by the ASHA for five cents an issue, used a phrase for the first time: the "American plan." Four times in the first two pages of the May 1919 issue, the authors referred to the Plan as such.[104] Whether this sudden terminological shift was the result of one writer's fancy or the careful decision of a team of ASHA strategists, it stuck. By July, the *Bulletin* was referring to the "American plan" without qualification, and by October both words were capitalized.[105]

The phrase "American Plan" was not new. Indeed, as early as 1885, physicians were writing of the "So-Called American Plan of the Treatment of Late Lesions of Syphilis."[106] The phrase was tied to a sense of national pride in Americans' belief in their ability to control and eliminate STIs. Physicians and policy makers used the phrase to distinguish it from the French Plan (initiated under Napoleon), the English Plan (embodied by the CD Acts), or the European or Continental Plan (regulationism in general).[107] "The name was evidently affixed to the Plan because it was different from that instituted by any other nation in the war," reflected one ASHA official.[108] Federal officials appear to have been using the phrase intermittently during World War I, but it did not become the go-to coinage for the government's anti-STI program until the spring of 1919.[109]

The new phrase signified a plan with "four lines of effort," as one Michigan promoter put it: (1) sex education; (2) recreation—to "[g]ive young people a right outlet for their natural energies and you are taking the first step to prevent their looking for the wrong outlet"; (3) medical measures—including private treatment, public clinics, and compulsory treatment; and (4) law enforcement—eliminating prostitution and incarcerating and treating spreaders of STIs.[110] Pamphlets began appearing, such as *The American Plan as Seen by an Englishwoman*, and the ASHA produced a film entitled *The American Plan*.[111] In just a matter of months, the phrase became commonplace.[112]

IT WAS THAT GOLDEN, jewel-bright hour before twilight, 4:00 or 5:00 p.m., and the two women were fleeing by way of streetcar. Together, Nina and Mary Loudenslager jolted along, over a bumpy gravel road, past the Park Hotel on their right, past a frame schoolhouse on their left, past a smattering of fields and houses and tiny lakes, and over a small iron bridge. They were headed to Shepherd, a train-stop village of just a few hundred people, a mere ten miles from Mt. Pleasant.[113] At least one of them was running for her freedom.

Upon arriving, the two women—who knew no one there—went straight to the town's hotel and checked in under the name Nina McCall Rock (or maybe just Nina Rock; later, she could not recall). They would spend the night there. Loudenslager paid the bill.[114]

"I was in Shepard [*sic*] running away from Miss Peck," Nina would testify.[115] She knew she couldn't stay there—so close to Alma—for long. So Nina and Loudenslager checked out the very next morning and traveled south to Ithaca, Michigan. They stayed that night at the homey Hotel Seaver (this time under Loudenslager's name). The Seaver lay just one block west of Ithaca's courthouse (which would soon be a site of high drama in Nina's life).[116] Determined to keep moving, they left the next morning and traveled to Alma, the belly of the beast, a mere handful of miles away. Nina returned again to her mother's home, this time to get a few more of her clothes and some other things she wanted for what was shaping up to be an extended trip.[117]

Once again, Nina remained in the house on Grover Avenue for just a moment. There was only enough time for mother and daughter to share a quick, worried word: "I told her Mrs. Peck had been there," Minnie recalled. "I told her Mrs. Peck was going to get her and she said she would send her to the House of Correction." Nina did not tell her mother where she was going, nor where she had been, possibly for her mother's own safety. Doubtless, Ida Peck would keep sniffing around.[118]

Probably too afraid to stay in Alma, Nina and Loudenslager continued on to St. Louis that same evening, where they checked into a hotel under Nina's married name. The next day, they left yet again, boarding a train and traveling along the Pere Marquette railroad, that vital artery of central Michigan, to Saginaw, a thriving port town and burgeoning industrial hub, not far from Bay City. The pair hid out in a hotel by the train station in Saginaw before parting ways the next day.[119] Nina boarded another train and made the boldest move of her flight: she set off on a one-hundred-mile journey south to Detroit, a city it appears she had never visited before. Loudenslager went elsewhere; Nina knew not where.[120]

Nina McCall had not begun the trip planning to end up in Detroit. She had intended to stay around Mt. Pleasant and find a job.[121] Just what motivated her to flee so far is a matter about which we can only speculate. Certainly, she had concluded that she had exhausted the job prospects in the small pocket of Michigan she knew so well: St. Louis, Alma, Ithaca, and Mt. Pleasant. "I went to Detroit because I could not do anything better," Nina would testify. "I could not work in Alma or any place."[122] But perhaps there were other reasons as well. Perhaps she feared staying so close to home, and thus to Ida Peck. Perhaps she had some sort of falling out with Mary Loudenslager (though there is no evidence of this: the two women's journey thus far had been purely ad hoc, following no logical route and returning to dangerous Alma twice in two days; it was not illogical for them to part ways). Perhaps Nina even held out hope that her husband, Clare Rock, residing in Detroit, would be able to assist her, to provide her with "protection" or possibly even affection.

Perhaps not. In any event, the nineteen-year-old Nina—hunted and haunted—hauling her few belongings in suitcases—boarded one last train and started out for Detroit, the same city her father had traveled to alone three years earlier, in an ill-fated attempt to "better himself."[123]

DETROIT IN 1919 was a city in a grand ferment. Trade unionists, bootleggers, suffragists, soapbox preachers, and wave after wave of assembly-line workers packed the city's increasingly crowded streets, all of them walking beneath the new slate-gray, steel-framed skyscrapers and matching sky. Workers in the ascendant auto industry—almost half the city's workforce—made $5 a day.[124] The Fisher Brody 21 plant had just opened at the edge of Poletown, and across the city, other auto plants—bearing names like Chrysler, Dodge, Studebaker, Cadillac, and the granddaddy of them all, Ford—were opening, expanding, and bustling with activity.[125] The city's population had doubled over the last decade, largely as a result of the influx of Poles, Germans, and other European pilgrims.[126] By 1920, Detroit was the fourth-largest city in America, and its borders had to literally expand to encapsulate all the new residents; the city had grown threefold in area over the last twenty years.[127] When the Great War closed the country's ports to European immigrants—immigration fell 90 percent from 1914 to 1918—the major industrial centers of America beckoned southward to fill their factories. Hundreds of thousands of blacks traveled north, to the booming cities of Chicago, New York, Pittsburgh, Gary, and Detroit, where black migrants packed into tiny, unsanitary boardinghouses in fetid, vibrant Black Bottom.[128] After the war ended, the black migration did not, but the flood from abroad started up again with a vengeance. The number of immigrants moving to Detroit more than tripled between 1918 and 1919, and Poletown, Corktown, and Germantown bulged.[129] Returning soldiers further swelled the city, happily removing their gas masks and replacing them with the less unwieldy face gear of factory workers.

It was into this cauldron of activity that Nina McCall rushed, early that spring. One of the first things she did upon arriving in the Motor City was send word to Clare Rock that she was in town. She was staying in a hotel not far from the train station, and she asked him to come there. Rock arrived, apparently with "a couple of other girls" in tow. A few days later, Nina moved into the boardinghouse where Rock was living. Together, they occupied rooms at 267-1/2 Baker Street, in a house belonging to James Mondas, a Greek-born autoworker, and Julia, his Kentucky-born wife. James, a stocky thirty-three-year-old, had avoided serving in the war because of a disabled trigger finger. Now he supplemented his income from Lincoln Motors by renting out rooms in his house; it appears that Julia did most of the interacting with the boarders. Nina still fully intended to separate from Rock, but apparently she had nowhere else to go. She wasn't sure if he knew she wanted to leave him—"I think he ought to have known it," she later reflected.[130]

Nina once again began the tricky task of finding a job. Detroit had the benefit of an exploding labor market, but it was also one of the most gender-imbalanced cities in the country, with 119 men for every 100 women in 1920. Women were thus in hot demand as brides or other sources of companionship; many chose or were forced to work as prostitutes. "In Detroit there exists a center of prostitution not equaled in any other American city today," thundered one University of Michigan professor a year before. Crowds of prostitutes reportedly took up residence right across the street from Detroit's armory and took to soliciting national guardsmen. Some Detroit women managed to find jobs in the tobacco plants and candy factories of the East Side, the pharmaceutical plants of Parke Davis and Stearns, the auto plants along the riverfront, and the sewing rooms of downtown department stores. Yet these women were still relative rarities in 1919, and plenty of unions excluded them. Many black women, immigrant women, and working-class women instead found their jobs in the service industry—waiting tables, cleaning houses, making hotel beds.[131]

Nina likely found some means of supporting herself in Detroit, for barely a week after moving in with Rock, she moved out again, relocating to a stand-alone boardinghouse on Beech Street belonging to a family whose name she later testified might have been Davis. She stayed there for a couple of weeks and then moved to 107 Ledyard Street, where she stayed with a family called Simons. From there, it was on to Park Boulevard, then Fourth Street, and then elsewhere, never staying more than two or three weeks at a place. Perhaps this constant moving, this near itinerancy, attests to Nina's precarious financial situation during this time. Perhaps it reflects her desire to not be found. She never returned to live with Clare Rock. We do not know how she supported herself in Detroit.[132]

Nina remained in the Motor City as the weather grew hotter, as May stretched into June, then July, then August, and into September. Then, a message arrived from home.

ON AUGUST 26, 1919, more than five hundred miles to the north of Detroit, six men walked beneath a jutting balcony and soaring columns, past a handsome neo-Renaissance façade, and into the prestigious Houghton Club. The

Houghton Club, located in hilly, chilly Houghton, Michigan, was further away from Nina McCall's boardinghouse than the boardinghouse was from the White House. Beyond mere geography, it was also a cultural world apart from an immigrant-owned bungalow. The club catered to northern Michigan's elite: white businessmen gathered there for stylish conventions; bankers with fine pedigrees dined there on the weekends.[133] And on that early autumn morning, the members of the Michigan Department of Health's advisory council—including the health commissioner, Olin—were there for their regular meeting.

For three hours, the councilors discussed the many topics that fell under their purview: how much to charge for "the examination of intoxicating liquors sent to the laboratory for analysis"; how best to regulate "public bath houses"; how a certain undertaker should be allowed to advertise his services, considering the fact that only his son was licensed to embalm. That in turn led to an extended, wide-ranging, mind-numbing conversation on the proper qualifications and certifications for embalmers. The men broke for lunch at noon and returned two hours later.[134]

The conversation moved to Act 272, Public Laws of 1919—formerly known as the Dunn bill, or the law drafted by Olin to fund and clarify the state's American Plan activities. The law, which was vital for the state to be eligible to receive federal funding, appropriated hundreds of thousands of dollars for state activities, but its scope was limited. Legislators concerned about civil liberties had eliminated the language enabling health officials to forcibly examine those merely "reasonably suspected" of carrying an STI. But now the department of health was going to draw up the "rules and regulations in regard to venereal diseases." They were going to determine how the law would be enforced.

After another discussion, the assembled men—all men—settled on five rules. The first held that, beginning on October 1, physicians would have to report all cases of STIs to the state not just by number, but with the names and addresses of the carriers. The third held that only active and infectious cases could be quarantined; the fourth addressed record keeping, and the fifth recommended the employment of female physicians for the examinations of young women. It was the second rule that would truly allow the American Plan to continue unabated in Michigan. "Any medical inspector or other authorized representative of the Michigan Department of Health or any local health officer who is a registered physician," read the rule, "is hereby empowered and directed to make an examination . . . of any suspected case of syphilis, gonorrhea or chancroid for the purpose of determining the fact."

Rule two went on: "All persons known to be common prostitutes or reasonably suspected and believed to be such, or any inmate of a house of ill fame or any man consorting with a common prostitute or an inmate of a house of ill-fame, shall be deemed to be suspected cases." And, finally, "If any person reasonably suspected by the health officer of being infected with any of the said diseases refuses to submit to the examination herein contemplated, such refusal shall be prima facie proof that such person is so infected, and shall authorize and justify the quarantining or isolation of any such person." Satisfied, the assembled men adjourned at 6:30 p.m.[135]

This was a coup. The department of health circumvented the clear intent of the legislators, who had excised such broad language. In fact, the new rules and regulations were even broader than the original Dunn bill had been. Yet it is worth noting that penalties for men remained—"any man consorting with a common prostitute." Perhaps there was hope for gender neutrality.

Hardly. A few months later, when Gardener M. Byington, director of the state's Division of Venereal Diseases, received a letter from C. C. Pierce, director of the US Public Health Service's Division of Venereal Diseases, warning him that certain "Women's organizations" were objecting to the American Plan in Michigan as discriminatory, Byington dismissed such concerns out of hand. He wrote back to Pierce that since November 1917, the state had received 10,541 reports of infected men and 4,929 reports of infected women. They had imprisoned and forcibly treated 69 men and 1,318 women (including Nina McCall). "I would like to state that while the above figures show we have hospitalized more females than males," Byington wrote, "we have been able to care for males thru' clinics and other organizations throughout the state"—that is to say, through voluntary outpatient treatment. "Our Department feels that a female can spread Venereal Disease a great deal more rapidly and, usually, it is easier to hospitalize a female than a male owing to the fact that the latter is a wage earner."

For Pierce's reference, Byington included a copy of the state's "new Rules and Regulations," and pointed his attention to rule two, underlining the part about examining "any man consorting with a common prostitute." Yet Byington—the very man who had proclaimed Nina free from infection—also felt the need to add that he and his department were certain that, in virtually every case, "the female was *the* source of infection [emphasis in original]."[136]

THE FACT THAT a federal official had felt the need to write to Byington in the first place reveals a key truth about the postwar American Plan: federal administrators continued to believe they had to provide guidance to state and local officials. Indeed, C. C. Pierce's subordinates were overseeing the bureaus of venereal diseases for nearly every state board of health.[137]

As the spring of 1919 turned into summer, the hundreds of male and female CTCA investigators were transferred to the Interdepartmental Social Hygiene Board, becoming the board's "field service." The transition wasn't entirely seamless, and funding troubles forced the board to rely on money from the Rockefeller Foundation (which was funneled to the government through the ASHA) to pay salaries for April, May, and June; higher-ups at the board laid off several members of the field service during those months.[138]

Still, the field agents worked—hundreds of them, in hundreds of communities across the nation. Upon arriving in a given town, field agents would familiarize themselves with local places of amusement (parks, theaters, dance halls, and "neighborhoods in which carriers of venereal disease are likely to be found"). They would canvass the brothels and suspicious hotels; talk to judges, police officers, health officers, and US Public Health Service agents; they would educate themselves regarding local laws and ordinances and inspect detention houses, jails, and reformatories. Once sufficiently edified, the field agents would urge the local authorities to identify, detain, examine, and forcibly treat suspicious women (and sometimes men). Certain members of the field service were called "under-cover investigators," and these were tasked with joining the police more directly in enforcing American Plan laws: identifying prostitutes, participating in raids, and so on.[139] While the transition from the CTCA to the board might on its surface appear bureaucratic and arcane, it was what allowed the federal government to extend its wartime American Plan activities into peacetime. "It is my understanding that the work of the Interdepartmental Social Hygiene Board will go on forever," one federal official wrote to another.[140]

Several other CTCA officials, including Bascom Johnson, returned to the ASHA.[141] William F. Snow returned as the association's general secretary, his salary partially paid by John D. Rockefeller, who continued funding the ASHA to the tune of hundreds of thousands a year.[142] Raymond Fosdick, meanwhile, served briefly as the undersecretary general of the League of Nations, until the United States refused to join the league. The dejected progressive then returned to New York, where he briefly practiced law before launching a professional relationship with Rockefeller that would span the next four decades. He quickly became Rockefeller's chief charitable advisor. Rockefeller "found wise philanthropy to be a heavy burden," wrote the historian Daryl Revoldt. "Although a Phi Beta Kappa, [Rockefeller] was neither a prolific reader nor a scholar." Fosdick, on the other hand, was "a careful investigator, skilled negotiator, efficiency-oriented, and intellectually flexible." In Revoldt's words, Fosdick "guarded the gate." He controlled access to Rockefeller, whom at least one supplicant called "Lady Bountiful."[143] In large part because of Fosdick's advice, Lady Bountiful continued giving generously to groups attempting to wipe out prostitution and STIs—most importantly, the ASHA.

The revived ASHA dispatched its own "expert investigators" into the field, performing much the same work as board field agents. At the ASHA's instruction, about seventy cities had set up "law enforcement committees," and workers under Johnson gave "aid and advice" to these committees "to vigorously assist in the reduction of commercial prostitution by legal means," as one internal report summarized. Workers drew up detailed maps of existing red-light districts, and pushed states and cities to crack down on them. Female protective workers were sent to Connecticut, Virginia, North Carolina, South Carolina, Kentucky, and Illinois. Other ASHA employees were assigned to promote American Plan legislation, printing and distributing the CTCA's model law and lobbying state legislatures in Pennsylvania, Rhode Island, Mississippi, Maryland, South Carolina, Georgia, Louisiana, and New Jersey that year.[144]

TO MANY OF THE WOMEN who had led the federal American Plan, however, its continuation at the hands of the board and ASHA was not especially welcome news.

During the summer, Maude Miner, who had returned to New York and the superintendency of her beloved detention house, received a number of letters urging her to push the American Plan to focus more on protective work, and less on repression. Miner began to consider this and passed the thought on to her former colleague, Ethel Sturges Dummer, who had become even more disillusioned than Miner.[145] "Is it not the crude and cruel treatment accorded one making the early mistake which really starts a girl downhill?" Dummer wrote to a friend around this time. "Would the shock result in disease, vice or crime were she not made to feel she had committed the unpardonable sin?"[146]

Jessie Binford, a CTCA and then Interdepartmental Social Hygiene Board (ISHB) administrator, echoed these concerns: "I cannot begin to tell you how distressed I am over the whole program," she told Dummer, "and the way we are going about it. We have plunged into the whole thing and we are not prepared for it in any way and the girls are suffering in consequence. . . . It is true here that under health regulations almost anyone can be examined for venereal disease if one has a right to suspect that she is diseased. You would be horrified at some of the things that are happening."[147] And another female CTCA-then-ISHB official wrote to a friend that the US Public Health Service was in danger of "defeat[ing] its purpose" by "playing up the health side" and "losing sight of the social service work which is necessary to prevent these girls from becoming repeaters."[148] It would only be a matter of time before these women began plotting a way to defeat the Plan from within.

Yet it is worth noting that these women would only go so far. They continued to promote "social service work," and one of Binford's primary concerns was that "we have no reformatories to commit [women] to when we have distinctly commitable cases."[149] Some more moderate women in the government called for "some other method outside of repression" in the same breath that they praised reformatory and protective work.[150] Even as they critiqued the American Plan, then, these women still believed that some women should be institutionalized and morally reformed. It just had to be the *right* women.

ALL THROUGHOUT the months of May, June, July, and August, Minnie McCall was forced to tolerate a constant barrage of visits from Ida Peck. As Minnie later testified, the welfare worker would show up uninvited "every little while"—in total, perhaps "five or six times; seven or eight." Every time, she asked Minnie where Nina was, what her address was. "I would not tell her; I didn't give her no addresses." Minnie had been in touch with her daughter. She knew how to reach her, though not her exact address; she also knew she wasn't living with Clare Rock. But she would not help Peck. In Minnie's telling, Peck told her that she "wanted to get her; she wanted to bring her back here. . . . I supposed it would be for the treatments." Peck apparently continued to maintain that Nina must take the mercury injections. She continued to tell Minnie that her daughter would be thrown in the house of correction if she didn't comply.[151]

Peck would testify that she "called on" Minnie "perhaps three or four times" while Nina was away. "My object in doing that was to find out where the girl was. I made every effort I could from that mother to find out her address." Yet Peck maintained—a tad unbelievably—that she was asking for Nina's address not in order to bring her back for treatment or imprisonment, but rather to help a St. Louis woman collect on a bill Nina supposedly owed her. Just why she would put so much effort into helping this woman—the jeweler's wife—collect on a debt for a diamond ring, Peck did not elaborate. (One wonders how the ostracized and chronically unemployed Nina could have qualified for credit in the first place.)[152] In any event, Peck's frequent visits surely provided at least some of the motivation for what Minnie did next.

"I sent for her to come home," Minnie would testify. "I thought I had some good news to tell her." A mysterious woman of some means—and with a strange religion—had come to see Minnie, and she had raised for Minnie an interesting possibility: Nina could sue the government to get its agents to stop harassing her. Minnie was intrigued, and she thought Nina might be too. So she sent a message summoning Nina back home.[153]

Mother and daughter had never before spoken of a lawsuit, per se. But, before Nina had left, they had talked of right and wrong. "We talked of what we thought ought to be right," Minnie would testify. "We felt that we had been injured." Perhaps the thought of a legal claim had crossed their minds, but they knew "we were not able to do that," Minnie recalled. At one point, Nina told her, "we will get even yet." "Now whether you would call that a suit or not," Minnie continued, "I don't know." Apparently, Nina had been considering resistance in her own unlettered way long before she found outside aid.[154]

Sometime early in September, shortly after receiving her mother's message, Nina McCall returned to Alma, determined to fight.

Chapter 8

"WHEN RIGHTEOUS WOMEN ARISE"

NINA MCCALL'S GUARDIAN ANGEL, Elizabeth Beverly Barr, was born in 1876 in Rockingham County, Virginia, a community of farmers and miners situated between the eastern peaks of the Allegheny Mountains and the western foothills of the Blue Ridge Mountains. She and her family soon moved from Appalachia to Baltimore, and then to Washington, DC. It was there, on September 3, 1900—the day after Nina was born six hundred miles away—that Elizabeth married John Githens, a New Jersey native several years her senior. The young couple relocated to St. Louis, Missouri, where John, an attorney, started working for Missouri Pacific Railroad. As a general freight agent for the railroad, he traveled around the country, becoming well known on the West Coast as well as in the Midwest. In 1912, he was promoted to the position of freight traffic manager. At some point in the next few years, though, John left the railroad to become a manager at Republic Motor Truck Company. This was, recall, the company that was based in Alma, Michigan; that employed Nina's brother, Vern; and that had attracted the soldiers who likely led to her detention.[1]

When John joined Republic, the company seemed unstoppable; during World War I, it had practically printed money. The Githenses moved to Alma to get in on the action, though it appears they also had a home in Chicago. (Many of the company's executives chose to live elsewhere, such as New York or Cleveland, not small, rural Alma.) John spent his time working for Republic, which was confidently expanding in the wake of its extraordinary wartime success. Elizabeth, meanwhile, filled her days consumed by a passion that she shared with no one else in her family or even her community: Christian Science. Founded just four decades before, Christian Science claimed to return to an earlier, more mystical Christianity. Adherents believed that everything in the physical world—including sickness—was a spiritual illusion. Thus, Christian Scientists eschewed nearly all forms of medicine and instead believed that, since sickness was an illusion, most illnesses could (and must) be cured by prayer alone. In the late nineteenth and early twentieth centuries, Christian Scientists were often ostracized as heretics or loons; many were persecuted or prosecuted when their children died as a result of being denied medical care. A century later, her great-granddaughter was at a loss to explain why Elizabeth joined this small, unusual, deeply spiritual sect.[2]

During the summer of 1919, while Nina was still hiding out in Detroit, Elizabeth Githens came to visit Minnie at her home in Alma. Minnie did not know "Mrs. Githens," as she invariably called her, and she had neither invited her nor had she known she was coming. Yet Mrs. Githens arrived at the small house on Grover Avenue bearing what Minnie later called "good news."[3] Mrs. Githens had somehow heard about Nina's predicament. "[E]verybody was talking [about] it," Nina later recalled, with palpable humiliation.[4] Mrs. Githens told Minnie "that the state of Michigan had no authority to quarantine anybody." She said "they had no right; no law" under which they could isolate women and send them to detention hospitals. Inspired, Minnie wrote to Nina, asking her to return home.[5]

Elizabeth Githens was a small woman. "I wouldn't call her pretty," one relative delicately stated decades later.[6] She was highly active in the Christian Science community, even though she was the sect's sole adherent in Alma.[7] And therein lay the roots of her opposition to the American Plan, and thus to Nina McCall's incarceration. Many Christian Scientists across the country apparently disliked the Plan not because they were unusually concerned about the welfare of women, but because they were fundamentally against the government mandating medical care for anyone, even suspected prostitutes. In New York, a CTCA official hoping to persuade the New York legislature to pass an American Plan law fretted over the presence of a Christian Science legislator.[8] In Los Angeles, it appears that several Christian Scientists signed a petition alleging that women imprisoned in the Los Feliz Detention Hospital were being "subjected to the most tyrannical and abusive compulsory medical treatment."[9] In Arizona, a number of Christian Scientists "have intimated opposition" to the Plan, reported one CTCA official, though he believed "it is not likely, in my opinion, that they will maintain such opposition when they learn that similar legislation is going through in other states."[10]

Shortly after Nina McCall returned home in September 1919, an invitation arrived at the Grover Avenue house from Mrs. Githens. Nina didn't know the iconoclastic Githens, yet she was interested (or desperate) enough to go visit her. "She told me they didn't have any right to pick me up or take me back," Nina recalled of that first meeting. "She told me I could sue for the damages they did to me." This was the first time Nina had ever contemplated a lawsuit. It was a captivating idea. "I didn't decide for sure then" to bring a lawsuit, she later claimed. But still—it was an idea to consider.[11]

OPPOSITION TO THE American Plan from those other than its victims was not limited just to Christian Scientists and the few women within the federal government who had witnessed its iniquities firsthand. Indeed, a small yet prominent handful of individuals, men as well as women, had for years been speaking out against the Plan with considerable fury.

One of the first of these individuals to oppose the Plan was H. L. Mencken. Already a curmudgeon at the age of thirty-seven, the famous journalist wrote a biting article in September 1917, savaging the Plan's administrators as "professional liars." "If patrols go out after suspicious women in the manner indicated by the press accounts," Mencken wrote, "a great many innocent women will be abominably persecuted."[12] A few months later, in Seattle, the International Workers of the World, known as the Wobblies—a radical labor union notorious for its fiery anticapitalist rhetoric and its promotion of social justice—dismissed the Plan as "the time-honored method of chasing the prostitutes around in circles." Many Wobblies, imprisoned for striking, expressed sympathy for the suspected prostitutes in jail alongside them—these "daughters of the working class."[13] A year after that, an eighty-year-old man in San Francisco scrawled a letter to Surgeon General Rupert Blue—an old acquaintance of his—to ask, "why if you are really braced up to real business, you do not deal with male carriers of this infection in the same way, and as publicly, as with women?"[14] Not too far away, in Sacramento, the editors of the *Bee* declared the American Plan an "outrage and an infamy," after twenty-two women were seized in a raid and twenty-one proved to be uninfected.[15]

Within weeks of Nina's meeting with Mrs. Githens, Edith Houghton Hooker—the radical suffragist who had successfully defeated New York's Section 79 a decade before—gave a speech before a gathering of nearly all of the American Plan's administrators and denounced the Plan to their faces as sexist and, perhaps just as importantly, futile. She recounted the story of a Baltimore woman who was detained, examined, and imprisoned for three months on the word of a single policeman. "What did it matter if that friendless woman, with no one to plead for her, were incarcerated?" she asked rhetorically. "It goes back to the primary question . . . because if we annihilated these women as they did the mosquitoes, if we hung by the neck until she were dead every prostitute in the world today, within a week we would have a new crop."[16]

Inarguably, the fiercest and most indefatigable opponent of the American Plan was a tall, slender, intense, gray-haired activist named Katharine Bushnell. Born in frigid, rural Illinois in 1855, Bushnell quickly proved herself to be a brilliant student, becoming—at the age of twenty-four—part of the first generation of female doctors.[17] As an undercover white slavery investigator for the Women's Christian Temperance Union (WCTU), she grew close to Josephine Butler and joined her in opposing the CD Acts, which remained in force throughout the British Empire in the late nineteenth century.[18] She first heard of the American Plan at the fateful July 1917 meeting of officials in San Francisco, and from that day on, she "began my protest."[19] Bushnell considered the Plan to be as damaging and discriminatory as the CD Acts, and she repeated this charge in dozens of eloquent, vitriolic pamphlets, brimming with religious rhetoric.[20] She started working through the night, staying up until 4:00 or 5:00 a.m. each morning, churning out anti-Plan tracts and mailing them to state legislators, US attorneys, military officials, physicians, every member of Congress, every member of the Cabinet, every minister in California, Raymond Fosdick, and hundreds of others.[21] She presciently blamed William F. Snow and his financial backer, John D. Rockefeller.[22] Her pamphlets began causing California officials "a lot of difficulty."[23]

At times, Bushnell despaired in her lonely task. "I am only working in a tiny section of this great country—utterly unable to reach out and do more." Yet she always told herself, "No I will *not* die, I will fight, and God will, if necessary resurrect me from the dead to fight."[24] She founded the Union to Combat the Sanitation of Vice, the only organization ever created explicitly to oppose the Plan, and issued a "Call to Arms" and, later, a "protest" addressed to the secretary of the treasury.[25] Among Bushnell's few allies were several elderly British reformers who had gotten their start battling the CD Acts alongside Josephine Butler decades before; now, they sent advice and money to Bushnell.[26]

In mid-1919, Bushnell decided to go undercover and investigate the Plan across California—a trip she believed would either end with a stunning report "or my own arrest as 'a vagrant with no visible means of support' (pretty near the truth), or something else desperate, to stop my mouth!"[27] She spoke with "repellant" health officers, cowardly judges, and dozens of incarcerated women.[28] Just weeks after Nina McCall's meeting with Mrs. Githens, Bushnell released the results of investigations in a thirty-six-page magnum opus entitled *What's Going On?* "This sort of quarantine," the pamphlet read, "deprives women of Constitutional rights which, if granted, would wreck the Federal measures. It is, practically, a quarantine from the Constitution." Bushnell hoped *What's Going On?*—which one American Plan administrator claimed caused "considerable harm"—would trigger a rebellion of women.[29]

Remarkably, in the final months of 1919, just as Nina was considering a lawsuit, Bushnell's long-sought opposition truly began to arise. "During the war, little was said by leading women relative to the apparent one-sidedness of the law enforcement campaign throughout the country, because of a possibility of confusing the issues, and also because of patriotic reasons," wrote one ASHA official in New York. "The time has now arrived when this issue must be met. Charges are being made by persons who are entitled to a respectful hearing, that the present system of law and law enforcement results in decided sex discrimination."[30] On the other side of the country, a group of eight leading Los Angeles men and women penned a letter to the city's mayor, decrying the "indignities and abuse" that women had suffered at the hands of the police and the health department. "Among these reports are that women arrested by the police department are compelled to submit to an examination in the horrible surroundings of the Los Angeles City Jail, an institution that has been characterized as unfit for human habitation, to say nothing of its total unfitness as a place of quarantine." The eight outraged Angelenos called for a "thorough and painstaking investigation" by a citizen committee to determine "whether or not women arrested and held by the police and health departments in the City Jail, Los Feliz Hospital and elsewhere are being denied their rights as American citizens and subjected to humiliation and abuse."[31] A few weeks later, a gathering of prominent San Diego women "proposed to do away with the hospital where women charged with moral offenses may be detained until they are non-infectious," as one federal official summarized it.[32]

This opposition was worrisome, to say the least. Yet such opposition—from elite journalists and reformers—was limited. Few of these self-righteous opponents took issue with the idea that genuine prostitutes or promiscuous or infected women should be incarcerated, treated, and morally reformed. Indeed, many promoted female reformatories; Bushnell had even founded and run one herself.[33] Rather, they took issue with the sex discrimination inherent in the American Plan's enforcement, and the routine denials of due process. They worried for the Plan's "innocent" victims, while never troubling the distinction between "innocent" and "guilty" women.

And their opposition didn't worry local or federal officials nearly as much as another form of opposition—incarcerated women suing the government.

ON NOVEMBER 3, 1919, almost a year to the day since Ida Peck had delivered Nina to the detention hospital, attorneys Seymour H. Person, Dean W. Kelley, and George P. Stone filed suit on behalf of Nina. The suit named health officer Thomas Carney, matron Mary Corrigan, and the hated Peck. The suit claimed that Nina was "without wrong or fault on her own part; and was reasonably free from any dangerous and communicable disease and from physical and mental disorder; and further was a person of good morals and of normal refinement, and was at all times a law abiding citizen of said County." However, the three defendants

> conspired and confederated together, to transgress the lawful rights, privileges and immunities of this Plaintiff as hereinafter alleged, and to deceive and defraud this Plaintiff in regard thereto; and by concerted schemes, devices, and wrongful assumption and pretense of power and authority and by misrepresentation, coercion and duress caused this Plaintiff to be assaulted, maltreated, abused, arrested, restrained and imprisoned, and grossly slandered, disgraced and humiliated. . . .
>
> [The Defendants] schemed, connived and confederated together among themselves and with divers[e] other persons both in official positions and without the shadow and shield of office . . . [and] commanded this Plaintiff to submit her body to an examination by [Carney], whereupon this Plaintiff refused to so submit herself, and that while said Plaintiff was in such condition of fear, restraint and duress, and without her lawful consent or the lawful consent of any person in her behalf, said Carney did then and there in a vulgar, rude and wrongful manner misuse, maltreat and abuse this Plaintiff in and about her body, and did then and there commit with force and arms an assault upon this Plaintiff thereby causing both physical and mental pain and suffering, and whereby she suffered great humiliation and disgrace, and a sense of degradation which has continued to this present day.

The petition continued in this vein for several pages. It was a starkly powerful (if wordy) indictment of the American Plan.[34]

Nina's three attorneys—Person, Kelley, and Stone—were not just any attorneys. They were among the most powerful lawyers in Michigan. Person had represented Lansing in the Michigan State House since 1915.[35] Perhaps it is significant that he had been working for the YMCA in France when the state legislature approved the Dunn bill—Michigan's American Plan law—and thus he hadn't voted for it.[36] Perhaps it is even more significant that he had personal experience with wrongful incarcerations; once, as a young lawyer in Lansing, he had been locked up when the police mistook him for the client he had been retained to represent. Seymour had fought back, kicking a police sergeant when he tried to search him.[37]

Kelley was a politically ambitious man who had first run for county prosecutor at the age of twenty-seven.[38] He won that election and later ran for state senator (a race he lost) but was appointed to his local school board the next year.[39] In 1914, the governor appointed him to serve a term as probate judge.[40]

Stone was the only one of Nina's attorneys from Gratiot County, yet he had no less august a reputation. Stone, who was several decades older than Person and Kelley, had also been a judge. He had served one term as a circuit court judge in Gratiot and Clinton Counties two decades before. "Judge Stone is most popular throughout the county, and at the time of his election was chosen as Democratic candidate by a large majority, though Gratiot and Clinton are usually sure Republican counties," reported one newspaper when his term expired at the end of 1905. "The judge owns a beautiful home in Ithaca"—just minutes from Alma and St. Louis—"and farms just out of the city. He will continue his law business and manage the affairs of his estate after his judgeship ceases."[41] Yet Stone quickly became restless and ran for state supreme court two years later.[42] When he lost that election, he settled into a comfortable life as a prominent local attorney.[43] In 1918, Stone ran for Gratiot County prosecutor. He lost again; Michigan really was a hard state for Democratic candidates.[44] Once again, he resigned himself to private practice. Stone—like Nina's other two lawyers—was well prepared for an epic fight.

The prominence of Nina's attorneys raises an intriguing question, one that consumed Michigan officials—how could she possibly have afforded them? The answer is unknowable at this late date. Certainly, the three might have taken the case pro bono; perhaps they agreed that a grave injustice had been done to her. Or perhaps Elizabeth Githens paid their bills; many government officials assumed this was the case. Setting this matter aside, it seems quite likely that Nina found the lawyers through Elizabeth Githens, whose husband was also a successful attorney. Nina and Mrs. Githens had remained in close contact since their first meeting several weeks before.

Sometime after that meeting, Mrs. Githens's housekeeper quit, and Nina took her place. The Githenses often had black domestic servants, yet apparently Elizabeth was fond of Nina and brought her on instead.[45] The formerly unemployable nineteen-year-old suddenly had a job. She did housework for the wealthy older woman for the next couple of months. After the Githenses bought a car in December, Nina also acted as Mrs. Githens's chauffeur. She did all of this for no pay, which Nina felt was only fair, since she lived with Mrs. Githens during this time. Besides, a lot of the driving was for Nina, anyway. "It was about the trial that she was taking me [by car]; she took me so I could get there," Nina recalled, perhaps meaning that she had taken the car to meet with her lawyers.

It is difficult to imagine how Nina could have brought her lawsuit without the aid of Mrs. Githens. "I asked her to help me. I asked her if she would stand by me." Mrs. Githens said yes. Nina considered her "a friend."[46]

Nina was able to live with Mrs. Githens because she was thoroughly alienated from her husband, Clare Rock. The two hadn't lived together since

Detroit, when he was busy running around with other women. Indeed, the serially philandering Rock had remarried in October 1919, to a twenty-two-year-old domestic servant named Rose, even though he was technically still married to Nina.[47] It appears he would cheat on Rose as well.[48] Obviously, he would provide no support to Nina during her legal odyssey.

Nina also could not live with her mother. Around this time, Minnie moved to Detroit. It is unclear why she did so, and she would soon return, but her motive may have been economic. Minnie, who it appears had never held a formal job before, was listed on the 1920 census as a music teacher. Significantly, she did not move with her husband, Henry Van Norman. Why the two remained apart is unclear, but the separation was permanent. For all intents and purposes, it appears that their marriage was over.[49]

In the coming days, Nina's lawyers filed much of the necessary paperwork for the lawsuit, and attorneys representing Peck, Carney, and Corrigan responded. For the next several weeks, little happened. The case crawled through the Gratiot County court system. It wasn't until many months later that Nina finally received a court date.[50] Yet, as a direct result of Nina filing suit, Alma authorities quickly suspended their enforcement of the American Plan. For months thereafter, the *Alma Record* later recounted, "little has been done locally, as officials were not certain of all of the legal questions that might be involved."[51]

MRS. GITHENS WAS A BUSY WOMAN. For weeks, she had been running around the state, interviewing young women, scribbling down their words in shorthand, collecting funds for these women, and discovering as much as she possibly could about the American Plan. Her opposition to the Plan had become an obsession, and she was determined to defeat it.[52]

Just days after Nina's lawyers filed her lawsuit, Mrs. Githens appeared in Battle Creek—home to Camp Custer, Michigan's military base—and met with a number of local residents, including the elderly Winfield S. Ensign and several of his sons. The Ensigns ran a mail-order patent medicine company, promising remedies for virtually every illness known to man, as well as for "bashfulness, disappointment in love and similar ailments," according to one medical journal. (Their medicine, one state investigation discovered, was sugar pills.) They also edited the *Truth-Teller*, a semimonthly publication dedicated to "medical freedom." The Ensigns and the *Truth-Teller* were especially opposed to animal cruelty in medical experimentation, as well as what they perceived as the diktats of the medical establishment, such as compulsory vaccinations. All this earned them the scorn and derision of the American

Medical Association, but it also surely endeared them to Elizabeth Githens, the dedicated Christian Scientist.[53]

Mrs. Githens told her audience all that she had discovered of the American Plan—and they were horrified. "The little city of Alma, Michigan, has less than 3,000 population," wrote one of the Ensigns in *Truth-Teller* soon thereafter, summarizing her speech. "Yet over one hundred young girls of that community have been railroaded to a 'detention home' as venereal cases or suspects. Some of these were not more than fourteen or fifteen years of age. Some of them were not only innocent of any disease, but thoroughly good girls, their only fault poverty and defenselessness." Githens told the shocked Battle Creek residents about the "menial toil," the vermin, and the "poor food" that Nina and the others had been forced to bear at Bay City.

> Worst of all were the medical examinations and treatment to which they were subjected. Sexual examination and treatment at the hands of three men, of a nature that sent girls out of the treatment room bitterly weeping at the gross indignities to which they had to submit, followed by the ribald laughter of the doctors, was a part of it. So oppressed by the horror of it were some of the girls that suicide was attempted and in one instance a tormented girl died of the poison she swallowed in the hope of escape.

She also told the Ensigns and others about Ida Peck.

> The method employed to get hold of the girls was as follows: A "nurse" in the employ of the health board would go to the home of a girl, walk boldly in without the formality of knocking at the door, and demand that the girl accompany her to the city health office. If she or her mother objected she was told that if she refused a sign with large letters would be place in the window, with the words, "Venereal Disease Exists in this House." . . . The girl was also told unless she went peaceably, the chief of police would be called and he would forcibly take her to the health office. Rarely did these threats fail of their object. Poor girls, or girls without one or both parents, were usually selected.

Almost every line of Mrs. Githens's speech echoed Nina's story.

After she finished speaking, an elderly man in the audience, identifying himself as Colonel Sol L. Long, stood up and declared, "Madam, you have told a terrible story, but I know it is tame in comparison with the actual facts, a good deal of which you have had to suppress." He claimed that he had known of these happenings for a long time, and that the only way to stop them was to shake up the entire medical establishment.

The Ensigns were apparently so moved by Mrs. Githens's speech that they printed a recounting of it in the *Truth-Teller*'s November 15 issue. A New York firm then reprinted their article as a pamphlet, entitled *Protecting the Public Health*, and distributed it widely across Michigan. Within days, it had reached Alma, where it caused a scandal. Some citizens were undoubtedly disturbed by the accusations contained in *Protecting the Public Health*; others were more miffed at the pall it cast upon Alma.

The editors of the *Alma Record* were especially irate. The pamphlet, they wrote on their front page and in an editorial, was "base slander . . . sent out promiscuously from New York City," which "reflects greatly upon the moral tone of the City of Alma. . . . It is evidently part of a propaganda, being circulated for some purpose. It is injuring Alma greatly no matter what the reason." The *Record* pointed out that Alma's population was eight thousand, not three thousand as the pamphlet had claimed, and they asserted that only twenty-five women had been examined and incarcerated, not one hundred. The paper admitted that some of these women had been as young as fourteen, but it endorsed this action, for these girls "are highly dangerous." The paper also rejected Mrs. Githens's assertion that some of the women were "not only innocent of a disease, but thoroughly good girls."

"[I]t is highly doubtful if thoroughly good girls would be in company that would bring them under suspicion of having such diseases," the editors scoffed.

The *Alma Record* took particular issue with the statement of Col. Sol L. Long. "We have not had the pleasure of meeting the enthusiastic Col. Sol L. Long," the editors wrote with bitter sarcasm, "but we would judge that his claim to the title of Colonel may be based upon the ability to shoot off his mouth, and let it run on forever like Tennyson's Brook. The fact that 'Col. Sol' should jump to his feet like a startled buck, and fly to the defense of this kind of slanderous propaganda would indicate that he is some bird, but some birds are queer anyhow."[54] Solomon Levy Long was, in fact, a fascinating figure, though whether or not he was truly a colonel is hard to tell. He claimed to have an MD and a PhD, to be a dentist, an artillery general, and a knight; he maintained that he had fought for the Confederate Army at the age of thirteen; been elected to the Kansas state legislature; served the Americans in the medical corps in Nicaragua and Guatemala; served the British as a sergeant in South Africa, Ireland, and India; served the French (at some point) as a brigadier general; and served the Texas Rangers as, yes, a colonel. He had, in truth, practiced law for many years, served as a Kansas state senator, and then given up law to write poetry and preach. The rest is harder to pin down.

Long was especially dedicated to "drugless systems of healing" and hated the medical establishment, which is almost certainly where his opposition to the American Plan came from.[55]

State authorities were so worried about the effects of this pamphlet that they soon dispatched Katharine Ostrander, the state's director of protective work for women, to Alma. Ostrander addressed a town meeting and informed the residents that their town was "no better, but no worse than the average community in this respect, but that the state desires a statewide cleanup of social diseases so far as possible, and the laws of the state and the regulations of the State Board of Health make it very evident that officials will have backing in the campaign." Carney's successor as health officer said that he was amenable to resuming examinations. Ostrander also addressed Nina's case directly. She said that the state "was very desirous of seeing the case carried through to the supreme court to settle such trouble for all time, and appeared very confident what the result would be, in view of the regulations of the State Board of Health, which back up the work of health officials of Michigan."[56]

ON NOVEMBER 19, 1919, Thomas J. Carney made a smart move. He formally hired O. L. Smith—Gratiot County's prosecutor—as his personal attorney.[57] Smith was something of a wunderkind: after graduating from the University of Michigan's law school in 1913, he practiced privately for just a year before becoming Gratiot's prosecutor in 1914. A photograph from his final year of law school shows a chubby-cheeked, cleft-chinned young man with prominent ears, a severe widow's peak, and a determined stare.[58] He was of average height and average weight, not an especially attractive man, yet possessed of a canny gaze and big, blue eyes.[59] In 1918, Smith ran for reelection as prosecutor against the man who had been his law partner for his year in private practice: George P. Stone. Smith defeated Stone. Surely this would provide a psychological advantage in the fratricidal battle Nina's trial was shaping up to be.[60]

Two months after being hired, on January 23, 1920, Smith wrote a letter to C. C. Pierce, head of the US Public Health Service's Division of Venereal Diseases and a member of the Interdepartmental Social Hygiene Board. "Will you kindly forward me at once any and all rules and measures adopted for the purpose of assisting the various States in caring for civilian persons whose detention, quarantine or commitment to institutions was found to be necessary for the protection of the military and naval forces of the United States against venereal diseases," he asked. "Dr. T. J. Carney of Alma, Michigan, was the committing officer for this County and suit has been instituted against him for what was claimed to be an unauthorized and illegal detention of the person committed to the detention hospital at Bay City. I am representing Dr. Carney in this matter and I am very anxious to have the material asked for in this letter immediately so that I may prepare proper plea and notice as this case is to be tried in the February term which begins in the second week."[61]

Pierce wrote back three days later, informing Smith about the Chamberlain-Kahn Act, the board, and federal appropriations to Michigan. He added that the federal government would "be glad to furnish any additional data you may need . . . in defending the action instituted against Dr. T. J. Carney" and provided Smith with a copy of a similar lawsuit from Texas that could help him in forming his argument. Copies of this suit had, Pierce noted, previously been mailed to "all prosecuting attorneys in the State of Michigan."[62]

This exchange was revealing. Federal officials like Pierce closely monitored cases like Nina's, for they knew that these cases were dangerous. If judges decided them the wrong way, they could spell the death of the American Plan.

Two of the first lawsuits challenging the Plan both appeared in the state of Washington in 1918. In the first, a young woman named Edna Woods was dragged from her hotel room and forced, "against her will and under protest," to submit to an STI examination; in the second, a young man named Francis Williams was similarly detained and examined. Both were found to be carrying STIs and both were locked in the city jail's hospital ward—a place one quarantined individual later called "most unsanitary and filthy, poorly ventilated and overcrowded." Both Woods and Williams sued for their freedom. A lower court quickly denied Woods's habeas petition, but, perhaps revealing a sexist double standard, a judge ordered that a panel of new physicians confirm Williams's diagnosis, as well as the diagnoses of the dozens of other individuals seeking habeas relief in Seattle, to see if they'd been "lawfully detained." Seattle's health officer, J. S. McBride, was furious and refused to comply. He decided to seek an order from the state supreme court to prevent local judges from second-guessing the health department's actions.[63]

The federal government was watching. In an attempt to persuade the state supreme court to rule in McBride's favor, US Surgeon General Rupert Blue asked an assistant attorney general to go to Olympia and advocate on McBride's behalf.[64] The assistant attorney general did so, and his advocacy worked beautifully.[65] The Washington State Supreme Court declared that the health officials' power to detain suspected individuals, examine them, and quarantine them was "not challenged"—and, indeed, could not be challenged; their actions were not even subject to judicial review. They could only be interfered with when they were "unreasonable and oppressive." Practically speaking, this endowed health officer McBride with virtually unlimited authority over his patients. "The immediate effect of the ruling at the local level," historian Nancy Rockafellar commented dryly, "was to cut off all legal action on behalf of quarantined inmates. Dr. McBride, confirmed in his authority, refused to allow patients to communicate further with any attorneys."[66]

The *McBride* case was hugely influential, heralded across the country by experts and journalists alike.[67] It would be cited in numerous cases challenging the validity of the American Plan.[68] In Texas, Nebraska, Ohio, Kansas, Alabama, and Oklahoma, appellate courts ruled that state laws allowing the examination of "reasonably suspected" women or the incarceration of these women were perfectly acceptable.[69] From 1919 to 1921, the court of appeal of California decided a handful of cases that together would set much of the precedent that allowed state and local governments to continue to isolate infected women for decades to come. Though petitioners won some of these cases, and the government won others, the court of appeal's cumulative message was that, so long as the state had reasonable suspicion, it could arrest, examine, and isolate individuals at will. Suspicion of prostitution or presence in a brothel was reasonable enough.[70] Even in a case in which the California justices ruled in favor of the imprisoned woman, they also made sure to write: "Where sufficient reasonable cause exists to believe that a person is afflicted with a quarantinable disease, there is no doubt of the right of the health authorities to examine into the case and, in a proper way, determine the fact."[71]

Federal officials closely monitored all these cases.[72] They also kept a careful eye on local lawsuits that had not yet reached appellate courts. When judges in these suits were not amenable to enforcing American Plan procedures, they would hear from irate federal officials, and those officials would be sure to send a report on the incident to their bosses.[73] Even local officials enforcing the Plan kept abreast of the lawsuits. In December 1919, just a few weeks before Smith wrote to Pierce about Nina's lawsuit, a Women's Court judge in New York wrote to the head of the Committee of Fourteen to discuss "the 'venereal disease-arrest' decisions." "It seems to me," the judge wrote, that the Seattle cases and the one in Nebraska "undoubtedly make reasonable suspicion a ground both for examination and detention until the period of infection is past."[74] These lawsuits thus had an influence far broader than just setting precedent; since they were so closely watched, they also dictated practices.

Federal officials even tried to prevent young women from being able to file suit in the first place. In mid-1919, just months before Nina initiated her lawsuit, a CTCA agent traveled to Chicago to meet with members of the American Bar Association's (ABA) executive committee, trying to persuade them to push the nation's lawyers not to oppose the American Plan. The CTCA man believed his meeting had been a success, writing that the ABA would adopt a resolution that would "remove some hindrances from the path of law enforcement and create a sentiment among lawyers against lending their efforts to those who are in opposition to the Government in this vital matter." Ultimately, the ABA declined to endorse so extreme a resolution. Its executive committee resolved only that "we cordially endorse and desire to cooperate with the efforts of the United States Government and the various State Governments and municipal authorities in stamping out venereal diseases throughout the United States."[75] Still, such a resolution did not bode well for young women hoping to find counsel to sue the government. It makes Nina's actions appear all the more extraordinary.

ON MARCH 2, 1920—a chilly, cloudy day—Robert Mundy, the mayor of Bay City, frantically called and then telegraphed Health Commissioner Richard Olin.[76] "Slight fire at Detention Hospital," he wrote. "Detain [elsewhere] any girls you expected to send [to Bay City] for a day or two. Will advise later."[77] The fire had apparently started in the attic and spread to the roof and third floor, destroying many of its interior decorations. No one had died, and the fire was eventually extinguished (presumably by the fire department), though much of the building was "thoroughly soaked with water" as one newspaper put it.[78] Mayor Mundy estimated that the detention hospital would be up and running again in about a week.[79] The police had the inmates in custody.[80]

According to the newspaper, "The fire is believed to have started from defective wiring in the attic."[81] Looking back, there is certainly no reason to believe otherwise; Mundy did not provide an explanation for the fire. However, it was not unprecedented for women incarcerated under the American Plan to resist their captivity by setting their sites of detention on fire. Indeed, it was common. Of the forty-three detention houses and reformatories for infected women funded by the federal government, five were destroyed by fires (almost certainly set by inmates).[82] "Fractious inmates" burned down the City Farm of Newport News, Virginia, five months after it opened in 1919. Quarantined women burned down the City Farm of Houston, Texas, not just once, but twice.[83] These fires sometimes had devastating consequences for the inmates themselves. After imprisoned women set the detention house in Lawton, Oklahoma, ablaze, there was no insurance and the inmates were transferred to the county jail, a "miserable place," in the words of a government employee.[84] Nonetheless, the fires represented genuine resistance on the part of the women.

Setting fires was not the only method of resistance for women incarcerated under the American Plan. In one wing of the horribly overcrowded Louisville jail, for instance, quarantined women staged a riot about once a week. (The CTCA official on site also noted their use of "terrible language.")[85] A woman incarcerated under the Plan in San Diego staged a three-day hunger strike to win her release.[86] Reformatory inmates sometimes assaulted their captors and engaged in what Maude Miner called "smashing out"—running down a hallway, breaking all the windows.[87] In Ponce, Puerto Rico, more than three hundred imprisoned women rioted after the prison director forbade family members from bringing them food and cigarettes; the women shouted insults to the US-appointed attorney general and refused to take their mercury injections. Only mass solitary confinement quelled the riot, but later thirty-eight inmates set fires in protest.[88] In Seattle, where conditions for quarantined women were especially vile, inmates attacked guards, clogged toilets, and destroyed the sewing machines that had just been installed for "vocational training." One day, fully half of the inmates lay in bed and refused to go to breakfast.[89] Such examples present a tempting, though ultimately speculative, explanation for the Bay City fire.

These women locked up under the American Plan were fighting back.

IT WAS DURING THE spring of 1920 that elite women—those connected to the federal government—began plotting their own (admittedly limited) campaign to fight back too.

After years of thinking, Ethel Sturges Dummer had formulated a novel hypothesis: "After reading of Shell shock cures, it occurred to me that much of the apparent feeblemindedness of women in reformatories might be a mental condition similar to shellshock and curable. Surely the curse of condemnation given to a very young girl having sex experience, followed by the often really indecent court procedure, is enough to wreck her mind."[90] It was a remarkably humane idea—that supposedly immoral women were, in fact, simply suffering from mental illness or trauma, both of which were treatable but which might be exacerbated by the harshness of the American Plan. The implication was that prostitutes and promiscuous women should be treated compassionately when they were locked up.

Dummer wrote to Jessie Binford—another Chicago female reformer—asking her what she thought about hosting a conference to promote this hypothesis. Binford, the Midwestern district supervisor for the Interdepartmental Social Hygiene Board, was spending her days attempting to implement the Plan in cities all across the Midwest—Detroit, Cleveland, Louisville, St. Louis, East St. Louis, Rockford, Des Moines, and Junction City—and supervising the board's field-workers in these cities.[91] Yet Binford felt that she was more detail-oriented than Dummer, and she too was worried by the severity of the Plan, so she began planning the conference. Then, however, Binford contracted influenza, and she had to return to her home in Iowa to convalesce. She advised Dummer to "wait until we are a little more sure of our ground" before holding the conference. Dummer assented.[92]

Just one month later, though, the restless Dummer, along with other women in the government, considered attempting to draw the ASHA and the board into a roundtable discussion at a springtime conference in Riverside, California, to "show them that in this law enforcement and lock hospital method, they are but following the European regulation which has proved a failure."[93] Yet Dummer ended up missing this conference when her sister-in-law fell ill.[94] It was almost as if her opposition were cursed. After the Riverside conference, Dummer, Martha Falconer, and other female feds began planning to use the National Conference of Social Work, to be held months later, to urge a more humane and scientific method of "social control" of female criminal offenders.[95]

Dummer also began making connections to opponents of the American Plan outside the government. Early in March 1920—just days after the Bay City Detention Hospital burned—she first read of Katharine Bushnell and her pamphlet, *What's Going On?* The former CPWG official eagerly struck up a correspondence with the Plan's most vocal critic. Dummer invited Bushnell to her conferences and expressed optimism that the conferences could effect change. "Surely," Dummer wrote, "if we women demand justice and opportunity for her, we may save much of this wreckage of life."[96] Bushnell was far less certain, yet she kept writing back, and the two developed a warm rapport. Bushnell even sent Dummer one of Edith Houghton Hooker's "admirable" articles condemning the "Federal scheme," which Dummer apparently enjoyed.[97] Dummer began showing *What's Going On?*—"practically the only open protest against our government's social hygiene program," she called it—to her fellow female reformers. Copies went out to Jessie Binford, Martha Falconer, Jane Addams, and several others. "I think it is very important," she told Binford, though she wished "Dr. Bushnell had made more promin[e]nt her appreciation of the rehabilitation work. We must all unite on that."[98]

In a way, Bushnell had predicted Dummer's small acts of resistance. In an extraordinary letter she wrote early in 1920 to a male federal official, Bushnell claimed that "thousands of women like myself" were ready

> to be on the alert to combat, and one day your abominable measures will, with the help of Almighty God get the *full force* of the unutterable hatred and scorn with which we view them, and in that day may God have pity for the framers of such measures! For when righteous women arise, it may be impossible for us to rise alone and do simply justice and no more, as we would wish, but every harlot that this system has manufactured, and every innocent woman whose virgin body has been raped by the

doctor's intruding hand, may take advantage of our rising—a great body of incarnate fiends and furies, and you men must take the consequences.

Such an uprising, she predicted, would be comparable to the French and Russian Revolutions. "Soon every woman who is not at heart a prostitute to the task of pleasing the male sex at cost of the virtue of other women will rise against your measures. You have stood a pyramid upon its apex, and I advise you to get out from under before it falls."[99]

Whether Dummer's civilized attempts at resistance would constitute this glorious uprising very much remained to be seen.

FINALLY, ON APRIL 1, 1920, Nina McCall's own attempt at resistance moved one step closer to fruition. On that day, her case was finally granted a place on the calendar of the Gratiot County Circuit Court. Her lawsuit would be heard on June 1—just two months away.[100] She was that much nearer to victory and vindication—or, of course, to bitter failure.

On May 27, just a week before Nina's trial opened, Alma's weekly newspaper ran a prominent story on the case—"it is now expected, and promises to be watched with interest over the entire state, being in the nature of a test case." The journalist who wrote the article briefly recounted the facts of the case and concluded, "The case promises to cover state laws, state board of health rulings, and to bring in the government act, which had as its end the protection of the American soldiers from diseased women. The case is an unusual one in Michigan, and is attracting wide attention, and it is more than possible that it will go to the supreme court for a decision, following the circuit court battle."[101]

Chapter 9

"HUNTING FOR GIRLS"

GAZING UP TO THE HEAVENS, Nina McCall would have seen darkening clouds and an ominous, gray sky. The weather presented a gloomy omen on that first day of the trial, Tuesday, June 1, 1920. The temperature was cool and comfortable but the forecasts called for rain that afternoon and evening— probably thunderstorms.[1] Despite the weather, Nina strode resolutely toward the Gratiot County Courthouse. Also making this short journey was her mother, Minnie, as well as her three powerful attorneys—Seymour H. Person, Dean W. Kelley, and George P. Stone. Person and Kelley were of a similar build and age—both were of medium height and girth, both were in their early forties, and both had bluish eyes, though Person's hair was already graying while Kelley's was still dark.[2] Stone, in contrast, was wrinkled and wizened, with sparse silver hair, already well into his seventies.[3] But surely he walked into the courthouse with a sense of comfort that his comrades could not match; a generation earlier, he had been the judge in this very courthouse. In fact, Stone himself had overseen the construction of the courthouse; no one had been more integral to its completion.[4]

The Gratiot County Courthouse was, according to one enthusiastic local historian, "one of the finest buildings of the kind in the state. . . . To say that its imposing appearance and its commodious appointments excite the admiration of all—citizens of the county, strangers and sojourners, alike—is but stating the bare fact, without exaggeration or embellishment."[5] The cornerstone had been laid on September 18, 1900, barely two weeks after Nina McCall's birth, on a glorious day, following the largest parade Ithaca had ever seen. Ithaca was the seat of Gratiot County, and, in spite of a formidable challenge from nearby Alma, it was the natural site for the location of the new courthouse. For the next two years, Judge Stone led battles against unscrupulous contractors and bondsmen even as he sat atop the bench in the old wooden courthouse just feet away from the hammering. In the summer of 1902, he and his staff moved into the new courthouse; in 1905, a clock was finally added to the handsome, 120-foot tower.[6]

Gazing up once more, Nina would have seen a courthouse that was two-and-a-half stories high, crowned with an elaborate, multitiered, octagonal-domed clock tower and belfry. The building was constructed of warm yellow-brown sandstone, elaborately carved with reliefs and flourishes. Spiral-fluted Corinthian columns and an arched entrance set off the front of the court-house. The columns featured reliefs of lions with disconcertingly human faces. Twin rows of trees flanked the path Nina and her lawyers walked up, surrounded on both sides by green carpets of grass.[7]

The two women and three men entered the courthouse, climbed a flight of iron steps, and found themselves in the courthouse's signature rotunda. It was a beautiful space—"frescoed walls and ceilings, the paneled wainscot-ing of polished oak, the tiled floor," gushed one local journalist. To the left was the county clerk, and to the right were the register of deeds, the county drain commissioner, the probate judge, and the county treasurer. Yet Nina's party proceeded up a second spacious staircase to the second floor. There, on the east end of the building, was the circuit courtroom—"large, finely and appropriately furnished and decorated, fitted up with tables, chairs, book-racks, and last but not least, an elaborate throne for the Judge."[8] The judge that day was Edward J. Moinet, a tall, strapping man with gray hair and brown eyes.[9]

There were seats for spectators on the inclined floor—"with opera chairs of the latest pattern." The courtroom was lit by electric bulbs, as well as light from the many tall windows looking out on Ithaca.[10] At some point, Nina's adversaries—Mary Corrigan, Ida Peck, and Thomas J. Carney—entered the courtroom as well, joined by their lawyers: James Kress, Alva M. Cummins, and O. L. Smith. Smith may well have come into the courtroom straight from the prosecutor's office, which was in the northwest corner of the second floor.[11]

The first order of business was jury selection. It appears not to have taken long, for testimony began that same day. Nina's jury, seated in a box to the side, facing the judge and witness stand, consisted of twelve men. After jury selec-tion, the first witness mounted the stand.[12]

Yet there was something oddly familiar about this whole tableau. A sense of déjà vu permeated the cool summer air. Many of the major players had been there before. Just two years earlier, in fact, lawyers George P. Stone and O. L. Smith had squared off in this very courtroom, in front of Judge Edward Moinet. They had been on the opposite sides of a sensational murder trial. A man named Albert Eichorn—a "big, burly fellow, who has the reputation of being something of a bully"—had been accused of killing sixteen-year-old Beatrice Epler, a young woman who was rumored to have spent a little too much time in Millerville, Alma's red-light district.[13] Stone stood for the defendant, while Smith was the prosecutor. Such a great crowd of spectators flocked into Judge Moinet's courtroom to see the two of them do battle that the floorboards began to sag and the plaster started to crack.[14]

Epler, the murdered young woman, and Nina shared a number of eerie similarities. They had been born within days of each other, and they had
lived just houses apart in Alma. In such a small town, the two certainly would
have known one another. At the murder trial in 1918, in spite of the testimony
of multiple alibi witnesses, it took the jury barely two hours to convict the
brawny Eichorn. Judge Moinet promptly handed down a life sentence, the
maximum penalty in Michigan. The Eichorn case made the front pages across
the state.[15] It was surely as thrilling a victory for Smith, the young prosecutor, as it was a crushing defeat for Stone, the former judge several decades
Smith's senior. Only years later would it emerge that the case against Eichorn
had been based on lies and greed. He, like Nina, had been wrongfully imprisoned. For the moment, though, in June 1920, two years after the Eichorn trial,
Stone and Smith were up against each other again. In the intervening time,
Smith had beaten Stone in the race for prosecutor. The trial of Nina McCall
was Stone's last chance at redemption. This was personal.

THE FIRST PERSON to walk across the dark hardwood floor and settle into the
witness stand, below the mural of Lady Justice, was nineteen-year-old Nina.[16]
She was just feet from the court clerk, from the jury, from the stenographer,
and from Judge Moinet himself, whose gaze surely intimidated her. He had an
arresting face—high forehead, fringe of graying hair, penetrating eyes staring
from behind rimless spectacles. A handsome, scholarly sort of face, but with
an intensity to it.[17]

Edward Julian Moinet had been born forty-seven years earlier in Stark
County, Ohio, the fourth child of a French father and an Ohioan mother.
When he was young, his family had moved to St. Johns, Michigan, the seat of
Clinton County, just to the south of Gratiot. Moinet attended public schools
and then the University of Michigan, from which he earned a law degree
in 1895. He practiced for a few years in Ithaca before returning to Clinton
County, where he soon became the county prosecutor.[18] On January 1, 1918,
he was one of fourteen new circuit judges to ascend to the bench, in the greatest judicial shakeup in the state's history.[19] It was a moment of triumph for the
ambitious Moinet, but this victory came just months after his seventeen-year-
old son fell into a water tank and died.[20] Determined in spite of this tragedy,
Moinet assumed the bench. He was something of a moralist, later railing in a
speech against the corrupting evils of the cigarette.[21] He was also a religious
man, keeping a copy of the Bible in his law library. His grandson, now an
Episcopal bishop, remembers him as a natty dresser, a good-looking, well-
respected jurist who loved the Detroit Tigers and double chocolate sundaes.
"Wherever he went, he would always whistle a little tune. A little Irish tune."[22]

Yet some who appeared before him remembered him more bitterly—he was "known as a reactionary, politically, and as a petty and mean man," recalled one lawyer years later.[23] Decades later, one Gratiot County judge would hear a rumor that Judge Moinet had owned a brothel. The judge didn't believe this rumor, but the very existence of the story is fascinating.[24]

With the eyes of Moinet—and everyone else—upon her, Nina commenced her testimony with a simple recitation of her life. "I am the Plaintiff here and I was nineteen years old on September 2nd, 1919," she began, in response to prompting by Dean Kelley. "I spent my girlhood in the country until I was about ten years old and then I moved to the village of St. Louis. My father died in 1916." She continued in this direct, unadorned style for a few more minutes. She had never met Carney, Peck, or Corrigan before her detention and incarceration. She had never before heard of the Bay City Detention Hospital either. Then she arrived at the point of her story. "On a certain occasion I was accosted by the sheriff, Mr. Martin," she stated. "I knew that he was stopping girls but I didn't know anything about the hospital then. I knew he was an officer."[25]

When Kelley asked what Martin had said to her, O. L. Smith rose to object for the first time. Any answer Nina gave "would be absolutely hearsay," Smith argued, "and would be prejudicial to these Defendants at this time." Judge Moinet agreed and sustained the objection. George Stone rose and tried to help out his junior colleague, but to no avail. The first round went to Smith, and the contents of the conversation that led to Nina's detention were lost forever.[26]

Nina continued her story largely uninterrupted for the next while: Deputy Sheriff Martin took her to health officer Carney, who told her that he wanted to examine her for STIs. When she refused, vehemently, Carney insisted it was the law.

"Did you believe what Dr. Carney told you about the law?" Kelley asked.

"Yes, I did."[27]

Carney examined the sobbing young woman and pronounced her infected. In a remarkable act of courage that she recounted in the same flat style, Nina called him a liar. Carney told her she would have to go to Bay City. After some persuading (and some lying on the health officer's part), Nina agreed to go. She recounted her first days in the detention hospital: her blood test, her painful treatments, her begging Miss Peck and Miss Corrigan to let her leave.[28]

"What liberties did you have in and about the hospital?"

"Well, we had to get permission to go out of doors; we used to go out in the yard once in a while. We never crossed—there was a ditch in front that we could never cross beyond that. I knew that we had to get permission because the nurses told us we would have to ask them. . . . I never asked to go outside or down town or away from the hospital because they said we couldn't. Some of the other women or girls that were there to my knowledge went away from the hospital; I mean left the hospital temporarily and got away from the ground and came back. There were 17 went away. To my knowledge that happened more than once. I know of punishment being accorded them for leaving the grounds."

"What do you know in that respect?"

"You mean of punishment?"[29]

At this point, Smith interrupted once again. Surely Carney was not connected with what happened at the detention hospital, he asserted. Without something to connect him to the goings-on there, there could be no conspiracy. The other lawyers also leaped up. Alva Cummins, another lawyer for the defendants, echoed Smith's claims. "Under the proof as it stands, this girl was asked to go to Dr. Carney's office for examination. For a week at least, Miss Peck has no knowledge or information concerning the matter so far as the evidence goes. There is no conspiracy between Miss Peck and Dr. Carney in the original investigation and examination. Miss Corrigan never knows anything about the case until some time after Miss Peck knows about it. There is no evidence of any conspiracy there. What do they seek to recover on?" Note that Peck and Corrigan both earned the prefix "Miss," but Nina was "this girl."[30]

Kelley countered that *of course* there was a conspiracy. "As to the proposition that Dr. Carney is liable for what happened at Bay City, it is our position and contention that he is liable for everything that happened at Bay City in connection with everything that happened before she got to Bay City. That [was] his design, his own design. . . . he cannot sidestep liability for anything that occurred at Bay City simply because he wasn't there."[31]

Judge Moinet sustained Smith's objection, declaring that the question about punishment in particular was irrelevant to proving conspiracy. Once again, Stone—the former judge—piped up after Moinet issued his ruling, and once again Moinet shut him down.[32]

Nina resumed her tale. She spoke again of the pain of the STI treatments, of the influenza she suffered, of her release, of Peck's stalking, and of her being forced to report to Dr. Carney for injections of mercury even once she was home. "I said I didn't see why I should; that I was negative in everything." Miss Peck "told me to go. I said I wouldn't at first." But Peck "said I had to obey or they would send me to the House of Correction. She said that then and there." Nina dutifully went to Dr. Carney's office. The shots hurt so much.

DEAN KELLEY returned to his seat and defense lawyer Alva Cummins rose in his place. Cummins was yet another ambitious Michigan attorney: he had served briefly as Ingham County prosecutor before spending the next several decades running for US representative, circuit judge, governor, state attorney general, and finally US senator. He would lose every race.[33]

Cummins asked Nina about her conversation with Deputy Sheriff Martin—a tad ironic, since he had just joined Smith in his earlier objection to her recounting their conversation. What was so special about Martin "talking with girls on the street" that she remembered it so vividly? he asked. Well, Nina replied, Martin wasn't usually one to "talk with ladies and girls very much."

"It was an unusual thing for him to speak to people on the street?"

"I said with girls."

"State what there was so startling about Mr. Martin talking with a girl on the street that it would impress itself on your mind."

"Because I just noticed that he was talking with these girls. I didn't know the purpose of it and what was done with those girls. I didn't know them; they were strangers to me; girls that were around St. Louis some; I had seen them around the street. I didn't know anything about them nor anything for or against them. When I saw him talking with them on the street I noticed it because I had never seen him talking with girls or ladies on the street much. He was a man that was always right along about his business. I had seen him talking with four or five girls in the last few days. In fact he said as much that he was picking up girls."[34]

At this point, Cummins turned to Judge Moinet. "I move to strike that out as not responsive."

"Strike it out," the judge replied.[35]

Under the barrage of questions that followed, Nina recounted many parts of the story she had told earlier that day: the examination at Dr. Carney's office, the blood test for syphilis, the treatments she had to endure after her release. She mentioned how bad the food was at Bay City, that the authorities there had censored her mail, and that she had avoided taking nearly all of the gonorrhea treatments in the detention hospital.[36]

On redirect, Kelley asked Nina more about what Carney had said to her. "Well, about Bay City, what I would have to do in Bay City, the law in Bay City, he said. He said obey the nurses, not run away, and he said if I did they would catch me and put me back in the House of Correction. . . . He didn't say anything about my signing a consent to go to Bay City. I didn't read those papers before I signed them." Carney had scared her. "In these conversations Dr. Carney said something about his power or authority. He said he had the power and authority to send me; that I had to go. He said he was Health Officer; that he got his power and authority from the Health Board. I did not have any knowledge of the powers of Health Officers. I believed what Dr. Carney told me."[37]

Cummins rose again to re-cross. He grilled her about her flight across the state with her friend Mary Loudenslager. He asked about her estranged husband, Clare Rock—"It didn't do any good having a husband to protect me," she said. Nina implied that Rock had wanted to prostitute her for money; she had refused.[38]

Cummins gradually arrived at two points that would consume the defense for the rest of the trial: the question of who was paying for Nina's lawyers, and Nina's history with men. First he asked about Mrs. Githens. "It is not true that Mrs. Githens has furnished me financial assistance," Nina claimed. "She didn't try to persuade me to start [the lawsuit]."[39]

Next he asked her the truly damning questions. Almost a century later, one can almost hear Nina's weariness. "It is not true that I was in very frequent association with the soldier boys. . . . I didn't have a great many different acquaintances among the soldier boys. . . . I knew [L]loyd Knap. I don't know Oren Strouse. It isn't true that I and Esther Morrow, [L]loyd Knapp and Oren Strouse spent the night together in my mother's home when they and no one else was there. . . . I never took any auto trips with a man I didn't know." The defense had clearly looked into her. Lloyd Knapp was the young soldier Nina had almost married. Wasn't it true that Nina had accepted a nineteen-mile ride home from some man? Cummins asked. No, it wasn't, Nina replied.[40]

"The accusation is made that you had improper relations with soldiers." "Well, I didn't."[41]

The defense was trying to prove that Nina was promiscuous, that she hung around with soldiers—possibly infecting them with her loose morals and her diseases—and that she went on automobile rides with them. This strategy was not mere character assassination. The defense sought to prove that the defendants had reasonable cause to suspect Nina of having an STI.

After another round of redirect and re-cross, and more insinuations about her interactions with soldiers, Nina finally left the stand.

NINA'S TRIAL CONTINUED for another three days. The yellowing trial transcript does not make clear when exactly one day began and another ended, but it is apparent from an article in the *Alma Record* that her testimony lasted into Wednesday, June 2.[42]

The next witness to mount the stand that Wednesday was Nina's mother, Minnie. Her testimony was largely a retelling of Nina's story, but from her own perspective. In nearly every respect, Minnie's story fit with Nina's version of events. She also added critical information, such as Peck's frequent visits to her home while Nina was in Detroit, and her own meeting with Mrs. Githens.

Her testimony is likewise striking in its defiance. Was it her contention that "the State had no authority to isolate patients and send them away to hospitals?" Alva Cummins asked on cross.

"Not against their will," Minnie replied.

A moment later: "You had no objection to her taking further treatments if further treatments were necessary?"

"I didn't think they were necessary."

When Cummins asked Minnie if Mrs. Githens was financing the lawsuit, Minnie said she was not. "The citizens finance it. I think the citizens are financing it."[43] She did not elaborate, but this terse statement suggests the possibility of some sort of local grassroots movement against the American Plan or perhaps simply in defense of local citizen Nina McCall. Yet it remains just a suggestion.

After Minnie came Mary Corrigan. She emphasized that she didn't know Dr. Carney, that she was simply following orders (from the state board of health). Kelley made sure to force her to admit that she had telephoned both Peck and Carney to notify them when Nina was being released. When Cummins started asking her about the authority of the state board of health and the necessity of Nina's medical treatments post-release, Nina's lawyers objected with a vengeance. They claimed every question was immaterial, calling for hearsay, or that Corrigan was incompetent to answer. Nina's lawyers objected fifteen times over the course of Corrigan's testimony and won exactly one of those objections.[44]

Corrigan attempted to rebut several of Nina's charges about life in the Bay City Detention Hospital. She asserted that she didn't think it possible that Nina hadn't been given any gonorrhea treatments for five weeks.[45] She also insisted that the inmates' movements were not as restricted as Nina had implied.[46]

One particular sticking point was food. While Nina had claimed in her testimony that her food was just red beets and potatoes "and such stuff as that," Corrigan asserted, "The girls were provided with suitable food, plain, wholesome, well cooked. . . . The bill of fare was meat, potatoes, vegetables, bread—beets and potatoes. We had red beets but that was not the exclusive bill of fare."[47] Corrigan continued that the food "was suitable in character and quantity for an institution of that kind" and that she couldn't recall Nina objecting to the meals while she was there.[48] Either Nina or Corrigan was exaggerating or outright lying, and it is impossible at this late date to know just who. Yet perhaps testimony from an inmate at another American Plan institution gives some insight. One man, locked in the Seattle jail's hospital ward for having an STI, claimed before city council, "The food was absolutely impossible to live on." There were worms in the mush, cockroaches in the soup, cigar butts in the meat, and ants in the peaches.[49]

Following Corrigan, Ida Peck rose to the stand. She admitted that, as part of her work for Dr. Carney, she followed only women suspected of having STIs but never men.[50] She also admitted seeing Nina and Minnie several times after Nina's release and insisting that Nina return to Dr. Carney's for treatment.[51] Yet Peck denied that Nina had complained about treatment at the detention hospital.[52] She denied that the food at Bay City had been bad.[53] She claimed that Nina had confided in her that "she had had sexual relations with L[l]oyd Knapp for some time."[54] And she denied bothering Nina as much as the young woman had said. In fact, Peck claimed, a major reason she had shown at up the McCall residence in the first place was not to insist on more treatment, but to collect on a bill. Nina had bought a diamond ring from a "Mrs. Scattergood of Alma, the jeweler's wife." Peck was "trying to collect for" Mrs. Scattergood. Just why Peck felt the need to do Mrs. Scattergood's bidding was left unspecified.[55]

In the course of denying the extent of her interactions with Nina and Minnie, Peck even contradicted herself. At one point, she testified, "I heard of the girl's being married. I did not go over there immediately after that. I don't know how long it was; perhaps a couple or three weeks. I think it was that long. It is not true that within 24 hours after I heard of the girl's being married I was over there to her mother's house." Yet a few minutes later, she admitted, "I saw her the day she was married. She was living in Alma part of the time. I would see her quite frequently." (Nina was married in St. Louis.)[56] Peck's last statement—"I would see her quite frequently"—also appears to contradict earlier testimony in which Peck claimed, "I perhaps saw her once a month, at least that often I would say."[57]

It was during a skillful and passionate examination by Nina's lawyer, Seymour Person, that the truly punitive and coercive nature of the American Plan's "protective work" became clear. "What was your business in 1918, in November, in Alma?" Person asked.

"I was in that school work and also welfare work," Peck replied.

"Hunting for girls?"

"I was not hunting. I was watching; looking for them; looking after them. That was my main activity. When I found her, if I thought she was a suspicious character I talked with her and if I thought it was necessary I requested her to go to the health officer, and that would be Dr. Carney."

"For what purpose?" Person pressed.

"For physical examination I meant."

"Now in 1918, November, your principal business was the getting of girls and sending them away?"

"I didn't get any girls and send them away."

"Finding them and sending them away?" Person repeated.

"I looked after them. As I said, if I found any suspicious ones why I requested them to go for physical examination with the object ultimately that they would be sent away if that was necessary for them to be sent away. The test was to determine that."[58]

Person's questioning was apparently damaging enough that O. L. Smith rose to walk Peck through a rebuttal. "You said you looked after the girls to find if they were suspicious characters," he asked, "suspicious in what respect?"

"In doing wrong, in sexual matters mostly," Peck blandly replied. "When I spoke of a person that I thought was suspicious, I meant a person that I thought was suspicious of having a venereal disease; if I saw them on the street, I watched them to see where they went and what they did. Yes sir, I have been out late at nights. Or girls habitually on the streets who have the reputation of not having a good character. Generally that is the class of girls that I was trying to help. I never had any other idea than that of helpfulness to those girls. I didn't have any bloodhounds or sleuths on their tracks dogging them."[59]

She was just trying to help.

AFTER PECK FINISHED SPEAKING, Person called Nina back up to the stand. He needed her to rebut Peck's charges. No, she hadn't told Peck that she'd been sleeping with Lloyd Knapp—"L[l]oyd Knapp was not mentioned in that conversation on that trip [to Bay City] only that I had been going with him, but as far as the other thing. . . . It is not true that I told her on that trip that I had sexual relations with this boy. I did not have sexual relations with him."[60]

Once again, Cummins did the cross-examination. Once again, the attempts to insinuate her promiscuity through his questions were obvious. No, she had never gone out with a man named Joe Johnson. No, she hadn't gone out with Jack Pope, either. No, she didn't know Roy Joslyn—she'd never been in a car with him. Nor had she told her friend Mary Loudenslager that she'd had sex with Johnson, Pope, and two other men.[61]

With these denials ringing in the ears of the twelve jurors, Cummins sat back down. Kelley stood up. "That is all," he said. "We rest."[62]

BY NOW, it was Thursday, June 3, the third day of the trial. It was the defense's turn, and Cummins immediately closed in for the kill. "We desire at this time to make a motion and I presume the jury will not be interested in the motion that I wish to make," he said.

"All right," replied Judge Moinet. "You may be excused, gentlemen, for a few moments. Just return to your rooms." The men of the jury filed out.

Cummins told the judge that Carney, Corrigan, and Peck couldn't have broken the law, since the law held STIs to be "dangerous communicable diseases"; thus, they had the "authority" to examine and imprison Nina. And even if they didn't have that authority, they could not have engaged in a conspiracy. Even if Carney, Corrigan, and Peck had done wrong, "they are three separate wrongs." They hadn't colluded.

"What do you say to that, gentlemen?" the judge asked Nina's lawyers.[63]

Kelley replied that Michigan's laws were "still insufficient to permit or authorize to be done what was done in this case; that there was no . . . explicit . . . statutory authority directly or indirectly which purported to authorize any health officer to examine the body or person of any individual against the consent or wish of that individual." Further, they denied that the statutory authority existed to imprison an infected woman in the Bay City Detention Hospital—"especially under the statute as it existed in 1918," before the 1919 American Plan law was enacted.[64]

"Doesn't the statute read that the State Board of Health shall have complete control and supervision of the public health of the state?" Moinet asked.

"Yes," Kelley responded, "there is no question about that."

Moinet called for a fifteen-minute recess. When court resumed, he announced his ruling. He ignored the issue of statutory authority for the moment and dwelt instead on the matter of conspiracy. "The Court has concluded upon the question of conspiracy that it is apparent from the evidence in the case that the measure of damages as to each of these defendants, if they are liable, would be entirely different as to each one, there not being any proof in my judgment which shows a conspiracy or confederation between the three of them, acting with a common purpose and a common inten[t] as charged in the declaration." He told Nina's lawyers to choose a single one of the defendants against whom to proceed. They chose Carney.

As to the question of statutory authority, Moinet continued, he would "defer it at the present time."[65]

THE JURY TROOPED BACK IN. The judge told them that there had been insufficient evidence to prove conspiracy, so the plaintiff was proceeding solely against Dr. Carney. Now it was the defense's turn to call witnesses. As it happened, they would only call one.[66]

Commissioner of Health Richard M. Olin strode up the aisle to the witness's seat and sat down. His girth and the physical strength he radiated made one forget he was only five feet eight and one-half inches tall. Two blue eyes stared out imperiously from an immense, bald head.[67] The trial was the first time he and Nina had ever been in the same room together. In fact, it may have been the first time he had ever intentionally been physically close to one of the women he had helped to lock up (outside of visits to detention hospitals).

Olin was there to establish the state's—and thus Dr. Carney's—authority to examine and imprison Nina. He had brought the minutes of the state board of health from October 11, 1917, when he and the other board members had mandated that all physicians report cases of STIs to the government, and from November 20, 1917, when he and the other board members formally declared STIs "dangerous communicable diseases" and decided to hire investigators to find cases of STIs and quarantine and treat their carriers.[68] Olin outlined the work of his department and its employees. "I know Dr. Carney," he said. "I did employ him. I appointed him on the 2nd of August, 1918. I made that appointment at the city of Alma in a conference or meeting with him. I employed Dr. Carney as a medical inspector for the purpose of the venereal disease campaign within his county, the County of Gratiot."

Kelley burst in to object, claiming Olin lacked "statutory authority" to appoint Carney as such. "We do claim there is statutory authority," Cummins countered. Judge Moinet allowed Olin to continue testifying.[69]

Over near-constant objections, Olin described instructing local health officers to enforce the Plan, entering into an agreement with Bay City authorities for use of the detention hospital, and clarifying the state's American Plan procedures. His testimony continued into the next day, June 4.[70] Cummins asked if these policies had arisen out of "war necessities?"

"Yes, sir," Olin replied.[71]

Later, during his cross-examination, Kelley asked how many of those who were reported as having STIs were locked up. Olin replied that he didn't know, but that more than two thousand people—he did not specify gender, but we know they were nearly all women—had been imprisoned across the state.[72] Kelley tried to get Olin to state that women like Nina were supposed to have the choice of "house or hospital quarantine." Olin would not give him a concrete answer. Kelley asked if women were to be given this choice under the new law, the 1919 American Plan law. Again, Olin was cagey.[73]

After Kelley finished, Cummins stood up. "There is a motion we would like to make at this time," he announced. Judge Moinet ordered the jury out of the room once more.[74]

"If your honor please," Cummins said, "it is the desire of the defense at this time to make a motion for a directed verdict upon the record as it now stands.

I realize that that is a rather unusual thing to do without fully and completely resting our case," but he didn't feel "that there is very much more that can be said. We contend as a matter of law that Dr. Carney was within his authority and that there is no cause here of an invasion of the rights of the plaintiff." Smith stood up and echoed his co-counsel.[75]

Kelley stood for the plaintiff. They held that Carney's actions violated the Fifth Amendment of the US Constitution, as well as Section 16 of Article 2 of the Michigan Constitution, by denying Nina due process. He agreed with Cummins that it was unnecessary to argue any further.[76]

Judge Moinet ordered the jury back into the room. He then proceeded to rule and, in addition, make his feelings plain to the jury. "This is a very important case," he declared, "and involves some very important legal principles. Michigan has never passed upon the question but there are some authorities from different states. The trend of the Courts seems to be, and in fact Michigan has held that the regulation of the public health is with the police power of the state; that the public health of the state is the first concern of the state. . . . It seems to me of necessity that within the statute the local health officer had the powers and acted within his authority at the time he did what is claimed in this case that he did do. You will therefore, by direction of the court, return a verdict here of no cause of action."[77]

Nina had lost. The judge ordered her to pay the defendants' legal fees.[78]

Perhaps spectators in the courtroom that final day recalled Nina's testimony, when she said she'd been so ashamed to go to Bay City that she had only told her mother and two aunts.[79] Now, newspapers across the state would print her name—worse still, her married name, Rock—and her crime, and her defeat.[80]

"In Nina McCall Rock, $10,000 damage suit against Dr. T. J. Carney and Misses Peck and Corrigan, Judge Moinet last Friday directed verdict of 'no cause of action,'" wrote a journalist on the front page of the *Gratiot County Herald* a week later. "He held Dr. Carney was acting within his legal powers as health officer, both in the examination of Mrs. Rock and in sending her to Bay City hospital for treatment. The case will be appealed and the power of a health officer in such a case thoroughly tested. This is well. If a health officer has the right to send persons afflicted with contagious or infectious diseases to a hospital for treatment both he and the public should know it so that he may not hesitate to do his duty from fear of prosecution for damages."[81]

A FEW MONTHS after Nina's trial ended, the elite women attempting to resist the American Plan in a very different way received a very interesting communiqué.

Jessie Binford, a dark-eyed forty-four-year-old social worker so dedicated she would later be nicknamed the "conscience of Chicago," was serving as Midwestern district supervisor for the Interdepartmental Social Hygiene Board. One day in October, she opened a letter inviting her to the Institute on Venereal Disease Control and Social Hygiene, to be held in Washington, DC, from November 22 to December 4, 1920, and then, following that, to the All-America Conference on Venereal Disease from December 6 to December 11. The institute was to be an educational meeting devoted to "intensive study," and Binford was invited to teach a course on "Protective Work for Girls."[82] The All-America Conference, on the other hand, was intended to "bring together recognized authorities in their respective fields, and especially to make possible a comparison and evaluation of the methods now being employed in various parts of the world of venereal diseases," according to a preliminary conference program.[83]

Binford was intrigued. This second event, the All-America Conference, could be just the opportunity she and Ethel Sturges Dummer had been waiting for to convince the American Plan's male bureaucrats of the error of their ways. Six days later, she and Dummer met in Chicago to discuss the invitation.[84] Dummer had been planning to use the 1921 National Conference of Social Work to try to convince the male leaders of the American Plan to make it less discriminatory, but the All-America Conference presented a much sooner chance. "I hope to go to Washington and am really looking forward to the possibility of seeing some genuine constructive measures suggested to the I.D.S.H. Board," she wrote to a friend shortly thereafter. "I tried to persuade several fine wom[e]n to go to Washington feeling that this opportunity to put in a strong plea for women must not be neglected."[85] In the coming weeks, Dummer and Binford collaborated with Maude Miner and some other prominent women to craft just those genuine, constructive suggestions.

These women ended up composing a series of resolutions that they desperately hoped the conference would adopt. These resolutions read, in part:

WHEREAS the compulsory examination and forcible detention of persons suspected of being carriers of venereal disease not convicted of a misdemeanor, constitutes a serious infraction of personal liberty and tends to deprive individuals of the usual legal safeguards, and

WHEREAS the enforcement of these health measures has resulted in confusion between disease and crime and in discrimination against girls and women, and

WHEREAS the purpose of protecting society from disease has not been accomplished by the examination and isolation of a small proportion of the carriers of disease who have returned to society after a short time, non-infectious but not rehabilitated . . .

BE IT RESOLVED that the All-America Conference on Venereal Diseases recommend:

THAT compulsory examination of persons suspected of being vene-real disease carriers and the forcible detention of suspected persons be abolished:

THAT everywhere adequate facilities for voluntary examination and treatment of venereal disease be provided together with a constructive program for re-education, industrially, morally, and socially,

THAT increased effort be made through protective and educational work to eliminate conditions that make for prostitution and disease to the end that youth be safeguarded and its exploitation prevented.[86]

These were powerful resolutions. If they were adopted, they would radically alter the American Plan, in theory making it far less discriminatory and far more just.

Months later, the Institute on Venereal Disease Control and Social Hy-giene—the event held just before the All-America Conference—went off without a hitch. Over six hundred "clinicians, physicians, health officers, nurses, educators, and social workers from all parts of the country" attended, according to one division report.[87] Speakers included numerous federal and ASHA officials (including William F. Snow and Martha Falconer), and ranged from renowned women's rights activist Anna Garlin Spencer to Charles Dav-enport, one of the nation's foremost eugenicists.[88]

"The Institute is over," Dummer wrote to a friend on the day between the end of the institute and the beginning of the All-America Conference. "It has been of great value to many, yet is considered by some not at all up-to-date." In spite of such impressions, Dummer was optimistic about the upcoming conference. "Rumor comes that the civilian program will be less fearful (filled with fear) than was that during the war. Let us hope so."[89]

To Dummer and her elite female allies, the All-America Conference was more than merely a meeting. It was a showdown. This showdown would play out politely and subtly, through parliamentary procedures rather than any show of force. But it was a showdown nonetheless—a battle between men and women to see who would control the future of government actions regulat-ing female bodies.

Nina had failed, but perhaps these women would succeed.

Chapter 10

"WE DEFEAT OURSELVES"

ON NOVEMBER 8, 1920, Clare Rock's philandering finally caught up with him. Rock was in Detroit, on his way to the theater. He was with his new wife, Rose (though, again, he was technically still married to Nina), as well as another woman, Rosella Caravalla. Rosella was just seventeen or eighteen years old, and she too was married. Why exactly she was accompanying Clare and Rose to the theater that day is obscured by accusations, insinuations, and the passage of time. Certainly, Rosella's husband believed Clare was trying to "wreck his home." At the very least, it seems that Rosella was not in a happy marriage. She had filed for divorce just a few days earlier, listing "Extreme Cruelty" and "Non-support" as the reasons.[1]

Her husband, James Caravalla, was a frightening man. He had a long record of arrests. In 1899, he had talked his way into a Detroit woman's home by posing as a plumber and then grabbed her by the throat; in 1901, he had been sentenced to six months for "smashing things in a Michigan avenue store"; in 1904, he had been arrested for robbing a saloonkeeper. As one article put it several decades before, Caravalla "has an extensive knowledge of the inner workings of the house of correction."[2] In the winter of 1920, Caravalla was middle-aged, a sometime bricklayer, salesman, and mechanic. He was about five feet six and a half inches tall with deep-set brown eyes, thinning chestnut hair, huge jug ears, a bulbous nose, and a generally pugnacious visage.[3] In other words, he was exactly the wrong man Clare should have wanted thinking he was trying to "wreck his home."

It was while the Rocks and Rosella were on the way to a show that Caravalla confronted Clare. An argument ensued. After the exchange of words, Caravalla pulled out a gun and shot Clare Rock. Then, Caravalla fled.[4]

Nina's erstwhile husband was dead. Whether she missed him and mourned his passage, or exulted in his comeuppance, or didn't even hear of his murder, is unknown. Nina's life during the last months of 1920 is a complete mystery.

Rock was not a significant man. One of the only newspapers to carry a story on his death was the *Ann Arbor Times News*, which ran a paragraph on the killing at the bottom of its front page.[5] There is no reason Nina would have subscribed to an Ann Arbor paper, but perhaps an acquaintance saw the story of her husband's death and sent a copy to her. If she saw the story of Clare's death, it is also possible she noticed the article directly above it: a brief story about a prominent Michigan public health expert receiving an invitation from William F. Snow to "become a member of a general conference of physicians to be held in Washington, D.C., December 6 to 11."[6] This was the All-America Conference, the very meeting at which the women of the federal government were planning to convince the men to make the American Plan less discriminatory. In the unlikely event that Nina saw this article, it was her only remote interaction with these elite women's attempts at resistance. She and they lived in worlds apart.

FINALLY, IT WAS MONDAY, December 6, 1920, and many of the nation's foremost reformers were gathering to talk about sex. It was a cool, cloudy day on the Mall in Washington, DC, and hundreds of well-dressed men and women walked into the New National Museum of the Smithsonian Institution.[7] Six towering pillars framed the main entrance to the museum, a grand building with high windows, surrounded by sweeping lawns, and topped with a massive, gleaming golden dome. So many important people were slated to attend this meeting: one governor, twelve mayors, nine judges, the former president of Stanford University and current dean of Harvard Law School, the US Surgeon General, the secretaries of war, the navy, and the treasury, and representatives from a dozen countries. There were physicians and religious leaders, eugenicists and captains of industry: five thousand attendees in total. Raymond Fosdick, William F. Snow, Bascom Johnson, and dozens of former CTCA and current Interdepartmental Social Hygiene Board and ASHA officials were there. John D. Rockefeller Jr. made it to the conference. Also in attendance were many well-known female reformers: Jessie Binford, Maude Miner, Ethel Sturges Dummer, Martha Falconer, and even the famous social worker Jane Addams. Twenty representatives from the state of Michigan had made it, including Gardener M. Byington, director of the state's Division of Venereal Diseases and the physician who had examined Nina and cleared her for release. All of these luminaries were there to register for the All-America Conference on Venereal Diseases.[8]

That evening, from 8:30 until 11:00 p.m., hundreds sat in the Hotel Washington's grand Hall of Nations for the conference's opening session.[9] M. W. Ireland, surgeon general of the army—that is, the senior medical officer in the army, and a member of the board—spoke that night. "I am sure we all appreciate the great importance of this Conference," he began. "I am also sure that all of us realize that this meeting is an epoch-making one. Five years ago it would have been impossible to have held such a meeting in the city of Washington."

Ireland was right. The war had ensured that STIs were destigmatized to the extent that they could be openly discussed in the nation's most hallowed halls. Ireland spoke of the "'all-American' plan of campaign against venereal disease," and claimed, "This plan was carried out very vigorously during the War and unquestionably proved that most gratifying results can be accomplished in community work on the social evil."[10] One wonders how Dummer, Miner, and their allies, sitting in the audience, felt about this pronouncement. Indeed, Ireland was being grossly misleading. The army's own internal statistics made clear that the American Plan had not substantially reduced the rate of STIs among the troops.[11]

The Plan's proudest nemesis, Katharine Bushnell, could not attend the All-America Conference, but allies of hers made sure to distribute a paper she had written for the occasion. "The New American Laws a Violation of the United States Constitution," proclaimed one subtitle. In this paper, Bushnell purported to demonstrate "the essential illegality of the whole process of the new laws." Her paper told the tale of a conference of the International Abolitionist Federation (a group founded by Josephine Butler), which had been held in Geneva, Switzerland, in September 1920. The ASHA's Walter Clarke (one of the few American Plan administrators not present for the All-America Conference) had attended on behalf of the Americans and, according to Bushnell, given a speech highlighting the educational aspects of the American Plan but "omit[ing] all references to the darker side of the subject." A British ally of Bushnell's posed three questions to Clarke: (1) "Was Major Snow, of the American Social Hygiene Society [sic], correct when he said recently in England in answer to a question that there were probably thousands of women in America under indeterminate sentence suspected of V.D.?" (2) "Was his further answer in near accordance with facts when he said that he did not know of one man who was so detained?" (3) "Is it also true that these women and girls could not be released until they had been subjected to several drastic surgical examinations?" Clarke immediately answered all three questions in the affirmative, though he objected to the word "drastic." Following Clarke's response, he became "the centre of a fire of questionings and arguments." Bushnell's recounting was powerful. There were, according to an ally of hers, "a sufficient number of copies struck off to circulate amongst the members of [the All-America] Conference." Bushnell believed that this paper made an impact on some of the attendees; certainly, it was the only paper she ever wrote that William F. Snow felt the need to rebut in a letter to her.[12]

From Tuesday to Friday, the regular conference goers met in morning and afternoon sessions to discuss topics ranging from manufacturing STI medication to the "colored population problem"—that is to say, the higher rate of STIs among African Americans, and the racist conclusions reformers drew from this higher rate. At the same time, in a separate location, members of the exclusive General Conference Committee—whose ranks included all the big male names (Snow, Fosdick, Johnson, Pierce, and Rockefeller, among dozens of others) as well as a handful of female ones (Miner, Falconer, and three others)—met to draft resolutions on these topics. During the lunch break, conference attendees could go on automobile trips to see many DC institutions, including the US Naval Observatory, the Government Hospital for the Insane, the Library of Congress, the Bureau of the Census, and Georgetown University. In the evenings, following dinner, the regular attendees would gather at 8:30 p.m. to vote on whether or not to adopt the General Conference Committee's suggestions.[13]

The debates regarding the methods of law enforcement weren't scheduled to begin until Thursday, December 9.[14] Until then, regular conference attendees discussed the latest STI treatments, the use of motion pictures in sex education, the importance of vice investigations, the place of women police, the power of Hull House, among much else. At the end of each session, general attendees adopted "resolutions or recommendations for reference" to the General Conference Committee.[15] Finally, on Thursday, December 9, the discussions of law enforcement methods began (both for the regular attendees and the General Conference Committee). Dummer, Binford, and the other women were planning to use the law enforcement methods general discussion to convince the attendees to adopt their resolutions. A number of questions regarding law enforcement had been posed to the delegates ahead of time, including, "Are the reformatory methods used with prostitutes effective in relation to the control of venereal disease?"; "Should fines ever be imposed on persons convicted of prostitution?"; and "Is there any discrimination against one sex in the enforcement of laws concerning prostitution in the United States?"[16] Such questions surely seemed to provide a perfect opening.

However, Dummer, who was exiled to the public meetings, was perplexed by her exclusion from the room where decisions were truly being made. "The Conference had staged certain debates to occupy the minds of the delegates until resolutions were presented to them," she later wrote, "and for one of these, the law enforcement question, one of the leading law enforcement men was shown on the program on the negative side."[17] This man was Bascom Johnson, former head of the CTCA's Law Enforcement Division and currently an ASHA executive. When she heard Johnson was slotted to decry the discriminatory nature of the American Plan, Dummer gasped and asked him, "You are to give the negative?" Johnson responded, "I understand the academic arguments against law enforcement, and can present them adequately."[18]

Dummer eventually realized that even this farce of a debate didn't matter. "The delegates," Dummer continued, "who were eager for open discussion, found they could offer their questions only through a special committee sitting separately, and as there was naturally delay in presenting surviving resolutions to the general meeting, people began to depart."[19] The staged debates and separation from the resolution-drafting committee worked; the women's resolutions never reached a vote in the evening sessions.[20] The General Conference Committee, so dominated by men, simply did not recommend them to be voted upon by the general attendees. Not only was Dummer excluded from the powerful committee, but Jessie Binford, Jane Addams, Edith Houghton Hooker, and the influential social worker Edith Abbott, among several others, had no voice in bringing resolutions to a vote. The few women who did have such a voice included Rockefeller ally Katharine Bement Davis, the notoriously pro-police Valeria Parker, and Martha Falconer—women who, out of all the women of the federal government, had been the least vocal in their opposition to the Plan.

Parker, in fact, was a former CTCA official who had personally overseen a squadron of five policewomen in Connecticut that detained and secured examinations for women they suspected of having STIs; infected women were committed to reformatories, detention houses, Christian rescue homes, and jails.[21] After the war, Parker had run the Connecticut State Farm for Women, an institution that housed women under the Plan.[22] Such a woman could hardly be expected to oppose the Plan.

Edith Hooker, furious at the turn of events, gave an impromptu speech in which she denounced Valeria Parker and another woman as members of "the opposition"—that is, opposing measures that all thinking women should support.[23] Her speech accomplished little. The conference did eventually end up adopting a resolution calling for "neither the laws themselves nor their enforcement [to] be discriminatory," but this was a far cry from the condemnation of exploitation and compulsory examinations that Dummer and her allies had proposed.[24] The conference's final report noted, "Considerable discussion was aroused by attempts to define the term 'reasonably suspected of having gonorrhea, syphilis, or chancroid.'" Some claimed that, as a result of the vagueness of the term, "innocent persons have been victimized and degraded by unwarranted detention and examination." The report continued, "Recognizing the value of the statute when properly utilized, yet insistent that the rights of innocent persons should be safeguarded," the conference goers adopted resolutions urging "further intensive study" with the purpose of "more precisely defining those who may be reasonably suspected."[25]

"The small group of women standing against law enforcement," Dummer concluded, "did, I think, carry some influence," but not "in securing the passing of a satisfactory resolution."[26] She and her allies had, in fact, been soundly defeated. The conference did not recommend making the American

Plan less discriminatory. The men of the government did not appear to have truly heard their voices at all.

FOLLOWING THE END of the All-America Conference, the reactions of its female attendees varied considerably. Binford and Dummer, for instance, both appear to have initially rationalized the defeat. In a letter to Alice Stone Blackwell, a prominent female doctor (and critic of the Plan), Jessie Binford wrote, "I am sorry we did not get all we wanted but I believe you will agree with me that this is a step in advance."[27] Dummer echoed this rhetoric. "There were some seeds sown in Washington which will bear fruit," she wrote to a friend on December 14.[28] "Of course," she wrote a month later to a female reformer in California, "we women didn't get all we went for, but I do think a slight impression was made upon the medical and military mind."[29] In a candid letter a month after that to Katharine Bushnell, Dummer wrote, "I was one of the few women opposed to the law enforcement work under the war program. I am sure you will be glad to know that many of the doctors are startled by the effect of their blunders during the war, and to let themselves off easily there was very free discussion as to what might be a wise civilian program." Once again, Dummer appears to be rationalizing the conference.[30]

Yet Dummer also wrote different letters to differently minded individuals, reflecting, perhaps, her political canniness. In a letter to avowed Plan critic Alice Stone Blackwell, Dummer likened the whole event to a "steam roller."[31] (Blackwell herself was "delighted to learn that an opposition had arisen," and hoped it heralded more resistance to come.[32]) However, in a letter to Martha Falconer, Dummer wrote, "What a wonderful meeting we had in Washington. Some day you will tell me truly, will you not, just how far ahead of the rest of us you are seeing, and how you attain your sphinx like expression and maintain silence, as you draw the rest of us after you. I gained new thought, and possibly not only further vision, but better understanding."[33]

Falconer wrote back with characteristic caution. "[W]hat I do see is the tremendous gain which we are constantly making," she wrote, "for which I am devoutly thankful and so anxious to keep the good-will of the leaders in order to help them to do more progressive things." Falconer warned Dummer not to be too aggressive in her future lobbying of male reformers. "If we antagonize continually, or if they lose confidence in us, then we defeat ourselves."[34]

Other women shared Falconer's reluctance to antagonize. One woman, Anna Garlin Spencer, wrote a lengthy letter to Edith Houghton Hooker, and copied Miner, Dummer, and several others. Spencer noted that Hooker had referred to her as part of the "opposition"; Spencer claimed, "[T]here was no opposition. . . . No one was 'against' any other." She continued that the conference "was the first time that the social workers and the ethical teachers had been asked to confer on this question with the doctors and legal workers, and [she] was profoundly grateful." While Spencer disliked the clause allowing for arrests and examinations of "suspected" persons and wished the conference had condemned it, she considered the American Plan laws "a great advance" and simply wanted to excise the reasonable suspicion clauses. She thought of the conference as a "priceless" opportunity to present ideas to influential officials and was optimistic about "the main tendencies of the men most in command."[35] Writing to Rachelle Yarros, a female board official, Spencer opined that if they all held Hooker's attitude, they "would shut the door opened so generously and give us again men in high authority working in secret for things we could not stop and we women battering outside the doors." She then reflected on the conference as a whole. "We got pretty far 'in' at Washington. I want to keep the doors open for such women as you and Dr. [Valeria] Parker and the rest to work from the inside out and long after I am gone. . . . It was a strenuous time and I felt it very much that we had to face the alternative presented. But on the whole the statements seemed to me such an advance upon anything we have ever had before that I feel happy over it."[36]

Yet others agreed with Hooker. On February 10, 1921, social worker and Hull House resident Edith Abbott wrote to Binford, "I am sure that you already understand that I belong with [Hooker] in the 'opposition.' As you have heard me discourse on this subject many times, you know that I feel strongly about it."[37] Writing directly to Anna Spencer, Abbott called Binford and Yarros—both female board officials—"well-meaning" but doing "a great deal of harm."[38]

ULTIMATELY, EDITH ABBOTT'S point was irrelevant. Binford's and Yarros's opportunities to do harm were nearing an end. On December 29, 1920, less than two weeks after the women of the government failed to bring their resolutions to a vote, the House of Representatives passed a version of Congress's annual appropriations bill to fund the government that failed to give the Interdepartmental Social Hygiene Board money to disburse to the states for anti-STI work.[39] Many apparently considered the board to have been just a wartime body whose time had passed. If this version of the bill were to become law, the board—and thus the federal government's main American Plan body—would be neutered.

Thomas Storey, an ASHA cofounder serving as the board's secretary, was shocked and mortified; he had not seen this coming.[40] Storey frantically tried to salvage the situation. He spent the days surrounding the New Year trying to get the board's members on the phone, in an effort to organize an emergency meeting.[41] A quarter century before, the stout, brown-haired Storey had met William F. Snow when both were undergraduates at Stanford; now Storey called on his old college buddy for help.[42] Snow leaped into battle, telling the secretary of the navy that he was "very greatly disturbed" by the funding vote—a "national calamity"—and offered to lobby Congress to reinsert the board's appropriations.[43] The secretary directed Storey to set things right with the Senate. Snow, meanwhile, wrote to every state health officer in the nation, urging them to wire their senators. One senator did attempt to secure some of the board's funding, but the committee on appropriations eventually decided as a whole to simply transfer the board's functions to the US Public Health Service, and thus dissolve the board as a separate entity. It was, Storey wrote to all members of the board in February 1921, a "disaster."[44]

Even some of Storey's female colleagues agreed. They had wanted to reform the board, not destroy it. "[I]f there is no change," Jessie Binford wrote to Ethel Sturges Dummer, "the Interdepartmental Board will go out of existence and no one knows what the Public Health Service will do with the money. I doubt very much if they will carry on the kind of protective work we have been doing."[45]

"The demise of the Interdepartmental Social Hygiene Board marked the first critical sign of the decline in efforts to combat venereal disease after the war," wrote the historian Allan Brandt. Though many claimed the US Public Health Service's Division of Venereal Diseases could continue the board's work, "the Division's budget was merely ten percent of the Board's."[46] With such limited resources, the division ceased all of the board's most hands-on activities.[47] Thomas Storey resigned from the government in disgust.[48] He was replaced with Valeria Parker (who, interestingly, would be paid $1,000 less a year than her male predecessor).[49] Parker had been tasked with steering a sinking ship. She continued to direct the board's field agents for more than a year, but by late 1922 she would remove its name from all government mailing lists, and by 1923 the board would close its doors for good.[50]

The federally administered American Plan was over. Popular opposition to the sexist and discriminatory elements of the federal Plan do not appear to have played a significant role in its demise; rather, opposition from a medical establishment terrified of government involvement in health care spurred Congress to neuter the board.[51] The American Medical Association, deeply suspicious of government-run health care, had lobbied hard against the board, denouncing it in a widely circulated editorial as superfluous and moralistic, a dictatorial, bureaucratic nightmare. It was socialized medicine at its worst.[52] Several male physicians had likewise written to Congress or federal officials to communicate their skepticism toward a federal board.[53]

These men had won where women had lost—in vanquishing a federally run American Plan. However, significantly, they had done nothing to oppose the Plan at the local level. And, because of the federal government's successful push to get states and cities to pass their own American Plan laws and to fund local American Plan institutions, the Plan could continue to thrive at a local level across the country. Indeed, in so many places, it would.

ONE PLACE IT WOULD NOT CONTINUE, ironically enough, was Bay City, Michigan. There, a local controversy would quickly engulf the city's detention hospital and soon shutter it for good. This controversy would suggest just how corrupt the local administration of the Plan had become.

Months before, state and federal officials had begun noticing some irregularities in Bay City's books; both the Michigan Department of Health and the Interdepartmental Social Hygiene Board had given Bay City officials thousands of dollars for the city's detention hospital, but they couldn't figure out what city officials were spending it on. Bay City's mayor stalled, writing placating letters to Health Commissioner Richard Olin and the feds.[54]

Bay Cityans had long thought of the detention hospital as a "big money maker" for the city.[55] It received, recall, $15 per patient per week from the state. But after the war ended, circumstances changed. Suddenly there was less furious impetus to arrest suspicious women; there were fewer soldiers to protect. The hospital's population dropped.

And then scandal struck. On a snowy January 24, 1921, at a meeting of the Bay City Common Council, Alderman Frederick Black announced that in July 1920, the detention hospital had treated "scores of patients" for STIs, "necessitating additional expense in the operation of this institution for the care of many sent here from various cities in Michigan for which the state paid liberally." At that point, the detention hospital had $16,000 on hand, but, somehow, just six months later, its administrators claimed to possess only $3,000. Where had the money gone? Since "the people of Bay City have been fed up on the repeated boast that the Detention hospital was a money-making proposition," Black was asking the mayor and board of health to "explain why the institution has been permitted to be operated at a continual loss to the taxpayers for the past few months without some action being taken to reduce the operating expenses."[56] An editorial two days later in the *Times Tribune* asserted, "Alderman Black is purely within his rights" in asking for a financial report, especially since everyone had heard that the detention hospital had made a "stack of money." "Now it is possible," the article continued, "that all of this money has gone into legitimate expenses, and then again, it may not have been handled in a business-like manner."[57]

On February 7, at the 7:30 p.m. meeting of the Common Council, Dr. J. A. Keho, secretary of the local board of health—and the man who had

administered Nina's gonorrhea treatments two years before—submitted a stu-
pefyingly detailed report accounting for the detention hospital's expenses. He
painstakingly traced its receipts, asserting that the institution had actually
gained $2,800 in the time Black examined. Keho concluded: "[T]he board of
health has nothing to cover up, neither has it endeavored to 'feed' the taxpayers on anything which was not authentic."[58]

Alderman Black does not appear to have responded at the meeting, at
least on the record. "Tells Council Detention Hospital Is And Has Been Big
Money-Maker," ran the front-page headline in the *Times Tribune*.[59] But Keho's
response was telling in another way. He noted that since 1919, the city had not
appropriated any amount for the detention hospital's upkeep, and that the
number of patients in the hospital had declined from as many as sixty to just
eight or nine.[60] Furthermore, the state had not yet appropriated any money to
care for sexually infected women in the coming year (dependent as the state
was on appropriations from the embattled Interdepartmental Social Hygiene
Board). The Bay City Detention Hospital was in trouble.[61]

The next week, Alderman Black struck back. He accused Keho of trying to
"fortify the board [of health] against public criticism" by inundating the Common Council with his "voluminous report . . . [produced] at huge expense to
the taxpayers . . . including a lot of data not called for in my resolution, and
wholly immaterial so far as the local situation is concerned." Furthermore,
Keho had accused him of "playing politics, which is false," and Black was offended. Since the state was withholding its funding, Black continued, he was
inviting the board of health to submit a statement "giving reasons why the
present extraordinary expenses at the detention hospital should not be reduced in proportion to the amount of service which it is being called upon to
render, and the corps of employes reduced accordingly."[62]

It appears that the board of health never took Alderman Black up on his
invitation. The next meeting of the Common Council was consumed with
a boisterous discussion of whether jitneys would be allowed to operate on
city streets; the detention hospital did not come up.[63] By the next month, the
detention hospital was housing "two Mexican women" suffering from tuberculosis. These women, as well as thirty other Mexican families recently arrived in town to work in the sugar-beet fields, Dr. Keho and Mayor Mundy
claimed, presented a "social calamity," spreading disease and demanding the
city's charity. The mayor wanted to ensure that "this influx of Mexicans and
other foreigners is nipped in the bud." Alderman Black expressed a desire to
ship the two women with tuberculosis back to Texas.[64]

By mid-1921, Bay City's days incarcerating women with STIs in the detention hospital were over. State anti-STI funding had evaporated in a cloud of
suspicion. Word had also likely reached Bay City about the Interdepartmental

Social Hygiene Board's funding difficulties, which would have eliminated any dreams of federal funding. Furthermore, many in town now suspected the detention hospital's finances were far from kosher. The public and the aldermen were watching closely. If the detention hospital's administrators had been less than scrupulous with their books before, they could not continue to do so under such close scrutiny. Besides, there were other individuals, suspected of having other infectious diseases, like these Mexican workers, to quarantine.

BY THIS POINT, it should be obvious that the American Plan was a thoroughly sexist program—and also a racist, classist, and xenophobic one as well. The Bay City brouhaha illustrates one additional fact: the Plan was inextricably linked to capitalism. Cities locked up women in part to make money.

As far back as the mid-nineteenth century, many of the most ardent supporters of rounding up suspected prostitutes were small businessmen, fearing that nearby brothels would hurt their businesses.[65] (Conversely, businessmen located far from a red-light district sometimes opposed closing brothels, since this might cause the prostitutes to relocate nearer to them.[66]) Early in the twentieth century, private antivice groups in New York and Chicago strong-armed hotels, saloons, and cabarets into banning women they suspected of prostitution from their premises by threatening to protest these establishments or have them prosecuted, and thus hurt their profits.[67] Members of local chambers of commerce had helped to found many of these private groups.[68] In the early 1910s, San Francisco shut down one of its red-light districts and targeted prostitutes because local businessmen had invested heavily in the upcoming Panama-Pacific International Exposition and needed the city to look "clean."[69] The next year, Bascom Johnson convinced property owners that it would be "to their financial advantage" to launch another "clean-up" in San Francisco.[70] A similar dynamic played out in Buffalo, Omaha, and some eighty cities across the country.[71]

By the time World War I arrived, this strategy was well established. Among the federal government's most effective tactics for getting local officials to enforce the Plan was to threaten to remove military camps, along with all the money the tens of thousands of soldiers brought to local businesses.[72] When, late in 1917, officials in Seattle refused to lock up infected women with sufficient vigor, the military placed the city "off limits" for the soldiers from Camp Lewis—presenting what one historian called a "grave threat to the local economy." Businessmen and others rebelled, very nearly impeaching the mayor and forcing him to launch a crackdown on suspected women.[73] When the War Department expressed doubts about the suitability of El Paso as a site for a potentially lucrative training camp (one newspaper estimated it would bring in half a million dollars every week), local authorities swore they would close the city's red-light district and the chamber of commerce hastily assembled a special delegation to go to Washington and persuade officials that the city would eliminate prostitution and STIs. As the *El Paso Herald* put it, "[T]he end of El Paso's 'wide open' period of tolerated debauchery may come suddenly and unanimously, now that the pocketbook is touched." El Paso police soon began launching nightly raids and arresting suspected prostitutes (and not their clients), and the city earned a coveted camp.[74] Each wanting to receive or retain their own training camp, Waco, San Antonio, Galveston, and Houston (as well as San Francisco) all followed suit.[75]

Authorities frequently emphasized the "sound business sense" of "aggressive tactics to eradicate venereal disease."[76] Even in Michigan, while trying to promote "venereal disease suppression," health officials planned "a series of talks to business men and manufacturers, appealing to them from an economic standpoint."[77]

In part because of such promotional efforts, in many cities, members of the chamber of commerce were among the Plan's most enthusiastic supporters. Local chambers gave the money to build detention houses in Montgomery, Alabama, and Houston, Texas, and pressured the government of Lawton, Oklahoma, to fork over the money to build its own.[78] Members of the chamber of commerce in El Paso helped to create that city's "purity squads"—what one historian called "vigilante groups that roamed the streets of south El Paso searching for 'undesirables.'"[79]

Bay City provides an example of a city directly profiting from the incarceration of women. Once the opportunity to make a profit disappeared, the city's thirst for locking up women disappeared along with it.

EVEN AS SCANDAL engulfed Bay City, Nina McCall simply lived her life. She had no choice but to do so. She worked, she rested, she had sex. She got pregnant. She got married.

On April 27, 1921, in the town of Saginaw, she married a young man named Norman Hess. At the time, Nina was twenty years old and Norman was twenty-three. He was a short, slender man with brown hair and brown eyes. On the surface, Norman's life story has all the characteristics of the classic, striving bildungsroman. He was the son of immigrants: his father, Jacob Hess, had come to the United States from Germany at the age of four and worked as a cigar maker; his mother, Anna Gunther, had likewise been born in Germany and emigrated in her youth. Jacob was a prominent Republican, and both were very active socialites on Saginaw's West Side: Jacob belonged to the Zion Lutheran Church and the Loyal Order of the Moose;

Anna belonged to various Ladies' Auxiliaries and the Daughters of Rebekah (the same charitable organization that counted Minnie McCall as a member). During the war, they bought bonds along with Saginaw's other patriotic citizens. Norman, their third son, had been born and raised in Saginaw. As a grade schooler, he made the honor roll virtually every year and had perfect attendance. After completing his education, he took up a respectable trade and became a plumber, at one point fixing pipes for the railroad.[80]

We know nothing about Norman and Nina's courtship—perhaps they had a slow, sedate engagement and then an elaborate nuptial; perhaps they had a torrid affair and then a shotgun wedding. Did she love him? Such a question is unanswerable. Yet Nina's marriage to Norman could be read, at least in part, as a disgraced woman making a bold, desperate jump into the respectable middle class. Norman had a solid job and an upright family; Nina had a dead laborer father, a dead Casanova husband, a remarried mother, and, most importantly, a notorious reputation. Perhaps it is significant that she did not marry a man from Gratiot County. Perhaps she couldn't find one who would have her.

The young couple settled in Norman's hometown of Saginaw, population approximately sixty-six thousand.[81] They moved in with his parents, into Norman's childhood home, a clapboard house on a leafy stretch of road just a few minutes' drive from the Saginaw River.[82] Saginaw was only fifteen miles from Bay City, and the two cities shared a dependence on the short, frigid, heavily polluted river for nearly all of their industry and commerce. Though Saginaw was an old town by Michigan standards, it was booming when Nina moved to it in the early 1920s. Hoping to cash in on the ascendant auto industry, a number of enterprising men had opened foundries and production plants in Saginaw; General Motors came to town with five separate plants. By 1922, the town boasted 135 miles of public sewers, 85 miles of paved roads, 125 factories, 58 churches, 31 schools, 5 banks, and 1 daily newspaper.[83] The next year, a state-of-the-art bus system replaced the old streetcars.[84] It was, all in all, not a bad place for a young couple starting a family.

Yet Nina had not forgotten the past. She had not lost her conviction that the government had wronged her. So, on June 23, 1921, her attorneys filed an appeal to the state supreme court, alleging that Judge Moinet committed thirty-six reversible errors. They asserted that he had been wrong to stop Nina from discussing her conversation with Deputy Sheriff Martin; that he had been wrong to stop her from talking about punishment at Bay City; that he had been wrong to allow Mary Corrigan to commit hearsay and speculation; that he had been wrong to allow Ida Peck to claim that Nina had told her she'd had sex with Lloyd Knapp; that he had been wrong to force Nina to choose one of the three defendants against whom to proceed; and that, ultimately, he had been wrong to direct a verdict in Carney's favor.[85] Just why they had waited more than a year to file the appeal is unclear.

This was a momentous week. Only six days later, on June 29, Nina gave birth to a son; she named him John, after both of her grandfathers. John died later that day.[86]

We have no record of the pain Nina and Norman surely felt, or the way their grief manifested. The passage of time has erased so much of their lives, and the vital detail that is their son John is no exception. Whatever tears were shed, prayers were said, or ceremony there was for a tiny boy in a tiny box has been lost to us. In twenty years of life, Nina had been married twice, imprisoned once, assaulted, stalked, and humiliated, and now she had borne and lost a child. Somehow, she kept going.

SIX MONTHS PASSED. Then, on December 21, 1921, the Michigan Supreme Court announced its decision: Judge Moinet had indeed erred. Justice Grant Fellows, writing for the majority, cited every case previously decided by an appellate court addressing American Plan laws. Together, these cases, as well as Michigan's own statutes, led him "irresistibly to the conclusion that we should hold: That the State board of health has validly determined that gonorrhea and syphilis are communicable diseases; that the power exists in the boards of health acting through their respective health officers to quarantine persons infected with these diseases either in their homes or in detention hospitals, such detention to continue so long as the diseases are in their infectious state; and that, subject to what will now be considered, such health officer has the power to make such examination as the nature of the disease requires to determine its presence."[87]

Yet, significantly, Fellows did not stop there. "I have said that I thought the health officer had the power to make the examination," he wrote. "When may that power be exercised? Indiscriminately? May he send for every man and woman, every boy and girl of the vicinage and examine them for these disorders? I think not."[88]

Fellows continued, "Dr. Carney had the power to make the examination but he could not exercise such power unless he had reasonable grounds to believe that plaintiff was infected. Such good faith on his part was a necessary prerequisite to the exercise of the power. I am unable to follow the contention of defendants' counsel that this record establishes such good faith." Therefore, the Michigan Supreme Court reversed the verdict and ordered a new trial.[89]

Fellows's opinion was accompanied by a concurrence, in part, from his colleague Justice Howard Wiest. Wiest, who had been appointed just months earlier, had not attended law school; in fact, he had not even graduated from high school. Nonetheless, he had read law at a Detroit firm and worked his way up through the state's legal hierarchy. This new justice was more skeptical than his other colleagues of the public health authorities' police power. He wrote that he was "not willing to go the whole length of the opinion of Mr. Justice FELLOWS relative to the powers of boards of health and health officers." He agreed with Fellows that, "if the health officer had power at all to examine plaintiff, he had no right to exercise it without reasonable cause," but he questioned whether the health officer should have the power to quarantine a duly examined and infected person in an institution if that person were willing to take medicine in her own home. "I recognize the need of full power to stay the spread of epidemic diseases," Wiest wrote, "and I find such power in the statute, but I cannot find there that, by the mere determination that a disease is dangerous and communicable, there follows power at the will of a health officer to refuse isolation in the home by quarantine and placard notice thereof and to commit the diseased person to a hospital. If the law conferred the power exercised by the health officer in this instance, then children with any one of the numerous diseases now declared dangerous and communicable could be taken from their homes and sent to a hospital."[90]

Wiest even questioned, to some extent, Carney's power to examine merely suspected individuals. "It would be an intolerable interference by way of officious meddling for health officers to assert and then assume the power of making physical examination of girls at will for venereal disease," he wrote. "The law of 1919 points out methods for bringing venereal cases to the attention of health officers, but does not sanction what plaintiff claims was done in this case, and surely the power of defendant [Carney] was not more without law upon the subject than it is now with law."[91] In these statements, Howard Wiest went further than any other appellate judge in America—before or since—in questioning the American Plan. Yet he would not go all the way. What did he think of the constitutionality of the 1919 American Plan law? Wiest would not say. "I do not deem it necessary to state in full the limitations upon the powers to be exercised by health officers," he wrote, "but leave decision thereon until the proper case arises. It is sufficient to pass upon what was done here and determine whether, under the evidence, a case was presented for the consideration of the jury."[92]

Nina was probably lucky that the Michigan Supreme Court of 1921 was not the Michigan Supreme Court of 1919. That year, Justice Wiest was not on the bench, but Justice Russell Ostrander was. Ostrander's daughter, Katherine, was one of the most powerful state officials enforcing the Plan. Perhaps he would not have looked so kindly on Nina's appeal. Fortunately, he had retired later that year.

For O. L. Smith, the court's decision was a simple misunderstanding. Smith had left Gratiot County a few months before to accept an appointment as assistant attorney general of Michigan.[93] In his new, vaunted position, he was openly dismissive of the court's ruling. He told the *Alma Record* that "the reversal in the case and the ordering of a retrial probably came from the fact that the supreme court record did not show that the officials had a previous knowledge of the condition of the girl." He told the newspaper that he welcomed a new trial.[94]

For Nina McCall Hess, the court's ruling was surely welcome news. At last, she had been vindicated. Yet for other women, it would prove to be a decidedly mixed bag. Justice Fellows had clearly stated, on behalf of the court, that Carney had the power to make the examination, and, indeed, impose quarantine, but that he had to act on "reasonable grounds." Since he had no reasonable grounds for suspicion in Nina's case, Carney had erred. Had he had such grounds, however, his actions would have been fine. Justice Wiest had waffled on Carney's power to examine and quarantine, but he would not outright condemn them.

Rock v. Carney, as the case became known, was one of a slew of judicial decisions that emerged from the American Plan. Several of these decisions immediately benefited the victims of the American Plan, as *Rock* did.[95] However, not a single one of these cases ever explicitly challenged the authority of the state to invasively examine women reasonably suspected of having venereal disease and to imprison those women. *Rock v. Carney* would eventually be cited by future decisions as supporting the proposition that "[i]t is a valid exercise of the police power not only to prevent the introduction and spread of infectious and contagious diseases but also to empower health boards to make regulations. . . . Such laws are to be liberally construed to effectuate the purpose of their enactment."[96] The ASHA would cite it as justifying the "right of the health officer to quarantine persons suffering with the venereal disease in an infectious state who constitute a menace to the public health."[97]

This is the ultimate irony of Nina McCall's story. Even though the court had delivered her a victory, in another sense it had been a defeat. The court blessed the laws and practices that resulted in her imprisonment. Nina's suit—the only one of its kind in Michigan history—ended up solidifying the basis on which the American Plan rested for years to come.

Chapter 11

"THE SITUATION SEEMS TO BE GETTING WORSE"

ON DECEMBER 27, 1921, just six days after the Michigan Supreme Court ruled in Nina's favor yet simultaneously upheld the state's American Plan law, the largest assembly of people ever to gather in opposition to the Plan met in Chicago. Dozens of men and women from five countries and twenty states made their way to the second floor of Chicago's Lexington Hotel, a massive building of brick and terra-cotta that had been hastily constructed to house pilgrims to the 1893 World's Fair. The Lexington would later become notorious after Al Capone supposedly stashed untold treasures within, but in 1921 no such infamy marked the building.[1] It was a chilly day, with temperatures below freezing, but inside the grand old hotel, the fires of reform burned hot.[2] The attendees were there for the International Purity Conference, a meeting hosted by the World's Purity Federation, a Wisconsin-based group dedicated to wiping out white slavery.[3]

Ethel Sturges Dummer had collaborated with the federation to boost attendance, and, likely as a result, three Interdepartmental Social Hygiene Board agents, including Jessie Binford, showed up.[4] For three glorious days, from December 27 to December 29, 1921, speakers spoke, preachers preached, and lecturers lectured. "All human liberty," the keynote speaker declared, "depends upon the legal rights of an immoral woman, equally with that of an immoral man, being treated with the same respect as that of an ambassador."[5] At the end of the conference, the attendees adopted resolutions condemning the "quarantine of women for vice maladies" as "absolutely unjust" and calling the sex discrimination inherent in the American Plan "absolutely absurd and futile from a scientific point of view."[6]

Following this conference, the World's Purity Federation's magazine, *The Light*, began running articles repudiating the Plan. "No greater outrage has ever been enacted into law," cried one.[7] The federation's head began attempting to raise $25,000 to purchase a new headquarters for the newly revitalized organization, so that it would be "fully equipped for aggressive and constructive work."[8] But such a campaign was too little, too late. The federal American

Plan was gone, and its local activities were too widespread, too variable, too entrenched in local communities to be rooted out without supreme effort. "The situation seems to be getting worse," one federation partisan would write to another late in 1923. He continued, "[W]e have reached a point where the people have got used to the thing, and so now but little protest is made."[9]

The federation's experience exemplifies what so many of the Plan's opponents went through in the early 1920s. Unable to stir a popular uprising, and fighting an increasingly diffuse foe, many simply gave up. Dummer, for one, largely dropped her opposition after 1921. So did Edith Houghton Hooker. That winter, Elizabeth Githens's husband, John, died at the age of sixty, and Mrs. Githens moved back to Chicago shortly thereafter. She appears to have ceased her crusade against the American Plan and rededicated herself to Christian Science.[10]

Even Katharine Bushnell, who once quipped that she could die and even then God would resurrect her to fight the Plan, also mostly stopped battling in the early 1920s. "The public generally refuses to heed warnings, and will only learn for itself," she wrote to Dummer in 1921.[11] A decade later, her eyesight failing, she would dedicate two pages of her twenty-eight-page autobiography to her struggles against the "Social Hygiene movement." After bitterly denouncing William F. Snow and his evil machinations, she arrived at the end. "So far as I know, we were completely beaten."[12]

ALL OF THESE DEMORALIZED opponents recognized a truth that has largely escaped modern historians: empowered by state and local laws, government officials had continued to enforce the American Plan all across the country. Health officers in places ranging from Akron, Ohio, to Jackson, Mississippi, to Casper, Wyoming, to San Francisco, California, continued to forcibly examine and imprison women merely "reasonably suspected" of having STIs or being prostitutes years after federal agents had packed up and left. Women continued to resist this treatment. An Akron woman sued for her freedom in late 1922, while women in Jackson and Casper sued in 1924 and one from San Francisco did likewise in 1925. The Jackson woman triumphed and won early release; the San Francisco, Casper, and Akron women lost and remained behind bars.[13]

In the small town of Lebanon, Pennsylvania, the police forcibly examined all women arrested for prostitution or similar offenses, isolating the infected ones. When three quarantined women escaped from captivity, it caused a minor scandal.[14] This scene played out elsewhere across Pennsylvania. In 1924 and 1925 (and beyond), state police continued to round up all women "reasonably suspected" of having STIs; as the state's director of the venereal disease division put it, "the entire [state police] force may be considered as being at the disposal of the department of health." The Keystone State had, the director continued, "32 places of detention within its borders in as many counties, where, particularly, the diseased promiscuous female is treated, controlled, and when possible rehabilitated." In Philadelphia and Reading, these detention facilities were Houses of the Good Shepherd—religious reformatories with hospitals tacked on. Pennsylvania authorities treated any "known prostitute" as "reasonably suspected" and would keep her under quarantine until she could be examined for STIs.[15] In 1926, the Philadelphia police detained some 2,471 women suspected of prostitution and examined them for STIs before any kind of trial; less than a quarter tested positive, but those who did were kept behind bars and forcibly treated.[16]

In Chicago, the police continued to partner with public health authorities and private organizations, including the female Juvenile Protective Association and the male Committee of Fifteen, to detain thousands of "reasonably suspected" women every year, examine them, and forcibly treat the infected ones in Lawndale Hospital, an old, decrepit detention hospital on the outskirts of town. The building was a fire hazard. It had guards, but there were still frequent escapes. Lawndale offered its inmates no education; throughout the 1920s, thousands of women spent their days cleaning the dormitories and preparing meals.[17] It appears that these inmates were disproportionately black.[18] When several former board agents living in Chicago, including Jessie Binford and Rachelle Yarros, sent an open letter to Chicago's health commissioner, asking him to reform the American Plan and not deny due process, he replied that state law not only justified his present actions, but made them mandatory.[19] When asked about the Plan's sex discrimination, the city's corporation counsel simply ignored the question.[20]

In Los Angeles, city officials likewise examined all women "reasonably suspected" of having STIs—before any criminal conviction. This included, of course, all women arrested for prostitution, vagrancy, disorderly conduct, and similar offenses, and included sometimes even men. In 1925, city authorities briefly lifted the "former rigid quarantine order" for women who could afford to be examined by private physicians, but following a "period of controversy," a new police chief (who had helped enforce the Plan years earlier) was appointed in 1926 and revived the Plan there. Los Angeles had a quarantine hospital for infected women (and a mere quarantine ward for infected men).[21] The quarantine site for infected women was the Los Feliz Detention Hospital, a squat, perpetually dilapidated structure surrounded by barbed wire and located on the northern slope of remote Elysian Park, a mile away from the nearest streetcar. In 1924, a grand jury condemned Los Feliz, citing the presence of "windows without glass or screens, a door without a screen, broken headers, kitchen floor worn through, leaky roof on a screen porch, and rotting door casings."[22] In spite of the condemnation, Los Feliz continued incarcerating infected women there unimpeded. These women were disproportionately working-class.[23]

The list of places where the Plan continued could go on and on—Salt Lake City, Utah; Tacoma, Washington; Hartford, Connecticut; San Antonio, Texas; Utica, New York.[24] This perpetuation did not happen on its own. Though the federal government no longer oversaw the Plan, the ASHA relentlessly strove to ensure the Plan's continuation. The association distributed its model law to lawmakers across the country, and its officials were "constantly called on . . . to aid in securing helpful legislation," as one report exultantly put it.[25] The ASHA worked with the US Bureau of Immigration "to coordinate the activities of the Federal and state official agencies dealing with immoral aliens, so that their deportation might be facilitated," in the words of another report.[26] It also continued to dispatch undercover investigators across the country to learn more about prostitution, STIs, and delinquency in various cities, and to pass that information on to the local police. ASHA staff members made more than three hundred field surveys in 1925.[27] They made thirty surveys in Rhode Island alone in 1926.[28] In 1927, field agents traveled three hundred thousand miles.[29] In 1928, field agents visited every state in the union.[30] The ASHA instructed its field agents to study the STI notification and treatment laws of a given city—"with a view to suggesting revisions and additions where necessary"—to study the STI prevalence and treatment practices, and to study the STI treatment facilities.[31]

The man who led the ASHA for the whole decade, and beyond, was William F. Snow. The man who directed the association's Department of Law Enforcement and Investigations, and thus oversaw its phalanx of undercover investigators, was Bascom Johnson—an investigator so dedicated he spent two years on the road without once seeing his wife and children.[32] And the man who continued to fund the ASHA's work was John D. Rockefeller Jr. In all, throughout the 1920s, Rockefeller gave nearly $2 million to the ASHA (the equivalent of more than $25 million in today's dollars).[33] The millionaire did this at the behest of his chief charitable advisor, Raymond Fosdick, who held both Johnson and Snow in high esteem.[34] In the end, it was the ASHA that would keep the torch of the American Plan burning as the first decade following the Great War passed into the second.

OF COURSE, the American Plan did not continue in every city and state. In many places, local officials lost funding and ceased to detain, examine, or imprison suspected women.

The state of Michigan, in fact, provides an instructive example of what happened when enforcement of the Plan dwindled along with federal appropriations. Michigan legislators had never been fire-breathing promoters of the Plan; many had been bored by the mountains of literature they received promoting it.[35] Without federal matching funds, and without the impetus of protecting the troops, they cut funding for STI control in 1922.[36] Throughout that year, the state department of health still promoted the "arrest and confinement" of infected women.[37] But by 1923, one state official could report, "the State no longer provides for hospitalization of venereally infected persons at State expense." Nonetheless, "Hospitalization has been continued to a somewhat greater extent than was expected through action of the counties."[38]

The continuation of the Plan in Michigan beyond 1923 depended in large part on the cooperation of physicians, who, under state law, had to report women with infections to the authorities. (They also had to report men, but men were never likewise detained en masse.) A year before, state health officials had attempted to individually survey every doctor in Michigan and ensure their commitment to the Plan.[39] But by the end of 1923, Health Commissioner Richard Olin feared this commitment might be shattering. "The Public Press has from time to time within the last few weeks contained stories relative to a decision in the Superior court at Grand Rapids that has led physicians to believe that the law requiring the reporting of venereal disease has been set aside," he wrote to every doctor in Michigan late that year. "This is not, by any means, true."[40] A local Grand Rapids judge had indeed declared the state's American Plan law unconstitutional, but the case was being appealed to the state supreme court. As Olin predicted, the higher court would overturn the local judge early in 1924 and uphold Act 272.[41] Nonetheless, this incident surely dampened physician support.

Local communities began halting their enforcement of the Plan. Take the city of Detroit. Back in 1921, a policewoman had looked around one Monday morning and observed some ninety-five women being held in the Women's Police Station, of whom sixty-four were there solely on suspicion of carrying an STI. Within thirty-six hours, these women would be sent to the health clinic, where they would be examined. The infected ones would be locked up; the uninfected ones would be released.[42] Just three years later, Detroit had abandoned this policy and adopted a tacit form of regulationism; hundreds of one-, two-, five-, and ten-dollar brothels operated across the city, well known to local health officers. The health department insisted that the prostitutes be regularly examined, and women were only detained and imprisoned when they did not report for their examinations. "Detroit does not find it necessary to compulsor[il]y isolate many infected prostitutes, because Detroit believes that an infected girl will not hustle while she is infected," wrote one disgusted observer.[43] After the ASHA condemned this regulationist setup in 1926, Detroit's police commissioner resigned in disgrace and the police shuttered three hundred brothels, arresting hundreds of alleged prostitutes and forcing prostitution underground. Still, even after this incident, the American Plan did not return to the Motor City.[44]

The cessation of the Plan was far less dramatic in Bay City, home of Nina's former detention hospital. In the spring of 1921, a member of the local board of health had proposed that the name of the detention hospital "be changed so that the words 'detention' or 'contagious' be omitted because of the gloomy reflection that these two words unnecessarily cast upon the surroundings of the place." The official clarified "that it was perfectly all right to have a place to which patients suffering with contagious or communicable diseases could be removed, but that the present hospital might be used to a much greater advantage by changing the name, and opening the place in the same manner as city hospitals are run in other cities."[45] A few weeks later, the Common Council voted unanimously to change the name of the detention hospital to General Hospital.[46]

No longer just for sexually infected women, the General Hospital was quickly remodeled and made "comfortable and convenient." An adulatory article in the *Times Tribune* recounted its metamorphosis: "This building is now in use as a contagious hospital. . . . The detention hospital got a bad reputation while it was under contract of the state. Young women from distant parts of the state were sent here for treatment and the city made a big profit out of the contract, aside from the good that was done during the war in ridding the state of venereal diseases. [There is, in fact, little evidence STI rates actually went down.] With the state contract finished, the hospital fell back upon the hands of the board of health which conceived the idea of making it a general hospital." Local dignitaries proudly toured the General Hospital. "No cleaner hospital can be found anywhere than the General hospital of Bay City," gushed the *Times Tribune*. "There is a clean, pure atmosphere everywhere, so different from the days when the state had its cases there."[47]

Filth had apparently been tolerated when the hospital was just for sexually infected women, but now that it was for men as well as women, most with far less stigmatized diseases, the hospital had to be nicer. Its facilities were soon modernized. The board of health began considering turning the hospital's grounds into a park—"not only for patients, but for the public who may enter Columbus avenue and rest upon seats scattered among the native trees."[48] This rapid change could not be explained by a change in personnel. Mary Corrigan was still the General Hospital's superintendent—a position she would retain until her death in 1924.[49] Rather, the change can only be explained by the shift in social status of the hospital's patients.

The Bay City Detention Hospital had changed—not with a bang, not with an inmate uprising, not with a fiery blaze, but with a quiet, gradual transformation. Across the country, several institutions that had been constructed to lock up women under the American Plan quietly transitioned away from this role in the early 1920s and became regular women's prisons or reformatories. No longer just for women with STIs, they survived as female prisons for decades; some continued to operate into the twenty-first century. In this way, the Plan laid the groundwork for the ambitious expansion of female incarceration in the twentieth century.[50]

Bay City authorities stopped mass-arresting women merely suspected of having STIs. Instead, as the *Times Tribune* recounted, they—along with officials across the state—adopted a procedure under which "all persons that are brought into the jails, especially for sexual crimes, be examined, and where it is deemed best treatments started."[51]

The American Plan's principal architects in Michigan also departed in the 1920s. Richard M. Olin, the man who had spearheaded the Plan in Michigan for years, left the department of health in 1927 to run the health center at Michigan State College (now Michigan State University). He would continue in this position until his untimely death in 1938; the MSU health center bears his name to this day.[52] Gardener M. Byington, director of the state's Division of Venereal Diseases and the man who had examined Nina before her release, had quit in 1921 after his wife died unexpectedly and he was too distraught to continue his work.[53] He resigned two months later, writing a letter to express his "regret [at] discontinuing this most interesting work."[54]

Still, in spite of all of these changes, the American Plan lived on in the attitudes that authorities retained about women, sex, and disease.

Consider the following case. In late 1922, Arthur Tuttle, a federal judge in eastern Michigan, began receiving a barrage of letters from an incarcerated woman and her family. The woman, Marie Hamilton, had been arrested a few weeks earlier for stealing a car, along with three young men, and driving it all the way from Nashville to Detroit. Hamilton pleaded guilty to the offense in the court of Judge Tuttle, and he sentenced her to "the heaviest sentence of any of the guilty occupants . . . because I thought she was worse than any of the others," as the judge later wrote. Hamilton was "a menace to society; she was leading young men astray, and more than that, she was scattering syphilis wherever she went." The judge wanted her in prison for two reasons: first, so that she could be cured of STIs, and second, so that she might learn "to lead a good, upright, clean, and honest life." Yet the judge discovered that "Marie is herself a voluminous letter writer and is able to induce many fine people to plead her case." Eventually, the entreaties wore Tuttle down. He agreed to recommend parole late in 1923, so long as she was rendered noninfectious, "reformed in her mind," and, above all, resolved to be a "good girl."[55]

At first glance, this case might not appear to have much in common with the American Plan—the same plan under which Nina McCall was isolated. Hamilton had been arrested for stealing a car and had pleaded guilty in a court of law. However, Hamilton's case embodies the philosophy and biases that were essential to the Plan: that young women were responsible for the indiscretions of young men; that promiscuity in women was worse than it was in men; that STIs merited jail time for women; that women could not merely serve their time as men did, but that they had to be cured of disease and be "reformed" in order to merit release. Marie Hamilton's case featured a representative of the government, endowed with the authority of his gender and his office, deciding to keep a woman behind bars because of an STI and because she was not yet a "good girl."

Hamilton's case reveals how easily the Plan became incorporated into the American penal system, even when women were not arrested under its laws per se. Until 1917, syphilis was not a condition for which Michigan authorities could incarcerate a woman. The Plan changed that. Further, it reinforced long-standing negative attitudes toward sexually active women and served to concretize discriminatory and paternalistic practices. The Plan embedded itself, subtly yet undeniably, into a broader American carceral tradition.

THROUGHOUT THE 1920s, Nina and Norman Hess continued to live with Norman's parents in their clapboard house at 1621 Ames Street in Saginaw. Norman continued to work as a plumber; Nina continued to work at home. Death slowly crept into their house. On April 2, 1929, Norman's mother, Anna, died at the age of sixty-four. Three days later, the family held a funeral for her in the house on Ames Street.[56] A few months after that, a census worker came around and recorded the remaining occupants of Norman's childhood home as Nina; Norman himself; Norman's brother, Herbert; and Norman's father, Jacob. Jacob was working as a truancy officer; Herbert was working as a pattern maker for an auto company; and Norman was still fixing pipes as a plumber.[57]

All in all, the three were pretty lucky to still be employed (especially Herbert). The Great Depression, which had begun around Anna's death, had struck Michigan especially hard. In the early 1930s, the state's unemployment rate was 34 percent, considerably higher than the national average of 26 percent. Michigan was particularly dependent on the auto industry, and between 1928 and 1932, General Motors was forced to fire half its employees. By 1933, the state's unemployment rate had climbed to an astonishing

46 percent.[58] Perhaps the economy is why Nina's mother, Minnie, was listed as a pickle-maker on the 1930 census. By then, Minnie was living with her son, Vern, and his wife, Irene, in Alma. It appears that Minnie had lived separately from her second husband, Henry Van Norman, after moving away from him in 1919.[59]

Nina spent her days performing domestic tasks. She would have shopped in one of Saginaw's immigrant-owned corner groceries, as well as its many dime stores, especially the two most important ones, Kresge's and Woolworths. A man in a horse-drawn carriage would have delivered her ice and milk in the morning. Clapboard houses like hers had "no insulation whatsoever," remembered Saginaw resident Robert Jackson Douglas. "Zero. We could hear the wind whistling through the cracks in the walls and floors and feel drafts that bordered on being hurricanes." Residents burned coal to stay warm, but this would inevitably soil the wallpaper. "It cost a lot to re-paper a room, so when the point was reached where we couldn't tell what the original color or pattern had been, we had a wall cleaning party." Housewives in Saginaw did their washing on Monday, as that was the day when they didn't light their stoves until late in the afternoon. Any other day, the burning coal would dirty the washing. Tuesday, therefore, was ironing day. Many Saginaw women baked bread on Friday, though, recalled Douglas, "they were becoming more and more inclined to buy it at the store." Very few in Saginaw had cars in those days, and horses meant a lot of upkeep, so most residents just walked or took the trolley.[60]

Yet, in spite of all of the complexities of daily life, Nina had not forgotten what the state did to her. After the Michigan Supreme Court granted her the right to a new trial, she had initially intended to try her luck again in court. On January 23, 1922, she filed suit again in Gratiot County. Yet that was all she did. Her case remained inactive and without a place on the court's docket for the next four years, until it was dismissed on November 26, 1925.[61] Perhaps she had decided she just wanted to move on.

SOME OF THE WOMEN who had helped to create and enforce the American Plan, however, could not move on. One woman, in particular, stands out as a fascinating—and tragic—case.

Ann Webster had trained as a social worker and come of age working at a women's reformatory in New York that housed women detained under the Plan. She joined the field staff of the Interdepartmental Social Hygiene Board in 1919 or 1920; she then led investigations in New Jersey and successfully lobbied the New Mexico legislature to pass the federal government's model law. Then, in 1921, Valeria Parker—the board's newly appointed executive secretary—asked Webster to join the League of Women Voters—specifically, its Social Hygiene Committee.[62]

The League of Women Voters had been formed in March 1919, to unite women from the fifteen states that allowed them to vote.[63] Its members were interested in promoting the American Plan from the very start, and they created a Social Hygiene Committee; in April, Parker was appointed the committee's chairman. Parker, along with the committee's early members, crafted a legislative program that the league would lobby states to pass. Among other measures, they agreed to support laws that allowed officials to examine suspected women and imprison the infected ones.[64] In 1920, Parker appointed committee chairmen (never called chairwomen), and these chairmen immediately began lobbying state legislatures across the nation to strengthen their American Plan laws. Many of these state chairmen, including Rachelle Yarros, were board agents.[65]

Webster assumed the committee's chairmanship in 1921 and initially supported the league's legislative program. "During the year 1921 a total of 152 measures bearing upon social hygiene were introduced in state legislatures," Webster later claimed, with obvious pride. "Of this number 55 were passed."[66] Yet she was growing increasingly worried that these laws—the ones she was helping to get passed—were discriminating against women. "During the war," she would reflect, "when we were all more or less hysterical over the safety of the armed forces, we all helped in enacting venereal disease control measures and other measures for the protection of men."[67] Webster's first chance to change the league's legislative program arrived at its annual convention in 1922. "The 'American plan' of no toleration of prostitution is succeeding," she told the throng of elite women, but then she endorsed a resolution: "The authorities shall not be empowered to compel women to undergo examination for venereal disease on suspicion before conviction." The resolution passed by a two-thirds vote.[68]

A few months later, Webster reflected that the "resolution was designed to overcome an abuse. Neither interference with, nor curtailment of, the basic powers of the health officer was intended."[69] She was thus in the uncomfortable position of endorsing the American Plan but rejecting the defining characteristics of its enforcement: sex discrimination and denial of due process. The next year, Webster traveled across Europe, where she was shocked by the curiosity about the Plan she found among women on the Continent. "We found women interested in our laws and in the 'American plan' everywhere we went," Webster recalled, and so she sent "copies of our model measures" to allies in each nation.[70] Her experience in Europe echoed that of another American woman, in Switzerland at this time, who reported that "certain Geneva people . . . have heard . . . that the policy of the United States

Government in the V.D. control work is to arrest women and forcibly detain them for examination, locking them up in lock-hospitals."[71] One American with close ties to Rockefeller and the ASHA worried that Webster had "misled the women of Europe."[72]

Upon her return, Webster embarked upon a fight for the nondiscriminatory enforcement of American Plan laws. After hearing that Toledo, Ohio, was examining suspected women, and that in 1923, "422 women were held for hospital examination whereas only one man was held," Webster immediately made plans to visit Toledo, where she would lead the local committee in "planning next steps" to combat the discrimination there.[73]

As the years passed, though, Webster grew increasingly distraught at her complicity in the continuing Plan. "You know that the chief object in providing detention homes during the war was the protection of the male and that women were outrageously discriminated against," she wrote to one female ally (another former board agent) in mid-1926. "We are slowly growing away from the war attitude bu[t] only slowly. I believe that if I referred to the war influence at all it would certainly be to admit that most of it was wrong."[74]

"You know I have worked in about thirty states for the government, with delinquents," she wrote to another acquaintance a year later, "and I know the way these things work out. I have been party to a procedure which deprived persons of their rights, I am ashamed to admit, in the name of their welfare." The Plan, she concluded, was "appalling."[75] In 1927, Webster informed the League of Women Voters that her committee's main function was no longer to promote a legislative agenda, but rather to oppose the existing one. "The keynote of the national program is the removal of discriminations against women in criminal law and in the enforcement of the criminal law, and the removal of discriminations against women in board of health regulations and in the administration of the regulations."[76] She had gone from co-conspirator to qualified supporter to tepid critic to despairing opponent. By 1930, shortly before she left the league on account of her health, Webster was advocating the decriminalization of prostitution.[77]

Ann Webster exemplifies the progress of many women who helped create the American Plan in the 1910s. After seeing what was happening to her fellow women on the ground, she gradually turned against the Plan, filled with feelings of horror and shame. And, typically, there was little she could do to stop it.

IN SPITE OF THIS FUTILITY, opposition to the Plan had never truly ceased. Women at the bottom—the Plan's victims, its survivors—remained its most dedicated antagonists.

Some women chose to sue. Other women—hundreds of them during the 1920s—escaped from the detention hospitals in which they were held.[78] One woman, who had been sent to Bedford Hills Reformatory under the Plan in 1926, then paroled, and then ordered to return for violating her parole, leaped from a moving train to avoid going back.[79] In Seattle, many women sought to escape the city's disgusting, dilapidated detention hospital by jumping out its high windows—"resulting," read one government report, "in serious accidents and one death."[80]

As the 1920s became the 1930s, the opposition from women at the top and at the bottom finally began to pay some dividends. The first place such opposition achieved real change was New York City. Throughout the 1920s, police officers and Committee of Fourteen investigators there had continued to arrest and examine thousands of women every year, quarantining hundreds of infected ones. Though New York may appear to have been more respectful of civil liberties than elsewhere, as it did not examine women for STIs until after they were convicted of prostitution, waywardness, vagrancy, or the like, this was just a façade. In reality, the police engaged in widespread entrapment and framing, often to settle a personal grudge, and the Women's Court magistrates convicted nearly everyone who went before them, usually on the word of a single cop. "Under present conditions," remarked one policewoman, "no woman is safe."[81] Each year, dozens of these women were sent to Bedford Hills; the inmates there, just like the women brought before the Women's Court, were disproportionately nonwhite and working class. A majority had worked one of just three jobs: factory worker, waitress, and domestic.[82]

Then the New York police made a mistake: they arrested a rich, prominent white woman. On May 12, 1930, a plainclothes vice squad officer detained Emma Swift Hammerstein—widow of famous Broadway producer Oscar Hammerstein—on charges of prostitution. Well-off society women immediately denounced the arrest of one of their own as a "frame-up." This led to a series of exposés in the *New Republic*, which in turn led Governor Franklin Roosevelt to order an investigation into the Women's Court.[83] Roosevelt appointed Samuel Seabury, an icily self-righteous former judge, to question thousands of witnesses; collectively, these witnesses revealed that hundreds of crooked cops and court officials had framed thousands women on various morals charges, targeting black women from Harlem in particular.[84] The Seabury investigations were media dynamite, generating headlines for months. One woman who had been framed for "immorality" and sentenced to Bedford was actually murdered before she could testify.[85] William F. Snow and Raymond Fosdick privately feared that disgruntled former ASHA investigators might reveal to Seabury the unsavory details of the association's "undercover methods."[86] They did not, but seventy-seven women wrongly committed to

Bedford on various trumped-up morals charges eventually won their release (though no restitution) as a result of other testimony.[87] Two Women's Court magistrates were forced off the bench.[88] The Committee of Fourteen, which had helped the cops and judges, was disgraced and quickly went out of existence.[89] The police commissioner announced that he had replaced the entire vice squad, and that from then on his fedora-wearing officers would only investigate women after ensuring that there were truly "reasonable grounds" to suspect them of morals crimes.[90] The remaining Women's Court judges would no longer convict women and have them examined on the uncorroborated testimony of a single officer.[91] Perhaps this was justice; perhaps the enforcement of the American Plan would get a little less unfair.

Such hints of reform spread to Chicago. There, a squadron of elite women—including former board agents Jessie Binford and Rachelle Yarros—compiled damning statistics to prove that the city's Morals Court railroaded thousands of women (especially black women) and denied them due process, as a result of Chicago's American Plan law.[92] These women made a list of lawsuits filed by women incarcerated under the Plan who had successfully won their freedom—including *Rock v. Carney*—and sent copies to city officials.[93] They held vigil in the Morals Court, witnessing dozens of women detained and examined without a shred of evidence.[94] Eventually, in the summer of 1931, these women pressured the city's assistant corporation counsel to declare that "mere *suspicion* . . . is not sufficient ground for subjecting [women] to a compulsory physical examination." In a ten-page opinion, the counsel cited a number of seminal American Plan lawsuits, including Nina's, which together established the principle that all women arrested for prostitution can be considered "reasonably suspected" and thus examined, but not all women arrested for *any* crime.[95] It took several more months of sweat and blood before the Chicago women finally forced the police commissioner to agree to not have women examined until after convictions.[96] In 1932, the Morals Court was changed to a Woman's Court, with a female prosecutor and bailiff, and Lawndale Hospital was converted to a children's hospital.[97]

Change also came to Los Angeles, but there it was driven by women who were anything but elite. On August 22, 1932, a cool, clear summer day, some seventy inmates at Los Feliz began to riot, "and within a few minutes the air was filled with flying missiles, such as cold-cream jars, pieces of furniture and the interior of the hospital was virtually wrecked before peace could be restored," reported the *Los Angeles Times*. One woman was struck over the head with a heavy vase. Administrators temporarily restored calm, but when prosecutors arrived, the "rioting again started." It took police officers to finally quell the furor. The inmates had been objecting to the disgusting conditions within Los Feliz, as well as overcrowding—seventy women were present to riot, though the hospital had an official capacity of only thirty.[98] Just six months later, almost certainly because of the riot and the bad press it engendered, Los Feliz was closed for good. By the middle of 1933, the city had largely stopped enforcing the Plan, having nowhere to house infected women.[99]

WOMEN IN NEW YORK, Chicago, and Los Angeles changed the enforcement of the Plan for the better in the early 1930s. The Great Depression, which struck with a sickening blow in 1929, further hindered enforcement of the Plan, as cities and states (and even the federal government) ceased to spend money on anti-STI measures or detention facilities for women.[100] The ASHA's budget plummeted from $262,957.68 in 1929 to $70,666.12 in 1935, forcing the association to depend more than ever on John D. Rockefeller's generosity.[101]

But women across the country could not celebrate the Plan's curtailment for too long. In the years to come, it became increasingly clear that their victories were Pyrrhic and hollow.

New York was the city to which the Plan returned the quickest. Samuel Seabury's investigation had "shocked New Yorkers," wrote the historian Elizabeth Alice Clement, but "it did not curb either police corruption or police violence over the long run." Clement concluded that it is possible that "judges as early as 1932 resumed the practice of taking unsupported police testimony as sufficient evidence for a conviction."[102] After a brief dip in arrests for prostitution, the number of arraignments began to rise rapidly again in 1932.[103] ASHA field agents (including Bascom Johnson) resumed their investigations of New York and handed over the names of dozens of suspected prostitutes to the vice squad.[104] Early in 1933, a new police commissioner took office and launched a crackdown on suspected streetwalkers.[105]

By 1934, one Women's Court judge would tell a journalist, "Every woman arrested, on any charge whatever, is given a physical examination in the House of Detention before arraignment." If infected women were convicted, the judge could have them imprisoned for treatment.[106] The city had returned to the relatively restrained pre-1932 American Plan, but it got worse in 1935. That year, the city hired Walter Clarke—a longtime ASHA investigator and former CTCA agent—to run its STI division, and he soon inaugurated a system under which all women would be examined, and his division could incarcerate the infected ones in the towering fourteen-story house of detention or Bedford Hills, regardless of whether they were convicted. To justify this, Clarke's department invoked the city's 1918 American Plan law.[107] The Plan was fully back. Several prominent women objected, but to no avail.[108]

New York provides an excellent example of an ASHA official pushing to perpetuate the Plan. Because "fundamental legislation is now in force in almost every state," wrote one observer, the ASHA was, by the mid-1930s, primarily focused on "hav[ing] local ordinances enacted and enforced."[109] The association's investigators routinely passed information on to local authorities, helping them "in determining the extent and nature of their problems and in focusing their attacks on the weak spots disclosed."[110] The ASHA's interventions could be even more direct. In 1935, Bascom Johnson successfully pushed the city of Gallup, New Mexico, to launch a system under which they arrested, examined, and imprisoned reasonably suspected Native American women, but not white women.[111]

The Plan also continued in many places even without the guiding hand of the ASHA, including Cincinnati, Ohio (until at least 1931); Seattle, Washington (until at least 1931); St. Louis, Missouri (until at least 1931); Kansas City, Missouri (until at least 1932); and a half-dozen locales across the state of Pennsylvania (until at least 1932).[112] Few cities locked up more people than San Francisco, where thousands of women were detained and examined every year, and hundreds of infected ones were locked away without due process in Ward L of the San Francisco Hospital, the iron-barred, overcrowded, police-guarded detention hospital wing the city had used for a decade and a half.[113] San Francisco finally closed the decrepit Ward L in early 1934, but officials continued enforcing its Plan ordinance (imprisoning infected women in the county jail) through at least the end of that year.[114]

Some places that had largely ceased to enforce the Plan even brought it back in the 1930s, Depression be damned. The booming (if corrupt) timber and shipping hub of Portland, Oregon, had mostly stopped enforcing the Plan in the mid-1920s.[115] But then in August 1934, just as San Francisco was winding down its enforcement, an enthusiastic physician in Portland's bureau of health began examining suspected prostitutes and "sources of infection" again, acting under the city's American Plan ordinance. Dozens, then hundreds, of suspected women were summarily rounded up and held without bail as they awaited the results of examinations; several sued the city for "injuries and familiarity" on the part of the male physicians poking and prodding their genitals; thereafter, female nurses had to be present for examinations. In just one year, between mid-1935 and mid-1936, Portland officials examined 44 men for syphilis and 41 men for gonorrhea, while at the same time examining 1,284 women for syphilis and 1,875 women for gonorrhea.[116]

Inarguably the most detailed records (which still exist) of the enforcement of the American Plan reside in Kansas. These records reveal that the Sunflower State enforced the Plan nonstop throughout the 1920s and 1930s (and beyond). Between 1918 and 1938, Kansas officials imprisoned 4,938 women, without due process, solely for violating the state's American Plan law.[117] These women were all sent to the Kansas State Industrial Farm for Women, a collection of small cottages high on a hill, overlooking endless farmlands and the muscular Missouri River. In the early years, the farm did not have running water or internal plumbing; it was crowded; there was little space for recreation.[118] By the mid-1920s, the farm's superintendent (chairman of the League of Women Voters' Social Hygiene Committee for the state) had introduced locks and heavy steel screens on the residential cottages and erected "punishment cells."[119] The women imprisoned there under the Plan were pumped with endless rounds of mercury and arsenic-based medications. In 1931, women from across Kansas flooded the governor with letters railing against the farm's injustices.[120] In 1933, a government commission condemned the farm as punitive, poorly run, and full of infected women who had been unjustly "railroad[ed]" by the police.[121] Nonetheless, the Plan continued there.

Still, the Plan was certainly in decline by the mid-1930s. It needed a savior. As if on cue, one arrived.

WITH HIS SLICK SWATCH of silver hair, dark mustache beneath a hooked nose, and intelligent eyes, Thomas Parran looked the part of a wise yet energetic surgeon general. Many historians have reprinted his biography—born in 1892 on a Maryland tobacco farm, attended Georgetown Medical School, quickly joined the US Public Health Service as a field investigator, was fascinated by STIs his entire life—but none have noted that he came of age enforcing the American Plan.[122] Late in 1918, as a young USPHS physician, he was assigned to northwestern Alabama, where he successfully pushed two towns to pass versions of the federal government's model American Plan law and saw to it that they were enforced.[123] This experience would prove to be quite formative.

Several years later, in 1926, Parran took over the USPHS's Division of Venereal Diseases. On just his second day as division chief, he received a request from another USPHS official for "studies on the subject of prostitution and its suppression." Parran responded by forwarding the man, among other things, the "ASHA's Legislative Manual" and "Model Laws and Ordinances."[124] Yet he was frustrated in this position, as the division had virtually no funding, and in 1930, he jumped at an opportunity to serve as New York governor Franklin Roosevelt's state health commissioner.[125] In this new job, Parran promoted sex education and public STI clinics, yet there are hints that he would have favored a more aggressive approach to preventing STIs if he thought such an approach were possible. When a friend asked his opinion about quarantining infected patients, Parran replied that the idea "appeals very strongly to me," and in a prestigious lecture at Johns Hopkins in 1931, he endorsed this more explicitly: "A certain proportion of the patients will be socially irresponsible and for them compulsory treatment or quarantine is necessary after other efforts have failed. The group of the population who come into the hands of the law, because of various crimes, should be examined as a routine measure for the prevalence of syphilis and prompt treatment must be carried out." The members of this latter group, his audience understood, were suspected prostitutes.[126]

Late in 1934, Parran was all set to deliver a talk on CBS radio entitled "Public Health Needs." Three minutes before the talk began, however, a CBS official told Parran that he could not say the word "syphilis" on the air. Appalled at this censorship, Parran folded up his papers and refused to speak at all.[127] This incident began Parran's rebellion against the so-called "conspiracy of silence." He became a passionate advocate for frank and open discussions of STIs and how to prevent them.[128] Just a few weeks later, in March 1935, President Franklin Roosevelt nominated Parran to be his surgeon general. Parran immediately began using his new bully pulpit to talk about STIs. He published a scandalously blunt article about syphilis in *Survey Graphic*, which was reprinted in *Reader's Digest* later that month.[129] Some readers objected to the provocative subject matter, but others approved of Parran's forthrightness.[130] "We have read your article on syphilis in the July Survey Graphic," a pair of physicians from Nina's home state of Michigan related, "and are keenly interested in the possibility of following it with actual, constructive work here in Detroit."[131] Encouraged by the responses to his article, Parran organized a national conference on STIs to be held in the nation's capital in December 1936.[132]

The surgeon general was prompting this racy national conversation at one of the most exciting moments in the history of STIs. After more than a decade of inaction by a nearly penniless Division of Venereal Diseases, the Social Security Act of 1935 had finally provided the federal government with almost a million dollars to disburse to states for anti-STI campaigns.[133] (Parran had helped to craft the act.)[134] And then, within days of Parran's national conference, newspapers across the country were flooded with stories about a new miracle drug, Prontosil, saving the life of Franklin Roosevelt Jr. These stories convinced millions of Americans of the curative benefits of "sulfa" drugs like Prontosil, the world's first widely used antibiotics. Sulfa drugs would quickly prove to be the first truly effective treatment for gonorrhea. Physicians like Parran were more confident than ever of their ability to cure STIs.[135]

On December 28, 1936, a thousand "expectant, even militant, observers from all parts of the United States" descended on the nation's capital for Parran's Conference on Venereal Disease Control Work, reported one excited medical journal.[136] Several of these conference goers had helped to enforce the Plan for decades.[137] Among other topics, the attendees discussed prostitution and promiscuity. "The only way to handle that problem is to repress prostitution and to take the profit out of it," Parran told the conference.

"Prostitutes and others who viciously and knowingly spread infection should be quarantined, either in jail or in a hospital." One female attendee rejected this proposition. "After all," she countered, "there is more clandestine prostitution than commercial. The intelligent way to handle the problem is through education."[138] Few agreed. By the end of the conference, the attendees voted to direct Parran to request $25 million in "emergency" funding from Social Security funds.[139] Parran pledged to request this money the very next week.[140]

A month after the conference ended, spurred by its success, an exultant ASHA held the first-ever National Social Hygiene Day to promote the fight against STIs. On February 3, 1937, there were more than 500 meetings across the country, 135 radio addresses, and what one observer called "a flood of newspaper and magazine publicity."[141] In Albany, Governor Herbert Lehman addressed a crowd of twenty-five hundred. In San Antonio, Texas, Bascom Johnson organized a "flying squadron" of speakers who went from meeting to meeting, giving addresses.[142] In New York City, the health commissioner proudly read a telegram of support from Eleanor Roosevelt; other speeches were given by Walter Clarke and Alan Johnstone (a former head of the CTCA's Law Enforcement Division).[143] In Chicago, the speeches and festivities were organized by former board agent Rachelle Yarros.[144] Dozens of radio stations broadcast addresses by Parran and ASHA president Ray Lyman Wilbur. William F. Snow had given a coast-to-coast lecture on radio station WOR the day before. The *Woman's Digest* reprinted an article by Valeria Parker.[145] Hundreds, possibly thousands, of ministers gave social hygiene–themed sermons. Speakers from women's clubs, the Lions, the Kiwanis club, the Rotarians, parent-teacher associations, the American Medical Association, the Social Security board, the Works Progress Administration, and, of course, city, county, and state medical boards all held events.[146]

"When February 3rd was over," recalled one ASHA official, "the weary staff at national headquarters dug themselves out from the avalanche of correspondence, newspapers clippings and shipping orders with a sigh of relief, but soon learned that though the principal date was past Social Hygiene Day continued to be a live issue. Requests and inquiries kept coming in, in almost as great numbers as before, and meetings continued to be planned." Dozens of cities set up new organizations "for social hygiene work."[147] Few of those making national addresses dwelt on the more punitive aspects of "venereal disease control"—including the repression of prostitution—instead mostly focusing on sex education and public clinics.[148] But for the first time in decades, momentum seemed to be on the ASHA's side.

Inspired by Parran's crusade, cities and states across the country began, with fits and starts, to reenforce the American Plan. In December 1936, Chicago officials began ramping up their raids on brothels and detaining dozens of alleged prostitutes and other women suspected of being promiscuous and examining them for STIs.[149] By the summer of 1937, the city's corporation counsel would inform judges that they could use the existing American Plan law to "provide for examination of persons suspected of suffering from venereal diseases, and for the quarantine of those infected," thus undoing the success of the women's campaign against the Plan in Chicago five years earlier.[150] "In the underworld, especially in the vice group," one observer reported in August, "the word has gone out, 'All the broads are being examined and those found infectious are being sent 'to the band house!' Now this is effective venereal control propaganda. The women are scared."[151]

That same August, two hundred miles away, a health officer in Indianapolis announced what he termed the "Indianapolis Plan," which called for the establishment of an "isolation ward at the city hospital" and requiring "vagrants to submit to examinations" for STIs. Authority for these measures, the health officer claimed, originated in the city's 1918 American Plan law.[152] A few days later, in California, the state's director of public health reestablished the state's Bureau of Venereal Diseases. Within months, the California State Board of Public Health would adopt new "regulations for the prevention of venereal diseases," which in fact simply reaffirmed the state's existing Plan practices. These regulations cited the state's almost twenty-year-old American Plan law and called for the examination of "persons reasonably suspected of having syphilis in the infectious stages or gonococcus infection. (Owing to the prevalence of such diseases among prostitutes, all such persons may be considered within the above class.)" They also called for the detention and treatment of such persons when it was "necessary to protect the public health."[153] Notably, both the Indianapolis health officer and the California director of public health had helped enforce the American Plan as far back as 1918. Indeed, the Indianapolis health officer had even served as superintendent of a detention hospital and personally secured the passage of the very law he now invoked to justify his new actions.[154]

Even Michigan—where an aging Nina McCall still resided—moved to reestablish the Plan. One evening that fall, the Michigan State Department of Health met in a Lansing hotel and adopted new "Regulations for the Control of Syphilis, Gonorrhea and Chancroid." These regulations called for compulsory reporting by physicians and compulsory contact tracing by public health officials; they allowed for "[p]lacarding, isolation, or quarantine" when "necessary" to "insure the public against infection" or to "make certain that the patient receives adequate treatment."[155] Significantly, while contact tracing theoretically involved tracking down the sexual contacts of anyone, male or female, with an STI, in practice it nearly always meant tracking down the female contacts of infected men, not the other way around.[156]

Toward the end of 1937, in October, a survey by the wunderkind poll-ster George Gallup found that a majority of Americans—especially the young ones—felt that STI treatment "should be obligatory." "By a majority of seven to three, young voters say the state should have power to punish any individ-ual who is knowingly afflicted and who nevertheless avoids treatment once it has been made available." Often, Gallup reported, his interviewers heard statements such as: "I'm in favor of any steps at all that would help control the disease. Nothing the government could do would be too drastic."[157]

Was there any limit to the people's support for extreme measures to com-bat this plague of STIs that was suddenly being openly discussed and enrap-turing the national media? There was. One had only look to the state of Kansas that October 1937 to discover it.

ON THE EVENING OF October 22, 1937, a slender, dark-haired former con-gresswoman with thoughtful eyes told a gathering of Democratic women in Wichita, Kansas, that their state had sterilized dozens of young women and girls. The women in the audience were shocked.[158] The speaker was Kathryn O'Loughlin McCarthy, a lawyer who had, extraordinarily, been elected to a term in Congress in 1932 as an unwed Democrat in a state full of Republi-cans.[159] The former congresswoman's charges made front pages across the state.[160] "Fifty-four girls were sterilized and eight unsexed, one of the last be-ing a girl nine years old," McCarthy announced two days later. These steriliza-tions were "done as a punishment."[161]

Though most of the young women sterilized had been inmates of the Be-loit industrial school for female juvenile delinquents, all of the sterilizations had been performed in the hospital of the Kansas State Industrial Farm for Women—home of the thousands of Kansas women imprisoned under the American Plan. Women incarcerated in the farm appear to have been ster-ilized there as early as 1922.[162] Of the sixty-two women whose sterilizations McCarthy revealed, at least four had not originally been sentenced to Beloit, but had instead been sent to the farm first under the American Plan. They had committed no offense other than testing positive for an STI.[163] Thus, we can see four clear examples of women incarcerated under the Plan being steril-ized. One of these women was a fourteen-year-old girl who had been detained because her mother was prostituting her; the girl had been suspected of car-rying an STI and thus had been duly examined and locked away. This girl was treated for her STI, then transferred to the industrial school at Beloit (despite having been convicted of no other crime). Soon, though, she was shipped back to the farm, where (though her IQ was well above the "feebleminded" range) she was sterilized. Her even younger sister—convicted not under the

Plan but, instead, of having "immoral associates"—was likewise "desexed."[164] And it appears that several other women locked up under the Plan, in addition to these four, also went under the knife.[165]

Sterilization had long been the dirty little secret of the American Plan— though, in fact, it was not terribly secret, at least among public health officials. Many women imprisoned under the Plan were eugenically sterilized, though exact numbers are impossible to determine, given the paltriness of sterilization records, the extensive use of euphemism in surviving records, and the restrictions on these records for reasons of medical privacy.

In Milwaukee, Wisconsin, for instance, one twenty-three-year-old prostitute went to see a doctor around this time because she had "such pains in my side I couldn't work." After the doctor examined her for STIs, she recounted, he "sent me to the hospital and said I was rotten from the clap. He took out both my tubes and my ovaries and a part of my womb. Goddam these doctors. After he took nearly everything out of me I went back to work." This young woman's statement is a rare sliver of evidence of what was surely a larger, if fragmentary, campaign to sterilize infected women detained for little more than their infection or perceived promiscuity. It also documents the pain and anger these sterilized women felt.[166]

In California, thousands of young women were eugenically sterilized in the 1910s and 1920s. Though it is unclear how many (if any) women detained under the Plan were then sterilized, it is quite likely that some were. A remarkable data set of thousands of sterilization records, compiled by Alexandra Minna Stern and her team at the University of Michigan and Arizona State University, reveals that 935 of 5,674 women sterilized in California between 1921 and 1937 (or 16.5 percent) were labeled "sexually delinquent." The records of 255 of the sterilized women (or 4.5 percent) noted that the women had an STI. There was overlap between the women with STIs and the women labeled sexual delinquents, but some women were labeled only as sexual delinquents, and some women had STIs who were not labeled as delinquents. Were any of the 935 sexually delinquent women, or any of the 255 sexually infected women, detained under California's American Plan laws? It is impossible to tell, but, given that authorities across the Golden State detained thousands of women under the Plan during those years, many of whom ended up in institutions that carried out sterilizations (often for no reason other than their perceived promiscuity), it seems probable they were. (Stern's data also underscore the racial disparities in eugenic sterilization; individuals with Hispanic surnames were more than three times as likely to be sterilized.)[167]

Even Nina McCall's state of Michigan, which had largely ceased to enforce the Plan as such, sterilized hundreds of women during these years, often because of promiscuity or STIs. Between 1923 and 1935, the University of

Michigan's hospital sterilized 36 men and 280 women. "All of these cases have been performed at the request of the Probate Courts," recalled the university's then record librarian, "because of feeble-mindedness, mental retardation, promiscuity associated with the above or venereal disease." Over roughly the same years, the Michigan Home and Training School at Lapeer sterilized 238 men and 776 women. Who were these sterilized inmates? As Lapeer's former director recollected, "The majority of these individuals were female patients who were suffering from chronic illness, which could cause any further pregnancies to endanger the life of the patient, or be detrimental to her health." This was likely code for STIs.[168] In Kansas, the sterilizations of the sixty-two girls—including, recall, a nine-year-old—became a scandal. Former congresswoman McCarthy embarked on a crusade to reform the state's eugenic sterilization law. Notably, she did not oppose all eugenic sterilizations, just those that were "a form of punishment" and for women with "normal" IQs and "negative report[s] on her Wasserman [sic] and slides." She feared that sterilizing non-feebleminded women would lead to more STIs—"With the fear of procreation removed, she may become worse than ever and become a menace in spreading social disease." And she repeatedly implied that she approved of authorities using an STI diagnosis as a factor in justifying sterilization.[169]

McCarthy's proposed law never passed. Eugenic sterilizations in Kansas would continue until 1961.[170] Yet sterilizations did cease for women held in Beloit. And by 1938, sterilizations appear to have ceased for women held at the farm as well. Certainly, no more sterilizations were listed in the farm's biennial reports.[171] Nonetheless, women continued to be held at the farm for no crime other than having syphilis or gonorrhea. The American Plan continued to be enforced in Kansas, and Kathryn McCarthy did not object, even after a 1938 federal commission condemned the farm for its "hopelessly inadequate and dangerous" hospital equipment.[172]

THE SCANDAL IN KANSAS, perhaps in large part because it was not really about STIs, did not dampen the public's enthusiasm for wiping them out by almost any means necessary. Recall that Surgeon General Thomas Parran had pledged to request $25 million to fight STIs. A Gallup poll in mid-1937 found that 79 percent of the public favored this.[173] Parran's request did not meet with success, but by the spring of 1938, five congressmen had proposed bills appropriating millions for "the control of venereal diseases." Four of those five congressmen were in their first term and perhaps saw STIs as their ticket to the big time.[174]

Meanwhile, Parran partnered with the ASHA and health officials from around the country to prepare yet another bill. This one called for an astonishing $271 million for anti-STI measures over the next thirteen years (more than $4.6 billion in today's dollars). The bill proposed that the federal government appropriate a modest $3 million for 1938, followed by $6 million for 1939, $12 million for 1940, and then $25 million a year for the next decade. As if to most unequivocally demonstrate the continuity of federal anti-STI efforts, this bill was proposed as an amendment to the twenty-year-old Chamberlain-Kahn Act, the seminal law (also written by the ASHA) that had expanded the American Plan and created the Division of Venereal Diseases and Interdepartmental Social Hygiene Board. The bill's drafters passed it on to Senator Robert M. La Follette Jr. (a Republican) and Representative Alfred L. Bulwinkle (a Democrat), who introduced it into the Senate and House, respectively, in January 1938.[175]

Parran and the ASHA worked to gin up support for the bill, but fears that it would stall led Congress to revise the bill to appropriate $15 million for the next three years and then "such sum as may be needed to carry out the purposes of this act" for the next ten years. The revised "Venereal Disease Control Act" passed both houses of Congress without a dissenting vote, and President Roosevelt happily signed it into law on May 24, 1938.[176] The Social Security Act had disbursed less than $1 million to the states for "venereal disease control." Now state health officers could request grants from a $15 million fund over the next three years. This money would prove vital as states and cities resumed or enhanced the American Plan in the following months.

Only one week after the Venereal Disease Control Act became the law of the land, the ASHA began requesting money from the newly flush Division of Venereal Diseases to conduct investigations. Bascom Johnson and Walter Clarke—the two longtime ASHA officials who had, twenty years earlier, been the CTCA's first two field investigators—secured this funding and launched studies that aimed to, among other things, investigate police and health policies toward prostitution and STIs and "indicate weaknesses . . . and suggest new provisions to meet present conditions." These investigations, which continued well into 1939, strengthened the ties between the federal government and the ASHA, as well as those between the ASHA investigators and the hundreds of local authorities they visited.[177]

The stage was set for the American Plan to return on a national scale.

THOMAS PARRAN had been remarkably successful. After four years as surgeon general, he had almost single-handedly revived the country's flagging campaign against STIs and their carriers. Yet there was a dark side to Parran's success: it helped resuscitate a federally run, countrywide American Plan.

Actually, there was another dark side to Parran's success: it ensured the continuation of the now infamous Tuskegee syphilis study.

In 1929, the Division of Venereal Diseases partnered with the Julius Rosenwald Fund—a philanthropic organization to promote the welfare of African Americans—to educate poor blacks in the rural South about STIs. After the Rosenwald Fund's stock portfolio began to decline in 1931, its leaders decided to stop funding this education program. Yet Taliaferro Clark, head of the division, decided to stay in one Southern community—Macon County, Alabama, home of the Tuskegee Institute, one of most prestigious sites of higher education for blacks in the nation—and study what would happen if they didn't treat syphilis in blacks, if, instead, they let the infection run its course. Public health officials believed syphilis progressed differently in blacks, and Clark thus felt that Macon County (82 percent black) "offered an unparalleled opportunity." Clark and his colleagues decided to confine the study to black men—"because," as Clark recorded in his notes, "it is next to impossible to get reliable information as to the date of infection of syphilis in the female." In late 1932, Clark dispatched a rather unattractive thirty-five-year-old STI specialist named Raymond Vonderlehr to Tuskegee to run the study.[178]

Vonderlehr, and another federal doctor named O. C. Wenger, took blood from hundreds of black men to find the subjects of their study. Vonderlehr decided they would compare nearly four hundred men with syphilis to two hundred men without syphilis who could serve as controls. No longer was there any talk at all of the men with syphilis receiving treatment. By March 1934, John R. Heller, a division employee, had located two hundred controls.[179] The study was, from a scientific point of view, abysmal—almost all of the men had received some treatment at some point, and some moved away; some of the controls became infected in the meantime, and division employees were not terribly good at keeping track of the men.

In 1935, Parran became surgeon general and thus was in charge of overseeing the Tuskegee study. Parran—who believed that "the Negro instinctively trusts the white man" and that Macon County was a "primitive" place and thus an "ideal location for such a study"—enthusiastically ensured that the study was continued through the 1930s and beyond.[180] Under his supervision, division employees gave the men useless elixirs and pink aspirin tablets but lied to the men and told them that these were syphilis cures; they coerced the men into undergoing painful and relatively dangerous spinal taps by claiming they were "free treatment"; they met with local doctors to ensure that the men would not receive treatment from any medical professional in Macon County. Eventually, many of the men began to die of complications from syphilis; others passed the infection on to their wives, who started to die as well.[181]

Never once mentioned in histories of the Tuskegee study is the fact that its creators—Taliaferro Clark and O. C. Wenger, among others—had played active roles in the American Plan of World War I. Clark had served during the war on assignment from the US Public Health Service as the head of the Red Cross's Bureau of Sanitary Service, which provided personnel and funds to assist the USPHS.[182] In this position, Clark requested—and received—$6,000 to train ten public health nurses to follow and scrutinize "infected persons."[183] He helped to enforce the American Plan near military bases across the country.[184] There are indications he may have personally helped incarcerate "women [who] are infected because of their immorality and possibl[y] infecting the men with whom they have intercourse."[185] He also may have played a role in attempting to establish "a venereal disease ward for the colored women" in Arkansas.[186] Wenger spent much of 1920 as a division field agent enforcing the Plan in Missouri. He personally "investigated vice conditions" in Kansas City, inspected "v.d. among the gypsies" in Ozark, and spoke with Joplin city officials "in regard to suppressing prostitution."[187] Then, as a division regional director in Arkansas, he oversaw the incarceration of infected women in the Little Rock jail.[188]

For anyone hoping to most fully understand how and why medical men could decide to not treat infected black men (and, by extension, their wives, as well as their children, who could become infected in utero), the Tuskegee study's founders' connections to the American Plan are significant. The study was overseen by physicians in the Division of Venereal Diseases, which had been created specifically to enforce the American Plan. The Plan reinforced for these physicians their authority and power over those whom they viewed as subordinate and inferior, especially women, especially (and disproportionately) women of color. The Plan reinforced for these physicians the unimportance of consent when it clashed with their ideas of what was best. His experience with the Plan led one USPHS official to state, in 1918, "The prevalence of gonorrhea in negroes and especially in women was an appalling factor in the inefficiency of the race. It is a current opinion among civilian practitioners who are in cities of the South near the camps that the incidence of venereal disease among the troops is largely due to their contact with negro women, who exercise little or no care in protecting themselves or in caring for themselves in the matter of gonorrhea."[189] Tellingly, these physicians decided not to examine black women because they were seen as *too* promiscuous; black men, on the other hand, were seen as perfect test subjects: too poor and ignorant to complain; too insignificant to merit treatment.

Just as significantly, the Tuskegee study's leaders in the years to come—Raymond Vonderlehr, John R. Heller, and others—would later play critical roles reinvigorating the Plan on a national level and overseeing it during World War II.

THE CONTINUATION of the American Plan, the sterilization of some of its victims, the Tuskegee syphilis study, Thomas Parran's crusade—these things changed the lives of countless thousands, but we still must remember that millions of Americans traipsed through life in the 1930s largely ignorant of the great war against STIs and promiscuity. Even if they glanced at headlines or walked a little more stiffly around health officers, they were more consumed with the goings-on of their daily lives.

Nina's mother, Minnie, had a much younger sister named Mary May. After Mary May married Roy Day, a World War I veteran, in 1919—just months after Minnie married for a second time and while Nina was still hiding out in Detroit—she became Mary May Day. It was a name like something out of a storybook. Mary May and Roy Day settled in St. Louis, and Mary May joined the local chapter of the Rebekahs—the same one that claimed Minnie as a member. In 1920, Mary May gave birth to a son, Robert Day; a daughter, Delma Mae, followed in 1924. Yet this storybook did not have a happy ending. In 1926, Roy died in an Alma hospital at the age of thirty-eight. "Mr. Day had been ill but a few days and his sudden demise was a severe shock to his family and friends," read his obituary. "He is survived by his widow and two small children." The tragedies kept coming. Just six years later, in 1932, Mary May died at the age of thirty-nine.

Robert Day was just twelve years old, and his sister, Delma Mae, was only eight. To take care of the two young orphans, Nina and Norman Hess left Saginaw and moved into the Days' home at 401 West Washington Street in St. Louis. Robert and Delma were Nina's first cousins. For the next decade, the childless Hesses raised the two Day children. Norman kept plumbing; Nina likely did much of the child rearing.[190]

These were tough times for everyone, even children. Wilmot F. Pruyne Jr., a slightly younger child who lived just down the street, recalled, "Now back in the mid-thirties, you didn't have a hell of a lot of fun. Cause there was no money to have it with. That was the middle of the Depression. You did what you could to get by, and that's that. If you went to a movie once a week, fine, it cost you a nickel. And an ice cream cone, if I recollect, cost a nickel." Asked what people in St. Louis did for fun, Pruyne immediately replied, "Survived."

Robert and Delma would have attended the same school as Pruyne. It was a small school for a small town, a little brick building—fairly tough, fairly pretty, but with "nothing fancy about it." There were no clubs, no school newspaper.

Pruyne remembered St. Louis as a "decent little place," a "common little grubby central Michigan town," with plenty of green spaces, a sugar refinery, an oil refinery, and other common industries like that. Pruyne's father was an electrician. "St. Louis and those were just little Michigan towns. Nobody had much of anything, except a few landed families. They were industrial, but industries weren't really running hot during that period. So people just simply got by." Still, residents found time for softball games, the occasional picnic, and plenty of church socials.[191]

Yet Nina Hess could never escape sadness for too long. On January 8, 1935, her old friend and comrade Mary Loudenslager died in St. Louis at the age of forty-six.[192] Three years later, on February 1, 1938, her mother, Minnie Scott McCall Van Norman, died at the age of fifty-nine. She died in the company of her in-laws, the Hesses, in the small clapboard house in Saginaw that Nina had called home for more than a decade. According to her obituary in the *Saginaw News*, her body was to be brought back to St. Louis and the funeral service was to be held in Nina's residence.[193]

The day after Minnie's death, a distraught Nina may have tried to distract herself by turning on the radio. If she did, and if she tuned into CBS or NBC, she would have heard Surgeon General Parran giving a speech to mark the second annual National Social Hygiene Day. "Scores of states and hundreds of communities now are mobilizing to fight syphilis," he declared. "A few states and communities already are organized and steadily gaining ground."[194] Nina knew better than most what that could mean.

Chapter 12

"A Total War"

AT ABOUT 4:40 A.M., on September 1, 1939, the Luftwaffe—the notorious German air force—bombarded the cozy Polish farming village of Wieluń, quickly killing as many as sixteen hundred of the town's sixteen thousand citizens. "There was hell over Wieluń," recalled one schoolboy. "Shooting, smoke, whining, crying—all this combined created a frightful scene." Seven minutes later, the German battleship *Schleswig-Holstein* began firing on a Polish military base on the peninsula of Westerplatte. Thick black smoke rose over decimated wooden buildings. Fires blazed. More died. As the morning progressed, some 1.5 million Nazi troops marched across Poland's border. World War II had begun.[1]

France and England immediately began to mobilize for war. President Roosevelt, on the other hand, asserted America's neutrality, yet he also declared what he called a "limited national emergency." This allowed him to add about a hundred thousand new men to the armed forces. Roosevelt then fled by train to his family home in Hyde Park.[2] At almost the exact same time that September 1939, a meeting took place among representatives of the army, the navy, several state health departments, the ASHA, and the Federal Security Agency—a cabinet-level department created a few months earlier to house a number of agencies, including the US Public Health Service, the Social Security board, and the Civilian Conservation Corps. United by the "limited national emergency," the representatives of these groups feared that the hundred thousand new troops might become infected with STIs. This meeting was an eerie echo of events twenty-two years earlier—STIs were suddenly no mere threat to morality; they were a threat to national security. Indeed, with Hitler's troops burning Poland, they could even be a threat to the future of the world.[3]

Together, these representatives reached what came to be known as the "Eight Point Agreement for the Control of the Venereal Diseases in Areas Where Armed Forces or National Defense Employees are Concentrated." The Eight Point Agreement called for

1. Early diagnosis and adequate treatment by the Army and the Navy of enlisted personnel infected with the venereal diseases.

2. Early diagnosis and treatment of the civilian population by the local health department.

3. When authentic information can be obtained as to the probable source of venereal disease infection of military or naval personnel, the facts will be reported by medical officers of the Army or Navy to the State or local health authorities as may be required. If additional authentic information is available as to extramarital contacts with diseased military or naval personnel during the communicable stage, this should also be reported.

4. All contacts of enlisted men with infected civilians to be reported to the medical officers in charge of the Army and Navy by the local or State health authorities.

5. Recalcitrant infected persons with communicable syphilis or gonorrhea to be forcibly isolated during the period of communicability; in civilian populations, it is the duty of the local health authorities to obtain the assistance of the local police authorities in enforcing such isolation.

6. Decrease as far as possible the opportunities for contacts with infected persons. The local police department is responsible for the repression of commercialized and clandestine prostitution. The local health departments, the State Health Department, the Public Health Service, the Army, and the Navy will cooperate with the local police authorities in repressing prostitution.

7. An aggressive program of education both among enlisted personnel and the civilian population regarding the dangers of the venereal diseases, the methods for preventing these infections, and the steps which should be taken if a person suspected that he is infected.

8. The local police and health authorities, the State Department of Health, the Public Health Service, the Army, and the Navy desire the assistance of representatives of the American Social Hygiene Association or affiliated social hygiene societies or other voluntary welfare organizations or groups in developing and stimulating public support for the above measures.[4]

The Eight Point Agreement proved to be a highly significant document. It would serve as a road map for the revitalization of a federally directed, federally funded American Plan. Importantly, this agreement demanded forcible isolation of infected persons, if necessary, and called on federal and military officials to work with local and state police and health authorities in the "repression of commercialized and clandestine prostitution."

This was a critical development. Yet some recognized that it was just one development along the long road that led to the revitalized federal Plan.

"Public health action has already begun," one federal official would note a few years later. "In 1936 Federal and state health authorities mapped a program for action. In 1937 the Venereal Disease Control Act made that program a national policy, and Congress provided funds for medical and public health attack. Doctors, clinics, and health departments were already attacking. The agreement of September 1939 merely moved to intensify this work to meet new problems posed by national defense."[5]

On September 30, William F. Snow—by now sixty-five years old—wrote to John D. Rockefeller Jr. (also sixty-five), "I have been spending some time in Washington the past weeks. I earnestly hope we are not going to repeat the days of 1917–18; but this so-called 'Limited National Emergency' calls for much to be done and planned for." Snow was again ready for war and reporting for duty. And, as before, he wanted Rockefeller's considerable aid. "It all brings back to me afresh what wise and timely assistance you and your immediate associates provided through so many channels."[6] A week later, Snow elaborated on his and the ASHA's role in the limited national emergency: "Behind the scenes and very quietly we are being of assistance in planning various steps and measures in the way of civilian cooperation in strategic areas, in the event that untoward circumstances make it necessary to again develop activities paralleling those of 1917–18 but adapted to the somewhat different conditions of 1939–40."[7]

Snow, Walter Clarke, and other ASHA veterans met with Thomas Parran and resolved to help the government in any way they could.[8] To test the "effectiveness" of the ASHA's "methods in dealing with flagrant prostitution conditions," Bascom Johnson traveled that December to the bustling mill town of Columbus, Georgia, which was rumored to be a den of iniquity and infection.[9] The tweedy ASHA man met with Columbus's mayor and a number of military, USPHS, state, county, city, religious, and chamber of commerce officials and warned them that conditions in their town were "of an unsavory nature," but that they "could be curbed."[10]

At his urging, Columbus, as well as Phenix City, Alabama, just across the Chattahoochee River, adopted resolutions demanding that police and health officials "vigorously enforce" Georgia's and Alabama's existing American Plan laws and "examine all persons who they have reasonable grounds for believing are infected with a venereal disease and who, by reason of their behavior (prostitution or other promiscuous conduct), have spread or are likely to spread the disease to others, particularly to soldiers." The resolutions also urged the health officials to place such persons "under isolation or quarantine, if necessary," and to make a special effort to target "prostitutes and other promiscuous persons for the purpose of making such examinations." The first arrests under the new resolutions were made on February 14—Valentine's Day.

In Columbus, eighty suspected prostitutes were arrested by the police and examined for STIs; twenty-five tested positive and were imprisoned for treatment in the county jail, without trials and without bail. In Phenix City, eighty-five suspected prostitutes were arrested.

Johnson's work in Columbus had proved to be a smashing success. After a few months there, he joined up with several USPHS and state public health officials (including American Plan veteran C. C. Pierce and Tuskegee study overseer John R. Heller) and traveled to western Louisiana and eastern Texas. In communities across the Gulf Coast, they convinced mayors and other officials to adopt the "program of measures [that] was substantially the same as that adopted in Columbus, where their efficiency had already been demonstrated."[11]

In the meantime, a squadron of ASHA officials—flush with a $10,000 infusion from Rockefeller—visited New York, Minnesota, Wisconsin, Washington, Virginia, Illinois, and elsewhere, and convinced local officials to adopt (or continue to enforce) the "program that had worked so well at Columbus." Raymond Vonderlehr, now head of the Division of Venereal Diseases, traveled across California promoting the American Plan. In some places, he found that officials needed prodding; in some places, like San Bernardino and Monterey County, he was delighted to discover that a program of mass arrests and examinations of hundreds of women was already well under way. Officials in all of these places began reenforcing their American Plan laws with a vengeance, detaining "reasonably suspected" women—"[l]local girls" as well as "prostitutes."[12] By the start of 1941, the ASHA had five investigators in the field. Of these men, only one—a thirty-one-year-old named George Gould—had not played a significant role enforcing the American Plan back in World War I.[13]

ON THE EVENING OF September 29, 1940, even as federal agents and ASHA investigators were fanning out across the country, Nina's cousin and adopted son, Robert Day, died at the tender age of twenty. Nina and her family could not escape tragedy.

Robert had attended St. Louis schools and had barely begun his life. On September 7, 1940, he had married Glenadine Lobsinger, a young Alma woman. Almost immediately thereafter, he had come down with a "serious illness." After three weeks of suffering, he passed. His funeral was held a few days later in Nina and Norman's home on Washington Avenue, where Robert had lived all his life.[14] Robert's widow, Glenadine, gave birth to his son seven months later. She named the baby Robert Jr. In yet another tragic turn, Robert Jr. would die at the age of twenty-four, just weeks before his own son, Robert, was born.[15]

In the fall of 1940, the deceased Robert Day's sixteen-year-old sister, Delma Mae, still lived with Nina and Norman in St. Louis. It is quite tempting to imagine Nina warning her teenaged charge to stay indoors and away from the authorities. For, all across Michigan, the American Plan was being resurrected.

Just four days after Robert's funeral, four thousand delegates gathered in a towering, ornate Detroit hotel for the sixty-ninth annual meeting of the American Public Health Association. Among the delegates were Raymond Vonderlehr and Bascom Johnson. The theme of the meeting was STI control, and several delegates emphasized the importance of the Plan. In the most widely reported speech, a retired major general and current health official called for the adoption of a "plan, parts of which already are in effect." This "plan" included "state and municipal health and police authorities acting under existing statutes and ordinances which in most localities authorize arrest, quarantine and treatment of prostitutes known to have venereal disease." Such a plan, the major general announced, had been "tested during the World War."[16]

A few days after the meeting ended, seventeen state and local health officials gathered in the chamber of commerce offices in Battle Creek—the town that housed Fort Custer (back in Nina's youth, it had been known as Camp Custer). The first draftees were scheduled to arrive at the fort in just a few weeks, and already, according to one observer, a "regular city of unpainted pine buildings has been erected and stretches almost as far as you can see." Together, the health officers drew up plans for "a rigid venereal disease control program" in Battle Creek and its environs. "The consensus of those attending," reported one Battle Creek journalist, "was that a plan of quarantine for all women found to be infected would be the most effective attack." State law already provided for this, they agreed.[17]

To ensure that the lofty goals of these meetings became reality, George Gould, the ASHA's most youthful investigator, arrived in Michigan in mid-December. Gould was horrified to discover that various Michigan officials were planning on regulating prostitution. One state health officer, he concluded in a "STRICTLY CONFIDENTIAL" report, "loves his job when it comes to rush all over the state checking on prostitutes," while another "just likes to tell prostitutes what to do." Undeterred, Gould crisscrossed the state, demanding that officials enforce the Plan. Within a matter of days, he had pushed Battle Creek authorities to do so; a few days after that, Gould had likewise succeeded in Jackson and Kalamazoo, and he had made headway with officials in all-important Detroit. Numerous officials had promised him they would "secure medical examinations for all cases and suspected cases . . . secure treatment for all infectious cases . . . [and] isolate or quarantine all infectious cases." The American Plan was back.[18]

These were thus dangerous times for Michigan sixteen-year-olds like Delma Mae. Nina certainly would have heard that her old antagonist, Dr. Thomas Carney, now almost completely bald, had salvaged his reputation in nearby Alma after the influenza imbroglio. He had founded Gratiot County's first general hospital, which expanded repeatedly and became known as the Carney-Wilcox Hospital. Carney had become a prominent Rotarian and was, in 1937, elected to Alma's city commission. He was serving out his second term when the Plan returned to Michigan, recently having promoted a municipal ordinance to bar young women from working in or even entering beer halls.[19]

Nina's other foes were likewise flourishing. O. L. Smith, one of Carney's defense lawyers back in the day, had served as US attorney for the Eastern District of Michigan in the late 1920s. Afterward, he became a prominent political grandee in Detroit, his slender frame gradually widening with indulgence. In the summer of 1940, just months after losing control of his car and injuring a fellow motorist, the aging Smith announced his candidacy for governor, bitterly denouncing "boss control." He won a number of key endorsements and returned to Gratiot County for some celebratory campaigning but was ultimately walloped by the bosses in the September Republican primary, just three days after Robert Day got married and three weeks before Robert Day died. Smith himself would be dead within two years. Today, a Dearborn middle school bears his name.[20]

Judge Edward J. Moinet had aged better. In July 1927, the tall, imposing jurist had accepted a lifetime appointment as a federal district court judge, towering over his fellow solomons as he took the oath of office. Within days of assuming the federal bench, Judge Moinet handed down the heaviest sentence in Detroit history for a Prohibition violation; liquor law crimes evidently became his passion.[21] Over the next decade, several defendants threatened to kill him. The judge was undeterred.[22] People who saw him coming would excitedly whisper, "Here comes the judge, here comes the judge." Especially after his wife died in 1940, his job was his life; he began to fade into dementia almost immediately upon retiring in 1946 and would die not long thereafter.[23] In 1940, though, Moinet's name was still regularly in the headlines—for instance, when he oversaw the arraignments of several former members of the Al Capone gang who were (allegedly) involved in the largest bootlegging operation since Prohibition.[24]

With all these men in positions of power and prestige, and with the papers bearing news of renewed anti-STI measures across Michigan, one can imagine the forty-year-old Nina Hess, perpetually in mourning, fretting over the fate of the sixteen-year-old orphan she was trying to keep safe.

ON JANUARY 20, 1941, Andrew May, a round-faced, jovial congressman from Kentucky, stood up in the House of Representatives to propose a bill. The bill, which had actually been drafted by members of the ASHA, copied significant chunks of Section 13 of the Selective Service Act of 1917 verbatim. Section 13, one of the foundational laws of the American Plan, had enabled the secretaries of war and the navy to take measures to eliminate prostitution near military bases during the First World War, and May's bill did the same for the Second.[25] Snow sent notes to ASHA members across the country, asking them to write a "letter of appreciation" to May, to demonstrate for him the broad national sentiment in favor of the bill.[26] Snow, Bascom Johnson, the leaders of the Boy Scouts, the Red Cross, the YMCA, and various women's clubs, as well as dozens of other individuals—including Fiorello La Guardia, New York's indomitable little mayor—urged Congress to pass the bill, which Congress did, unanimously, that summer.[27]

La Guardia, for one, was thrilled. He told a cheering New York crowd of the bill and its importance. There was a danger, he said, in women "found infected with venereal disease. They must be cured. . . . Therefore, following an arrest, whether convicted or not, if the woman is found infected with venereal disease, provision must be made for her complete cure."[28] By this point, such a "cure" usually involved sulfa drugs for gonorrhea, which were certainly more effective than previous treatment, though they were far from perfect and many people were resistant to them; for syphilis, a "cure" usually involved years of painful injections of arsenic- and bismuth-based drugs, which could not, in fact, achieve a cure.[29]

In the spring of 1941, a few months before the May bill became the May Act, federal public health and military officials created a new federal agency—the Social Protection Division (SPD)—to spur local officials to locate, incarcerate, and treat prostitutes and other promiscuous women whose sexual proclivities might prove to be a threat to the soldiers. Unlike the federal agencies of World War I, the SPD did not have to push state and local legislators to pass new laws. Rather, as the division's first director put it, the SPD sought "to persuade local officials to enforce their own laws."[30]

That first director was none other than Bascom Johnson. Such an appointment was only natural; the ASHA had lobbied for the establishment of the SPD and Johnson had spent the last several decades traveling around the country and the world, cultivating relationships and urging officials to eliminate prostitution.[31] There was perhaps no one on earth more qualified for the job. Making use of his contacts at the ASHA, Johnson secured much of the association's field staff (men he had "personally trained for 25 years") to work as the SPD's investigators. Since Congress was reluctant to pay the ASHA agents, federal officials and Snow approached Raymond Fosdick to inquire about securing Rockefeller Foundation funds. Rockefeller ultimately demurred, but he helped persuade the newly founded United Service Organizations (USO) to give $50,000 to the ASHA "for the investigation work in connection with Bascom Johnson's program." Significantly, Rockefeller gave hundreds of thousands to, and repeatedly used his connections to raise millions for, the USO. Therefore, he continued to indirectly support the ASHA. In the future, Rockefeller would continue to ensure that the USO gave tens of thousands to the ASHA each year.[32]

In spite of this success, however, federal and ASHA officials privately doubted Johnson's abilities as a leader; they felt he was a better lieutenant than a general. Walter Clarke wanted Johnson replaced by Snow, but when the ASHA secretary passed on the job, federal officials cast a wide net and eventually settled on one of the most famous law enforcement officers in American history: Eliot Ness.[33] Born in Chicago in 1903, Ness is now principally remembered as the relentless, pugnacious, "untouchable" federal agent who took down Al Capone, but he had actually spent several years afterward as a Cleveland law enforcement officer, targeting suspected prostitutes with "blitzkrieg tactics," leading rabid men armed with sledgehammers into suspected brothels.[34] At one point, Ness hit a small roadblock when a female judge refused to convict women of prostitution because Ness had hired "citizen cadets" to arrest the prostitutes—cadets who, the judge claimed, "corrupted themselves" in obtaining evidence.[35] Ness found a way around this by charging the women with a slightly different crime.[36] He was so focused on this work that his marriage collapsed; he began drinking heavily. Snow and others thought he was perfect.[37] Johnson was quietly ushered out the door and asked to "look the situation over" in the Pacific Northwest.[38]

For the rest of 1941, Eliot Ness pushed "local authorities" to adopt the SPD's program "as a permanent policy."[39] He personally traveled to San Antonio, Texas, where, at his urging, police immediately began rounding up dozens of suspected women, giving them what Raymond Vonderlehr noted was "a very poor examination" and then dumping the infected ones in the "very bad" jail, where they languished on bare mattresses.[40]

Ness's underlings did likewise. In California, SPD officials met with the state's handsome, idealistic attorney general, Earl Warren. Now revered as a liberal US Chief Justice, Warren was known at the time for his enthusiastic prosecutions of alleged prostitutes as a young district attorney.[41] Now state attorney general, he heartily endorsed the SPD's agenda and personally persuaded military authorities stationed across the state to pledge "their cooperation in getting rid of prostitutes." Warren organized a conference of dozens of district attorneys and county sheriffs and pushed them to do likewise—all to wipe out STIs. At his insistent urging, several cities—from Vallejo to Stockton to Sacramento—immediately began rounding up and examining suspected women.[42] Following his election as California's governor two years later, Warren would enthusiastically oversee the American Plan.[43] As one colleague recalled in an oral history decades later, "Warren supported that venereal disease control very heartily."[44]

By the end of 1941, New York City had locked up more than five hundred infected women.[45] Kansas officials too had continued to enforce the Plan, forcing the disproportionately working-class and nonwhite inmates of the State Industrial Farm for Women to produce doilies, aprons, ties, and even Santa Claus suits, which the state sold for a profit.[46]

At the same time, officials at all levels of government were debating how and where to use the newly enacted May Act, which empowered the feds to suppress prostitution. Citizens from Fayetteville, North Carolina, for instance, asked for the act "to be invoked by bringing in the FBI people and put[ting] some of the load off on the Federal Government. Wilmington also wants the bill invoked, but wants to go right in and clean things up, themselves, thereafter."[47] SPD higher-ups met with the FBI, which was to enforce the May Act, but the G-men decided they would need nearly $2.5 million to begin such work, and discussions of immediately invoking the act stalled.[48] Surgeon General Parran felt strongly that the government "ought to go into more definite offensive action on the May Bill, use a couple of places as an example by having Justice go in and really do some enforcing."[49] Others in the government, however, considered the May Act to be "in the nature of a Federal threat to hold in reserve and be invoked only after all other local measures had failed."[50] In Tacoma, Washington, for instance, army officials had threatened to invoke the act if local authorities did not do something to combat prostitution in their community. Within days, the police had closed down almost every brothel in town.[51]

Frustrated that the act had yet to be invoked, Parran and Vonderlehr literally wrote a book attacking the secretaries of war and the navy for not invoking it. This outraged William F. Snow, alarmed President Roosevelt, enraged the American Medical Association (which claimed the book was advocating socialized medicine), and drew praise from Raymond Fosdick. "I went through this business in the last war and I can speak from personal experience," he wrote to Parran. "More strength to your elbow!" Officials in twenty-four states called on the federal government to invoke the May Act. Roosevelt suggested that had Parran been in the military, he would have "been liable to immediate court martial."[52]

Yet just two days later, that controversy abruptly died down. That day, December 7, 1941, something happened that was so terrifying, so enraging, so monumental that it silenced the internal debates and, to a large extent, united government officials as to the urgency of repressing prostitution and suppressing STIs.[53] That fateful day, the Japanese attacked the American military base of Pearl Harbor. Within a day, the United States would declare war on Japan. Germany and Italy would declare war on the United States a few days later, and the United States would enthusiastically reciprocate.

THE ATTACK ON PEARL HARBOR and the American entrance into the war dispelled any reluctance to enforce the American Plan as vigorously as possible.[54] In January, New York police began partnering with military men to arrest even more women.[55] In February, San Francisco officials began holding all suspected women for seventy-two hours, to ensure that STI examinations were sufficiently thorough.[56] It was not until late March that federal officials began seriously planning the invocation of the May Act, and it was not until late May that the act was finally invoked for the first time, in twenty-seven Tennessee counties famed for their thriving sex trade.[57]

Hundreds of agents of the FBI descended on Tennessee. Working out of the Memphis and Nashville offices, squadrons of G-men partnered with local police officers, and all hit the streets to find young women. In Nashville, the FBI agents and police united to form a "May Act squad." According to a federal report, the federal and local officials "worked out a cooperative arrangement whereby women suspected of prostitution were arrested by the police on local charges. One or more Federal Bureau of Investigation Agents worked with them. They interviewed the women picked up and if they felt there was a May Act case, took it over for prosecution in the Federal Court." Regular Nashville patrolmen and vice squad officers stepped up their arrests of "women suspected to be prostitutes." All such women—indeed, all women arrested for any crime other than "minor traffic violations"—were taken to the jail and examined for STIs. Those found infected were often quarantined and forcibly treated.[58] All across Tennessee, local and federal authorities detained, examined, and imprisoned women—disproportionately black women—without due process.[59] The FBI's actions were personally monitored by the bureau's legendary director, J. Edgar Hoover.[60]

The second place where the federal government invoked the May Act was central North Carolina. The state's health officer, its governor, and a contingent of prominent women had spent the summer publicly calling for the act to be enforced.[61] As in Tennessee, hundreds of FBI agents partnered with local police to arrest hundreds of people—mostly women, though a handful of johns, pimps, and procurers as well. (ASHA agents also came to North Carolina to investigate prostitution.)[62] Ultimately, North Carolina was the final place where the act would be invoked, but it nonetheless remained a successful cudgel in persuading the rest of the country to arrest women. Perhaps the ASHA put it best when, in one publication, the association compared the existence of the May Act to "the threat of the atomic bomb."[63]

By the beginning of June 1942, Eliot Ness was able to report that the SPD had helped secure the closure of red-light districts in two hundred twenty cities (though a hundred of these were in California alone).[64] That very month, El Paso had initiated an "effective repression program."[65] Oklahoma City would detain nine hundred women in June alone.[66] By the end of the summer, New York was arresting and examining hundreds of women every month. "We are engaged in a total war," the governor declared.[67]

As in World War I, the American Plan remained inextricably linked to local businessmen's desires to make money. When attempting to persuade cities to open detention facilities for infected women, one SPD official emphasized the profits these facilities might bring.[68] In May 1942, after the federal government threatened to place Nashville, Tennessee, "off limits" to soldiers, thus threatening to starve businesses of the soldiers' wages, the city immediately cracked down on suspected women.[69] This pattern was repeated across the country.[70] One particularly arresting example is the city of Phoenix, Arizona. After the federal government placed Phoenix "out of bounds," the city's merchants rebelled.[71] In a stunningly audacious move, the Phoenix Chamber of Commerce assembled a slate of new individuals who they felt would run the city in a way that adequately addressed Phoenix's "vice conditions." The chamber of commerce directors then held a six-hour meeting with the city's chief of police, clerk-magistrate, and city manager, and, as the Associated Press put it, "bluntly demanded action." They insisted that the city officials resign, which, remarkably, they did. And the chamber of commerce's selections for the new positions assumed control.[72] Three days after the government was replaced, the military placed Phoenix back "in bounds."[73] Hundreds of arrests, examinations, and incarcerations followed.[74]

Also as in World War I, the American Plan extended to American territories and holdings abroad. Bascom Johnson Jr., son of one of the Plan's founding fathers and a federal health officer, personally spurred Juarez, Mexico, to close its brothels by June and implement a "conscientious policy of repression."[75] Meanwhile, in the territory of Hawaii, the military governor issued an order supplementing the regulations of the board of health; these demanded the examination of "suspected sources" of STIs and "[e]ffective quarantine of contagious cases with hospitalization when necessary."[76] A similar scheme was put into effect in Trinidad as well as in Puerto Rico, where Surgeon General Parran personally promoted the "rigid repression of prostitution."[77]

The conditions in these territories were of particular concern because American troops were stationed there, and federal officials considered the dark-skinned natives to be especially prone to promiscuity and infection. "Because of the degeneracy of the natives," wrote one major in the medical corps stationed in Trinidad, "there is little value placed on virtue."[78] Another official felt that Puerto Ricans were "like some of our colored brethren in the South" when it came to "promiscuity."[79] A few months later, one federal committee adopted resolutions on "the Caribbean and [Panama] Canal Zone," which read, in part: "the extensive patronage by white soldiers of elderly professional prostitutes, often black and lacking in attractiveness, is one evidence of deterioration of morale."[80]

Among the federal government's many attempts to improve the STI situation in these territories were efforts to spur the creation of "quarantine hospitals." In December 1941, Parran and others had begun attempting to fund several such hospitals in Panama, efforts that continued over the next six months.[81] Indeed, all across the continental United States, cities began running out of space for all of the women they were incarcerating—exactly as had happened in the previous war.[82] To remedy this, SPD officials in the summer of 1942 started trying to acquire several dozen abandoned Civilian Conservation Corps (CCC) camps for use as quarantine facilities. The CCC had been one of the premier New Deal agencies, employing hundreds of thousands of young men in manual jobs, housing them in camps across the United States. When the CCC lost funding following Pearl Harbor, there were hundreds of abandoned camps. Some would later be used to house prisoners of war, Americans of Japanese and German descent, and conscientious objectors. But American Plan administrators wanted some to be used for housing infected women. The camps already had barracks, hospitals, fences, and plenty of space.[83]

There followed, one official recorded in his diary, a "tremendous scramble for these camps from various sources."[84] A rumor circulated that the air force wanted all of them.[85] Finally, on August 6, Ness and others met with some army officials "who are now controlling the CCC camps." They settled on an agreement whereby the CCC would give them thirty abandoned CCC camps, which "will be operated throughout the states by local state governments, who will be furnished [federal public housing] funds."[86]

Officials in communities all over the nation clamored for one of the abandoned camps near them to become a "concentration camp" for women.[87] The first such camp opened in Leesville, Louisiana, a small, poor, rural hamlet not far from the sixty thousand troops living in Camp Polk. It was, as *Collier's* magazine put it, a "mud-splattered little place."[88] Leesville officials had watched in horror as young women followed the troops into town. "Girls who had been raised in one-room swamp cabins—and for whom sex held no sweet mysteries—moved to town," the *Collier's* journalist wrote. "Camp followers swarmed in from every state in the Union. Local police were helpless. Much of the activity was outside town limits. The local jail—small, filthy, windowless— wasn't big enough to care for even a small fraction of the traffic."[89] Following a visit from Bascom Johnson, however, local public health officials swung into action. One health officer "dug up an invaluable piece of legislation passed in 1918. This was a quarantine act that permitted isolation of people with communicable diseases." They scoured the countryside, eventually settling on the deserted Union Hotel, and leased it. The army built a fence around it, and the state police supplied guards.[90]

The Leesville detention hospital had a dining room, a kitchen, a rec room, a gatehouse for the police, a separate structure for the nurses, and a two-story hospital ward: one floor for black women, one floor for whites. Leesville officials quickly built 120 beds out of rough lumber. Then, as *Collier's* reported, "the big roundup began. . . . All agencies co-operated—Army, local police, parish, health officers, state police."[91] As one editorial in a local newspaper noted, officials across Rapides Parish arrested and examined hundreds of women for prostitution and hundreds more for vagrancy (when they didn't have proof of prostitution). An additional 848 "suspected prostitutes" were summoned to the Rapides Health Unit for an examination. Infected ones were sent off to Leesville.[92] In its first year, the Leesville detention hospital treated around five hundred women. The *Collier's* journalist estimated that "not more than 5 per cent" of these prisoners were "professional prostitutes." Most were "amateurs"—"young girls who, caught by the excitement of war, have left home seeking adventure."[93]

In fact, many were nothing of the sort. The historian Marilyn Hegarty recounted the travails of one Mrs. A, a twenty-nine-year-old white waitress who was detained "on suspicion," apparently for simply sitting by herself to eat lunch at a Leesville restaurant. "Charged with vagrancy (for dining alone?)," wrote Hegarty, "she remained in jail for seven days until the local health department convinced her to commit herself voluntarily to the isolation hospital. Mrs. A had, however, tested negative for venereal disease." Hegarty noted that waitressing was a profession "marked" for suspicion: "For example, out of 709 women arrested in a two-month period in the Southwest, more than 600 were waitresses." When authorities saw Mrs. A dining alone, they apparently suspected that she was waiting for a man—and that was enough "reasonable suspicion" to upend her life.[94]

On November 29, 1942, Surgeon General Parran, Vice President Henry Wallace, and dozens of other luminaries braved the rain and the cold to open a massive quarantine hospital in Chicago. This facility—which could house twenty-five hundred women a year (a majority of whom would be "infected prostitutes," reported the *New York Times*)—was the first of what became known as "rapid treatment centers."[95] Rapid treatment centers were so named for the "rapid therapy" that physicians performed within them: most women were given often-toxic arsenic-bismuth treatments for syphilis (i.e., neoarsphenamine) and sulfa drugs for gonorrhea, though, as the historian John Parascandola noted, more unusual treatments like heat therapy and malaria-induced fever therapy were also occasionally used. The syphilis drugs were delivered through either an intravenous drip or a series of injections; such rapid treatment could take anywhere from a few days to six weeks. Rapid treatment centers disproportionately housed women. "There was no similar system of quarantine hospitals established for infected men," Parascandola wrote. "Although these facilities were sometimes referred to as quarantine hospitals for prostitutes, it is clear that any infected woman who was deemed a threat to the war effort could be confined in a rapid treatment center and made to undergo therapy."[96]

Many of the first rapid treatment centers were built in the former CCC camps the American Plan's administrators had obtained. Most were racially segregated and, like other detention hospitals, they often had barbed wire, armed guards, and even electric-charged fences.[97] They were also required to have space for "wholesome recreation" and vocational training. Parran and Vonderlehr believed that reformed prostitutes could provide some badly needed labor for war industries. Predictably, however, the vocational training often involved jobs that were considered "women's work," like cooking, cleaning, or sewing.[98] As more and more rapid treatment centers popped up across the country in years to come, some accepted men and women (who sometimes went there voluntarily), but dozens accepted only women committed there under American Plan laws.[99]

By the start of 1943, there were more than a dozen rapid treatment centers up and running across the country, and abroad. That summer, there were thirty. They were in major metropolises like Chicago, Phoenix, Denver, and Indianapolis, as well as such decidedly out-of-the-way places like Monnet, Missouri; Rush Springs, Oklahoma; and Goldville, South Carolina. They were also in Aguidilla and Caguas, Puerto Rico, and St. Thomas, Virgin Islands. They ranged in capacity from 350 (Chicago) to 25 (St. Thomas).[100] A year later, New York City opened its first rapid treatment center in a wing of the storied Bellevue Hospital.[101]

These facilities enabled the further expansion of the American Plan, yet they worried some federal officials. Raymond Vonderlehr feared the "undue publicity given to the 'prostitute prison camp' aspect of the Rapid Treatment Centers."[102] Several other officials held a conference to discuss "the lack so far of rehabilitation and efforts at employment for the girls who come out of the hospitals."[103] Eliot Ness, on the other hand, felt the centers were too

focused on infected women. He wanted to lock up uninfected yet promiscuous women. "Ness said what about the girls who are not infected—they still
don't have any places to put them," a colleague recorded in his diary, "—need
some strictly detention places [*sic*]."[104] Rapid treatment centers were designed
to be rapid, yet some in the federal government still wanted women held long
term. One SPD regional supervisor, stationed in Texas, wrote a memo to Ness
spelling out the importance of incarcerating women for up to a year. "Such
commitments would serve a dual purpose," he wrote. "(1) They would remove
disease spreaders from the community and (2) they would be for the welfare
of those persons engaged in such activities in that sufficient time would be
given for health treatment and their retraining for useful occupations."[105]

ON JUNE 9, 1943, First Lady Eleanor Roosevelt attended a meeting with Eliot Ness and various other federal officials for a discussion of "Woman's Role
in Social Protection." Representatives of many of the nation's most important women's organizations were present, such as the YWCA, the General
Federation of Women's Clubs, the National Council of Catholic Women, the
National Council of Jewish Women, the American Association of University Women, the American Medical Women's Association, the National Congress of Parent-Teachers, the Women's Auxiliary to the Congress of Industrial
Organizations, and the Girls' Friendly Society.[106] Ness and other men spoke
about "what our program is"—they talked about "quarantine hospitals" and
their efforts to detain women who "had drifted into a kind of promiscuity
which was not professional prostitution." The first of their female guests to
speak was Roosevelt.

She spoke about social protection in England. "I think the English people have decided, and we have decided, that venereal disease is not, strictly
speaking, a war problem. It is a peace problem. It is a problem that is with us
all the time. It is with Great Britain all the time," she declared in her high, affected accent. "And the real roots of the problem lie in the fact that we do not
face our community conditions." The First Lady called for better "community
services," more sex education, and speaking about STIs like "any other health
problem."[107] What she was calling for was a classic social protective agenda:
positive, protective programs, not negative, repressive ones like mass arrests
and imprisonment.

Because of this short speech, the historian Marilyn Hegarty claimed that
Roosevelt "represented a singular resistant voice in the campaign as she tried
to turn the discussion in a direction that was not completely focused on repression of female sexuality."[108] Yet this is an overstatement for two reasons.
First, Roosevelt was hardly "resistant." At the end of the meeting, the women

present unanimously adopted resolutions giving their "hearty endorsement" to the American Plan. Whether Roosevelt cast a vote on these resolutions is unclear, yet even if she did not, she neither uttered nor wrote a single word openly critical of the American Plan—which she obviously knew was going on, since Ness and others had just explained it in no uncertain terms. (Indeed, in 1949, the ASHA considered Eleanor Roosevelt for its highest honor, the William Freeman Snow Award, in recognition of "her interest in and appreciation of the work of the Association."[109]) Second, and more importantly, Roosevelt's voice was not a singular one. Over the past three decades, women such as Maude Miner, Ethel Sturges Dummer, and Katharine Bushnell had been calling for just such a positive, social protective turn in the campaign against STIs; some women, Jessie Binford and Rachelle Yarros among them, had continued making these calls even as the nation entered World War II.[110]

At a meeting back in 1941, for instance, Binford told male officials they were making "a mistake if you think the majority of these girls have to be forcibly restrained. In all the experience of the last war we found they are perfectly amenable to good case-work, if it is good enough, and to the kind of treatment they would get in these places."[111] In a letter to Bascom Johnson later that year, Yarros—who had fought alongside Binford against the Plan in Chicago—cautioned, "There is still very little understanding of the need of real protection and care of young girls." She added mournfully, "I am not strong enough to struggle as I did in the past for these unpopular causes."[112]

Yet like Roosevelt, Binford and Yarros remained complicit in the Plan's cruelties. Binford and other Chicago women tried to obtain funding for a "House of Detention" in the "Women's Court."[113] She and the Juvenile Protective Association, the women's organization she helped run, mostly confined their activities to advocating for "increased social protective measures; the object being to arrive at some concerted action to correct those conditions which threaten and demoralize our young people as well as the boys in uniform," yet this framed the campaign in sexist terms, accepting the premise that women were a danger to men. Furthermore, they never repudiated the Plan outright as they had in the 1930s.[114] Yarros likewise coupled her calls for protective measures with praise for the Plan, even telling Johnson she wished she were back in Washington, so she could work for him.[115]

This dynamic—elite women calling for positive work while neglecting to repudiate the negative—could be observed again and again throughout the war. When a committee of women in New York, led by a prominent female judge, condemned that city's Women's Court for "case fixing, bail-bond deals and other irregularities," the committee members also complimented "the military, naval and health authorities [for] their splendid venereal disease program."[116] When the women of the Social Hygiene Committee of

the prominent National Council of Women—led by none other than Valeria Parker—repeatedly lobbied the government for more "protective work for
young girls," they also "pledge[d] all possible support to the Government program for law enforcement against prostitution."[117] When Rhoda Milliken, a
well-respected Washington, DC, policewoman, told a group of male police
officials that many of them were holding suspected women for too long and
that they should be examining men too, she still did not object to the Plan's
denial of due process. In the end, she was ignored.[118]

Sometimes women actively promoted the Plan's darker elements. Indeed,
one woman who had fought the Plan back in 1920 now ran a Massachusetts
reformatory that imprisoned women under it in 1942.[119] In New York, the
Girls' Service League—the protective organization founded (under a slightly
different name) and run by Maude Miner—still operated a detention home
and filled it with dozens of "wayward" women each year, many detained by
the police. All new admits to the detention home were examined for STIs
and "required to occupy the isolation room" until they received a diagnosis.
The new head of the league, wrote one federal official, "expressed real interest
in the [federal] program."[120] One prominent women's group that was more
equivocal than most about the Plan was the Girl Scouts. In 1943, recounted
an observer, the group's "Board members were quite disturbed and horrified when they learned a 'girl scout' in a southern city had been arrested and
placed in 'jail' on a sex delinquency charge." Nonetheless, the Girl Scouts sent
a representative to the June 9 meeting attended by the First Lady and pledged
themselves to promoting protective work.[121]

Meanwhile, the General Federation of Women's Clubs—representing more
than two million women—took more concrete steps to aid in the incarceration
of women. First, in July of 1942, this group formally endorsed the American
Plan. Then, at an October meeting, the General Federation urged clubwomen
across the country to assist in the passage of laws "which will outlaw all phases
of prostitution," advocate for "Federal aid in the establishment of rehabilitation
centers," support the Eight Point Agreement and the invocation of the May
Act, and "[s]eek law enforcement which is continuous, vigorous, honest, and
without regard for the power or prominence of offenders." The General Federation's leaders were especially complimentary of the "proposed utilization of
former CCC camps as isolation and treatment centers for careless and uncoop-
erative cases" and "[i]nstitutions for the long term commitment of prostitutes
for reeducation, training and rehabilitation."[122]

JUST AS IN YEARS PAST, stronger opposition to the Plan had to come, instead,
from women at the bottom. These women—among the most marginalized

in the country—were, after all, the ones subject to the Plan's cruelties and indignities. And there were cruelties and indignities. Beyond the denials of due process, the sexual and racial discrimination, the poisonous treatments, the unpleasant, unsanitary, or overcrowded detention facilities surrounded with armed guards, there was also an undeniable element of assault inherent in the Plan. In Redding, California, for instance, one suspected woman was examined in what a state official called "an unsatisfactory manner" to ascertain whether or not she was a virgin.[123] In the District of Columbia, one woman was walking past three drunk soldiers outside a saloon when, according to a judge, the three men "accosted" her. When one of the soldiers later claimed the woman had given him an STI, *she* was arrested.[124]

So, as before, these women rebelled. In Puerto Rico, a crowd of 105 women in their pajamas escaped from the Troche Venereal Disease Hospital during a torrential downpour; in the Virgin Islands, 10 women attempted escape from the rapid treatment center, requiring officials to "have the whole hospital wired like a hen house."[125] In Kansas, between 1942 and 1944, some 410 women were locked in the State Industrial Farm for Women simply for having an STI; four of these managed to escape.[126] An additional 217 women were quarantined at the farm from 1944 to 1946, of whom a whopping 15 escaped.[127]

One study of "promiscuous women" in San Francisco in 1943 and 1944 found: "Much resentment was expressed toward those in authority who were responsible for the girls' apprehension and detention, especially in those instances where arrests were made or sentences imposed upon suspicion and not fact." This resentment led to "hostility" and, to the horror of local officials, was "used in some instances as an excuse for subsequent promiscuous behavior."[128]

Women also sued the government to try to win their freedom. In Atlanta, seven women brought suit against the city just one month after municipal officials started strictly enforcing the Plan again.[129] In Kansas, two women sued the state for locking them up—their incarceration, they claimed, would cause them to be "disgraced, humiliated and embarrassed" and would "follow them and each of them to their grave."[130] In Chattanooga, Tennessee—where, according to an ASHA investigator, the "police are exceedingly active"—a woman named Rachel Kennedy, who felt she was wrongly imprisoned under the Plan, escaped. This was not uncommon, as Chattanooga's rapid treatment center was an unpleasant place from which women frequently escaped. After Kennedy was recaptured and incarcerated, she sued.[131] Not one of these women prevailed in court.

In Seattle, when Betty Sader, the wife of a well-regarded naval officer, was threatened with arrest in her hotel room—by two "insolent domineering" detectives with "loud and boisterous tones"—the navy brass rushed to her defense. An admiral called the city's health commissioner, "all worked up about the Sader case," the commissioner recalled, "protesting our 'persecution' of Mrs. Sader." The brouhaha scared the police and "arrests of promiscuous women" dropped to only 110 that month.[132] Sader subsequently sued (for $10,000, the same amount as Nina McCall), which Eliot Ness feared could be "very harmful to the program."[133] A judge eventually declared that Sader had been framed by "someone who had it in for her." Nonetheless, he still ruled that "no damage had been done and that the officers were within their rights in making the investigation."[134] The American Plan in Seattle continued; the city opened a rapid treatment center; and police and health officials resumed detaining and examining hundreds of "promiscuous women" every month.[135] During one eight-month period, authorities arrested and examined more than two thousand women.[136]

Perhaps the most striking case of resistance took place in Arkansas, where a woman named Billie Smith sued the government for trying to lock her up in what she called a "concentration camp." A Little Rock judge ruled in Smith's favor, calling the city health officer's authority "dictatorial," but the Arkansas Supreme Court disagreed, writing that Smith's status as infected "affects the public health so intimately and so insidiously, that consideration of delicacy and privacy may not be permitted to thwart measures necessary to avert the public peril. . . . [T]he private rights of appellee, if any, must yield in the interest of the public security."[137] Yet Little Rock authorities soon realized to their horror that they had accidentally released Smith from jail, and she had vanished. Two days later, her name appeared on the front page of the *Arkansas Gazette* next to the words, "Whereabouts Not Known," and the sheriff's office began searching for her.[138] The sheriff issued a warrant for her arrest, and one policeman told the press she was hiding in Colorado.[139] It was another month before Smith was captured in a Memphis hotel and fined $127 for several crimes, including prostitution. Smith was sent to "an isolation unit in Shelby county" for STI treatment. It wasn't until the end of the year that she was returned to the Pulaski County jail, and then finally to the Hot Springs Venereal Disease Clinic—the institution she had called a "concentration camp."[140]

That still wasn't the end of Billie Smith's saga. After just a few days in the Hot Springs facility, Smith and another woman attempted to escape, and, after this, the Hot Springs authorities refused to take them back. A municipal judge sentenced her to thirty days in jail for the escape attempt.[141] The case of Billie Smith illustrates the ongoing resistance of women incarcerated under the American Plan. She attempted to defy the Arkansas authorities in almost every conceivable way: by suing them, by fleeing the state, and then by trying to break out of her detention hospital. Perhaps even more significant, her invocation of the phrase "concentration camp"—the only record we have of her own voice—reveals a notable degree of worldliness. It also suggests that women being held against their will under the auspices of the Plan connected themselves to a larger pattern of resistance against governmental violence and disdain.[142] Perhaps Smith had seen the headlines the very day she was released from jail. The *New York Times* had reported that more than a million Jews had been murdered by the Nazis.[143]

SITTING IN HER SMALL HOME on West Washington Street in St. Louis, just two blocks away from the Pine River, Nina McCall may have felt a mounting sense of anxiety for her young charge, Delma Mae Day. All across Michigan, the American Plan was tightening its stranglehold on the lives of young women. By the end of 1941, Battle Creek had a "well organized repression program" going, according to an SPD investigator. Infected women were given a choice between the "old frame house" used as a detention hospital and the county jail; this allowed authorities to claim that "almost all of the women 'voluntarily' accept quarantine." In spite of this voluntary language, women escaped in droves—in just one week, nine broke out. Detroit, meanwhile, had a detention hospital that was "obsolete and a fire hazard."[144] Still, by mid-1942, Detroit authorities were arresting thirty or forty reasonably "suspicious" women a night. Policewomen patrolled twenty-four hours a day, "identifying youth who needed protection."[145] And still, the federal government wanted more. One SPD investigator visiting Michigan recommended enhancing "police methods of *harassment* of resident prostitutes who are 'known' to be operating but who skillfully avoid flagrant violations that make the placing of formal charges practicable [emphasis in original]."[146]

Women quarantined in Michigan were overwhelmingly young, like Delma Mae. In one sample of seventy-four incarcerated women, twenty were between the ages of fourteen and eighteen, and only fourteen were over the age of twenty-five. Unlike Delma Mae, they were also disproportionately black.[147] In Saginaw, authorities spoke of the "unusually bad situation in the First Ward, the Negro district."[148] In Battle Creek, the SPD feared an influx of "negro girls visiting Battle Creek to find husband, friends or sweethearts."[149] To one investigator, the "negro community of about 3,000 or 4,000 population in Battle Creek presents special problems. It is almost an isolated island in Battle Creek and almost anything can go on within its boundaries."[150] Authorities arrested prostitutes with special venom, yet by the beginning of 1942, they had realized that most arrested women were not prostitutes but just what they termed "loose women."[151]

For women in Michigan, as for women across the country, the war radically upended life. "Because of its duration and the extent of civilian participation it fostered," the historian Karen Anderson has written, "no war in American history has had as profound an effect on American society and American women."[152] With the men away in Europe, women once again stepped up to fill gaps in the labor market. Some labored away in munitions factories and some knitted hats; some became mechanics for fighter jets and some sold sex to soldiers.[153] Many women in Alma and St. Louis began working for local factories and refineries, while others contributed to the war effort by carpooling, growing gardens, canning foods, and the like.[154] In Detroit, the Ford Motor Company, which had historically excluded women, now had to hire them by the hundreds.[155] The number of women in the workforce jumped almost 50 percent from 1940 to 1944. And, since the government pushed industries to hire married women, their young daughters were less supervised than ever before.[156]

Responding to their own passions, their newfound freedom, and the government's constant calls to help the war effort, many of these women "volunteered to entertain—to provide pleasurable companionship for—the troops," recounted the historian Marilyn Hegarty. As a result, some women became what some observers called "patriotutes"—patriotic prostitutes. Or, more accurately, young women having sex with soldiers.[157] It is important to note that dating, oral sex, premarital sex, "petting"—all of these unsettling trends had been increasing for decades, a shift that was accentuated and exacerbated—but not created—by the war. By the time the fighting began, almost 50 percent of all young women were having premarital sex. It was during World War II that such behavior came to be viewed as "the norm."[158]

Male officials, as well as privileged female collaborators, had to put a stop to this. Such immorality would beget more immorality—and more STIs—and harm the troops! As Anderson wrote, these rapid changes "created considerable anxiety about the stability and durability of the family, as working mothers were blamed by many for a rising divorce rate, child neglect, an ostensibly increasing rate of juvenile delinquency, and a host of other ills supposedly exacerbated by women's newly acquired independence." Such anxieties inevitably resulted in a "renewed vigilance regarding women's sexual conduct and an increasing resort to psychological and social welfare authorities to explain and regulate women's behavior."[159] This vigilance manifested itself in many ways, but few were more repressive, more regressive, or more important than the expanded American Plan.

It is unclear if the Plan reached Alma and St. Louis as it had back in 1918, yet Nina still would have had ample reason to think it might. Surely she had watched with horror as, on April 8, 1941, her old nemesis Thomas J. Carney was elected mayor of Alma. Bespectacled, bald, and now seventy-one years old, Carney entered office amid laudatory profiles proclaiming him a "public health crusader" with a "record of civic service." Days after Pearl Harbor, Mayor Carney called a meeting of the Gratiot County Council of Defense to plan a response in case the nation's enemies attacked rural Michigan. He served out his two-year term and was sufficiently popular to be reelected in 1943; he would not be ousted until an anti-incumbent sweep in 1945 cost him the mayor's office by fewer than a hundred votes.[160]

Once again, grief would abruptly replace worry in the life of Nina Hess. On November 9, 1943, after just a few days of suffering, Delma Mae Day died in Nina's home. It was almost twenty-five years to the day since Nina was brought to the Bay City Detention Hospital at the age of eighteen. Delma Mae was just nineteen years old when she passed. Perhaps it is significant that the local St. Louis newspaper and her official death certificate identified Delma Day as "Delma Mae Hess" and listed Nina and Norman Hess as her "parents." Though there is no record of Nina and Norman formally adopting Delma, perhaps this indicates the closeness of their relationship. Another family had lost another daughter.[161]

Nina had buried a biological son, an adopted son, an adopted daughter, a mother, a father, and a mother-in-law. She was just forty-three years old.

IN OCTOBER 1943, a veteran US Public Health Service doctor named John F. Mahoney gave a talk before a meeting of the American Public Health Association. The audience members strained to hear what he said; his words, recalled one listener, were "electrifying," and his speech "overwhelming."[162] At first glance, this might seem odd. The doctor had merely told a group of his peers about injecting mold into a sorry lot of rabbits and a handful of sailors. But this wasn't just any mold. It was penicillin, destined to become the most important antibiotic in history. Penicillin was far more effective than the sulfa drugs, developed a few years earlier. Like the sulfa drugs, it could cure gonorrhea; unlike the sulfa drugs, it could also cure syphilis. More than anything else, penicillin would change the American Plan forever.

The magic mold had been discovered entirely by accident in a London basement in 1929. By 1940, scientists were aware of penicillin's power to "kill" pneumococci, meningococci, streptococci, and several other bacteria.[163] Officials began planning to use the new drug to protect men stationed abroad, but penicillin remained notoriously difficult to mass-produce. "The yield is very low," one public health official in Michigan wrote to the governor in 1943. "Approximately one gram is recovered from 100 liters (25 gallons) of culture liquid."[164] Eventually, following a search that spanned the globe, an Illinois lab assistant discovered the best strain of penicillin growing on a moldy cantaloupe. Margaret Hutchinson Rousseau, the first woman to receive a doctorate in chemical engineering from MIT, designed the first commercial-scale plant to produce the drug, using enormous fermentation tanks. Soon, pharmaceutical companies were making hundreds of billions of units of penicillin every month.[165]

In the spring of 1943, Dr. Mahoney read that researchers at the Mayo Clinic had discovered that penicillin could treat sulfa-resistant gonorrhea. This led Mahoney and his team on Staten Island to test penicillin on syphilitic rabbits, and then syphilitic humans. Penicillin was, Mahoney found, the very cure he had been looking for.[166]

Within weeks of Mahoney's monumental October 1943 announcement, a federal official reached out to him, seeking his expertise. "We are presented with a rather serious note and as yet unsolved problem in the treatment of supposedly sulfa-resistant cases of gonorrhea essentially confined to the females in the several Rapid Treatment Centers being operated by State Health Departments and the Public Health Service," he wrote. "We would appreciate the assistance of yourself or members of your staff in visiting a number of these Rapid Treatment Centers."[167]

A few weeks later, rapid treatment centers began receiving shipments of penicillin.[168] At the time, the drug was not widely available to the public, and some health officials felt they must keep their possession of it secret lest the public demand access. For this reason, and also because of a general disregard of the norms of consent, patients were sometimes not told what exactly they were receiving injections of. "This has caused quite a bit of curiosity among the patients," recalled one USPHS official, "and in one instance a patient referred to the new treatment as the 'kill or cure' treatment."[169]

As penicillin became somewhat more widespread in rapid treatment centers, the need to imprison women for months or weeks at a time became less pressing. Physicians delighted in how quickly they could treat their patients. Nonetheless, some felt that women should still be held for extended periods of time, in order to reform them.[170] At a conference in 1944, Walter Clarke of the ASHA told the audience that "the venereal disease problem cannot be solved by the 'find them and treat them' method alone," reported the *New York Herald Tribune*. "More stringent methods must be employed by the authorities, he said, in repressing the tendency to sex promiscuity."[171]

Throughout 1944, penicillin still remained scarce. By the end of that year, there were some sixty-three rapid treatment centers scattered across the country (and in American holdings around the world).[172] Even in this period when penicillin was increasingly accessible, about half of these centers still accepted only women.[173]

THE COMPLICITY of some of the foremost paragons of twentieth-century liberalism in the World War II phase of the American Plan should, by this point, be obvious. Earl Warren, Franklin Roosevelt, Fiorello La Guardia, even, to some extent, Eleanor Roosevelt—all supported the Plan. Even the liberal *Nation* magazine praised the Plan.[174] To this list we must add two revered liberal institutions, the American Bar Association (ABA) and the American Civil Liberties Union (ACLU), as well as another revered liberal politician, Edmund "Pat" Brown.

Recall that during World War I, federal and local officials had closely followed lawsuits challenging the Plan (such as Nina's). Officials at all levels of government had tried to stymie lawyers representing incarcerated women; the CTCA had even threatened local judges and pressured the ABA to urge its members not to represent them. World War II saw a repeat of this dynamic. Indeed, recalled one SPD supervisor, after the city of San Antonio imprisoned hundreds of women under the Plan, "there was one attorney who had consistently appeared for them, and a man down there would give his personal bond and get the girls out. [The police commissioner] said to him, 'If you do that again, I am going to throw you in jail.' Well, he did it again, and he was thrown in jail."[175]

Early on the morning of August 18, 1942, Eliot Ness and another official visited George Maurice Morris, the soon-to-be ABA president, who was "very much interested in their suggestions."[176] At the urging of the feds, the ABA created the Committee on Courts and Wartime Social Protection—"to study the questions of judicial procedure involved in the handling of prostitution, liquor, and gambling in the vicinity of Army camps, Naval stations, and war industry."[177] For the committee's chairman, SPD officials secured the appointment of John Marshall Goldsmith, a former prosecutor and police judge from Virginia.[178] The committee held its first meeting on November 5. Present were Goldsmith and Morris, as well as Bascom Johnson, Timothy Pfeiffer (a longtime ASHA member and former CTCA agent), and John Henry Wigmore, a law professor still remembered today for writing the definitive treatise on the law of evidence. At this meeting, the assembled members agreed to draft "model laws" for the use of cities and states. While all of the states already had American Plan laws on the books, many cities did not, and even those that did (as well as the states) could always strengthen their laws—by, for instance, adopting laws mandating fingerprinting.[179] They also agreed to put pressure on local district attorneys to enforce the Plan.[180] On December 11, an SPD official read a paper by ABA committee member Wigmore to a conference of local law enforcement officials. In his paper, Wigmore stressed the importance of "liberal interpretation of the laws and ordinances." "In time of war," he wrote, "there need be no stress laid on the technicalities of criminal procedure. Those technicalities were meant to prevent oppression by civil authorities in time of peace. But there is no danger of such oppression here today." Such a comment was startling both in its implications (coming from one of the nation's foremost legal scholars) and in how blinded it was by Wigmore's privilege. "Let the judges," Wigmore concluded, "having in mind the beneficent purpose of protecting our armed forces from the terrible enemy of disease—let the judges so conduct the trials that all technicalities be brushed aside and substantial justice be done upon all who seek to evade it." An SPD representative wrote to Wigmore a few days later that his paper received "many favorable comments."[181]

Finally, on January 16, 1943, the ABA's board of governors endorsed a report authored by Goldsmith and his committee. The ABA declared that all "reasonably suspected" persons should be examined—especially prostitutes, promiscuous women, and their ilk—and health officers should quarantine those "who have, or are reasonably suspected of having," STIs, if in their opinion it "is necessary for the protection of the public health."[182] The nation's largest and most influential collection of lawyers and legal scholars had spoken. The American Plan was sound. Indeed, it was necessary.

In the months that followed, John Marshall Goldsmith and the ABA continued to work closely with the ASHA and SPD. When the Cincinnati police were troubled by the lawsuit of a "known prostitute," who was challenging the state's American Plan law, the SPD got legal advice from the ABA; when Walter Clarke of the ASHA feared the Georgia legislature might not pass a strong antiprostitution bill, he called a federal official, who called Goldsmith; when a fed considered intervening in a Florida legislative debate, he consulted Goldsmith first; when Ness wanted the May Act enforced more stringently in Nashville, he sent Goldsmith to Tennessee. In East St. Louis, Illinois, Goldsmith personally spearheaded the city's successful defense of its American Plan law against a woman suing for her freedom. In the spring of 1943, Goldsmith met with a number of doctors and lawyers from Michigan and was impressed by their enthusiasm for enforcing the Plan. The SPD would use Goldsmith's report and the ABA's clout to further lobby states to enforce the Plan.[183]

For most of the war, meanwhile, the ACLU had done nothing to oppose the Plan. Indeed, Roger Baldwin, the group's cofounder and executive director, had even sent a memorandum to all ACLU local branches, encouraging them to cooperate with the police in the enforcement of the Plan.[184] But in January 1944, Ernest Besig, the brash, young executive director of the ACLU of Northern California began to take a different approach. Besig had heard about San Francisco's policy of holding all suspected women for seventy-two hours while they were examined, and he found this "patently in conflict with the requirements of our Penal Code."[185] Besig was unafraid to take unpopular stands like this. Indeed, at the same time he decided to oppose the Plan, he was representing a young Japanese American man named Fred Korematsu who had been sent to an internment camp because of his ethnicity. Though a majority of ACLU members supported the internment of Japanese Americans, Besig encouraged Korematsu to sue the government, in what would become one of the most significant lawsuits of the twentieth century.[186]

There were some connections between the World War II–era internment of infected women and the concomitant internment of more than 110,000 Japanese Americans. At the Rohwer internment camp in southeastern Arkansas, for instance, every one of the thousands of inmates of the camp was examined for STIs upon entering. Those who were infected were treated in the camp's 150-bed hospital. When several local residents and some of the military officers guarding the camp contracted STIs, local officials blamed the nearby community's "large Negro population . . . which is uncontrollable as far as law enforcement is concerned." Nonetheless, an SPD agent repeatedly visited Rohwer and the nearby Jerome internment camp. She too concluded that the "Japs" were not to blame, and that few of them were infected, even though their internment had "disrupted [their] home life."[187] Ernest Besig may well have drawn a parallel between the two carceral schemes.

On January 18, Besig met with Pat Brown, San Francisco's impetuous district attorney, to voice his concerns. The denial of due process bothered Besig, as did reports that women were not being allowed to speak with their attorneys. Brown assured Besig of the government's "good intentions," but ultimately brushed him off.[188] Brown, who would one day become a beloved governor of California, counseled patience. "I am sure it will take at least six months to perfect a satisfactory program," he wrote to Besig.[189]

When, six months later, nothing had changed, Besig wrote a letter to the editor of the *San Francisco News*, decrying police for quarantining "innumerable girls without any reasonable grounds for believing they are infected with a venereal disease." He appealed to groups like the San Francisco Lawyers Guild and the San Francisco Bar Association, in an attempt to find allies in having "the present practice changed." Yet such appeals yielded no changes. And Besig would only go so far in expressing his sympathy. "We recognize, of course, that there is a reasonable basis for quarantining known prostitutes," he wrote, "but the majority of the girls that are picked up are NOT in that class as health department records will show." He also pronounced himself "hopeful" that a rapid treatment center would soon open in California.[190] Pat Brown responded with his own letter to the editor, making clear that "[n]o one is quarantined unless there is probable cause to believe that they might be infected. This probable cause is determined by observation of the suspects and their behavior with different men over a period of time." (His phrasing—"their behavior with different men"—betrayed the fact that only women were targeted.) That some women were wrongfully detained was "unfortunate," but "in this war effort there are many dislocations and the test must be the greater good for the greater number."[191]

When, late in 1944, San Francisco's police chief and public health director proposed a new ordinance to empower the police to arrest any person (male or female) whom they "suspected"—it did not say "reasonably suspected"—Besig called on Brown again, demanding that the word "reasonably" be inserted.[192] The proposed ordinance was so extreme that it united strange bedfellows in their opposition. The ABA's John Goldsmith believed it to be overbroad—"a bad law, unconstitutional and . . . vicious"—and a prominent Christian Scientist objected to the fact that it did not "guarantee rights to anyone desiring to rely on prayer for healing."[193] Yet an amended version of the ordinance passed the board of supervisors on November 27.[194]

Over the course of eighteen months in 1943 and 1944, San Francisco officials examined 1,402 women—of whom 311 were prostitutes, 283 were alcoholics, 57 were drug addicts, and a whopping 751 were simply (thought to be) promiscuous.[195] Only in 1945 did Besig and the ACLU begin defending these women on an individual basis. At a conference with various city officials, and then in follow-up letters, Besig recounted his visits to the city's Women's Court, where he saw women who weren't even promiscuous being repeatedly detained and examined. Still, his critiques only went so far. "We are, of course, not opposed to a venereal disease control program in San Francisco," Besig told the men, "and, indeed, I am sure that our membership is heartily in favor of some kind of control. At the same time, we are concerned about procedures involved in the present control program."[196] Unsurprisingly, such objections did not change San Francisco's enforcement of the Plan.[197] Within a few months, Besig's chapter of the ACLU had largely given up the fight.[198]

AND SO, women continued to be imprisoned. Indeed, some were imprisoned in ways strikingly similar to Nina a quarter century earlier.

Take the case of Bettie May James, who was arrested in the north end of Beaumont, Texas, one Saturday evening in 1944. Like Nina, James was an eighteen-year-old who lived with her widowed mother (coincidentally named Alma). A police officer who later claimed to have seen James dancing with soldiers and generally carousing, picked her up on the instruction of his superior. Like Dr. Carney, a Beaumont physician took smears from James's urethra and cervix and pronounced her infected with gonorrhea. He sent her to the women's cell on the second floor of Beamont's jail, where infected women were quarantined. The women's cell was a single room about twelve feet by fourteen feet, with ten or twelve bunks. There was one toilet, one sink, and nowhere to bathe.

Eventually, James (through her mother) filed suit against the government, just as Nina had. Just like Nina's lawyers, James's lawyers tried to prove that she was respectable, that she could afford medical treatment herself, and that the police had not had sufficient grounds to arrest her. Just like Judge Moinet, the judge in James's case shot them down. "Gentlemen," he ruled, "the enforcement of this law might seem to some people as severe but in passing it the Legislature had in mind the protection not only of the individual infected with disease, but the public generally, and especially soldier boys visiting the town." Just like Nina, James appealed, claiming Texas's Plan statute was "unconstitutional and void."[199]

Yet here the similarities stop. For there was a key difference between Nina McCall and Bettie Mae James. Nina was white, while Bettie Mae was black. And though it is impossible to tell definitely, it is possible that this racial difference explains, in part, why Nina prevailed in her appeal, while Texas's highest court quickly denied James's appeal, citing several American Plan cases from the 1910s as precedent.[200]

The case of Bettie Mae James reflects one of the more sinister realities of the American Plan: through the decades, the Plan had remained stubbornly racist at every stage. James's arrest, detention, and losses in court are obviously a product of her gender, but they are also inextricably a product of her race. James was a black woman living in Beaumont, Texas—which meant she was a second-class citizen, constantly subject to suspicion and even hatred.

When the officer who arrested James claimed he had seen her with soldiers, he specified that he had seen her in several "negro dives." Every inmate in the jail cell in which James and other infected Beaumont women were locked was black. Indeed, in SPD investigators' first meeting with town officials (years before James was arrested), they recommended that the city fathers ask the military that the "colored sections of the City of Beaumont be placed off-limits for white soldiers." Beaumont's leaders immediately obliged, as did the military.[201] Shortly thereafter, at the urging of Ness and others, Beaumont implemented a policy of "repression against commercialized prostitution," shutting down its decades-old red-light district and arresting many of the women found within.[202] City health officials examined women arrested for vagrancy, prostitution, and the like, and in some cases they quarantined infected ones in the jail, but they allowed most infected women to seek treatment as outpatients.[203]

That changed once Artie Pollock became chief of police on December 1, 1943. Pollock accepted the appointment as chief after gaining assurances from the city council that "no limitations" would be imposed on him. Pollock told an SPD investigator "that he will resign his position if he is ever told to ease up on any person or group of persons." Pollock immediately fired a dozen officers he deemed insufficiently vigilant and began enforcing Texas's laws against prostitution and vagrancy with a vengeance. Suspected women were examined, and those found to be infected were quarantined. Pollock maintained a strict policy of racial segregation: infected white women were held in the county building, while infected black women were held in the city jail.[204]

Such segregation was justified on sanitary as well as racial grounds. In the 1940s, experts widely believed that STIs were more dangerous in blacks than in whites. "The Negro is not to blame because his syphilis rate is six times that of the white," Surgeon General Thomas Parran himself once said,

> It is not his fault that the disease is biologically different in him than in the white; that his blood vessels are particularly susceptible so that late syphilis brings with it crippling circulatory diseases, cuts his working usefulness in half, and makes him [an] unemployable burden upon the community in the last years of his shortened life. It is through no fault of hers that the colored woman remains infectious two and one-half times as long as the white woman.[205]

Pollock and other police chiefs like him in Texas were so enthusiastic in their enforcement of the American Plan that it even worried the SPD. At a regional meeting in San Antonio just days after James was arrested, the assembled SPD representatives agreed "that civil liberties are probably being violated with considerable frequency in most large communities in the arrest of girls and women in the repression program." According to notes from this meeting, the SPD's regional supervisor "did not urge the members of the staff to undertake a special campaign for the preservation of the civil liberties of these girls and women, but he declared that the Social Protection Division could not go on record as advocating illegal practices."[206] There is no record that SPD officials made any attempts to stop the denial of civil liberties, and Pollock continued his aggressive campaign untrammeled.[207]

And the racial problems in Beaumont went deeper than discriminatory policing. Since the war had begun, the town had been flooded with industrial shipbuilding workers and soldiers on leave from nearby Camp Polk.[208] After President Roosevelt ordered the defense industry desegregated, white shipbuilders had to labor alongside blacks. This caused tension in hot, overcrowded Beaumont. Many workers had to live in trailer camps scattered along the city limits, without water, sewer, or garbage disposal facilities.[209] There was a food shortage and not enough buses to accommodate all the workers. One black man was shot for refusing to move to the back of a bus.[210] When, not even a year before James was arrested, white shipbuilders heard a rumor (a false one, it later emerged) that a black man had raped a white woman, a mob of thousands gathered at the jail. The white "victim" appeared and told the throng of whites that her assailant wasn't there. For the next three days, Beaumont's whites rioted, razing black neighborhoods and murdering or mutilating scores of black citizens. One black girl, just fourteen years old, later recalled that she was walking back from the store during the riot when six white men in a pickup pulled up alongside her and threatened her. No one was ever prosecuted for these crimes.

As Pamela Lippold, a scholar of the riot, recounted, "A mass exodus of African Americans ensued with approximately 2,500 leaving by any means available, including walking." Rumors swirled of black bodies floating in the Neches River in the days following the riot. Hundreds of whites wrote to the governor of Texas calling for the government "to keep them [blacks] in their place." Months later, FBI director J. Edgar Hoover was still receiving reports of brutality directed toward Beaumont blacks.[211]

In this climate, it is hardly even surprising that Bettie Mae James was arrested.

RACIAL BIGOTRY was endemic to the Plan during World War II. More than half of the 861 women locked up in Detroit under the Plan during one year were black (though blacks made up barely 10 percent of Motor City residents).[212] In South Carolina, there was one rapid treatment center for blacks and one for whites; the one for blacks was "more dilapidated" and "less convenient as to facilities for care of patients."[213] In San Francisco, one woman was detained for being in the presence of "a colored man."[214] Two other San Francisco women were detained on suspicion of prostitution solely because they had been seen repeatedly in a restaurant favored by Filipinos.[215] According to one study, women arrested under the May Act were disproportionately Native American.[216]

Prominent blacks did object to the Plan. According to the influential black newspaper, the *Pittsburgh Courier*, black leaders in Texas were "indignantly aroused" by the "alleged mistreatment of Negro women by municipal authorities in the police departments of several cities and towns since the recent Government order to prevent prostitution in defense areas." The *Courier* continued, "A smoldering resentment is growing in the minds and hearts of thousands of race patriots over the unfair and outrageous treatment of Negro womanhood as an aftermath of the Government's order. Many have expressed understanding of having such an order issued for the protection of every citizen, but voiced their protest at being subjected to the actions of police who allegedly have used no discretion whatsoever in their tactics." This was a powerful renunciation, yet even these black leaders made clear that they objected primarily to the outrages against "respectable women."[217]

More consistent opposition came from the bottom. In one Florida rapid treatment center, a black female inmate got into an argument with a male carpenter, and he slapped her. In response, the black inmates "began to assemble and howl," reported one observer. Even after the carpenter was suspended, the black and white inmates began fighting at the canteen. "The colored patients then paraded the hospital area abusing with utmost profanity the matrons and workers on the area. Assemblies were broken up many times, but race hatred was demonstrated in many ways." The sheriff had to be called in, since "anything could happen with colored women in that frame of mind."[218]

When considering the racism of the Plan's federal administrators, it is instructive to recall the ongoing Tuskegee syphilis study. Raymond Vonderlehr, head of the Division of Venereal Diseases early in the war, had been the first federal official to run the study. After Vonderlehr stepped down as head of the division in 1943, he was replaced by John R. Heller, who had located the Tuskegee study's "controls" and who had handed the unlettered black sharecroppers tablets of aspirin, leading them to believe they were receiving treatment. Being head of the division, Heller recalled decades later, was "quite a delightful and stimulating experience."[219]

The Tuskegee syphilis study had continued into the 1940s and beyond. During World War II, army draftees were examined for STIs, and those found to be infected were treated. Yet when several of the men in the study were drafted, the division sent a list of their names to the draft board asking that the men on it not be treated, and the board complied.[220] After a rapid treatment center opened in Birmingham, some of the study participants sought to go. One later recalled that he "was told by a nurse that because I was in this study I could not go." Another, Herman Shaw, made it all the way to Birmingham, but a nurse in the rapid treatment center heard his name and sent him home. "You're not supposed to be here," she told him.[221]

That the Tuskegee study continued even after the widespread availability of rapid treatment and penicillin is one of its cruelest realities. The Oslo Study of untreated syphilis in white men half a century earlier, on which the Tuskegee study was based, had ceased once Salvarsan became available; the Tuskegee subjects could, and should, have received penicillin, a far more effective treatment than Ehrlich's magic bullet.[222] Instead, they were repeatedly misled and denied the drugs, and they—along with their spouses and children—began to die as a result of syphilis.

Interestingly, in spite of the deliberate denial of penicillin, more than half of the surviving subjects did eventually receive penicillin over the next couple of decades. This appears to have been because the study was so sloppily run and many local doctors did not realize these men were in it. Herman Shaw himself received some penicillin in the 1950s when he was hospitalized for pneumonia. Nonetheless, only a fraction of the men received "what could be considered adequate doses," in the words of the historian Allan Brandt; many had infections that were, by the 1940s, far too advanced to be cured by penicillin. Besides, many were already dead by the time penicillin became available.[223] Just like the American Plan, the Tuskegee syphilis study continued.

IT WAS THE HAPPIEST BIRTHDAY Harry S. Truman ever had. He had been elevated to the presidency not even a month earlier, after Franklin Roosevelt's death from a cerebral hemorrhage. Just a few weeks later, Roosevelt's nemesis, Adolf Hitler, had committed suicide, buried in his bunker below bombarded Berlin. Now, finally, on May 8, 1945—Truman's sixty-first birthday—Nazi Germany's supreme military commander signed an act of unconditional surrender. The war in Europe was over. The Allies were victorious. Ecstatic crowds massed all over the world.

Many of the leaders of the ASHA and SPD had been planning for the end of the war long before Soviet bombs rained down on Berlin like hail and Hitler blasted a bullet into his brain. As early as January 1945, ASHA executive director Walter Clarke had written a memorandum to association members entitled "Postwar Social Hygiene Problems and Strategy."[224] Throughout that year, the ASHA, and especially William F. Snow, fought for both the May Act and the SPD to be extended past 1945. They succeeded in persuading Congress to pass laws enabling this.[225]

Two weeks after Germany surrendered, at an SPD meeting, federal officials celebrated in Washington's Hotel Statler, basking in self-congratulation. Yet John Heller made clear that their work was far from done. STIs could increase when the millions of young troops returned from overseas. "It is apparent that the repression of prostitution must be carried on to an even greater extent than has been true during the war," Heller declared.[226]

Two months after that, American pilots dropped a uranium bomb on the Japanese city of Hiroshima; three days later, the Americans dropped a plutonium bomb on the city of Nagasaki. Mushroom clouds illuminated the sky as hundreds of thousands burned alive. World War II was finally over. Without it, could the Plan possibly go on?

Chapter 13

"Venereal Disease Was Not Our Concern"

YES, THE AMERICAN PLAN COULD GO ON, even as the war ended.

As the 1940s continued, dozens of locales still detained "reasonably suspected" women, examined them, and imprisoned them. As we shall see, these locales included cities in California, Colorado, Indiana, Kansas, New York, Ohio, Oklahoma, Pennsylvania, Texas, Utah, Virginia, Washington, and elsewhere.

In Michigan, for instance, the Plan continued in many places for at least a year after the fall of Germany. In 1946, undercover SPD investigators in Flint worried about "lax enforcement against negro prostitution" and urged stricter adherence to the "8-point agreement." Yet they were cheered by a "most fearless and trustworthy" sheriff and a local judge and prosecutor who helped ensure ninety-nine arrests in a single month.[1] In Muskegon, SPD reps were thrilled when a former FBI agent became police chief, while a policewoman assigned to the health department closely monitored local dance halls.[2] In Nina's former hometown of Saginaw, prostitution was vigorously repressed—and had been since autumn 1944, when the local press reported that the deputy health officer, Dr. Georgia Mills, launched a crusade to "ferret out and hospitalize all venereally-infected brothel habitués." Two years later, an SPD agent exulted, "There simply is no enforcement problem; the city is one of the cleanest in the U.S." Just as exciting: "A new detention home is nearing completion."[3]

In Oklahoma City, a woman was arrested in May 1947 under the state's 1919 American Plan law. She sued for her freedom—and lost, and Oklahoma continued enforcing the Plan for at least three more years.[4] In September 1947, two women in a Stockton, California, motel were dragged from their beds and quarantined in the "greatly crowded" jail as reasonably suspected. They too sued and lost. After they were examined and released as uninfected, both tried in vain to recover the $500 they had posted as bond—five years later, one woman was still trying (the other had died in a car accident).[5] Los Angeles continued enforcing the Plan throughout the late 1940s (even though city officials admitted its quarantine "facilities are poor," and the ASHA concluded they were "not all that could be desired"), as did Sacramento, Oakland, Fresno, and Richmond.[6] In 1947, a pair of drunk San Francisco police officers threatened to have a woman "vagged [likely meaning examined vaginally] and quarantined" unless she gave them "some dough."[7] In 1949, four Berkeley cops stopped a black woman trying to catch a taxi and asked her, "What have you been doing with your big black belly?" Then they detained her and held her in jail for three days, only releasing her when she tested negative.[8] In 1950, San Francisco actually stepped up its enforcement of the Plan.[9]

Yet times were changing. In New York, the state's American Plan law empowered local officials to examine "all persons arrested on charges of prostitution or offenses relating to prostitution." The enforcement of this law was predictably sexist. In 1947, New York City forcibly examined 3,174 women and just 21 men. As one ASHA document put it, "Following arraignment, no matter what the plea, the woman or girl is removed to the Women's House of Detention for five days to await the result of the health examination." Of those examined, 1,335 women (and 2 men) proved to be infected; of these, 206 women were imprisoned for treatment. Those with gonorrhea were held in the house of detention or the Euphrasian Residence (a religious detention house), while those with communicable syphilis were taken to the rapid treatment center at Bellevue Hospital.[10]

Yet those same numbers reveal that a striking change was under way in New York City. The next year, in 1948, even more people were examined—3,684 women and 7 men, of whom 1,211 women and zero men proved to be infected. Yet, whereas 206 women had been forcibly imprisoned the year before, now only 58 were.[11] The year after that, in 1949, roughly the same number of people were again examined—3,225 women and 2 men, of whom 961 women and zero men had syphilis or gonorrhea. Yet this time, just 31 women were forcibly hospitalized.[12]

These numbers present a question: what had changed? The answer is shockingly simple: penicillin. Rapid treatment centers had begun receiving shipments of the miracle drug in January 1944; the army had adopted the miracle drug as the routine treatment for syphilis in June of that year.[13] "At first supplies were limited and mostly reserved for military use," wrote the historian John Parascandola, "but by 1944 innovations introduced in American government, university and industry laboratories had greatly increased the yield and available supply of penicillin. In April 1945"—just before VE Day—"all restrictions on its distribution in the United States were removed."[14] By the late 1940s, authorities were aware that a single injection of penicillin could cure gonorrhea, and it took just ten to fourteen days of outpatient care to cure syphilis.[15] In 1950, the state of Louisiana stopped distributing any anti-STI drugs other than penicillin.[16]

Because penicillin was such a quick and effective treatment, it made long stretches of time in isolation pretty much unnecessary. Thus, New York authorities felt they had to "forcibly hospitalize" 206 women in 1947 but just 31 in 1949. They were still examining these women and then demanding they accept treatment, but treatment was now a single injection (or series of injections), so most women acquiesced. "The simplicity and short duration of treatment has reduced the numbers with infectious disease who refused treatment and were forcibly removed to hospitals," wrote New York health officials a year later. "Only 12 such patients were so removed during 1950."[17]

Such a development spelled death for rapid treatment centers. In the summer of 1953, the country's last rapid treatment center closed its doors.[18] Instead of maintaining these centers, many locales began focusing their attention and funds on locating infected individuals. "[P]enicillin therapy has now obviated the need for highly elaborate case-holding activities," wrote Illinois public health officials in 1947. "The emphasis has thus been switched to case-finding, time and effort for which have been provided by reduction in case-holding activities."[19] Throughout the late 1940s and early 1950s, in Chicago, Boston, Los Angeles, San Francisco, New York, and Seattle, public health investigators sought out thousands of suspected women to hold and examine each year—and virtually no men.[20]

Still, many places continued enforcing some form of the Plan, including at least a few days of quarantine and imprisonment. They now only quarantined women long enough to thoroughly examine them for STIs—usually just a few days—but still they denied women due process and enforced their laws discriminatorily. As late as November 1950, officials in Dallas, Texas, kept detaining and quarantining suspected women for forty-eight hours while they were examined.[21] Cops in Cleveland, Ohio, did similarly at least through 1951.[22] It is unclear when, exactly, Dallas and Cleveland ceased to enforce their American Plan laws in this way. We know of each city's continued Plan activities at this late date only because of a single record from each location. Since the federal government no longer oversaw the Plan, it no longer kept records of its enforcement. The silence surrounding the Plan in the 1950s and beyond is nearly impenetrable. Nearly, yet not always.

THE DRIVING FORCE behind the perpetuation of the Plan was, predictably, the ASHA.

In the months following the war's end, William F. Snow, Walter Clarke, Eliot Ness, John Heller, and the other fathers of the Plan desperately strategized how to perpetuate the SPD's work beyond the summer of 1946, when it was set to expire.[23] An ASHA member serving in Congress introduced a bill to keep funding the SPD; the bill won endorsements from the Salvation Army, the General Federation of Women's Clubs, the National Council of Jewish Women, and the governors of twenty-eight states, including California governor Earl Warren, who sent a telegram demanding that "everything possible be done to suppress prostitution and the spread of venereal disease." He had ordered the officials of his state to focus on this "critical problem," he concluded.[24] As Congress debated this bill, a panel of federal officials—including Fred Vinson, who would become US chief justice just weeks later—met to revise the Eight Point Agreement and make it more draconian, in one place replacing the phrase "infected persons" with "persons reasonably suspected of being infected."[25] Army chief of staff Dwight D. Eisenhower enthusiastically endorsed the new agreement.[26]

Yet on July 16, 1946, Congress defeated the bill to fund the SPD in a vote that shocked the ASHA.[27] Enthusiasm for federal oversight of the nation's morality had waned considerably now that the war was over; this was a matter of states' rights. Several representatives asserted that "the folks could take care of their own sex problems, without the help of federal snoopers."[28]

ASHA members were distraught—"You cannot imagine how sorry we all are," one wrote to a friend in the SPD.[29] The division's death made the association more important than ever. It had to keep investigating prostitution and STIs, to keep pressuring local officials to enforce the Plan. The ASHA quickly established field offices near each of the major army camps across the country; it added former SPD officials to its staff and stepped up investigations.[30] Such activities weren't cheap, however. So, late in 1946, the association embarked on an ambitious fund-raising campaign. At a tony luncheon at the Hotel Astor, Eleanor Roosevelt made a pitch for the ASHA, telling guests that the association was "an important thing for our young people, and for all of us." The world's reigning heavyweight champ, Joe Louis, appeared before a crowd of a thousand people in front of New York's city hall to swing his famous left hook at a cloth dummy labeled "VD" and urge donations to the ASHA. Louis leaned into the microphone (broadcasting live on WNYC) and declared, "There's only one thing that can 'kayo' VD and that's good clean living, and you know I mean that."[31]

Ultimately, such public appeals, creative though they were, would not raise nearly enough money for the ASHA to continue its ambitious work, and it would rely heavily on the USO, then the Community Chests (later known as the United Way) for most of its annual budget.[32] Snow urged the ASHA to reach back out to Rockefeller, but the aging billionaire evidently wasn't in a generous mood and repeatedly declined to give.[33] The ASHA's work was further hampered by the retirements of two of its most important leaders, William F. Snow and Bascom Johnson, after the war.[34] Both would remain active in lobbying for the Plan until their deaths in 1950 and 1954, respectively. Their passings were heralded by laudatory and widely reprinted obituaries.[35]

Money was similarly drying up at a federal level. The Division of Venereal Diseases had $18 million to give to the states for anti-STI work in 1949, but just $7 million the next year, and a mere $3 million by the mid-1950s.[36] And, in the spring of 1948, Thomas Parran failed to secure reappointment as surgeon general and decamped to become the founding dean of the University of Pittsburgh's Graduate School of Public Health.[37]

Still the ASHA kept trying. In the summer of 1948, a squadron of ASHA investigators descended on Alaska and examined the territory for signs of prostitution. They focused their investigations especially on Native American women and ultimately concluded that conditions in Alaska were "very bad." They urged the enforcement of the American Plan there. However, in spite of expressions of support from Attorney General Tom Clark, this effort yielded little fruit.[38] That same year, the ASHA investigated prostitution on the Mexican side of the Texas border and urged Secretary of State George Marshall to instruct the Mexican government to crack down on the "vicious conditions" there.[39] Indeed, in 1950, association investigators scrutinized prostitution and vice in two hundred cities, and had a backlog of dozens of cities clamoring for their services.[40] The next year, ASHA representatives went to 228 cities, about 90 percent of them near military establishments. These visits, the association's annual report claimed, served "to stimulate better law enforcement against commercialized prostitution and allied vice."[41] In 1952, ASHA investigators traveled to a whopping 343 towns and cities.[42]

In February 1951, an ASHA investigator journeyed to San Antonio, Texas, where he noted that city officials continued to detain women (and underage girls) and hold them in the local jail, without access to lawyers, for up to a week while they examined them repeatedly for STIs. Even Walter Clarke, the ASHA's executive director after Snow's departure, concluded this "probably is not on a sound legal basis." In the age of penicillin, San Antonio's enforcement of the Plan could be construed as a "dangerous invasion of personal liberty."[43]

The ASHA's rhetoric did transform to match the changing times. In 1950, Clarke penned a widely praised article on how to safeguard social hygiene in the event of an "atom-bomb attack." (He advocated strict enforcement of the Plan as a preemptive measure.)[44] Then the United States sent hundreds of thousands of troops to Korea, and the ASHA once again found itself urging local officials near the newly thrumming military training camps to enforce the Plan. In Norfolk, Virginia, home to the one of the country's largest naval training sites, among other sites across the country, the ASHA successfully pushed officials to stop "[a]ny woman found roaming the street at night or early A.M.," quarantine and examine reasonably suspected ones, and immediately treat those who proved to be infected. Of course, men were not treated likewise.[45]

Even after the Korean War ended in 1953, the ASHA kept on investigating prostitution and STIs in hundreds of communities a year, strong-arming towns from Galveston, Texas, to Laramie, Wyoming, into cracking down on prostitution.[46] Yet as the years passed, the association's core mission hardly changed at all. "The American Social Hygiene Association believes that although there may be some shifts in emphasis, the future program for venereal disease control requires no new approaches," an aging yet still active Walter Clarke wrote in 1955. "Despite satisfactory conditions in some areas, there are many scattered pockets of high prevalence. . . . The lessons of the past revealed in the adverse effects of undue complacency should be remembered."[47]

IN 1949, Nina and Norman Hess left Gratiot County forever. Gratiot had been Nina's home for nearly all her life. She had been born in the county, raised in the county, detained and examined in the county; it was in Gratiot that she had sued the government and been married; it was in Gratiot that she had buried two adopted children. Yet in 1949, for reasons that are, sadly, lost to history, she and Norman moved fifty miles to the northeast, to Bay City. This was, of course, the city in which Nina had been imprisoned more than three decades before. Just how she felt about the move to a site of profound sadness in her life is an unsolvable mystery.[48]

Yet this Bay City would have been hardly recognizable compared to any memories Nina had of it. By the late 1940s, the city had shrunk slightly from 11.05 square miles to 10.5. Telephone wires now draped every street, and enormous new factories belched smoke. The number of hotels had dropped from thirty to eight, while the miles of paved road had grown from 50 to 110. These roads now teemed with long, sleek cars. There were hundreds fewer factories, but the surviving ones had swelled and consolidated. Thirty years before, thousands of residents had worked in beet-sugar processing plants, local fisheries, and one of the largest knitting works in the world; now the dominant town industries were dedicated to producing automobile parts, steel cranes, iron, steel, and magnesium casings, and other metal goods. Dow Chemical also employed many locals. "Bay City is not a town of portable citizens," the chamber of commerce wrote in the late 1940s. "It is a city of thrifty homeowners (approximately 80%) who take justifiable pride in building their community into a more pleasant and profitable place to live."[49] Such citizens surely would have noticed the newcomers in their midst.

The Hesses moved into 201 McGraw Avenue, a small clapboard house in the south of town, mere steps from the Saginaw River and a little outcropping of land known locally as Skull Island. Bay Cityans recall this neighborhood as somewhat poorer and perhaps less reputable, home to many immigrants living on the outskirts of town.[50] It was a collection of one- and two-story residential homes, lined by trees, just to the east of the brief stretch where the Saginaw River temporarily splits in two. One man who lived just a few houses down from the Hesses in the 1950s, John Runberg, recalled that the street "wasn't very well-paved." His washing machine was pretty balky—"It kind of walked across the floor on a couple of occasions." The homes were on the older side, though very pretty. "And they were not in the greatest state of repair." Some had linoleum rather than rugs. Whatever its reputation or drawbacks, Nina and Norman Hess made this neighborhood their home.[51]

As she had in St. Louis, Nina kept house. Norman continued to work as a plumber. This was a respectable and highly useful trade, though it provided far from steady work. "Well, he was on strike and laid off half the time," recalled Barbara Schweinsberg, whose husband, Lloyd, was also a plumber in Bay City in the early fifties.[52] Throughout the 1950s, Norman remained a plumber, though his employer changed every few years, perhaps attesting to the tenuousness of the work: he moved from Fitch Plumbing to Saginaw Plumbing to Miller Davis Plumbing to Associated Services of Midland.[53]

Both John Runberg and Barbara Schweinsberg still vividly recall one Bay City institution, even all these decades later: the Bay City General Hospital. John once spent time there as a patient; Barbara gave birth to one of her sons there. "It was just a nice hospital," Barbara recalled. "I remember getting good care." In her eyes, it was big. John has similar recollections. The Bay City General Hospital might have been of particular interest to Nina, since back in her day it had been known as the Bay City Detention Hospital. Now it was cleaner and more modern, yet its exterior had not changed too much; undeniably it was the institution in which she'd been imprisoned. During World War II, patients with STIs could go to the General Hospital for outpatient treatment, though it appears to have no longer quarantined infected women. In the 1940s, it had eighty-four beds.[54] Beginning in 1951, the hospital was without a full-time director, a troublesome situation that lasted until 1954, when a Citizens Hospital Association launched a $250,000 fund-raising campaign and then assumed control of the General Hospital, signed a twenty-year lease, and pledged to upgrade and enlarge it. All this was covered on the front page of the *Bay City Times*. One can only imagine Nina reading such a story or being asked to contribute to the fund-raising effort.[55]

On the day before Christmas 1953, Nina's brother, Vern, died at the age of fifty-one. Sometime in the last decade, he and his wife, Irene, had moved from St. Louis, where he'd worked as a truck driver, to Grayling, Michigan, a small fishing village known for its annual canoe marathon. There he'd found work as a well driller. Whether Nina made the hour-and-a-half journey north for his funeral is unknown; Vern left the world just as he'd entered and occupied it: largely unnoticed. He left behind no children.[56]

Nina and Norman continued to live in their small clapboard house by the river. Then, in early 1957, Nina fell ill. She may have experienced nausea or vomiting, seizures or difficulty speaking; she may have had trouble walking or speaking or even understanding what Norman said to her. She had a glioblastoma—a tumor growing on the left parietal lobe of her brain. Soon, Norman could no longer take care of her, and Nina moved into the Colonial Nursing Home. It was just a fifteen-minute drive west from her old home, across the Saginaw River, yet the move fundamentally upended her and Norman's life. Now alone, he moved into a smaller house at 2627 Broadway. For four and a half months, Nina dwindled in the Colonial Home, another institution that failed to cure her of a medical condition doctors told her she had. This time, at least, they were right.

Nina died at 3:30 p.m. on Sunday, July 21, 1957, at the age of fifty-six. Two days later, her body was transported back to Bay City, and the next day, at 2:00 p.m., was her funeral—in Woodside Avenue Methodist Church, to which she had belonged. Her obituary in the *Bay City Times* was just six sentences long. One of them was, "Her husband is the only surviving relative."[57]

NINA WAS NOT the only woman affected by the American Plan to die around this time. Nearly all of the women who had helped to create and enforce the Plan also began to pass away.

In 1941, Martha Falconer died just a few months shy of her eightieth birthday; in 1953, Jane Deeter Rippin, another female Plan administrator, died at the age of seventy-one; and in 1954, Ethel Sturges Dummer succumbed at eighty-eight. Rachelle Yarros died in 1964, Jessie Binford in 1966. Maude Miner survived the longest—until 1967. All of these prominent women were praised and mourned in death; each of their obituaries was far longer than Nina's sad little paragraph.

There is evidence that each regretted her service to the American Plan. Many, including Miner and Dummer, had vigorously opposed the Plan at meetings like the All-America Conference of 1920. Yarros and Binford had continued to fight the Plan in Chicago for the next two decades. Shortly before her death, Falconer visited Westfield Farm—formerly known as the Bedford Hills Reformatory. On this visit, Falconer dwelt, in the recollection of a friend, on the "various problems which continually arise in [such] an institution."[58] Late in her life, Jane Deeter Rippin, an influential former Plan administrator, gave a series of interviews to a woman who was planning a (never completed) biography of her. The would-be biographer recorded little of Rippin's time running the Plan, but one of the insights she gleaned from the old woman was a telling one: "First emphasis was to protect women then it was changed to protect the boys."[59]

Ethel Sturges Dummer wrote her autobiography, published in 1937, and in it she attacked the Plan in no uncertain terms. Nonetheless, she also wrote of her continued faith in "protective work," in locking wayward young women in reformatories.[60] In 1942, when the ASHA reached out to Dummer, asking her to donate money, she replied by calling the association's activities "rather stupid." "I argued with Dr. Snow and Bascom Johnson about the unwisdom of their procedure," the elderly woman wrote to the ASHA, but to no avail. "Disapproving as I do, I cannot contribute to the American Social Hygiene Association."[61] The next year, in the midst of World War II, she sent Surgeon General Parran a copy of her book, urging him to focus on "protective work" and "rehabilitation."[62]

He didn't listen.

Even Katharine Bushnell, the California radical who had once been the Plan's most fervent foe, did not forget her opposition as she neared her ninetieth year. All alone and nearly blind, her hands shaking uncontrollably, she continued seeking recruits in her war against "the hypocritical 'Social Hygiene' movement, [funded by] John D. Rockefeller Jr.'s millions." Loyal as ever to the memory of British abolitionist Josephine Butler—the woman who had defeated the English Plan—Bushnell wrote to one Nevada woman in 1943, "[I]f I could interest you in the cause [Butler] fought for, I have a quantity of literature for your help. I am too old to do much any more. . . . The work is sadly needed in America, at the present time."[63] Her correspondent demurred, and Bushnell died, defeated and forgotten, shortly after World War II ended. "Her work was like a rock dropped to the bottom of the ocean," recalled her pastor. "Kerplunk, it was gone, the end of it."[64]

ON JULY 30, 1957, exactly one week after Nina Hess's funeral, El Paso's City-County Health Unit director—essentially its chief health officer—announced a "'new' venereal disease program" for his city. "Under it," reported the *El Paso Herald-Post*, "suspects would first have to be convicted of either vagrancy or prostitution. Health Department doctors would then be asked if they wanted to examine them. . . . However, if suspects fail to report for examination or treatment the Health Department can issue a warrant for 'detention quarantine.'"[65] The *Herald-Post* immediately denounced the new program's respect for due process in a bitter editorial. "Every person who goes into the City and County jails should be examined, and treated if necessary, whether the offense is speeding or prostitution," the paper pontificated. "Nobody will object to that. If, perhaps, one does, then he should be examined for lunacy."[66] In spite of this protest, El Paso's city officials soon accepted the new program.[67] The Plan in this blazing westernmost spot of Texas had fundamentally changed.

Such a development was mirrored around the country. Officials in various locales in Pennsylvania appear to have enforced the Plan until about 1952, when state health authorities adopted a new system using "appointment clinics." Under this system, suspected individuals would usually not be arrested but would rather be given appointments for STI exams at a local clinic.[68]

Or take the state of Kansas. Between 1946 and 1952, 121 women were imprisoned under the Plan in the Sunflower State (even though Kansas's American Plan facility, the State Industrial Farm for Women, was condemned in 1951).[69] Yet commitments under the Plan slowed to a trickle in the 1950s. The final woman locked up under the Plan in that state was admitted on December 23, 1955, and released twelve days later.[70] Still, even though women in Kansas were no longer being detained under the American Plan, public officials continued to police women's conduct. As the number of women committed to the farm under Chapter 205 (the state's Plan law) dropped to zero in the decade after the war, the number of women committed to the farm because of prostitution, lewd and lascivious conduct, and vagrancy increased.[71]

The example of Kansas illustrates that officials remained focused on locking up women even as they abandoned the Plan as a tool in their arsenal. The example of El Paso illustrates a related truth: that, even in the age of penicillin, there was still widespread support for the Plan as a method of combating female promiscuity. In El Paso, the newspaper had editorialized in the Plan's favor. Across the country in Fresno, the city had largely ceased to enforce the Plan in late 1945.[72] However, in October 1953, after many in town were enraged by a flood of Mexican farmworkers entering the community without proper documentation, and after the head of the local border patrol claimed these Mexicans led to the presence of prostitutes and spread STIs, the town's mayor ordered its health officer to revive the American Plan.[73] The mayor "asserted if women arrested for prostitution are kept in jail until they can be checked for disease, they will stay out of Fresno thereafter," summarized the *Fresno Bee*. The police chief announced his support. Yet the health officer dismissed this as "unlawful" and refused to go along, and the Plan was not resurrected there.[74]

The Plan remained tempting for many city officials. As late as 1967, Indianapolis's mayor called for the revival of the American Plan in his city, claiming that doing so "would result in the mass departure of nearly all the 200 known street-walking prostitutes in Indianapolis."[75] In 1968, Frank Roberts, an elderly Tennessee health officer who had been working since 1923 (and thus almost certainly had experience with the Plan), made headlines when he declared that STIs were primarily spread through "just plain old promiscuity."[76] In 1972, the *Atlanta Constitution* reported that Roberts "has dusted off an antique Memphis city ordinance, a quarantine law, to aid in surveillance of the VD situation." Sadly the paper did not elaborate, and just what Roberts did is lost to history.[77]

The example of El Paso also demonstrates a remarkable naiveté on the part of some of the Plan's proponents. "Nobody will object to that," the editors had confidently asserted about compulsory STI examinations. As the 1950s became the 1960s, this sentiment would come to look increasingly absurd.

THE SEXUAL REVOLUTION was a long one. Though most people associate it with the 1960s, the liberalization and destigmatization of sex had, in fact, begun far earlier.

In 1948, an unassuming Indiana scientist named Alfred Kinsey, known until then primarily for his research into the North American gall wasp, published *Sexual Behavior in the Human Male*. This dry, 804-page academic treatise by the doughy-faced former Sunday school teacher became an immediate and sensational best seller. Based on thousands of interviews, it revealed that about half of adult men were at least somewhat attracted to other men (and more than a third had acted on this attraction); that nearly 90 percent of men had had sex before marriage; that 50 percent had committed adultery; and that almost 70 percent had slept with a prostitute at least once.[78] Five years later, in 1953, Kinsey published a follow-up, *Sexual Behavior in the Human Female*. These findings were, if anything, even more shocking. About 50 percent of women had engaged in premarital sex, and more than 25 percent had engaged in extramarital sex.[79]

The two reports upended the way Americans talked about sex. Kinsey appeared on the cover of *Time* and journalists raced to write about sex; academics held hundreds of conferences on the studies, and copycats published dozens of related books. The ASHA dedicated its annual conference to discussing Kinsey's findings.[80] Yet astounding as they were, the reports did not actually reveal that a shift was under way. Rather, noted the historian James Gilbert, "the most important change was probably a shift in approval. Sex habits among American young people had not rapidly changed; instead public opinion had begun to catch up with practices initiated decades before. The result was the appearance of sudden revolution."[81] As a result of urbanization, the entrance of women into the workplace, the establishment of the weekend and other forms of free time that came along with a shortened workday, and the advent of a racy popular culture and an addictive consumer culture—with its attendant restaurants, bars, drugstores, movie theaters, and the like—the sexual revolution had already occurred.[82] Kinsey's reports documented several decades of promiscuous, if undiscussed, sex.

It was in the 1950s and 1960s that popular opinion began to catch up with reality. *Playboy* appeared in newsstands; articles on sex proliferated; the Supreme Court contracted the definition of obscenity; and, most importantly, in 1960 the birth control pill hit shelves. "Just as the availability of penicillin in the 1940s had seemed to separate sex from the danger of venereal disease once and for all," wrote the historian David Allyn, "the invention of the birth control pill finally appeared to divorce sex from the unwanted pregnancy."[83] In 1963, a college student, beatnik, and proto–flower child named Jefferson Poland cofounded the Sexual Freedom League in New York. This group practiced and preached "free love"—including wild sex orgies—and made headlines across the country. In 1966, Poland legally changed his middle name to Fuck.[84]

The sexual revolution had not only transformed the way people felt about sex, but it began to change the way they thought about prostitution. In 1964, Poland and his fellow league members held a "speak-out" at Columbia University, trying to persuade college students to support the legalization of prostitution.[85] Over the next couple years, as activists in the burgeoning second-wave feminist movement began marching for and demanding equal rights and privacy, a chorus of prominent women too started to call for the decriminalization of sex work.[86]

In this era of the civil rights, women's liberation, and anti–Vietnam War movements, even stigmatized people started to rebel. Part- or full-time prostitutes—male and female—along with gay men, lesbians, transgender individuals, and drag queens, started fighting back against police violence and harassment. In 1959, a group of these marginalized individuals rioted in the streets of Los Angeles; in 1965 and again in 1966, they did so in San Francisco; finally, in 1969, prostitutes and other sex workers joined gay people in the famous uprising at the Stonewall Inn.[87] As the historian Susan Stryker has argued, trans women— among the most marginalized members of the queer community, and often the instigators of these riots and uprisings—were so discriminated against in employment and housing that nearly all were forced to sell sex at one point or another.[88] It was they who led the 1960s-era efforts at resistance.

The uprisings of queers, trans women, hustlers, and prostitutes may have even begun to enjoy some modicum of public support. Consider the case of Cynthia Scott in Detroit, Michigan. At 3:00 a.m. on July 5, 1963, two police officers approached St. Cynthia, as she was known—a six-foot-tall, two-hundred-pound black prostitute who had previously been arrested for her trade seven times. After an altercation with the police left Scott dead—shot through the heart—she became a martyr to Detroit's black community. Hundreds massed at her funeral, and an even larger crowd picketed outside police headquarters later that day. As the historian David Maraniss has documented, Winifred X, Malcolm's sister, addressed the marchers, and the black-owned *Michigan Chronicle* wrote that Scott was "not a felon but a known prostitute. . . . The situation did not warrant extreme measures." The Nation of Islam partnered with a prominent black reverend to call for the police commissioner's ouster, and one cop later recalled an inspector telling him, "Somebody shot the whore over here and now everyone's going crazy and she was a good young girl and should not have been shot."[89]

Yet if prostitution was slowly losing some of its stigma, and if prostitutes themselves were rising up (as they had done behind prison walls for generations), STIs remained as hated and stigmatized as ever. Though rates of STIs had fallen after the war, they began to rise once more in the late 1950s and throughout the 1960s. Public health experts blamed the three "p's": permissiveness, promiscuity, and the Pill. "Even as sexual mores were liberalized in the 1960s, attitudes towards the venereal diseases proved more resistant to change," wrote the historian Allan Brandt. "Even the American Medical Association, which instituted a publicity campaign for the control of syphilis and gonorrhea in the 1960s, deleted these words from its advertisements."[90]

During the 1950s and 1960s, the specter of STIs was raised to stand in the way of social progress. After the 1954 decision of *Brown v. Board of Education*, an organization called Separate Schools denounced the black community as "a vast reservoir of infectious venereal diseases" and claimed that integration would lead to more infected whites.[91] When black female citizens in Birmingham, Alabama, tried to register to vote, they were sometimes asked if they had STIs. One justification Birmingham whites gave for segregation was, as one man put it in 1963, "that Negroes carry a very high rate of venereal diseases. . . . And myself, I don't wish to catch 'em."[92] Even a black rape survivor could be dismissed by white authorities as "nothing but a whore" who "had been treated for some time . . . for venereal disease."[93]

STIs were still stigmatized. And even with penicillin, they had not gone away. As one ASHA publication put it, "drugs alone do not stop venereal disease."[94] Thus, as late as 1962, the ASHA still published model laws, urging states and cities to pass or beef up legislation allowing authorities to examine women "reasonably believed" to be infected, and to isolate infected individuals.[95] When President John F. Kennedy signed an executive order that year, listing diseases that warranted quarantine, he included syphilis and gonorrhea—even though public health officials had been aware for a generation that both were easily and quickly cured with penicillin.[96]

IN SPITE of THIS STIGMA, it was marginalized women themselves—in this age of uprisings—who led some of the final campaigns against the remnants of the American Plan.

On February 19, 1965, an eighteen-year-old woman with dark eyes and bushy black hair was arrested at an antiwar demonstration outside the United Nations. The young woman's name was Andrea Dworkin, and she would later become one of the best-known and most controversial feminist writers in the world (and a fiery foe of the legalization of prostitution). At the time, she was a member of the Student Peace Union at Bennington College, where she was a freshman. Since neither Dworkin nor her two teenaged companions had enough money for bail, they were sent to the dreaded house of detention at 2:00 a.m. "While in jail," Dworkin later wrote of her stay in the house of detention,

> in addition to the many strip-searches by hand that police and nurses made into my vagina and anus, I was brutalized by two male doctors who gave me an internal examination, the first one I ever had. They pretty much tore me up inside with a steel speculum and had themselves a fine old time verbally tormenting me as well. I saw them enjoy it. I witnessed their pleasure in doing it. I couldn't understand why they would like to hurt me. I began to bleed right after. When I came out of jail I was mute from the trauma.

Dworkin would continue to bleed for days afterward. When her family doctor examined her, the doctor burst into tears.[97]

The assault that Dworkin was forced to endure was, in fact, an STI examination enabled under New York's American Plan law. As Dworkin later recalled, before they began the examination, one of the doctors explained to her "that they were examining us for venereal disease."[98] The brutality of the examination was not an unprecedented indignity inflicted upon those who challenged the social order. Dworkin had been protesting the Vietnam War; at roughly the same time, black Civil Rights activists marching for change in Birmingham feared "crude examinations for venereal disease" at the hands of the police.[99] A few years later, police would demand that Black Panthers in Sacramento submit to "V.D. examinations" as part of a concerted harassment campaign.[100] We might also note that Dworkin was, like Nina, an eighteen-year-old forced to yield to her first gynecological exam.

Dworkin, a survivor of childhood sexual abuse, was furious over her treatment, so she contacted a reporter. "So what?" was the response. Dworkin then approached her male colleagues in the antiwar movement. They "laughed at me." Yet she refused to let the story die. "I mounted a protest against the prison," she later wrote.[101] "I had been sexually brutalized and had turned the internal examinations of women in that place into a political issue that would eventually topple the ancien régime, the callous, encrusted Democrats."[102] The *New York Times*, *New York Post*, and *Daily News* ran stories on the incident. They highlighted Dworkin's fear and complaints about the examination, as well as her gripe that the "homosexuality was rampant and pretty hard to take" in her cellblock, and that she had been denied access to her lawyer. These stories stirred up such a controversy that the house of detention's superintendent was forced to issue a statement claiming that the STI exams were routine and conducted "with the greatest dignity and decorum."[103]

The controversy refused to die. By the next month, one of physicians who had examined Dworkin had resigned, and the other was suspended.[104] Four different investigative committees would scrutinize the house of detention, and a grand jury quickly convened.[105] The sustained media attention focused on the treatment of female prisoners, and especially their STI examinations, coupled with the coincidental passage of a new state law reducing penalties for prostitution, finally conquered the surviving remnants of New York's American Plan as well. On June 30, 1967, the city closed the clinic in which it had examined all reasonably suspected women for decades. "Starting last night," reported the famed journalist J. Anthony Lukas in the *New York Times*, "women arraigned on prostitution charges were asked to sign a form pledging to be examined within 48 hours either by their own doctors or by one of the city's 12 social hygiene clinics. The change was designed to meet charges that the old system discriminated unfairly against women accused of prostitution." In a statement that would have been unthinkable a generation earlier, the chief of the city's health department asserted "that prostitutes were less important in the spreading of venereal disease than was commonly believed." Exceedingly few actually had either syphilis or gonorrhea.[106]

THE FIGHT NEXT MOVED to San Francisco, which presents the most compelling example of women on the ground themselves vanquishing the American Plan.

One Thursday back in the spring of 1954, members of the San Francisco Police Department raided an apartment house at 1275 Bay Street. The officers quickly arrested a squat, dark-haired woman named Mabel Malotte— the apartment's owner. Beneath where Malotte had been found, the officers discovered, was a trapdoor, which led to a secret chamber. On the apartment's back porch, the officers found a blue notebook containing names and addresses, "99 percent of them men," claimed San Francisco's district attorney. Some of the men, he continued, tantalizingly, had "very prominent names—especially one." Malotte, the cops believed, was a madam. That same day, they also arrested two young women—twenty and twenty-two years old, respectively—whom the police claimed Malotte had sent to a downtown hotel to sleep with officers. Malotte and the two younger women were booked on a variety of morals charges, yet when city officials attempted to follow routine protocol and examine them for STIs, they refused to submit. Instead, the three women obtained attorneys and filed petitions for writs of habeas corpus, challenging San Francisco's American Plan laws' constitutionality.[107]

A couple of weeks later, a superior court judge ruled in the women's favor, stating that examining all women merely arrested for prostitution—and not yet convicted—was improper. "It would be up to the health department," the *San Francisco Chronicle* summarized, "to make its own investigation to show whether there is reasonable grounds to believe the arrested person is afflicted with VD, he said." The city's director of public health told the *Chronicle* that "the decision probably will mean a revision of quarantine procedures which have been followed here for a dozen years."[108]

Yet nothing of the sort ended up happening. San Francisco police simply continued detaining and examining merely suspected women—for decades. The women who proved to be infected would no longer have to be isolated for lengthy stretches of time, as they had in the past. Instead, they would usually be held for just seventy-two hours. But, still, San Francisco continued to enforce this distinctly modern iteration of the American Plan throughout the 1950s and 1960s.

Then, one evening in the winter of 1972, the San Francisco Police Department raided an upscale bordello. The cops were in full riot gear, recorded Margo St. James, a local activist and former prostitute.[109] She thought they were "high, really up, turned on, their eyes sparkling, nostrils flaring. Uniformed cops in their riot squad helmets complete with chin straps ran from room to room like hounds, while the more cool plainclothesmen postured in front of mirrors, peeked into closets and made off with 60-odd bottles of booze from the bar." St. James claimed that the madam "had leaped or was pushed from a third story window to the cement courtyard below." She was left lying there for twenty minutes. "The woman survived but there is a question whether she will ever walk again."

To St. James, "The issue is not whether she is guilty of soliciting the men—she isn't; they came to her—but rather one of do licensed thugs have the right to barge into a woman's home, a place where certain 'respectable' men take great pleasure in coming, and literally frightening her out of the window." St. James noted that a man was almost never arrested for prostitution ("unless he was black"), while female prostitutes (and suspected prostitutes) were routinely arrested and held in jail. "Half the women in the county jail are there on sex charges—political prisoners, arbitrarily chosen by society to pay dues for its sexual guilt. Most of them are black, another aspect of the discrimination—minority women being forced to work on the street due to the fact that the hotels and massage parlors are owned by white folks who won't hire them or let them hang over."

Well, St. James wasn't going to take it anymore. As she wrote in a December 1972 article in the *Realist* (a nationally circulated countercultural monthly), "*Coyote*, a Loose Woman's Organization" had risen up to protest the treatment of suspected women. Coyote, St. James continued, "is providing legal assistance, court clothes and alternative means of survival to those women being discriminated against." She claimed that the nascent organization had already successfully pressured the city into releasing women charged with prostitution on their own recognizance.[110]

St. James's article marked the first time "Coyote" was referred to in print. Her announcement of the new group caused a minor splash. The pioneering second-wave feminist Kate Millett announced her support for the new group shortly thereafter. Then Jefferson Poland (by then calling himself Jefferson Clitlick) wrote to St. James, "I want to help, if I can, your efforts to decriminalize prostitution and unionize hookers."[111] Coyote would quickly transform into COYOTE, an acronym standing for "Call Off Your Old Tired Ethics." It is generally regarded as the world's first sex workers' rights organization—with the colorful St. James as its trailblazing leader. Within a year, COYOTE claimed a thousand members.[112] The group soon inspired spinoff and sister organizations across the country.[113] Though COYOTE is sometimes remembered today in academic histories and feminist tracts, its role in opposing the surviving remnants of the American Plan has been largely forgotten. For the early members of COYOTE, though, the mistreatment of women suspected of having STIs was central to their organizing.

On May 1, 1973—also known as May Day, or International Workers' Day—St. James issued a press release on new COYOTE letterhead, a howling dog beside the spiky text. "COYOTE proclaims Mayday as the beginning of an effort to change the policy of enforcement of sumptuary laws governing prostitution in San Francisco." The new organization demanded an end to police entrapment; it decried the sexist double standard under which female prostitutes were arrested and male johns were not; it recommended issuing citations rather than arresting women for street solicitation; and it repudiated the "racism that exists . . . with the poor women of racial minorities making up the majority of those arrested."

The press release also condemned San Francisco's enforcement of the American Plan. For decades, the SFPD had been holding all women arrested for prostitution and similar offenses for seventy-two hours in jail while they were examined for STIs. "Considering the purpose of coercing prostitutes into unnecessary treatment for VD (9 out of 10 are clean) is to protect the innocent wives," St. James wrote, "the husband should also be deemed promiscuous and at least examined and quarantined as women are. (Under the threat of spending three days in jail waiting for the results of the culture, most people opt for being shot up!). COYOTE is against treatment unless proven necessary and feels the use of the quarantine is in direct conflict with the interests of the public."[114]

St. James moved quickly to follow up this proclamation. Two weeks later, on Mother's Day, she again condemned the American Plan in a press release.[115] A longtime friend got a job as a "jail doctor" so that St. James could have "inside information as well as gossip from the women he examined."[116] Then, on June 20, she wrote a letter to "V.D. doctors" across the nation, asking for information on their city's "procedure regarding examination for VD in persons charged with 'sex crimes'" and also informing them that San Francisco's procedure was a "real 'pain in the ass.'"[117] Armed with information from the doctors' replies, as well as whatever was provided to her by her mole inside the jail, St. James issued another statement on Labor Day, again denouncing the quarantine and STI examinations. (She signed it, "Soliciting! Jacking Some Dude Off!")[118] In the weeks that followed, COYOTE (with the backing of the ACLU) began negotiating with the city to end its enforcement of the Plan. Members of the health department expressed sympathy for St. James's complaints, but the police and municipal judges refused to go along.[119]

So, on January 9, 1974, ACLU attorney and St. James ally Deborah Hinkel filed suit in San Francisco Superior Court, demanding that the city's enforcement of the Plan cease immediately. "The quarantine and inspection of prostitutes is unconstitutional," one newspaper summarized, "because it violates a person's right to be free from unreasonable searches, denies him or her equal protection, due process, bail, the right of privacy and freedom from cruel or unusual punishment." If San Francisco police wanted a woman examined, they would have to establish "a pattern of behavior . . . such as previous arrests" to justify this.[120]

Less than a month later, a superior court judge issued a preliminary injunction, halting the city's Plan enforcement for the first time in decades.[121] An exultant COYOTE began suing for broader decriminalization of prostitution. St. James proclaimed 1974 to be the "Year of the Whore."[122] ACLU attorney Hinkel also challenged the Plan in nearby Oakland, the seat of Alameda County, where arrested women (disproportionately black) spent up to eight days in jail undergoing STI examinations. Again, she won an injunction.[123]

The Alameda County authorities appealed to the state's highest court and waited. In the meantime, California's acting state health department director issued a statement condemning practices such as Oakland's as "obviously absurd." There was no evidence that prostitutes had a higher rate of STIs than members of the general public, he said. "The Department of Health cannot support actions disguised as preventive health measures that are actually intended to achieve law-enforcement objectives, particularly when they appear to constitute a denial of basic rights."[124] Finally, several months later, the Court of Appeal of California issued its ruling. Though they declined to rule on the overall constitutionality of a law criminalizing prostitution, the judges held that the Oakland authorities would have to enforce it equally against both men and women—including the quarantine provision. "[W]hen it was ordered that the practice of quarantining those arrested for violations of [the prostitution law] be equally applied to customers, requiring several men to spend 5 days in jail awaiting the results of their venereal disease tests," summed up an article in the *California Law Review*, "the practice was immediately discontinued."[125]

THROUGHOUT THE turbulent 1960s and into the 1970s, Norman Hess continued to live in his small house at 2627 Broadway in Bay City. At some point, he retired from his work as a plumber. Then, late in the winter of 1971, he fell ill. Norman was taken to Bay City's General Hospital. One truly wonders if he appreciated the irony of going for care to the institution that had imprisoned and tortured his late wife. The Bay City General Hospital had expanded considerably late in the 1950s. "After it moved out of the status of a 'pest-house' for the care of highly contagious disease sufferers," ran an article in the *Bay City Democrat*, just two months after Nina's death, "it grew rapidly and made fine progress for a number of years." Additions and extra beds were added to the hospital. On March 22, 1971, Norman died there.

Two days later he would be buried next to Nina in the Floral Gardens Cemetery—a flat, green expanse of land, surrounded by pine trees, about a five-minute drive from the former Bay City Detention Hospital.[126]

THE LATE 1960s AND 1970s represented one of the true seismic shifts of American history, and the American Plan was hardly immune from this shift. In 1972, the ASHA finally ceased its signature undercover investigations of prostitution. The next year, it launched its "first modern public awareness campaign," called "VD Is for Everybody." In the years that followed, the ASHA would come to focus less on syphilis and gonorrhea and more on herpes.[127]

On July 18, 1972, Raymond Fosdick died at the age of eighty-nine. The *New York Times* covered his tidy, respectable death in its tidy, respectable way.[128] Exactly one week later, the *Times* broke the story of the Tuskegee syphilis study, which by then had led to as many as 107 deaths.[129] When a massive public uproar ensued, the federal government hastily ended the study and appointed a high-profile panel to investigate it. Yet without consulting archival records, and without access to any of the study's surviving subjects, the panel issued a weak and misleading report—claiming, for instance, that the study's subjects had knowingly "volunteered." It took a young Columbia University graduate student named Allan Brandt to venture into the stacks of the National Archives to expose the true duplicity, coerciveness, and racism of the study.[130]

The day the Tuskegee story broke, most of the ASHA's leaders were on vacation, but they were alarmed to read the news in the papers. The association's director hastily issued a statement, instructing members that the ASHA's "stance on this whole thing . . . is simple and unqualified: '*No comment*, because ASHA was neither involved, nor responsible for it, at any time.'"[131] This was untrue. For instance, Thomas Parran, who oversaw the Tuskegee study for more than a decade and had helped shaped it from the beginning, had served the ASHA in various capacities for decades, including many years on its board of directors.[132]

Tuskegee became one of the best-known (albeit least understood) examples of medical abuse in American history. The very word has become a stand-in for medical racism. Brandt and others have done an admirable job placing Tuskegee in the context of its times. They have examined its connections to broader racism in society and in the medical community; to other studies of untreated STIs; and to the virtual nonexistence of informed consent. Yet none included the American Plan in their discussions of the roots of Tuskegee. And none were likely aware that, even in the late 1960s and early 1970s, the laws created by the Plan continued to be enforced.

The city of Terre Haute, Indiana, for instance, had vigorously applied its American Plan law since World War II a quarter century before. By the late 1960s, the county health commissioner had hired an investigator who "seeks out suspected cases of venereal disease." The county then "orders the suspected carriers in for checkups and the police can arrest them if they refuse." It appears that women arrested for prostitution were automatic STI suspects.[133]

In Salt Lake City, Utah, city officials—fearing that "hippies" were spreading STIs—began reusing a previously discontinued Plan law and started detaining "suspected" women in August 1968, and apparently continued to do so until 1976, when a county attorney ruled that the state's Plan law "only would allow carriers to be kept at a hospital or at home," but not in jail.[134] The city of Denver, Colorado, continued to enforce its American Plan ordinance as late as 1972, forcing some "reasonably suspected" women to remain in jail for forty-eight hours for an STI exam. When one woman sued, the Tenth Circuit Court of Appeals upheld this ordinance, citing numerous Plan precedents and declaring, "It is not illogical or unreasonable, and on the contrary it is reasonable, to suspect that known prostitutes are a prime source of infectious venereal disease."[135]

It appears that Denver nonetheless ceased this practice as a result of the lawsuit, but Colorado Springs, some seventy-five miles away, continued to enforce a version of the Plan until at least as late as the end of 1977.[136] "Women arrested on local streets for prostitution are held in jail if they have not been tested for VD in the preceding 30 days," reported the *Colorado Springs Gazette-Telegraph* that December. "Until the women are tested and found not to have VD or are treated, they are held in jail without bond." Colorado Springs had done this continuously since 1970, when the district attorney dusted off a "rarely-used statute allowing health officials to order the detention of persons suspected of having communicable diseases." The purpose of the enforcement of these laws, the district attorney admitted, was "to get prostitutes off the streets and jail them temporarily."[137]

As late as 1982, when officials in Atlantic City, New Jersey, launched an "all-out war" on boardwalk prostitution, the mayor floated the idea of calling on the legislature to enact "tougher laws and a 'quarantine' of prostitutes found spreading venereal disease."[138]

Even where the Plan was no longer enforced, the ideology that undergirded it—that prostitutes were uniquely infected and had to be controlled, civil liberties be damned—remained. In late 1977 in Fresno and Monterey County, California, for example, police demanded that prostitutes periodically report to a "VD clinic" for examinations; if they failed to do so, they could be locked up and forcibly examined. "State law gives county health officers broad powers to fight venereal disease, including the right to force a person to submit to an examination," noted the *Los Angeles Times*. "In effect, the health officer may arrest and quarantine a person who refuses to comply." This system was classic regulationism, yet with an undeniably coercive twist. In explaining the system, one Monterey County police commander gave a quote to the *Times* admitting its true aims, and, in so doing, inadvertently admitted the true aims of American Plan laws that enabled it.

"Venereal disease was not our concern. Cleaning up the streets was our concern," the police commander told the newspaper. "More than anything else, it was a harassing technique that falls within legal parameters for the police, so that we don't have to worry about civil liberties union or the public defender's office or somebody like that issuing a court order against us."[139]

Nonetheless, by the end of the 1970s, momentum was decidedly against the remnants of the Plan and other policies to harass marginalized women. In

October 1975, a poll indicated that half of Californians favored legalizing prostitution.[140] Then, in the summer of 1981, physicians began noticing a spate of very rare cancers in gay men in California and New York.

FROM THE EARLIEST DAYS of the HIV/AIDS epidemic in the United States, the plague's sufferers feared the prospect of compulsory testing and quarantine. Gay activists heard the same concern repeated over and over again, with dread: "AIDS might be used as a medical pretext to round up homosexuals and put them in concentration camps."[141] Yet for the first few years of the epidemic, serious attempts to institute quarantine were rare. In large part, this was because the epidemic was not especially well understood, and few thought AIDS affected anyone other than Haitians, hemophiliacs, heroin users, and, above all, homosexuals. Yet some had an idea of what was coming. "In 1984, heterosexuals were still going on their merry way, not caring or even knowing about safe sex, thinking of AIDS as something that happened to *those people*," Dolores French, an outspoken sex workers' rights advocate, later wrote. "But we prostitutes knew that, sooner or later, AIDS would spread into the heterosexual community and that when it did not only would we be blamed, but if history were any guide, we would also be arrested, quarantined, and worse."[142]

As it became clear that straight people could indeed get AIDS, and that women might be able to transmit HIV to men, the calls for quarantine began. First, in New Haven, Connecticut, then in San Francisco, rumors of infected female prostitutes who refused to stop sleeping with clients led to frantic calls to lock these women up.[143] The army released a report claiming that infected female prostitutes accounted for a huge proportion of infected servicemen; once again, these women posed a possibly significant threat to national security. (That closeted gay soldiers might be lying about where they got the infection apparently didn't occur to army physicians.)[144] First Connecticut, and then dozens of other states, passed laws specifically adding AIDS to the list of conditions that could merit quarantine or simply making it easier to lock up those with the dreaded plague; sometimes these laws were amendments to American Plan laws.[145] State legislators across the country considered proposals to compulsorily examine women merely accused of prostitution.[146] By the end of 1985, one poll found that a majority of Americans favored quarantining those with AIDS.[147]

Facing such a drastic threat, prostitutes rose up and fought back. They testified before local and federal government panels, repeatedly presenting evidence that prostitutes were not significant risk factors for spreading HIV/AIDS.[148] Sex workers' rights advocates spread the word about safe sex and collaborated with public health experts to study the links between prostitution and HIV themselves; their findings confirmed that female prostitutes were not common vectors for the virus, since female-to-male vaginal transmission is so rare.[149] Other marginalized individuals, including gay men, took to the streets, chanting slogans like, "No way! No tracing, no quarantine, no lying!"[150] Their marches and protests successfully blocked several attempts at quarantine and compulsory testing.[151]

For those opposing quarantine and compulsory testing, history was a vitally important weapon in their arsenal. And little history was more relevant than that of the American Plan. Journalists, scholars, and activists frequently brought up the Plan in condemning the calls for quarantine.[152] "In response to widespread fear, legislators nation-wide have introduced AIDS-related bills calling for the testing of those 'suspected' of infection, and the quarantining of known AIDS carriers under broad-based state police powers over public health," noted one scholar and activist in 1987. "The language of these bills is strikingly similar and frequently identical to that of quarantine and testing provisions written nearly a century ago."[153] Allan Brandt, the historian who had exposed the duplicity of Tuskegee a decade earlier, wrote a groundbreaking study of STIs in America; in 1987, he reissued his book with a new chapter on AIDS. Brandt noted that the fears surrounding AIDS "are reminiscent of those that surrounded syphilis at the turn of the century. . . . As was the case in the early twentieth century, public health measures that require dramatic infringements of civil liberties are again being proposed."[154] Many AIDS activists contacted Brandt around this time, hoping to better understand the history of mandatory testing, quarantine, and their effectiveness. It struck him that so many of those learning this history were those for whom it was most personally relevant.[155]

This history only made these individuals more resolute. "During World War I, Congress approved over $1 million to incarcerate 30,000 prostitutes, for the purposes of ending the spread of VD. The effort was not successful— VD rates continued to climb," wrote one HIV-positive man around this time. "Existing public health statutes give health officers the authority necessary to intervene on a case by case basis with individuals who are known to be infected and who continue to engage in behaviors which could spread HIV to others. . . . There are just three words which I use to explain why quarantine won't work: I WON'T GO."[156]

Yet others wielded the history of the American Plan for very different reasons. "Health officials have legal authority to test anyone they 'reasonably suspect' of carrying a sexually transmitted disease," noted one journalist in 1985.[157] "All you got to do is look at every plague that's ever hit this country," claimed a South Carolina government employee debating quarantine in

1989. "And the only way they've gotten rid of it is quarantine."[158] When public health officials did quarantine a handful of individuals with HIV during the 1980s and 1990s—mostly prostitutes and others who were deemed "recalcitrant"—courts frequently cited American Plan laws and precedents to uphold these actions.[159] One decision from 1990 relied on a 1919 Plan case that declared the quarantine of a woman who allegedly had gonorrhea "a reasonable and proper, indeed the usual, measure taken to prevent the increase and spread thereof."[160]

It would be a stretch to call the movement to quarantine HIV/AIDS patients (and the few cases of actual quarantine) a direct continuation of the American Plan. The Plan dealt with syphilis and gonorrhea, not HIV/AIDS. Furthermore, many of the individuals examined or quarantined for HIV/AIDS were prosecuted under new HIV/AIDS-specific laws. And it would appear that most of those convicted on HIV/AIDS-related charges were accorded somewhat greater due process protections than were victims of the Plan. Yet in many respects the two campaigns are similar, and the response to HIV/AIDS is an obvious intellectual, legislative, and judicial successor to the American Plan. Both campaigns instituted penalties—quarantine and mandatory treatment—for STIs; both campaigns relied on stereotypes about prostitutes, nonwhite individuals, and supposedly promiscuous people. Both campaigns assumed—incorrectly—that prostitutes were disproportionately responsible for spreading disease.[161]

Each of the laws that enabled the American Plan—those laws passed at federal behest in 1917, 1918, and 1919—remains on the books, in some form, to this day. Not one of them has ever been struck down by an appeals court.[162] Yet the Plan's legacy is not merely these laws and these precedents. It is the philosophy they helped to cement: that women and promiscuous people are dangerous and morally inferior; that they need to be stopped, locked up, and reformed. This philosophy, and the practice of policing the sex lives of stigmatized groups, especially women, has a long history. This philosophy endures to this day.

EPILOGUE

ON SEPTEMBER 27, 2011, I was a freshman in college, taking notes in a lecture course called Media and Medicine in Modern America. It was a massive class, and throngs of students, most of them still bleary-eyed at 10:30 a.m., crowded Yale's cavernous, windowless Davies Auditorium. The professor was talking about how government officials attempted to combat the dreaded specter of STIs—syphilis and gonorrhea—even as rules, written and unwritten, prevented them from being able to even mention these conditions publicly. During the 1910s, the campaign against prostitution, he told us, was the one lens through which officials could publicly discuss STIs.

Then, almost as an afterthought, he said something to the effect of: "There were even concentration camps in this country for prostitutes."

The line caught me off guard. What? I took a break from my note taking and pulled up Google. I typed in, "concentration camps for prostitutes." Nothing. I went to Wikipedia and entered the same search. Nothing. This was strange.

Slightly more sophisticated Googling after class yielded slightly more information, but only slightly. I stumbled across a few mentions of something called the Chamberlain-Kahn Act. Later, I would learn that this was one of the federal laws that enabled a national American Plan. At the time, I only knew that the 1918 law had authorized the secretaries of war and the navy to assist states "in caring for civilian persons whose detention, isolation, quarantine, or commitment to institutions may be found necessary for the protection of the military and naval forces of the United States against venereal diseases."[1] I was intrigued.

I entered the Chamberlain-Kahn Act into a database that searched through the collections of Yale's libraries. I came up with a few odd titles, which I resolved to check out that day. Later, I would learn that employees of the library would retrieve books for students, but it was my first month of college, and I was ignorant. So I set off on my own. Sometime that afternoon, I ventured deep into the dark, claustrophobic stacks of the towering Sterling Memorial Library to find these books that might resolve what was still for me just a tickling curiosity. Happily, the books were not hard to find; most of them were clustered together on a shelf that looked like it contained titles relating to the history of prostitution—not a subject I had ever considered before.

I pulled the books I had sought off the shelves and settled onto the dusty ground to peruse them. I wasn't sure I really wanted to check them out and lug them back up five flights of stairs to my dorm room. I opened one at random. It was *The Response to Prostitution in the Progressive Era*, by Mark Thomas Connelly, a classic in the field. I flipped to the index, found the Chamberlain-Kahn Act, and opened the book to the correct page. Connelly's book contained a few pages about the government's campaign against STIs—and their supposed carriers—during the World War I era. It was fascinating. At the end of one particularly juicy paragraph, there was an endnote. I dutifully turned to the notes section and found the appropriate citation. At the end of it, Connelly had written, "This domestic aspect of World War I deserves further and more detailed study."[2]

In that moment, sitting on the floor of the stacks, holding a thirty-year-old book in my lap, I felt like I had just received my marching orders. Years later, after reading thousands of books and articles and having passed countless hours in archives across the country, after having spent the better part of my college career researching the American Plan and having decided to devote myself to this research full-time following college, I would know that the Plan was far more than just a domestic aspect of World War I. I would know that it continued for decades beyond the scope of Connelly's book. I would know that many historians had also heeded Connelly's call before me, but that there was still so much research left to do. The Plan was vast; it contained multitudes. But even as I buried myself in research, having begged or wheedled or, occasionally, paid to obtain copies of deteriorating documents from archives across the country and around the world, and even as I wrote, I would always remember that moment on the floor.

I wrote about the American Plan, so far as I understood it, in the five-to-seven-page essay I had to do for Media and Medicine in Modern America. I kept researching. In the years that followed, professors generously allowed me to research and write about the Plan for a great many classes. In one seminar on the history of pollution, my final paper compared the rhetoric of anti-pollution activists in Bay City with that of anti-STI activists; for a class on the global uprisings of 1968, my paper compared the stigmatization of prostitution and STIs in the late '60s with their stigmatization in the late 1910s. I began choosing classes—Writing History; American Captivity Narratives; Public Health in America—specifically because they might allow me to continue my research.

At first I believed that the American Plan was merely a World War I–era program and that, as one historian wrote rather vaguely, "the work continued in many cases on the state and local level throughout the 1920s."[3] Anything after that, I thought, was surely a different program altogether. Yet an independent study in my junior year allowed me to examine lawsuits filed by women (like Nina) who challenged their incarceration under the Plan. Creating a list of these lawsuits, I noticed something odd: they didn't stop in the 1920s. They continued into the 1930s, 1940s, and 1950s. There was even one in the early 1970s. Perhaps some places hadn't stopped enforcing the Plan after all. I decided to examine the local laws that enabled city and state authorities to police "reasonably suspicious" women after the Great War ended. I noticed that these laws had never been repealed. I realized the women who had brought the lawsuits I was examining had been locked up under the same American Plan laws—even the women imprisoned decades after these laws were passed. The Plan was longer and larger than anyone had realized.

As I was finishing that independent study, I vented frustration to the professor overseeing it about how few sources there were in which I could locate the voices of incarcerated women themselves. She suggested that I write to state archives across the country, to see if they had any records of any American Plan cases. Perhaps they would have trial transcripts! So, over the course of one whirlwind afternoon, I dutifully sent out fifty e-mails. The very first reply I received was from the Archives of Michigan, which had one yellowing transcript for me. It turned out to be Nina's. The rest, as they say, was history (quite literally).

Finally, I had found the voice of a woman who was actually incarcerated under the Plan, as well as the voices of her mother, her lawyers, and her captors. Furthermore, Nina's case was located far from New York or Chicago or San Francisco or any of the other cities where studies of prostitution, STIs, and incarceration are often located. She lived in central Michigan—a rural, remote place, to be sure, yet also one with a smattering of daily and weekly newspapers. Her case would illustrate the decentralized nature of the Plan, how it operated independent of federal oversight. In all these ways, Nina made for an ideal protagonist.

Yet there were also drawbacks to focusing on her. She was a white woman, and the Plan disproportionately affected nonwhite women. Nearly all the records of Michigan's department of health were inadvertently destroyed long ago. And, remarkable for a woman of her generation, Nina left behind no direct descendants, nor did her brother, her husband, or anyone close enough to her to be of any narrative value. Nina's one biological child and two adopted children all died young. She herself died young—more than a half century before I started working on this book. I contacted every distant relative of Nina's I could find (various cousins of various removals have scattered from Ohio to Arizona); I interviewed dozens of elderly residents of St. Louis and Bay City;

I even scraped together the money to hire a professional genealogist in Michigan—and still, I could find no one living who had known Nina.

Nonetheless, Nina's voice captivated me. It is hard to overstate just how bold an eighteen-year-old woman would have had to be in 1918 to call a male authority figure a liar, as she did to Dr. Carney the very first time she met him. And so I plunged into the story of Nina McCall and all the trials she was forced to endure.

After I had completed the bulk of the archival research, and as I began the process of writing this book, I spoke on the phone with a best-selling author—the uncle of a childhood friend. At one point during our conversation, he asked me, "Who are your antagonists?" I paused, sputtered, and eventually said, "Well, I guess everyone was kind of an antagonist. Except the women on the ground." The men who had created and run the Plan were obviously responsible for its discrimination and its cruelty. So too were the women who helped them enforce it, at both a federal and a local level, and who themselves also greatly expanded the Plan through their misguided attempts at "protective" work. Even the journalists, reformers, and activists who opposed the Plan were complicit in its cruelties, for they never fought—and often promoted—the idea that truly infected or promiscuous women should be locked up to be reformed; rather, they disliked the sexism of only locking up women, and they objected to the denials of due process and other indignities incarcerated women were forced to bear. By fighting for the Plan's "innocent" victims, they tacitly condemned its "guilty" victims to ignominy.

I found inspiration in the resistance of other women—the other women on the ground, those locked up as a result of the Plan. These were the women who had fought the Plan from the beginning, who had filed lawsuits and escaped from detention hospitals, who had launched hunger strikes and leapt from moving trains and set fires—many fires—and even assaulted their captors. It was the resistance of these women, I realized, that had been most forgotten, and it was their resistance that was most important to remember.

Over time, it dawned on me that the American Plan is not ancient history. The Plan helped create the infrastructure and rationale for an explosion of the female prison population that continues to this day. We still imprison women for selling sex while temporarily locking up only a small fraction of the men who purchase their services. And the women arrested and convicted of prostitution and other crimes related to sex work are still disproportionately poor and nonwhite.

Further, as I was writing this book, controversies arose over whether to quarantine those with Ebola or the Zika virus. Quarantine can be a valid public health tool. But I felt that I had seen what could happen when decisions to quarantine were informed by stereotypes or fear or simple hatred of women. Further, I kept reading news reports that syphilis and gonorrhea were growing increasingly resistant to antibiotics, and that rates of both were increasing rapidly. "Gonorrhea Is Now One Antibiotic Away from Being Untreatable," read one headline in 2012. As the director of STD Prevention at the Centers for Disease Control remarked, "It's only a matter of time" before we have no treatment left for these infections.[4] What will authorities do then, especially since American Plan statutes remain the law of the land? One may consider the case of Salt Lake City, where, in late 1976, authorities threatened "arrest and forced treatment of suspected carriers of a strain of venereal disease that is resistant to penicillin treatment."[5]

Yet the American Plan being resuscitated in such a doomsday, post-antibiotic scenario is not my only concern. I am, if anything, more bothered by the deafening silence that continues to surround the Plan. Over the six years I spent researching and writing this book, I came across virtually no one who had ever heard of it. I believe this history is vitally important. It has informed the way that women and disease are perceived to this day; the Plan laid the groundwork for a terrifying expansion of state surveillance, women's prisons, and the policing of sexuality, to say nothing of the Tuskegee study or the response to the AIDS epidemic. I want the Plan taught, understood, and remembered.

The American Plan was never a secret, per se. During the years that it operated, it was well covered in the pages of local and national newspapers; politicians like Fiorello La Guardia spoke of it to roaring crowds; it was widely discussed. Supporters of the Plan often remarked on the widespread knowledge and fear of the Plan among women.[6] Even men had opinions on it. "Much complaint is heard from 'the man on the street' about the practice on the part of the police of 'picking up any strange girl and taking her to the Health Department for examination'; and 'the town is overrun with whores they never touch,'" recounted one CTCA agent stationed in Petersburg, Virginia.[7]

Some even grasped the Plan's continuity. "As you are aware, the venereal disease control program of the official health agencies was not born after Pearl Harbor," one California public health official told an audience in 1942. "This program really had its birth in the first round of this world conflict back in 1917. It developed into a robust youth at that time. For some fifteen years after that first World War, however, the civilian control program was so poorly nourished that it came near dying of starvation. But it did not die. In a few isolated areas of the country and in the offices of the U.S. Public Health Service and the American Social Hygiene Association the program remained very much alive, albeit terribly undernourished."[8]

Yet sometime between the end of World War II and our own day, the American Plan has been forgotten. To be sure, a handful of historians have done vitally important work on the Plan, and in this corner of the academy, it is somewhat remembered. None have quite grasped its longevity or its scope, and none have centered their work on the Plan's survivors, as I have tried to do in this book—but still, I could never have begun to write this book but for the remarkable work of previous historians. In the wider world, however, pretty much no one has heard of the American Plan. It is not taught in high schools, as it should be. No one in the federal government has ever apologized for the Plan, as President Bill Clinton did for Tuskegee in 1997. Neither has the League of Women Voters, the Rockefeller Foundation, the US Chamber of Commerce, nor the American Bar Association. Nor has the ASHA—which still exists to this day, though it is now known as the American Sexual Health Association. The modern ASHA is largely devoted to promoting sex education. Its website contains an extensive, highly sanitized, and entirely uninformative history.

For a long time, I thought the story was this simple: the Plan had been forgotten, as many injustices of the past inevitably are. Yet I gradually came to realize that this was not quite the case. Rather, the true and full history of the Plan was intentionally obscured, as certain voices were deliberately silenced.

In the winter of 2014, I traveled, along with my father, to Michigan for the first time. I was there to scour a few archives, and also to see the places where Nina lived, where she was incarcerated, and where she died. On our last day in the state, my dad and I drove along icy roads, through frankly treacherous conditions, to see the clapboard house where Nina and Norman shared their life, the street on which Deputy Sheriff Martin first approached her, and the sprawling mega-hospital that the Bay City Detention Hospital has become. In the hospital's parking lot, I stood outside in swirling snow and tried to feel Nina's presence. Mostly, I felt cold. Finally, we drove to the pine-lined cemetery in which Nina resides today and forevermore. We were there to see Nina's grave and pay our respects. However, the snow was simply too heavy, and the grave markers were all covered in white powder. We couldn't find Nina.

My father was visibly disappointed, but I saw a silver lining to the whole situation. This scene—looking for Nina, yet being unable to find her—could be a great closing act for this book. It would serve as a metaphor to illustrate how Nina—and by extension the American Plan—has been obscured by the thick snows of time. Yet then I realized I was wrong. This scene would convey a message precisely at odds with the truth. A blizzard is a natural phenomenon. The erasure of the Plan was deliberate and man-made; it was unnatural.

Acknowledgments

THIS BOOK would have been impossible without my parents. As I spent more than two years following college writing and researching full-time, my parents, Howard Stern and Rhonda Wasserman, allowed me to live at home, rent-free, and they were endlessly helpful in a million ways I truly cannot adequately recognize. When I needed a place to work, my mother (a law professor) found me an often-unused office in her building. All of this was an extraordinary privilege and one for which I can never be sufficiently grateful.

Yet to do this project justice, to fully understand how the American Plan worked, I needed to travel to archives all across the country, from Topeka, Kansas, and Madison, Wisconsin, to Portland, Oregon. So I dipped into my savings (money dutifully squirreled away from several work-study jobs I had in college). Just as my bank account fell below $100 and I started to panic, John Bradley, the associate head of my residential college at Yale, called me out of the blue and told me that a woman named Wendy Hamilton wanted to speak with me. She had admired some of the op-ed columns criticizing the Yale administration I had written during college. In an unlikely turn of events, Wendy offered to finance my further travel. I had never met Wendy at the time. This project would not have been possible without her generosity. Truly, I am blessed.

With this infusion of cash, I was able to take more ambitious research trips than I had thought possible, including a lengthy one to Minnesota, and an even lengthier one to London. Her assistance also allowed me to reach out to dozens of archives in places I could not visit, from Wyoming to Georgia, and pay librarians or students to copy documents for me. I simply cannot thank her enough.

In the meantime, my neighbor, Sam Prepelka, had heard that I was looking for a literary agent. He mentioned that a friend of his from high school, PJ Dempsey, was an experienced editor and a generous person who was knowledgeable about the publishing industry. He put us in touch, and PJ graciously answered several of my questions about this mysterious world. She then offered to put me in touch with a friend of hers, Susan Lee Cohen, a literary agent. I gratefully accepted PJ's offer. The next day, I sent Susan what I'd written so far. A few days later, we spoke on the phone, and she offered to represent me.

Susan is everything anyone could want in a literary agent—kind, erudite, ridiculously knowledgeable, a fabulous editor, and an endlessly encouraging friend. At her suggestion, and after months of her patient prodding, I radically revised my book proposal, dividing it into two books, one for a general audience that focused on Nina (this is the book you've just read) and another, much longer one (without Nina) aimed at an academic readership. (Look out for it at some point in the hopefully not-too-distant future.) Susan eventually placed the Nina book with Beacon Press and in the hands of its director, Helene Atwan. From our very first phone call, Helene was warm, supportive, blessedly patient, and the best editor I've ever met. She was working with a naive first-time author and helped me turn an unwieldy manuscript into the book you have before you.

In the spirit of staying within my word-count—Helene could tell you how much of a challenge that is for me—I must begin to thank the legions of other people who helped make this book possible.

First, the remarkable professors, librarians, staff members, and other teachers at Yale: John Warner first introduced me to the American Plan, and helped guide this project before it was even conceived. Heidi Knoblauch was the first person ever to read anything I wrote on the Plan, and her thoughtful critiques helped convince me to continue my research. Birgit Brander Rasmussen accepted me into her wonderful Captivity Narratives seminar and later allowed me to do an independent study with her; it was her advice that led me to fully understand the length and scope of the American Plan. It was also her advice that led me to find Nina. She was, and is, one of the kindest and best teachers I've ever had. Crystal Feimster was one of my earliest mentors in college, and she remained an advisor and a friend throughout my time at Yale. Glenda Gilmore allowed me to design not one but two independent studies under her tutelage, the second on the American Plan, and she has been a fount of wisdom when it came to all things research, writing, and publishing. Joanne Meyerowitz advised my senior essay on the Plan, and her guidance and edits helped me focus what was at the time a most unfocused project; her warmth and advice further helped make this book real. When I couldn't find someone to advise yet another independent study on the Plan, Stephen Pitti graciously offered to oversee it, and his generosity as an advisor inside and outside the classroom has been unmatched. John Demos helped teach me narrative history writing, and his books are the model I strive in vain to replicate; he also answered my repeated questions about book publishing. Others at Yale who advised papers I wrote on the Plan, taught classes that shaped my understanding of it, or offered advice include Naomi Rogers, Kelly O'Donnell, David Huyssen (who also answered my repeated frantic questions about graduate school), Becky

Conekin, Greta LaFleur, John Gaddis (who graciously answered many entreaties about publishing), Kathryn Dudley, Alison Kanosky, Jean Cherniavksy, Alejandra Dubcovsky, and Melissa Grafe. David Gary deserves a special mention for his years of kind and diligent assistance in finding documents, even after we both left Yale.

Several Yale American Studies and history undergrad and graduate students read pieces of this book back when they were essays for various classes, and I thank each of them: Teresa Logue, Andrea Villena, Viet Trinh, Justin Randolph, Nicole Nelson, George MacDonnell, and Lucy Caplan. Other friends in Branford also read pieces of it, even if they don't remember this, and they and my suitemates kept me sane (no small task): Matthew Glover, Justin Young, Gordon McCambridge, Cody Pomeranz, Tayo Ajayi, Victor Hicks, Moktar Jama, Michael Wu, Sam Goldstein, Liz Rodriguez-Florido, Jane O'Bryan, Emma Schmidt, and many others. Mitchell Nobel provided critical assistance with legal research.

A number of historians generously spoke or corresponded with me as I researched and wrote, and I am in their debt: Allan Brandt, Antoinette Burton, Kristin Kobes Du Mez, Karin Zipf, Anne Gray Fischer, Michael Willrich, Nicole Perry, Erin Wuebker, and Christopher Lovett. The students in Birgit's seminar at SUNY Binghamton were among the very first to read part of my manuscript, and their feedback was quite helpful. Alexandra Minna Stern, Kate O'Connor, and the rest of their team were stunningly generous in helping me better understand eugenic sterilization.

When this project was quite young, several writers and professors offered me indispensable advice on agents, publishers, and the like. These include David Garrow, Kenneth Gormley, Mitchell Zuckoff, Glenda Gilmore, John Demos, John Gaddis, and Joanne Meyerowitz.

During the years that I was back home writing this book, I was blessed to have so many friends to encourage me, force me to take a break and be social, watch movies with me, and listen to my endless anxieties about life, romance, and "the future": Joanne Gilligan, Meghan McNeil, Zacchiaus McKee, Sam Shrivastava, Maddie Camerlengo, Elena Leib, Tara Gangwar, Jill Jaycox, Lindsey Milisits, Jack Mulligan, Josh Orange, Ariel Rascoe, Aryel Abramovitz, and Darya Fischbach, among others.

In Ithaca, Michigan, Jeff Martlew, Randy Tahvonen, and several others were kind enough to show me around the courthouse where Nina's trial took place. Without David McMacken's decades of research and writing on Alma and St. Louis, I could never have completed this book. He graciously answered my repeated questions, and he and his whole family were remarkably kind when I visited Alma for the centennial of the town's entrance into the Great War. Jan E. Tripp provided key assistance with Michigan genealogy.

Several individuals spoke with me over the years about their experiences decades ago fighting for sex workers and other marginalized women, including Margo St. James, Norma Jean Almodovar, Priscilla Alexander, Marilyn Haft, and the few who wished their stories to remain off the record. All those who have generously spoken with me about the case of Carlotta Locklear will be acknowledged in a future publication—wait and see!

A veritable platoon of friends from all periods of my life hosted me during my travels to archives across the country and around the world. These include Taylor Lawson, Michelle Taylor (and Rhonda Wasserman) in Boston; Sara Samuel, Justin Young, Tara Gangwar, Michael Wu, Noah Schoen, and Geng Ngarmboonanant in New York; Yael Wollstein in Princeton; Noah Schoen, Justin Young, Danielle Zucker (and her housemates), Cody Pomeranz, and Zac Krislov in Washington, DC; Matt Glover and Eric Stern in Chicago; Evi Steyer in London; Jordan Konell in Oxford; Emily Wolfson and Jake Stockman in Madison; and Sumil Thakrar (as well as Shan Kothari and Claire Milsted) in Minneapolis.

Then there were the zillions of people who assisted me in oh so many archives. I will acknowledge all that I can, but please forgive me and my abysmal memory for names: Graham Ambrose in New Haven; Cindy Atman in Seattle; Louisa and Meredith McCambridge in Dallas (and Gordon McCambridge, for putting us in touch); Katherine Richter at Northwestern (and Rachel Weingart, for putting us in touch); Annie Fryman and Amelia Fisher in San Francisco (and Aileen Lerch, for putting us in touch); Zaharina Velazquez-Ramos in Sacramento (and Matt Glover, for putting us in touch); Cameron Green in Wyoming (and the rest of the staff of the American Heritage Center); John Stoltenberg for allowing me to see the Andrea Dworkin Papers; John Fierst at Central Michigan University; Lee Anne Titangos at the University of California at Berkeley; the staff of the University of Michigan's Bentley Historical Library (especially Karen Jania, Emma Hawker, Diana Bachman, and Eryn Killian); the staff of the Archives of Michigan (especially Brice Sample, Mark Harvey, Jill Arnold, and Kris Rzepczynski); Simon Fowler in London; Megan Keller and David Greenstein at the University of Illinois at Chicago; Kate Evans, Emma Pizarro, and others at the Women's Library of the London School of Economics; Linnea Anderson at the Social Welfare History Archives of the University of Minnesota; Carole Powers and the other volunteers at the Bay County Historical Society; Jessica Pigza and the staff of the New York Public Library; Melodi Andersen, Jessica Herrick, and others at the California State Archives; Tab Lewis and James Kelling, among many others, at the National Archives in College Park, Maryland; Catherine Miller at the National Archives in Atlanta; Ellen Shea, Hannah Weinberg, Natalie Kelsey, and the rest of the staff of the Schlesinger Library at Radcliffe; Patricia Johnson at the

Center for Sacramento History; Kevin Kimura and others at the University of Chicago; Melissa Atkinson and Lisa McQuillan at the Library of the Society of Friends in London; Helen Koo at UCLA; Yevgeniya Gribov at the Girl Scout National Historic Preservation Center; Lin Fredericksen and many others at the Kansas State Archives; Anne Frantilla at the Seattle Municipal Archives; Rebecca Pixler at the King County Archives; David Olson at Columbia; Alex Asal, Amy Hague, and others at the Sophia Smith Collection; Jacques Oberson at the United Nations Archives at Geneva; Vince Lee and Jeff Warner in Houston; Margaret A. Hogan, Amy Fitch, and the rest of the staff of the Rockefeller Archive Center; Darla Brock at the Tennessee State Library and Archives; Tony Black at the Texas State Library and Archives; Lupita Lopez at the Washington State Archives; David Sigler and Joanne Wyse at Oviatt Library of California State University, Northridge; Joanna Black at the Gay, Lesbian, Bisexual, Transgender Historical Society; Meg Langford at the Oregon Health & Science University; Tom Carey at the San Francisco History Center; David Uhlich at the UCSF Archives; and Scott Daniels at the Oregon Historical Society.

The staff of the Carnegie Library of Pittsburgh also deserves my eternal gratitude. David and Becky Harris and Dee and John Seiffer helped me out by patronizing my expert dog-sitting services. At the University of Pittsburgh School of Law, Linda Tashbook, Bernard Hibbitts, and Deborah Brake also provided crucial advice as I was beginning to research the history and legacy of American Plan laws and cases. Elena Baylis graciously allowed me to squat in her office for more than two years; my thanks also to Matthew Shames and Chuck Cohen. Indeed, innumerable members of the staff and administration of the University of Pittsburgh School of Law assisted me throughout this journey.

In addition to my editor, Helene, the entire staff of Beacon Press was an absolute dream come true. They included Maya Fernandez, Gayatri Patnaik, Alyssa Hassan, Tom Hallock, Susan Lumenello, Marcy Barnes, and my tireless publicist, Nicholas DiSabatino. My film agent, Jody Hotchkiss, helped me to see that Nina's story had potential that reached far past the page.

Many, many thanks to my younger brother, Benny (who graduates college nine days after the release of this book—a hearty mazel tov to him!), and my twin brother, Eric. Finally, I must thank my parents yet again, for far more than just the material assistance. My father was my indefatigable traveling companion, and he was, and is, the most optimistic and encouraging person I know. Often his faith in me, and in this book, strained the bounds of rationality, but it meant more to me than he could know. My mother was, and always has been, my most trusted editor; she was the only person I allowed to see my first drafts. She provided levelheaded advice at every stage of this project. She

Notes

ARCHIVES CONSULTED

ACLUNCR	American Civil Liberties Union of Northern California Records, California Historical Society
ADP	Andrea Dworkin Papers, Schlesinger Library, Radcliffe Institute
AEHC	Addie E. Hill Collection, Clarke Historical Library, Central Michigan University
AGSP	Anna Garlin Spencer Papers, Peace Collection, Swarthmore College
AJTP	Arthur J. Tuttle Papers, Bentley Historical Library, University of Michigan
AKPAJA	Anna Kross Papers, American Jewish Archives, Cincinnati
AKPSS	Anna Kross Papers, Sophia Smith Collection, Northampton, Massachusetts
AM	Archives of Michigan
AMSHR	Association for Moral & Social Hygiene Records, Women's Library, London School of Economics
ASHAR	American Social Hygiene Association Records, Social Welfare History Archives, University of Minnesota
BCGR	Bay City Government Records, Bentley Historical Library, University of Michigan
BCHS	Bay County Historical Society, Bay City, Michigan
BLRP	Ben Lewis Reitman Papers, University of Illinois at Chicago
C14R	Committee of Fourteen Records, New York Public Library
CDPHR	California Department of Public Health Records, California State Archives
CHL	Clarke Historical Library, Central Michigan University
COYOTER	COYOTE Records, Schlesinger Library, Radcliffe Institute
CPTP	Charles P. Taft Papers, Library of Congress
CSA	California State Archives
CSH	Center for Sacramento History
CWEP	Charles William Eliot Papers, Harvard University
DHDC	Dallas Health Department Collection, Dallas Public Library
EGPP	Elizabeth G. Pritchard Papers, National Library of Medicine
ESDP	Ethel Sturges Dummer Papers, Schlesinger Library, Radcliffe Institute
FAPSRP	Friends' Association for the Promotion of Social Purity, Library of the Society of Friends, London
FHP	Franklin Hichborn Papers, Charles E. Young Research Library, University of California at Los Angeles
FPBP	Frances Payne Bolton Papers, Western Reserve Historical Society
GSUSAR	Girl Scouts of the United States of America Records, Girl Scout National Historic Preservation Center, New York
HHWP	Harry H. Woodring Papers, Kansas State Archives
HKP	Harry Kelly Papers, Archives of Michigan
JAP	Jane Addams Papers, Ramapo College of New Jersey

JDP   Josephus Daniels Papers, Library of Congress
JFMP   John F. Miller Papers, University of Washington
JHWP   John Henry Wigmore Papers, Northwestern University
JPAR   Juvenile Protective Association Records, University of Illinois at Chicago
JSP   John Sundwall Papers, Bentley Historical Library, University of Michigan
KCA   King County Archives, Seattle
KEOMP   Kathryn Ellen O'Loughlin McCarthy Papers, Kansas State Archives
KISGC   Kansas Industrial School for Girls Clippings, Kansas State Archives
KSA   Kansas State Archives
KSBHR   Kansas State Board of Health Records, Kansas State Archives
KSIFWR   Kansas State Industrial Farm for Women Records, Kansas State Archives
LDWP   Lillian D. Wald Papers, Columbia University
LWVR   League of Women Voters Records, Library of Congress
MBHR   Minnesota Board of Health Records, Minnesota Historical Society
MFCP   Minnie Fisher Cunningham Papers, University of Houston
MVWP   Miriam Van Waters Papers, Schlesinger Library, Radcliffe Institute
MWIP   Merritte W. Ireland Papers, National Library of Medicine
NA   National Archives, College Park, Maryland
NLM   National Library of Medicine
NYPL   New York Public Library
NYSA   New York State Archives
NYSL   New York State Library
OHSU   Oregon Health & Science University
OSHSR   Oregon Social Hygiene Society Records
PBPP   Paul Bowman Popenoe Papers, American Heritage Center, University
           of Wyoming
RAC   Rockefeller Archive Center, New York
RBFP   Raymond Blaine Fosdick Papers, Seeley G. Mudd Manuscript Library,
           Princeton University
RMLFP   Robert M. La Follette Papers, Library of Congress
SMA   Seattle Municipal Archives
SPBP   Sophonisba P. Breckinridge Papers, University of Illinois at Chicago
TEXSLA   Texas State Library and Archives
TPP   Thomas Parran Papers, University of Pittsburgh
TSLA   Tennessee State Library and Archives
VDPS   Venereal Disease Program Scrapbook, Oviatt Library, California State
           University Northridge
WASP   Wilbur A. Sawyer Papers, National Library of Medicine
WSA   Washington State Archives

INTRODUCTION: "YOUNG LADY, DO YOU MEAN TO CALL ME A LIAR?"
   1. Transcript of Record at 1, 42, Rock v. Carney, 185 N.W. 798 (Mich. 1921), Case File 29600,
Box 54, RG 96–175, AM. Hereafter, this transcript will be referred to by the last name of witness,
page number.
   2. "The Weather," *Bay City Times Tribune*, Oct. 31, 1918; "The Weather," *Saginaw News*, Oct.
31, 1918.

3. To get a sense of the St. Louis downtown architecture, see David McMacken, *A St. Louis Album: A Pictorial History of St. Louis, Michigan* (St. Louis, MI: Middle of the Mitten Association, 2012), 156–68.

4. "St. Louis, Michigan," sheet 4, 1910, Sanborn Fire Insurance Maps, 1867–1970—Michigan; "St. Louis, Michigan," sheet 2, 1924, Sanborn Fire Insurance Maps, 1867–1970—Michigan.

5. McCall, 2.

6. "Ithaca," *Saginaw News*, Aug. 11, 1918.

7. 1920 US Census, St. Louis, Gratiot County, MI, sheet 26, family 877, lines 3–5, Mar. 5, 1920; McCall, 15.

8. McCall, 17–18.

9. Ibid., 16.

10. McCall, 2–3. Though a lawyer asked McCall, during her civil trial against several government officials, "What did Mr. Martin say to you if anything?" the defendants' lawyers objected to the question, and the judge sustained the objection.

11. McCall, 1, 17; Van Norman, 42. The garage's owner was thirty-one-year-old Glenn Kane. 1920 US Census, St. Louis, Gratiot County, MI, sheet 24, family 618, lines 22–25, Jan. 28, 1920.

12. McCall, 17; Van Norman, 42.

13. Van Norman, 42.

14. McCall, 3; Van Norman, 42, 44.

15. 1920 US Census, Alma, Gratiot County, MI, p. 20A, family 209, lines 46–47, Jan. 15, 1920. Carney's anti-influenza methods will be discussed in ch. 6.

16. McCall, 3–4; Van Norman, 42.

17. Van Norman, 44.

18. McCall, 4; Van Norman, 43.

19. McCall, 4.

20. Van Norman, 43.

21. McCall, 4.

22. McCall, 18, 89; Van Norman, 42.

23. Using one's fingers would have been standard procedure at the time. See Letter from Katharine Bushnell to Maurice Gregory, quoted in Maurice Gregory, Appended Papers on Venereal Disease Control, Nov. 1918, Box 123, 3AMS/D/51/04, AMSHR.

24. McCall, 28.

25. McCall, 5, 18, 89; Van Norman, 42–43, 48.

26. McCall 5, 18–19; Van Norman, 43.

27. McCall, 5. In Minnie's recollection, Nina replied, "Yes, Dr. Carney, if you say I have a disease." Van Norman, 45.

28. McCall, 5, 19–21; Van Norman, 44.

29. "Copy of Large Red Card," Michigan State Board of Health, Box 124, 3AMS/D/51/05, AMSHR; McCall, 5, 19–20; Van Norman, 44.

30. McCall, 5, 19–20; Van Norman, 44.

31. McCall, 6, 20.

32. Ibid., 6–7.

33. Mary Macey Dietzler, *Detention Houses and Reformatories as Protective Social Agencies, in the Campaign of the United States Government Against Venereal Diseases* (Interdepartmental Social Hygiene Board, 1922), 75.

34. State ex rel. Kennedy v. Head, 185 S.W.2d 530, 530 (Tenn. 1945).

35. See Scott Wasserman Stern, "The Long American Plan: The U.S. Government's Campaign Against Venereal Disease and Its Carriers," *Harvard Journal of Law & Gender* 38 (2015): 378–79 and appendices.

36. "The Weather," *Bay City Times Tribune*, June 1, 1920.

CHAPTER 1: "WILLING TO GO TO JAIL FOR SUCH A CAUSE"

1. Josephine Butler, *Personal Reminiscences of a Great Crusade* (London: Horace Marshall, 1896), 48–49.

2. Butler speaking at Nottingham, Mar. 8, 1870, reprinted in *Josephine Butler and the Prostitution Campaigns: Diseases of the Body Politic, Vol. II: The Ladies' Appeal and Protest*, ed. Jane Jordan and Ingrid Sharp (London: Routledge, 2003), 114–15.

3. Jane Jordan, *Josephine Butler* (London: John Murray, 2001), 112–16.

4. Ibid., 110.

5. Charles Walter Clarke, *Taboo: The Story of the Pioneers of Social Hygiene* (Washington, DC: Public Affairs Press, 1961), 17.

6. Butler, *Personal Reminiscences of a Great Crusade*, 44–51.

7. Jill Harsin, *Policing Prostitution in Nineteenth-Century Paris* (Princeton, NJ: Princeton University Press, 1985), xvi. On Napoleon's virginity, see Oscar Browning, *Napoleon: The First Phase* (London: John Lane, 1905), 287, quoted in Andrew Roberts, *Napoleon: A Life* (New York: Viking, 2014), 23; F. M. Kircheisen, ed., *Napoleon's Autobiography* (New York: Duffield, 1931), 22–23.

8. Though he would later bear the lion's share of the blame for this policy, Napoleon did not actually create it. See Katharine Bushnell, "Plain Words to Plain People," 1918, Box 122, 3AMS/D/51/01, AMSHR; Katharine Bushnell, "The Medical Protest Against the Compulsory Treatment of Women," *Light* 147 (Jul.–Aug. 1922): 44; Edith Houghton Hooker, "The Page Bill," *Survey* 24 (Aug. 13, 1910): 710; Clarke, *Taboo*, 14; Katherine Anthony, "Feminism in Foreign Countries: The Woman Movement in France," *Suffragist* 9.1 (Jan.–Feb. 1921): 357; Stephanie A. Limoncelli, "International Voluntary Associations, Local Social Movements and State Paths to the Abolition of Regulated Prostitution in Europe, 1875–1950," *International Sociology* 21.1 (Jan. 2006): 33. Nonetheless, Napoleon's authoritarian, strictly secular dictates and his faith in public hygiene paved the way for the policy of regulation and examination, and he approved of it; he trusted that it would protect his soldiers, and he would later expand the policy into virtually every place his armies conquered. In spite of his personal distaste for prostitutes, the emperor firmly believed that their profession was not only inevitable, but that it served a valuable societal purpose. "Without them men would assault decent girls in the streets," he wrote in his memoirs. Kircheisen, *Napoleon's Autobiography*, 155.

9. Yves Guyot, *Prostitution Under the Regulation System: French and English: A Study in Social Physiology*, trans. Edgar Truman (London: G. Redway, 1884), 29; Julia Christine Scriven Miller, "The 'Romance of Regulation': The Movement Against State-Regulated Prostitution in France, 1871–1946," PhD diss., New York University, 2000, 6–7; Harsin, *Policing Prostitution in Nineteenth-Century Paris*, xvi, 7, 10, 90, 194–95, 212–15, 256, 266; David Pivar, *Purity Crusade: Sexual Morality and Social Control, 1868–1900* (Westport, CT: Greenwood Press, 1973), 53; Jordan, *Josephine Butler*, 150–51; Vern Bullough, *The History of Prostitution* (New Hyde Park, NY: University Books, 1964), 167. See also David Wright, "State Regulation of Vice in Nineteenth-Century France," master's thesis, University of Wisconsin, 1979, 71–81; Alain Corbin, *Women for Hire: Prostitution and Sexuality in France After 1850*, trans. Alan Sheridan (Cambridge, MA: Harvard University Press, 1990), 89–93, 228.

10. John Parascandola, *Sex, Sin, and Science: A History of Syphilis in America* (Westport, CT: Praeger, 2008), 16–18.

11. Allan Brandt, *No Magic Bullet: A Social History of Venereal Disease in the United States Since 1880* (New York: Oxford University Press, 1985), 11–12; Parascandola, *Sex, Sin, and Science*, 16–18, 57–58, 77–78; James F. Gardner Jr., "Microbes and Morality: The Social Hygiene Crusade in New York City, 1892–1917," PhD diss., Indiana University, 1974, 178–79; Philippa Levine, *Prostitution, Race, and Politics: Policing Venereal Disease in the British Empire* (New York: Routledge, 2003), 123; Nicole Hahn Rafter, *Partial Justice: Women in State Prisons, 1800–1935* (Boston: Northeastern University Press, 1985), 218n49.

12. Linda Kollar and Brian Shmaefsky, *Gonorrhea* (Philadelphia: Chelsea House Publishers, 2005), 21.

13. See "Gonorrhea—CDC Fact Sheet," Centers for Disease Control and Prevention, Oct. 14, 2015, http://www.cdc.gov/std/gonorrhea/stdfact-gonorrhea.htm.

14. Herbert Shelton, *Syphilis: Werewolf of Medicine* (1962; Pomeroy, WA: Health Research Books, 1996), 16–20; Katherine Crawford, *European Sexualities, 1400–1800* (Cambridge, UK: Cambridge University Press, 2007), 129–35; John Mann, *The Elusive Magic Bullet: The Search for the Perfect Drug* (New York: Oxford University Press, 1999), 8–9. For a good discussion of the historiography surrounding the origins of syphilis, see Kristina Oldenburg, "'All the Prostitutes May Be Made Subject to Supervision and the Spread of Disease Infinitely Reduced': Implications of Alexandre Parent-Duchâtelet and William Acton's Regulatory Proposals," master's thesis, Simon Fraser University, 2006, 4n12. For more on the contested history of syphilis, see Mario M. Castro et al., "Thoracic Aortic Aneurysm in a Pre-Columbian (210 BC) Inhabitant of Northern Chile: Implications for the Origins of Syphilis," *International Journal of Paleopathology* 13 (June 2016): 20–26; Kristin N. Harper et al., "On the Origin of the Treponematoses: A Phylogenetic Approach," *Neglected Tropical Diseases* (Jan. 15, 2008), http://journals.plos.org/plosntds/article?id=10.1371/journal.pntd.0000148; George J. Armelagos et al., "The Science Behind Pre-Columbian Evidence of Syphilis in Europe: Research by Documentary," *Evolutionary Anthropology* 21.2 (Mar.–Apr. 2012): 50–57. These studies were excellently synthesized in Cari Romm, "A New Skeleton and an Old Debate About Syphilis," *Atlantic*, Feb. 18, 2016, http://www.theatlantic.com/health/archive/2016/02/the-neverending-story-of-the-origins-of-syphilis/463401.

15. See "Syphilis—CDC Fact Sheet," Centers for Disease Control and Prevention, Nov. 12, 2015, http://www.cdc.gov/std/syphilis/stdfact-syphilis.htm.

16. Brandt, *No Magic Bullet*, 9.

17. Petra de Vries, "'The Shadow of Contagion': Gender, Syphilis and the Regulation of Prostitution in the Netherlands, 1870–1914," in *Sex, Sin and Suffering: Venereal Disease and European Society Since 1870*, ed. Roger Davidson and Lesley A. Hall (London: Routledge, 2001), 44–47.

18. See International Abolitionist Federation, *Actes du Congrés de Genéve* (Neuchatel: Bureau du Bulletin Continental, 1878), ch. 1; Limoncelli, "International Voluntary Associations," 35.

19. Butler, *Personal Reminiscences of a Great Crusade*, 146–47.

20. Harsin, *Policing Prostitution in Nineteenth-Century Paris*, 205–6 and also 114–24, 142–48, 207–12, 229.

21. Ibid., 30. See also Corbin, *Women for Hire*, 104–7.

22. Corbin, *Women for Hire*, 228.

23. Sadly, the race of the women arrested under the French Plan has been woefully understudied. Miller, "The 'Romance of Regulation,'" 8–9; Corbin, *Women for Hire*, 228; Bullough, *The History of Prostitution*, 167.

24. Jordan, *Josephine Butler*, 157. Significantly, the examination for venereal disease (at the time syphilis and gonorrhea were believed to be one and the same) was often inaccurate, depending as it did on hasty visual scrutiny of the genitals. This was before the organisms that caused either infection had been isolated, so physicians could not examine slides under a microscope or perform a blood test; rather, they looked for telltale symptoms. Yet many conditions (some of them benign) can cause bumps or rashes or excretions, and, furthermore, syphilis and gonorrhea can present variably and asymptomatically.

25. Subsequent acts passed in 1866 and 1869. Paul McHugh, *Prostitution and Victorian Social Reform* (New York: St. Martin's Press, 1980), 35–38; Judith Walkowitz, *Prostitution and Victorian Society: Women, Class, and the State* (Cambridge, UK: Cambridge University Press, 1980), 74–77.

26. Walkowitz, *Prostitution and Victorian Society*, 159, 178. See also McHugh, *Prostitution and Victorian Social Reform*, 39–52

27. Walkowitz, *Prostitution and Victorian Society*, 61, 201–2, 214.

28. Ibid., 1–6.

29. "The Ladies' Appeal and Protest," *Daily News*, Dec. 31, 1869, reprinted in Jordan and Sharp, *Josephine Butler and the Prostitution Campaigns, Vol. II*, 45–50; Butler, *Personal Reminiscences of a Great Crusade*, 10–11; Clarke, *Taboo*, 14–16.

30. See Parascandola, *Sex, Sin, and Science*, 36; Pivar, *Purity Crusade*, 55–90.

31. Butler, *Personal Reminiscences of a Great Crusade*, 10–11, 44–51; Clarke, *Taboo*, 14–17.

32. See John C. Burnham, "The Social Evil Ordinance—A Social Experiment in Nineteenth-Century St. Louis," *Bulletin of the Missouri Historical Society* 27 (1971): 204–7; John C. Burnham, "Medical Inspection of Prostitutes in America in the Nineteenth Century: The St. Louis Experiment and Its Sequel," *Bulletin of the History of Medicine* 45 (1971): 205–7; Duane Sneddeker, "Regulating Vice: Prostitution and the St. Louis Social Evil," *Gateway Heritage* 11.2 (Fall 1990): 23–24; James Wunsch, "Prostitution and Public Policy: From Regulation to Suppression, 1858–1920," PhD diss., University of Chicago, 1976, 42–48; James Wunsch, "The Social Evil Ordinance," *American Heritage* 33 (Feb. 1982): 53–54.

33. Burnham, "Medical Inspection of Prostitutes in America in the Nineteenth Century," 209; Burnham, "The Social Evil Ordinance," 213. For a discussion of attempts at regulationism in all of the following cities, see International Abolitionist Federation, *Actes du Congrés de Genéve*, 203–24.

34. Henry J. Wilson and James P. Gledstone, *Report of a visit to the United States, as delegates from the British, continental, and general federation for the abolition of government regulation of prostitution* (Sheffield, UK: Leader and Sons, 1876), 3–4.

35. Marion Horan, "Trafficking in Danger: Working-Class Women and Narratives of Sexual Danger in English and United States Anti-Prostitution Campaigns, 1875–1914," PhD diss., SUNY Binghamton, 2006, 46–47.

36. Pivar, *Purity Crusade*, 57–58; Burnham, "The Social Evil Ordinance," 214.

37. Wilson and Gledstone, *Report of a visit to the United States*, 4–5.

38. Burnham, "The Social Evil Ordinance," 214–15; ibid., 5.

39. Wilson and Gledstone, *Report of a visit to the United States*, 5–6.

40. Neil Larry Shumsky, "Tacit Acceptance: Respectable Americans and Segregated Prostitution, 1870–1910," *Journal of Social History* 19.4 (Summer 1986): 665.

41. James R. McGovern, "'Sporting Life on the Line': Prostitution in Progressive Era Pensacola," *Florida Historical Quarterly* 54.2 (Oct. 1975): 134; Shumsky, "Tacit Acceptance," 666–67; Neil Larry Shumsky and Larry M. Springer, "San Francisco's Zone of Prostitution, 1880–1934," *Journal of Historical Geography* 7.1 (1981): 74–76; Ivan Light, "From Vice District to Tourist Attraction: The Moral Career of American Chinatowns, 1880–1940," *Pacific Historical Review* 43.3 (Aug. 1974): 368–76; Wunsch, "Prostitution and Public Policy," 159; Timothy J. Gilfoyle, *City of Eros: New York City, Prostitution, and the Commercialization of Sex, 1790–1920* (New York: Norton, 1992), 209–10.

42. Andrew Michael Bourn, "Secularizing San Francisco: Religion, Prostitution, and Public Policy, 1848–1917," PhD diss., University of California, Santa Barbara, 2012, 26–27.

43. Mara L. Keire, "Vice in American Cities, 1890–1925," PhD diss., Johns Hopkins University, 2001, 63–64.

44. See Wilson and Gledstone, *Report of a visit to the United States*.

45. Wunsch, "The Social Evil Ordinance," 54–55; Burnham, "Medical Inspection of Prostitutes in America in the Nineteenth Century," 208–10; Wunsch, "Prostitution and Public Policy," 50–56. The "two historians" referred to are John D'Emilio and Estelle B. Freedman, authors of *Intimate Matters: A History of Sexuality in America* (New York: Harper & Row, 1988), 139.

46. David Pivar, *Purity and Hygiene: Women, Prostitution, and the "American Plan," 1900–1930* (Westport, CT: Greenwood Press, 2002), 3.

47. In 1880, a crop of "new men"—radicals devoted to the repeal of the CD Acts—had been elected to Parliament, and they infiltrated the power structure of the Liberal Party, effectively

converting its members to the cause. At the same time, radical workingmen in the East End and middle-class women in the West End both increased their lobbying efforts. These two forces led to the suspension. McHugh, *Prostitution and Victorian Social Reform*, 263; Walkowitz, *Prostitution and Victorian Society*, 98–99. See also McHugh, *Prostitution and Victorian Social Reform*, chs. 5–9.

48. "Weather Indications," *Jackson Citizen-Patriot*, Mar. 30, 1883.

49. Certificate of Death, John Henry McCall, Bethany, Gratiot, MI, June 18, 1906, *Michigan, Deaths and Burials, 1800–1995*, FHL film number 985692.

50. 1880 US Census, Bethany Township, Gratiot County, MI, p. 455, family 66, lines 20–31, June 8, 1880.

51. John H. McCall, Oath of Citizenship, Gratiot County, MI, Mar. 30, 1883, Reel 8770, volume 2, p. 246, Naturalization Records, RG 94–341, AM.

52. David McMacken, *St. Louis at 150: The Story of the Middle of the Mitten* (St. Louis: Concept Communications, 2003), 5.

53. Willard Davis Tucker, *Gratiot County, Michigan: Historical, Biographical, Statistical* (Saginaw, MI: Seemann & Peters, 1913), 226.

54. 1880 United States Non-Population Census, Productions of Agriculture in Bethany Township, Gratiot County, MI, p. 5, farm 4, June 8, 1880.

55. Addie E. Hill, "Reflections," p. 11, 1980, AEHC.

56. Kathleen Anne Mapes, "Defining the Boundaries: Family Farmers, Migrant Labor, Industrial Agriculture, and the State in the Rural Midwest, 1898–1938," PhD diss., University of Illinois, Urbana-Champaign, 2000, 26–27; Glenn Worth Britton, "'Improving' the Middle Landscape: Conservation and Social Change in Rural Southern Michigan, 1890 to 1940," PhD diss., UCLA, 2005, 226–27; Tucker, *Gratiot County, Michigan*, 27, 225–26, 924, 927–28.

57. 1880 US Census, Bethany Township, Gratiot County, MI, p. 455, family 63, lines 10–13, June 8, 1880. This census record suggests she was born in 1870 or 1871, but other records contradict this. A later census records Minnie as having married at the age of 18, and Minnie's testimony suggested that she had married in about 1898, which would put her birth at about 1880. This is supported by her obituary. See 1930 US Census, Alma, Gratiot County, MI, p. 5A, family 91, lines 37–39, Apr. 10, 1930; "Mrs. Minnie S. Van Norman," *Saginaw News*, Feb. 2, 1938. Nonetheless, an 1894 census record lists Abraham and Minnie McCall living together in Bethany Township, and lists Minnie's age as twenty-three, meaning she would have been born in 1870 or 1871. This presents the reader with two possibilities: either she and Abraham ran away together when she was shockingly young (and ran only to an adjoining farm), or she married at a more conventional age and was older than she later led people (including court officials) to believe. (She told the court in 1920 that she had married "about twenty-two years" ago, which would be 1898, or four years after she and Abraham were listed as living together, sharing a last name.) 1894 Michigan Census, Bethany Township, Gratiot County, MI, p. 220, family 2, lines 3–4, June 29, 1894.

58. Tucker, *Gratiot County, Michigan*, 1343–48.

59. Howard Jacob Karger and Joanne Levine, "Social Work Practice with European Immigrants," 168, in *Social Work Practice with Immigrants and Refugees*, ed. Pallassana R. Balgopal, (New York: Columbia University Press, 2000); Leonard Dinnerstein and David M. Reimers, *Ethnic Americans: A History of Immigration* (New York: Columbia University Press, 2009), 56.

60. Karger and Levine, "Social Work Practice with European Immigrants," 168; Dinnerstein and Reimers, *Ethnic Americans*, 56–58.

61. Brandt, *No Magic Bullet*, 20–21; Parascandola, *Sex, Sin, and Science*, 37–38.

62. Committee of Fifteen, *The Social Evil, With Special Reference to Conditions Existing in the City of New York* (New York: G.P. Putnam's Sons, 1902), 196. Initially, the term had been a synonym for wage slavery, used by activists decrying the hard labor of the working class. Hugo transformed it into a usage it still retains today.

63. Horan, "Trafficking in Danger," 112–38; Jordan, *Josephine Butler*, 189–92.

64. The quotations come from Kelli Ann McCoy, "Claiming Victims: The Mann Act, Gender, and Class in the American West, 1910–1930s," PhD diss., University of California, San Diego, 2010, 39–40. See Egal Feldman, "Prostitution, the Alien Woman and the Progressive Imagination, 1910–1915," *American Quarterly* 19.2 (Summer 1967): 192–206; David J. Langum, *Crossing Over the Line: Legislating Morality and the Mann Act* (Chicago: University of Chicago Press, 1994), 28–47; Mara L. Keire, *For Business & Pleasure: Red-Light Districts and the Regulation of Vice in the United States, 1890–1933* (Baltimore: Johns Hopkins University Press, 2010), 87–88; Mara L. Keire, "The Vice Trust: A Reinterpretation of the White Slavery Scare in the United States, 1907–1917," *Journal of Social History* 35.1 (Autumn 2001): 5–6; Rafter, *Partial Justice*, 54; James A. Monroe, *Hellfire Nation: The Politics of Sin in American History* (New Haven, CT: Yale University Press, 2003), 268–70; Wunsch, "Prostitution and Public Policy," 126–27; Hiroyuki Matsubara, "Unsettled Controversies: The Anti-Prostitution Movement and the Transformation of American Political Culture, 1910–1919," PhD diss., University of Santa Cruz, 2005, 21–38; Mary de Young, "Help, I'm Being Held Captive! The White Slave Fairy Tale of the Progressive Era," *Journal of American Culture* 6.1 (Spring 1983): 97–99; Pamela Roby, "Politics and Prostitution: A Case Study of the Formulation, Enforcement and Judicial Administration of the New York State Penal Laws on Prostitution, 1870–1970," PhD diss., New York

University, 1971, 133; McCoy, "Claiming Victims," 15–40; Barbara Meil Hobson, *Uneasy Virtue: The Politics of Prostitution and the American Reform* (New York: Basic Books, 1987), 143.

65. William T. Stead, "The Maiden Tribute of Modern Babylon I," *Pall Mall Gazette*, Jul. 6, 1885.

66. William T. Stead, "The Maiden Tribute of Modern Babylon IV," *Pall Mall Gazette*, Jul. 10, 1885.

67. William T. Stead, *Why I Went to Prison*, 1910, p. 7, 3AMS/B/11/12, AMSHR; Bridget O'Donnell, *Inspector Minahan Makes a Stand, or The Missing Girls of England* (London: Picador, 2012), 171, 216–17; Walkowitz, *Prostitution and Victorian Society*, 246; Mary Odem, *Delinquent Daughters: Protecting and Policing Adolescent Female Sexuality in the United States, 1885–1920* (Chapel Hill: University of North Carolina Press, 1995), 12.

68. Sharon D'Cruze and Louise A. Jackson, *Women, Crime and Justice in England Since 1660* (London: Palgrave MacMillan, 2009), 73; Josephine Butler, *Ladies National Association Circular*, Aug. 17, 1885, reprinted in Jane Jordan and Ingrid Sharp, eds., *Josephine Butler and the Prostitution Campaigns, Vol. IV: Child Prostitution and the Age of Consent* (New York: Routledge, 2003), 274–76; Walkowitz, *Prostitution and Victorian Society*, 99.

69. Letter from Josephine Butler to Stanley Butler, Apr. 25, 1886, reprinted in Jane Jordan and Ingrid Sharp, eds., *Josephine Butler and the Prostitution Campaigns: Diseases of the Body Politic, Vol. III: The Constitution Violated: The Parliamentary Campaign* (London: Routledge, 2003), 99.

70. Judith R. Walkowitz, "Male Vice and Female Virtue: Feminism and the Politics of Prostitution in Nineteenth-Century Britain," in *Powers of Desire: The Politics of Sexuality*, ed. Ann Snitow, Christine Stansell, and Sharon Thompson (New York: Monthly Review Press, 1983), 425–27.

71. The amendment also criminalized homosexual sex, a proscription that would last until 1967. Walkowitz, *Prostitution and Victorian Society*, 211. Also, see ibid., 242–46.

72. McCall, 1, 15; Van Norman, 41. We know they moved after May 6, as a census taker encountered the McCalls in St. Louis on that date. See 1910 US Census, Bethany Township, Gratiot County, MI, p. 18A, family 307, lines 5–8, May 6, 1910.

73. US Bureau of the Census, *Census of Population and Housing, 1910: vol 2 Population: Reports by States Alabama–Montana* (Washington, DC: Government Printing Office, 1910), 908.

74. Abe McCall, 1901, roll 59, *U.S., Indexed County Land Ownership Maps, 1860–1918*. On the location of the railroad, see the map on Tucker, *Gratiot County, Michigan*, 225.

75. See 1930 US Census, Alma, Gratiot County, MI, p. 5A, family 91, lines 37–39, Apr. 10, 1930.

76. John McCall, 1901, roll 59, *U.S., Indexed County Land Ownership Maps, 1860–1918*; John Scott, 1901, roll 59, *U.S., Indexed County Land Ownership Maps, 1860–1918*.

77. 1894 Michigan Census, Bethany Township, Gratiot County, MI, p. 220, family 2, lines 3–4, June 20, 1894. In this census, Minnie and Abraham are listed living together, without John (while John appears in the 1900 census); 1900 US Census, Bethany Township, Gratiot County, MI, supervisor's district no. 11, enumeration district no. 46, sheet 15, family 315, lines 24–26, June 25, 1900. John's wife, Barbara (nee List) had died in 1892. Certificate of Death, Barbara McCall, Bethany, Gratiot, MI, Apr. 5, 1892, *Michigan, Deaths and Burials Index, 1867–1995*, FHL film number 985691. John died on June 26, 1906, at the age of seventy-three. See Tucker, *Gratiot County, Michigan*, 243.

78. McCall, 1.

79. Certificate of Birth, Vern McCall, Bethany Township, Gratiot County, MI, Feb. 15, 1902, *Michigan Births, 1867–1902*, FHL film number 2363037.

80. Van Norman, 41.

81. 1910 US Census, Bethany Township, Gratiot County, MI, sheet 18A, family 307, lines 5–8, May 6, 1910.

82. Van Norman, 41.

83. Hill, "Reflections," 2, 5.

84. Ibid., 4.

85. Ibid., 11.

86. Elizabeth A. Ramey, *Class, Gender, and the American Family Farm in the 20th Century* (New York: Routledge, 2014), 42–51; John J. Fry, *The Farm Press, Reform and Rural Change, 1895–1920* (New York: Routledge, 2005), 140; Pamela Riney-Kehrberg, *Childhood on the Farm: Work, Play, and Coming of Age in the Midwest* (Lawrence: University Press of Kansas), 36–42; David B. Danbom, *Born in the Country: A History of Rural America* (Baltimore: Johns Hopkins University Press), 90.

87. Pamela Riney-Kehrberg, "Rural Childhood and Youth," 141, in *The Routledge History of Rural America*, ed. Pamela Riney-Kehrberg (New York: Routledge, 2016).

88. Anne Effland, "Rural Labor," in Riney-Kehrberg, *The Routledge History of Rural America*, 319.

89. "The Life of an Illinois Farmer's Wife," in *The Female Experience: An American Documentary*, ed. Gerda Lerner (New York: Oxford University Press, 1977), 126–29.

90. Riney-Kehrberg, *Childhood on the Farm*, 47.

91. Ramey, *Class, Gender, and the American Family Farm in the 20th Century*, 45.

92. Sara Egge, "'When We Get to Voting': Rural Women, Community, Gender, and Woman Suffrage in the Midwest," PhD diss., Iowa State University, 2012, 1–20, 70–71, 76. On overt political

activity, see Mary Jo Wagner, "Farms, Families, and Reform: Women in the Farmers' Alliance and Populist Party," PhD diss., University of Oregon, 1986.

93. Hill, "Reflections," 14.

94. Rachel Erin Kleinschmidt, "'What to Do with Our Girls': Prescriptive Literature and the Girl Problem in the Rural Midwest, 1865–1900," PhD diss., Iowa State University, 2013.

95. Ibid., 227.

96. Joan M. Jensen, "The Death of Rosa: Sexuality in Rural America," *Agricultural History* 67.4 (Autumn 1993): 6–8.

97. McCall, 1; Van Norman, 41.

98. McMacken, *St. Louis at 150*, 19–22; Tucker, *Gratiot County, Michigan*, 925–27, 987.

99. Van Norman, 41.

100. "County Correspondence: Emerson and Bethany," *St. Louis Leader*, Mar. 3, 1910, CHL. The first telephone line in the county had arrived in 1878, in St. Louis. See Tucker, *Gratiot County, Michigan*, 1340. For more on that telephone line, see Hill, "Reflections," 10.

101. Mark Thomas Connelly, *The Response to Prostitution in the Progressive Era* (Chapel Hill: University of North Carolina Press, 1980), 31.

102. Jenny Barker Devine, "Rural Women," 129, in Riney-Kehrberg, *The Routledge History of Rural America*.

103. Ruth M. Alexander, *The "Girl Problem": Female Sexual Delinquency in New York, 1900–1930* (Ithaca, NY: Cornell University Press, 1995), 18–21; Odem, *Delinquent Daughters*, 24.

104. Joanne J. Meyerowitz, *Women Adrift: Independent Wage Earners in Chicago, 1880–1930* (Chicago: University of Chicago Press, 1988), xx, 5, 102.

105. Cynthia M. Blair, *I've Got to Make My Livin': Black Women's Sex Work in Turn-of-the-Century Chicago* (Chicago: University of Chicago Press, 2010), 27–29; Elizabeth Alice Clement, *Love for Sale: Courting, Treating, and Prostitution in New York City, 1900–1945* (Chapel Hill: University of North Carolina Press, 2006), 5, 78–86; Hobson, *Uneasy Virtue*, 35–36, 88–94; Ruth Rosen, *The Lost Sisterhood: Prostitution in America, 1900–1918* (Baltimore: Johns Hopkins University Press, 1982), 79–81.

106. Clement, *Love for Sale*, 1; Blair, *I've Got to Make My Livin'*, 3, 11, 48. For the quote from the Kentucky woman, see Pauline Tabor, *Memoirs of the Madam on Clay Street* (New York: Touchstone, 1971), 23, 39. For the laughter and quote from the crowd of prostitutes, see "Women of Redlight District Make Plea for Fair Play," *San Francisco Chronicle*, Jan. 26, 1917. For more on this shifting dynamic, see Meyerowitz, *Women Adrift*; Alexander, *The "Girl Problem"*; Kathy L. Peiss, "'Charity Girls' and City Pleasures: Historical Notes on Working-Class Sexuality, 1880–1920," in Snitow et al., *Powers of Desire*; Kathy L. Peiss, *Cheap Amusements: Working Women and Leisure in Turn-of-the-Century New York* (Philadelphia: Temple University Press, 1987); Daniel Scott Smith, "The Dating of the American Sexual Revolution: Evidence and Interpretation," in *The American Family in Social-Historical Perspective*, ed. Michael Gordon (New York: St. Martin's, 1978); Rosen, *The Lost Sisterhood*; Odem, *Delinquent Daughters*; Connelly, *The Response to Prostitution in the Progressive Era*.

107. See ch. 2 in Connelly, *The Response to Prostitution in the Progressive Era*.

108. See Maude E. Miner, *Slavery of Prostitution: A Plea for Emancipation* (New York: Mac-Millan, 1916), 144.

109. Pivar, *Purity Crusade*, 91.

110. For an excellent example, see Madison Ivan, "'The City's Shame': Prostitution in Cleveland, 1866–1915," master's thesis, Case Western Reserve University, Mar. 2014, 46–49. Ivan cited Daniel Kerr, "'The Reign of Wickedness': The Changing Structures of Prostitution, Gambling and Political Protection in Cleveland from the Progressive Era to the Great Depression," master's thesis, Case Western Reserve University, 1998. Also see more classic studies, including Rosen, *The Lost Sisterhood*, 32; Clement, *Love for Sale*, 134–38.

111. Pivar, *Purity and Hygiene*, 25; Corbin, *Women for Hire*, 88, 99–101, 246–52.

112. Paul de Kruif, *Microbe Hunters* (New York: Harcourt, Brace, 1926), 326–32, 345–48; Thomas Hager, *The Demon Under the Microscope: From Battlefield Hospitals to Nazi Labs, One Doctor's Heroic Search for the World's First Miracle Drug* (New York: Harmony Books, 2006), 78–84; John Parascandola, "The Theoretical Basis of Paul Ehrlich's Chemotherapy," *Journal of the History of Medicine* (Jan. 1981): 24–25; Clarke, *Taboo*, 45–46; Nancy Tomes, *The Gospel of Germs* (Cambridge, MA: Harvard University Press, 1998), 252; Allan M. Brandt, "The Syphilis Epidemic and Its Relation to AIDS," *Science* 239.4838 (Jan. 22, 1988): 376; Martha Marquardt, *Paul Ehrlich* (New York: Henry Schuman, 1951), 188–206.

113. See Paul Starr, *The Social Transformation of American Medicine* (New York: Basic Books, 1982), 79–145; Corbin, *Women for Hire*, 246–52.

114. George E. Worthington and Ruth Topping, *Specialized Courts Dealing with Sex Delinquency: A Study of the Procedure in Chicago, Boston, Philadelphia and New York* (New York: F. H. Hitchcock, 1925), 293.

115. Alice L. Woodbridge, "Section 79 and Its Career," *Vigilance* 24.8 (Aug.–Sept. 1911): 9–10; Val Marie Johnson, "Defining 'Social Evil': Moral Citizenship and Governance in New York City, 1890–1920," PhD diss., New York University, 2002, 507, 519–20; Judith Lee Vaupen Joseph, "The

Nafkeh and the Lady: Jews, Prostitutes and Progressives in New York City, 1900–1930," PhD diss., SUNY Stony Brook, 1986, 142; Gardner, "Microbes and Morality," 176, 190; Edwin R. A. Seligman, ed., *The Social Evil, with Special Reference to Conditions Existing in the City of New York*, 2nd ed. (New York: G. P. Putnam's Sons, 1912), 232; Pivar, *Purity and Hygiene*, 104.

116. Pivar, *Purity and Hygiene*, 102. See also Gardner, "Microbes and Morality," 139–40.

117. "Suffragettes Start Fight on New Court," *New York Times*, Sept. 2, 1910.

118. Cooper Union meeting, "Resolutions," Jan. 19, 1911, Folder 6.3, Box 91, LDWP.

119. Sarah Emerson, "Working of the Page Law," *New York Tribune*, Mar. 10, 1911.

120. "Report on Page Law Out," *New York Tribune*, Mar. 1, 1911.

121. Matsubara, "Unsettled Controversies," 89.

122. "Ehrlich's Remedy a Medical Wonder," *New York Times*, Sept. 11, 1910; Gardner, "Microbes and Morality," 176; "Experience with '606' (Salvarsan)," *American Journal of Clinical Medicine* 18.2 (Feb. 1911): 219–21.

123. Exhibit A, Case File, People ex rel. Barone v. Fox, 202 N.Y. 616 (N.Y. 1911), Series J2002, NYSL; Miner, *Slavery of Prostitution*, 185–86, 225; Johnson, "Defining 'Social Evil,'" 519–20; Gardner, "Microbes and Morality," 199–200, 282; George E. Worthington and Ruth Topping, "The Women's Day Court of Manhattan and the Bronx, New York City," *Journal of Social Hygiene* 8.4 (Oct. 1922): 473; Henry Bischoff, Opinion, and Bertha Rembaugh, Demurrer to Return, Case File, People ex rel. Barone v. Fox, 202 N.Y. 616 (N.Y. 1911), Series J2002, NYSL; "Women Win in Court," *New York Times*, Nov. 26, 1910; Woodbridge, "Section 79 and Its Career," 11; People ex rel. Barone v. Fox, 202 N.Y. 616 (N.Y. 1911); Woodbridge, "Section 79 and Its Career," 12–13; "The End of Clause 79," *Survey* 26 (Jul. 8, 1911): 552–53; "The Page Bill," *American Journal of Nursing* 11.12 (Sept. 1911): 1002–3.

124. Matsubara, "Unsettled Controversies," 129; Untitled transcript, p. 1, Red-Light Abatement—Municipal Clinic for Women Folder, Box 120, FHP.

125. Julius Rosenstirn, *Our Nation's Health Endangered by Poisonous Infection Through the Social Malady: The Protective Work of the Municipal Clinic of San Francisco and its Fight for Existence* (San Francisco: Town Talk Press, 1913), 19–22; Brenda Elaine Pillors, "The Criminalization of Prostitution in the United States: The Case of San Francisco, 1854–1919," PhD diss., UC Berkeley, 1982, 149; Shumsky and Springer, "San Francisco's zone of prostitution," 81–82; Matsubara, "Unsettled Controversies," 129–130; Pivar, *Purity and Hygiene*, 107; Nancy Moore Rockafellar, "Making the World Safe for Soldiers of Democracy: Patriotism, Public Health and Venereal Disease Control on the West Coast, 1910–1919," PhD diss., University of Washington, 1990, 113–20; Franklin Hichborn, "The Anti-Vice Movement in California: I. Suppression," *Social Hygiene* 6.2 (Apr. 1920): 214; Untitled transcript, pp. 2–3, Red-Light Abatement—Municipal Clinic for Women Folder, Box 120, FHP.

126. Rockafellar, "Making the World Safe for Soldiers of Democracy," 120–21.

127. Matsubara, "Unsettled Controversies," 170–216; Rockafellar, "Making the World Safe for Soldiers of Democracy," 122–23; Josh Sides, *Erotic City: Sexual Revolutions and the Making of Modern San Francisco* (New York: Oxford University Press, 2009), 22–23.

128. Untitled transcript, pp. 2–4, Red-Light Abatement—Municipal Clinic for Women Folder, Box 120, FHP.

129. See Rosenstirn, *Our Nation's Health*, 38–43; "Board Sanctions Municipal Clinic," *San Francisco Chronicle*, June 10, 1913; *San Francisco Chronicle*, June 12, 1913; Hichborn, "The Anti-Vice Movement in California," 214.

130. See Sides, *Erotic City*, 22–23; Shumsky and Springer, "San Francisco's Zone of Prostitution," 84–85; Herbert Asbury, *The Barbary Coast: An Informal History of the San Francisco Underworld* (New York: Knopf, 1933), 302–6; Matsubara, "Unsettled Controversies," 130, 170–75; Rockafellar, "Making the World Safe for Soldiers of Democracy," 123–27; Rosenstirn, *Our Nation's Health*, 56; Hichborn, "The Anti-Vice Movement in California, 217–18; Teresa Hurley and Jarrod Harrison, "'Awed by the Women's Clubs': Women Voters and Moral Reform, 1913–1914," in *California Women and Politics: From the Gold Rush to the Great Depression*, ed. Robert W. Cherny, Mary Ann Irwin, and Ann Marie Wilson (Lincoln: University of Nebraska Press, 2011), 242–47; Franklin Hichborn, "California's Fight for a Red Light Abatement Law," *Social Hygiene* 1.1 (Dec. 1914): 7; Franklin Hichborn, "The Organization That Backed the California Red Light Abatement Bill," *Social Hygiene* 1.2 (Mar. 1915): 194–95; Rosen, *The Lost Sisterhood*, 52; Woods, "A Penchant for Probity," 102; Heather A. Clemmer, "'The City That Knows How': San Francisco, The Great War, and Urban Identity," PhD diss., University of Oklahoma, 2008, 125; Bascom Johnson, "Moral Conditions in San Francisco and at the Panama-Pacific Exposition," *Social Hygiene* 1.4 (Sept. 1915): 602–3.

131. Pivar, *Purity and Hygiene*, 160–61.

132. Wilbur A. Sawyer, "His Early Years in California," *Journal of Social Hygiene* 36.9 (Dec. 1950): 388–90; William F. Snow, "Pioneer Experiences," *Social Hygiene* 5.4 (Oct. 1919): 579–80; Clarke, *Taboo*, 70–74; Minutes of the California State Board of Health, June 26, 1909, CSA.

133. Snow, "Pioneer Experiences."

134. Minutes of the California State Board of Health, Feb. 5, 1910, CSA; Minutes of the California State Board of Health, Oct. 1, 1910, CSA; Wilbur A. Sawyer, "The California Program for the Prevention of Venereal Diseases," *Social Hygiene* 4.1 (Jan. 1918): 26.

135. New York's law passed on Feb. 20, 1912, effective May 1. Gardner, "Microbes and Morality," 305–8; Pivar, *Purity and Hygiene*, 110, 161. See also Rockafellar, "Making the World Safe for Soldiers of Democracy," 56; Eric Anderson, "Prostitution and Social Justice: Chicago, 1910–15," *Social Service Review* 48.2 (June 1974): 219–20; "Social Hygiene Legislation in 1915," *Social Hygiene* 2.2 (Apr. 1916): 245–56.To some, this was inadequate. As George Gould noted years later, "The venereal diseases had been made reportable either by statute or regulations of state board of health in only thirteen states prior to Jan. 1, 1917." George Gould, *Twenty Years' Progress in Social Hygiene Legislation: Developments in the Adoption of State Laws for the Prevention and Control of the Venereal Diseases and for Repression of Prostitution from the year 1925 to November 1, 1944*, p. 13, Folder 2, Box 214, Series 7, ASHAR.

136. "GRAND JURY FOR JANUARY TERM—1910"; Thomas O'Sullivan, "THE COURT'S CHARGE TO THE GRAND JURY," Jan. 3, 1910—both of these are in Folder 56, Box 8, Series O, RAC; John William Klein, "The Role and Impact of Rockefeller Philanthropy During the Progressive Era," PhD diss., Fordham University, 1980, 200–201.

137. Albert Frederick Schenkel, "The Rich Man and the Kingdom: John D. Rockefeller, Jr., and the Protestant Establishment, 1900–1960," PhD diss., Harvard University, 1990, 35–43; Ron Chernow, *Titan: The Life of John D. Rockefeller, Sr.* (New York: Random House, 1998), 347–56; Raymond Fosdick, *John D. Rockefeller, Jr.: A Portrait* (New York: Harper & Bros., 1956), 60, 110–20; Raymond Fosdick, *The Story of the Rockefeller Foundation* (New York: Harper & Brothers, 1952), 1–20; Margaret J. Kavounas, "Feeblemindedness and Prostitution: The Laboratory of Social Hygiene's Influence on Progressive Era Prostitution Reform," master's thesis, Sarah Lawrence College, 1992, 67–68; Pivar, *Purity and Hygiene*, 120; Klein, "The Role and Impact of Rockefeller Philanthropy," 199–200; Fosdick, *The Story of the Rockefeller Foundation*, 1–20; John Ensor Harr and Peter J. Johnson, *The Rockefeller Century* (New York: Scribner, 1988), 108–10. For more on Rockefeller funding research into prostitution, see Letter from William H. Baldwin Jr. to John D. Rockefeller, Jan. 15, 1901; Letter from George F. Peabody to John D. Rockefeller, Jan. 21, 1901; Letter from Finance Committee of the Committee of Fifteen to John D. Rockefeller, Mar. 14, 1901; Letter from George F. Peabody to John D. Rockefeller, Mar. 23, 1901; Letter from William H. Baldwin Jr. to John D. Rockefeller Jr., Aug. 29, 1901—all of these are in Folder 40, Box 6, Series O, RAC; Letter from Starr Murphy to the New York Society for the Suppression of Vice, Apr. 7, 1905; Letter from Anthony Comstock to Starr Murphy, Dec. 11, 1905—both of these are in Folder 131, Box 17, Series K, RAC.

138. Fosdick, *John D. Rockefeller*, 137.

139. Ibid., 137–38; Johnson, "Defining 'Social Evil,'" 304–5; John D. Rockefeller Jr., "MEMORANDUM," May 6, 1910, Folder 56, Box 8, Series O, RAC; Fosdick, *John D. Rockefeller*, 140.

140. Jennifer Fronc, *New York Undercover: Private Surveillance in the Progressive Era* (Chicago: University of Chicago Press, 2009), 21–25.

141. John P. Peters, "The Story of the Committee of Fourteen of New York," *Social Hygiene* 4.3 (Jul. 1918): 356–60; Thomas C. Mackey, *Pursuing Johns: Criminal Law Reform, Defending Character, and New York City's Committee of Fourteen, 1920–1930* (Columbus: Ohio State University Press, 2005), 16–17; Fronc, *New York Undercover*, 33–51; Letter from William H. Baldwin Jr. to John D. Rockefeller Jr., Aug. 29, 1901, Folder 40, Box 6, Series O, RAC. The investigators' reports are held in the Committee of Fifteen Records, NYPL.

142. Committee of Fifteen, *The Social Evil*, 65–78.

143. Letter from Lawrence Veiller to Howard H. Russell, Jan. 10, 1905, Committee Minutes, Mar. 1905–1913, Box 86, C14R; Fronc, *New York Undercover*, 66; Mackey, *Pursuing Johns*, 19–20; Roby, "Politics and Prostitution," 125–27.

144. Fronc, *New York Undercover*, 66–94; Committee of Fourteen, *The Social Evil in New York City: A Study of Law Enforcement* (New York: Andrew H. Kellogg, 1910), 37 f1.

145. See Investigator's Report, Dec. 8, 1906; Investigator's Report, Dec. 18, 1906; Investigator's Report, May 29, 1908; Investigator's Report, June 25, 1908—all are in 1906-07-09 Folder, Box 28, C14R; Mackey, *Pursuing Johns*, 21–24; Johnson, "Defining 'Social Evil,'" 491; Roby, "Politics and Prostitution," 129–30; Quinn, "Revisiting Anna Moscowitz Kross's Critique of New York City's Women's Court," 108–12; Pivar, *Purity and Hygiene*, 121; Peters, "The Story of the Committee of Fourteen of New York," 373–76.

146. Pivar, *Purity and Hygiene*, 105; Mackey, *Pursuing Johns*, 24; Keire, "Vice in American Cities," 126–27.

147. On funding the Committee of Fourteen, see Letter from John P. Peters to John D. Rockefeller Jr., Oct. 25, 1907; Letter from Frederick Whitin to John D. Rockefeller Jr., Nov. 18, 1907; "COMMITTEE OF FOURTEEN"; Letter from John D. Rockefeller Jr. to Louis Slade, Dec. 7, 1910—all in Folder 40, Box 6, Series O, RAC. On Rockefeller's father funding the Committee of Fifteen, see Letter from William H. Baldwin Jr. to John D. Rockefeller, Jan. 15, 1901; Letter from George F. Peabody to John D. Rockefeller, Jan. 21, 1901; Letter from Finance Committee of the Committee of Fifteen to John D. Rockefeller, Mar. 14, 1901; Letter from George F. Peabody to John D. Rockefeller, Mar. 23, 1901; Letter from William H. Baldwin Jr. to John D. Rockefeller Jr., Aug. 29, 1901—all in Folder 40, Box 6, Series O, RAC.

148. "JDR, JR. SCRAPBOOKS," pp. 2–4, RAC; Gretchen Soderlund, *Sex Trafficking, Scandal, and the Transformation of Journalism, 1885–1917* (Chicago: University of Chicago Press, 2013), 149–51, 158; Roby, "Politics and Prostitution," 140; Harr and Johnson, *The Rockefeller Century*, 111.

149. Klein, "The Role and Impact of Rockefeller Philanthropy," 209–17; Jennifer Gunn, "A Few Good Men: The Rockefeller Approach to Population, 1911–1936," in *The Development of the Social Scientists in the United States and Canada: The Role of Philanthropy*, ed. Theresa Richardson and Donald Fisher (New York: Ablex Publishing, 1999), 102–3. Gunn called the BSH "a family affair." Letter from James Bronson Reynolds to John D. Rockefeller Jr., Jul. 8, 1910, Folder 59, Box 8, Series O, RAC; Letter from James Bronson Reynolds to John D. Rockefeller Jr., Jul. 14, 1910; Letter from James Bronson Reynolds to John D. Rockefeller Jr., Aug. 9, 1910; Letter from James Bronson Reynolds to John D. Rockefeller Jr., Aug. 26, 1910—these last three are in Folder 57, Box 8, Series O, RAC.

150. Letter from John D. Rockefeller Jr. to Clifford Roe, Jan. 26, 1911; Letter from Clifford Roe to John D. Rockefeller Jr., Jan. 30, 1911; Memorandum from John D. Rockefeller Jr. to Charles O. Heydt, Mar. 31, 1911; Letter from Clifford Roe to the Committee of Three, Apr. 1, 1911–Apr. 1, 1912—all of these are in Folder 42, Box 7, Series O, RAC.

151. Letter from John D. Rockefeller Jr. to Clifford Barnes, Dec. 19, 1912, Folder 38, Box 6, Series O, RAC; Letter from John D. Rockefeller Jr. to Edward L. Keyes Jr., June or Jul. 1913, Folder 30, Box 6, Series O, RAC. For Rockefeller's funding of the American Vigilance Association (leader of the social purity forces—and abolitionists), see Letter from John D. Rockefeller Jr. to Clifford Roe, Jan. 26, 1912; Letter from John D. Rockefeller to Dean Sumner, Mar. 6, 1912—both in Folder 30, Box 6, Series O, RAC. For his funding of the American Federation for Sex Hygiene (leader of the social hygiene forces—and neoregulationists), see Letter from Prince A. Morrow to John D. Rockefeller Jr., Sept. 20, 1910; Letter from John D. Rockefeller Jr. to Prince A. Morrow, Oct. 3, 1910—both in Folder 130, Box 16, Series K, RAC. See more such grant requests in Folder 130.

152. See Gardner, "Microbes and Morality," 181–86.

153. This analysis comes from Pivar, *Purity and Hygiene*, 125. See Pivar's insightful chapter, "Rockefeller Reshapes Social Hygiene."

154. See the extensive correspondence in Folder 30, Box 6, Series O, RAC.

155. See Letter from John D. Rockefeller Jr. to Clifford Roe, Oct. 16, 1912; Letter from Clifford Roe to John D. Rockefeller Jr., Aug. 5, 1912—both in Folder 30, Box 6, Series O, Office of the Messrs. Rockefeller records, Rockefeller Boards, RAC.

156. Letter from John D. Rockefeller to Dean Sumner, Mar. 6, 1912, Folder 30, Box 6, Series O, RAC; Letter from John D. Rockefeller Jr. to Prince A. Morrow, Mar. 18, 1912, Folder 130, Box 16, Series K, RAC; Meeting minutes, Bureau of Social Hygiene, Apr. 3, 1912, Folder 24, Box 2, Series 1, RAC; Letter from John D. Rockefeller Jr. to Clifford Barnes, Apr. 23, 1912; Letter from John D. Rockefeller Jr. to Edith McCormick, June 13, 1912; Letter from Clifford Roe to Charles Heydt, Aug. 10, 1912—these last three are in Folder 30, Box 6, Series O, Office of the Messrs. Rockefeller records, Rockefeller Boards, RAC.

157. Letter from John D. Rockefeller Jr. to Edward L. Keyes Jr., Jul. 18, 1913, Folder 30, Box 6, Series O, RAC; Pivar, *Purity and Hygiene*, 127–28.

158. See Letter from Jerome D. Greene to John D. Rockefeller Jr., Sept. 2, 1913; Letter from Charles Eliot to John D. Rockefeller Jr., Sept. 9, 1913—both of these are in Folder 30, Box 6, Series O, Office of the Messrs. Rockefeller records, Rockefeller Boards, RAC; Pivar, *Purity and Hygiene*, 129.

159. Clarke, *Taboo*, 74.

160. Kayla Jo Blackman, "Public Power, Private Matters: The American Social Hygiene Association and the Policing of Sexual Health in the Progressive Era," master's thesis, University of Montana, May 2014, 34–35.

161. Meeting Minutes, American Social Hygiene Association, Feb. 13, 1914, Folder 2, Box 5, Series 2, ASHAR; Blackman, "Public Power, Private Matters," 35–69. For more information on the ASHA's activities, see Letter from James Bronson Reynolds and William F. Snow to Executive Committee, Nov. 19, 1915, American Social Hygiene Association 1913–1915 Folder 1, Box 89, CWEP.

162. Letter from William F. Snow to Frederick Whitin, Sept. 24, 1914; Letter from William F. Snow to Frederick Whitin, Sept. 24, 1914; Letter from William F. Snow to Frederick Whitin, Oct. 28, 1914; Letter from William F. Snow to Frederick Whitin, Feb. 1, 1915—all of these are in Box 9, C14R; Letter from William F. Snow to Mary Cobb, Apr. 11, 1914, Folder 5, Box 1, Series 1, ASHAR; American Social Hygiene Association, *First Annual Report: 1913–1914* (New York: ASHA, 1915), p. 8–9, Folder 5, Box 19, Series 2, ASHAR; Bascom Johnson, "Moral Conditions in San Francisco and at the Panama-Pacific Exposition," *Social Hygiene* 1.4 (Sept. 1915): 589–90; Letter from James Bronson Reynolds to John D. Rockefeller Jr., Feb. 17, 1915, Folder 55, Box 7, Series O, RAC.

163. "Proposed Plan for Investigation of Certain Special Phases of the Social Evil in San Francisco," Redlight Abatement—Proposed San Francisco Investigation Folder, Box 120, FHP; Letter from Thomas Eliot to Franklin Hichborn, Nov. 7, 1914, Eliot, Thomas D. 1914 Folder, Box 158, FHP.

164. Johnson, "Moral Conditions in San Francisco and at the Panama-Pacific Exposition," 596–97.

165. B. B. Blake, Transcript of investigation, Mar. 22, 1915, Panama-Pacific Exposition Folder, Box 63, FHP.

166. See Hennigan, "Property War," 123–25. Hennigan cites affidavits and investigator reports from Johnson and Eliot that appear to have been refiled in Boxes 210 and 211, Series 7, ASHAR. See also "From Our Files," *Journal of Social Hygiene* 12.8 (Nov. 1926): 483–91.

167. Pivar, *Purity and Hygiene*, 208.

CHAPTER 2: "LESS FORTUNATE SISTERS"

1. *Fourth International Congress on School Hygiene: Transactions*, vol. 2, 405–12.

2. Tucker, *Gratiot County, Michigan*, 1024.

3. The business classes were part of a "Commercial" curriculum students could choose. Tucker, *Gratiot County, Michigan*, 1025–28; McMacken, *St. Louis at 150*, 37–38; "Advantages of the St. Louis High School," *St. Louis Leader*, June 8, 1911, CHL.

4. Van Norman, 41; Tucker, *Gratiot County, Michigan*, 1028–29.

5. McCall, 14.

6. See Hill, "Reflections," 22.

7. *Annual Reports of the School Districts of the Township of Bethany, County of Gratiot, Michigan, for the School Year Ending July 8, 1912*, Box 150, RG 55–11, AM.

8. At trial, her mother noted that McCall worked as an eighteen-year-old but did not mention her working any earlier. Van Norman, 47. As previously mentioned, it also would have been against the law for her to work in lieu of school.

9. Tucker, *Gratiot County, Michigan*, 923, 1030–38, 1053–60.

10. Ibid., 1303, 1322–23.

11. Ibid., 1312.

12. The article's title was cut off by a blemish. See *St. Louis Leader*, June 8, 1911, CHL.

13. Tucker, *Gratiot County, Michigan*, 245, 1022.

14. Quoted in ibid., 922.

15. McCall, 15.

16. Van Norman, 41. For more information on the hardware store, see Tucker, *Gratiot County, Michigan*, 1058; for more information on the grain elevator, see ibid., 1062.

17. Tucker, *Gratiot County, Michigan*, 1040.

18. Ibid., 1218–19.

19. *Sixteenth Biennial Report of the Michigan State Industrial Home for Girls for the Years 1907–1908* (Lansing, MI: Wynkoop, Hallenbeck, Crawford, 1915), 87–88, 93–95. For background, see Georgina Hickey, "Rescuing the Working Girl: Agency and Conflict in the Michigan Reform School for Girls, 1879–1893," *Michigan Historical Review* 20.1 (Spring 1994): 1–28.

20. *Eighteenth Biennial Report of the Michigan State Industrial Home for Girls for the Years 1913–1914* (Lansing, MI: Wynkoop, Hallenbeck, Crawford, 1915), 13–14, 20–22, 31.

21. Ibid., 15, 26–27.

22. *Sixteenth Biennial Report of the Michigan State Industrial Home*, 81–82.

23. *Eighteenth Biennial Report of the Michigan State Industrial Home*, 19.

24. One illustrative case can be found in Tucker, *Gratiot County, Michigan*, 1319–20.

25. Estelle Freedman, *Their Sisters' Keepers: Women's Prison Reform in America, 1830–1930* (Ann Arbor: University of Michigan Press, 1981), 15; Rafter, *Partial Justice*, 7.

26. Freedman, *Their Sisters' Keepers*, 22.

27. Regina G. Kunzel, *Fallen Women, Problem Girls: Unmarried Mothers and the Professionalization of Social Work, 1890–1945* (New Haven, CT: Yale University Press, 1993), 1–2; Freedman, *Their Sisters' Keepers*, 19–20; Janis Appier, *Policing Women: The Sexual Politics of Law Enforcement and the LAPD* (Philadelphia: Temple University Press, 1998), 12; Rafter, *Partial Justice*, xxviii.

28. Rafter, *Partial Justice*, 29–35.

29. Kunzel, *Fallen Women, Problem Girls*, 10. See also Hobson, *Uneasy Virtue*, ch. 5.

30. Odem, *Delinquent Daughters*, 118.

31. Rafter, *Partial Justice*, 159.

32. For the physical description of Bedford, see Paul W. Garret and Austin H. MacCormick, eds., *Handbook of American Prisons and Reformatories* (New York: National Society of Penal Information, 1929), 654; *Salient Facts About the New York State Reformatory for Women, Bedford Hills, N.Y.*, Folder 32, Box 6, Series O, RAC; Miner, *Slavery of Prostitution*, 231–32; Gardner, "Microbes and Morality," 282.

33. Mabel Jacques Eichel, "Katharine Bement Davis: The Story of a Woman of Action, Whose Career Has Included Problems Presented by Teaching, Food Demonstration, Earthquakes, Wars, Delinquent Girls and City Departments," *Woman's Journal* 13 (Apr. 1928): 20–21, 41; A. S. Gregg, "A State Home for Delinquent Females," *Light* 119 (Jan.–Feb. 1918): 35–36; Alexander, *The "Girl Problem,"* 74; Kavounas, "Feeblemindedness and Prostitution," 31; Freedman, *Their Sisters' Keepers*, 117; Miner, *Slavery of Prostitution*, 231–32, 239; Johnson, "Defining 'Social Evil,'" 484–85.

34. Letter from Katharine Bement Davis to John D. Rockefeller Jr., Sept. 13, 1911, Folder 40, Box 6, Series O, RAC. See also Klein, "The Role and Impact of Rockefeller Philanthropy," 222–23.

35. *Recommendations of the Laboratory of Social Hygiene Affiliated with New York State Reformatory for Women at Bedford Hills, N.Y. for Disposition of First One Hundred Cases Studied* (1914);

Letter from Rufus Cole to Starr Murphy, Jan. 22, 1914—both of these are in Folder 31, Box 6, Series O, RAC; Kavounas, "Feeblemindedness and Prostitution," 29; Brandt, *No Magic Bullet*, 39–40.

36. As the historian Nicole Hahn Rafter concluded, the studies at Bedford resulted in "an increase in state power over prisoners" and "helped persuade the public that crime was a disease and that criminals therefore should be confined until medical experts pronounced them cured." Rafter, *Partial Justice*, 73–74.

37. Clement, *Love for Sale*, 81.

38. Cheryl D. Hicks, "'Bright and Good Looking Colored Girl': Black Women's Sexuality and 'Harmful Intimacy' in Early Twentieth-Century New York," *Journal of the History of Sexuality* 18.3 (Sept. 2009): 426.

39. Odem, *Delinquent Daughters*, 119–20; Janie Porter Barrett, *Fifth Annual Report of the Industrial Home School for Colored Girls* (Peake's Turnout, Hanover County, VA, 1920), 12, 14; Cheryl Hicks, *Talk with You Like a Woman: African American Women, Justice, and Reform in New York, 1890–1935* (Chapel Hill: University of North Carolina Press, 2010), ch. 3; Alexander Pisciotta, "Race, Sex, and Rehabilitation: A Study of Differential Treatment in the Juvenile Reformatory, 1825–1900," *Crime and Delinquency* 29.2 (1983): 256–57; Katherine Mellen Charron, *Freedom's Teacher: The Life of Septima Clark* (Chapel Hill: University of North Carolina Press, 2009), 135. Thanks to Rebecca Steinberg for providing me with her unpublished thesis, which pointed me to several of these sources. See also Christina Simmons, "African Americans and Sexual Victorianism in the Social Hygiene Movement, 1910–1940," *Journal of the History of Sexuality* 4.1 (Jul. 1993): 51–75.

40. Maude Miner Hadden, *Quest for Peace: Personal and Political* (Washington, DC: Farrar Publishing Co., 1968), 1–49; Rheta Childe Dorr, "The Prodigal Daughter," *Hampton's Magazine* 24 (Jan. 1910–June 1910): 526–28; "Work Miss Miner Is Doing," *Idaho Statesman*, June 22, 1910; Odem, *Delinquent Daughters*, 113–14; State of New York, *Proceedings of the Commission to Inquire into the Courts of Inferior Criminal Jurisdiction in Cities of the First Class*, vol. 4, 3864–66.

41. Letter from Maude Miner to John D. Rockefeller Jr., Jul. 5, 1910; Charles O. Heydt, "Memorandum," Jul. 6, 1910; Letter from Maude Miner to John D. Rockefeller Jr., Feb. 14, 1911—all of these are in Folder 39, Box 4, Series R, RAC. See Folder 39 for more on Rockefeller's financing of Waverley over the decades.

42. "New York Probation and Protective Association," pamphlet, 1916, Folder 11, Box 6, MFCP.

43. Odem, *Delinquent Daughters*, 113–14; Miner, *Slavery of Prostitution*, 189.

44. Johnson, "Defining 'Social Evil,'" 309–10.

45. Ibid., 503–4; Pivar, *Purity and Hygiene*, 4.

46. Odem, *Delinquent Daughters*, 111–12; Mary Odem, "City Mothers and Delinquent Daughters: Female Juvenile Justice Reform in Early Twentieth-Century Los Angeles," in *California Progressivism Revisited*, ed. William Deverell and Tom Sitton (Berkeley: University of California Press, 1994), 178–79; Appier, *Policing Women*, 4–10; AnneMarie Kooistra, "Angels for Sale: The History of Prostitution in Los Angeles, 1880–1940," PhD diss., University of Southern California, 2003, 74–75.

47. James W. Hurst, *Pancho Villa and Black Jack Pershing: The Punitive Expedition in Mexico* (Westport, CT: Praeger, 2008), 20–29; Herbert Molloy Mason Jr., *The Great Pursuit: General John J. Pershing's Punitive Expedition Across the Rio Grande to Destroy the Mexican Bandit Pancho Villa* (New York: Random House, 1970), 3; Eileen Welsome, *The General and the Jaguar: Pershing's Hunt for Pancho Villa: A True Story of Revolution and Revenge* (New York: Little, Brown, 2006), 81.

48. Hurst, *Pancho Villa and Black Jack Pershing*, 20–29; Clarence Clendenen, *The United States and Pancho Villa: A Study in Unconventional Diplomacy* (Port Washington, NY: Kennikat Press, 1961), 157–58.

49. Frederick Palmer, *Newton D. Baker: America at War*, vol. 1 (New York: Dodd, Mead, 1931), 7–10.

50. C. H. Cramer, *Newton D. Baker: A Biography* (Cleveland: World Publishing, 1961), 83.

51. Welsome, *The General and the Jaguar*, 287; Ann R. Gabbert, "Prostitution and Moral Reform in the Borderlands: El Paso, 1890–1920," *Journal of the History of Sexuality* 12.4 (Oct. 2003): 576, 596–602; Letter from Raymond Fosdick to Newton Baker, Aug. 10, Folder 1, Box 23, RBFP; James A. Sandos, "Prostitution and Drugs: The United States Army on the Mexican-American Border, 1916–1917," *Pacific Historical Review* 49.4 (Nov. 1980): 629. On Pershing's gonorrhea, see Donald Smythe, *Pershing: General of the Armies* (Bloomington: Indiana University Press, 1986), 250.

52. Fosdick to Baker, Aug. 10, 1916, RBFP; Bascom Johnson, "What Some Communities of the West and Southwest Have Done for the Protection of the Morals and Health of Soldiers and Sailors," p. 8, June 21, 1918, Box 1635, RG 287, NA.

53. Brandt, *No Magic Bullet*, 53; Raymond B. Fosdick, *Chronicle of a Generation: An Autobiography* (New York: Harper Bros., 1958), 135–36.

54. For more on Fosdick's early life, see Fosdick, *Chronicle of a Generation*; Daryl L. Revoldt, "Raymond B. Fosdick: Reform, Internationalism, and the Rockefeller Foundation," PhD diss., University of Akron, 1982; Roy S. Durstine, "College Men Who Are Making Good," magazine unknown, Folder 2, Box 25, RBFP; Untitled memorandum, June 7, 1915, Panama-Pacific Exposition Folder, Box 63, FHP. On his ties to Rockefeller and the ASHA, see Revoldt, "Raymond B. Fosdick," 85–86; the correspondence in Folder 18, Box 2, Series 1, RAC; Meeting minutes, Bureau of Social Hygiene,

Feb. 6, 1913, Folder 25, Box 2, Series 1, RAC; Meeting Minutes, American Social Hygiene Association, Apr. 2, 1914, Folder 2, Box 5, Series 2, ASHAR. The "dialect stories" anecdote comes from Fosdick, *Chronicle of a Generation*, 47–49.

55. Fosdick, *Chronicle of a Generation*, 136.

56. Meeting Minutes, Bureau of Social Hygiene, May 9, 1919, Folder 31, Box 3, Series 1, RAC.

57. Fosdick to Baker, Aug. 10, 1916, RBFP.

58. Ibid.

59. Ibid.

60. Fosdick, *Chronicle of a Generation*, 139.

61. For more on the office, see Cramer, *Newton D. Baker*, 23; Palmer, *Newton D. Baker*, 10–11.

62. This was Baker's customary habit of sitting. See Cramer, *Newton D. Baker*, 19.

63. Fosdick, *Chronicle of a Generation*, 141.

64. Van Norman, 41. I claim that Abraham worked in a factory there because the "establishment in which employed" is listed in his death certificate as "factory," and he had never worked in factory, so far as I can tell, in St. Louis or in Bethany Township (where his farm had been).

65. See Olivier Zunz, *The Changing Face of Inequality: Urbanization, Industrial Development, and Immigrants in Detroit* (Chicago: University of Chicago Press, 1982), 286–92.

66. Van Norman, 41.

67. Zunz, *The Changing Face of Inequality*, 286.

68. Van Norman, 41.

69. Certificate of Death, Abraham McCall, St. Louis, Gratiot County, MI, Sept. 18, 1916, *Michigan, Deaths and Burials, 1800–1995*, FHL film number 985692.

CHAPTER 3: "WAGING WAR ON THE WOMEN"

1. McCall, 40.

2. Ibid.

3. This description comes from the beautiful narrative at the beginning of Robert H. Ferrell, *Woodrow Wilson and World War I: 1917–1921* (New York: Harper & Row, 1985), 1–2.

4. Ibid., 2; David M. Kennedy, *Over Here: The First World War and American Society* (New York: Oxford University Press, 1980), 13.

5. Ferrell, *Woodrow Wilson and World War I*, 2. For more on Wilson's decision to enter World War I, see Robert W. Tucker, *Woodrow Wilson and the Great War: Reconsidering America's Neutrality, 1914–1917* (Charlottesville: University of Virginia Press, 2007), 188–92.

6. See, for instance, *Report of the Special Committee on Investigation of the Munitions Industry* (Nye Report), US Congress, Senate, 74th Cong., 2nd Sess., Feb. 24, 1936, pp. 3–13; Smedley D. Butler, *War Is a Racket* (New York: Round Table Press, 1935).

7. Fosdick, *Chronicle of a Generation*, 142.

8. See Letter from Newton Baker to Joseph Lee, Apr. 18, 1917; Letter from Newton Baker to Malcolm McBride, Apr. 16, 1917—both of these are Doc. 26829, Box 55, Entry 393, RG 165, NA.

9. Franklin H. Martin, ed., *Digest of the Proceedings of the Council of National Defense During the World War* (Washington, DC: Government Printing Office, 1934), 149–50.

10. "Records for Twenty-Four Hours," *Evening Star*, Apr. 26, 1917; "Weather in Various Cities," *Evening Star*, Apr. 26, 1917.

11. Meeting Minutes, Apr. 26, 1917, Doc. A1909, Box 2, Entry 403, RG 165, NA.

12. Fosdick, *Chronicle of a Generation*, 145.

13. Senator Jones, speaking on H.R. 3545, on May 1, 1917, 65th Cong., 1st Sess., *Congressional Record* 55, pt. 2, p. 1615. See also Letter from W. L. Jones to Newton Baker, May 7, 1917, Doc. 26829, Box 55, Entry 393, RG 165, NA.

14. Fosdick, *Chronicle of a Generation*, 144–45.

15. The adoption of Section 12 was far more controversial than that of Section 13. For more surrounding this debate, see John Dickinson, *The Building of an Army: A Detailed Account of Legislation, Administration and Opinion in the United States, 1915–1920* (New York: Century Co., 1922), 208–14.

16. Selective Service Act, Pub. L. 65–12, 40 Stat. 76 (May 18, 1917).

17. Letter from Newton Baker to various mayors, Aug. 14, 1917, Folder 807, Box 50, TPP.

18. Ferrell, *Woodrow Wilson and World War I*, 14–16.

19. There is evidence that blacks were slightly overrepresented in the draft. As Paul T. Murray wrote, "Although blacks constituted only 9.63% of the total registration, they were 13.08% of those drafted. While 34.10% of all black registrants were ultimately inducted, only 24.04% of the whites were drafted." See Paul T. Murray, "Blacks and the Draft: A History of Institutional Racism," *Journal of Black Studies* 2.1 (Sept. 1971): 58.

20. Ferrell, *Woodrow Wilson and World War I*, 17–19; YMCA, *Summary of the World War Work of the American Y.M.C.A.* (New York: YMCA, 1920), 9.

21. Ferrell, *Woodrow Wilson and World War I*, no page.

22. Abigail Claire Barnes, "Pure Spaces and Impure Bodies: The Detention of Prostitutes in the U.S. During World War I," PhD diss., UCLA, 2010, 44–46; Memorandum from the Surgeon General

of the Army to the Department Surgeon of the Southeastern Department, "Detection of Venereal Diseases," Apr. 29, 1918, Box 423, Entry 29A, RG 112, NA. (This document spelled out the inspection procedures used in the army since 1916.)

23. Van Norman, 48.

24. Ibid., 41–42.

25. Telephone interview with David McMacken, Jan. 13, 2017; "Cleaning Up Alma Heights," *Alma Record*, Jul. 15, 1915.

26. Hill, "Reflections," 31.

27. David McMacken, "Over There: The Great War Comes to Gratiot County," Apr. 8, 2017, e-mailed to the author.

28. Ibid.; "Gratiot County's Men Are Leaving," *Alma Record*, Sept. 6, 1917.

29. See Maurine Weiner Greenwald, *Women, War, and Work: The Impact of World War I on Women Workers in the United States* (Ithaca, NY: Cornell University Press, 1980).

30. Telephone interview with David McMacken, Jan. 13, 2017.

31. Susan Ferentinos, "An Unpredictable Age: Sex, Consumption, and the Emergence of the American Teenager, 1900–1950," PhD diss., Indiana University, 2005, 233.

32. "Mich. Cantonment Is Named Camp Custer," *Jackson Citizen Patriot*, Jul. 20, 1917; "Camp Custer Being Rushed to Completion for Uncle Sam's New Army," *Kalamazoo Gazette*, Aug. 13, 1917.

33. J. S., "Parlor Houses of Prostitution," Oct. 1, 1917, Michigan Folder, Box 9, Entry 395, RG 165, NA.

34. "'Y' at Camp Custer Soon to Be Opened," *Jackson Citizen Patriot*, Jul. 23, 1917.

35. "Saginaw Company Is at Camp Custer," *Saginaw News*, Jul. 30, 1917.

36. Letter from Walter Clarke to Raymond Fosdick, June 25, 1917, Doc. 1162, Michigan Folder, Box 9, Entry 395, RG 165, NA.

37. "Saginaw Club May Be Moved to Alma," *Saginaw News*, June 19, 1917; "Locals Still Hold Lead in League by Trimming Alma," *Bay City Times Tribune*, Jul. 2, 1917; "Bold Burglar Gang Corralled at Last," *Daily Telegraph* (Adrian, MI), June 9, 1917; "Great Crowd," *Alma Record*, Sept. 6, 1917.

38. For more biographical information on Clarke, see "BIOGRAPHICAL NOTES," Oct. 20, 1943, Folder 2, Box 48, Series 4, ASHAR; documents in CLARKE, Charles W., MD, Folder, Box 231, Series 2, ASHAR.

39. Meeting Minutes, American Social Hygiene Association, May 10, 1917; Letter from William F. Snow to the Executive Committee of the ASHA, 10 May 1917—both in Folder 6, Box 5, Series 2, ASHAR.

40. Meeting Minutes, American Social Hygiene Association, June 21, 1917, Folder 6, Box 5, Series 2, ASHAR.

41. On Johnson's background, see American Social Hygiene Association, *Honorary Life Membership: Bascom Johnson, M.D.* (1942), Folder 988, Box 57, RPP; "No International Meet," *Riverside Daily Press*, Apr. 11, 1900; "Superintendent Hall Returns from Trip," *Riverside Independent Enterprise*, Nov. 18, 1910; "S.F. Moves a Subject for Discussion," *San Francisco Chronicle*, Aug. 4, 1915.

42. Bascom Johnson, "Moral Conditions in San Francisco, Apr. 25th, 1917," May 3, 1917; Bascom Johnson, "Preliminary Report on Moral Conditions in California, June 24th to July 21st 1917 by Bascom Johnson"—both in California Folder, Box 5, Entry 395, RG 165, NA.

43. Letter from William T. Seibels to William F. Snow, Sept. 17, 1917, Doc. 6252, Box 1, Entry 393, RG 165, NA; Alan Johnstone, Report on Montgomery, Alabama, Dec. 15, 1917, General Storage Folder, Box 129, Entry 29A, RG 112, NA; Letter from Bascom Johnson to Raymond Fosdick, Aug. 27, 1917, Doc. 8508, Box 6, Entry 393, RG 165, NA; Paul Wooton, "War Department Will Watch Vice in New Orleans," *New Orleans Times-Picayune*, Nov. 18, 1917. For more on the closure of Storyville, see Letter from Raymond Fosdick to Josephus Daniels, Sept. 11, 1917, Box 458, JDP; Emily Epstein Landau, *Spectacular Wickedness: Sex, Race, and Memory in Storyville New Orleans* (Baton Rouge: Louisiana State University Press, 2013), 188–90; Letter from Newton Baker to Raymond Fosdick, Apr. 21, 1917, Doc. 26829, Box 55, Entry 393, RG 165, NA; Gary Krist, *Empire of Sin: A Story of Sex, Jazz, Murder, and the Battle of Modern New Orleans* (New York: Crown, 2014), 252–55.

44. "Cleanup of Vice Started in Douglas," *Tucson Citizen*, June 25, 1917; "Alexandria Abolishes Red Light District," *New Orleans States*, Sept. 5, 1917.

45. Letter, *New York Evening Journal*, Jan. 27, 1914, cited in Rosen, *The Lost Sisterhood*, 31.

46. "Women of Redlight District Make Plea for Fair Play," *San Francisco Chronicle*, Jan. 26, 1917; "Women of Underworld Storm Vice Crusader's Church," *Evening Tribune* (San Diego), Jan. 26, 1917.

47. *Law Enforcement Division*, 2, Box 2, Entry 404, RG 165, NA.

48. Fosdick, *Chronicle of a Generation*, 145; Letter from Raymond Fosdick to William C. Gorgas, Oct. 10, 1917, Doc. 8504, Box 6, Entry 393, RG 165, NA.

49. Fosdick, *Chronicle of a Generation*, 145.

50. *Law Enforcement Division*, 2–3; Timothy N. Pfeiffer, "Social Hygiene and the War," *Social Hygiene* 4.3 (Jul. 1918): 423–24; "Outline of Social Hygiene Work for Sanitary Corps," NA. On the racism, see Letter from Raymond Fosdick to George Nesbitt, Sept. 14, 1917, Doc. 6092; Letter from Harold Keats to Raymond Fosdick, Aug. 31, 1917, Doc. 4686—both in Washington, DC, Folder, Box 10, Entry 395, RG 165, NA; Nancy K. Bristow, *Making Men Moral: Social Engineering During the*

Great War (New York: NYU Press, 1996), 159–61; Landau, *Spectacular Wickedness*, 190. For a few examples of flouting this rule, see Barnes, "Pure Spaces and Impure Bodies," 169–70. For more on Philadelphia, see James H. Adams, *Urban Reform and Sexual Vice in Progressive-Era Philadelphia: The Faithful and the Fallen* (Lanham, MD: Lexington, 2015), 140–45; *Law Enforcement Division*, pp. 16–17, Box 26, Entry 399, RG 165, NA.

51. See Letter from Allison T. French to Bascom Johnson, Oct. 18, 1917, Doc. 8513; Letter from Allison T. French to Matthew J. Brady, Oct. 25, 1917—both in Doc. 8510, Box 6, Entry 393, RG 165, NA; Letter from W. A. Sawyer to the Oregon Social Hygiene Society, Nov. 2, 1917, Box 438, RG 62, NA.

52. Rockafellar, "Making the World Safe for Soldiers of Democracy," 223.

53. Letter from Allison T. French to Bascom Johnson, Oct. 17, 1917, Doc. 8516, Box 6, Entry 393, RG 165, NA.

54. Letter from John W. Davis to Newton Baker, Sept. 6, 1917, Doc. 27362, Box 57, Entry 393, RG 165, NA. See also Letter from William L. Martin to Raymond Fosdick, Aug. 6, 1917, case #8000–3794, pp. 125–26, Old German Files, 1909–21, Records of the Federal Bureau of Investigation, RG 65, NA, retrieved from www.fold3.com/image/#2163125 and www.fold3.com/image/#2163130; Letter from A. Bruce Bielaski to Edmund R. Beckwith, Aug. 16, 1917, case #8000–3794, p. 127, Old German Files, 1909–21, Records of the Federal Bureau of Investigation, RG 65, NA, retrieved from www.fold3.com /image/#2163137. For more on the Bureau of Investigation/Federal Bureau of Investigation, and how its history is indelibly linked to the repression and policing of women, see Jessica Pliley, *Policing Sexuality: The Mann Act and the Making of the FBI* (Cambridge, MA: Harvard University Press, 2014).

55. Eventually, the BOI would divide the country into 174 enforcement districts. See *Law Enforcement Division*, p. 45, Box 26, Entry 399, RG 165, NA; E. B. Sisk, "In Re: Blanche Mason Alleged Violation Section 13, Act May 18, 1917," Nov. 26, 1917, case #8000–91132, Old German Files, 1909–21, Records of the Federal Bureau of Investigation, RG 65, NA, retrieved from www.fold3.com/image/#1098288; F. L. Garbarino, "In Re: ENFORCEMENT SECTIONS 12 & 13 CONSCRIPTION ACT—Vicinity of Camp Dix," Dec. 3, 1917, case #33658, p. 103, Old German Files, 1909–21, Records of the Federal Bureau of Investigation, RG 65, NA, retrieved from www .fold3.com/image/#953687; Letter from Raymond Fosdick to Josephus Daniels, Oct. 31, 1917, Box 458, JDP; Letter from Raymond Fosdick to A. B. Bielaski, Sept. 29, 1917, Doc. 6413, Box 1, Entry 393, RG 165, NA.

56. See, for instance, Robert L. Skiles, "In re general matters," Dec. 9, 1917, case #24382, p. 95, Old German Files, 1909–21, Records of the Federal Bureau of Investigation, Record Group 65, NA, retrieved from www.fold3.com/image/#2288070.

57. In Chicago, this group was called the Committee of Fifteen; in San Francisco, it was the Law Enforcement League; in Oregon, it was the Oregon Social Hygiene Society. Bascom Johnson, "Address: Extra Cantonment Zones," Oct. 23, 1917, Doc. 8311, Box 5, Entry 393, RG 165, NA.

58. Meeting minutes, Sept. 5, 1917; Committee of Fourteen, *Annual Report for 1917* (New York: 1918), 15–26, 55—both in Box 86, C14R; Letter from Bascom Johnson to Timothy Pfeiffer, Oct. 16, 1917, Box 24, C14R.

59. For Chicago's Committee of Fifteen, see Melissa Hope Ditmore, ed., *Encyclopedia of Prostitution and Sex Work*, vol. 1 (Westport, CT: Greenwood Press, 2006), 97. For New York's Committee of Fourteen, see Johnson, "Defining 'Social Evil,'" 596–97.

60. American Social Hygiene Association, "A List of Contributors for the Fiscal Year 1917–1918," Folder 121, Box 15, Series K, RAC. See also Gardner, "Microbes and Morality," 350.

61. Meeting Minutes, Rockefeller Foundation, June 7, 1917, Folder 154, Box 15, Series 200, RG 1.1, RAC.

62. "The American Social Hygiene Association: A Brief Historical Statement," 1948, Folder 1, Box 1, Series 1, ASHAR. See also *Report of Work of the American Social Hygiene Association For the Year 1919*, Folder 6, Box 19, Series 2, ASHAR; Meeting Minutes, American Social Hygiene Association, Dec. 14, 1917, Folder 6, Box 5, Series 2, ASHAR; Meeting Minutes, American Social Hygiene Association, Jan. 11, 1918, Folder 7, Box 5, Series 2, ASHAR; Gardner, "Microbes and Morality," 351–52.

63. Meeting Minutes, Bureau of Social Hygiene, May 9, 1919, Folder 31, Box 3, Series 1, RAC; American Social Hygiene Association, "Budget for the Fiscal Year 1917–1918," Folder 6, Box 5, Series 2, ASHAR; Barnes, "Pure Spaces and Impure Bodies," 133.

64. Letter from Raymond Fosdick to Ethel Sturges Dummer, Sept. 20, 1917, Folder 377, Box 24, A-127, ESDP; Linda Sharon Janke, "Prisoners of War: Sexuality, Venereal Disease, and Women's Incarceration During World War I," PhD diss., SUNY Binghamton, 2006, 68; Bristow, *Making Men Moral*, 114. For information of Dummer's background, see Ethel Sturges Dummer, *Why I Think So: The Autobiography of an Hypothesis* (Chicago: Clarke-McElroy Publishing, 1937) (hereafter *Autobiography of an Hypothesis*); Ethel M. Lichtman, *Ethel Sturges Dummer: A Pioneer of American Social Activism* (Bloomington, IN: iUniverse, 2009).

65. Letter from Ethel Sturges Dummer to Raymond Fosdick, Sept. 27, 1917, Folder 377, Box 24, A-127, ESDP.

66. Miner to Dummer, Sept. 26, 1917, ESDP. Later, they would move to the sixth floor. See Letter from Maude Miner to Ethel Sturges Dummer, Oct. 25, 1917, Folder 378, Box 24, A-127, ESDP.

67. See Letter from Maude Miner to Ethel Sturges Dummer, Oct. 24, 1917; Letter from Maude Miner to Ethel Sturges Dummer, Oct. 30, 1917—both in Folder 378, Box 24, A-127, ESDP.

68. Letter from Ethel Sturges Dummer to Maude Miner, Nov. 8, 1917, Folder 378, Box 24, A-127, ESDP.

69. Raymond Fosdick, untitled memorandum, Oct. 8, 1917, Doc. 6211, Box 1, Entry 393, RG 165, NA.

70. Winthrop D. Lane, "Girls and Khaki: Some Practical Measures of Protection for Young Women in Time of War," *Survey*, Dec. 1, 1917, 237; Letter from Ethel Sturges Dummer to Julia Lathrop, Oct. 30, 1917, Folder 874, Box 39, A-127, ESDP.

71. Janke, "Prisoners of War," 82.

72. See Letter from Jessie Binford to Ethel Sturges Dummer, Dec. 22, 1917, Folder 402, Box 25, A-127, ESDP.

73. Janke, "Prisoners of War," 84–88. For an example of CPWG workers realizing young girls were, for the most part, not passive victims, see "Committee on Protective Work for Girls," Feb. 20, 1918, Doc. 26908, Box 56, Entry 393, RG 165, NA.

74. Jane Deeter Rippin, "Outline of Organization and Methods: Section on Women and Girls, Law Enforcement Division, War and Navy Department Commissions on Training Camp Activities," Jul. 1, 1918, Misc. Corr. Probation Folder, Box 1, Entry 396, RG 165, NA.

75. Maude Miner, "Report of the Committee on Protective Work for Girls: October 1, 1917 to April 1, 1918," Doc. 25812, Box 53, Entry 393, RG 165, NA; Maude Miner, "Protective Work for Girls in War Time," *Proceedings of the National Conference of Social Work* 45 (1918): 657–59; "Committee on Protective Work for Girls," (likely author Raymond Fosdick) Oct. 1917, Doc. 6211, Box 1, Entry 393, RG 165, NA; Report, Northeastern District, Committee on Protective Work for Girls, Jan. 21, 1918, Folder 381, Box 24, A-127, ESDP; Hobson, *Uneasy Virtue*, 177. On the racially segregated nature of the officers' work, see Report, Eastern District, Committee on Protective Work for Girls, Jan. 21, 1918; Report, Southwestern District, Committee on Protective Work for Girls, Jan. 21, 1918—both in Folder 381, Box 24, A-127, ESDP; Jane Deeter Rippin, "Section on Women and Girls: Report and Personnel Sheet, Based on the reports covering the period from June 16 to June 30, 1918," Doc. 33441, Box 78, Entry 393, RG 165, NA; Miner, "Protective Work for Girls in War Time," 661; Miner, "Report of the Committee on Protective Work for Girls," NA; Martha Falconer, "Industrial Schools for Girls and Women," *Social Hygiene* 3.3 (Jul. 1917): 329.

76. Report, Central District, Committee on Protective Work for Girls, Jan. 21, 1918, Folder 381, Box 24, A-127, ESDP.

77. Miner, "Report of the Committee on Protective Work for Girls," NA.

78. Janke, "Prisoners of War," 105.

79. Miner, "Report of the Committee on Protective Work for Girls," NA.

80. Dietzler, *Detention Houses and Reformatories*, 88–91.

81. Ibid., 23.

82. E. A. Beals, "Weather Report," *San Francisco Chronicle*, Jul. 21, 1917.

83. Wilbur A. Sawyer, "The California Program for the Prevention of Venereal Diseases," *Social Hygiene* 4.1 (Jan. 1918): 27; "Fight Waged Against Disease in Army Life," *San Jose Mercury News*, Jul. 23, 1917.

84. Wilbur A. Sawyer, Diary, Vol. XIV, pp. 115–16, Jul. 21, 1917, Box 6, WASP.

85. Letter from W. A. Sawyer to Attorney, State Board of Health, Jul. 24, 1917, Box 124, 3AMS/D/51/05, AMSHR.

86. "California Sets Example in Dealing with Problem," *Bay City Times Tribune*, Feb. 27, 1918.

87. Sawyer to Attorney, State Board of Health, Jul. 24, 1917; "Fight Waged Against Disease in Army Life," 4.

88. Minutes of the California State Board of Health, Sept. 1, 1917, CSA.

89. Lewis Michelson, quoted in *Twenty-Fifth Biennial Report of the State Board of Health of California for the Fiscal Years from July 1, 1916, to June 30, 1918* (Sacramento: California State Printing Office, 1919), 172.

90. Minutes of the California State Board of Health, Sept. 1, 1917, CSA.

91. See Cal. Pol. Code § 266 (Kerr 1919). For the sodomy statute, see § 286.

92. Wilbur A. Sawyer, Diary, Vol. XIV, p. 121, Sept. 6, 1917, Box 6, WASP.

93. Wilbur A. Sawyer, Diary, Vol. XIV, p. 122, Sept. 10, 1917; Wilbur A. Sawyer, Diary, Vol. XIV, p. 123, Sept. 12, 1917—both in Box 6, WASP. For more on San Diego's enforcement of the Plan, see Letter from W. F. Schwermeyer to Mayor and City Council Members of San Diego, Sept. 15, 1917, doc. 8451, Box 6, Entry 393, RG 165, NA.

94. Meeting Minutes, 1919–1921 volume, p. 20, FAPSRP.

95. Wunsch, "Prostitution and Public Policy," 17; Rafter, *Partial Justice*, 73–74; Brandt, *No Magic Bullet*, 39–40, 72. See also Connelly, *The Response to Prostitution in the Progressive Era*, ch. 4.

96. New York State Board of Health, "Venereal Diseases," Doc. 25474, Box 52, Entry 393, RG 165, NA.

97. Allan J. McLaughlin, "Pioneering in Venereal Disease Control," *American Journal of Obstetrics and the Diseases of Women and Children* 80 (Dec. 1919): 639.

98. George Chauncey, *Gay New York: Gender, Urban Culture, and the Makings of the Gay Male World, 1890–1940* (New York: Basic Books, 1994), 85.

CHAPTER 4: "REACHING THE WHOLE COUNTRY"

1. "Segregation Is to Be Considered," *Bay City Times*, Sept. 11, 1917; "Conference Opens, About Fifty Present," *Jackson Citizen-Patriot*, Sept. 12, 1917; "State Commission Urged for Control of Sex Maladies," *Jackson Citizen-Patriot*, Sept. 13, 1917; "Discuss Fighting Sex Diseases of Army Men," *Muskegon Chronicle*, Sept. 13, 1917.

2. "Jackson Plans to Prevent Outbreak of Army Sex Ills," *Jackson Citizen-Patriot*, Sept. 4, 1917.

3. "State Commission Urged for Control of Sex Maladies."

4. "Let Soldiers Alone Is Plea," *Evening News* (Sault Ste. Marie), Sept. 14, 1917.

5. Ibid.; Letter from William F. Martin to William F. Snow, Sept. 23, 1917, Box 424, Entry 29A, RG 112, NA.

6. "Let Soldiers Alone Is Plea."

7. Paul B. Johnson, "Social Hygiene and the War," *Social Hygiene* 4.1 (Jan. 1918): 109–10.

8. Richard M. Olin, *Forty-Sixth Annual Report of the Secretary of the State Board of Health of the State of Michigan for the Fiscal Year Ending June 30, 1918* (Lansing, MI: Wynkoop, Hallenbeck, Crawford Co., State Printers, 1919), 10.

9. Letter from Richard M. Olin to Michigan doctors, Nov. 12, 1917, Box 311, Entry 42, RG 90, NA.

10. Johnson, "Social Hygiene and the War," 112. Johnson reproduced the form.

11. Meeting Minutes, Nov. 20, 1917, *Minutes of the State Board of Health/State Council of Health, 1903–1937, Minutes, 1912–1919*, vol. 2, Lot number 25, RG 75–36, AM.

12. Johnson, "Social Hygiene and the War," 113; "Druggists Pledge Their Cooperation," *Bay City Times Tribune*, Nov. 20, 1917. These over-the-counter medications could include mercury pills or solutions, arsenical drugs (which were rebranded as arsphenamine or neoarsphenamine when the Germans refused to sell the Allies Salvarsan or Neosalvarsan), and a wide variety of "quack" remedies.

13. "Physicians Urge Clean Up of the City as War Move," *Saginaw News*, Nov. 21, 1917.

14. Johnson, "Social Hygiene and the War," 113.

15. American Social Hygiene Association, "Social Hygiene Legislation Manual," Publication No. 812 (New York, 1921), 52. See Chapter 259, "Offenses Against Chastity, Morality and Decency, Compiled Laws of the State of Michigan, 1915."

16. Edwin Kirk Piper, *United States World War I Draft Registration Cards, 1917–1918*, Battle Creek, Michigan, FHL film number 1675065; "'Pep and Fun' Urged to Assure Business Success," *Cincinnati Post*, May 31, 1916.

17. Letter from Bascom Johnson to Edwin K. Piper, Oct. 30, 1917, Doc. 8609, Box 6, Entry 393, RG 165, NA.

18. Quoted in Letter from George Nesbitt to Raymond Fosdick, Sept. 28, 1917, Doc. 5959, Michigan Folder, Box 9, Entry 395, RG 165, NA.

19. Memorandum from William F. Snow to Edwin K. Piper, "Assignment to Duty," Oct. 16, 1917, Doc. 8607, Box 6, Entry 393, RG 165, NA.

20. Memorandum from Sidney F. Morgan to Raymond Fosdick, "Assignment to duty of Edwin K. Piper of Battle Creek, Mich.," Oct. 22, 1917, Doc. 8607; Memorandum from Edwin K. Piper to William C. Gorgas, Oct. 25, 1917, Doc. 8703; Letter from Bascom Johnson to W. E. Kellogg, Oct. 30, 1917, Doc. 8578; Letter from Bascom Johnson to Edwin K. Piper, Oct. 31, 1917, Doc. 8608—both in Box 6, Entry 393, RG 165, NA.

21. Edwin K. Piper, "Report of Lieut. Edwin K. Piper, Sanitary Corps, U.S.N.A., week ending November 10th, 1917," Doc. 12392, Michigan Folder, Box 9, Entry 395, RG 165, NA.

22. "Payroll at Camp Custer Is $20,000," *Kalamazoo Gazette* (Kalamazoo, MI), July 19, 1917, 2.

23. Olin, *Forty-Sixth Annual Report*, 12.

24. Brandt, *No Magic Bullet*, 98–99.

25. Edwin K. Piper, "Report of Lieut. Edwin K. Piper, Sanitary Corps, U.S.N.A., week ending November 10th, 1917," Doc. 12392, Michigan Folder, Box 9, Entry 395, RG 165, NA.

26. Letter from Edwin K. Piper to Bascom Johnson, Nov. 23, 1917, Michigan Folder, Box 9, Entry 395, RG 165, NA. Sadly, only weekly reports from November and December appear to have survived. See Edwin K. Piper, "Report of Lieut. Edwin K. Piper, Sanitary Corps, U.S.N.A., week ending November 24, 1917"; Edwin K. Piper, "Report of Lieut. Edwin K. Piper, Sanitary Corps, U.S.N.A., week ending December 1, 1917"; Edwin K. Piper, "Report of Lieut. Edwin K. Piper, Sanitary Corps, U.S.N.A., week ending December 22, 1917"—all are in Box 9, Entry 395, RG 165, NA.

27. Letter from Provost Marshal to Commanding General 85th Division, Nov. 20, 1917, Michigan Folder; Edwin K. Piper, "Report of Lieut. Edwin K. Piper, Sanitary Corps, U.S.N.A., week ending November 24, 1917"—both in Box 9, Entry 395, RG 165, NA.

28. Memorandum from Edwin K. Piper to Bascom Johnson, Nov. 18, 1917, Doc. 12540, Michigan Folder, Box 9, Entry 395, RG 165, NA.

29. Letter from Bascom Johnson to Edwin Piper, Nov. 24, 1917, Doc. 12540, Michigan Folder, Box 9, Entry 395, RG 165, NA.

30. See Edwin K. Piper, "Report of Lieut. Edwin K. Piper, Sanitary Corps, U.S.N.A., week ending December 1st, 1917"; Edwin K. Piper, "Report of Lieut. Edwin K. Piper, Sanitary Corps, U.S.N.A., Week Ending December 8th, 1917"; Edwin K. Piper, "Report of Lieut. Edwin K. Piper, Sanitary Corps, U.S.N.A., Week Ending December 15th, 1917"; Edwin K. Piper, "Report of Lieut. Edwin K. Piper, Sanitary Corps, U.S.N.A., Week Ending December 22nd, 1917"—all of these in Michigan Folder, Box 9, Entry 395, RG 165, NA.

31. E. R. Beckwith, "Conditions at Camp Custer, Battle Creek, and Kalamazoo," Dec. 22, 1917, Michigan Folder, Box 9, Entry 395, RG 165, NA.

32. See Johnson, "Social Hygiene and the War," 91–98; William H. Zinsser, "Social Hygiene and the War," *Social Hygiene* 4.4 (Oct. 1918): 501–2; William H. Zinsser, "Working with Men Outside the Camps," *Annals of the American Academy of Political and Social Science* 79 (Sept. 1918): 194–98; Brandt, *No Magic Bullet*, 77–78; *Hearings Before the Committee on Military Affairs, United States Senate*, pp. 61–64 (June 18, 1918), 65th Cong., 2nd Sess.

33. Clarke, *Taboo*, 70; Program for Dinner in Honor of William F. Snow, Oct. 1, 1937, Folder 446, Box 36, TPP.

34. Snow's committee was called the Committee for Civilian Cooperation in Combating Venereal Diseases (CCCCVD). "Section on Men's Work," pp. 1–3, *Social Hygiene Division*, Box 2, Entry 404, RG 165, NA; Meeting Minutes, American Social Hygiene Association, 13 Sept. 1917, Folder 6, Box 5, Series 2, ASHAR; Zinsser, "Social Hygiene and the War," 501–3; Brandt, *No Magic Bullet*, 78–80.

35. Reprinted in Johnson, "Social Hygiene and the War," 97–98. This was sent at the direction of Franklin Martin.

36. Ibid., 99–101.

37. Ibid., 102–3.

38. C. C. Pierce, "Summary of Venereal Disease Work of the U.S. Public Health Service From Jan. 1, 1918 to June 30, 1924," Folder 308.2, Box 174, Entry 42, RG 90, NA; "Memorandum for Dr. Allan J. McLaughlin: Summary of Progress in Venereal Disease Control up to July 1, 1918," Folder 304.2, Box 174, Entry 42, RG 90, NA; Paul Popenoe, "Second Report on Prostitution and the Sale of Liquor to Soldiers," Jan. 15, 1918, Folder 1, Box 47, PBPP.

39. See Wilbur A. Sawyer, Diary, Vol. XIV, p. 140, Oct. 23, 1917; Wilbur A. Sawyer, Diary, Vol. XIV, p. 143, Nov. 16, 1917; Wilbur A. Sawyer, Diary, Vol. XIV, p. 143, Nov. 21, 1917—all are in Box 6, WASP.

40. Wilbur A. Sawyer, Diary, Vol. XIV, p. 152, Jan. 22, 1918, Box 6, WASP.

41. Wilbur A. Sawyer, Diary, Vol. XIV, p. 153, Jan. 31, 1918, Box 6, WASP. For Sawyer's love letters, see Folders 16 and 17, Box 1, WASP.

42. Wilbur A. Sawyer, Diary, Vol. XIV, p. 154, Feb. 4, 1918, Box 6, WASP.

43. Letter from Wilbur A. Sawyer to J. W. Duke, Feb. 26, 1918, Box 423, Entry 29A, RG 112, NA.

44. Letter from William F. Snow to officers of the Medical Reserve Corps, Feb. 1918, Box 423, Entry 29A, RG 112, NA.

45. See Letter from S. L. Jepson to William F. Snow, Feb. 22, 1918; Letter from W. C. Gorgas to Mark H. Wiseman, Feb. 28, 1918—both in Box 423, Entry 29A, RG 112, NA; Sawyer to Duke, Feb. 26, 1918, NA.

46. Gertrude Seymour, "A Year's Progress in Venereal Disease Control," *Social Hygiene* 5.1 (Jan. 1919): 49.

47. Summary text in Division of Venereal Diseases, "Memorandum for Dr. Allan J. McLaughlin: Summary of Progress in Venereal Disease Control up to July 1, 1918," Folder 304.2, Box 174, Entry 42, RG 90, NA. Original in "Suggestions for State Board of Health Regulations for the Prevention of Venereal Disease," *Public Health Reports* 33.13 (Mar. 29, 1918): 435–39.

48. "Memorandum for Dr. Allan J. McLaughlin," NA. See also Letter from Wilbur A. Sawyer to W. A. Stoecks, Apr. 2, 1918, Box 423, Entry 29A, RG 112, NA.

49. Letter from T. W. Gregory to US Attorneys, Apr. 3, 1918, Box 318, Entry 42, RG 90, NA.

50. T. W. Gregory, "Memorandum on the Legal Aspects of the Proposed System of Medical Examination of Women Convicted Under Section 13, Selective Service Act," Apr. 3, 1918, Box 318, Entry 42, RG 90, NA. Gregory sent a follow-up letter a month later to clear up "[s]ome misunderstanding" about where women could be incarcerated. See Letter from T. W. Gregory to United States District Judges and United States Attorneys, May 10, 1918, Folder 5, Box 47, PBPP.

51. Memorandum from T. W. Gregory to US District Judges, Apr. 3, 1918, Mar./Apr. 1918 Folder, Box 129, Entry 29A, RG 112, NA.

52. See Memorandum from Frank Osborne to Frederick Whitin, "New York State legislation re control and treatment of prostitutes," Mar. 6, 1918, Box 24, C14R.

53. Letter from Frederick Whitin to Frank Osborne, Mar. 8, 1918, Box 24, C14R.

54. "AN ACT To amend the public health law, in relation to certain contagious diseases," Mar. 27, 1918, Venereal Disease Folder, Box 63, C14R; for federal lobbying, see Joseph A. Warren, "Venereal Disease Control Under the Provisions of Chapter 264 of the Laws of 1918," *Health News* 13.10

(Oct. 1918): 272; Chapter 264, Laws of 1918, passed on Apr. 17, 1918. See N.Y. Consol. Laws Ann. Cm. Supp. §§343-m-t (1920); "Progress in Venereal Disease Control," *Weekly Bulletin of the Department of Health, City of New York* 7.35 (Aug. 31, 1918): 271–76; Janke, "Prisoners of War," 289.

55. Janke, "Prisoners of War," 230–31; Inmate #2504, Folder 5, Box 2, RG 14610–77B, NYSA. See also Willoughby Cyrus Waterman, *Prostitution and Its Repression in New York City, 1900–1931* (New York: Columbia University Press, 1932), 54–55; *Annual Report for 1919*, pp. 30–31, Box 86, C14R; Worthington and Topping, *Specialized Courts Dealing with Sex Delinquency*, 334–42; Pivar, *Purity and Hygiene*, 106; Edith R. Spaulding, *An Experimental Study of Psychopathic Delinquent Women* (New York: Patterson Smith, 1923), 271–72.

56. "The Weather," *Bay City Times Tribune*, Feb. 9, 1918.

57. US Bureau of the Census, *Fourteenth Census of the United States Taken in the Year 1920*, vol. 3: Composition and Characteristics of the Population by States (Washington, DC: Government Printing Office, 1910), 488.

58. Julie Reinhart, "The Belles of Bay City Beckoned," *Bay City Times*, Aug. 3, 1980, held in CHL.

59. "Vice Problem Considered in Mayor's Office," *Bay City Times Tribune*, Feb. 9, 1918. See also "City Restaurants Periled by Vice," *Detroit Free Press*, Feb. 10, 1918.

60. Edwin K. Piper, "Report of Lieut. Edwin K. Piper, Sanitary Corps, U.S.N.A., Week Ending December 22nd, 1917," Michigan Folder, Box 9, Entry 395, RG 165, NA.

61. Olin, 101; Richard Milo Olin, *United States World War I Draft Registration Cards, 1917–1918*, Lansing, MI, FHL film number 1675768; 1920 US Census, Lansing, Ingham County, MI, sheet 4B, family 88, line 70, Jan. 6, 1920; *Polk's Battle Creek City Directory, 1899–1900* (Detroit: R. L. Polk, 1901), 276.

62. "Vice Problem Considered in Mayor's Office," *Bay City Times Tribune*, Feb. 9, 1918.

63. "Daughter of Chief Justice Offered Job," *Bay City Times Tribune*, Jan. 9, 1918.

64. See Letter from Raymond Fosdick to Katharine Ostrander, Jan. 26, 1918, Doc. 16390, Box 30, Entry 393, RG 165, NA.

65. Memorandum from Raymond Fosdick to Commanding Officer of Camp McClellan, "Duties of Lieut. Edwin K. Piper, San. Corps, N.A.," Jan. 25, 1918, Doc. 17042, Box 31, Entry 393, RG 165, NA.

66. *American Medical Directory* 7 (American Medical Association, 1921), 743; "Men and Women Inspect the Local Vice Hospital," *Bay City Times Tribune*, Mar. 21, 1919.

67. "Vice Problem Considered in Mayor's Office," *Bay City Times Tribune*, Feb. 9, 1918.

68. Johnson, "Social Hygiene and the War," 110–11.

69. Van Norman, 41–42

70. Fosdick, *Chronicle of a Generation*, 147–48; *Law Enforcement Division*, n.d., pp. 17–18, Box 2, Entry 404, RG 165, NA. Newport News had been enforcing the Plan since at least Nov. 1917. See Memorandum from Paul Popenoe to W. C. Gorgas, "Report," Nov. 20, 1917, Folder 7, Box 46, PBPP.

71. Letter from Bascom Johnson to Raymond Fosdick, Feb. 1, 1918, Doc. 20448, Box 40, Entry 393, RG 165, NA

72. Draft letter from Raymond Fosdick to Newton Baker, Jan. 30, 1918, Doc. 20448; Letter from Bascom Johnson to Raymond Fosdick, Feb. 1, 1918, Doc. 20448; Letter from Maude Miner to Raymond Fosdick, Feb. 4, 1918, Doc. 20448—all in Box 40, Entry 393, RG 165, NA.

73. Olin, 108–9.

74. "The Common Council," *Bay City Times Tribune*, Apr. 16, 1918.

75. See "Camp Sevier," *Greenville County Library System Digital Collections*, http://encore .greenvillelibrary.org/iii/cpro.

76. "Rescue Workers Hold Conference," *News and Courier*, May 23, 1919.

77. See Letter from C. S. Webb to Newton Baker, Aug. 18, 1917, Doc. 4129, Box 574, Entry 393, RG 165, NA; Nancy K. Bristow, "Creating Crusaders: The Commission on Training Camp Activities and the Pursuit of the Progressive Social Vision During World War One," PhD diss., UC Berkeley, 1989, 370–71, 449n54. For background information on the CTCA in South Carolina, see Box 10, Entry 395, RG 165, NA; Benjamin S. Warren, Charles F. Bolduan, Barry S. Levy, and Victor W. Sidel, "War Activities of the United States Public Health Service," *Public Health Reports* 34.23 (June 6, 1919): 119–20; Report, Southeastern District, Committee on Protective Work for Girls, Jan. 21, 1918, Folder 381, Box 24, A-127, ESDP.

78. Martha Falconer, "Work of the Section on Reformatories and Houses of Detention," *Proceedings of the National Conference of Social Work* 45 (1919): 668; Martha Falconer, "The Part of the Reformatory Institution in the Elimination of Prostitution," *Social Hygiene* 5.1 (Jan. 1919): 2–3; Dietzler, *Detention Houses and Reformatories*, 24; *Law Enforcement Division*, pp. 24–25, Box 2, Entry 404, RG 165, NA; Dickinson, *The Building of an Army*, 216. The exact number of girls who were arrested in this episode is surprisingly tricky to pin down. Dietzler and Falconer pegged it at 19; John Dickinson, who quoted Fosdick speaking about the episode just weeks later, put the number at 24. A roughly contemporaneous CPWG report gave the number 15. See "Committee on Protective Work for Girls," Feb. 20, 1918, Doc. 26908, Box 56, Entry 393, RG 165, NA.

79. For information on Framingham (also called Sherborn), see Rafter, *Partial Justice*, 34; Freedman, *Their Sisters' Keepers*, 68–70.

80. "Committee on Protective Work for Girls," Feb. 20, 1918, Attachment B. Nancy Bristow has analyzed this document in her excellent dissertation and monograph, but she appears not to have connected it with the creation of Committee on Reformatories (later the Section on Reformatories and Detention Houses). See Bristow, *Making Men Moral*, 118–19; Bristow, "Creating Crusaders," 349–51.

81. Mabel Ruth Fernald, Mary Holmes Stevens Hayes, Almena Dawley, and Beardsley Ruml, *A Study of Women Delinquents in New York State* (New York: Century Co., 1920), 380–81.

82. Indeed, in one 1919 study of 131 "delinquent girls" imprisoned in Chicago, social worker June Purcell-Guild noted that thirty-five of the girls had been raped, and rape had been the "sole sex experience" for nineteen of them. "It may seem unfair to count these nineteen girls as delinquents," she wrote, "until it is stated that, with one exception, these girls were all guilty of other lesser delinquencies, such as running away from home, larceny, and so forth, which brought them to the institution." June Purcell-Guild, "Study of One Hundred and Thirty-One Delinquent Girls Held at the Juvenile Detention Home in Chicago, 1917," *Journal of Criminal Law and Criminology* 10 (Nov. 1919): 443–44.

83. Dietzler, *Detention Houses and Reformatories*, 35. See also: Falconer, "Work of the Section on Reformatories and Houses of Detention," 668; Falconer, "The Part of the Reformatory Institution in the Elimination of Prostitution," 2–3; Letter from Raymond Fosdick to Martha Falconer, Mar. 25, 1918, Doc. 27532, Box 58, Entry 393, RG 165, NA.

84. Miner, "Report of the Committee on Protective Work for Girls," NA; Letter from Raymond Fosdick to Martha Falconer, Mar. 25, 1918, Doc. 27532, Box 58, Entry 393, RG 165, NA; Janke, "Prisoners of War," 101.

85. Letter from Raymond Fosdick to William F. Snow, Mar. 26, 1918, Doc. 26189, Box 53, Entry 393, RG 165, NA; *Law Enforcement Division*, 9; Letter from Raymond Fosdick to Katharine Davis, Mar. 26, 1918, Doc. 26749, Box 55, Entry 393, RG 165, NA; Letter from Katharine Bement Davis to John D. Rockefeller Jr., Mar. 23, 1918, Folder 44, Box 7, Series O, RAC.

86. Janke, "Prisoners of War," 105; Martha Falconer, "The Segregation of Delinquent Women and Girls as a War Problem," *Annals of the American Academy of Political and Social Science* 79 (Sept. 1, 1918): 160–66.

87. Falconer, "The Part of the Reformatory Institution in the Elimination of Prostitution," 3–4.

88. Keire, *For Business & Pleasure*, 109.

89. Dietzler, *Detention Houses and Reformatories*, 74–76. This is brilliantly synthesized in Odem, *Delinquent Daughters*, 126.

90. Janke, "Prisoners of War," 127–28; Memorandum from Virginia Murray to Jane Deeter Rippin, Apr. 25, 1918, Doc. 25703, Box 52, Entry 393, RG 165, NA; Letter from H. S. Braucher to E. Dana Caulkins, May 28, 1918, Doc. 31025; Letter from E. Dana Caulkins to H. S. Braucher, May 31, 1918, Doc. 31025—both in Box 70, Entry 393, RG 165, NA. For other examples of this disparity, see Memorandum from Wilbur Sawyer to J. G. Wilson, Taliaferro Clark, and Martha Falconer, May 14, 1918, Box 423, Entry 29A, RG 112, NA; Bristow, *Making Men Moral*, 161–62; Dietzler, *Detention Houses and Reformatories*, 91–95, 162–65, 180–82, 208–11, 219–23; Wilbur A. Sawyer, *Second Report to the American Social Hygiene Association on the Social Hygiene Demonstration in the Hampton Roads District*, Dec. 1, 1918, Folder 6, Box 19, Series 2, ASHAR; Parascandola, *Sex, Sin, and Science*, 126.

91. See, for instance, Waukegan's Lake County General Hospital and Baltimore's Morrow Hospital. Dietzler, *Detention Houses and Reformatories*, 116–18, 124–29.

92. Letter from Maude Miner to Raymond Fosdick, Feb. 16, 1918, Doc. 23551, Entry 393, RG 165, NA. Quoted in Janke, "Prisoners of War," 107, and also in Letter from Maude Miner to Raymond Fosdick, Apr. 9, 1918, Doc. 26056, Box 53, Entry 393, RG 165, NA.

93. Letter from Maude Miner to Raymond Fosdick, Apr. 9, 1918, Doc. 26056, Box 53, Entry 393, RG 165, NA.

94. Letter from Raymond Fosdick to Maude Miner, Apr. 15, 1918, Doc. 26056, Box 53, Entry 393, RG 165, NA.

95. Letter from Maude Miner to Ethel Sturges Dummer, Apr. 17, 1918, Folder 378, Box 24, A-127, ESDP.

96. Bristow, *Making Men Moral*, 126.

97. Rippin, "Section on Women and Girls," NA.

98. Letter from Maude Miner to John D. Rockefeller Jr., June 17, 1918, Folder 39, Box 4, Series R, RAC; *Eleventh Annual Report of the New York Probation and Protective Association for the Year Ending September 30, 1919*, 7, 27.

99. David McMacken, "Republic trucks put Alma on the map," *Morning Sun*, June 13, 2013, http://www.themorningsun.com/article/MS/20130613/LIFE01/130619834; David McMacken, *Flash and Fizzle: The Rise and Fall of the Republic Motor Truck Company of Alma, Michigan* (Alma, MI: Alma Public Library, 2011), 1–92.

100. McMacken, *Flash and Fizzle*, 93–96; "8,000 Motor Trucks Are Ordered for the Army: Fifteen Manufacturers, Including Detroit and Alma Factories, Given Shares of Big Order," *Daily Telegram* (Adrian, MI), May 25, 1918; Telephone interview with David McMacken, Jan. 13, 2017; Van Norman, 48.

101. McMacken, *Flash and Fizzle*, 96–98; Telephone interview with David McMacken, Jan. 13, 2017; "$10,000 Suit Tests War Health Laws," *Detroit Free Press*, June 3, 1920; "City Interested in Suit at Alma: Woman Sent to Detention Hospital Asks $10,000 from Health Officer," *Bay City Times Tribune*, June 3, 1920.

102. "Action Is Needed," *Alma Record*, May 16, 1918.

103. "Clean Up," *Alma Record*, May 16, 1918.

104. "Alma Loses Dr. Thomas Carney, Health Crusader and Civic Leader," *Alma Record*, Jan. 6, 1949; Telephone interview with David McMacken, Jan. 13, 2017; David McMacken, "T.J. Carney: Determined Doctor," Nov. 3, 2016, article e-mailed to the author by McMacken; "Health Department Will Enforce Ordinances to the Letter says Dr. Carney," *Alma Record*, Jul. 26, 1916; "Health Campaign to Continue Despite Opposition," *Alma Record*, Aug. 17, 1916; "Germ-Chaser to Rule City," *Detroit Free Press*, Apr. 20, 1941.

105. "Weather," *Evening Star*, Jul. 9, 1918; "Cool Weather Due to 'High Pressure,'" *Evening Star*, Jul. 9, 1918.

106. "Smashing Blow Again Delivered Against Huns," *Evening Star*, Jul. 9, 1918.

107. *Hearings Before the Committee on Military Affairs, United States Senate* (June 18, 1918), 65th Congress, 2nd Session.

108. Chamberlain-Kahn Act, Pub. L. No. 65–193, 40 Stat. 845 (1918).

109. Seymour, "A Year's Progress in Venereal Disease Control," 55–56; *Hearings Before the Committee on Military Affairs*, pp. 77–78.

110. Lloyd Bill, 1918; and Moore Bill, 1918—both in Folder 9, Box 1, JFMP. See also Letter from Wilbur A. Sawyer to Allan McLaughlin, Apr. 12, 1918, Box 423, Entry 29A, RG 112, NA; Memorandum from Franklin Martin to John F. Miller (signed by H. H. Moore), "Legislation re venereal diseases and prostitution," Apr. 27, 1918, Folder 5, Box 1, JFMP; Letter from John F. Miller to H. H. Moore, May 3, 1918, Folder 7, Box 1, JFMP.

111. See testimony in *Hearings Before the Committee on Military Affairs, United States Senate*.

112. Letter from H. G. Irvine to Lewis Michelson, Aug. 2, 1918, Various Important Items Regarding Early VD Work–Minn–1918–1924 Folder, Box 28, MBHR.

113. Rockafellar, "Making the World Safe for Soldiers of Democracy," 273–75; "Work of the Division of Venereal Diseases of the United States Public Health Service," *American Journal of Syphilis* 3.3 (Jul. 1919): 500–501, quoting Rupert Blue; Laurence Schmeckebier, *The Public Health Service: Its History, Activities, and Organization* (Baltimore: Johns Hopkins University Press, 1923), 153–54; "Division of Venereal Diseases," *Annual Report of the Surgeon General for the Fiscal Year 1919* (Washington, DC: Government Printing Office, 1919), 234–25; "Report of Antivenereal Campaign," *Public Health Reports* 34.1 (Jan. 3, 1919): 2–3; *Hearings Before the Committee on Military Affairs*, pp. 74–75.

114. C. C. Pierce, "The Public Health Service Campaign Against Venereal Diseases," *Social Hygiene* 5.4 (Oct. 1919): 436.

115. Minutes of the ISHB, Jul. 16, 1918, Box 1, Entry 30, RG 90, NA; "Memoranda relation to the meeting of The Interdepartmental Social Hygiene Board," Aug. 2, 1918, Box 8, Entry 30, RG 90, NA; "Minutes of an informal meeting of several members of the Interdepartmental Social Hygiene Board preceding the first meeting of the Interdepartmental Social Hygiene Board called on August 2, 1918," Box 8, Entry 30, RG 90, NA; Meeting minutes, ISHB, Aug. 8, 1918, Box 8, Entry 30, RG 90, NA; William F. Snow, "Report of the Executive Committee to the Interdepartmental Social Hygiene Board," Aug. 12, 1918, Box 463, JDP; William Gibbs McAdoo, "Regulations Governing Allotment of Funds for Venereal Disease Prevention Work," Sept. 4, 1918, Box 5, Entry 30, RG 90, NA.

116. Interdepartmental Social Hygiene Board, *Manual for Various Agents of the Board* (Washington, DC: 1920), 46.

117. Eileen J. Suárez Findlay, *Imposing Decency: The Politics of Sexuality and Race in Puerto Rico, 1870–1920* (Durham, NC: Duke University Press, 1999), 176–97.

118. C. C. Pierce, "Venereal Disease Control in Civilian Communities," *American Journal of Public Health* 9.5 (1918): 341; "Necessary to a Real 'Clean-Up,'" *Honolulu Star-Bulletin*, Apr. 11, 1918; "Regulation of Vice Diseases Is War Measure," *Honolulu Star-Bulletin*, Apr. 22, 1918.

119. Rebecca Lord, "Quarantine in the Fort Ozama Dungeon: The Control of Prostitution and Venereal Disease in the Dominican Republic," *Caribbean Quarterly* 49.4 (Dec. 2003): 12–29.

120. Jeffrey W. Parker, "Sex at a Crossroads: The Gender Politics of Racial Uplift and Afro-Caribbean Activism in Panama, 1918–1932," *Women, Gender, and Families of Color* 4.2 (Fall 2016): 196–97; "Note and Comment," *Social Hygiene* 5.2 (Apr. 1919): 259–64; "Note and Comment," *Social Hygiene* 6.4 (Oct. 1920): 620–22; American Social Hygiene Association, *Social Hygiene Legislation Manual*, 18.

121. Luis C. Dery, "Prostitution in Colonial Manila," *Philippine Studies* 39.4 (Fourth Quarter 1991): 481–83; John Andrew Byers, "The Sexual Economy of War: Regulation of Sexuality and the U.S. Army, 1898–1940," PhD diss., Duke University, 2012, 157–59.

122. Examples of these men include C. C. Pierce, Allan J. McLaughlin, W. C. Gorgas, Rupert Blue, and L. M. Maus. Warwick Anderson, *Colonial Pathologies: American Tropical Medicine, Race, and Hygiene in the Philippines* (Durham, NC: Duke University Press, 2006). For the defecation example, see ibid., 101, 119–20.

123. McCall, 36–37, 88; Certificate of Marriage, Nina McCall and Lloyd Knapp, May 11, 1918, *Michigan Marriages, 1868–1925*, FHL film number 2342726.

124. Falconer, "The Segregation of Delinquent Women and Girls," 162.

125. Rippin, "Social Hygiene and the War: Work with Women and Girls," 130.

126. Telegram from Marion Dummer to William and Ethel Dummer, Dec. 29, 1917, Folder 36, Box 3, A-127, ESDP.

127. Certificate of Marriage, Nina McCall and Lloyd Knapp, May 11, 1918. I am indebted to Jan E. Tripp for pointing this out to me.

128. McCall, 88.

129. McCall, 37; Peck, 81.

130. Van Norman, 41–42; McCall, 1.

131. "Girls Taken in Tow by Officer," *Alma Record*, Aug. 1, 1918; "Got Away," *Alma Record*, Aug. 8, 1918.

132. Olin, 104.

133. "Carney Suit Will Start Next Week," *Alma Record*, May 27, 1920; McMacken, "T. J. Carney."

134. "Girls Taken in Tow by Officer," 1. McMacken, *Flash and Fizzle*, 99.

135. "Got Away."

136. "Caught Again," *Alma Record*, Aug. 15, 1918.

137. Katharine Bushnell, *What's Going On? A Report of Investigations by Katharine C. Bushnell, M.D., Regarding Certain Social and Legal Abuses in California That Have Been in Part Aggravated and in Part Created by the Federal Social Hygiene Program* (1919), p. 16, Box 122, 3AMS/D/51/01, AMSHR.

138. Ibid., 4–5.

139. Paul Popenoe, "Fourth report on prostitution and the sale of liquor to soldiers," Mar. 3, 1918, Folder 3, Box 47, PBPP.

140. Inmate No. 2003, Inmate Interview Forms, ID #194418, KSIFWR; Inmate No. 2098, Inmate Interview Forms, ID #194418, KSIFWR.

141. Inmate No. 2199, Inmate Interview Forms, ID #194418, KSIFWR; Inmate No. 2100, Inmate Interview Forms, ID #194418, KSIFWR.

142. Inmate No. 2200, Inmate Interview Forms, ID #194418, KSIFWR; Inmate No. 3799, Inmate Interview Forms, ID #194418, KSIFWR.

143. Inmate No. 3798, Inmate Interview Forms, ID #194418, KSIFWR; Inmate No. 2465, Inmate Interview Forms, ID #194418, KSIFWR.

144. Inmate No. 3420, Inmate Interview Forms, ID #194418, KSIFWR.

145. Inmate No. 3022, Inmate Interview Forms, ID #194418, KSIFWR.

146. For example, Inmate No. 2400, Inmate Interview Forms, ID #194418, KSIFWR; Inmate No. 2525, Inmate Interview Forms, ID #194418, KSIFWR. See also Inmate No. 2044, Inmate Interview Forms, ID #194418, KSIFWR; Inmate No. 3119, Inmate Interview Forms, ID #194418, KSIFWR.

147. Inmate No. 2000, Inmate Interview Forms, ID #194418, KSIFWR.

148. Paul Popenoe, "Report on prostitution and sale of alcohol at Columbus, N.M.," Nov. 12, 1917, Folder 6, Box 46, PBPP.

149. Memorandum from Paul Popenoe to Law Enforcement Division, "Columbus, N.M.," Apr. 1, 1918, Folder 4, Box 47, PBPP.

150. Inmate No. 2002, Inmate Interview Forms, ID #194418, KSIFWR; Inmate No. 2074, Inmate Interview Forms, ID #194418, KSIFWR; Inmate No. 2081, Inmate Interview Forms, ID #194418, KSIFWR; Inmate No. 2199, Inmate Interview Forms, ID #194418, KSIFWR; Inmate No. 2300, Inmate Interview Forms, ID #194418, KSIFWR; Inmate No. 2704, Inmate Interview Forms, ID #194418, KSIFWR.

151. Inmate No. 2470, Inmate Interview Forms, ID #194418, KSIFWR.

152. Inmate No. 2852, Inmate Interview Forms, ID #194418, KSIFWR.

153. Inmate No. 2929, Inmate Interview Forms, ID #194418, KSIFWR; Inmate No. 3301, Inmate Interview Forms, ID #194418, KSIFWR.

154. Inmate No. 3030, Inmate Interview Forms, ID #194418, KSIFWR.

155. Inmate No. 2926, Inmate Interview Forms, ID #194418, KSIFWR.

156. Peck, 73–74.

157. "The Weather," *Jackson Citizen-Patriot*, Sept. 23, 1918.

158. Peck, 73–74.

159. Ibid., 86–87.

160. Ibid., 74–75.

161. Ibid., 86.

162. Ibid., 75.

CHAPTER 5: "IT WAS TOO LATE"

1. McCall, 6.

2. Peck, 75.

3. McCall, 6.

4. McCall, 89.
5. Ibid., 6.
6. Ibid., 19.
7. Ibid., 29.
8. See "Alma," *Saginaw News*, Nov. 6, 1918; "Local News Items," *Alma Record*, Nov. 7, 1918.
9. McCall, 7.
10. Peck, 75.
11. "Ithaca," *Saginaw News*, Nov. 5, 1918.
12. McCall, 8, 25; Corrigan, 56.
13. McCall, 8.
14. Corrigan, 55–57. For other copies of two of these forms, see Voluntary Commitment Order, Michigan State Board of Health, Box 124, 3AMS/D/51/05, AMSHR, and "Commitment Order of the Michigan State Board of Health," Box 124, 3AMS/D/51/05, AMSHR.
15. McCall, 8.
16. McCall, 8; Van Norman, 45.
17. McCall, 8.
18. Hobson, *Uneasy Virtue*, 168–69.
19. Maurice Gregory, Appended Papers on Venereal Disease Control, Nov. 1918, Box 123, 3AMS/D/51/04, AMSHR.
20. Rupert Blue, "Venereal Disease Control: Standards for Discharge of Carriers," *Public Health Reports* 33.29 (Jul. 19, 1918): 1190.
21. Odem, *Delinquent Daughters*, 114, 144–45; Ruth Topping and George E. Worthington, "A Study of Specialized Courts Dealing with Sex Delinquency: The Misdemeanants' Division of the Philadelphia Municipal Court," *Journal of Social Hygiene* 8.1 (Jan. 1922): 43–45.
22. Walkowitz, *Prostitution and Victorian Society*, 201–2; Horan, "Trafficking in Danger," 32; Hobson, *Uneasy Virtue*, 168–69.
23. Walkowitz, "Male Vice and Female Virtue," 421.
24. Letter from Katharine Bushnell to Maurice Gregory, Apr. 8, 1918, Box 123, 3AMS/D/51/04, AMSHR; Letter from Katharine Bushnell to Maurice Gregory, Apr. 11, 1918, Box 123, 3AMS/D/51/04, AMSHR.
25. "Arrests Halted After Innocent Women Taken," *Sacramento Bee*, Feb. 26, 1919.
26. "American Neo-Regulation Built on the Thin Crust of a Volcano: Three Cases in Women's Courts in the United States," *Light* 145 (May–June 1922): 28.
27. Richard M. Olin, *Forty-Seventh Annual Report of the Secretary of the State Board of Health of the State of Michigan for the Fiscal Year Ending June 30, 1919* (Fort Wayne, IN: Fort Wayne Printing Co., 1920), 29.
28. Rockafellar, "Making the World Safe for the Soldiers of Democracy," 432.
29. Barnes, "Pure Spaces and Impure Bodies," 86–87.
30. *In re Habeas Corpus, Clara Mongerson*, Aug. 6, 1918, Dance Halls Folder, Box 328, Entry 42, RG 90, NA.
31. McCall, 6–8, 21; Peck, 76–77.
32. "Medical News: Michigan," *Journal of the American Medical Association (JAMA)* 58.2 (Jan. 13, 1912): 124; "The Detention Hospital," *Bay City Times Tribune*, Oct. 30, 1920, 4; American Medical Association, *American Medical Directory* 7 (1921): 743; "Men and Women Inspect the Local Vice Hospital," 10; "Detention Hospital Burned in Bay City," *Ann Arbor Times News*, Mar. 6, 1920; "City Officials Inspect New City Hospital," *Bay City Times Tribune*, Oct. 6, 1921; Corrigan, 58.
33. 1920 US Census, Bay City, Bay County, MI, p. 7A, family 154, lines 39–46, Apr. 19, 1910; *Polk's Medical Register of the United States and Canada* 14 (New York: Polk, 1917), 782.
34. Letter from Richard M. Olin to Helen Fraser, Jul. 6, 1918, Box 124, 3AMS/D/51/05, AMSHR; Katharine Ostrander, "Social Service and the Venereal Carrier," *Public Health* 7.1 (Jan. 1919): 17.
35. 1900 US Census, Bay City, Bay County, MI, p. 6, family 130, lines 96–100, June 5, 1900; 1920 US Census, Bay City, Bay County, MI, p. 4A, family 79, lines 24–50, Jan. 13, 1920.
36. Corrigan, 71.
37. Ibid., 62.
38. Peck, 77.
39. McCall, 8.
40. McCall, 29.
41. Fosdick, *Chronicle of a Generation*, 172.
42. Quoted in Bascom Johnson, "DEMOBILIZATION PROGRAM—Law Enforcement," Nov. 21, 1918, Doc. 43136, Box 119, Entry 393, RG 165, NA.
43. William H. Zinsser quoted in Bristow, *Making Men Moral*, 181. Zinsser wrote a letter with nearly identical wording to John D. Rockefeller Jr., and 35,000 other "correspondents," on Dec. 5, 1918 (found in Folder 54, Box 7, Series K, RAC).
44. "St. Louis and Alma Have Big Celebration," *Saginaw News*, Nov. 9, 1918; "Alma in Wild Celebration," *Alma Record*, Nov. 14, 1918.
45. "Bay City Goes Wild over the News of Peace," *Bay City Times Tribune*, Nov. 11, 1918.

46. McCall, 9, 21–22. Official documents indicate that this test may have occurred several days earlier than McCall testified it did, perhaps on November 7. See Corrigan, 66.

47. Richard M. Olin, *Forty-Fourth and Forty-Fifth Annual Report of the Secretary of the State Board of Health of the State of Michigan for the Fiscal Years Ending June 30, 1916, and June 30, 1917* (Lansing, MI: Wynkoop, Hallenbeck, Crawford Co., State Printers, 1917), 15; Olin, *Forty-Sixth Annual Report*, 9.

48. Olin, *Forty-Sixth Annual Report*, 58–59.

49. Janke, "Prisoners of War," 243.

50. Robert M. Kaplan and Dennis P. Saccuzo, *Psychological Testing: Principles, Applications, and Issues*, 8th ed. (Belmont, CA: Wadsworth, 2013), 14–15.

51. Rafter, *Partial Justice*, 68.

52. Ferrell, *Woodrow Wilson and World War I*, 20–21.

53. Robert J. Cynkar, "Buck v. Bell: 'Felt Necessities' v. Fundamental Values?," *Columbia Law Review* 81 (Nov. 1981): 1423; Margaret J. Kavounas, "Feeblemindedness and Prostitution: The Laboratory of Social Hygiene's Influence on Progressive Era Prostitution Reform," master's thesis, Sarah Lawrence College, 1992, 39–40.

54. Paul Mertz, "Mental Deficiency of Prostitutes: A Study of Delinquent Women at an Army Port of Embarkation," *JAMA* 72.22 (May 31, 1919): 1598.

55. Jennifer Gunn, "A Few Good Men: The Rockefeller Approach to Population, 1911–1936," in *The Development of the Social Scientists in the United States and Canada: The Role of Philanthropy*, ed. Theresa Richardson and Donald Fisher (New York: Ablex Publishing, 1999), 108.

56. "Minutes of the State Board of Health/State Council of Health, 1903–1937," Feb. 21, 1919, pp. 241–50, vol. 2, Lot no. 25, RG 75–36, AM.

57. Wendy Kline, *Building a Better Race: Gender, Sexuality, and Eugenics from the Turn of the Century to the Baby Boom* (Berkeley: University of California Press, 2001), 45–46.

58. Mertz, "Mental Deficiency of Prostitutes," Pivar, *Purity and Hygiene*, 94.

59. Sidney Morgan, Maude E. Stearns, and Mary E. Magee, "General analysis of the answers given in 15,010 case records of women and girls who came to the attention of field workers of the United States Interdepartmental Social Hygiene Board, and of its predecessors, the War Department and the Navy Department Commissions on Training Camp Activities," Reprint from the Annual Report of the Board, June 30, 1921 (Washington, DC: Government Printing Office, 1922), 175.

60. Miner, "Report of the Committee on Protective Work for Girls," NA.

61. Olin, *Forty-Sixth Annual Report*, 32–33; Katharine Ostrander, "At Work in Michigan," *Social Hygiene Bulletin* 5.9 (Sept. 1918): 1; Lutz Kaelber, "Michigan," *Eugenics: Compulsory Sterilization in 50 American States*, https://www.uvm.edu/~lkaelber/eugenics/MI/MI.html; Jeffrey Alan Hodges, "Dealing with Degeneracy: Michigan Eugenics in Context," PhD diss., Michigan State University, 2001, 314. Sometimes funding prevented the state from institutionalizing "feebleminded" women it otherwise would have locked up. See Ostrander, "At Work in Michigan," 1.

62. McCall, 40.

63. Quoted in Kline, *Building a Better Race*, 49.

64. Kline, *Building a Better Race*, 50; Hodges, "Dealing with Degeneracy," 130.

65. Joseph Mayer, "Social Hygiene Legislation in 1917," *Social Hygiene* 5.1 (Jan. 1919): 68–69.

66. Kline, *Building a Better Race*, 51–55.

67. Harriet A. Washington, *Medical Apartheid: The Dark History of Medical Experimentation on Black Americans from Colonial Times to the Present* (New York: Doubleday, 2006), 203.

68. Hodges, "Dealing with Degeneracy," 144–46.

69. Christopher Capozzola, *Uncle Sam Wants You: World War I and the Making of the Modern American Citizen* (New York: Oxford University Press, 2008), 134; Kline, *Building a Better Race*, 47–60. Later chapters will further document women being sterilized under the Plan.

70. Hobson, *Uneasy Virtue*, 191–92.

71. McCall, 9.

72. Corrigan, 71.

73. Miriam Van Waters, "Where Girls Go Right: Some Dynamic Aspects of State Correctional Schools for Girls and Young Women," *Survey* 48.9 (May 27, 1922): 367. Reformatories are distinct from detention hospitals; reformatories were designed more explicitly to "reform" young women and, therefore, to house them for longer periods of time. However, the activities of women inside both types of institutions did not vary much during the years of the American Plan. See Dietzler, *Detention Houses and Reformatories*.

74. Corrigan, 71.

75. Bristow, *Making Men Moral*, 121.

76. Alexander, *The "Girl Problem,"* 4.

77. Jessie Hodder, speech before the National Committee on Prisons and Prison Labor, Feb. 3, 1919, Folder 231, A-71, MVWP.

78. "Men and Women Inspect the Local Vice Hospital," 10; Corrigan, 73.

79. Corrigan, 57.

80. "Men and Women Inspect the Local Vice Hospital," 10.

81. McCall, 21.
82. Corrigan, 73.
83. McCall, 11.
84. Alexander, *The "Girl Problem,"* 94–95; "Denies Brutality at Reformatory," *New York Times*, Nov. 23, 1919; "Asks Reformatory Heads Be Ousted," *New York Times*, Mar. 19, 1920.
85. Van Waters, "Where Girls Go Right," 374. Van Waters surveyed several dozen institutions for girls and young women; many of these were used to house women under the American Plan, including Sleighton Farms (Pennsylvania), Samarcand Manor (North Carolina), the Sauk Centre (Minnesota), the Virginia State School for Colored Girls, and the Kansas State Industrial Farm for Women.
86. Corrigan, 71.
87. Ibid., 57.
88. Brandt, *No Magic Bullet*, 89. Also, seventeen out of thirty-two detention hospitals that received federal funding had barbed wire, armed guards, or both, according to Dietzler, *Detention Houses and Reformatories*, 75. Detention hospitals were meant to be more temporary than reformatories, but they were often used interchangeably for venereal women.
89. Franklin Hichborn, "The Anti-Vice Movement in California," *Social Hygiene* 6 (Jul. 1920): 369; and Dietzler, *Detention Houses and Reformatories*, 74–76. This is succinctly summarized in Odem, *Delinquent Daughters*, 126.
90. Janke, "Prisoners of War," 197; Diezler, *Detention Houses and Reformatories*, 174–77.
91. McCall, 10.
92. McCall, 23A.
93. Barbara W. Sanborn, "An Analysis of the Population of the Reformatory for Women at Framingham, Mass.," *Journal of the American Institute of Criminal Law and Criminology* 16.1 (May 1925): 148–50. For other examples of censorship, see Alexander, *The "Girl Problem,"* 112–14; Diezler, *Detention Houses and Reformatories*, 55, 101, 106.
94. This form is in many Bedford case files. See, for instance, Inmate #2781, Folder 36, Box 2, RG 14610–77B, NYSA.
95. Brandt, *No Magic Bullet*, 89.
96. Diezler, *Detention Houses and Reformatories*, 118–22; 149–54.
97. *Twentieth Biennial Report of the Michigan State Industrial Home for Girls for the Years 1917–1918* (Fort Wayne, IN: Fort Wayne Printing Co., 1919), 13.
98. McCall, 10.

CHAPTER 6: "WHY SHOULD A WOMAN BE IMPRISONED FOR A DISEASE?"
1. "The Weather," *Bay City Times-Tribune*, Nov. 7, 1918; "The Weather," *Bay City Times-Tribune*, Nov. 9, 1918; "The Weather," *Bay City Times-Tribune*, Nov. 11, 1918; "The Weather," *Bay City Times-Tribune*, Nov. 13, 1918; "The Weather," *Bay City Times-Tribune*, Nov. 15, 1918; "The Weather," *Bay City Times-Tribune*, Nov. 17, 1918; "The Weather," *Bay City Times-Tribune*, Nov. 19, 1918; "The Weather," *Bay City Times-Tribune*, Nov. 21, 1918.
2. McCall, 9, 21, 93–95.
3. Charles Franklin Craig, *The Wassermann Test* (St. Louis: C. V. Mosby, 1918), 162.
4. *In the Matter of the Petition of Mary Main, for a Writ of Habeas Corpus*, Nov. 18, 1918, Dance Halls Folder, Box 328, Entry 42, RG 90, NA.
5. Barnes, "Pure Spaces and Impure Bodies," 90–93.
6. Corrigan, 66–67.
7. McCall, 21–22.
8. Ibid., 94–95.
9. Ibid., 9, 13, 21–24, 94–95.
10. Clarke, *Taboo*, 46; Tomes, *The Gospel of Germs*, 252.
11. Thomas Parran, *Shadow on the Land: Syphilis* (Baltimore: Waverly Press, 1937), 80–81.
12. Gardner Jr., "Microbes and Morality," 178–79; Levine, *Prostitution, Race, and Politics*, 123; Rafter, *Partial Justice*, 218n40.
13. McCall, 9.
14. Ibid., 13.
15. Ibid., 94.
16. Rockafellar, "Making the World Safe for the Soldiers of Democracy," 348.
17. Rafter, *Partial Justice*, 218n40.
18. For instance, of 412 infected women held between 1919 and 1921 by The Hospice—a detention facility in Jacksonville, Florida—"136 were discharged as noninfectious, 80 escaped, 3 died, 1 married; there is no record of what happened to the remaining 188," in the words of one government investigator. Dietzler *Detention Houses and Reformatories*, 107.
19. Barnes, "Pure Spaces and Impure Bodies," 3–4.
20. "The Weather," *Bay City Times-Tribune*, Nov. 30, 1918.
21. Peck, 77, 82–83.
22. McCall, 10.

23. McCall, 10; Peck, 77, 82–83. A little later, Peck suggested that McCall asked her to ask Minnie "to send her something to eat. Most of the girls requested that." See Peck, 86.

24. Van Norman, 45–48.

25. McCall, 10.

26. Peck, 82.

27. Peck, 82–83.

28. Corrigan, 71.

29. Letter from R. M. Olin to Robert Mundy, Dec. 20, 1918, Mayor's and City Attorney's file Dec. 1918, BCGR.

30. 1920 US Census, Bay City, Bay County, MI, pp. 4A–4B, dwelling 78, lines 24–59, Jan. 13, 1920.

31. "Men and Women Inspect the Local Vice Hospital," 10.

32. Clement, *Love for Sale*, 79–86; 177–78; Hobson, *Uneasy Virtue*, 36–37, 99; Rosen, *The Lost Sisterhood*, 79–81.

33. Clement, *Love for Sale*, 86, 202–3; Hobson, *Uneasy Virtue*, 35.

34. Pivar, *Purity and Hygiene*, 191; Katherin N. Hallgren, "Mothers Raise the Army: Women's Politics, Popular Culture and the Great War in America, 1914–1941," PhD diss., CUNY, 2012, 138–39.

35. Isadore Dyer," State Committee of National Defense Medical Section," Feb. 11, 1918, Doc. 26748, Box 55, Entry 393, RG 165, NA.

36. Bristow, *Making Men Moral*, 160.

37. Ibid., 162. This racial disparity predated, and would outlast, the CTCA. See Clement, *Love for Sale*, 209–10; Waterman, *Prostitution and Its Repression in New York City*, 51; Letter from Harold Keats to Raymond Fosdick, Aug. 31, 1917, Doc. 4686, Washington, DC, Folder, Box 10, Entry 395, RG 165, NA.

38. Memorandum from Allison T. French to William F. Snow, "Summary of reports from Military Police," Dec. 29, 1917, Jan. Folder, Box 129, Entry 29A, RG 112, NA; Bascom Johnson, "Section on Vice & Liquor Control. Summary of Reports From Field Representatives for Week Ending April 26, 1918," Mar./Apr. 1918 Folder, Box 129, Entry 29A, RG 112, NA; Memorandum from Bascom Johnson to Representatives of the Section on Vice and Liquor Control, "Venereal Disease Among Colored Troops and Colored Civilian Population," May 29, 1918, Folder 5, Box 47, PBPP.

39. Alice M. Hill, "Psychiatric Studies of Delinquents: Part III. Social and Environmental Factors in the Moral Delinquency of Girls Committed to the Kansas State Industrial Farm," *Public Health Reports* 35.26 (June 25, 1920): 1503, 1513, 1517, 1527; Nicole Perry, "Diseased Bodies and Ruined Reputations: Venereal Disease and the Construction of Women's Respectability in Early 20th Century Kansas," PhD diss., University of Kansas, 2015, 98–101.

40. Clement, *Love for Sale*, 85; Hallgren, "Mothers Raise the Army," 140; Bristow, *Making Men Moral*, 161–62.

41. Dietzler, *Detention Houses and Reformatories*, 165–68, 178–80.

42. Irma Victoria Montelongo, "Illicit Inhabitants: Empire, Immigration, Race and Sexuality on the U.S.-Mexico Border, 1891–1924," PhD diss., University of Texas, El Paso, 2014, 77–84.

43. Estelle B. Freedman, "The Prison Lesbian: Race, Class, and the Construction of the Aggressive Female Homosexual, 1915–1965," *Feminist Studies* 22.2 (Summer 1996): 397–423; Diezler, *Detention Houses and Reformatories*, 68–69; Clement, *Love for Sale*, 85–86; Alexander, *The "Girl Problem*," 92–95; Hicks, *Talk with You Like a Woman*, 223–32.

44. Bristow, *Making Men Moral*, 160.

45. Diezler, *Detention Houses and Reformatories*, 174–77.

46. 1920 US Census, Alma, Gratiot County, MI; p. 10B, family 248, line 87; Jan. 7, 1920; "Return Relative to Divorces from the Circuit Court, County of Gratiot, State of Michigan, for the Year Ending December 31, 1918," Record 180, Sept. 17, 1918; McCall, 30–31, 41.

47. Meeting Minutes, Dec. 20, 1918, Doc. A1909, Box 2, Entry 403, RG 165, NA.

48. Meeting Minutes, Dec. 20, 1918, NA.

49. Bristow, *Making Men Moral*, 184–85.

50. Letter from Edwin R. Embree to William F. Snow, Nov. 8, 1918, in Meeting Minutes, American Social Hygiene Association, Dec. 14, 1918, Folder 7, Box 5, Series 2, ASHAR.

51. Dummer, *Why I Think So*, 81–83; Lichtman, *Ethel Sturges Dummer*, 52; Letter from Jessie Binford to Ethel Sturges Dummer, Dec. 22, 1917, Folder 402, Box 25, A-127, ESDP.

52. Letter from Jessie Binford to Ethel Sturges Dummer, May 8, 1918, Folder 402, Box 25, A-127, ESDP.

53. Letter from Ethel Sturges Dummer to Jessie Binford, Dec. 24, 1918, Folder 402, Box 25, A-127, ESDP.

54. McCall, 9, 23–24.

55. Corrigan, 63, 72.

56. McCall, 23, 95.

57. Jennifer Lisa Koslow, *Cultivating Health: Los Angeles Women and Public Health Reform* (New Brunswick, NJ: Rutgers University Press, 2009), 143.

58. McCall, 23, 95.

59. Ibid., 23.

60. Janke, "Prisoners of War," 211. Janke recounts a report that "women incarcerated at Ward L of the County Hospital [in San Francisco] were taking part in a study prompted by 'previous unsatisfactory results in the treatment of chronic gonorrhea.' This study included a 'compulsory surgical intervention of infected Bartholinian and Skene's glands, together with cauterization of infected cervices rebellious to medical treatment.' Supposedly these surgeries never happened without 'consent of the patient,' but [the official's] report reveals that those who refused to participate had an additional six months attached to their sentence."

61. Brandt, *No Magic Bullet*, 12. See also "40D," *Lancet* (Aug. 17, 1918): 211–12. Here, the eminent British medical journal noted, "And this conclusion is entirely in harmony with the admitted difficulty—some experienced clinicians go so far as to call it impossibility—of curing gonorrhea in the female."

62. McCall, 23–24.

63. Clement, *Love for Sale*, 140–41.

64. "The Weather," *Bay City Times-Tribune*, Dec. 13, 1918; "The Weather," *Bay City Times-Tribune*, Dec. 18, 1918.

65. "The Weather," *Bay City Times-Tribune*, Dec. 24, 1918.

66. "Needy Children Given Xmas Cheer," *Bay City Times-Tribune*, Dec. 25, 1918.

67. "102 Deaths from Grip on Tuesday," *Bay City Times-Tribune*, Dec. 25, 1918.

68. Letter from R. M. Olin to Robert Mundy, Dec. 20, 1918, Mayor's and City Attorney's file Dec. 1918, BCGR.

69. Corrigan, 72.

70. Nancy Bristow, *American Pandemic: The Lost Worlds of the 1918 Influenza Epidemic* (New York: Oxford University Press, 2012), 3.

71. Ibid., 44.

72. Olin, *Forty-Seventh Annual Report*, 135.

73. Executive Order, Michigan, Oct. 19, 1918, Mayor's and City Attorney's file Oct. 1918, BCGR.

74. Leslie E. Arndt, "Flu Epidemic in 1918 Paralyzed Bay County," *Bay City Times*, Nov. 1974, BCHS.

75. "To Be or Not to Be, That Is the Question," *Saginaw News*, Oct. 23, 1918; "Trouble Started Over Influenza," *Alma Record*, Oct. 24, 1918; Certificate of Birth, Albert Worden, Alma, Gratiot County, MI, Dec. 29, 1897, *Michigan Births, 1867–1902*, FHL film number 2322712; Certificate of Death, Albert Worden, Alma, Gratiot County, MI, Oct. 25, 1918, *Michigan Deaths and Burials, 1800–1995*, FHL film number 985692; "Violate Flu Quarantine, Guard Called," *Muskegon Chronicle*, Oct. 24, 1918.

76. Olin, *Forty-Seventh Annual Report*, 135.

77. "Reports Indicate Crest of Epidemic Has Been Passed," *Saginaw News*, Jan. 4, 1919.

78. "Alma Makes New Health Officer," *Saginaw News*, Dec. 4, 1918; "Health Officer Carney Resigns," *Alma Record*, Dec. 5, 1918.

79. "Alma May Not Get Physician Officer," *Saginaw News*, Dec. 7, 1918; "Alma Is Without Health Officer," *Saginaw News*, Dec. 6, 1918; "Alma Finally Gets Health Officer," *Saginaw News*, Dec. 12, 1918.

80. McCall, 13.

81. Letter from Rupert Blue to G. M. Byington, Jan. 20, 1919, Law Enforcement Folder (220.7), Box 56, Entry 42, RG 90, NA.

82. Letter from Frederick Whitin to W. Bruce Cobb, Jan. 16, 1919, Hon W. Bruce Cobb Folder, Box 64, C14R.

83. Letter from Alan Johnstone wrote to Richard M. Olin, Jan. 11, 1919, Doc. 44580, Box 125, Entry 393, RG 165, NA.

84. Commissions on Training Camp Activities, *Standard Forms of Laws for the Repression of Prostitution, the Control of Venereal Diseases, the Establishment and Management of Reformatories for Women and Girls, and Suggestions for a Law Relating to Feeble-Minded Persons* (Washington, DC: Government Printing Office, Aug. 20, 1919), 12–19.

85. W. J. V. Deacon, *A Brief History of the Michigan Dept. of Health Under Commissioner Richard M. Olin, 1917–1927*, picture following p. 4, Box 1, RG 75–40, AM.

86. Letter from G. M. Byington to C. C. Pierce, Jan. 27, 1919, Law Enforcement Folder (220.7), Box 56, Entry 42, RG 90, NA.

87. "A BILL to protect the public health, to prevent the spreading of venereal diseases, to prescribe the duties and powers of the State Board of Health and of local health officers and health boards with reference thereto, and to make an appropriation to carry out the provisions hereof," 1919, Law Enforcement Folder (220.7), Box 56, Entry 42, RG 90, NA; "For New State Laws," *Social Hygiene Bulletin* 6.2 (Feb. 1919): 3.

88. *Law Enforcement Division*, p. 48, Box 26, Entry 399, RG 165, NA.

89. Act No. 272, Compiled Laws of the State of Michigan (May 13, 1919), p. 474.

90. "The Weather," *Bay City Times-Tribune*, Jan. 27, 1919.

91. Letter from C. C. Pierce to Richard M. Olin, Dec. 18, 1918, Michigan Folder (220.1), Box 55, Entry 42, RG 90, NA; Letter from Rupert Blue to Carter Glass, Dec. 18, 1918, Personnel Folder (220.3), Box 55, Entry 42, RG 90, NA.

92. Letter from Rupert Blue to G. M. Byington, Jan. 20, 1919, Law Enforcement Folder (220.7), Box 56, Entry 42, RG 90, NA; Letter from C. C. Pierce to G. M. Byington, Jan. 18, 1919; Letter from Thomas Storey to G. M. Byington, Jan. 14, 1919—these last two are in Michigan Folder (220.1), Box 55, Entry 42, RG 90, NA.

93. "Dr. Byington to Do State Health Work," *Jackson Citizen-Patriot*, Sept. 20, 1919; Certificate of Death, Mason Byington, Charlotte, Eaton County, MI, Sept. 6, 1927, *Michigan, Deaths and Burials Index, 1867–1995*, FHL film number 1973231.

94. Letter from G. M. Byington to C. C. Pierce, Jan. 27, 1919; "A BILL to protect the public health, to prevent the spreading of venereal diseases, to prescribe the duties and powers of the State Board of Health and of local health officers and health boards with reference thereto, and to make an appropriation to carry out the provisions hereof," 1919—both in Law Enforcement Folder (220.7), Box 56, Entry 42, RG 90, NA.

95. McCall, 24; Corrigan, 52–54, 68–69.

96. Corrigan, 53.

97. McCall, 24–25.

98. Corrigan, 69.

99. Corrigan, 68; Peck, 77.

100. McCall, 13.

101. McCall, 30; "Ithaca," *Saginaw News-Courier*, Jan. 17, 1919; Certificate of Marriage, Minnie McCall and Henry Van Norman, Jan. 18, 1919, *Michigan Marriages, 1868–1925*, FHL film number 2342730; Certificate of Marriage, Blanche Thornton and Henry Van Norman, Sept. 29, 1905, *Michigan Marriages, 1868–1925*, FHL film number 2342672; 1900 US Census, New Haven township, Gratiot County, MI, sheet 9B, family 213, lines 66–68, June 18, 1900; 1910 US Census, New Haven township, Gratiot County, MI, sheet 4A, family 65, lines 26–29, Apr. 22, 1910.

102. McCall, 14.

103. Parascandola, *Sex, Sin, and Science*, 78.

CHAPTER 7: "WE WILL GET EVEN YET"

1. McCall, 25.

2. Ibid., 29.

3. John Dunnewind, "Adrian Home D—Disgrace, Says Head of Trustees," *Detroit Free Press*, Jan. 24, 1919; "Girls' Treatment at Adrian School Disgrace to State," *Jackson Citizen Patriot*, Jan. 24, 1919; John Dunnewind, "Adrian Home Warps Lives," *Detroit Free Press*, Jan. 28, 1919; "Girls, Ill, Get Scant Care at Adrian 'Home,'" *Detroit Free Press*, Jan. 29, 1919; John Dunnewind, "Girl at Adrian Is Going Blind; And 'Too Dear,'" *Detroit Free Press*, Jan. 31, 1919.

4. Dietzler, *Detention Houses and Reformatories*, 135–38, 193–200.

5. "But One Nurse at Girls' Home, Board Learns," *Ann Arbor News*, Jan. 29, 1919.

6. "Girls, Ill, Get Scant Care at Adrian 'Home.'"

7. Peck, 77.

8. Ibid., 85.

9. Ibid.

10. McCall, 13.

11. Ibid., 13–14.

12. Peck, 83.

13. McCall, 14; Peck, 85.

14. McCall, 14.

15. Ibid.

16. Van Norman, 46.

17. McCall, 14.

18. Ibid., 25.

19. Ibid., 33.

20. Alexander, *The "Girl Problem*," 4; Bristow, *Making Men Moral*, 121.

21. Rafter, *Partial Justice*, 63.

22. Dietzler, *Detention Houses and Reformatories*, 213–16. For more on racism in the parole system for women, see Hicks, *Talk with You Like a Woman*, chs. 8 and 9.

23. Janke, "Prisoners of War," 275. For an amazing week-by-week account of this parole system and how it applied to women imprisoned under the Plan, see the voluminous reports on the inmates of the Cedars, in Meeting Minutes, 1918–1921, Boxes 7 and 8, OSHSR.

24. Alexander, *The "Girl Problem*," 125.

25. Quoted in Paul B. Johnson, "Social Hygiene and the War," *Social Hygiene* 4.1 (Jan. 1918): 109–10.

26. "Adrian Trades Outside State," *Detroit Free Press*, Feb. 5, 1919; "Adrian Jolts Mrs. Palmer," *Detroit Free Press*, Feb. 26, 1919.

27. John H. Dunnewind, "Found—A Heart in 1 Girl Ruler," *Detroit Free Press*, Feb. 7, 1919; "Inmates Kneel to Show 'Love,'" *Detroit Free Press*, Feb. 11, 1919; Sleeper Going to See Adrian," *Detroit Free Press*, Feb. 12, 1919.

28. John Dunnewind, "Adrian Taboos Family Photos," *Detroit Free Press*, Feb. 16, 1919.

29. "Sleeper Going to See Adrian," 13.

30. "Sleeper Going to See Adrian," 13; Harriet Culver, "Adrian Head Is Detroiter," *Detroit Free Press*, Mar. 7, 1919.

31. "Probers of the Adrian Home Call Witnesses Today," *Bay City Times Tribune*, Feb. 27, 1919.

32. W. J. V. Deacon, *A Brief History of the Michigan Dept. of Health Under Commissioner Richard M. Olin, 1917–1927*, picture following p. 4, Box 1, RG 75–40, AM.

33. "Minutes of the State Board of Health/State Council of Health, 1903–1937," Feb. 21, 1919, pp. 241–50, vol. 2, Lot no. 25, RG 75–36, AM.

34. "The Weather," *Bay City Times Tribune*, Mar. 21, 1919.

35. "Men and Women Inspect the Local Vice Hospital," 10.

36. McCall, 30; Van Norman, 46; Peck, 79.

37. McCall, 33.

38. Van Norman, 46; "Republic Co. Enjoys Brisk Trade Abroad," *Flint Journal*, Mar. 15, 1919.

39. Peck, 78–79, 84.

40. Van Norman, 46–47.

41. McCall, 31–32.

42. Alexander, *The "Girl Problem,"* 124.

43. Falconer, "The Segregation of Delinquent Women and Girls as a War Problem," 165. See also Miner, *Slavery of Prostitution*, 244.

44. Janke, "Prisoners of War," 272–76. As mentioned earlier, for an amazing week-by-week account of this parole system and how Peck-like female workers interacted with women imprisoned under the Plan, see the voluminous reports on the inmates of the Cedars, in Meeting Minutes, 1918–1921, Boxes 7 and 8, OSHSR.

45. Alexander, *The "Girl Problem,"* 125. See "THE CEDARS: Report for 2 weeks ending August 30, 1918"; "THE CEDARS: Report for week ending Sept. 13, 1918"; "THE CEDARS: Report for week ending October 4, 1918"—all in Meeting Minutes, 1917–1918 volume, Box 7, OSHSR; "THE CEDARS: Report December 1 to 12, 1918"; "THE CEDARS: Report for week ending Jan. 24, 1919"; "THE CEDARS: Report for week ending August 8, 1919"; "THE CEDARS: Report for week ending September 19, 1919"—all in Meeting Minutes, 1918–1919 volume, Box 8, OSHSR.

46. See Hicks, *Talk with You Like a Woman*, ch. 8.

47. Rafter, *Partial Justice*, ch. 5 and pp. 159–62. See "THE CEDARS: Report for week ending December 20, 1918"; "THE CEDARS: Report for week ending Feb. 7, 1919"—both in Meeting Minutes, 1918–1919 volume, Box 8, OSHSR.

48. Hicks, *Talk with You Like a Woman*, 239.

49. Quoted in Letter from Ethel Sturges Dummer to Miriam Van Waters, Jul. 30, 1920, Folder 818, Box 37, A-127, ESDP.

50. Sheldon and Eleanor T. Glueck, *Five Hundred Delinquent Women* (New York: Knopf, 1934), 231; Alexander, *The "Girl Problem,"* 125.

51. Dennis E. Alward and Charles S. Pierce, *Michigan Legislative Handbook* (Fort Wayne, IN: Fort Wayne Printing Company, 1919).

52. Gurd M. Hayes, "10 Days Will Bring End of Legislature," *Flint Journal*, Apr. 14, 1919.

53. "State Lawmakers Assembled for Session of 1919," *Jackson Citizen-Patriot*, Jan. 1, 1919.

54. "Governor Sleeper's Inaugural Message," *Daily Telegram*, Jan. 2, 1919.

55. "Eugenics Bill Again Before Legislature," *Flint Journal*, Jan. 15, 1919; "'Eugenics Marriage' Bill Is Introduced," *Bay City Times Tribune*, Jan. 16, 1919.

56. "Believes Measure Would Help Erase Venereal Diseases," *Bay City Times Tribune*, Mar. 5, 1919.

57. John Dunnewind, "Legislators May Work Overtime," *Detroit Free Press*, Apr. 10, 1919.

58. Alward and Pierce, *Michigan Legislative Handbook*, 81.

59. "Equal Wage Bill Passes Lower House," *Bay City Times-Tribune*, Mar. 12, 1919.

60. "Steam Lines Fight High Trolley Fare," *Detroit Free Press*, Apr. 11, 1919. See also "No More Bills to Be Introduced This Session," *Saginaw News*, Apr. 12, 1919.

61. "Senate Speeds Up for Last Week of Present Session," *Bay City Times Tribune*, Apr. 22, 1919; "Dunn Health Bill Goes to Governor," *Detroit Free Press*, Apr. 23, 1919.

62. Alice Stone Blackwell, "The Legislature and the Social Evil," *Woman Citizen* 3.34 (Jan. 8, 1919): 687–88.

63. Alice Stone Blackwell, "Dangerous Legislation," *Woman Citizen* 3.41 (Mar. 8, 1919): 839.

64. Alice Stone Blackwell, "Danger for Women," *Woman Citizen* 3.42 (Mar. 15, 1919): 866–67.

65. "Industrial Farm for Women to be Urged," *San Francisco Chronicle*, Jan. 22, 1919; "Opposition to Vice Fight at Capitol Opens," *San Francisco Chronicle*, Feb. 27, 1919; "Combat Vice Methods Abroad," *Oakland Tribune*, Feb. 28, 1919.

66. "Industrial Farm Urged Before House Committee," *San Diego Union*, Mar. 23, 1919.

67. "Delinquent Farm Bill in Assembly," *Riverside Daily Press*, Apr. 19, 1919; "Dramatic Scenes Enliven Closing Hours of State Assembly; Charges Fly," *Evening Tribune*, Apr. 24, 1919.

68. "Legislature Closes Work for Session," *Bay City Times Tribune*, Apr. 26, 1919; "Dr. Olin Is Head of New Health Board," *Flint Journal*, May 2, 1919.

69. Act No. 272, Compiled Laws of the State of Michigan (May 13, 1919), p. 474.

70. "New Michigan Acts Aid Labor," *Detroit Free Press*, Apr. 28, 1919.

71. See Stern, "The Long American Plan," 433–34; Bess Furman (in consultation with Ralph C. Williams), *A Profile of the United States Public Health Service, 1798–1948* (Washington, DC: US Government Printing Office, 1973), 321.

72. McCall, 32.

73. "Return of Marriages in the County of Gratiot for the Quarter Ending June 30, 1919," Apr. 28, 1919. Minnie Van Norman's testimony further suggests this: see Van Norman, 46–47.

74. McCall, 40.

75. Ibid., 32.

76. Ibid., 33.

77. Ibid., 30.

78. McCall, 31–32; Van Norman, 46–47.

79. Peck, 84.

80. 1910 US Census, Alma, Gratiot County, MI, sheet 2A, family 33, lines 23–25, Apr. 16, 1910.

81. McCall, 32.

82. Sidney J. King, *King's Official Route Guide: Automobile Routes of Michigan and Northern Indiana* (Chicago: Fred Klein Co., 1920), 446–47.

83. McCall, 32, 40.

84. Ibid., 39.

85. "The Weather," *Bay City Times Tribune*, Apr. 30, 1919.

86. 1920 US Census, Alma, Gratiot County, MI, p. 10B, family 248, line 87, Jan. 7, 1920; Certificate of Divorce, Mary Loudenslager and Samuel Loudenslager, *Michigan, Divorce Records, 1897–1952*, Sept. 17, 1918, record no. 180.

87. McCall, 31.

88. Ibid., 39.

89. Ibid., 30–32, 39–40.

90. Ibid., 40.

91. Ibid., 39–41.

92. Ibid., 32.

93. Ibid.

94. Dietzler, *Detention Houses and Reformatories*, 170–73.

95. Ibid., 107.

96. Ibid., 187–90.

97. Katharine Ostrander, "At Work in Michigan," *Social Hygiene Bulletin* 5.9 (Sept. 1918): 1.

98. "Men and Women Inspect the Local Vice Hospital," 10.

99. Rockafellar, "Making the World Safe for the Soldiers of Democracy," 348.

100. "Five Wmen [*sic*] Break Out of Hospital," *Los Angeles Times*, June 5, 1919.

101. American Social Hygiene Association, "Social Hygiene Legislation Manual," 72. This manual was based on the Laws of Connecticut, 1917, Chapter 358.

102. Prisoner Record, May 5, 1925, Folder 233, A-71, MVPW.

103. Koslow, *Cultivating Health*, 146–48.

104. "National Agencies Collaborate," *Social Hygiene Bulletin* 6.5 (May 1919): 1; "Texas Reports," *Social Hygiene Bulletin* 6.5 (May 1919): 1; "Tennessee Falls Out," *Social Hygiene Bulletin* 6.5 (May 1919): 1; "For Quarantine of Infected Men," *Social Hygiene Bulletin* 6.5 (May 1919): 2.

105. "Colonel Snow Describes Social Hygiene Abroad," 1; "Sex Equality," *Social Hygiene Bulletin* 6.10 (Oct. 1919): 6.

106. F. N. Otis, "Concerning the So-Called American Plan of the Treatment of the Late Lesions of Syphilis by Large Doses of Iodide of Potassium," *Medical Record* (Jan. 17, 1885): 82–84.

107. Stern, "The Long American Plan," 433–34.

108. Timothy N. Pfeiffer, "Community Social Hygiene: A Program of Action," Apr. 9, 1920, Folder 6, Box 18, Series 2, ASHAR.

109. For a 1918 usage, see Hugh Young, "Brief Summary of Report byMajor Hugh H. Young of Investigation at Blois," May 20–21, 1918, Folder 3, Box 1, RBFP.

110. Marjorie Delavan, "American Made," *Public Health* 8.2 (Feb. 1920): 61–65. As the historian Courtney Q. Shah noted, this plan was quite similar to a four-part anti-VD plan proposed by the USPHS in 1909 for use in the Philippines. Courtney Q. Shah, *Sex Ed, Segregated: The Quest for Sexual Knowledge in Progressive-Era America* (Rochester, NY: University of Rochester Press, 2015), 81, 87.

111. Edith Picton-Turbervill, "The American Plan: As Seen by an Englishwoman," 1919, Folder 5, Box 171, Series 11, ASHAR; "Police Chiefs Meet in Annual Convention," *Social Hygiene Bulletin* 7.8 (Aug. 1920): 9; Letter from Thomas Storey to Josephus Daniels, Nov. 15, 1920, Box 463, JDP.

112. For the clearest evidence of this change, compare issues of *Social Hygiene Bulletin* from 1918, 1919, and 1920.

113. McCall, 31–32.

114. Ibid., 31–34.

115. Ibid., 31.

116. Sidney J. King, *King's Official Route Guide: Automobile Routes of Michigan and Northern Indiana* (Chicago: Fred Klein Co., 1919), 317; McCall, 31, 33-34.

117. McCall, 34.

118. McCall, 34; Van Norman, 47.

119. McCall, 31, 34.

120. Ibid., 30-31, 33-34.

121. McCall, 41.

122. Ibid., 33.

123. Van Norman, 41.

124. Scott Martelle, *Detroit: A Biography* (Chicago: Chicago Review Press, 2012), 76; Olivier Zunz, *The Changing Face of Inequality: Urbanization, Industrial Development, and Immigrants in Detroit* (Chicago: University of Chicago Press, 1982), 286.

125. Martelle, *Detroit*, 100; Zunz, *The Changing Face of Inequality*, 292-96.

126. Reynolds Farley, Sheldon Danziger, and Harry J. Holzer, *Detroit Divided* (New York: Russell Sage Foundation, 2000), 22-23.

127. Zunz, *The Changing Face of Inequality*, 286.

128. Isabel Wilkerson, *The Warmth of Other Suns: The Epic Story of America's Great Migration* (New York: Random House, 2010), 160-62; Martelle, *Detroit*, 85-93.

129. Zunz, *The Changing Face of Inequality*, 291; Martelle, *Detroit*, 85-86.

130. McCall, 32-33, 35; *Polk's Detroit City Directory* (Detroit: R. L. Polk., 1919), 1479; 1920 US Census, Detroit, Wayne County, MI, p. 1A, family 20, lines 1-2, Jan. 2, 1920; James Nickelson Mondas (misspelled Mandas), *United States World War I Draft Registration Cards, 1917-1918*, Detroit, MI, FHL film number 2024110. Later, James Mondas remarried. See 1930 US Census, Detroit, Wayne County, MI, p. 1B, family 20, lines 78-81, Apr. 2, 1930.

131. Steve Babson (with Ron Alpern, Dave Elsila, and John Revitte), *Working Detroit: The Making of a Union Town* (Detroit: Wayne State University Press, 1986), 45-47; Alfred Scott Warthin, "Combating Venereal Diseases in a State During War Time," *Light* 120 (Mar.-Apr. 1918): 26; William F. Snow and Wilbur A. Sawyer, "Venereal Disease Control in the Army," *JAMA* 71.6 (Aug. 10, 1918): 462.

132. McCall, 34-35.

133. See Arthur W. Thurner, *Strangers and Sojourners: A History of Michigan's Keweenaw Peninsula* (Detroit: Wayne State University Press, 1994), 177.

134. "Minutes of the State Board of Health/State Council of Health, 1903-1937," Aug. 26, 1919, pp. 10-13, vol. 3, Lot no. 25, RG 75-36, AM.

135. Ibid., 13-15.

136. Letter from G. M. Byington to C. C. Pierce, Nov. 29, 1919, Woman Question Folder, Box 331, Entry 42, RG 90, NA.

137. "Report of Antivenereal Campaign," *Public Health Reports* 34.1 (Jan. 3, 1919): 2-3.

138. Letter from Edwin R. Embree to William F. Snow, Nov. 8, 1918, in Meeting Minutes, American Social Hygiene Association, Dec. 14, 1918, Folder 7, Box 5, Series 2, ASHAR; *Report of the United States Interdepartmental Social Hygiene Board for The Fiscal Year Ended June 30, 1921* (Washington, DC: Government Printing Office, 1921), 176-179; Memorandum from Thomas A. Storey to Jason Joy, Mar. 17, 1919, Doc. 48080, Box 140, Entry 393, RG 165, NA.

139. *Report of the United States Interdepartmental Social Hygiene Board*, 180-83.

140. Memorandum from Jason Joy to Henrietta Additon, May 19, 1919, Doc. 49055, Box 144, Entry 393, RG 165, NA.

141. Meeting Minutes, American Social Hygiene Association, Mar. 10, 1919, Folder 8, Box 5, Series 2, ASHAR; Meeting Minutes, Bureau of Social Hygiene, May 9, 1919, Folder 31, Box 3, Series 1, RAC; "A.S.H.A. Meets," *Social Hygiene Bulletin* 6.8 (Aug. 1919): 7; "Experts Discuss Problems," *Social Hygiene Bulletin* 6.11 (Nov. 1919): 7.

142. Letter from John D. Rockefeller Jr. to William F. Snow, Jul. 5, 1919, Folder 122, Box 15, Series K, RAC; Letter from John D. Rockefeller Jr. to the Bureau of Social Hygiene, Oct. 30, 1919, Meeting Minutes, Bureau of Social Hygiene, Dec. 31, 1919, Folder 31, Box 3, Series 1, RAC; Meeting Minutes, Bureau of Social Hygiene, Mar. 26, 1921, Folder 32, Box 3, Series 1, RAC; Meeting Minutes, Bureau of Social Hygiene, May 9, 1919, Folder 31, Box 3, Series 1, RAC; "Contributions from BUREAU OF SOCIAL HYGIENE, INC. to AMERICAN SOCIAL HYGIENE ASSOCIATION," Folder 124, Box 15, Series K, RAC; "PLEDGES AND CONTRIBUTIONS to the AMERICAN SOCIAL HYGIENE ASSOCIATION with covering correspondence for the period 1919-1929," Folder 124, Box 15, Series K, RAC.

143. Revoldt, "Raymond B. Fosdick," 313-15.

144. *Report of the American Social Hygiene Association for the Year 1919*, Folder 6, Box 19, Series 2, ASHAR.

145. Letter from Maude Miner to Ethel Sturges Dummer, Jul. 31, 1919, Folder 384, Box 24, A-127, ESDP.

146. Letter from Ethel Sturges Dummer to William Healy, May 19, 1919, Folder 874, Box 39, A-127, ESDP.

147. Letter from Jessie Binford to Ethel Sturges Dummer, Oct. 22, 1918, Folder 402, Box 25, A-127, ESDP. Also quoted in Janke, "Prisoners of War," 132–33.

148. Quoted in Janke, "Prisoners of War," 133–34.

149. Binford to Dummer, Oct. 22, 1918, ESDP.

150. Letter from Elizabeth McManus to Ethel Sturges Dummer, 21 Jan. 1919, Folder 385a, Box 24, A-127, ESDP.

151. Van Norman, 47, 50.

152. Peck, 78.

153. Van Norman, 49.

154. Ibid., 49–50.

CHAPTER 8: "WHEN RIGHTEOUS WOMEN ARISE"

1. Certificate of Birth, Elizabeth Barr, Rockingham County, VA, Sept. 19, 1876, *Rockingham County, Virginia Births, 1866–84*, p. 297; 1880 US Census, Baltimore City, MD, p. 21, family 177, lines 13–17, June 7, 1880; 1900 US Census, Washington, DC, sheet 17, family 276, lines 28–30, June 11, 1900; Certificate of Death, Elizabeth Githens, Casco, Allegan County, MI, Sept. 24, 1950, *Michigan, Deaths and Burials Index, 1867–1995*, FHL film number 2110085; Certificate of Burial, Elizabeth Githens, Chicago, IL, Sept. 27, 1950; *Michigan, Deaths and Burials Index, 1867–1995*, FHL film number 2110154; Certificate of Marriage, Elizabeth Beverly Barr and John Nichols Githens, Sept. 3, 1900, *District of Columbia, Compiled Marriage Index, 1830–1921*, FHL film number 2108219; "Marriage Licenses," *Evening Star*, Sept. 4, 1900; "J. N. Githens Promoted," *San Francisco Chronicle*, Aug. 27, 1912; 1910 US Census, Bonhomme Township, St. Louis, MO, sheet 1A, family 8, lines 22–25, Apr. 15, 1910; Telephone interview with Catherine Thaler, Mar. 22, 2016.

2. Certificate of Death, John N. Githens, Chicago, Cook County, IL, Jan. 28, 1921, *Illinois Deaths and Stillbirths, 1916–1947*, FHL film number 1852953; Telephone interview with Catherine Thaler, Mar. 22, 2016.

3. Van Norman, 49.

4. McCall, 38.

5. Van Norman, 49–50.

6. Telephone interview with John Daggett, Mar. 22, 2016.

7. "Christian Science Practitioners: Michigan," *Christian Science Journal* 39.1 (Apr. 1921): xxxii. Ida Peck had encountered Elizabeth Githens at the Christian Science Reading Room. See Peck, 84.

8. Janke, "Prisoners of War," 289–90.

9. Letter from Allen Winter to Rupert Blue, Nov. 6, 1919, Law Enforcement Folder (204.7), Box 21, RG 90, NA.

10. Paul Popenoe, "Plans of state board of health for combatting venereal diseases," Feb. 15, 1918, Folder 6, Box 47, PBPP.

11. McCall, 36–38.

12. H. L. Mencken, "'Reformers' Oppose Sanitary Measures Against Disease," *Evening Mail*, Sept. 18, 1917.

13. Quoted in Rockafellar, "Making the World Safe," 318–20.

14. Letter from Edward F. Adams to Rupert Blue, Jan. 28, 1919, Miscellaneous Folder (204.8), Box 21, Entry 42, RG 90, NA.

15. "An Outrage and an Infamy upon Innocent Women," *Sacramento Bee*, Feb. 27, 1919. For a remarkable minute-by-minute account of this raid, see Sacramento City Police Register, p. 102, Feb. 25, 1919, CSH. Much further coverage can be found in the *Bee*.

16. *Proceedings of the International Conference of Women Physicians*, vol. 6 (New York: The Women's Press, 1920), 81–96.

17. Dana Hardwick, *Oh Thou Woman That Bringest Good Tidings: The Life and Work of Katharine C. Bushnell* (St. Paul, MN: Christians for Biblical Equality, 1995), 13–16; Katharine Bushnell, *Dr. Katharine C. Bushnell: A Brief Sketch of Her Life Work* (Hartford, CT: Rose & Sons, 1932), 3; Kristin Kobes Du Mez, *A New Gospel for Women: Katharine Bushnell and the Challenge of Christian Feminism* (New York: Oxford University Press, 2015), 24.

18. On Bushnell's white slavery investigations in the British Empire, see Katharine Bushnell and Elizabeth Andrew, *The Queen's Daughters in India* (London: Morgan and Scott, 1899); Elizabeth Andrew, "A Winter's Purity Campaign in India," *Union Signal*, May 11, 1892; Antoinette Burton, *Burdens of History: British Feminists, Indian Women, And Imperial Culture, 1865–1915* (Chapel Hill: University of North Carolina Press, 1994), 158–62; Katharine Bushnell and Elizabeth Andrew, *Indian Journal* (1892), 3HJW/F/05, HJWP; Du Mez, *A New Gospel for Women*, 70; Hardwick, *Oh Thou Woman That Bringest Good Tidings*, 43–61; "The Outcome of a Noble Work," *Union Signal*, Oct. 5, 1893; "Pastor and People," *Daily Inter Ocean* (Chicago), Apr. 22, 1893. On Bushnell's white slavery investigations in the US, see "Current Events," *Northern Christian Advocate*, Jan. 10, 1889; Katharine Bushnell, "Work in Northern Wisconsin," *W.C.T.U. State Work* 3 (Nov. 1888): 2–5; Bushnell, *Dr. Katharine C.*

Bushnell, 6–7; Du Mez, *A New Gospel for Women*, 58; "Saturday's Sessions," *Union Signal*, Nov. 8, 1888; Katharine Bushnell, "The Facts in the Case," *Union Signal*, Mar. 17, 1889; Pivar, *Purity Crusade*, 137; Hardwick, *Oh Thou Woman That Bringest Good Tidings*, 30; "Those Alleged Dives," *Wisconsin State Journal*, Jan. 18, 1889; "Wisconsin Dens," *Trenton Evening Times*, Mar. 17, 1889; J. P. Gledstone, "Mrs. Andrew and Dr. Kate Bushnell of the World's Women's Christian Temperance Union," *Christian*, June 1, 1893. On Bushnell's connections to Butler, see Bushnell, *Dr. Katharine C. Bushnell*, 8–11; Letter from Josephine Butler to "Dear Friends," Mar. 9, 1891, 3JBL/30/13, JBLC; *Union Signal*, Dec. 25, 1890; Du Mez, *A New Gospel for Women*, 66; Kristin Kobes Du Mez, "The Forgotten Woman's Bible: Katharine Bushnell, Lee Anna Starr, Madeline Southard, and the Construction of a Woman-Centered Protestantism in America, 1870–1930," PhD diss., University of Notre Dame, 2004, 60.

19. Letter from Katharine Bushnell to Ethel Sturges Dummer, Apr. 12, 1920, Folder 484, Box 28, A-127, ESDP.

20. Letter from Katharine Bushnell to Alison Neilans, Aug. 16, 1917, Box 122, 3AMS/D/51/01, AMSHR.

21. Letter from Katharine Bushnell to Alison Neilans, Nov. 1, 1917; "Statement of Account re Anti-Regulation Work, July 1917 to August 1918," 1918; Katharine Bushnell, "Physician, Heal Thyself"; Katharine Bushnell, "Plain Words to Plain People," 1918; Letter from Katharine Bushnell to Alison Neilans, Apr. 24, 1919—these are all in Box 122, 3AMS/D/51/01, AMSHR; Letter from Katharine Bushnell to Raymond Fosdick, Mar. 6, 1918, Doc. 23245, Box 47, Entry 393, RG 165, NA; "Opposition to Vice Fight at Capitol Opens," *San Francisco Chronicle*, Feb. 27, 1919; "Combat Vice Methods Abroad," *Oakland Tribune*, Feb. 28, 1919.

22. Letter from Katharine Bushnell to Fanny Forsaith, Nov. 20, 1917; Letter from Katharine Bushnell to Alison Neilans, Feb. 11, 1918; Letter from Katharine Bushnell to Alison Neilans, Aug. 2, 1918; Bushnell to Neilans, Apr. 24, 1919; Letter from Katharine Bushnell to Alison Neilans, Apr. 28, 1928—these are all in Box 122, 3AMS/D/51/01, AMSHR.

23. Letter from Allison French to Bascom Johnson, Sept. 6, 1917, Doc. 8528, California Folder, Box 5, Entry 395, RG 165, NA.

24. Bushnell to Forsaith, Nov. 20, 1917, AMSHR.

25. Bushnell to Neilans, Feb. 11, 1918; Katharine Bushnell, *The Union to Combat the Sanitation of Vice: Principles*; "A protest addressed to Secretary of the Treasury, William Gibbs McAdoo, head of the Public Health Service, by the Union to Combat the Sanitation of Vice, state of California," Jul. 7, 1918—these are all in Box 122, 3AMS/D/51/01, AMSHR.

26. These allies included Maurice Gregory of the Friends' Association for the Promotion of Social Purity and Fanny Forsaith, Charles J. Tarring, Helen Wilson, and Alison Neilans of the Association for Moral and Social Hygiene (the descendant of Butler's Ladies' National Association). Her extensive correspondence with them is in FAPSRP and Boxes 122–124, AMSHR.

27. Bushnell to Neilans, Apr. 24, 1919, AMSHR.

28. Katharine Bushnell, *What's Going On?*, 18–21, AMSHR.

29. Ibid., 14; Letter from Ethel M. Watters to U.S.P.H.S. Surgeon General, Oct. 22, 1919, Box 329, Entry 42, RG 90, NA.

30. Letter from George Worthington to Frederick Whitin, Nov. 17, 1919, Box 9, C14R.

31. This was the petition mentioned before the Christian Scientists appear to have signed. Letter from Marguerite A. Chappell, Tom C. Thornton, Mrs. Felicia H. Webb, George Starr White, Paula E. Dunnigan, Thomas P. White, Mrs. H. S. Darling, and Estelle L. Lindsey to Meredith F. Snyder, Oct. 1, 1919, Law Enforcement Folder (204.7), Box 21, RG 90, NA.

32. Letter from Allen Winter to Lillian Prey Palmer, Nov. 3, 1919, Law Enforcement Folder (204.7), Box 21, RG 90, NA; "Find Institutions Treat Women Well," *Los Angeles Times*, Nov. 4, 1919.

33. See *Union Signal*, Mar. 4, 1886; Katharine Bushnell, "The Woman Condemned," *Voice Extra* 1.19 (Dec. 1886): 12; Hardwick, *Oh Thou Woman That Bringest Good Tidings*, 20; Frances Willard, ed., *A Woman of the Century* (Buffalo: Moolton, 1893), 141; Frances Willard, "Our White-Ribbon Anchorage," *Union Signal*, Oct. 20, 1892; Du Mez, *A New Gospel for Women*, 52; Frances Willard, "Our White-Ribbon Anchorage," *Union Signal*, Oct. 20, 1892.

34. Petition, Transcript of Record, Rock v. Carney, 185 N.W. 798 (Mich. 1921), Case File 29600, Box 54, RG 96–175, AM.

35. "Republicans Have a Majority in the Legislature," *Daily Telegram*, Nov. 5, 1914; "Michigan's Next Legislature," *Ann Arbor News*, Nov. 30, 1914; "Ingham Sends Person Back to Legislature," *Jackson Citizen Patriot*, Nov. 9, 1916; Alward and Pierce, *Michigan Legislative Handbook*, 64.

36. Gurd M. Hayes, "Legislature Takes Final Adjournment," *Muskegon Chronicle*, May 15, 1919.

37. "Peninsula Paragraphs," *Flint Journal*, May 30, 1907.

38. "Clinton County Democrats Hold a Big Convention," *Saginaw News*, Sept. 29, 1904; 1910 US Census, St. Johns, Clinton County, MI, sheet 10B, family 208, lines 68–71, Apr. 26, 1910.

39. "Campaign in Branch County," *Kalamazoo Gazette*, Apr. 2, 1909; "Candidates on Three Tickets Who Qualified," *Ann Arbor News*, Aug. 3, 1912; "Dean Kelley Is Now School Board Member," *Grand Rapids Press*, Jul. 16, 1913.

40. "Day's News of a Busy State Boiled Down," *Ann Arbor News*, Sept. 9, 1914.

41. "Honor Judge Stone," *Grand Rapids Press*, Dec. 4, 1905.

42. "Democratic Party Is Virile After Its Many Defeats," *Saginaw News*, Feb. 28, 1907.
43. "The Last Election," *Bay City Times*, Apr. 25, 1907.
44. "Ithaca," *Saginaw News*, Aug. 11, 1918.
45. Telephone interview with Catherine Thaler, Mar. 22, 2016.
46. McCall, 36–37.
47. "Return of Marriages in the County of Wayne for the Quarter Ending December 31, 1919," Oct. 10, 1919.
48. The circumstances of his murder would make this clear.
49. 1920 US Census, Detroit, Wayne County, MI, sheet 4B, family 87, lines 85–88, Jan. 1920.
50. Calendar entries, Transcript of Record, Rock v. Carney, 185 N.W. 798 (Mich. 1921), Case File 29600, Box 54, RG 96–175, AM; Case No. 3957, Calendar, Gratiot County Circuit Court, RG 2007–19, AM.
51. "Increase Activity," *Alma Record*, Mar. 4, 1920.
52. "Grave Reflection Is Cast upon the City of Alma," *Alma Record*, Dec. 11, 1919.
53. "The Propaganda for Reform," *JAMA* 79.5 (Jul. 29, 1922): 395–98; "Periodicals in the City Many," *Battle Creek Enquirer*, Jan. 30, 1921; "Editorial Comment: Exit Vivisection," *Colorado Medicine* 19.11 (Nov. 1922): 217.
54. "Grave Reflection Is Cast upon the City of Alma," 1; "Slandering the City," *Alma Record*, Dec. 11, 1919.
55. "Knight, Soldier and Gentleman of South Is Colonel Sol Long," *Morning Star* (Rockford, IL), Dec. 6, 1927; "District Court," *Sedan Lance*, Oct. 27, 1898; "Looks Like Corruption!" *Sedan Lance*, Nov. 3, 1898; "Long Fixing His Fences," *Kansas City Star*, Sept. 25, 1904; "Does Evangelistic Work," *Sedan Times-Star*, Mar. 12, 1909; "Chiropractors in Parade," *Fort Wayne News Sentinel*, Aug. 3, 1920; Sol L. Long, *Rights, Legal and Ethical of Practitioners of Drugless Systems of Healing* (Oklahoma City: Harlow-Ratcliff, 1912).
56. "Increase Activity," 1.
57. Notice of Retainer, Nov. 19, 1919, Rock v. Carney case file, Case No. 3957, Box 127, RG 2007–19, AM.
58. "Law Seniors," *Michiganensian* 17 (1913): 152.
59. Ora Lynn Smith, *United States World War I Draft Registration Cards, 1917–1918*, Gratiot County, MI, FHL film number 1675660. See also photographs in the possession of the author.
60. "Ithaca," *Saginaw News*, Aug. 11, 1918.
61. Letter from O. L. Smith to C. C. Pierce, Jan. 23, 1920, Law Enforcement Folder (220.7), Box 56, Entry 42, RG 90, NA.
62. Letter from C. C. Pierce to O. L. Smith, Jan. 26, 1920, Law Enforcement Folder (220.7), Box 56, Entry 42, RG 90, NA.
63. Respondent's Return, p. 7; Petition, pp. 1–3, *State ex rel. Woods v. Mackintosh*, 169 P. 990 (Wash. 1918), Washington State Archives; Rockefellar, "Making the World Safe," 325–30; Stern, "The Long American Plan," 391–93; State ex. rel. McBride v. Superior Court for King Cnty., 174 P. 973, 974 (Wash. 1918); Application for Writ of Prohibition, Washington State Supreme Court Case File #14913, WSA.
64. Letter from J. S. McBride to Newton Baker, Mar. 18, 1918, Mar./Apr. 1918 Folder, Box 129, Entry 29A, RG 112, NA; "Health Quarantine Upheld," *Seattle Daily Times*, Aug. 28, 1918.
65. Clarence L. Reames, Amicus Curiae brief, Washington State Supreme Court Case File #14913, WSA. An allusion on the first page of his brief suggests that Reames either appeared before the justices or his presence was mentioned to them.
66. Stern, "The Long American Plan," 392–93; Rockafellar, "Making the World Safe for Soldiers of Democracy," 335.
67. Rockafellar, "Making the World Safe for Soldiers of Democracy," 335.
68. See, e.g., *In re* Application of Johnson, 180 P. 644, 645 (Cal. Ct. App. 1919); People *ex rel.* Baker v. Strautz, 54 N.E.2d 441, 443 (Ill. 1944); People *ex rel.* Barmore v. Robertson, 134 N.E. 815, 817 (Ill. 1922); Rock v. Carney, 185 N.W. 798, 803 (Mich. 1921); *Ex parte* Lewis, 42 S.W.2d 21, 22 (Mo. 1931); *Ex parte* Hardcastle, 208 S.W. 531, 532 (Tex. Crim. App. 1919).
69. Wragg v. Griffin, 170 N.W. 400 (Iowa 1919); *Ex parte* Brooks, 212 S.W. 956 (Tex. Crim. App. 1919); *Ex parte* Brown, 172 N.W. 522 (Neb. 1919); *Ex parte* Mason, 30 Ohio Dec. 139 (1919); *Ex parte* McGee, 185 P. 14 (Kan. 1919); Dowling v. Harden, 88 So. 217 (Ala. Ct. App. 1921).
70. Stern, "The Long American Plan," 398–400.
71. *Ex parte* Dillon, 186 P. 170, 172 (Cal. Dist. Ct. App. 1919).
72. See Letter from P.A. Surgeon in Charge, Des Moines, IA to C.C. Pierce, Jan. 23, 1919; Letter from H. C. Hall to Division of Venereal Diseases, Jan. 23, 1919; Letter from R. W. Feezer to C. C. Pierce, Jan. 25, 1919; Memorandum from Bascom Johnson to C. C. Pierce, Feb. 8, 1919—all in Folder 409.1, Box 224, Entry 42, RG 90, NA.
73. See Memorandum from Jane Deeter Rippin to Bascom Johnson, Nov. 22, 1918; Letter from W. A. Brumfield to Rupert Blue, Dec. 18, 1918—both in Box 224, Entry 42, RG 90, NA.
74. Letter from W. Bruce Cobb to Frederick Whitin, Dec. 19, 1919, Hon W. Bruce Cobb Folder, Box 64, C14R.

75. Barnes, "Pure Spaces and Impure Bodies," 162-63. The South Carolina Bar Association endorsed the Plan far more explicitly. See "Venereal Disease Control Regulations," *Public Health Reports* 33.38 (Sept. 20, 1918): 1575-79.

76. "The Weather," *Bay City Times-Tribune*, Mar. 2, 1920.

77. Telegram from Robert Mundy to R. M. Olin, Mar. 2, 1920, BCGR.

78. "Detention Hospital Burned in Bay City," *Ann Arbor Times News*, Mar. 6, 1920; "Wenona Pavement to Cost $111,589," *Bay City Times Tribune*, Mar. 7, 1921.

79. Letter from Robert Mundy to R. M. Olin, Mar. 8, 1920, BCGR.

80. "Detention Hospital Burned in Bay City," 7.

81. Ibid.

82. Dietzler, *Detention Houses and Reformatories*, 3.

83. Ibid., 170-73, 180.

84. Ibid., 146-49.

85. Janke, "Prisoners of War," 178-79.

86. "Hunger Strike Wins Woman's Freedom," *Los Angeles Times*, Sept. 26, 1920; Dietzler, *Detention Houses and Reformatories*, 95-99.

87. Kavounas, "Feeblemindedness and Prostitution," 48-49; Alexander, The *"Girl Problem,"* 93-95.

88. Findlay, *Imposing Decency*, 190.

89. Rockafellar, "Making the World Safe for Soldiers of Democracy," 348-49. These incidents, and others, are recorded in Transcript of Proceedings, "INVESTIGATION of complaints and petitions containing charges preferred against Health, Sanitation and Police Departments in the matter of the arrest and detention of persons alleged to be suffering from certain contagious diseases," Apr. 21, 1919, File 73358, SMA.

90. Letter from Ethel Sturges Dummer to Katharine Bushnell, Mar. 13, 1920, Folder 484, Box 28, A-127, ESDP.

91. Paul Gerard Anderson, "The Good to Be Done: A History of Juvenile Protective Association of Chicago, 1898-1976," PhD diss., University of Chicago, 1988, 399-403; Jessie Binford, "Weekly Report of Supervisor," Mar. 31, 1919-Apr. 7, 1919, Folder 402, Box 25, A-127, ESDP.

92. Letter from Ethel Sturges Dummer to Jessie Binford, Mar. 16, 1920, Folder 403, Box 25, A-127, ESDP; Letter from Ethel Sturges Dummer to Adolf Meyer, 1920, Folder 375, Box 24, A-127, ESDP.

93. Letter from Ethel Sturges Dummer to Alice Hamilton, Apr. 8, 1920, Folder 382, Box 24, A-127, ESDP.

94. Letter from Ethel Sturges Dummer to Jessie Binford, May 9, 1920, Folder 403, Box 25, A-127, ESDP.

95. This idea appears to have been originally proposed by journalist Winthrop Lane. Letter from Winthrop Lane to Martha Falconer, June 4, 1920, Folder 375, Box 24, A-127, ESDP; Letter from Ethel Sturges Dummer to Winthrop Lane, June 17, 1920, Folder 385, Box 24, A-127, ESDP; Letter from Ethel Sturges Dummer to Jane Deeter Rippin, Aug. 21, 1920, Folder 387, Box 24, A-127, ESDP.

96. Letter from Ethel Sturges Dummer to Katharine Bushnell, Mar. 7, 1920, Folder 484, Box 28, A-127, ESDP.

97. Letter from Katharine Bushnell to Ethel Sturges Dummer, Apr. 12, 1920, Folder 484, Box 28, A-127, ESDP; Letter from Ethel Sturges Dummer to Jessie Binford, Mar. 16, 1920, Folder 403, Box 25, A-127, ESDP.

98. Dummer to Binford, Mar. 16, 1920, ESDP; Letter from Jessie Binford to Ethel Sturges Dummer, May 21, 1920, Folder 403, Box 25, A-127, ESDP; Letter from Ethel Sturges Dummer to Katharine Bushnell, June 18, 1920, Folder 484, Box 28, A-127, ESDP; Letter from Adolf Meyer to Ethel Sturges Dummer, Mar. 24, 1920, Folder 375, Box 24, A-127, ESDP; Letter from Ethel Sturges Dummer to Alice Hamilton, Apr. 8, 1920, Folder 382, Box 24, A-127, ESDP; Letter from Ethel Sturges Dummer to Katharine Bushnell, Apr. 8, 1920, Folder 484, Box 28, A-127, ESDP.

99. Letter from Katharine Bushnell to David Robinson, Feb. 14, 1920, Box 329, Entry 42, RG 90, NA.

100. Calendar entries, Transcript of Record, Archives of Michigan; Case No. 3957, Calendar, AM.

101. "Carney Suit Will Start Next Week," *Alma Record*, May 27, 1920.

CHAPTER 9: "HUNTING FOR GIRLS"

1. "The Weather," *Flint Journal*, June 1, 1920; "The Weather," *Bay City Times-Tribune*, June 1, 1920.

2. Dean Wellington Kelley, *United States World War I Draft Registration Cards, 1917-1918*, Lansing, MI, FHL film number 1675767; Seymour Howe Person, *United States World War I Draft Registration Cards, 1917-1918*, Lansing, MI, FHL film number 1675768.

3. See the portrait of Stone in the Gratiot County Courthouse.

4. Tucker, *Gratiot County, Michigan*, 1235.

5. Ibid., 1234.

6. Ibid., 1234-50; John Fedynsky, *Michigan's County Courthouses* (Ann Arbor: University of Michigan Press, 2010), 64-65.

7. Ibid.; observations from personal visit to the Gratiot County Courthouse. See roughly contemporaneous photographs on Tucker, *Gratiot County, Michigan*, 1246–47.

8. Ibid., 1249.

9. Edward Julien Moinet, *United States World War I Draft Registration Cards, 1917–1918*, Clinton County, MI, FHL film number 1675134.

10. Tucker, *Gratiot County, Michigan*, 1249.

11. Ibid.

12. Edward J. Moinet, untitled memorandum, June 1, 1920, Transcript of Record, AM; Case No. 3957, Calendar, AM.

13. "Man Arrested Here for Alma Murder," *Saginaw News*, Dec. 17, 1917; "Alma Is Stirred by Developments in Epler Murder," *Saginaw News*, Dec. 18, 1917; "Who Can Claim Capturing of Criminal Now?" *Muskegon Chronicle*, Dec. 19, 1917; "Eichorn Has an Alibi; Was Visiting a Widow on Night of Murder," *Ann Arbor News*, Dec. 20, 1917; "Farmer Accused of Murder Offers Alibi," *Grand Rapids Press*, Dec. 20, 1917; "Woman in Murder Mystery Arraigned," *Grand Rapids Press*, Dec. 26, 1917; "Unraveling Mystery," *Morning Sun*, Sept. 17, 2006, http://www.themorningsun.com/20060917/unraveling-mystery.

14. "Unraveling Mystery."

15. "Eichorn Trial Nears Conclusion," *Saginaw News*, May 17, 1918; "Eichborn [*sic*] Starts Life Term," *Daily Telegram*, May 21, 1918; "Eichorn Begins Life Term at Marquette For Murder of Girl of Seventeen," *Jackson Citizen-Patriot*, May 21, 1918; "Albert Eichorn Gets Life Term," *Kalamazoo Gazette*, May 21, 1918.

16. For the floor: observations from personal visit to the Gratiot County Courthouse. For the mural: recollections of Judge Jeffrey Martlew.

17. Photographs e-mailed to the author by Alden Moinet Hathaway, Jan. 17, 2016.

18. S. B. Daboll, *Past and Present of Clinton County, Michigan* (Chicago: S. J. Clarke, 1906), 75–76.

19. "Michigan's Bench Shake-Up Greatest in State History," *Muskegon Chronicle*, Jan. 1, 1918.

20. Telephone interview with Alden Moinet Hathaway, Jan. 17, 2016.

21. Daboll, *Past and Present of Clinton County*, 75–76; "Judge Moinet Hits Evil of Cigarette," *Saginaw News-Courier*, Apr. 21, 1922.

22. Telephone interview with Alden Moinet Hathaway, Jan. 17, 2016.

23. Quoted in Ernest Goodman, "The Spanish Loyalist Indictments: Skirmish in Detroit," *Guild Practitioner* 36 (1979): 2.

24. Recollections of Judge Randy Tahvonen. Judge Tahvonen emphasized that he doubted this rumor's veracity.

25. McCall, 1–2.

26. Ibid., 2–3.

27. Ibid., 3–4.

28. Ibid., 4–10.

29. Ibid., 11.

30. Ibid., 11–12.

31. Ibid., 12–12A.

32. Ibid., 12A-13.

33. See "Tour Genesee County," *Flint Journal*, Oct. 19, 1910; "Ferris to Tour County Tomorrow," *Flint Journal*, Sept. 30, 1912; "Democratic Ticket," *Bay City Times-Tribune*, Nov. 4, 1922.

34. McCall, 15–17.

35. Ibid., 17.

36. Ibid., 17–26.

37. Ibid., 27–28.

38. Ibid., 29–33.

39. Ibid., 35–36.

40. Ibid., 36–37.

41. Ibid., 39.

42. "Anti-Vice Case Is Being Tried," *Alma Record*, June 3, 1920.

43. Van Norman, 41–50.

44. Corrigan, 51–73. Objections can be found on pp. 55 and 59–69. Nina's lawyers' sole victorious objection came on p. 63.

45. Ibid., 63.

46. Ibid., 71.

47. McCall, 21; Corrigan, 71.

48. Corrigan, 72.

49. Transcript of Proceedings, 144–45, Apr. 21, 1919, SMA.

50. Peck, 73–77.

51. Ibid., 77–78, 84–85.

52. Ibid., 81–82.

53. Ibid., 84.

54. Ibid., 81.

55. Ibid., 77–80.
56. Ibid., 78, 84.
57. Ibid., 78.
58. Ibid., 86–87.
59. Ibid., 87–88.
60. McCall, 88–89.
61. Ibid., 95.
62. Ibid.
63. Ibid., 96–98.
64. Ibid., 98–99.
65. Ibid., 99–100.
66. Ibid., 100–101.
67. Olin, *United States World War I Draft Registration Cards, 1917–1918.*
68. Olin, 101–3.
69. Ibid., 104.
70. Ibid., 105–11. For the day, see ibid., 111.
71. Ibid., 111.
72. Ibid., 114–15.
73. Ibid., 115–16.
74. Ibid., 116–17.
75. Ibid., 117–18.
76. Ibid., 118–19.
77. Moinet, 121.
78. Ruling of the Judge, Transcript of Record, Rock v. Carney, 185 N.W. 798, Case File 29600, Box 54, RG 96–175, AM.
79. McCall, 29.
80. See "Court Dismisses Suit to Recover $10,000," *Flint Daily Journal*, June 5, 1920; "$10,000 Suit Tests War Health Laws," *Detroit Free Press*, June 3, 1920; "City Interested in Suit at Alma," *Bay City Times Tribune*, June 3, 1920; "Alma," *Saginaw News Courier*, Nov. 27, 1919.
81. "Judge Moinet Takes Rock Case," *Gratiot County Herald*, June 10, 1920.
82. Letter from C. C. Pierce to Jessie Binford, Oct. 1, 1920, Folder 403, Box 25, A-127, ESDP.
83. "All-America Conference on Venereal Diseases, Washington, DC, December 6 to 11, 1920: Preliminary Program," Box 1, MWIP.
84. Letter from Jessie Binford to Ethel Sturges Dummer, Oct. 8, 1920, Folder 403, Box 25, A-127, ESDP.
85. Letter from Ethel Sturges Dummer to Miriam Van Waters, Oct. 30, 1920, Folder 818, Box 37, A-127, ESDP.
86. The resolutions were suggested by "Miss Mine, Mrs. Dummer, Dr. Van Waters, Jessie Binford *and others*" (emphasis mine). "Resolutions suggested by Miss Miner, Mrs. Dummer, Dr. Van Waters, Jessie Binford and others, at the All America Conference on Venereal Disease, Washington, DC, December, 1920," Folder 390, Box 24, A-127, ESDP.
87. "Division of Venereal Diseases, Report of Activities for the Fiscal Years 1919–1922," draft, pp. 5–6, Folder 304.2, Box 174, Entry 42, RG 90, NA.
88. "Preliminary Announcement With Tentative Schedule of Courses: Institute on Venereal Disease Control and Social Hygiene, Washington, DC, November 22 to December 4, 1920," US Public Health Service, Folder 390, Box 24, A-127, ESDP; Kenneth M. Gould, "Progress, 1920–21," *Social Hygiene* 7.3 (Jul. 1921): 314.
89. Letter from Ethel Sturges Dummer to W. I. Thomas, Dec. 5, 1920, Folder 785, Box 36, A-127, ESDP.

CHAPTER 10: "WE DEFEAT OURSELVES"
1. "Cops Stop Man in Detroit; Is Killed," *Ann Arbor Times-News*, Nov. 9, 1920; "'The Lone Wolf' Admits Killing Man in Detroit," *Illinois State Register*, Oct. 15, 1921; "Captive Admits Killing Charge," *Springfield Sunday Journal*, Oct. 16, 1921; Certificate of Marriage, James Carrovall and Rosella Mack, Detroit, Wayne County, MI, Apr. 26, 1920, *Michigan Marriages, 1868–1925*, FHL film number 2342740; Certificate of Divorce, James Carravallah and Rosella Carravallah, *Michigan, Divorce Records, 1897–1952*, Mar. 7, 1921, record no. 80854.
2. "Lively Chase: Butchers and Patrolman Burke Caught Alleged Assaulter," *Detroit Free Press*, Oct. 1, 1899; "Caravallah in More Trouble," *Detroit Free Press*, Apr. 25, 1901; "First Victim of 'Parade,'" *Detroit Free Press*, Apr. 25, 1904.
3. Inmate No. 11308, James Barnett (alias), Record of Prisoners, Southern Michigan Prison, RG 64–50, AM; Inmate No. 33816–11308, James Carravalla, Michigan Department of Corrections, RG 94–196, AM; 1920 US Census, Detroit, Wayne County, MI; sheet 4A, family 68, lines 19–37, Jan. 5, 1920.
4. "Cop Stops Man in Detroit; Is Killed."
5. Ibid.

6. "Warthin Enters Big Drive on Disease," *Ann Arbor Times News*, Nov. 9, 1920.

7. "Weather," *Evening Star* (Washington, DC), Dec. 6, 1920; Untitled conference program, Folder 390, Box 24, A-127, ESDP. The New National Museum is now known as the National Museum of Natural History.

8. "Members All-America Conference on Venereal Diseases—980," Oct. 21, 1920, Folder 400-a.3 (10F2), Box 229, Entry 42, RG 90, NA; "All-America Conference on Venereal Diseases, December 6–11, 1920, Washington, DC: Announcement," W6 P3 v.7481, Box 122, no. 10, NLM.

9. "All-America Conference on Venereal Diseases, December 6–11, 1920, Washington, DC: Announcement," NLM.

10. M. W. Ireland, Speech at All-America Conference on Venereal Disease, Box 1, MWIP.

11. Brandt, *No Magic Bullet*, 77–81, 115–17.

12. Maurice Gregory, "Order of Events" and attachments, Box 123, 3AMS/D/51/04, AMSHR. See also Letter from Chrystal Macmillan to Jane Addams, Aug. 11, 1920, Reel 13, JAP; Meeting Minutes, Executive Committee of the Friends' Association for the Promotion of Social Purity, Oct. 8, 1920, Box 123, 3AMS/D/51/04, AMSHR.

13. "All-America Conference on Venereal Diseases, December 6–11, 1920, Washington, DC: Announcement," NLM; "Outstanding Administrative Details of the Sessions of the General Conference Committee of Fifty," Folder 410 (10F2), Box 229, Entry 42, RG 90, NA; Untitled conference program, Folder 390, Box 24, A-127, ESDP; "The All-America Conference on Venereal Diseases," *JAMA* 75.26 (Dec. 25, 1920): 1790–91; Charles Bolduan, "All-America Conference on Venereal Diseases: Report on the Proceedings and the Resolutions of the General Conference Committee," *Public Health Reports* 36.28 (Jul. 15, 1921): 1632–34. For the machinations shaping the Committee of Fifty's (later General Conference Committee's) membership, see also, "Minutes: Meeting of Administrative Committee All-America Conference on Venereal Diseases," Nov. 4, 1920, Folder 410 (10F2), Box 229, Entry 42, RG 90, NA.

14. "All-America Conference on Venereal Diseases, Washington, DC, December 6 to 11, 1920: Preliminary Program," MWIP.

15. "All-America Conference on Venereal Diseases, December 6–11, 1920," Washington, DC: Announcement," NLM.

16. "Revised to November 29, 1920: Problems Relating to Law Enforcement and Protective Social Measures," Folder 410 (10F2), Box 229, Entry 42, RG 90, NA; "All-America Conference on Venereal Diseases, Washington, DC, December 6 to 11, 1920: Preliminary Program," MWIP.

17. Letter from Ethel Sturges Dummer to Alice Stone Blackwell, Jan. 22, 1921, reprinted in Dummer, *Autobiography of an Hypothesis*, 105–6.

18. Letter from Ethel Sturges Dummer to W. I. Thomas, Jan. 27, 1921, Folder 786, Box 36, A-127, ESDP.

19. Dummer to Blackwell, Jan. 22, 1921, reprinted in Dummer, *Autobiography of an Hypothesis*, 105–6.

20. See Hobson, *Uneasy Virtue*, 182.

21. Katharine Bement Davis, "Social Hygiene and the War: Women's Part in Social Hygiene," *Social Hygiene* 4.4 (Oct. 1918): 534; Mrs. Philip North Moore, "Health and Recreation," *Annals of the American Academy of Political and Social Science* 79 (Sept. 1918): 252; Letter from Valeria Parker to Raymond Fosdick, Apr. 22, 1918, Doc. 26891, Box 55, Entry 393, RG 165, NA.

22. *Proceedings of the Annual Congress of the American Prison Association* (New York: Wynkoop, Hallenbeck, Crawford, and Co., 1921), 294; Mina C. Van Winkle, "Work of the Woman's Bureau of the Metropolitan Police Department," *Proceedings of the Annual Congress of Correction* (New York: Buford, 1919), 396–97.

23. Letter from Anna Garlin Spencer to Edith Houghton Hooker, Dec. 18, 1920, Folder 403, Box 25, A-127, ESDP.

24. Bolduan, "All-America Conference on Venereal Diseases," 1624.

25. Ibid., 1611–12, 1626. For the original draft of this report (which structured the discussion of the "reasonably suspected" kerfuffle differently), see Charles Bolduan, "Reports of the General Conference Committee," Folder 410 (10F2), Box 229, Entry 42, RG 90, NA.

26. Dummer to Blackwell, Jan. 22, 1921, reprinted in Dummer, *Autobiography of an Hypothesis*, 105–6.

27. Letter from Jessie Binford to Alice Stone Blackwell, Jan. 3, 1921, Reel 13, JAP.

28. Letter from Ethel Sturges Dummer to Miriam Van Waters, Dec. 14, 1920, Folder 818, Box 37, A-127, ESDP.

29. Letter from Ethel Sturges Dummer to Elizabeth McManus, Jan. 11, 1921, Folder 385a, Box 24, A-127, ESDP.

30. Letter from Ethel Sturges Dummer to Katharine Bushnell, Feb. 9, 1921, Folder 484, Box 28, A-127, ESDP.

31. Dummer to Blackwell, Jan. 22, 1921, reprinted in Dummer, *Autobiography of an Hypothesis*, 105–6.

32. Letter from Alice Stone Blackwell to Jessie Binford, Feb. 25, 1921, Folder 403, Box 25, A-127, ESDP.

33. Letter from Ethel Sturges Dummer to Martha Falconer, Dec. 17, 1920, Folder 385, Box 24, A-127, ESDP.

34. Letter from Martha Falconer to Ethel Sturges Dummer, Jan. 6, 1921, Folder 385, Box 24, A-127, ESDP.

35. Letter from Spencer to Hooker, Dec. 18, 1920, ESDP.

36. Letter from Anna Garlin Spencer to Rachel Yarros, Dec. 18, 1920, Folder 403, Box 25, A-127, ESDP.

37. Letter from Edith Abbott to Jessie Binford, Feb. 10, 1921, Box 1, AGSP.

38. Letter from Edith Abbott to Anna Garlin Spencer, Feb. 10, 1921, Box 1, AGSP.

39. Letter from Thomas A. Storey to Hugh Cumming, Apr. 5, 1921, Box 4, Entry 30, RG 90, NA.

40. Quoted in Letter from C.C. Pierce to Ann Webster, Jan. 19, 1922, Box 1, Entry 30, RG 90, NA.

41. Letter from Thomas A. Storey to Hugh Cumming, Apr. 5, 1921, Box 4, Entry 30, RG 90, NA. See also Letter from Josephus Daniels, Carter Glass, and Newton Baker to George Chamberlain and S. H. Dont, Jan. 16, 1919, Box 2, Entry 30, RG 90, NA.

42. Thomas Andrew Storey, *United States World War I Draft Registration Cards, 1917–1918*, New York, New York, FHL film number 1786810; O .E. Byrd, G. S. Luckett, and J. P. Mitchell, "Memorial Resolution: Thomas Andrew Storey (1875–1943)," Stanford Historical Society, http://histsoc.stanford.edu/pdfmem/StoreyT.pdf; Frederik Ohles, *Biographical Dictionary of Modern American Educators* (Westport, CT: Greenwood Press, 1997), 309; H. Spencer Turner and Janet L. Hurley, eds., *The History and Practice of College Health* (Lexington: University of Kentucky Press, 2002), 6.

43. Letter from William F. Snow to Josephus Daniels, Jan. 1, 1921. Box 4, Entry 30, RG 90, NA; Letter from William F. Snow to Millard Knowlton, Jan. 6, 1921, Box 185, Entry 42, RG 90.

44. Telegram from William F. Snow to State Health Officers, Jan. 1, 1921, Box 185, Entry 42, RG 90, NA; "Meeting of Executive Committee," Mar. 12, 1921, Box 4, Entry 30, RG 90, NA; Letter from Thomas A. Storey to the various agents of the ISHB, Feb. 7, 1921; Untitled memorandum; Letter from Carter Glass to Francis Warren, Dec. 31, 1920; "Memorandum for the Secretary," May 5, 1921; Letter from E. R. Stitt to Hugh S. Cummings, Apr. 12, 1921—all in Box 1, Entry 30, RG 90, NA.

45. Letter from Jessie Binford to Ethel Sturges Dummer, Feb. 14, 1921, Folder 403, Box 25, A-127, ESDP.

46. Brandt, *No Magic Bullet*, 123.

47. As historian John Parascandola noted, the DVD lost nearly all of its funding, decreasing from $4 million in 1920 to less than $60,000 in 1926, making action virtually impossible. Parascandola, *Sex, Sin, and Science*, 74.

48. Letter from Thomas A. Storey to C. C. Pierce, June 27, 1921, Box 5, Entry 30, RG 90, NA.

49. M. W. Ireland, "Memorandum for U.S. Interdepartmental Social Hygiene Board," June 25, 1921, Box 4, Entry 30, RG 90, NA.

50. Letter from M. W. Ireland to Division of Venereal Diseases, Sept. 8, 1922, Box 3, Entry 30, RG 90, NA; Letter from Mark J. White to C. R. Horner, Aug. 16, 1923, Box 1, Entry 30, RG 90, NA.

51. Rockafellar, "Making the World Safe," 496–97.

52. "The Passing of the Interdepartmental Social Hygiene Board," *JAMA* 76.2 (Jan. 8, 1921): 117.

53. I. H. Dillon, "The Passing of the Interdepartmental Social Hygiene Board," *JAMA* 76.3 (Jan. 15, 1921): 195; Letter from Ellis Bashore to C. C. Pierce, Nov. 3, 1920, Box 3, Entry 30, RG 90, NA.

54. Letter from C. C. Pierce to Robert Mundy, June 21, 1920; Letter from Robert Mundy to C. C. Pierce, June 24, 1920; Letter from R. M. Olin to Robert Mundy, June 30, 1920; Letter from Robert Mundy to R. M. Olin, Aug. 4, 1920; Letter from Robert Mundy to C. C. Pierce, Aug. 4, 1920—all in Mayor's and City Attorney's file Jul.–Dec. 1920, BCGR.

55. "The Common Council," *Bay City Times Tribune*, Apr. 16, 1918; "The Detention Hospital," *Bay City Times Tribune*, Oct. 30, 1920.

56. "Motions and Resolutions," *Bay City Times Tribune*, Jan. 25, 1921.

57. "The Detention Hospital," *Bay City Times Tribune*, Jan. 26, 1921.

58. "The Common Council," *Bay City Times Tribune*, Feb. 8, 1921.

59. "Board Asserts Hospital Isn't Losing Money: Tells Council Detention Hospital Is And Has Been Big Money-Maker—Shows Gain of $2,800 Since Last July—Less Patients," *Bay City Times Tribune*, Feb. 8, 1921.

60. "The Common Council," 10.

61. "May Change Hospital Name," *Bay City Times Tribune*, May 28, 1921.

62. "Common Council," *Bay City Times Tribune*, Feb. 15, 1921.

63. "Carnival Spirit in Council Chamber Monday Night; 'Jitneys' May Now Operate on City Streets," *Bay City Times Tribune*, Feb. 22, 1921; "The Common Council," *Bay City Times Tribune*, Feb. 22, 1921.

64. "The Common Council," *Bay City Times Tribune*, Mar. 15, 1921; "Mexicans Now Are City and County Wards," *Bay City Times Tribune*, Mar. 15, 1921.

65. Hobson, *Uneasy Virtue*, 25.

66. Wunsch, "Prostitution and Public Policy," 150.

67. Fronc, *New York Undercover*, 65–69, 93; Clifford W. Barnes, "The Story of the Committee of Fifteen of Chicago," *Social Hygiene* 4.2 (Apr. 1918): 151–52.

68. Peters, "The Story of the Committee of Fourteen of New York," 357; Johnson, "Defining 'Social Evil,'" 55.

69. Josh Sides, "Excavating the Postwar Sex District in San Francisco," *Journal of Urban History* 32.3 (Mar. 2006): 359; Sides, *Erotic City*, 22–23; Shumsky and Springer, "San Francisco's zone of prostitution," 84; Rosen, *The Lost Sisterhood*, 16–17; Clemmer, "'The City That Knows How,'" 43–44.

70. Bascom Johnson, "The Moral Revolution in San Francisco," 1917, Doc. 5331, California Folder, Box 5, Entry 395, RG 165, NA.

71. Keire, *For Business & Pleasure*, 87–88.

72. Keire, *For Business & Pleasure*, 107; Barnes, "Pure Spaces and Impure Bodies," 158.

73. Rockafellar, "Making the World Safe for Soldiers of Democracy," 236–41.

74. Ann R. Gabbert, "Prostitution and Moral Reform in the Borderlands: El Paso, 1890–1920," *Journal of the History of Sexuality* 12.4 (Oct. 2003): 597–99; Garna L. Christina, "Newton Baker's War on El Paso Vice," *Red River Valley Historical Review* 5 (1980): 55–67.

75. David C. Humphrey, "Prostitution in Texas: From the 1830s to the 1960s," *East Texas Historical Journal* 33 (1995): 31; Clemmer, "'The City That Knows How,'" 87, 134–36; Memorandum from C. B. Hudspeth to Bascom Johnson, "Clean-up—El Paso," Dec. 20, 1917, Folder 1, Box 47, PBPP.

76. Alexandra M. Lord, *Condom Nation: The U.S. Government's Sex Education Campaign from World War I to the Internet* (Baltimore: Johns Hopkins University Press: 2009), 30; C. C. Pierce, "Venereal Disease Control: Methods, Obstacles, and Results," *American Journal of Public Health* 10.2 (Feb. 1920): 136; *Social Hygiene Division*, p. 2, Box 2, Entry 404, RG 165, NA.

77. Olin, *Forty-Sixth Annual Report*, 11.

78. Miner, "Report of the Committee on Protective Work for Girls," NA; Report, Southwestern District, Committee on Protective Work for Girls, Jan. 21, 1918, Folder 381, Box 24, A-127, ESDP; Dietzler, *Detention Houses and Reformatories*, 146–49; *Report of the United States Interdepartmental Social Hygiene Board*, 39.

79. Montelongo, "Illicit Inhabitants," 78. For examples of other local chambers' enthusiasm, see Letter from F. B. Barnet to Walter Clarke, Aug. 18, 1917, Doc. 8542, Box 6, Entry 393, RG 165, NA; Frank J. Osborne, "The Law Enforcement Program Applied," *Social Hygiene* 5.1 (Jan. 1919): 85–91.

80. "Hess, Jacob," *Saginaw News*, Oct. 21, 1950; "HESS," *Saginaw Daily News*, Apr. 3, 1929; 1900 US Census, Saginaw, Saginaw County, MI, sheet 8, family 168, lines 33–37, June 7, 1900; Certificate of Birth, Norman Hess, Saginaw, Saginaw County, MI, Dec. 10, 1897, *Michigan, Births and Christenings Index, 1867–1911*, FHL film number 967183; 1920 US Census, Saginaw, Saginaw County, MI; sheet 10A, family 223, lines 1–2, Jan. 9, 1920; Certificate of Marriage, Norman Hess and Nina McCall, Saginaw, Saginaw County, MI, Apr. 27, 1921, *Michigan Marriages, 1868–1925*, FHL film number 2342745. On Norman's school attendance, see "Honor Roll of the West Side Public Schools," *Saginaw News*, June 11, 1904; "Honor Roll of West Side Schools," *Saginaw News*, June 19, 1907; "Honor Roll of W.S. Public School Pupils," *Saginaw News*, June 23, 1909; "Roll of Honor of W.S. Schools," *Saginaw News*, June 21, 1910. For more on Norman's parents socializing (and Republicanism), see "Hundreds Are Expected," *Saginaw News*, Aug. 3, 1901; "Personal Mention," *Saginaw News*, Jul. 14, 1904; "The A.U.V. Messe," *Saginaw News*, Aug. 22, 1904; "Golden Jubilee of O-Saw-Wah-Bun," *Saginaw News*, June 22, 1905; "Additional Society," *Saginaw News*, Oct. 15, 1907; "Saginaw Social Life," *Saginaw News*, Oct. 28, 1907; "The Committees Have Been Named," *Saginaw News*, Mar. 9, 1908; "Arbeiter Bund Opens Annual Session Here," *Saginaw News*, June 8, 1908; "Political News," *Saginaw News*, Oct. 20, 1908; "Committees for the Anniversary," *Saginaw News*, Dec. 13, 1909; "Odd Fellows Meet; Dedicate Hall," *Saginaw News*, Nov. 17, 1911; "Arbeiters Name Delegates to Their State Convention," *Saginaw News*, May 7, 1914; "In Society," *Saginaw News*, Oct. 5, 1915; "Liberty Loan Subscriptions," *Saginaw News*, Oct. 30, 1917; "Victory Loan Honor Roll," *Saginaw News*, Apr. 27, 1919.

81. *Polk's Saginaw City Directory* (Detroit: R. L. Polk., 1922), 27.

82. *Polk's Saginaw City Directory*, 1922, 452; *Polk's Saginaw City Directory* (Detroit: R. L. Polk, 1923), 438; 1930 US Census, Saginaw, Saginaw County, MI, sheet 8B, family 178, lines 54–57, Apr. 8, 1930.

83. *Polk's Saginaw City Directory*, 1922, 28, 31–32.

84. Robert Jackson Douglas, *Saginaw* (Bloomington, IN: AuthorHouse, 2005), 33.

85. Assignments of Error, Rock v. Carney, 185 N.W. 798, Case File 29600, Box 54, RG 96–175, AM.

86. Certificate of Death, John Charles Hess, June 29, 1921, Saginaw, Saginaw County, MI, June 29, 1921, *Michigan Death Certificates, 1921–1952*, FHL film number 1937080.

87. Rock v. Carney, 185 N.W. 798, 804 (Mich. 1921).

88. Ibid.

89. Ibid.

90. Ibid., 798–99.

91. Ibid., 800.

92. Ibid., 798.

93. "Prosecutor O. L. Smith to Resign," *Gratiot County Herald*, June 9, 1921.

94. "Carney-Rock Case Is Back in Lower Court," *Alma Record*, Dec. 29, 1921.

95. For example, see Wragg v. Griffin, 170 N.W. 400, 400 (Iowa 1919); In re Application of Milstead, 186 P. 170, 170–71 (Cal. Ct. App. 1919).

96. State v. Vachon, 140 Conn. 478, 481–82 (Conn. 1953).

97. "Notes on Venereal Disease Decisions," Dec. 16, 1922, Folder 12, Box 215, ASHAR.

CHAPTER 11: "THE SITUATION SEEMS TO BE GETTING WORSE"

1. David K. Fremon, *Chicago Politics, Ward by Ward* (Bloomington: Indiana University Press, 1988), 24; Hank Klibanoff, "The Opening of Al Capone's Vault," *Philadelphia Inquirer*, Apr. 20, 1986; "Report, International Purity Conference," *Light* 144 (Mar.–Apr. 1922): 5–7.

2. "Detailed Weather Report," *Daily Illinois State Register*, Dec. 27, 1921.

3. "Report, International Purity Conference," 5.

4. Letter from B. S. Steadwell to Ethel Sturges Dummer, Nov. 4, 1921, Folder 766, Box 36, A-127, ESDP; Letter from Ethel Sturges Dummer to B. S. Steadwell, Nov. 11, 1921, Folder 380, Box 24, A-127, ESDP.

5. Maurice Gregory, "State-Regulation of Vice; Its Various Forms," *Light* 144 (Mar.–Apr. 1922): 25–26.

6. "How to Test All Legislative Proposals for Dealing with Venereal Disease," *Light* 144 (Mar.–Apr. 1922): 27.

7. Ethel Sturges Dummer, "The Responsibility of the Home," *Light* 147 (Jul.–Aug. 1922): 50–54; ". . . With the Editor . . ." *Light* 147 (Jul.–Aug. 1922): 54; "The Injustice in American 'Justice,'" *Light* 147 (Jul.–Aug. 1922): 61; Katharine Bushnell, "'Understood But Not Expressed,'" *Light* 148 (Sept.–Oct. 1922): 31–33; Katharine Bushnell, "Human Rights and 'Women's Rights': Real Significance of Recent 'Compulsory' Measures in Dealing with Venereal Diseases," *Light* 149 (Nov.–Dec. 1922): 19–23.

8. B. S. Steadwell, "Sustaining and Promotion Fund for the W.P.F.," *Light* 147 (Jul.–Aug. 1922): 3.

9. Letter from B. S. Steadwell to Maurice Gregory, Oct. 16, 1923, reprinted in "Both Sides of the Atlantic!," n.d., Box 123, 3AMS/D/51/04, AMSHR.

10. Certificate of Death, John N. Githens, Chicago, Cook, IL, Jan. 28, 1921, *Illinois, Deaths and Burials Index, 1916–1947*, FHL film number 1852953; Telephone interview with Catherine Thaler, Mar. 22, 2016; *Chicago Central Business and Office Building Directory: 1925* (Chicago: Winters, 1925), 148, 455.

11. Letter from Katharine Bushnell to Ethel Sturges Dummer, May 20, 1921, Folder 484, Box 28, A-127, ESDP.

12. Bushnell, *Dr. Katharine C. Bushnell*, 26–27.

13. *Ex parte* Company, 139 N.E. 204 (Ohio 1922); Jackson v. Mitchell, 100 So. 513 (Miss. 1924); *In re* Fisher, 239 P. 1100 (Cal. Ct. App. 1925); "Judge Refuses Writ to Venereal Suspect," *JAMA* 82.25 (June 21, 1924): 2059.

14. "Three Women Escaped from Pest House," *Lebanon Semi-Weekly News*, Feb. 12, 1923; "Public Forum," *Lebanon Daily News*, Jul. 20, 1923.

15. Edgar S. Everhart, "Venereal Disease Control in Pennsylvania: Plan Utilizing State Police—Genito-Urinary Division," *Venereal Disease Information* 5.1 (Jan. 20, 1924): 1–2; Letter from Hugh Cumming to Gertrude Seymour, Oct. 23, 1925, Box 224, Entry 42, RG 90, NA.

16. H. G. Fretz, "Problems of Venereal Disease Control in Philadelphia," *Venereal Disease Information* 8.9 (Sept. 20, 1927): 361–62; Malcolm Cowley, "The Vice Squad Carries On: No Woman Is Safe," *New Republic* 63.813 (Jul. 2, 1930): 177.

17. Worthington and Topping, *Specialized Courts Dealing with Sex Delinquency*, 30–31; Herman Bundesen, "Venereal Disease Control," pp. 51–52, in *Report of the Department of Health of the City of Chicago for the Year 1922* (Chicago: Nov. 1923); *Sixteenth Annual Report of the Committee of Fifteen for the Year Ended December 31, 1924*, Folder 38, Box 6, Series O, RAC; Nels Anderson, "MONTHLY REPORT," Jan. 1923, Folder 92, Box 6, JPAR; *Seventeenth Annual Report of the Committee of Fifteen for the Year Ended December 31, 1925*, Folder 38, Box 6, Series O, RAC; Edith Abbott and Sophinisba Breckinridge, "Outline of a Proposed Study of the Morals Court of Chicago Through the Method of Experimentation," Aug. 19, 1931, Folder 202, Box 10, Series 3, RAC; Walter Reckless, *Vice in Chicago* (Montclair, NJ: Patterson Smith, 1969), 243; Michael Willrich, *City of Courts: Socializing Justice in Progressive Era Chicago* (Cambridge, UK: Cambridge University Press, 2003), 202.

18. Ditmore, *Encyclopedia of Prostitution and Sex Work*, 97. See also Mary Linehan, "Vicious Circle: Prostitution, Reform and Public Policy in Chicago, 1830–1930," PhD diss., Notre Dame University, 1991, 294–95.

19. "Forcible Cure of Victims of Vice Raids Hit," *Chicago Daily Tribune*, June 3, 1923.

20. "Single Standard to Curb Disease Gets Knockout," *Chicago Daily Tribune*, June 24, 1923.

21. Alida C. Bowler, "A Police Department's Social Hygiene Activities," *Journal of Social Hygiene* 15.9 (Dec. 1929): 530–34.

22. "Crime Board's Work Indorsed," *Los Angeles Times*, Feb. 14, 1924; "City Hospital Is Condemned," *Los Angeles Times*, Oct. 29, 1924; Koslow. *Cultivating Health*, 154.

23. Jennifer Lisa Koslow, *Cultivating Health: Los Angeles Women and Public Health Reform* (New Brunswick, NJ: Rutgers University Press, 2009), 144–47.

24. On Salt Lake City, see "Stringent Health Rule Is Enforced," *Ogden Standard-Express*, Feb. 15, 1925; "The Law of Quarantine as Applied to Venereal Disease," *Venereal Disease Information* 6.1 (Jan. 20, 1925): 1–4. On Tacoma, Hartford, and San Antonio, William F. Snow, Susan B. Bristol, and

Mary S. Edwards, "Venereal Disease Control," 1927, p. 223, Folder 1, Box 116, Series 8, ASHAR. On Utica, see Waterman, *Prostitution and its Repression in New York City*, 38; George E. Worthington and Ruth Topping, *Specialized Courts Dealing with Sex Delinquency: A Study of the Procedure in Chicago, Boston, Philadelphia and New York* (New York: F.H. Hitchcock, 1925), 334–35; Committee of Fourteen, *Annual Report for 1920*, p. 24, Box 86, C14R.

25. American Social Hygiene Association, *The Association's Tenth Year, 1914–1924*, p. 2, Folder 6, Box 19, Series 2, ASHAR.

26. American Social Hygiene Association, *Summary of Activities for 1925*, p. 9, Folder 6, Box 19, Series 2, ASHAR.

27. American Social Hygiene Association, *Summary of Activities for 1925*, p. 1.

28. American Social Hygiene Association, *Summary of Activities for 1926*, p. 3, Folder 6, Box 19, Series 2, ASHAR.

29. American Social Hygiene Association, *Summary of Activities for 1927*, p. 1, Folder 6, Box 19, Series 2, ASHAR.

30. American Social Hygiene Association, *Summary of Achievements for 1928*, p. 8, Folder 6, Box 19, Series 2, ASHAR.

31. "Office of the Medical Measures Section of a Social Hygiene Survey," Dec. 1, 1928, Folder 12, Box 209, Series 7, ASHAR.

32. Ruth Topping, "SURVEY OF TRAFFIC IN WOMEN AND CHILDREN," Aug. 23, 1932, Folder 203, Box 10, Series 3, RAC.

33. Letter from John D. Rockefeller Jr. to William F. Snow, Jan. 6, 1926, in Meeting Minutes, Bureau of Social Hygiene, Jan. 12, 1927, Folder 39, Box 3, Series 1, Bureau of Social Hygiene Records, RAC; Letter from Charles O. Heydt to John D. Rockefeller Jr., Feb. 8, 1926, Folder 44, Box 7, Series O, RAC; Bureau of Social Hygiene, "Treasurer's Annual Report of Bureau of Social Hygiene, Inc. For the year ending Dec. 31, 1926," Folder 39, Box 3, Series 1, RAC; Meeting Minutes, Bureau of Social Hygiene, Jan. 12, 1927, Folder 39, Box 3, Series 1, RAC; Bureau of Social Hygiene, *A Report to the Trustees Covering the Years 1928, 1929, 1930*, pg. 53, Folder 1, Box 1, Series 1, RAC.

34. See, for instance, Memorandum from Ruth Topping to the Executive Committee of the Bureau of Social Hygiene, "SURVEY OF TRAFFIC IN WOMEN AND CHILDREN IN THE FAR EAST," Dec. 21, 1929, Folder 73, Box 9, Series O, RAC.

35. Letter from G. M. Byington to C. C. Pierce, Dec. 28, 1920, Box 311, Entry 42, RG 90, NA.

36. Telegram from W. J. V. Deacon to C. C. Pierce, Aug. 18, 1922, Finances Folder (220.1), Box 141, Entry 42, RG 90, NA.

37. See Letter from W. J. V. Deacon to C. C. Pierce, Apr. 24, 1922, Reports Folder (220.4), Box 141, Entry 42, RG 90, NA; "Gogebic Worst in Venereal Diseases," *Ironwood Daily Globe*, Oct. 16, 1922; Letter from W. J. V. Deacon to Mark J. White, Dec. 8, 1922, Legal Folder (220.7), Box 141, Entry 42, RG 90, NA.

38. Letter from W. J. V. Deacon to Mark J. White, Mar. 2, 1923, Legal Folder (220.7), Box 141, Entry 42, RG 90, NA.

39. W. H. Fraser, "Report of Eleven Days' Work in Kalamazoo, Calling on Physicians in the Interest of Venereal Disease Reports," Oct. 15, 1921; Letter from C. C. Pierce to W. J. V. Deacon, Oct. 26, 1921; Letter from W. J. V. Deacon to C. C. Pierce, Apr. 24, 1922—all in Reports Folder (220.4), Box 141, RG 90, NA.

40. Letter from Richard M. Olin to the Physicians of Michigan, Nov. 15, 1923, Michigan Dept. of Health, 1923 Folder, Box 5, JSP.

41. People v. Wohlford, 197 N.W. 558 (Mich. 1924).

42. Letter from C. C. Pierce to Virginia Murray, Mar. 1, 1921, Box 311, Entry 42, RG 90, NA.

43. Letter from Ben Lewis Reitman to Herman Bunesen, Oct. 27, 1924, Folder 54, Box 4, BLRP; "Detroit, Michigan, Jan. 4 to Feb. 4, 1926, and Mar. 4 to June 4, 1926, Report on Prostitution, the Police, the Law, and the Courts," p. 10, Folder 9, Box 99, Series 7, ASHAR.

44. "Detroit Police Chief Resigns Under Fire," *St. Louis Globe-Democrat*, Jul. 16, 1926, in Folder 409.1, Box 224, Entry 42, RG 90, NA; American Social Hygiene Association, *Summary of Activities for 1926*, p. 3; American Social Hygiene Association, *Summary of Activities for 1927*, p. 2; American Social Hygiene Association, *Summary of Achievements for 1928*, p. 9—these three are in Folder 6, Box 19, Series 7, ASHAR.

45. "May Change Hospital Name," *Bay City Times Tribune*, May 28, 1921.

46. "City Commission," *Bay City Times Tribune*, June 21, 1921.

47. "City Officials Inspect New City Hospital," *Bay City Times Tribune*, Oct. 6, 1921.

48. Ibid.

49. "Board of Health and Hospital Receipts," *Bay City Times Tribune*, Oct. 15, 1921; "Bay City Hospital Head Died After Long Illness," *Battle Creek Enquirer*, Nov. 15, 1924.

50. These include Samarcand Manor, Bedford Hills Reformatory (later Westfield Farm), Newport News City Farm (later a men's prison), Fairwold Home for Delinquent Girls (later Wilkinson Home for Underprivileged Orphans), Connecticut State Farm for Women (later Niantic prison).

51. "May Change Hospital Name," 10.

52. A. M. Moak, Memorandum, Feb. 2, 1927, Personnel Folder (220.3), Box 141, RG 90, NA; "History of Student Health Services," *Michigan State University*, 2012, http://www.olin.msu.edu /aboutus/history.htm.

53. Letter from W. H. Fraser to C. C. Pierce, Mar. 24, 1921, Miscellaneous Folder (220.8), Box 56, Entry 42, RG 90, NA.

54. Letter from G. M. Byington to C. C. Pierce, June 21, 1921, Personnel Folder (220.3), Box 55, RG 90, NA.

55. Letter from Arthur Tuttle to Heber H. Votaw, Dec. 19, 1923; Letter from Arthur Tuttle to Mrs. James Guffee, Dec. 19, 1923—both in Box 42, AJTP.

56. Certificate of Death, Anna Hess, Saginaw, Saginaw, MI, Apr. 2, 1929, *Michigan Death Certificates, 1921–1952*, FHL film number 1973084; Obituary, *Saginaw News*, Apr. 3, 1929.

57. 1930 US Census, Saginaw, Saginaw County, MI, sheet 8B, family 178, lines 54–57, Apr. 8, 1930.

58. Susan Stein-Roggenbuck, *Negotiating Relief: The Development of Social Welfare Programs in Depression-Era Michigan, 1930–1940* (Columbus, OH: Ohio University Press, 2008), 20–21.

59. 1920 US Census, Alma, Gratiot County, MI, sheet 4B, family 87, lines 85–88, Jan. 1920; 1930 US Census, Alma, Gratiot County, MI, sheet 13A, family 91, lines 37–39, Apr. 10, 1930.

60. Douglas, *Saginaw*, 37, 40, 42, 70, 77, 79.

61. Case No. 3957, Calendar, Gratiot County Circuit Court, RG 2007–19, AM.

62. "Introducing Mrs. Webster," *Woman Citizen* 6.6 (Aug. 13, 1921): 18; "Identification or Discovery of Individuals Who Are Carriers of Venereal Diseases," *Mimeogram* 6 (Sept. 1920), in Alcohol and Vice Control—Interdepartmental Social Hygiene Board 1920 Aug.–Oct. Folder, Box 463, JDP; "Search for Foci of Venereal Diseases," *Mimeogram* 7 (Oct. 1920), in Alcohol and Vice Control—Interdepartmental Social Hygiene Board 1920 Aug.–Oct. Folder, Box 463, JDP; "Identification or Discovery of Individuals who are Carriers of Venereal Diseases," *Mimeogram* 7 (Oct. 1920), in Alcohol and Vice Control—Interdepartmental Social Hygiene Board 1920 Aug.–Oct., Folder, Box 463, JDP; Letter from Valeria Parker to Ann Webster, May 31, 1921, Social Hygiene Folder, Box II:7, LWVR; Letter from Valeria Parker to Mrs. Scott Campbell, Jul. 26, 1921, Social Hygiene—State Corres. Folder, Box II:18, LWVR.

63. See Jacqueline Van Voris, *Carrie Chapman Catt: A Public Life* (New York: Feminist Press at CUNY, 1987), 153–54.

64. "League of Women Voters at Work," *Woman Citizen* 4.11 (Aug. 16, 1919): 273; "Trumpet Call to Action from the Social Hygiene Committee of the National League of Women Voters," *Woman Citizen* 4.43 (May 15, 1920): 1260–61.

65. "Trumpet Call to Action," 1256–58.

66. Ann Webster, "Recommendations of the Social Hygiene Committee," Social Hygiene Folder, Box II:7, LWVR.

67. Letter from Ann Webster to Mrs. Herman P. Strater, Jan. 22, 1923, Social Hygiene—State Corres. Folder, Box II:18, LWVR.

68. This resolution was proposed by Alice Stone Blackwell. Webster, "Recommendations of the Social Hygiene Committee," LWVR; Webster to Strater, Jan. 22, 1923, LWVR; Webster, untitled memorandum, Oct. 9, 1922, LWVR.

69. Webster, untitled memorandum, Oct. 9, 1922, LWVR.

70. "Mrs. Anne Webster Tells of Mission to International Conference at Rome," *Tennessean*, Aug. 19, 1923.

71. Letter from Gertrude Seymour to Hugh Cumming, Oct. 3, 1925, Box 224, Entry 42, RG 90, NA.

72. Letter from Charles O. Heydt to John D. Rockefeller Jr., Jan. 11, 1926, Folder 44, Box 7, Series O, RAC.

73. Letter from Olive A. Colton and Charlotte Price Frohlich to Bernard F. Brough, Nov. 5, 1924, Social Hygiene Committee Folder, Box II:191, LWVR; Letter from Ann Webster to William F. Snow, Dec. 16, 1924, Box II:30, LWVR.

74. Letter from Ann Webster to Adena Rich, May 10, 1926, Social Hygiene Commission Folder, Box II:123, LWVR.

75. Letter from Ann Webster to Charlotte Sherrard, Feb. 14, 1927, Social Hygiene Commission Folder, Box II:123, LWVR.

76. Memorandum from Ann Webster to Mrs. Neff, "Social Hygiene Committee," Social Hygiene Comm. Folder, Box II:123, LWVR.

77. Ann Webster, "The Double Standard in the Penal Code," *New Republic* 63.819 (Aug. 13, 1930): 374.

78. For instance, nine women escaped from the Kansas State Industrial Farm for Women between 1922 and 1924, and fifty-four women escaped from Bedford Hills reformatory in 1925, followed by forty-three women in 1926. *Fourth Biennial Report of the Industrial Farm for Women, Lansing, Kansas, for the Two Years Ending June 30, 1924* (Topeka: Kansas State Printing Plant, 1925), 30; *Twenty-Fifth Annual Report of the New York State Reformatory for Women, Bedford Hills, N.Y., for the Year Ending June 30, 1925*, 8; *Twenty-Sixth Annual Report of the New York State Reformatory for Women, Bedford Hills, N.Y., for the Year Ending June 30, 1926*, 12.

79. Inmate #4044, Folder 3, Box 10, RG 14610–77B, NYSA.

80. *Beginnings, Progress and Achievement in the Medical Work of King County, Washington* (1931), 93–95, KCA.

81. Committee of Fourteen annual reports, Box 86, C14R; Cowley, "The Vice Squad Carries On: No Woman Is Safe," 177–80; Malcolm Cowley, "The Vice Squad Carries On: Mrs. Hammerstein and the Inspector's Men," *New Republic* 63.812 (June 25, 1930): 148–49; Waterman, *Prostitution and Its Repression in New York City*, 54; Vincenzo Pascale, "A Study of the Service for the Control of Venereal Diseases Among Sex Offenders in New York," *Journal of Social Hygiene* 19.3 (Mar. 1933): 111–42; Adolph Jacoby, "Activities of the New York City Health Department in the Prevention and Control of Syphilis and Gonorrhea," *Journal of Social Hygiene* 19.3 (Mar. 1933): 160–61; "American Neo-Regulation Built on the Thin Crust of a Volcano: Three Cases in Women's Courts in the United States," *Light* 145 (May–June 1922): 29–30; Letter from Frederick Whitin to Alison Neilans, Nov. 20, 1922, Alison Neilans Folder, Box 11, C14R; Raymond Moley, *Tribunes of the People: The Past and Future of the New York Magistrates' Courts* (New Haven, CT: Yale University Press, 1932), 132–35; Hicks, "'Bright and Good Looking Colored Girl,'" 442–43; Henry Hirschberg's statement upon appeal, in People v. Johnson, 169 N.E. 619 (N.Y. 1930) case file, NYSA.

82. See *Twenty-Fifth Annual Report of the New York State Reformatory for Women, Bedford Hills, N.Y., For the Year Ending June 30, 1925*, 15–17; *Twenty-Sixth Annual Report of the New York State Reformatory for Women, Bedford Hills, N.Y., For the Year Ending June 30, 1926*, 19.

83. "Bails Mrs. Hammerstein," *New York Times*, May 14, 1930; "Mrs. Hammerstein Heard," *New York Times*, May 21, 1930; "Hammerstein Case Off," *New York Times*, May 23, 1930; "Hears Mrs. Hammerstein," *New York Times*, May 30, 1930; "Mrs. Hammerstein Is Found Guilty," *New York Times*, June 7, 1930; Joseph, "The Nafkeh and the Lady," 329–33; "Nurse Found Guilty of Vagrancy After Frameup Charge," *Brooklyn Daily Eagle*, Aug. 23, 1930; "Vice Squad Detectives Accused by Society," *Brooklyn Daily Eagle*, Sept. 28, 1930; "Bay Ridge Woman Devotes Life to Solving Troubles of Others," *Brooklyn Daily Eagle*, Dec. 16, 1931; "Report on Vice Awaited byWomen as Basis of Court Reform Program," *New York Herald Tribune*, Mar. 1, 1931; Cowley, "The Vice Squad Carries On: No Woman Is Safe"; Cowley, "The Vice Squad Carries On: Mrs. Hammerstein and the Inspector's Men."

84. See William B. Northrop and John B. Northrop, *The Insolence of Office: The Story of the Seabury Investigations* (New York: G. P. Putnam's Sons, 1932); Herbert Mitgang, *The Man Who Rode the Tiger: The Life and Times of Judge Samuel Seabury* (New York: J. B. Lippincott, 1963); Walter Chambers, *Samuel Seabury: A Challenge* (New York: Century, 1932); Herbert Mitgang, *Once Upon a Time in New York: Jimmy Walker, Franklin Roosevelt, and the Last Great Battle of the Jazz Age* (New York: Free Press, 2000); Samuel Seabury, *Final Report of Samuel Seabury, Referee, in the Matter of the Investigation of the Magistrates' Courts in the First Judicial Department and the Magistrates Thereof, and of Attorneys-at-Law Practicing in Said Courts* (New York: Mar. 28, 1932). The testimony of damning witnesses, including John Weston and Chile Mapocha Acuna, was covered extensively in New York's dailies, especially the *Times*.

85. "Woman Vice Case Witness Found Strangled in Park; Her Lawyer Arrested," *New York Times*, Feb. 27, 1931.

86. Memorandum from Ruth Topping to Lawrence B. Dunham, "VICE INVESTIGATORS," Jan. 3, 1931; Lawrence B. Dunham, "VICE INVESTIGATORS," Jan. 8, 1931—both in Folder 164, Box 7, Series 3, RAC.

87. "Bondsmen Examined on Underworld Link," *New York Times*, Mar. 7, 1931; High Courts Rule Twice for Seabury," *New York Times*, Apr. 8, 1931.

88. Chambers, *Samuel Seabury*, 266–75; Northrop and Northrop, *The Insolence of Office*, 82–91; Mitgang, *The Man Who Rode the Tiger*, 191–93; "Mrs. Norris Admits She Convicted Girl Without Evidence," *New York Times*, June 25, 1931; "Mrs. Norris Ousted as Unfit for Bench; Guilty on 5 Charges," *New York Times*, June 26, 1931; "Silbermann Ousted for Bench Favors; Cleared of Graft," *New York Times*, Jul. 3, 1931.

89. "Vice Crusading Committee of Fourteen Quits," *New York Herald Tribune*, Nov. 25, 1932; Letter from William H. Baldwin to John D. Rockefeller Jr., June 10, 1931, Folder 40, Box 6, Series O, RAC.

90. "Mulrooney Replaces Entire Vice Squad; A New General Order Bars Informers to Cure Abuses Revealed by Seabury," *New York Times*, Apr. 12, 1931; "The Vice Squad Walks the Streets," *New Republic* 66.855 (Apr. 22, 1931): 662.

91. See Clement, *Love for Sale*, 196.

92. Anya Jabour, "Prostitution Politics and Feminist Activism in Modern America: Sophonisba Breckenridge and the Morals Court in Prohibition-Era Chicago," *Journal of Women's History* 25.3 (2013): 146–51; Letter from Sophonisba Breckinridge to Jessie Binford, Mar. 2, 1929, Correspondence Mar. 1929 Folder, Box 743, Reel 5, SPBP; Abbott and Breckinridge, "Outline of a Proposed Study of the Morals Court," Aug. 19, 1931, RAC; Meeting Minutes, Citizens' Committee on Social Work in the Municipal Court, May 23, 1931, Correspondence May—Jul. 1931 Folder, Box 744, Reel 5, SPBP.

93. Jabour, "Prostitution Politics and Feminist Activism in Modern America," 152–53. The court cases include Rock v. Carney, 185 N.W. 798 (Mich. 1921); *Ex Parte Dillon*, et al., 186 Pac. 170 (Calif.

1919); and *Ex parte Arata*, 198 P. 814 (Calif. 1921), all found in Miscellany 1928–1931 Folder, Box 775, Reel 34, SPBP.

94. Letter from Sophonisba Breckinridge to Frederic Siedenburg, Aug. 1, 1931; Letter from Sophonisba Breckinridge to John Swanson, Aug. 6, 1931; Letter from Pearl Hart to Sophonisba Breckinridge, Aug. 13, 1931—all in Correspondence Aug. 1931 Folder, Box 744, Reel 5, SPBP.

95. Letter from Carl J. Appel to Herman Bundesen, Aug. 26, 1931; Letter from Herman Bundesen to Sophonisba Breckinridge, Aug. 28, 1931—both in Correspondence Aug. 1931 Folder, Box 744, Reel 5, SPBP.

96. Letter from James Allman to Commanding Officers, Feb. 23, 1932; General Order 113, Feb. 23, 1932—both in Correspondence Feb. 19–29, 1932 Folder, Box 745, Reel 6, SPBP; Jabour, "Prostitution Politics and Feminist Activism in Modern America," 153. See also Frank L. Hayes, "Change in Court Policy Gives Woman Prisoners the Same Rights as Men," *Chicago Daily News*, Mar. 1, 1932, in Correspondence Mar. 1–10, 1932 Folder, Box 745, Reel 6, SPBP; Letter from Pearl Hart to Sophonisba Breckinridge, Feb. 29, 1932, Correspondence Feb. 19–29, 1932 Folder, Box 745, Reel 6, SPBP; Letter from Sophonisba Breckinridge to John Sonsteby, Mar. 16, 1932, Correspondence Mar. 16–25, 1932 Folder, Box 745, Reel 6, SPBP.

97. "Municipal Court Will Open New Women's Branch," *Chicago Daily Tribune*, Sept. 14, 1932; "Women's Court, An Innovation, To Open Today," *Chicago Daily Tribune*, Oct. 3, 1932; "Bertha Delin Is Prosecutor for Women's Court," *Chicago Daily Tribune*, Oct. 18, 1932; Letter from Pearl Hart to Sophonisba Breckinridge, Dec. 1, 1932, Correspondence Dec. 1931 Folder, Box 744, Reel 5, SPBP.

98. "Hard to Believe, But: Girls Will Be Girls, They Say," *Los Angeles Times*, Aug. 23, 1932; "The Weather Report," *Los Angeles Times*, Aug. 23, 1932; "Warm Weather Forecast Today," *Los Angeles Times*, Aug. 23, 1932; "Quarantine Conditions Criticised," *Los Angeles Times*, Aug. 18, 1932; "Women Inmates Housing Sought," *Los Angeles Times*, Aug. 25, 1932.

99. "Step Taken to Care for Diseased Women," *Los Angeles Times*, Feb. 1, 1933; "Hospital Site Park Addition Furthered," *Los Angeles Times*, Feb. 27, 1933; *Annual Report of the Department of Health, City of Los Angeles, California, for the Fiscal Year Ended June 30, 1933*, pp. 15–17; *Annual Report of the Department of Health, City of Los Angeles, California, for the Fiscal Year Ended June 30, 1934*, pp. 4, 47–48. In the coming years, journalists and public health officials repeatedly demanded that the city resuscitate the Plan, but this took several more years. See *Annual Report of the Department of Health, City of Los Angeles, California, for the Fiscal Year Ended June 30, 1934*, p. 4; *Annual Report of the Department of Health, City of Los Angeles, California, for the Fiscal Year Ended June 30, 1935*, p. 14; *Annual Report of the Department of Health, City of Los Angeles, California, for the Fiscal Year Ended June 30, 1936*, pp. 12, 27; Tom O'Connor, "Trace 400 Syphilitic Cases to Prostitute," *Evening News*, Dec. 28, 1936, on p. 5 of VDPS and pp. 1–6 of VDPS.

100. Brandt, *No Magic Bullet*, 125–26; Rafter, *Partial Justice*, 82. For a dramatic revelation of the effects of the Depression on anti-STI measures, see *Public Health Survey Records*, Collection 2004-025, OHSU. Further examples of these cities/states include Pennsylvania, Cincinnati, San Francisco, and Seattle. Seattle and San Francisco, as well as Los Angeles and Chicago, all closed their detention facilities for women held under the Plan in the early 1930s. All of these examples will be discussed in the text shortly.

101. "The American Social Hygiene Association: A Brief Historical Statement," 1948, Folder 1, Box 1, Series 1, ASHAR; Memorandum from Ruth Topping to Lawrence B. Dunham, "THE AMERICAN SOCIAL HYGIENE ASSOCIATION," Oct. 26, 1931, Folder 164, Box 7, Series 3, RAC.

102. Clement, *Love for Sale*, 196.

103. Roby, "Politics and Prostitution," 202–3; Anna Kross, "Report on Prostitution and the Women's Court," p. 6, Folder 14, Box 37, AKPAJA.

104. Memorandum for John D. Rockefeller Jr., "A.S.H.A.—DIVISION OF LEGAL AND PROTECTIVE MEASURES; INTERVIEW WITH DR. SNOW AND MR. KINSEY, APRIL 25, 1932," RAC; Bascom Johnson, Report on conditions at Yorkville Bellevue District, Oct. 20, 1932, Folder 164, Box 7, Series 3, RAC.

105. American Social Hygiene Association, *Commercialized Prostitution in New York City in 1933*, Dec. 31, 1933, Folder 164, Box 7, Series 3, RAC.

106. Zelda Popkin, "Sociological Court Is Urged for Women," *New York Times*, Nov. 25, 1934.

107. Walter Clarke, "The New York City Plan for Combating Syphilis," *JAMA* 109.13 (Sept. 25, 1937): 1023; Marguerite Marsh, *Prostitutes in New York City: Their Apprehension, Trial, and Treatment, July 1939–June 1940* (New York: Research Bureau, Welfare Council of New York City, June 1941), 92–95, 143–44; Clarice Feinman, "Imprisoned Women: A History of the Treatment of Women Incarcerated in New York City, 1932–1975," PhD diss., New York University, 1976, 74–78. For an example of a woman being sent to Bedford just for having an STI, see Inmate #6072, Reel 4, RG 14610-77B, NYSA.

108. "Social Plan Urged to End Vice Racket," *New York Times*, June 17, 1936.

109. Memorandum for John D. Rockefeller Jr., "A.S.H.A.—DIVISION OF LEGAL AND PROTECTIVE MEASURES; INTERVIEW WITH DR. SNOW AND MR. KINSEY, APRIL 25, 1932," RAC.

110. Bascom Johnson, "Facing an Old Problem: How American Communities Are Dealing with Commercialized Prostitution," *Journal of Social Hygiene* 21.1 (Jan. 1935): 24.

111. Bascom Johnson, "Law and Order and Related Problems of Navajo Indians at Gallup, New Mexico," 1935, Folder 9, Box 100, Series 7, ASHAR.

112. *In re* Jarrell, 28 Ohio N.P. (n.s.) 473 (Ohio N.P. 1930); *Fourteenth Annual Report of the Cincinnati Social Hygiene Society* (June 1930—May 1931), pp. 4–5, in Folder 1, Box 4, OSHSR; *Beginnings, Progress and Achievement in the Medical Work of King County, Washington* (1931), 93–95, KCA; *Ex parte* Lewis, 42 S.W.2d 21 (Mo. 1931); Calvin L. Cooper, "Activities of the Kansas City Health Department in Relation to Social Hygiene," *Journal of Social Hygiene* 18.3 (Mar. 1932): 155–57; "Quarantines 350 in Six Hospitals," *New Castle News*, Feb. 18, 1931; "Quarantines 350 in Six Hospitals," *Daily Notes* (Canonsburg, PA), Feb. 11, 1931; "Report on Field Trip by Valeria H. Parker, M.D., to Pittsburgh, Pa.," Dec. 1–15, 1932, p. 1, Folder 1, Box 109, Series 7, ASHAR. For more details on Cincinnati, see "To the Friends and Members of the Cincinnati Social Hygiene Society," Oct. 1923, Folder 7, Box 4, OSHSR. Astoundingly, officials from the state of Pennsylvania claimed to have quarantined 4,401 individuals with STIs in 1930 alone (of whom the "larger portion" were prostitutes, though "a definite number" were merely promiscuous women). See "Quarantines 350 in Six Hospitals."

113. "Confinement in Ward L of the San Francisco Hospital is not a pleasant experience," admitted even the ASHA in one report. "Ward L is a gloomy, crowded place with normal accommodations for 25 beds. It has at the present time 43 beds and nearly all of these were occupied at the time of this study. The inmates of the ward have little or nothing to do, and, as they are mostly ambulatory cases, great boredom is suffered. It is not difficult to understand why the prostitutes of San Francisco dread commitment to Ward L." ASHA, *Report of a Survey of Medical Aspects of Social Hygiene in San Francisco, California, 1931*, pp. 67–68, 78, 84.

114. See Letter from J. C. Geiger to Members of the Health Advisory Board, Jan. 22, 1934; Minutes of the Joint Meeting of the Advisory Board of Health and S.F. County Medical Society, Feb. 6, 1934—both in Folder 12, Box 10, San Francisco Department of Public Health Records, San Francisco History Center; Letter from William J. Quinn to Anna Kross, Nov. 30, 1934, Folder 3, Box 20, AKPAJA. See also George V. Kulchar and Erla I. Ninnis, "Tracing the Source of Infection in Syphilis," *Journal of Social Hygiene* 22.8 (Nov. 1936): 370–71.

115. "Social Hygiene Choked Off," *Telegram*, Feb. 17, 1923, in Box 15, OSHSR. City officials did this in large part because they felt that the "taxpayers of Oregon do not get value for their money in operating The Cedars"—the city's detention hospital. "Cedars Is Tax Waste, Say Critics," *Oregon Journal*, Jan. 23, 1923; "The Cedars," *Oregon Journal*, Jan. 23, 1923—both in Box 15, OSHSR. Every now and then, however, officials would crack down on prostitution or detain a suspected woman. See "Police Take 200 in Vice Cleanup," *Oregonian*, Dec. 1, 1929, in Box 16, OSHSR; "Report of the Executive Secretary, Oregon Social Hygiene Society," May 1933, Folder 2, Box 4, OSHSR.

116. Meeting Minutes, Oct. 16, 1934; "Report of the Executive Secretary, Oregon Social Hygiene Society," Oct. 1934; Oregon Social Hygiene Society, *Annual Report*, 1934; "Report of the Executive Secretary, Oregon Social Hygiene Society," June 1936—all in Folder 4, Box 1, OSHSR; Thomas A. Davis, "City Venereal Disease Control," Sept. 17, 1935; Memorandum from Thomas A. Davis to R. Earl Riley, "Venereal Disease Section Report, Health Bureau, City of Portland," Jul. 13, 1936—both in Folder 7, Box 4, OSHSR.

117. See the Farm's biennial reports, held in the KSA.

118. Van Waters, "Where Girls Go Right," 374; Dietzler, *Detention Houses and Reformatories*, 191; *Report of the Public Welfare Temporary Commission, State of Kansas*, p. 223, Jan. 15, 1933, KSA.

119. *Fifth Biennial Report of the Industrial Farm for Women, Lansing, Kansas, for the Two Years Ending June 30, 1926* (Topeka: Kansas State Printing Plant, 1927), 7, 22; Perry, "Diseased Bodies and Ruined Reputations," 170.

120. See the numerous letters in Box 24.16, Correspondence File, HHWP.

121. *Report of the Public Welfare Temporary Commission, State of Kansas*, pp. 223–24, KSA.

122. Brandt, *No Magic Bullet*, 125; "Roosevelt Picks Parran to Head Health Service," *Washington Post*, Mar. 24, 1936; Lynne Page Snyder, "New York, the Nation, the World: The Career of Surgeon General Thomas J. Parran, Jr., MD, (1892–1968)," *Public Health Reports* 110.5 (Sept.–Oct. 1995): 630; "PARRAN, Thomas," *Biographical Directory of the United States Congress*, http://bioguide.congress .gov/scripts/biodisplay.pl?index=P000077; "Thomas Parran, Jr. (1936–1948)," SurgeonGeneral.gov, US Department of Health & Human Services, Jan. 4, 2007, http://www.surgeongeneral.gov/about /previous/bioparran.html. There is currently no book-length biography of Parran; one is desperately needed.

123. W. G. Stromquist, "Report on Activities of the United States Public Health Service in the Muscle Shoals Sanitary District from March 15, 1918, to June 30, 1919," Folder 216, Box 23, TPP.

124. Memorandum from Thomas Parran to B. J. Lloyd, Sept. 20, 1926, Folder 409.1, Box 224, Entry 42, RG 90, NA.

125. Brandt, *No Magic Bullet*, 126.

126. By this point, Salvarsan and Neosalvarsan had largely replaced mercury as the standard treatment. Letter from John Stokes to Thomas Parran, Dec. 22, 1930, Folder 34, Box 4, TPP; Letter

from Thomas Parran to John Stokes, Jan. 3, 1931, Folder 34, Box 4, TPP; Thomas Parran, "The Eradication of Syphilis as a Practical Public Health Objective," Mar. 3, 1931, Folder 328, Box 31, TPP.

127. "Talk Censored, Dr. Parran Quits Radio Council," *New York Herald-Tribune*, Nov. 21, 1934; Brandt, *No Magic Bullet*, 122; Doris Darmstadter, untitled memorandum; Letter from William F. Snow to William S. Paley, Nov. 20, 1934—both in Folder 4, Box 70, Series 5, ASHAR.

128. "To Fight Social Disease," *New York Times*, Feb. 26, 1936; Letter from Thomas Parran to John Stokes, Feb. 18, 1936; Letter from John Stokes to Thomas Parran, Feb. 27, 1936—both in Folder 34, Box 4, TPP.

129. Thomas Parran, "Why Don't We Stamp Out Syphilis," *Survey Graphic*, Jul. 1936, Folder 961, Box 54, TPP.

130. See Letter from A Taxpayer to Franklin D. Roosevelt, Aug. 25, 1936, Box 532, GCR IX, RG 90, NA.

131. Letter from Roger M. Dolese and Thomas M. Courtis to Thomas Parran, Jul. 18, 1936, Box 532, GCR IX, RG 90, NA.

132. "The Venereal Disease Conference," *American Journal of Public Health* 27.2 (Feb. 1937): 178.

133. Brandt, *No Magic Bullet*, 143. See also Letter from Hugh Cumming to Joseph Earle Moore, Jan. 28, 1935; Letter from Joseph Earle Moore to Thomas Parran, Feb. 21, 1935—both in Folder 23, Box 3, TPP.

134. "Roosevelt Names Social Study Aides," *New York Times*, November 11, 1934.

135. Hager, *The Demon Under the Microscope*, 186–204, 270; "President's Son Fought for Life, Doctor Reveals," *New York Herald-Tribune*, Dec. 17, 1936.

136. "The Venereal Disease Conference," 178.

137. These included Lawrence T. Price, Walter Clarke, and Earle Brown.

138. "Finish Battle Opened Against Social Disease," *Washington Post*, Dec. 31, 1936.

139. *Proceedings of Conference on Venereal Disease Control Work, Washington, D.C., December 28–30, 1936* (Washington, DC: Government Printing Office, 1937), 77, Folder 898, Box 52, TPP.

140. "Finish Battle Opened Against Social Disease."

141. Ibid., 105.

142. Ibid., 109.

143. "Clinics Urged Free to All to Curb Syphilis," *New York Herald Tribune*, Feb. 4, 1937.

144. "City and Nation Sound Call for War on Syphilis," *Chicago Daily Tribune*, Feb. 4, 1937.

145. Jean B. Pinney, "The First National Social Hygiene Day, Feb. 3, 1937," *Journal of Social Hygiene* 23.3 (Mar. 1937): 115.

146. Ibid., 111.

147. Ibid., 117.

148. See, for instance, Ray Lyman Wilbur and Thomas Parran, "A Social Hygiene Message to All Americans," *Journal of Social Hygiene* 23.3 (Mar. 1937): 127–33.

149. "Health and Law Forces Unite in War on Syphilis," *Chicago Daily Tribune*, Dec. 3, 1936; "Tests Ordered by Court Reveal Syphilis Spread," *Chicago Daily Tribune*, Dec. 4, 1936.

150. Arthur Evans, "Statutes Allow Forced Care of Syphilis Carrier," *Chicago Daily Tribune*, Aug. 11, 1937; Ben Lewis Reitman, "More Prostitutes Are Examined in the Womans Court," VDC #101, p. 533; Ben Lewis Reitman, VDC #104, p. 536—both in Folder 334, Box 26, BLRP.

151. Ben Lewis Reitman, "The Whores and the Pimps Are Afraid of the House of Correction," VDC #106, p. 553, Folder 335, Box 26, BLRP.

152. "'Indianapolis Plan' Of Fighting Against Venereal Disease," *Washington Post*, Aug. 8, 1937.

153. California State Department of Public Health, "Venereal Disease Regulations," Jan. 10, 1938, General 1942 Folder, Box 32, Entry 3, RG 90, NA; Minutes of the California State Board of Health, Nov. 6, 1937, CSA; Minutes of the California State Board of Health, Dec. 31, 1937, CSA.

154. On the Indianapolis health officer (Herman Morgan), see "Dr. Morgan Marks Quarter Century of Service on Board of Health Today," *Indianapolis Star*, Aug. 26, 1937; "News Notes and Personals," *Journal of the Indiana State Medical Association* 11.10 (Oct. 15, 1918): 389–90. See also "Medical News: Indiana," *JAMA* 71.11 (Sept. 14, 1918): 915; "Public Health Service Campaign Against Venereal Diseases," *New York Medical Journal* 109.1 (Jan. 4, 1919): 20. On the California director of public health (Walter Dickie), see Letter from Allen Winter to Rupert Blue, Nov. 6, 1917, Law Enforcement Folder (204.7), Box 21, Entry 42, RG 90, NA; "Ask Home for Street Women," *Los Angeles Times*, May 5, 1918; Letter from Walter Dickie to C. C. Pierce, Feb. 15, 1921, Finance Folder (204.1), Box 20, Entry 42, RG 90, NA; Letter from James Earle Moore to Raymond Vonderlehr, Dec. 27, 1935, Folder 204.8, Box 131, Entry 42, RG 90.

155. "Minutes of the State Board of Health/State Council of Health, 1903–1937," Nov. 10, 1937, p. 141, Vol. 3, Lot no. 25, RG 75–36, AM.

156. See Clement, *Love for Sale*, 244; Barnes, "Pure Spaces and Impure Bodies," 172–73.

157. George Gallup, "Survey Reveals U.S. Eager for War on Syphilis," *New York Herald Tribune*, Oct. 10, 1937, Venereal Disease Data Folder, Box I: C469, RMLFP.

158. "For Sterilization Probe," *Kansas City Times*, Oct. 23, 1937, vol. 1, KISGC.

159. Anna Derrell, "The Women of Reform: Kansas Eugenics," master's thesis, University of Missouri-Kansas City, 2014, 58–59; Biographical Sketch, KEOMP.

160. See, for instance, "Sterilization of 61 Ordered, Records Show," *Hutchinson News*, Oct. 23, 1937; "Woman Demands Investigation of Sterilization," *Iola Register*, Oct. 23, 1937.

161. "McCarthy Will Press For An Investigation," *Hutchinson News*, Oct. 24, 1937; "Sterilizing at Girls' School Raises a Stir," *Abilene Reflector*, Oct. 24, 1937, KISGC.

162. *Third Biennial Report of the Industrial Farm for Women, Lansing, Kansas, for the Two Years Ending June 30, 1922* (Topeka: Kansas State Printing Plant, 1923), 20–21.

163. Inmates No. 5500, No. 5559, No. 5704, and No. 5889 were all held at the farm for violating Chapter 205 and were subsequently transferred to Beloit. Their names all appear on McCarthy's list of the Beloit sterilizations. See List of sterilizations, attached to Letter from Blanche Peterson to Kathryn McCarthy, Section 11, KEOMP.

164. See Inmate No. 5500 and Inmate No. 5502, Inmate Records, ID #193819, KSIFWR; List of sterilizations, KEOMP.

165. Telegram from Joseph F. McDonald to Kathryn McCarthy, Oct. 25, 1937, Section 11, McCarthy Papers; *Tenth Biennial Report of the Industrial Farm for Women, Lansing, Kansas, for the Two Years Ending June 30, 1936*, 8; *Eleventh Biennial Report of the Industrial Farm for Women, Lansing, Kansas, for the Two Years Ending June 30, 1938* (Topeka: Kansas State Printing Plant, 1939), 13; Inmate No. 6068, Inmate Records, ID #193819, KSIFWR.

166. Ben Lewis Reitman, "How They Treat the Whores in Detroit. It's Dangerous to Be a Whore in Most Big Cities Except in Chicago," VDC #266, p. 1283, Folder 357, Box 28, BLRP.

167. Many thanks to Alexandra Minna Stern and Kate O'Connor for their generous assistance. See Eugenic Rubicon—a joint University of Michigan-Arizona State University project being prototyped at http://scalar.usc.edu/works/the-eugenic-rubicon/index; Alexandra Minna Stern, "When California Sterilized 20,000 of Its Citizens," *Zócalo*, Jan. 6, 2016, http://www.zocalopublicsquare.org/2016/01/06/when-california-sterilized-20000-of-its-citizens; Kline, *Building a Better Race*, 47–60; e-mail from Kate O'Connor to Scott Stern, Apr. 28, 2016; Paul Popenoe, "Eugenic Sterilization in California," *Journal of Social Hygiene* 13.5 (May 1927): 257–68.

168. Hodges, "Dealing with Degeneracy," 166, 168, 182, 185. STIs also justified sterilizations in North Carolina. See Susan K. Cahn, *Sexual Reckonings: Southern Girls in a Troubling Age* (Cambridge, MA: Harvard University Press, 2007), 168.

169. Kathryn McCarthy, "Arguments for Amending the Sterilization Law of Kansas," Section 12, KEOMP; Letter from Kathryn McCarthy to Rose Wilson, Nov. 13, 1937, Section 11, KEOMP.

170. Lutz Kaelber, "Kansas," *Eugenics: Compulsory Sterilization in 50 American States*, 2009, http://www.uvm.edu/~lkaelber/eugenics/KS/KS.html.

171. See, for instance, *Twelfth Biennial Report of the Industrial Farm for Women, Lansing, Kansas, for the Two Years Ending June 30, 1940* (Topeka: Kansas State Printing Plant, 1941), 23.

172. Prison Industries Reorganization Administration, *The Prison Labor Problem in Kansas* (Kansas Legislative Council, Aug. 1938).

173. "Pre-Marital Medical Examination Favored," *Indianapolis Star*, May 9, 1937.

174. Memorandum from Raymond Vonderlehr to Thomas Parran, Jul. 14, 1937, Box 532, GCR IX, RG 90, NA; "Backers Fear Delay of Venereal Control by 'Enthusiasm,' Meaning Plethora of Bills," *Washington Post*, Apr. 13, 1938.

175. Clarke, *Taboo*, 81; "By Reading This You Might Save Your Child's Life," draft, 1938, Folder 275, Box 28, TPP; *We Face a New Day in Public Health: Three Social Hygiene Radio Addresses by Surgeon General Thomas Parran, General John J. Pershing, President Ray Lyman Wilbur*, Folder 466, Box 36, TPP; "Congress Asked for Funds to Fight Venereal Diseases," *St. Louis Post-Dispatch*, Jan. 20, 1938.

176. *We Face a New Day in Public Health*; Debate on S. 3290, on Mar. 31, 1938, 75th Cong., 3rd sess., *Congressional Record* 83, p. 4444; Letter from Administrative Assistant to Bruce Gould, Mar. 29, 1938, Folder 275, Box 28, TPP; Robert La Follette, "History of the La Follette-Bulwinkle Act," Venereal Disease 1939–40 Folder, Box I:C469, RMLFP; "Venereal Bill Wins Approval of House Unit," *Washington Post*, Apr. 21, 1938; "Signs Bill for Fight on Venereal Disease," *New York Times*, May 26, 1938.

177. The extensive records of these investigations are in Folder 11, Box 132, Series 9.4, ASHAR. See also: Walter Clarke, "The American Social Hygiene Association," *Public Health Reports* 70.4 (Apr. 1955): 424; Memorandum from Raymond Vonderlehr to Chief, Personnel Records Section, June 22, 1938, Box 532, GCR IX, RG 90, NA.

178. James Jones, *Bad Blood: The Tuskegee Syphilis Experiment* (New York: Free Press, 1993), 53–112; Susan M. Reverby, *Examining Tuskegee: The Infamous Syphilis Study and its Legacy* (Chapel Hill: University of North Carolina Press, 2009), 27–46; Taliaferro Clark, *The Control of Syphilis in Southern Rural Areas: A Study by the United States Public Health Service and Certain State and Local Departments of Health in Cooperation with the Julius Rosenwald Fund* (Chicago: Rosenwald Fund, 1932), 17.

179. Jones, *Bad Blood*, 126–50; Reverby, *Examining Tuskegee*, 46–50; Taliaferro Clark, "Weekly Report, Division of Venereal Diseases, Week Ending May 6, 1933"; Taliaferro Clark, "Weekly Report, Division of Venereal Diseases, Week Ending June 3, 1933"—both in Box 174, Entry 42, RG 90, NA.

180. Thomas Parran, *Shadow on the Land: Syphilis* (New York: Reynal & Hitchcock, 1937), 160–81; Thomas Parran, "Macon County, Alabama," Jan. 15, 1932, Folder 164, Box 17, TPP.

181. Jones, *Bad Blood*, 113–63; Reverby, *Examining Tuskegee*, 41–61; Taliaferro Clark, "Weekly Report, Division of Venereal Diseases, Week Ending October 22, 1932"; Taliaferro Clark, "Weekly Report, Division of Venereal Diseases, Week Ending May 6, 1933"; Taliaferro Clark, "Weekly Report, Division of Venereal Diseases, Week Ending June 3, 1933"—all in Box 174, Entry 42, RG 90, NA.

182. "Dr. Taliaferro Clark Appointed," *Red Cross Bulletin* 2.9 (Feb. 25, 1918): 2; "Red Cross Shock Troops Battle Against Germ Army," *Idaho Statesman*, Mar. 10, 1918; "Canadian Officer Sells House Here," *Evening Star*, June 22, 1918; American Red Cross, *The Work of the American Red Cross: Report by the War Council of Appropriations and Activities from Outbreak of War to November 1, 1917* (Washington, DC, 1918), 49–51.

183. Lavinia Dock, Sarah Elizabeth Pickett, Clara D. Noyes, Fannie F. Clement, Elizabeth G. Fox, and Anna R. Van Meter, *History of American Red Cross Nursing* (New York: Macmillan, 1922), 1286–87.

184. C. C. Pierce, "Public Health Service Problem for the Nation-Wide Control of Venereal Diseases," *Transactions of the Ninth Annual Meeting of the American Association for Study and Prevention of Infant Morality* (Baltimore: Franklin Printing, 1919), 167–68.

185. Letter from William F. Snow to Taliaferro Clark, Aug. 31, 1918, Jul.–Aug. 1918 Folder, Box 129, Entry 29A, RG 112, NA.

186. Memorandum from Wilbur Sawyer to J. G. Wilson, Taliaferro Clark, and Martha Falconer, May 14, 1918, Box 423, Entry 29A, RG 112, NA.

187. Letter from O. C. Wenger to C. C. Pierce, Aug. 21, 1920; Letter from O. C. Wenger to C. C. Pierce, Aug. 29, 1920; Letter from O. C. Wenger to C. C. Pierce, Sept. 5, 1920—all are in Box 205, Entry 42, RG 90, NA.

188. Memorandum from O. C. Wenger to C. C. Pierce, "Report on Little Rock, Arkansas," Sept. 18, 1920, Box 205, Entry 42, RG 90, NA.

189. Isadore Dyer, "State Committee of National Defense Medical Section," Feb. 11, 1918, Doc. 26748, Box 55, Entry 393, RG 165, NA.

190. Obituary, *St. Louis Leader & Breckenridge American*, Mar. 4, 1926; "Death Comes to St. Louis Woman Early Monday," *St. Louis Leader*, Aug. 11, 1932; *Polk's Saginaw City Directory* (Detroit: R. L. Polk, 1931), 240; 1920 US Census, St. Louis, Gratiot County, MI, sheet 10A, family 256, lines 22–24, Jan. 10–12, 1920; 1930 US Census, St. Louis, Gratiot County, MI, sheet 4A, family 87, lines 9–13, May 8, 1930; 1940 US Census, St. Louis, Gratiot County, MI, sheet 15A, family 352, lines 24–27, Apr. 18, 1940. It appears that this house's number changed from 402 to 401. One can see this by comparing the 1920, 1930, and 1940 censuses—none of the other house numbers change, but 402 disappears and 401 appears.

191. Telephone interview with Wilmot F. Pruyne Jr., Sept. 7, 2016. For images of the St. Louis schools, see McMacken, *A St. Louis Album*, 24.

192. "Mary Loudenslager," memorial number 87679811, *Find a Grave*, Mar. 30, 2012, https://www.findagrave.com/cgi-bin/fg.cgi?page=gr&GRid=87679811.

193. Certificate of Death, Minnie Van Norman, Saginaw, Saginaw, MI, Feb. 1, 1938, *Michigan Death Certificates, 1921–1952*, FHL film number 1973086; "Mrs. Minnie S. Van Norman," *Saginaw News*, Feb. 2, 1938.

194. *We Face a New Day in Public Health: Three Social Hygiene Radio Addresses by Surgeon General Thomas Parran, General John J. Pershing, President Ray Lyman Wilbur*, Folder 466, Box 36, TPP.

CHAPTER 12: "A TOTAL WAR"

1. See Richard Hargreaves, *Blitzkrieg Unleashed: The German Invasion of Poland, 1939* (Mechanicsburg, PA: Stackpole Books, 2008), 97–123.

2. Robert J. Brown, *Manipulating the Ether: The Power of Broadcast Radio in Thirties America* (Jefferson, NC: McFarland, 1998), 91–92; "Text of Emergency Edict," *Christian Science Monitor*, Sept. 8, 1939; "Emergency Proclaimed by President," *Los Angeles Times*, Sept. 9, 1939.

3. Marilyn Hegarty, *Victory Girls, Khaki-Wackies, and Patriotutes: The Regulation of Female Sexuality During World War II* (New York: New York University Press, 2008), 13–14; Eliot Ness, "Venereal Disease Control in Defense," *Annals of the American Academy of Political and Social Science* 22 (Mar. 1942): 89; C. Walter Clarke, "The American Social Hygiene Association," *Public Health Reports* 70.4 (Apr. 1955): 424; Minutes of June 14, 1941 Meeting, Advisory Committee of the Division of Social Protection, Box 1, Entry 41, RG 215, NA.

4. "An Agreement by the War and Navy Departments, the Federal Security Agency, and State Health Departments on Measures for the Control of the Venereal Diseases in Areas Where Armed Forces or National Defense Employees are Concentrated," May 7–13, 1940, Policy Memoranda to FSA and Related Units, Jul. 1941–Oct. 1944 Folder, Committee Meetings, Box 1, Entry 41, RG 215, NA.

5. Ness, "Venereal Disease Control in Defense," 90.

6. Letter from William F. Snow to John D. Rockefeller Jr., Sept. 30, 1939, Folder 126, Box 16, Series K, RAC.

7. Letter from William F. Snow to John D. Rockefeller Jr., Oct. 7, 1939, Folder 126, Box 16, Series K, RAC.

8. Meeting Minutes, American Social Hygiene Association, Nov. 6, 1939, Folder 986, Box 57, TPP.

9. "A Demonstration at Columbus, Georgia, and Phenix City, Alabama," in Memorandum from Walter Clarke to Paul McNutt, Jan. 21, 1941, Policy Memoranda to FSA and Related Units, Jul. 1941–Oct. 1944 Folder, Box 1, Entry 41, RG 215, NA; Memorandum from Raymond Vonderlehr to Thomas Parran, Dec. 21, 1939, Box 149, GCR II, RG 90, NA.

10. "Drive Against Vice Promised for Columbus," *Columbus Daily Enquirer*, Dec. 22, 1939.

11. "A Demonstration at Columbus, Georgia, and Phenix City, Alabama," NA; C. C. Pierce, "Memorandum for the Surgeon General," Mar. 11, 1940, Box 149, GCR II, RG 90, NA.

12. Bascom Johnson, "The Work of the Association in Connection with Military Maneuvers, 1940," in Memorandum from Walter Clarke to Paul McNutt, Jan. 21, 1941, Policy Memoranda to FSA and Related Units, Jul. 1941–Oct. 1944 Folder, Box 1, Entry 41, RG 215, NA; Otis L. Anderson, "Trip Report—Little Falls, Minn., August 19–21, 1940," Box 167, GCR II, RG 90, NA; R.R. Sullivan, "Minnesota Venereal Disease Control Program in Connection with Military Maneuvers," *Journal of Social Hygiene* 26.8 (Nov. 1940): 371–76; M. Trautmann, "A PROGRAM FOR PREVENTING DISEASE IN A MILITARY CONCENTRATION," Sept. 11, 1940, Box 167, GCR II, RG 90, NA; "Third Service Command," Dec. 1940, Venereal Disease Control—General—District 2 Folder, Box 3, EGPP, National Library of Medicine; George Gould, "Report of Activities in Chicago, Ill.," Dec. 16, 1940, Region VI—Illinois—ASHA Material Folder, Box 95, Entry 3, RG 215, NA. On Rockefeller's funding, see Letter from John D. Rockefeller Jr. to Arthur W. Packard, Jul. 24, 1940; Letter from Arthur W. Packard to William F. Snow, Jul. 26, 1940—both in Folder 121, Box 15, Series K, RAC. On Vonderlehr's trip to California, see Memorandum from Raymond Vonderlehr to Thomas Parran, Feb. 8, 1941, 1941 Folder, Box 722, Entry 42, RG 90, NA; Memorandum from Malcolm H. Merrill to Bertram P. Brown, "Visit to San Bernardino, December 11," Dec. 19, 1940; Memorandum from Malcolm H. Merrill to Bertram P. Brown, "Weekly Report—Jan. 27 to Feb. 1," Feb. 4, 1941; Memorandum from Malcolm H. Merrill to Bertram P. Brown, "Summary Report—Bureau of Venereal Diseases— For the two week period Jan. 20 to Feb. 1 inclusive," Feb. 4, 1941—all are in Series 52, R384, CDPHR.

13. "Activities of American Social Hygiene Association representatives in areas adjacent to military and naval establishments, from September 1, 1939, to January 1, 1941," Jan. 10, 1941, from Memorandum from Walter Clarke to Paul McNutt, Jan. 21, 1941, Policy Memoranda to FSA and Related Units, Jul. 1941–Oct. 1944 Folder, Committee Meetings, Box 1, Entry 41, RG 215, NA; Letter from Raymond Vonderlehr to Knox E. Miller, Jan. 2, 1941, 1941 Folder, Box 722, Entry 42, RG 90, NA.

14. "Brief Illness Is Fatal to Young Man," *St. Louis Leader & Breckenridge American*, Oct. 3, 1940; Certificate of Death, Robert Leroy Day, St. Louis, Gratiot, MI, Sept. 29, 1940, *Michigan Death Certificates, 1921–1952*, FHL film number 1972722.

15. "Robert LeRoy Carter Sr.," memorial number 54485790, *Find a Grave*, Jul. 4, 2010, https://www.findagrave.com/cgi-bin/fg.cgi?page=gr&GRid=54485790.

16. "Health Studied as Defense Aid," *Detroit Free Press*, Oct. 7, 1940; "Plan for Venereal Disease Control for Army Proposed," *Battle Creek Enquirer and News*, Oct. 10, 1940; "Experts Study Army's Health," *Detroit Free Press*, Oct. 11, 1940.

17. "Disease Control Plans Discussed at Meeting," *Battle Creek Enquirer and News*, Oct. 16, 1940; Letter from Sidney P. Howell to Bascom Johnson, Nov. 28, 1940, Region V—Michigan—ASHA Material Folder, Box 133, Entry 3, RG 215, NA.

18. See Gould's numerous reports in Region V—Michigan—ASHA Material Folder, Box 133, Entry 3, RG 215, NA.

19. McMacken, "T.J. Carney"; "Alma Electorate Routs Incumbents," *Lansing State Journal*, Apr. 6, 1937; "Tavern Girl Issue Confronting Alma," *Lansing State Journal*, Feb. 16, 1937; "Alma Electors Vote for Complete Change in City Administration Monday," *Alma Record*, Apr. 8, 1937; "Rotarians Honor Alma Physician at Convention Here," *Times Herald* (Port Huron, MI), June 7, 1938; "Extra Candidate to Cost Alma $400," *Lansing State Journal*, Feb. 14, 1939.

20. "O. L. Smith Figures in Auto Accident," *News-Palladium* (Benton Harbor, MI), Feb. 28, 1940; "Detroiter Seen as G.O.P. Entry," *Detroit Free Press*, May 4, 1940; "O. L. Smith Joins Governor's Race," *Lansing State Journal*, Jul. 3, 1940; "We Need More of Them," *Detroit Free Press*, Jul. 4, 1940; "Osborn Says Dickinson Is Not 'His Man,'" *Battle Creek Enquirer and News*, Jul. 9, 1940; "O.L. Smith's Supporters to Celebrate Wednesday," *Detroit Free Press*, Jul. 14, 1940; "Dickinson and Van Wagoner Nominated," *Times Herald*, Sept. 11, 1940.

21. "On Federal Branch," *Battle Creek Enquirer and News*, Jul. 10, 1927; "Judges See Moinet Become U.S. Jurist," *Detroit Free Press*, Jul. 10, 1927; "Two-Year Term Given Rummer," *Detroit Free Press*, Jul. 27, 1927; "Moinet Applies 6 Dry Padlocks," *Detroit Free Press*, Oct. 4, 1927; "Ex-Coal Dealer Jailed as Rummer," *Detroit Free Press*, Oct. 6, 1927; "3 Men Are Fined as Dry Violators," *Detroit Free Press*, Feb. 11, 1928; newspapers carried dozens of such articles over the next two decades.

22. See "Thief in Court Threatens Life of Judge Moinet," *Detroit Free Press*, Mar. 25, 1939; "Nabbed for Threat to Kill Judge," *Times Herald* (Port Huron, MI), Jul. 14, 1939.

23. Telephone interview with Alden Moinet Hathaway, Jan. 17, 2016; "Democrats Scramble for Judgeships," *Detroit Free Press*, Feb. 22, 1946; "Former Judge Dies," *Battle Creek Enquirer*, Dec. 24, 1952.

24. "Defendant Denies Rum-Ring Charge," *Detroit Free Press*, Feb. 7, 1940; "Suspect Indicted on Liquor Charge," *Detroit Free Press*, Apr. 24, 1940.

25. H.R. 2475, "A BILL To prohibit prostitution within such reasonable distance of military and/or naval establishments as the Secretaries of War and/or Navy shall determine to be needful to the efficiency, health, and welfare of the Army and/or Navy," Jan. 20, 1941, Folder 5, Box 210, Series 7, ASHAR; Thomas H. Sternberg, Ernest B. Howard, Leonard A. Dewey, and Paul Padget, "Chapter X: Venereal Diseases," 142, in *Preventive Medicine in World War II: Volume V: Communicable Diseases Transmitted Through Contact or byUnknown Means*, ed. John Boyd Coates (Office of the Surgeon General, Department of the Army, Jan. 1, 1960).

26. Letter from William F. Snow to ASHA, Jan. 22, 1941, Folder 5, Box 210, Series 7, ASHAR.

27. See Table of Contents, *Hearings to Prohibit Prostitution Within Reasonable Distance of Military and Naval Establishments*, Committee on Military Affairs, House of Representatives (Mar. 11, 12, and 18, 1941).

28. Fiorello La Guardia, "An Address," *Journal of Social Hygiene* 27.7 (Oct. 1941): 321–26.

29. See Parascandola, *Sex, Sin, and Science*, 78, 121–22.

30. Bascom Johnson, "Mobilization for Social Protection," *Journal of Social Hygiene* 27.7 (Oct. 1941): 348. See also George Gould, "Twenty Years' Progress in Social Hygiene Legislation," *Journal of Social Hygiene* 30.8 (Nov. 1944): 469.

31. Clarke, "The American Social Hygiene Association and World War II," 170.

32. See the correspondence and memoranda in Folder 127, Box 16, Series K, Office of the Messrs. Rockefeller, Medical Interests, RAC; Charles Taft, Daily Activities Diary, Apr. 14, 1941, Box I:1, CPTP; Charles Taft, Daily Activities Diary, Apr. 15, 1941, Box I:1, CPTP; Charles Taft, Daily Activities Diary, May 8, 1941, Box I:1, CPTP; Charles Taft, Daily Activities Diary, May 12, 1941, Box I:1, CPTP; Meghan Kate Winchell, "Good Food, Good Fun, and Good Girls: USO Hostesses and World War Two," PhD diss., University of Arizona, 2003, 26–27; "WHAT JOHN D. ROCKEFELLER, JR.'S ASSOCIATION WITH USO MEANT TO IT," 1954, RAC; Letter from John D. Rockefeller Jr. to W. Spencer Robertson, Apr. 27, 1942, Folder 125, Box 15, Series K, RAC; James Brunot, "EFFECT OF USO PLANS ON 1949 BUDGETS OF: AMERICAN SOCIAL HYGIENE ASSOCIATION, NATIONAL TRAVELERS AID ASSOCIATION," Aug. 11, 1948, Folder 127, Box 16, Series K, RAC; "The American Social Hygiene Association: A Brief Historical Statement," 1948, Folder 1, Box 1, Series 1, ASHAR; Clarke, "The American Social Hygiene Association and World War II," 170–71, 177; Minutes of June 14, 1941 Meeting, Advisory Committee of the Division of Social Protection, Box 1, Entry 41, RG 215, NA.

33. Charles Taft, Daily Activities Diary, Jul. 24, 1941; Charles Taft, Daily Activities Diary, Aug. 8, 1941; Charles Taft, Daily Activities Diary, Aug. 19, 1941; Charles Taft, Daily Activities Diary, Aug. 29, 1941; Charles Taft, Daily Activities Diary, Sept. 2, 1941; Charles Taft, Daily Activities Diary, Sept. 8, 1941—all are in Box I:1, Taft Papers.

34. Burton Benjamin, "One Man Gang War Puts Gamblers on the Spot," *Georgia Magazine*, Jul. 27, 1941, 6; Douglas Perry, *Eliot Ness: The Rise and Fall of an American Hero* (New York: Viking, 2014), 140–41.

35. "Judge Will Refuse 'Corrupt' Evidence," *Cleveland Plain Dealer*, Aug. 24, 1937.

36. According to one journalist, "Warrants charging 'directing a person to rooms for immoral purposes' will supplant those for 'keeping.' Both charges carry the same penalty, one to three years in the workhouse, and vice squad detectives believe the new charge may be easier to prove." "Police Adopt New Vice Case Charges," *Cleveland Plain Dealer*, Aug. 26, 1937.

37. Charles Taft, Daily Activities Diary, Oct. 7, 1941, Box I:1, CPTP.

38. Charles Taft, Daily Activities Diary, Jul. 28, 1941, Box I:1, CPTP.

39. "Division of Social Protection Announces Program," *Journal of Social Hygiene* 27.9 (Dec. 1941): 433–35.

40. Charles Taft, Daily Activities Diary, Sept. 24, 1941, Box I:1, CPTP; Memorandum from Henry W. Waltz to Eliot Ness, "Report on San Antonio, Texas," Oct. 3, 1941, San Antonio, Texas, 1942 Folder, Box 214, Entry 3, RG 215, NA; Charles Taft, Daily Activities Diary, Nov. 3, 1941, Box I:1, CPTP; Whicomb H. Allen, "Report on the Repression and Venereal Disease Control Program in San Antonio, Texas, Covering a Period From October, 1941 to December 31, 1943," Repression Studies Folder, Box 6, Entry 43, RG 215, NA; "S.A. Police Reverse Police; Lid Clamped Down on Vice," *San Antonio Light*, Nov. 30, 1941; Letter from Eliot Ness to Alice Clements, Dec. 1, 1941; Telegram from Charles P. Taft to P. L. Anderson, Dec. 2, 1941; "Washington Approves Closing of Vice Area," *San Antonio Express*, Dec. 2, 1941; "Police Warring on Vice Arrest; 19 Women, 2 Gaming Suspects," unknown newspaper, Dec. 2, 1941; Raymond Vonderlehr, "Survey of the Venereal Disease Control Program in San Antonio, Texas," Jan. 13, 1942—these last six are in Region X Texas, San Antonio, 1941–1942, Folder, Box 214, Entry 3, RG 215, NA.

41. G. Edward White, *Earl Warren: A Public Life* (New York: Oxford University Press, 1982), 27, 49, 221–22.

42. Roy E. Dickerson, "Follow-up Commercialized Prostitution Conditions in Monterey and Adjacent Counties, California," Feb. 17, 1941, California ASHA Material Folder, Box 51, Entry 3, RG 215, NA; Memorandum from Malcolm H. Merrill to Bertram P. Brown, "Special Report—Conference

in office of Attorney General Warren, Monday afternoon, Feb. 17," Feb. 26, 1941, Series 52, R384, CD-PHR; Warren, *Memoirs of Earl Warren*, 150–51; Telegram from William F. Snow to Bascom Johnson, May 27, 1941, General 1942 Folder, Box 32, Entry 3, RG 215, NA; Telegram from Paul McNutt to Bertram Brown, May 27, 1941, General 1942 Folder, Box 32, Entry 3, RG 215, NA; "War on Vice Threatened by Army," *San Luis Obispo Telegram-Tribune*, May 30, 1941; "Vallejo Will Wage War on Vice Resorts," *Sacramento Bee*, May 31, 1941; "Lid Is Clamped on Vice in Stockton," *Sacramento Bee*, May 31, 1941; Officialdom Declares War on Social Diseases," *Los Angeles Times*, Nov. 2, 1941; Letter from Thomas Parran to Paul McNutt, Nov. 23, 1941, Folder 807, Box 50, TPP; "Women Are Freed as Cured of Venereal Ill," *Sacramento Bee*, Nov. 7, 1941; Daily calendar, May 29, 1941, Folder 315, EWP. For a list of those present, see the list of names appended to Letter from Earl Warren to Bertram Brown, May 26, 1941, Folder 359, EWP.

43. See Letter from Wilton L. Halverson to Esteban Ramirez, Aug. 26, 1943, Folder 3229, EWP, and correspondence in Folders 3232 and 3233, EWP.

44. Oral History of Russel VanArsdale Lee, "Pioneering in Prepaid Group Medicine," p. 19, *Earl Warren and Health Insurance: 1943–1949* (1970), OH W-11, CSA.

45. *Department of Health: Annual Report, 1941–1948* (New York: Department of Health, City of New York), 171.

46. *Thirteenth Biennial Report of the Industrial Farm for Women, Lansing, Kansas, for the Two Years Ending June 30, 1942* (Topeka: Kansas State Printing Plant, 1943), 8, 25–27; Kansas State Board of Health, Division of Venereal Diseases, *Annual Report: June 30, 1940—July 1, 1941*, pp. 4–6, ID #215254, KSBHR.

47. Charles Taft, Daily Activities Diary, Aug. 11, 1941, Box I:1, CPTP.

48. Letter from Otis L. Anderson to Raymond Vonderlehr, Aug. 12, 1941, Oct.–Dec. 1941 Folder, Box 722, Entry 42, RG 90, NA; Charles Taft, Daily Activities Diary, Aug. 18, 1941, Box I:1, CPTP.

49. Charles Taft, Daily Activities Diary, Jul. 30, 1941, Box I:1, CPTP.

50. Letter from A. J. Aselmeyer to Donald G. Evans, Aug. 7, 1941, Oct.–Dec. 1941 Folder, Box 722, Entry 42, RG 90, NA.

51. Letter from William F. Snow to Ray Lyman Wilbur, Board of Directors, and Executive Committee, Oct. 31, 1941, Folder 985, Box 57, TPP; Letter from William F. Snow to Mr. and Mrs. Charles Babcock, Oct. 15, 1941, Folder 127, Box 16, Series K, RAC.

52. Thomas Parran and Raymond Vonderlehr, *Plain Words About Venereal Disease* (New York: Reynal & Hitchcock, 1941), 89–91; Brandt, *No Magic Bullet*, 162; "Report of Conference held in Dr. Parran's office between Dr. Vonderlehr, Mrs. Parran, Dr. Snow and Dr. Baehr," Nov. 10, 1941, Folder 805, Box 49, TPP; Memorandum from Franklin Roosevelt to Paul McNutt, Nov. 18, 1941, Folder 807, Box 50, TPP; "American Medical Association Challenges Parran-Vonderlehr Book on Venereal Disease; Journal Charges 'Increased Federal Power' in Local Health Problems Sought," *Science Service*, Nov. 26, 1941, Folder 806, Box 49, TPP; Charles Taft, Daily Activities Diary, Nov. 22, 1941, Box I:1, CPTP; Letter from Raymond Fosdick to Thomas Parran, Nov. 24, 1941, Folder 805, Box 49, TPP; "American Medical Association Challenges Parran-Vonderlehr Book on Venereal Disease; Journal Charges 'Increased Federal Power' in Local Health Problems Sought," *Science Service*, Nov. 26, 1941, Folder 806, Box 49, TPP; Charles Taft, Daily Activities Diary, Nov. 22, 1941, Box I:1, CPTP; Letter from Raymond Fosdick to Thomas Parran, Nov. 24, 1941, Folder 805, Box 49, TPP; "24 States Ask U.S. Aid Against Vice at Camps," *Baltimore Sun*, Dec. 3, 1941, Folder 807, Box 50, TPP; Letter from Thomas Parran to Paul McNutt, Nov. 23, 1941, Folder 807, Box 50, Parran TPP; Letter from Franklin Delano Roosevelt to Paul McNutt, Dec. 5, 1941, Folder 807, Box 50, TPP. Letter from Thomas Parran to Paul McNutt, Nov. 23, 1941; Letter from Franklin Delano Roosevelt to Paul McNutt, Dec. 5, 1941—both in Folder 807, Box 50, TPP.

53. Brandt, *No Magic Bullet*, 163.

54. See "Prostitution Is an Axis Partner," *American Journal of Public Health* 32.1 (Jan. 1942): 85–86.

55. See the testimony of Albert Williams and Peter M. Horn in *Transcript of Proceedings, Conference on Venereal Disease Control*, Nov. 19, 1945, in Box 1, Entry 44, RG 215, NA.

56. Memorandum from Edwin Cooley to Eliot Ness, "Constructive Interest in Prevention and Reduction of Prostitution and Venereal Disease," Feb. 6, 1942, General 1942 Folder, Box 32, Entry 3, RG 215, NA.

57. Kathryn Close, "In May Act Areas," *Survey Midmonthly* 79.3 (Mar. 1943): 1; Charles Taft, Daily Activities Diary, Mar. 28, 1942, Box I:1, CPTP; Charles Taft, Daily Activities Diary, Mar. 27, 1942, Box I:1, CPTP; J. Lacey Reynolds, "Anti-Prostitution Move Hits Davidson, 26 Midstate Counties," *Nashville Tennessean*, May 21, 1942; Robert G. Spinney, "Municipal Government in Nashville, Tennessee, 1938–1951: World War II and the Growth of the Private Sector," *Journal of Southern History* 61.1 (Feb. 1995): 84–85; W. C. Williams and G. F. McGinnes, "Plans for Handling Special Health and Other Problems Incident to the Army Maneuvers in Tennessee," *Public Health Reports* 56.43 (Oct. 24, 1941): 2069–70; "Report on Repression Program in Nashville, Tennessee," Repression Studies Folder, Box 6, Entry 43, RG 215, NA.

58. Close, "In May Act Areas," 2; Spinney, "Municipal Government in Nashville," 86; "Report on Repression Program in Nashville, Tennessee," NA.

59. "Bedford, Franklin, Coffee Raids Are Made by FBI," *Nashville Tennessean*, June 4, 1942; Close, "In May Act Areas," 1–3; "Report on Repression Program in Nashville, Tennessee," NA.

60. See J. Edgar Hoover, "MAY ACT," Oct. 9, 1942, Reel 18C, Box J, Classification 18, RG 65, NA.

61. "Woman's Health Education Group Asks Sheriff to Stamp Out Vice; Meeting Called for Tuesday Night," *Robesonian*, June 4, 1942; "Lax Law Enforcement Is Scored by Reynolds," *High Point Enterprise*, June 12, 1942; Close, "In May Act Areas," 2.

62. "May Act Invoked in the Counties Around Ft. Bragg," *Statesville Record and Landmark*, Aug. 3, 1942; "RAIDS!," *Robesonian*, Aug. 10, 1942; "54 Arrested in Fort Bragg Area Under May Act," *Asheville Citizen-Times*, Aug. 10, 1942; "Sheriff E. C. Wade Releases Statement About May Act," *Robesonian*, Aug. 11, 1942; "All but 13 Are Released in May Act Actions Here," *Robesonian*, Aug. 14, 1942; Close, "In May Act Areas," 1; Hegarty, *Victory Girls, Khaki-Wackies, and Patriotutes*, 39–40. For the ASHA's involvement, see American Social Hygiene Association, "Survey of Commercialized Prostitution Conditions," Kinston, NC, Jan. 1943, Box 1, Entry 41, RG 215, NA.

63. American Social Hygiene Association, "The War Against Prostitution Must Go On," *Journal of Social Hygiene* 31.8 (Nov. 1945): 502.

64. Minutes of June 2, 1942 Interdepartmental Committee Meeting, Box 1, Entry 41, RG 215, NA.

65. "Report on Repression Program in El Paso, Texas," Repression Studies Folder, Box 6, Entry 43, RG 215, NA.

66. Hegarty, *Victory Girls, Khaki-Wackies, and Patriotutes*, 12.

67. Roby, "Politics and Prostitution," 217–18; "800 Arrested in Drive on Vice, Hogan Says," *New York Times*, Jul. 26, 1942; "Curran and Hogan Lock Horns in Feud," *New York Times*, Aug. 8, 1942.

68. Memorandum from J. R. Heller to Mary E. Switzer, July 8, 1943, Jan. 1943 Folder, Box 772, Entry 42, RG 90, NA.

69. Close, "In May Act Areas," 1–2; "Report on Repression Program in Nashville, Tennessee," NA.

70. Amanda Hope Littauer, "Unsanctioned Encounters: Women, Girls, and Non-Marital Sexuality in the United States, 1941–1963," PhD diss., University of California, Berkeley, 2006, 73–74; Amanda H. Littauer, *Bad Girls: Young Women, Sex, and Rebellion* (Chapel Hill: University of North Carolina Press, 2015), 56–58.

71. Charles F. Blankenship, "Trip Report—Various Points in Arizona and to Las Vegas, Nevada," Dec. 16, 1942, Box 172, GCR II, RG 90, NA; "Army Extends Drastic Ban Against Arizona Capital," *Riverside Daily Press*, Dec. 1, 1942; "Report of the Activities of 5th U.S. Public Health Service District, Fiscal Year Ending June 30, 1943," Box 172, GCR II, RG 90, NA.

72. "Phoenix Ousts City Regime to Spur Vice Drive," *New York Herald Tribune*, Dec. 18, 1942; "Phoenix Ousts Officials in War to Clean Up Vice," *Chicago Daily Tribune*, Dec. 18, 1942; Memorandum from Edwin Cooley to Eliot Ness, "Ousting of City Officials Over City Vice—Phoenix, Arizona," Dec. 18, 1942, Phoenix, AZ, Folder, Box 47, Entry 3, RG 215, NA.

73. "Air Force Ban on Phoenix to End Tomorrow," *Chicago Daily Tribune*, Dec. 20, 1942; Blankenship, "Trip Report—Various Points in Arizona and to Las Vegas, Nevada," NA.

74. See memoranda in Phoenix, AZ, Folder, Box 47, Entry 3, RG 215, NA.

75. Letter from Thomas Parran to Bascom Johnson Jr., Aug. 4, 1942, Mexican Border Folder, Box 723, Entry 42, RG 90, NA; Bascom Johnson Jr., "Prostitution in the Spread of Venereal Disease in an Army Cantonment Area," *Journal of Social Hygiene* 28.9 (Dec. 1942): 525–35.

76. Elliott G. Colby and Samuel D. Allison, "Venereal Disease in Wartime Hawaii," Venereal Disease—General—District 10 Folder, Box 3, EGPP.

77. Letter from W. J. Pennell to C. S. Stephenson, Nov. 27, 1942, Box 7, Entry 49B, RG 52, NA; Letter from Thomas Parran to O. C. Wenger, Mar. 23, 1942, Folder 38, Box 5, TPP. For more on Trinidad, see Memorandum from Senior Medical Officer to Commandant, US Naval Operating Base, Trinidad, "Policy on Control of Venereal Disease and the Repression of Prostitution," June 9, 1942, Box 7, Entry 49B, RG 52, NA. For more on Puerto Rico, see Dr. Ury, "Rapid Treatment Centers in Puerto Rico: General Statement," Jul. 22, 1943; Letter from V. M. Hoge to Florence Kerr, Dec. 4, 1943—both in Rapid Treatment Centers—Porto Rico Folder, Box 188, Entry 3, RG 215, NA.

78. Memorandum from Dean M. Walker to Adjutant, Trinidad Base Command, June 5, 1941, Box 7, Entry 49B, RG 52, NA.

79. Minutes of June 2, 1942 Interdepartmental Committee Meeting, Committee Meetings, Box 1, Entry 41, RG 215, NA.

80. Resolutions of Interdepartmental Committee on Venereal Disease, Nov. 17, 1942, Committee Meetings, Box 1, Entry 41, RG 215, NA.

81. Charles Taft, Daily Activities Diary, Dec. 30, 1941, Box I:1, Taft Papers; Charles Taft, Daily Activities Diary, Mar. 21, 1942; Charles Taft, Daily Activities Diary, May 22, 1942—both in Box I:1, TPP.

82. See, for instance, Littauer, "Unsanctioned Encounters," 62–65; Spinney, "Municipal Government in Nashville," 87; "Four Girls Flee Isolation Hospital," *Nashville Tennessean*, Sept. 22, 1943.

83. Charles Taft, Daily Activities Diary, May 22, 1942, Box I:1, CPTP; Charles Taft, Daily Activities Diary, May 25, 1942, Box I:1, CPTP; Minutes of the National Advisory Police Committee on Social Protection, June 30, 1942, Box 2, Entry 41, RG 215, NA. Memorandum from Otis L. Anderson

to Raymond Vonderlehr, Aug. 8, 1942, Box 149, GCR II, RG 90, NA; Charles Taft, Daily Activities Diary, Jul. 22, 1942, Box I:1, CPTP.

84. Charles Taft, Daily Activities Diary, Jul. 22, 1942, Box I:1, CPTP.

85. Charles Taft, Daily Activities Diary, Jul. 14, 1942; Charles Taft, Daily Activities Diary, Jul. 17, 1942—both in Box I:1, CPTP.

86. Proceedings of Aug. 7, 1942 Meeting, National Advisory Police Committee for Social Protection, Committee Meetings, Box 1, Entry 41, RG 215, NA; Memorandum from Otis L. Anderson to Raymond Vonderlehr, Aug. 8, 1942, Box 149, GCR II, RG 90, NA.

87. Charles Taft, Daily Activities Diary, Aug. 26, 1942, Box I:1, Taft Papers; Memorandum from James B. Marley to Paul McNutt, "Establishment of Quarantine Hospitals in Abandoned CCC Camps," Sept. 3, 1942, Rapid Treatment Centers Folder, Box 26, Entry 3, RG 215, NA; Charles Taft, Daily Activities Diary, Sept. 15, 1942, Box I:1, CPTP; Memorandum from Leland J. Hanchett to Raymond Vonderlehr, Sept. 24, 1942, Box 531, GCR IX, RG 90, NA; "Will Intern Prostitutes," *Baltimore Afro-American*, Aug. 15, 1942.

88. J. D. Ratcliff, "The War Against Syphilis," *Collier's*, Apr. 10, 1943, 15; "Interview with Dr. A. B. Price, May 28, 29, and 31, 1946," in Venereal Disease Control: General District 4 Folder, Box 3, EGPP.

89. Ratcliff, "The War Against Syphilis," 15.

90. "Interview with Dr. A. B. Price, May 28, 29, and 31, 1946," NA; Ratcliff, "The War Against Syphilis," 15, 72; Memorandum from Whitcomb H. Allen to Eliot Ness, "Detention Hospitals for Patients with Venereal Disease at CCC Camps and Other Sites," Nov. 24, 1942, Rapid Treatment Centers Folder, Box 26, Entry 3, RG 215, NA; "Girl 'Pick-Ups' in Bars Causing Grave Problems," *Weekly Town Talk* (Alexandria, LA), Mar. 20, 1943.

91. Ratcliff, "The War Against Syphilis," 15.

92. "City Policeman Is Your Minister, Lawyer, Banker," *Daily Town Talk* (Alexandria, LA), Apr. 10, 1943.

93. Ratcliff, "The War Against Syphilis," 72.

94. Hegarty, *Victory Girls, Khaki-Wackies, and Patriotutes*, 86. See also the documents in Leesville Study Folder, Box 6, Entry 43, RG 215, NA.

95. Thomas Parran, speech dedicating the Chicago Intensive Treatment Center for Venereal Diseases, Nov. 29, 1942, Folder 610, Box 44, TPP; "Venereal Center Opened in Chicago," *New York Times*, Nov. 30, 1942; clipping from *Time*, Dec. 14, 1942, in Chicago Folder, Box 95, Entry 3, RG 215, NA.

96. Parascandola, *Sex, Sin, and Science*, 121–22; John Parascandola, "Presidential Address: Quarantining Women: Venereal Disease Rapid Treatment Centers in World War II America," *Bulletin of the History of Medicine* 83.3 (Fall 2009): 434–35, 442–44.

97. Parascandola, *Sex, Sin, and Science*, 126–28; Letter from Raymond Vonderlehr to W. C. Williams, June 26, 1943, Box 531, GCR IX, RG 90, NA.

98. Parascandola, "Presidential Address: Quarantining Women," 447–48.

99. See Erin Wuebker, "Taking the Venereal out of Venereal Disease: The Public Health Campaign Against Syphilis, 1934–1945," PhD diss., CUNY, 2015, 46; Parascandola, *Sex, Sin, and Science*, 121–22.

100. Memorandum from Raymond Vonderlehr to Thomas Parran, Jan. 12, 1943, Box 149, GCR II, RG 90, NA; Letter from Thomas Parran to F. T. Hines, Sept. 30, 1943, Jan. 1943 Folder, Box 772, Entry 42, RG 90, NA.

101. "Venereal Center Is Dedicated Here," *New York Times*, Apr. 2, 1944.

102. Memorandum from Raymond Vonderlehr to Thomas Parran, June 11, 1943, Box 531, GCR IX, RG 90, NA.

103. Charles Taft, Daily Activities Diary, Jul. 15, 1943, Box I:2, CPTP.

104. Charles Taft, Daily Activities Diary, Jul. 22, 1943, Box I:2, CPTP.

105. Memorandum from Whitcomb H. Allen to Eliot Ness, "The Need for Providing State Training Schools for Delinquent Girls," May 3, 1943, Rapid Treatment Centers Folder, Box 26, Entry 3, RG 215, NA.

106. Charles Taft, Daily Activities Diary, June 9, 1943, Box I:2, CPTP.

107. Minutes of the Social Protection Conference, "The Woman's Role in Social Protection," June 9, 1943, Committee Meetings, Box 2, Entry 41, RG 215, NA.

108. Hegarty, *Victory Girls, Khaki-Wackies, and Patriotutes*, 150.

109. In the end, Roosevelt did not receive this award, apparently because the last year's winner had been a woman and the Association was reluctant to give it to two women in a row. Letter from John H. Stokes to Frances Payne Bolton, Nov. 14, 1949, Folder 1419, Container 80, FPBP.

110. Minutes of the Social Protection Conference on "The Woman's Role in Social Protection," NA.

111. Minutes of June 14, 1941 Meeting, Advisory Committee of the Division of Social Protection, Box 1, Entry 41, RG 215, NA.

112. Letter from Rachelle Yarros to Bascom Johnson, Sept. 28, 1941, General 1942 Folder, Box 32, Entry 3, RG 215, NA.

113. Meeting minutes, JPA Board of Directors, Apr. 11, 1941, Folder 31, Supplement I Box 6, JPAR. See also Juvenile Protective Association, *Annual Report* (1941), Folder 126, Box 9, JPAR.

114. Letter from Emily W. Dean to Board of Directors, Apr. 14, 1943; Meeting minutes, JPA Board of Directors, Apr. 9, 1943; Meeting minutes, JPA Board of Directors, Apr. 29, 1943, Folder 31—all are in Supplement I Box 6, JPAR.

115. Yarros to Johnson, Sept. 28, 1941, NA.

116. "Deny Case Fixing in Women's Court," *New York Times*, Jul. 21, 1942; Women's Court Committee of the Social Service Bureau, "Women's Court: Immediate Recommendations to Improve the Service," June 8, 1942, Folder 1, Box 31, AKPAJA.

117. Valeria H. Parker, "The National Council of Women of the United States," *Journal of Social Hygiene* 29.1 (Jan. 1943): 33–35.

118. Minutes of Meeting of the Special Committee on Enforcement of the National Advisory Police Committee on Social Protection, Nov. 20, 1942, Committee Meetings, Box 1, Entry 41, RG 215, NA.

119. Sub-Committee for Committee on Social Protective Measures of the Boston Committee on Public Safety, *Survey of Social Protection in Problem in Boston* (Mar. 1942), pp. 18–19, Region I—Massachusetts—Boston Folder, Box 127, Entry 3, RG 215, NA. This woman was Miriam Van Waters, who ran the Massachusetts Reformatory for Women at Framingham. Two decades before, she had been among the women to draft resolutions opposing the Plan at the All-America Conference. During World War II, Van Waters wholeheartedly supported cracking down on prostitution and female promiscuity: at one meeting of military officials discussing "the 'teen-age girl' problem in relationship [sic] to venereal disease," Van Waters told the crowd "that prostitution can be stopped, and that every [female sexual] contact which is apprehended prevents greater trouble." Van Waters still believed that penal facilities for women should be reformative, but she also definitely believed in the importance of incarceration as a form of social uplift (albeit a discriminatory form). Memorandum from Robert F. Ott to Eliot Ness, "Meeting of Police Mobilization Coordinators and Advisory Committee, for a general discussion of the 'teen-age girl' problem," Jul. 19, 1943; Memorandum from Janet S. Burgoon to Eliot Ness, "Massachusetts Reformatory for Women," Apr. 26, 1943—both in Region I—Massachusetts—General Folder, Box 127, Entry 3, RG 215, NA.

120. Memorandum from Alice S. Clements to Eliot Ness, "Interview June 30, 1943, with Miss Helma Newman," Jul. 14, 1943, Girls Service League of America Folder, Box 3, Entry 45, RG 215, NA.

121. Memorandum from Alice S. Clements to Eliot Ness, "Visit to the National Office of the Girls Scouts, Inc.," Jul. 1943; Letter from Mrs. Lewis A. DeBlois to Charles P. Taft, May 28, 1943—both in National Girl Scouts Inc. Folder, Box 5, Entry 45, RG 215, NA.

122. "Women Declare 'Total War' on Venereal Disease," *Washington Post*, Jul. 17, 1942; "Women Will War on Social Diseases," *New York Times*, Oct. 18, 1942.

123. Memorandum from Max R. Kiesselbach to A. Frank Brewer, "Field Trip to Shasta County for Institution of Venereal Disease Control Program, July 5, 1944," Jul. 11, 1944, Series 51, R384, CDPHR.

124. Huffman v. District of Columbia, 39 A.2d 558, 559–63; "Woman Fined for Violating Health Order," *Washington Post*, June 2, 1944.

125. Hegarty, *Victory Girls, Khaki-Wackies, and Patriotutes*, 149–50.

126. *Fourteenth Biennial Report of the Industrial Farm for Women, Lansing, Kansas, for the Two Years Ending June 30, 1944* (Topeka: Kansas State Printing Plant, 1945), 21.

127. *Fifteenth Biennial Report of the Industrial Farm for Women, Lansing, Kansas, for the Two Years Ending June 30, 1946* (Topeka: Kansas State Printing Plant, 1947), 19–20.

128. Ernest G. Lyon, Helen M. Jambor, Hazle G. Corrigan, and Katherine P. Bradway, *An Experiment in the Psychiatric Treatment of Promiscuous Girls* (San Francisco Department of Public Health, 1945), in Box 1, Entry 44, RG 215, NA.

129. "Army, Navy May Invoke U.S. Vice Act Here," *Atlanta Constitution*, Aug. 4, 1942; "Murphy Urges Internment in Venereal Cases," *Atlanta Constitution*, Aug. 5, 1942; "Complaint Here Attacks Legality of Health Law," *Atlanta Constitution*, Aug. 7, 1942; "4 More Women Seek to Avoid Health Program," *Atlanta Constitution*, Aug. 8, 1942; "Hearing Slated on Interned Women Here," *Atlanta Constitution*, Aug. 9, 1942; "Around Atlanta," *Atlanta Constitution*, Aug. 10, 1942; "Health Law Test Cases Dropped," *Atlanta Constitution*, Aug. 11, 1942. In September, Atlanta's city council passed an ordinance clarifying the municipal authority to enforce the American Plan. (Previously, this authority had come from a state law.) "Council Passes to Deny Bail to Moral Suspects," *Atlanta Constitution*, Sept. 22, 1942.

130. Noland v. Gardner, 136 P.2d 233, 233–34 (Kan. 1943). See also "Petition for Writ of Habeas Corpus"; "Brief of Petitioner"—both in Case File 35927, Noland v. Gardner, KSA.

131. Petition for Habeas Corpus, State ex rel. Kennedy v. Head, Feb. 8, 1944, in Supreme Court Trial Case File, TSLA; Undercover investigation, Chattanooga, TN, Mar. 1944, Region VII—Tennessee—Chattanooga Folder, Box 204, Entry 3, RG 215, NA; Memorandum from Arthur Fink to Eliot Ness, "Special ASHA Report on Chattanooga, Tennessee," Dec. 22, 1943, Region VII—Tennessee—ASHA Material Folder, Box 204, Entry 3, RG 215, NA; State *ex rel.* Kennedy v. Head, 185 S.W.2d 530, 531–32 (Tenn. 1945).

132. Letter from Ragnar Westman to Thomas Parran, Sept. 24, 1943, Region XII—Washington—Seattle Folder, Box 229, Entry 3, RG 215, NA; "Laws Prevent Drive on Vice," *Seattle Times*, Aug. 31, 1943; "Navy Officer, Wife Sues Police Vice Probers," *Seattle Times*, Sept. 24, 1943; "Wife Sues City Over V.D. Raid," *Seattle Times*, Mar. 21, 1944.

133. Charles Taft, Daily Activities Diary, Oct. 14, 1943, Box I:2, CPTP.

134. "Court Dismisses Vice Probe Suit," *Seattle Times*, Apr. 11, 1944.

135. Memorandum from Edwin Cooley to Eliot Ness, "VD Conditions in Seattle, Washington—March 1944," Apr. 22, 1944, Region XII—Washington—Seattle Folder, Box 229, Entry 3, RG 215, NA; "Raps Federal Vice Control," *Seattle Times*, Apr. 15, 1944; "Social Disease Lower in Sept., Says Westman," *Seattle Times*, Oct. 10, 1944; "Social Disease Cases Increase," *Seattle Times*, Dec. 15, 1944; "Interview with Dr. Hesbacher," Apr. 19, 1946, Venereal Disease Control—General—District 5 Folder, Box 3, EGPP.

136. "Services Offered Arrested Girls, Seattle, Washington," 1945, Social Treatment Folder, Box 11, Entry 37, RG 215, NA.

137. City of Little Rock v. Smith, 163 S.W.2d 705, 705–09 (Ark. 1942); "City Fights to Preserve Quarantine," *Arkansas Gazette*, June 24, 1942; "City Appeals Denial of Quarantine," *Arkansas Gazette*, June 25, 1942.

138. "NEWS on Inside Pages," *Arkansas Gazette*, Jul. 15, 1942; "Billie Smith Whereabouts Not Known," *Arkansas Gazette*, Jul. 15, 1942.

139. "Warrant for Arrest of Billie Smith," *Arkansas Gazette*, Jul. 25, 1942.

140. "Billie Smith in Custody in Memphis," *Arkansas Gazette*, Aug. 16, 1942; "Principal in Vice Case Returned Here," *Arkansas Gazette*, Dec. 8, 1942; "Billie Smith Will Go to Health Center," *Arkansas Gazette*, Dec. 13, 1942.

141. "Two Flee From Health Center and Now Can't Return," *Arkansas Gazette*, Jan. 5, 1943.

142. See Stern, "The Long American Plan," 414–15.

143. "1,000,000 Jews Slain by Nazis, Report Says," *New York Times*, June 30, 1942.

144. Memorandum from Irving K. Furst to Raymond F. Clapp, "Field Trip to Battle Creek, Lansing, and Fort Custer, Michigan," Sept. 17, 1941, Region V—Michigan—Battle Creek Folder, Box 133, Entry 3, RG 215, NA.

145. Memorandum from Irving K. Furst to Alice S. Clements, "Detroit, Michigan—June 8–9, 1942," June 22, 1942, Region V—Michigan—Detroit Folder, Box 133, Entry 3, RG 215, NA; "Law Enforcement and Legislation Relating to Prostitution," *Journal of Social Hygiene* 29.5 (May 1943): 278–86.

146. Memorandum from Irving K. Furst to M. F. Amen, "Report on Prostitution Conditions in Battle Creek, Michigan," Dec. 11, 1941, Region V—Michigan—Battle Creek Folder, Box 133, Entry 3, RG 215, NA.

147. Memorandum from Irving K. Furst to Eliot Ness, "Supplement to Report of October 10, 1941," Oct. 25, 1941, Region V—Michigan—Battle Creek Folder, Box 133, Entry 3, RG 215, NA.

148. Memorandum from Irving K. Furst to Eliot Ness, "Field Trip to Saginaw, Michigan—June 11–17, 1942," June 25, 1942, Region V—Michigan—Saginaw Folder, Box 135, Entry 3, RG 215, NA.

149. Memorandum from Irving K. Furst to Eliot Ness, "Field Trip to Battle Creek and Fort Custer, Michigan, March 21, 1942," Region V—Michigan—Battle Creek Folder, Box 133, Entry 3, RG 215, NA.

150. Memorandum from Irving K. Furst to M. F. Amen, "Report on Prostitution Conditions in Battle Creek, Michigan," Dec. 11, 1941, Region V—Michigan—Battle Creek Folder, Box 133, Entry 3, RG 215, NA.

151. "Supplementary to Report of 12/11/41," Feb. 11, 1942, Region V—Michigan—Battle Creek Folder, Box 133, Entry 3, RG 215, NA.

152. Karen Anderson, *Wartime Women: Sex Roles, Family Relations, and the Status of Women During World War II* (Westport CT: Greenwood Press, 1981), 4.

153. For a female fighter plane mechanic in Michigan, see Scott Atkinson, "Michigan Honors: Flint Woman, 91, Recalls Time as Fighter Plane Mechanic During World War II," *Michigan Live*, Jul. 4, 2014, http://www.mlive.com/entertainment/flint/index.ssf/2014/07/i_was_the_only_girl_flint_woma.html.

154. Telephone interview with David McMacken, Jan. 13, 2017.

155. Sherrie A. Kossoudji and Laura J. Dresser, "Working Class Rosies: Women Industrial Workers During World War II," *Journal of Economic History* 52.2 (June 1992): 434; Anderson, *Wartime Women*, 26.

156. Anderson, *Wartime Women*, 4–5.

157. Hegarty, *Victory Girls, Khaki-Wackies, and Patriotutes*, 8.

158. Clement, *Love for Sale*, 213, 242–43.

159. Anderson, *Wartime Women*, 10, 76; Hegarty, *Victory Girls, Khaki-Wackies, and Patriotutes*, 8.

160. "Hospital Founder Elected in Alma," *Lansing State Journal*, Apr. 8, 1941; "Carney Elected Mayor, Church and Niles Win Commissioners Berths," *Alma Record*, Apr. 10, 1917; "Germ-Chaser to Rule City," *Detroit Free Press*, Apr. 20, 1941; "County Defense Council Meeting in Alma Tonight,"

Alma Record, Dec. 11, 1941; "Primary Election Assured in Alma," *Lansing State Journal*, Jan. 26, 1943; "Alma's Voters Upset Regime," *Lansing State Journal*, Apr. 3, 1945.

161. "Delma Mae Hess," *St. Louis Leader & Breckenridge American*, Nov. 11, 1943; Certificate of Death, Delma Mae Hess, St. Louis, Gratiot, MI, Nov. 9, 1943, *Michigan Death Certificates, 1921–1952*, FHL film number 1972724.

162. Quoted in John Parascandola, "John Mahoney and the Introduction of Penicillin to Treat Syphilis," 12 (2001), https://lhncbc.nlm.nih.gov/files/archive/pub2001051.pdf; Robert Bud, *Penicillin: Triumph and Tragedy* (New York: Oxford University Press, 2007), 58.

163. Waldemar Kaempffert, "Science in the News," *New York Times*, Oct. 20, 1940.

164. Memorandum from C. C. Young to Arlon G. Ley, "Penicillin," Nov. 19, 1943, Folder 16, Box 22, RG 42, HKP.

165. Howard Markel, "The Real Story Behind Penicillin," *NewsHour*, PBS, Sept. 27, 2013, http://www.pbs.org/newshour/rundown/the-real-story-behind-the-worlds-first-antibiotic.

166. Parascandola, "John Mahoney and the Introduction of Penicillin to Treat Syphilis," 9–10; Lennard Bickel, *Rise Up to Life: A Biography of Howard Walter Florey, Who Gave Penicillin to the World* (New York: Scribner, 1972), 187–90.

167. Letter from Otis L. Anderson to J. F. Mahoney, Dec. 9, 1943, Box 531, GCR IX, RG 90, NA.

168. See untitled article, *Washington Post*, Jan. 4, 1944; "Many Penicillin Units Received at Augusta Center," *Atlanta Constitution*, Jan. 24, 1944.

169. Memorandum from Manfred Willmer to C. L. Wiliams, Mar. 18, 1944, Box 169, GCR II, RG 90, NA.

170. Parascandola, "Presidential Address: Quarantining Women," 448–49.

171. "Physician Says Penicillin Could Eliminate Syphilis," *New York Herald Tribune*, May 26, 1944.

172. Federal Security Agency, "Milestones in Venereal Disease Control," 1949, Folder 1, Box 1, Series 1, ASHAR.

173. Wuebker, "Taking the Venereal out of Venereal Disease: The Public Health Campaign Against Syphilis, 1934–1945," 46.

174. See Albert Deutsch, "DANGER! VENEREAL DISEASE," *Nation*, June 22, 1945, in DANGER-VENEREAL DISEASE, ALBERT DEUTSCH Folder, Box 2, Entry 45, RG 215, NA.

175. Minutes of the Meeting of the National Venereal Disease Committee, Sept. 13, 1945, pp. 1–11.

176. Charles Taft, Daily Activities Diary, Aug. 18, 1942, Box I:1, CPTP.

177. Letter from Charles P. Taft to John Henry Wigmore, Aug. 27, 1942, Folder 1, Box 22, JHWP. See also Charles Taft, Daily Activities Diary, Aug. 19, 1942, Box I:1, CPTP; Charles Taft, Daily Activities Diary, Aug. 26, 1942, Box I:1, CPTP.

178. Charles Taft, Daily Activities Diary, Sept. 17, 1942, Box I:1, CPTP; Charles Taft, Daily Activities Diary, Sept. 18, 1942, Box I:1, CPTP; Letter from Charles P. Taft to John Henry Wigmore, Sept. 24, 1942, Folder 4, Box 43, JHWP.

179. Letter from Eliot Ness to Charles Hough, Nov. 18, 1942, Folder 5, Box 43, JHWP. Fingerprinting had first been introduced in some places decades before. It allowed police to identify recidivists and suspects using false names. New York officials had controversially used fingerprinting while enforcing Section 79 back in 1912. Pivar, *Purity and Hygiene*, 100. As the historian Barbara Meil Hobson noted, "New York was a pioneer in the use of fingerprinting, and prostitutes were the first criminal types to be sentenced under this fool-proof scientific way of identifying a recidivist." Hobson, *Uneasy Virtue*, 160.

180. Charles Taft, Daily Activities Diary, Nov. 5, 1942, Box I:1, CPTP.

181. "Regional Conference, Social Protection Division," Dec. 11, 1942; Letter from John Henry Wigmore to Janet S. Burgoon, Nov. 23, 1942; Letter from Janet S. Burgoon to John Henry Wigmore, Dec. 14, 1942—all are in Folder 5, Box 43, JHWP.

182. American Bar Association, *Venereal Disease, Prostitution and War* (Washington, DC, Feb. 1943). For Goldsmith's first draft, see "First Draft of the Report of the Committee of the American Bar Association on Courts and Wartime Social Protection," Folder 5, Box 43, JHWP.

183. *Hearings Before Subcommittee No. 3 of the Committee on the Judiciary, House of Representatives, Seventy-Ninth Congress, Second Session on H.R. 5234, A Bill to Authorize the Federal Security Administrator to Assist the States in Matters Relating to Social Protection, and for Other Purposes*, Mar. 18, 1946 (Washington, DC: Government Printing Office, 1946), 19; Letter from Eliot Ness to John M. Goldsmith, June 29, 1943, Region VII—Tennessee—General Folder, Box 204, Entry 3, RG 215, NA; Charles Taft, Daily Activities Diary, Mar. 17, 1943; Charles Taft, Daily Activities Diary, Apr. 29, 1943; Charles Taft, Daily Activities Diary, May 19, 1943—all are in Box I:2, CPTP. For more on Goldsmith's influence in Tennessee, see material in Region VII—Tennessee—Bar Committee Folder, Box 204, Entry 3, RG 215, NA. For more on the East St. Louis case, see memoranda in Region VI—Illinois—East St. Louis Folder, Box 96, Entry 3, RG 215, NA. For Goldsmith in Michigan, see Letter from John M. Goldsmith to James J. Dunn, May 31, 1943, Region V—Michigan—Battle Creek Folder, Box 133, Entry 3, RG 215, NA.

184. Anderson, *Wartime Women*, 109.

185. Letter from Ernest Besig to Edmund Brown, Jan. 19, 1944, Folder 776, Carton 36, ACLUNCR.

186. Lorraine K. Bannai, *Enduring Conviction: Fred Korematsu and His Quest for Justice* (Seattle: University of Washington Press, 2015), 7–85.

187. Memorandum from Melba M. Foltz to Eliot Ness, "Initial Field Report—McGehee, Arkansas," Sept. 23, 1942; Memorandum from Melba M. Foltz to Eliot Ness, "Field Report—McGehee, Arkansas," Jul. 28, 1943—bother are in Region IX—Arkansas—McGehee and Jerome Folder, Box 50, Entry 3, RG 215, NA.

188. Besig to Brown, Jan. 19, 1944, ACLUNCR; Letter from Ernest Besig to Edmund Brown, Feb. 18, 1944, Folder 776, Carton 36, ACLUNCR.

189. Letter from Edmund Brown to Ernest Besig, Feb. 24, 1944, Folder 776, Carton 36, ACLUNCR.

190. Letter from Ernest Besig to Editor, *San Francisco News*, June 23, 1944; Letter from Ernest Besig to Barney Dreyfus, Apr. 1, 1944; Letter from Ernest Besig to Alfred D. Martin, Apr. 3, 1944; Letter from Alfred D. Martin to Ernest Besig, May 3, 1944—all in Folder 776, Carton 36, ACLUNCR.

191. Letter from Edmund Brown to Editor, *San Francisco News*, June 30, 1944, Folder 776, Carton 36, ACLUNCR.

192. "City Battles Rising Venereal Rate: Arrest of Disease Suspects Is Asked," *San Francisco Chronicle*, Oct. 20, 1944; Letter from Ernest Besig to Bert Levitt, Nov. 11, 1944, Folder 776, Carton 36, ACLUNCR. For the text of the ordinance, see "An ordinance relating to and providing for the preservation of the public health . . ." Folder 777, Carton 36, ACLUNCR.

193. Letter from John M. Goldsmith to Edwin Cooley, Nov. 13, 1944, San Francisco, California Folder, Box 1, Entry 40, RG 215, NA; "New City Law to Control Venereal Disease Studied," *San Francisco News*, Nov. 17, 1944, in Folder 777, Carton 36, ACLUNCR.

194. "Committee Irons Out Kinds in Venereal Disease Plan," *San Francisco News*, Nov. 23, 1944, in Folder 777, Carton 36, ACLUNCR; "V.D. Control Ordinance Up Today," *San Francisco Chronicle*, Nov. 27, 1944.

195. Richard A. Koch and Ray Lyman Wilbur, "Promiscuity as a Factor in the Spread of Venereal Disease," *Journal of Social Hygiene* 30.9 (Dec. 1944): 521–25.

196. "Conf. with Geiger et al, Jan. 12, '45 at 10^{30} AM"; Letter from Ernest Besig to J. C. Geiger, Jan. 16, 1945—both in Folder 776, Carton 36, ACLUNCR.

197. See Ann Ray, Women's Court records, 1945, Folder 777, Carton 36, ACLUNCR.

198. Letter from Ernest Besig to Edwin Cooley, Jul. 24, 1945, Folder 777, Carton 36, ACLUNCR.

199. "Statement of Facts," State of Texas v. Bettie Mae James, Apr. 14, 1944, in case file, Ex parte James, TexSLA; Brief for Appellant, Ex parte James, Apr. 11, 1944, in case file, Ex parte James, TexSLA.

200. *Ex parte* James, 181 S.W.2d 83, 84 (Tex. Crim. App. 1944).

201. Memorandum from Christopher J. French to Eliot Ness, "Beaumont, Texas, etc.," Mar. 17, 1942, Region X—Texas—Beaumont Folder, Box 209, Entry 3, RG 215, NA.

202. See Letter from Paul McNutt to George Morgan, Mar. 12, 1942; Letter from Eliot Ness to George Morgan, Mar. 23, 1942; "Taken from Page 69 of the Composite Report on BEAUMONT-PORT ARTHUR-PORT NECHES WAR PRODUCTION AREA, Jefferson County, Texas," June 30, 1942—these three are in Region X—Texas—Beaumont Folder, Box 209, Entry 3, RG 215, NA; Memorandum from Whitcomb H. Allen to Eliot Ness, "Completion of attached tabulation," Jul. 16, 1942, Community Study Re Prostitution Folder, Box 7, Entry 43, RG 215, NA.

203. Memorandum from Fred R. Kearney to Eliot Ness, "Supplementary Report—Beaumont," Mar. 24, 1943, Region X—Texas—Beaumont Folder, Box 209, Entry 3, RG 215, NA.

204. "Supplementary Report on Beaumont, Texas," Apr. 5, 1944, Region X—Texas—Beaumont Folder, Box 209, Entry 3, RG 215, NA.

205. Quoted in Alankaar Sharma, "Diseased Race, Racialized Disease: The Story of the Negro Project of American Social Hygiene Association Against the Backdrop of the Tuskegee Syphilis Experiment," *Journal of African American Studies* 14.2 (June 2010): 250. For more on the racialization of syphilis, see ibid., 254–55.

206. Regional Staff Meeting, Region X, Social Protection Division, Office of Community War Services," Apr. 12, 13, 15, 1944, 1944 Folder, Box 26, Entry 3, RG 215, NA.

207. See Memorandum from Franklyn C. Hochreiter to Eliot Ness, "Beaumont, Texas—Interim Report," Jul. 7, 1944, Region X—Texas—Beaumont Folder, Box 209, Entry 3, RG 215, NA.

208. Memorandum from Fred R. Kearney to Eliot Ness, "Beaumont, Texas," Mar. 3, 1942, Region X—Texas—Beaumont Folder, Box 209, Entry 3, RG 215, NA.

209. "Action Summary of Inter-Agency Meeting of March 4, 1944," Box 27, Entry 3, RG 215, NA; James A. Burran, "The Beaumont Race Riot, 1943," master's thesis, Texas Tech University, 1973, 23, 31–35.

210. Burran, "The Beaumont Race Riot," 43.

211. See Pamela Lippold, "Recollections: Revisiting the Beaumont Race Riot," honors thesis, Lamar University, 2005; James A. Burran, "Violence in an 'Arsenal of Democracy': The Beaumont Race Riot of 1943," *East Texas Historical Journal* 14 (Spring 1976): 39–47; Burran, "The Beaumont Race Riot."

212. Charlotte Rolison, "Social Case Work Among Venereally Infected Females in a Quarantine Hospital," *Journal of Social Hygiene* 32.1 (Jan. 1946): 18.

213. Hegarty, *Victory Girls, Khaki-Wackies, and Patriotutes,* 77.

214. Untitled memoranda, Jan. 1945, Folder 776, Carton 36, ACLU of Northern California Records.

215. Letter from Ernest Besig to J. C. Geiger, Jan. 16, 1945, Folder 776, Carton 36, ACLUNCR.

216. Helen Hironimus, "Survey of 100 May Act Violators Committed to the Federal Reformatory for Women," *Federal Probation* 7 (Apr.–June 1943): 31–34.

217. "Texas Police Are Accused of Mistreatment: Women Subjected to Humiliation in Police Questioning," *Pittsburgh Courier,* Jul. 18, 1942.

218. Parascandola, "Presidential Address: Quarantining Women," 455–56.

219. Wyndham D. Miles, "Dr. John R. Heller: An Oral History," Oct. 26, 1964, transcribed Dec. 1, 1988, National Institutes of Health, https://history.nih.gov/archives/downloads/hellerjohn.pdf.

220. Allan Brandt, "Racism and Research: The Case of the Tuskegee Syphilis Study," *Hastings Center Report* 8.6 (1978): 25–26.

221. Jones, *Bad Blood,* 162–63; Reverby, *Examining Tuskegee,* 122–24. Reverby demonstrates that in the second case, that of Herman Shaw, more innocent factors may have contributed to the nurse's decision to send him away.

222. Brandt, "Racism and Research," 23.

223. Reverby, *Examining Tuskegee,* 124–28; Brandt, "Racism and Research," 26.

224. Walter Clarke, "Postwar Social Hygiene Problems," *Journal of Social Hygiene* 31.1 (Jan. 1945): 4–5.

225. Letter from William F. Snow to Andrew J. May, Apr. 10, 1945; Letter from William F. Snow to persons interested in the May Act, Apr. 20, 1945; Memorandum from Thomas Parran to Alanson W. Willcox, "H.R. 2992, a bill 'To extend the provisions of the Act of July 11, 1941' (Public Law 163, Seventy-seventh Congress)," Apr. 30, 1945—these three in Folder 702, Box 47, TPP; Letter from William F. Snow to Ray Lyman Wilbur, May 17, 1945; Letter from William F. Snow to Thomas Parran, May 30, 1945; Thomas Parran, Testimony at hearings of the Social Protection Division, June 14, 1945—these three are in Folder 705, Box 47, TPP.

226. Minutes of Meeting of the National Advisory Police Committee on Social Protection, May 23, 1945, Committee Meetings, Box 1, Entry 41, RG 215, NA.

CHAPTER 13: "VENEREAL DISEASE WAS NOT OUR CONCERN"

1. Walter Hixenbaugh, Memorandum on Flint, Oct. 1945; Walter Hixenbaugh, Memorandum on Flint, Feb. 1946; Walter Hixenbaugh, Memorandum on Flint, Mar. 1946—all in Flint Folder, Box 5, Entry 40, RG 215, NA.

2. Walter Hixenbaugh, Memorandum on Muskegon, Apr. 1946, Muskegon Folder, Box 5, Entry 40, RG 215, NA.

3. Walter Hixenbaugh, Memorandum on Saginaw, Mar. 1946; Reprint of "Council Shuts 'Line' Houses," *Saginaw News,* Oct. 24, 1944—both in Saginaw Folder, Box 5, Entry 40, RG 215, NA.

4. *Ex parte* Fowler, 184 P.2d 814, 814–20 (Okla. Crim. App. 1947); *Ex parte* Woodruff, 210 P.2d 191 (Okla. Crim. App. 1949); Hill v. Hilbert, 222 P.2d 166 (Okla. Crim. App. 1950).

5. In re Martin, 188 P.2d 287, 288–93 (Cal. App. 1948); Testimony of James C. Malcolm, p. 34, Sept. 13, 1947; Petition for Writ of Habeas Corpus, Sept. 11, 1947; Amended Sheriff's Return, Oct. 1, 1947 Letter from Harold Wyatt to George N. Didion, May 15, 1948, and related correspondence—all in case file, In re Martin, CSA.

6. Malcolm H. Merrill, "Venereal Disease Prevention in Wartime: An Evaluation of Progress Under the Eight Point Agreement of May, 1940," *Journal of Social Hygiene* 29.2 (Feb. 1943): 80–88; "Vice Crackdown: City Moves to Check Army, Navy Disease Rate," *San Francisco Chronicle,* August 12, 1942; *Annual Report of the Department of Health, City of Los Angeles, California, for the Fiscal Year Ended June 30, 1943,* p. 76; *Annual Report of the Department of Health, City of Los Angeles, California, for the Fiscal Year Ended June 30, 1948,* pp. 103, 113; *Annual Report of the Department of Health, City of Los Angeles, California, for the Fiscal Year Ended June 30, 1949,* p. 146; Walter Clarke, "Some Social Hygiene Problems of Los Angeles," *Journal of Social Hygiene* 34.7 (Oct. 1948): 313–22; American Social Hygiene Association, "Los Angeles County Social Hygiene Survey," 1948, Folder 3, Box 98, Series 7, ASHAR; "Wallace Denies Vice Accusation," *Fresno Bee,* Feb. 19, 1948; Ernest Besig, press release, Oct. 21, 1946; and Letter from Martin Mills to Wayne E. Thompson, Dec. 31, 1949—both in Folder 776, Carton 36, ACLUNCR.

7. "Three Cops Close Bar Wrong Way," *San Francisco Chronicle,* Jul. 16, 1947, in Folder 777, Carton 36, ACLUNCR. It appears "vagged" could also refer to being charged with vagrancy, which had a much lower threshold of proof than prostitution. Littauer, "Unsanctioned Encounters," 66.

8. Letter from Bertram Edises to Ora E. Rhodes, May 9, 1949, Folder 776, Carton 36, ACLUNCR.

9. Untitled clipping, *San Francisco Chronicle,* Apr. 18, 1950, in Folder 777, Carton 36, ACLUNCR.

10. *Department of Health: Annual Report, 1941–1948* (New York: Department of Health), 166–68, 171; "The Specialized Courts in New York City Dealing with Woman Sex Offenders," n.d. but a note saying "1948 or later." Folder 17, Box 209, Series 7, ASHAR.

11. *Department of Health: Annual Report,* 167–68, 171.

12. *Department of Health: Annual Report, 1949* (New York: Department of Health), 157, 159.

13. See untitled article, *Washington Post*, Jan. 4, 1944; "Many Penicillin Units Received at Augusta Center," *Atlanta Constitution*, Jan. 24, 1944; Parascandola, *Sex, Sin, and Science*, 130.

14. Parascandola, *Sex, Sin, and Science*, 128.

15. See Thomas B. Turner, "Penicillin in the Venereal Disease Control Program," *Journal of Social Hygiene* 34.5 (May 1948): 205–6; Seattle-King County Department of Public Health, *Road to Health: 1954.*

16. *Health: Biennial Report: Louisiana State Board of Health, 1950–1951*, 39–41.

17. *Department of Health: Annual Report, 1950* (New York: Department of Health), 155.

18. Parascandola, *Sex, Sin, and Science*, 137.

19. *Thirtieth Annual Report of the Department of Public Health, July 1, 1946 to June 30, 1947*, 51.

20. See ibid., 54–58; Nicholas J. Fiumara, "The Police Role in Contact Investigation," *Journal of Social Hygiene* 37.6 (June 1951): 276; Seattle-King County Department of Public Health, *Report: 1952–1955*, 20–21. See also Patrick Kelley, Field Report, Seattle, WA, Mar. 12, 1951, Folder 7, Box 111, Series 7, ASHAR.

21. Letter from J. W. Bass to L. B. Woods, Nov. 10, 1950, Folder 5, Box 9, DHDC.

22. Carl C. Bare, "A Clean Slate for Cleveland," *Journal of Social Hygiene* 39.2 (Feb. 1953): 92–93.

23. Minutes of the Meeting of the National Venereal Disease Committee [*sic*], Sept. 13, 1945, Box 2, Entry 41, RG 215, NA.

24. *Hearings Before Subcommittee No. 3 of the Committee on the Judiciary, House of Representatives, Seventy-Ninth Congress, Second Session on H.R. 5234, a Bill to Authorize the Federal Security Administrator to Assist the States in Matters Relating to Social Protection, and for Other Purposes*, Mar. 18, 1946 (Washington, DC: Government Printing Office, 1946), 1–10, 53–63.

25. Robert Patterson, Fred Vinson, James Forrestal, Watson Miller, "The New Eight Point Agreement of 1946: An Agreement of Measures for the Control of Venereal Disease, April 1946," Folder 1183, Box 82, TPP.

26. Dwight D. Eisenhower and Edward F. Witsell, "REPRESSION OF PROSTITUTION," Apr. 5, 1946, Army and Navy Folder, Box 1, Entry 37, RG 215, NA.

27. Telegram from William F. Snow to Frances Payne Bolton, Jul. 18, 1946; Letter from Frances Payne Bolton to William F. Snow, Jul. 19, 1946—both in Folder 111, Container 7, FPBP.

28. "Washington as Seen by Fred Othman," United Press, Jul. 17, 1946, in Folder 111, Container 7, FPBP.

29. Percy Shostac, American Social Hygiene Association Press Release, Jul. 16, 1946; Letter from Esther Emerson Sweeney to Thomas Devine, Jul. 17, 1946—both in American Social Hygiene Association Folder, Box 1, Entry 37, RG 215, NA.

30. American Social Hygiene Association, "Description of Projects in Proposed Budget for Period from October 1, 1945 to September 30, 1946, Inclusive," Folder 2, Box 22, Series 3, ASHAR; Walter Clarke, "The American Social Hygiene Association," *Public Health Reports* 70.4 (Apr. 1955): 425; "SUGGESTION FOR USO CLIP SHEET," Nov. 9, 1948, and the other correspondence/reports in Folder 2, Box 45, Series 3, ASHAR. For a close look at the ASHA's activities near military bases in the late 1940s, see "Monthly Report of Defense Program," May 9, 1949, Folder 1419, Container 80, FPBP.

31. "Drive Against VD Begins Tomorrow," *New York Times*, Oct. 7, 1946; "Anti-VD Campaign Proclaimed Here," *New York Times*, Oct. 8, 1946; "Control of VD Now Urged by M'Intire," *New York Times*, Oct. 9, 1946; "Stamp Out VD Campaign Luncheon Held at Hotel Astor on October 8, 1946, Under the Auspices of American Social Hygiene Association," Folder 4, Box 24, Series 3, ASHAR.

32. See the voluminous correspondence in Folders 3–4, Box 31, Series 3, and Folders 2–9, Box 45, Series 3, ASHAR; "The American Social Hygiene Association: A Brief Historical Statement," 1948, Folder 1, Box 1, Series 1, ASHAR; Philip R. Mather, "The Community in Action," *Journal of Social Hygiene* 33.7 (Oct. 1947): 326; Memorandum from Arthur W. Packard to John D. Rockefeller Jr., "American Social Hygiene Association, Inc. Special Project Negro Leadership Training," Dec. 11, 1946, Folder 127, Box 16, Series K, RAC; Orel J. Myers, "Report of the Finance Committee: American Social Hygiene Association: Jan. 1, 1950—Dec. 31, 1950," Jan. 26, 1951, Folder 3, Box 22, Series 2, ASHAR.

33. Letter from William F. Snow to Ray Lyman Wilbur, n.d., Folder 2, Box 45, Series 3, ASHAR; American Social Hygiene Association: Summary Annual Report: August, 1950," Folder 128, Box 16, Series K, RAC.

34. Walter Clarke, *1946—A Year of Transition from War to Peace: Annual Report of the American Social Hygiene Association*, Folder 985, Box 57, TPP.

35. "Dr. Snow, Leader in Public Health," *New York Times*, June 13, 1950; "Bascom Johnson, 76, Dies; Helped Shut Barbary Coast," *New York Herald Tribune*, Oct. 21, 1954; "Vice Crusader Bascom Johnson Is Dead at 76," *Atlanta Constitution*, Oct. 21, 1954.

36. Parascandola, *Sex, Sin, and Science*, 137; Brandt, *No Magic Bullet*, 176.

37. Snyder, "New York, the Nation, the World," 632; "Thomas Parran, Jr. (1936–1948)," SurgeonGeneral.gov, US Department of Health & Human Services, Jan. 4, 2007, http://www.surgeongeneral.gov/about/previous/bioparran.html; "$13,600,000 Mellon Gift for Pitt Health School," *Pittsburgh Press*, Sept. 22, 1948.

38. "Progress Report on National Defense Activities of the American Social Hygiene Association," Folder 1183, Box 82, TPP. See the investigator's confidential reports and correspondence in Alaska—Social Hygiene Problems, 1948 Folder, Box I:84, CPTP. See also Folders 6–10, Box 164, Series 11, ASHAR.

39. Letter from Philip R. Mather to George C. Marshall, Sept. 1, 1948, Folder 2, Box 45, Series 3, ASHAR.

40. American Social Hygiene Association, *In Defense of the Nation: Three Times in 33 Years*, 1950, Folder 4, Box 20, Series 2, ASHAR.

41. American Social Hygiene Association, *The True Strength: A Record of Activities During 1951*, Folder 4, Box 20, Series 2, ASHAR.

42. Off-Limits . . . And the Heat's On!," *Journal of Social Hygiene* 38.4 (Apr. 1952): 171–72.

43. Walter Clarke, "Venereal Disease Control Activities in San Antonio," pp. 17–19, Feb. 14, 1951, Folder 6, Box 102, Series 7, ASHAR; ASHA Field Notes, San Antonio, 1950, Folder 7, Box 102, Series 7, ASHAR.

44. Walter Clarke, "Venereal Disease Control in Atom-Bombed Areas," Oct. 23, 1950, Folder 1, Box 165, Series 11, ASHAR. See the correspondence concerning this article in this folder.

45. Thomas C. Edwards, Field Report, Norfolk, VA, Jan. 9, 1950; Thomas C. Edwards, Field Report, Norfolk, VA, Jan. 10, 1950—both in Folder 5, Box 111, Series 7, ASHAR. For another example, see Sidney S. Lee, "Military + Civilian = Control," *Journal of Social Hygiene* 38.8 (Nov. 1952): 363–70, which is about Camp LeJeune in North Carolina.

46. See ASHA, "HIGHLIGHTS of 1953," ASHA Records; Untitled ASHA report, "early 1954"; "Social Protection Services," *Social Hygiene News* 30.4 (Apr. 1955); *What the American Social Hygiene Association Did in 1955*—all in Folder 5, Box 20, Series 2, ASHAR. On Galveston, see field reports in Folder 8, Box 110, Series 7, ASHAR; Jean M. Brown, "Free Rein: Galveston Island's Alcohol, Gambling, and Prostitution Era, 1839–1957," master's thesis, Lamar University, 1998. On Laramie, see field reports in Folder 2, Box 112, Series 7, ASHAR; John P. Woodward, "'The Taming of Front Street': Prostitution in Southeastern Wyoming, 1930–1960," master's thesis, University of Wyoming, 2010, 67–86.

47. Walter Clarke, "The American Social Hygiene Association," *Public Health Reports* 70.4 (Apr. 1955): 426.

48. "Hess," *Bay City Times*, Jul. 21, 1957.

49. *Polk's Bay City Directory, 1916–1917* (Detroit: R. L. Polk & Co., 1918), 11–12; *Polk's Bay City Directory, 1948* (Detroit: R. L. Polk & Co., 1949), 12–13.

50. Thanks to the volunteers of the Bay County Historical Society for pointing this out.

51. Telephone interview with John V. Runberg, Sept. 7, 2016.

52. Telephone interview with Barbara Schweinsberg, Sept. 19, 2016.

53. *Polk's Bay City Directory, 1952* (Detroit: R. L. Polk & Co., 1953), 120; *Polk's Bay City Directory, 1956* (Detroit: R. L. Polk & Co., 1957), 153; *Polk's Bay City Directory, 1958* (Detroit: R. L. Polk & Co., 1959), 153; *Polk's Bay City Directory, 1960* (Detroit: R. L. Polk & Co., 1961), 146.

54. "Inspection Report—Relief Station: Bay City, Michigan," 1940, Box 167, GCR II, RG 90, NA.

55. "New Hospital Lease Signed," *Bay City Times*, Aug. 26, 1954, BCHS.

56. 1940 US Census, St. Louis, Gratiot County, Michigan, sheet 13B, family 342, lines 61–62, Apr. 15, 1940; Certificate of Death, Vern McCall, Grayling, Crawford, Michigan, Dec. 24, 1953, *Michigan, Deaths and Burials Index, 1867–1995*, FHL film number 965633.

57. "Hess," 4; Certificate of Death, Nina Hess, Bay City, Bay, MI, Jul. 21, 1953, *Michigan, Deaths and Burials Index, 1867–1995*. Thanks to Jan E. Tripp for finding this for me.

58. Letter from Henrietta Additon to Miriam Van Waters, Mar. 19, 1942, Folder 506, A-71, MVWP.

59. Vera Watson Schmidt, typed biographical notes of interview with Jane Deeter Rippin, Box 1599, GSUSAR.

60. Dummer, *Autobiography of an Hypothesis*.

61. Letter from Ethel Sturges Dummer to Clarence Randall, Feb. 14, 1942, Folder 400, Box 25, A-127, ESDP.

62. Letter from Ethel Sturges Dummer to Thomas Parran, Apr. 10, 1943, Folder 403, Box 25, A-127, ESDP.

63. Letter from Katharine Bushnell to Anne Henrietta Martin, Aug. 12, 1943; Letter from Katharine Bushnell to Anne Henrietta Martin, Sept. 2, 1943—both in Folder 16, Box 2, MSS P-G 282, AHMP.

64. Ruth Hoppin, "The Legacy of Katherine Bushnell," *Priscilla Papers* 9.1 (Winter 1995): 9.

65. "Health Checkup Policy Changed," *El Paso Herald-Post*, Jul. 30, 1957.

66. "Fighting Disease in El Paso," *El Paso Herald-Post*, Aug. 1, 1957.

67. "Mayor Approves Health Plan," *El Paso Herald-Post*, Aug. 5, 1957. The article said, "The Health Department already has workable procedures for examining VD suspects before conviction," but this likely referred to suspects who had refused examinations—as comments by the city attorney on June 5 make clear. The article further noted that health officers and state investigators "have authority to issue report-for-examination notices to venereal suspects."

68. "Uncover New VD Control Procedures," *Indiana Gazette*, Apr. 24, 1952. On Pennsylvania's enforcement into the early 1950s, see Arrest 10 Girls in Farrell Raid," *Record-Argus* (Greenville, PA), Mar. 18, 1950; *Biennial Report of the Department of Health of the Commonwealth of Pennsylvania, Fiscal Period, June 1, 1948—May 31, 1950* (Harrisburg, PA), 103; *Biennial Report of the Department of Health of the Commonwealth of Pennsylvania, Fiscal Period, June 1, 1950—May 31, 1952* (Harrisburg, PA), 42.

69. *Fifteenth Biennial Report of the Industrial Farm for Women*, 20; *Sixteenth Biennial Report of the Industrial Farm for Women, Lansing, Kansas, for the Two Years Ending June 30, 1948* (Topeka: Kansas State Printing Plant, 1949), 19; *Seventeenth Biennial Report of the Industrial Farm for Women, Lansing, Kansas, for the Two Years Ending June 30, 1950* (Topeka: Kansas State Printing Plant, 1951), 16; *Eighteenth Biennial Report of the Industrial Farm for Women, Lansing, Kansas, for the Two Years Ending June 30, 1952* (Topeka: Kansas State Printing Plant, 1953), 2–5, 12–13.

70. Case Number 8719, Inmates Discharged Register, Jan. 1956, ID #193822, KSIFW Records; *Twentieth Biennial Report of the Industrial Farm for Women* (Topeka: Kansas State Printing Plant, 1957), 61; *Twenty-First Biennial Report of the Industrial Farm for Women* (Topeka: Kansas State Printing Plant, 1959), 89.

71. To see this, compare the biennial reports. Detentions for prostitution were zero until 1950–52, when there was 1; there were 8 in 1954–56. Detentions for lewd and lascivious conduct and vagrancy increased from 4 in 1946–48 to 14 in 1950–52, then to 16 in 1952–54 (and 14 in 1954–56). (Even when these numbers remained relatively stable, this still represented a greater proportion of morals arrests, since Farm's population declined over this decade: 333 in 1944–46; 164 in 1946–48; 138 in 1948–50; 99 in 1950–52; 93 in 1952–54, before briefly rising again to 106 in 1954–56.)

72. Memorandum from Max R. Kiesselbach to A. Frank Brewer, "Trip to Fresno City and County—October 10," Nov. 5, 1945, Series 51, R384, CDPHR; "Wallace Denies Vice Accusation," *Fresno Bee*, Feb. 19, 1948.

73. "Border Patrol Head Urges Alien Hiring Penalty," *Fresno Bee*, Oct. 10, 1948.

74. "Dunn Says Health Officer Hamstrings City's Effort to Wipe Out Prostitution," *Fresno Bee*, Oct. 28, 1953.

75. Rick Johnson, "Barton Urges New Law to Halt V.D.," *Indianapolis Star*, Sept. 13, 1967.

76. Judy Sims, "Gonorrhea: Ancient Disease Making Comeback," *Delta Democrat-Times*, Nov. 11, 1968; "Gonorrhea Rise Reported in Memphis," *Tennessean*, Oct. 9, 1969. For more on Roberts, see Frederick M. Culp and Mrs. Robert E. Ross, "The Health Department," *Gibson County: Past and Present* (Trenton, TN: Gibson County Historical Society, 1961), 316.

77. "Spearheads VD Fight," *Atlanta Constitution*, Apr. 27, 1972.

78. D'Emilio and Freedman, *Intimate Matters*, 285; Alfred C. Kinsey et al., *Sexual Behavior in the Human Male* (Philadelphia: W. B. Saunders, 1948); Clement, *Love for Sale*, 211.

79. Alfred C. Kinsey et al., *Sexual Behavior in the Human Female* (Philadelphia: W. B. Saunders, 1953).

80. D'Emilio and Freedman, *Intimate Matters*, 286–87; "Our History: 1948: The Kinsey Report," American Sexual Health Association, 2017, http://www.ashasexualhealth.org/who-we-are/312-2.

81. James Gilbert, *A Cycle of Outrage: America's Reaction to the Juvenile Delinquent in the 1950s* (New York: Oxford University Press, 1986), 22.

82. See, for instance, Alan Petigny, "Illegitimacy, Postwar Psychology, and the Reperiodization of the Sexual Revolution," *Journal of Social History* 38.1 (Autumn 2004): 63–79.

83. David Allyn, *Make Love, Not War: The Sexual Revolution; an Unfettered History* (New York: Little, Brown, 2000), 33.

84. Ibid., 41–53.

85. Ibid., 46.

86. Heather Dean, "Free Woman," *San Francisco Express Times* (1966); Untitled poster, Sept. 12, 1967, Folder 124, Carton 2, COYOTER; Gail King, "Us All," *No More Fun and Games: A Journal of Female Liberation* 1 (Oct. 1968); "An Independent Women's Liberation Movement," *Women* 1.1 (Fall 1969): 59; Ellen Strong, "The Hooker," in *Sisterhood Is Powerful: An Anthology of Writings from the Women's Liberation Movement*, ed. Robin Morgan (New York: Random House, 1970), 289–90; Roxanne Dunbar, "'Sexual Liberation': More of the Same," *No More Fun and Games* 1.3 (Nov. 1969): 49–56.

87. Lillian Faderman and Stuart Timmons, *Gay L.A.: A History of Sexual Outlaws, Power Politics, and Lipstick Lesbians* (New York: Basic Books, 2006), 1–2; Susan Stryker, *Transgender History* (Berkeley, CA: Seal Press, 2008), 60–64; John D'Emilio, *Sexual Politics, Sexual Communities: The Making of a Homosexual Minority in the United States, 1940–1970* (Chicago: University of Chicago Press, 1983), 193–95; Lynn Witt and Eric Marcus, eds., *Out in All Directions: The Almanac of Gay and Lesbian America* (New York: Warner Books, 1995), 210; Mack Friedman, *Strapped for Cash: A History of American Hustler Culture* (Los Angeles: Alyson Books, 2003), 111–50.

88. Stryker, *Transgender History*, 66–68; Friedman, *Strapped for Cash*, 128–33.

89. David Maraniss, *Once in a Great City: A Detroit Story* (New York: Simon & Schuster, 2015), 197–203.

90. Brandt, *No Magic Bullet*, 174–76.

91. Cahn, *Sexual Reckonings*, 283.

92. Diane McWhorter, *Carry Me Home: Birmingham, Alabama, and the Climactic Battle of the Civil Rights Revolution* (New York: Simon & Schuster, 2001), 246, 405.

93. Danielle L. McGuire, *At the Dark End of the Street: Black Women, Rape, and Resistance—a New History of the Civil Rights Movement from Rosa Parks to the Rise of Black Power* (New York: Vintage Books, 2010), 39.

94. Brandt, *No Magic Bullet*, 177.

95. "Forms and Principles of State Social Hygiene Laws Prepared by Division of Legal and Protective Services American Social Hygiene Association," 1962, Box 124, 3AMS/D/51/05, AMSHR.

96. Exec. Order No. 11,070, 27 Fed. Reg. 12,393 (Dec. 14, 1962).

97. "Andrea Dworkin, 1946–," 14, in *Contemporary Authors Autobiography Series*, vol. 21, ed. Joyce Nakamura (New York: Gale, 1995); Feinman, "Imprisoned Women," 130; William E. Farrell, "Inquiry Ordered at Women's Jail," *New York Times*, Mar. 6, 1965; Ariel Levy, "The Prisoner of Sex," *New York Magazine*, June 2005, http://nymag.com/nymetro/news/people/features/11907/index1.html.

98. Quoted in James A. Weschler, "Who Sinned?," *New York Post*, Mar. 8, 1965, in Folder 16, Box 38, ADP.

99. Taylor Branch, *Parting the Waters: America in the King Years 1954–63* (New York: Simon & Schuster, 1988), 763.

100. Earl Caldwell, "Sacramento Mayor 'Shocked' at Damage by Police to Panther Headquarters," *New York Times*, June 18, 1969.

101. Dworkin, *Contemporary Authors Autobiography Series*, 15.

102. Andrea Dworkin, *Heartbreak: The Political Memoir of a Feminist Militant* (London: Continuum, 2006), 62

103. Farrell, "Inquiry Ordered at Women's Jail," 27; Feinman, "Imprisoned Women," 131; Memorandum from Mary Lindsay to Anna Kross, "REPORT OF INVESTIGATION REGARDING ALLEGATIONS BY FORMER INMATE ANDREA DWORKIN CONTAINED IN A LETTER DATED MARCH 2, 1965 TO ANNA M. KROSS," Mar. 9, 1965, Folder 8, Box 4, AKPSS.

104. "Accused Physician Has Resigned Post at Women's Prison," *New York Times*, Mar. 31, 1965.

105. Feinman, "Imprisoned Women," 131–33; Edith Evans Asbury, "Fourth Group Begins Inquiry into Women's Jail," *New York Times*, Mar. 19, 1965; Sydney H. Schanberg, "Control of Jails by State Urged," *New York Times*, Mar. 23, 1965; Dworkin, *Heartbreak*, 62–64. The Committee of Outraged Parents also sprang up to advocate for the closure of the house of detention and against the "dehumanization of the internal examination." See the correspondence in Folder 16, Box 38, ADP; John Morrin, "Prison Notes," *New York Post*, Apr. 28, 1965, in Folder 6D, Box 4, AKPSS.

106. J. Anthony Lukas, "Court V.D. Clinic Is Closed by City," *New York Times*, July 1, 1967.

107. "SF Call House Raid Reveals Big Operation," *Sacramento Bee*, Mar. 12, 1954; "Quarantine Spared Three," *San Francisco Examiner*, Mar. 18, 1954, in Folder 777, Carton 36, ACLUNCR.

108. "Call-Girl Quarantine Procedure Held Illegal," *San Francisco Chronicle*, Mar. 30, 1954.

109. Melinda Chateauvert, *Sex Workers Unite: A History of the Movement from Stonewall to SlutWalk* (Boston: Beacon Press, 2013), 50–56; Margo St. James, "Preface," xvii, in *A Vindication of the Rights of Whores*, ed. Gail Pheterson (Seattle: Seal Press, 1989); Laura Renata Martin, "Precarious City: Marginal Workers, the State, and Working-Class Activism in Post-Industrial San Francisco, 1964–1979," PhD diss., University of California, Santa Cruz, 2014, 345. Some would later question whether or not St. James ever actually worked as a prostitute. (See Kirsten Pullen, "Performing Prostitution: Agency and Discourse, Actresses and Whores," PhD diss., University of Wisconsin, 2001, 265–66.) Years later, her friend and longtime COYOTE colleague Priscilla Alexander would say, "I don't think she [sold sex] in any great quantity, you know, for any extended period of time, but she was around North Beach in the period in which the lines between casual sex and informal prostitution weren't so great. That whole hippie period. And so I think she did some [sex] work then, but it wasn't a lot. But she had enough experience that she knew what it was." Telephone interview with Priscilla Alexander, Aug. 18, 2015.

110. Margo St. James, "Prostitutes as Political Prisoners," *Realist*, Dec. 1972, Folder 259, Reel 1, M143, COYOTER.

111. Letter from Jefferson Clitlick to Margo St. James, Mar. 16, 1973, Folder 124, Carton 2, COYOTER.

112. Valerie Jenness, "From Sex as Sin to Sex as Work: COYOTE and the Reorganization of Prostitution as a Social Problem," *Social Problems* 37.3 (Aug. 1990): 407.

113. Martin, "Precarious City," 343–44; Jenness, "From Sex as Sin to Sex as Work," 403n1; Gail Pheterson, "Not Repeating History," in Pheterson, *A Vindication of the Rights of Whores*, 5.

114. Margo St. James, "Mayday 1973 San Francisco," Folder 254, Box 6, COYOTER.

115. Margo St. James, "Mothers' Day 1973," Folder 254, Box 6, COYOTER.

116. St. James, "Preface," xviii.

117. Form letter from Margo St. James to "City Prison Doctor," June 20, 1973, Folder 110, Carton 2, COYOTE Records.

118. Margo St. James, "Whore as Metaphor: Prostitute as Political Prisoner," Aug. 10, 1973, Folder 254, Box 6, COYOTER.

119. Ernest Lenn, "Scott raps lifting of prostitutes quarantine," *San Francisco Examiner*, Oct. 31, 1973; "COYOTE: A Loose Woman's Organization," *San Francisco Mental Health Newsletter*, Nov. 1973; Ernest Lenn, "VD Quarantine Plan Opposed—and Upheld," *San Francisco Examiner*, Dec. 6, 1973; Harriet Katz Berman, "Quarantine: Policing Prostitution," *Civil Liberties*, Mar. 1974—all in Folder 261, Reel 1, M143, COYOTER.

120. "Prostitutes Backed by ACLU," *Santa Cruz Sentinel*, Jan. 10, 1974.

121. "An Order to Halt VD Exams," *San Francisco Chronicle*, Feb. 8, 1974, in Folder 261, Reel 1, M143, COYOTE Records; "VD Check Is Halted," *Times* (San Mateo, CA), Feb. 8, 1974; "New Prostitute Rule," *San Francisco Examiner*, Feb. 8, 1974.

122. Letter from Margo St. James to COYOTE members, Jan. 1975, Folder 131, Carton 3, COYOTER.

123. "ACLU Wins Major Victory Against Prostitution Laws," Feb. 27, 1975, Folder 905, Carton 17, COYOTER; Philip Hager, "Prostitute Patron Also Faces Jail," *Los Angeles Times*, Feb. 28, 1975; Jerome H. Skolnick, *Justice Without Trial: Law Enforcement in Democratic Society* (New York: John Wiley & Sons, 1966), 99–108. (On Skolnick's "Westview" being Oakland, see Geoffrey C. Hazard, "Book Reviews," *University of Chicago Law Review* 34 (1966): 226; Wayne R. La Fave, "Books Reviews," *Fordham Law Review* 36.1 (1967): 145; Kenneth Culp Davis, *Discretionary Justice: A Preliminary Inquiry* (Baton Rouge: Louisiana State University Press, 1969), 171–72.

124. "Jailing Prostitutes for VD Tests Denounced," *Independent* (Long Beach, CA), Mar. 19, 1975.

125. Kathleen Hendrix, "Prostitution: Part II: The Law vs. a Changing Moral Climate: Unequal Application of Penal Code Changed," *Los Angeles Times*, Feb. 9, 1976; M. Anne Jennings, "The Victim as Criminal: A Consideration of California's Prostitution Law," *California Law Review* 64.5 (Sept. 1976): 1252 n103; Chateauvert, *Sex Workers Unite*, 68–69.

126. "Hess, Norman H.," *Bay City Times*, Mar. 23, 1971; "This Week," *Bay City Democrat*, Sept. 19, 1957, BCHS.

127. See American Social Health Association, *The Association's Annual Report of 1971*; American Social Health Association, *The Association's Annual Report of 1972*—both in Folder 5, Box 20, Series 2, ASHAR; American Sexual Health Association, "Who We Are," 2017, http://www.ashasexual health.org/who-we-are. See also Kramer, Blum and Associates, "Final Report of the Evaluation and Action Planning Committee to the American Social Health Association Board of Directors," Nov. 1974, Box 233, Series 2, AHSAR.

128. "Raymond B. Fosdick Dies at 89; Headed Rockefeller Foundation," *New York Times*, Jul. 19, 1972.

129. Jean Heller, "Syphilis Victims in U.S. Study Went Untreated for 40 Years," *New York Times*, Jul. 26, 1972.

130. Washington, *Medical Apartheid*, 169, 173; Reverby, *Examining Tuskegee*, 90–94, 196–97; Brandt, "Racism and Research," 27.

131. Memorandum from Earle Lippincotte to Regional Directors and Division Directors, "The Tuskegee Study," Aug. 23, 1972, Tuskegee Study 1972 Folder, Box 188, Series 2, ASHAR.

132. See the documents in Folders 985–988, Box 57, TPP.

133. "Examinations Urged Here to Combat V.D.," *Indianapolis Star*, Nov. 30, 1967. See also "Seven Women Held in Raids to Face Court," *Terre Haute Tribune*, May 29, 1964; "Dr. Duckwall Airs Problems Facing City," *Terre Haute Tribune*, Aug. 1, 1968.

134. "Hippies Just Laugh at VD, Won't Stop Making Love," *Salt Lake Tribune*, May 3, 1968; "Despite Constant Police Efforts Prostitution Flourishes in S.L.," *Salt Lake Tribune*, May 27, 1968; "Hold Till Cured: Police Order Exams in Sex Arrests," *Salt Lake Tribune*, Aug. 11, 1968; "Ruling Empowers City to Detain Prostitutes," *Salt Lake Tribune*, Aug. 14, 1968; "First Arrest Under V.D. Rule Test," *Salt Lake Tribune*, Aug. 22, 1968; "Judge to Study Case in S.L. Morals Charge," *Salt Lake Tribune*, Sept. 15, 1968; "Suspected Sex Offenders to Get VD Test," *Daily Herald* (Provo, UT), May 20, 1969; "Attorney Slams Law on Venereal Disease," *Ogden Standard-Examiner*, May 31, 1969; "Venereal Disease Rate Gains Tenfold in S.L.," *Ogden Standard-Examiner*, Sept. 18, 1969; "Arrests Made For Venereal Disease in S.L.," *Daily Herald*, Sept. 22, 1969; "Salt Lake City May Arrest Carriers of New VD Strain," *San Bernardino County Sun-Telegram*, Dec. 14, 1976.

135. Peter Ney, *Getting Here: From a Seat on a Train to a Seat on the Bench* (Bloomington, IN: iUniverse, 2009), 173–75; Reynolds v. McNichols, 488 F.2d 1378, 1380–82; Stern, "The Long American Plan," 417.

136. Ney, *Getting Here*, 175.

137. Doug Hardie, "D.A., Health Officials to Crackdown [*sic*] on Prostitution," *Colorado Springs Gazette-Telegraph*, Jul. 3, 1970; Marianne Salcetti, "Prostitution, Military Linked to High Rate of Gonorrhea," *Colorado Springs Gazette-Telegraph*, Dec. 18, 1977.

138. "'All-Out War' on Prostitution Brings About Stiffer Sentences," *Hartford Courant*, Jan. 5, 1982.

139. Steven Emmons, "Streetwalkers Target of Economic Boycott," *Los Angeles Times*, Dec. 17, 1977.

140. Jack Thomas, "Nation Takes New Look at Prostitution Laws," *Boston Globe*, Oct. 5, 1975.

141. Randy Shilts, *And the Band Played On: Politics, People, and the AIDS Epidemic* (New York: St. Martin's Press, 1987), 228.

142. Chateauvert, *Sex Workers Unite*, 93, 95–96.

143. For the New Haven case, see Hampton Sides, "Lana: A Story of Scarlet Letters, Private Lives and Public Health," *New Journal* 16.3 (Dec. 9, 1983): 16–20; numerous articles on Carlotta Locklear (aka Lana) in Folder 883, Carton 17, COYOTER; Richard L. Melchreit, "HIV Infection in Connecticut, 1980–1990," *Connecticut History* 38.1 (Fall 1997–Spring 1999): 45–46; Christine Guilfoy, "Connecticut Quarantine Law Out of Committee," *Gay Community News* 11.42 (May 12, 1984): 3; Christine Guilfoy, "Quarantine Bill Passes in Connecticut," *Gay Community News* 11.45 (June 2, 1984): 3; P.A. 84–336, § 1, 1984 Conn. Acts—(Reg. Sess.) (amending CONN. GEN. STAT. 19a-221: An Act Concerning Quarantine Measures); Ronald Bayer, *Private Acts, Social Consequences: AIDS and the Politics of Public Health* (New York: Free Press, 1989), 177. For the San Francisco case, see Shilts, *And the Band Played On*, 508–10; Randy Shilts, "Working Prostitute Waits for Test: A 'Monster' Dilemma on AIDS," *San Francisco Chronicle*, Jan. 5, 1985; "Prostitute May Have AIDS, But Says She Will Still Work," *Journal News* (White Plains, NY), Jan. 6, 1985; Marilyn Chase, "Doctors' Efforts to Control AIDS Spark Battles Over Civil Liberties," *Wall Street Journal*, Feb. 8, 1985; Lawrence K. Altman, "Heterosexuals and AIDS: New Data Examined," *New York Times*, Jan. 22, 1985.

144. William A. Check, "Heterosexual AIDS Risk Studied," *Washington Post*, Apr. 17, 1985; Rosemary Goudreau, "AIDS Hits New Group of Victims Drug-Using Prostitutes Suspected as Carriers," *Orlando Sentinel*, Apr. 18, 1985; Edward Barnes and Anne Hollister, "The New Victims: AIDS Is an Epidemic That May Change the Way America Lives," *Life*, Jul. 1985; Shilts, *And the Band Played On*, 511–13; Chateauvert, *Sex Workers Unite*, 85; "Researcher Testifies Soldiers Getting AIDS from Prostitutes," *Houston Chronicle*, Sept. 26, 1985. See also Donna King, "'Prostitutes as Pariah in the Age of AIDS': A Content Analysis of Coverage of Women Prostitutes in the *New York Times* and the *Washington Post*, Sept. 1985–April 1988," *Women & Health* 16, nos. 3–4 (1990): 155–76.

145. Melchreit, "HIV Infection in Connecticut," 46; Tamar Lewin, "Rights of Citizens and Society Raise Legal Muddle on AIDS," *New York Times*, Oct. 14, 1987; Ronald Bayer and Amy Fairchild-Carrino, "AIDS and the Limits of Control: Public Health Orders, Quarantine, and Recalcitrant Behavior," *American Journal of Public Health* 83.10 (Oct. 1993): 1471–75; Stern, "The Long American Plan," 427.

146. See Warren King, "AIDS Test Set for Prostitutes in County Jail," *Seattle Times*, Oct. 19, 1985; Bayer, *Private Acts, Social Consequences*, 174, 182; Mary Irvine, "From 'Social Evil' to Public Health Menace: The Justifications and Implications of Strict Approaches to Prostitutes in the HIV Epidemic," *Berkeley Journal of Sociology* 43 (1998–99): 66; Ronald Sullivan, "AIDS Test Is Weighed in Sex Cases," *New York Times*, Nov. 21, 1987.

147. "Poll Indicates Majority Favors Quarantine for AIDS Victims," *New York Times*, Dec. 20, 1985. See also Bayer, *Private Acts, Social Consequences*, 176.

148. See Testimony of Priscilla Alexander before the San Francisco Human Rights Commission, Feb. 5, 1986; Testimony of Priscilla Alexander Before the Senate Select Committee on Substance Abuse and Senate Select Committee on AIDS, Oct. 20, 1987; Testimony of Priscilla Alexander before the Senate Judiciary Committee in Opposition to AB 2319, Feb. 23, 1988—all in Folder 1, Carton 1, COYOTER.

149. Chateauvert, *Sex Workers Unite*, 83–84, 102; Melinda Chateauvert, "Resisting the Virus of Prejudice: Sex Workers Fight the AIDS Panic," *Beacon Broadside*, July 20, 2016, http://www.beaconbroadside.com/broadside/2016/07/resisting-the-virus-of-prejudice-sex-workers-fight-the-aids-panic.html; Constance Wofsy et al., "Isolation of AIDS-Associated Retrovirus from Genital Secretions of Women with Antibodies to the Virus," *Lancet* 8.1 (Mar. 1986): 527–29; Constance Wofsy, "Human Immunodeficiency Virus Infection in Women," *JAMA* 257.15 (Apr. 17, 1987): 2074–76.

150. "Myers, Dr. Woodrow," videotape, Jan. 18, 1990, I.B1 ACT UP Actions, Testing the Limits Records, NYPL.

151. See, for instance, James Colgrove, *Epidemic City: The Politics of Public Health in New York* (New York: Russell Sage Foundation, 2011), 193–94; Timothy Stewart-Winter, *Queer Clout: Chicago and the Rise of Gay Politics* (Philadelphia: University of Pennsylvania Press, 2016), 200–201.

152. See Wendy E. Paremt, "AIDS and Quarantine: The Revival of an Archaic Doctrine," *Hofstra Law Review* 14 (1985–86): 66–69, 75, 90; Lewin, "Rights of Citizens and Society Raise Legal Muddle on AIDS"; Debi Brock, "Prostitutes Are Scapegoats in the AIDS Panic," *Resources for Feminist Research* 18.2 (Sept. 1989): 13; Mark Blumberg, "The Limits of Quarantine as a Measure for Controlling the Spread of AIDS," in *AIDS: The Impact on the Criminal Justice System*, ed. Mark Blumberg (Columbus, OH: Merrill, 1990), 143; Elizabeth Fee, "Sin versus Science: Venereal Disease in Twentieth-Century Baltimore," 121–46, in *AIDS: The Burdens of History*, ed. Elizabeth Fee and Daniel M. Fox (Berkeley: University of California Press, 1988); Testimony of Priscilla Alexander before the President's Commission on AIDS, Mar. 24, 1988, Folder 1, Carton 1, COYOTER.

153. Beth Bergman, "AIDS, Prostitution, and the Use of Historical Stereotypes to Legislative Sexuality," *John Marshall Law Review* 21 (1987–1988): 777–806.

154. Brandt, *No Magic Bullet*, 195, 201–2.

155. Telephone interview with Allan Brandt, Mar. 24, 2017.

156. Untitled memorandum, Quarantine Folder, Box 8, Stanley Hadden Papers, Gay, Lesbian, Bisexual, Transgender Historical Society.

157. King, "AIDS Test Set for Prostitutes in County Jail."

158. "ACT UP Protests Against Quarantine Laws," videotape, Apr. 21, 1989, Entry 01304, AIDS Activist Videotape Collection, NYPL.

159. See 226 Cal. App. 3d 736 (Cal. Ct. App. 1990); Dunn v. White, 880 F.2d 1188. Also, People v. McVickers, 840 P.2d 955 (Cal. 1992); Fosman v. State of Florida, 644 So. 2d 1163 (Fla. Dist. Ct. App. 1995); People v. Adams, 597 N.E. 2d 574 (Ill. 1992); Stern, "The Long American Plan," 427.

160. 226 Cal. App. 3d 736, 746–48 (Cal. Ct. App. 1990); In re Application of Johnson, 180 P. 644, 645 (Cal. Ct. App. 1919).

161. Stern, "The Long American Plan," 427–29; Christian Klesse, *The Spectre of Promiscuity: Gay Male and Bisexual Non-Monogamies and Polyamories* (New York: Routledge, 2007), 59; Irvine, "'Social Evil' to Public Health Menace," 66, 84.

162. See Stern, "The Long American Plan," 378–79 and appendices.

EPILOGUE

1. Chamberlain-Kahn Act, Pub. L. No. 65–193, 40 Stat. 845 (1918).

2. Connelly, *The Response to Prostitution in the Progressive Era*, 209n18.

3. Bristow, *Making Men Moral*, 197.

4. See Cord Jefferson, "Gonorrhea Is Now One Antibiotic Away from Being Untreatable," *Gawker*, Aug. 9, 2012, http://gawker.com/5933459/gonorrhea-is-now-one-antibiotic-away-from -being-untreatable; James Hamblin, "Here It Comes: Super Gonorrhea," *Atlantic*, Aug. 9, 2012, https://www.theatlantic.com/health/archive/2012/08/here-it-comes-super-gonorrhea/260937/; Samuel Sarmiento, "3 Common STDs Becoming Untreatable: How Worried Should We Be?" *NBC News*, Sept. 2, 2016, http://www.nbcnews.com/health/sexual-health/3-common-stds-becoming -untreatable-what-happens-now-n642161.

5. "Salt Lake City May Arrest Carriers of New VD Strain," *San Bernardino County Sun-Telegram*, Dec. 14, 1976; "VD Epidemic Is a Fact," *Times* (San Mateo, CA), Apr. 19, 1977.

6. See Memorandum from Paul Popenoe to Director, Section on Vice and Liquor Control, "Newport News, Virginia," Jan. 7, 1919, Folder 6, Box 47, PBPP; Reitman, "The Whores and the Pimps Are Afraid of the House of Correction."

7. Paul Popenoe, Observations of Petersburg, VA, Jan. 6, 1919, Folder 6, Box 47, PBPP.

8. Merrill, "Venereal Disease Prevention in Wartime," 80–88.

Index

Abbott, Edith, 167, 169
abolitionism, abolitionists: and the closing of red light districts, 15, 24, 48; Criminal Law Amendment penalties, 20; embracing of my American medical journals, 24; opposition to regulatory approaches, 14, 16; views on police abuse of power, 19–20; views on prostitution, 11, 14–15; and white slavery, 18–19. *See also* American Social Hygiene Association (ASHA); Bureau of Social Hygiene, New York City; regulationism
Act 272, Public Laws of 1919 (Dunn bill), 117, 125, 183
"Action Is Needed" editorial (*Alma Record*), 72
African Americans/African American women: assumptions of promiscuity among, 79; conditions during incarceration, 70, 98–99; disproportionate detention and incarceration of, 50, 52, 79, 97–98, 181, 193, 216–17, 225, 233; disproportionate sterilization of, 90; and IQ tests, 88–89; as focus of CTCA enforcement activities, 49–50; investigative work for the Division of Venereal Disease, 74; monitoring/stalking of parolees, 115; objections to the Plan, 235–36, parolee work opportunities, 91, 111; targeting of by CPWG workers, 52. *See also* Hispanic women; Native American women; racism
Alabama: American Plan laws/enforcement efforts, 49, 143, 208; Montgomery detention house, 174; Parran's experience in, 194; rationales for segregation in, 250; State Training School for Girls, 120. *See also* Tuskegee syphilis study
Alaska, antiprostitution activities, 242
Albion reformatory, New York, parolee work opportunities, 111
alcohol use: association with female promiscuity, 39, 47–49, 59, 78, 232; control of during World War I, 44–45
Aldrich, Thomas Bailey, 18
Alexander, Priscilla, 272, 338n109
All-America Conference on Venereal Disease, Washington, DC, 161–67
Allyn, David, 249
Alma, Michigan: celebrations of the armistice, 87; detention of suspect women in, 1–2, 77; election of Carney as mayor, 226–27; employment of women during World War I, 47; Githens family move to, 131; growth during World War I, 71; influenza in, 103–4; McCall family in, 46, 114; Millerville district, 46–47; organized entertainments in, 48, 72; responses to

quarantine measures, 104; response to *Protecting the Public Health* in, 140–41; suspension of Plan enforcement during NM's trial, 138
Alma Record: "Action Is Needed" editorial, 72; reports of arrests and incarceration of Franklin and Marvin, 77; response to *Protecting the Public Health*, 140; stories about the McCall case, 147, 178
American Bar Association (ABA): active support for the Plan, 143–44; Committee on Courts and Wartime Social Protection, 229; model laws and ordinances proposed by, 229–30; support for the Plan, 229
American Civil Liberties Union (ACLU): backing for COYOTE, 255; Besig's role with, 232; tacit support for the Plan, 230–31
American Medical Association (AMA): opposition to regulationism, 16; opposition to the Interdepartmental Social Hygiene Board, 170; views on venereal disease, 250
the American Plan: components, 121 and debates about HIV/AIDS, 260–61; first official use of the term, 121; funding sources, 49–50, 128, 182; historical obscurity of, reasons and implications, 261–68; impact of the Great Depression on, 192; legal authority for, 54–55, 57–58, 62–66, 104–5, 125, 142–43, 178, 182, 197, 229–30, 261; misogyny of/targeting of women, 55, 58, 67, 71, 78–79, 91–92, 97–98, 112, 114, 134–35, 165, 179, 186, 189, 299n85; public support/ praise for, 161–62, 165, 174, 188, 194–95, 214, 222, 229–31, 243, 266; as punitive and coercive, 114, 145, 156–57; racism of, 79, 216–17, 233, 235–36; resistance/opposition to, 26, 50, 145, 117, 132–36, 168, 177, 179–80 189–90, 245, 254–55; and the Tuskegee study, 202–3, 236–37, 257; scope and scale of, 5–7, 31–32, 59–60, 74–75; state and local enforcement approach, 6–7, 127, 170, 173, 180–81, 192, 196–98, 240, 257–58; following World War I, 87, 100, 117; during World War II, 206–9, 215–16. *See also* American Social Hygiene Association (ASHA); Commission on Training Camp Activities (CTCA), War Department; due process violations; examinations, forced; protective work for girls/women; quarantines, compulsory; "reasonable suspicion" concept *and specific states and localities.*
American Public Health Association, 210, 227
American Social Hygiene Association (ASHA): agenda and strategy, 31; award considered for Eleanor Roosevelt, 221; cessation of undercover investigations, 256;

342